THE DANUBE

BOOKS BY ERWIN LESSNER

CRADLE OF CONQUERORS: SIBERIA

AT THE DEVIL'S BOOTH

PHANTOM VICTORY: THE FOURTH REICH

BLITZKRIEG AND BLUFF: THE LEGEND OF NAZI INVINCIBILITY

FAMOUS AUTO RACES AND RALLIES

THE DANUBE

The Dramatic History of the
Great River and the People
Touched by Its Flow

Erwin Lessner

WITH THE COLLABORATION OF

ANN M. LINGG LESSNER

DOUBLEDAY & COMPANY, INC.

GARDEN CITY, NEW YORK

1961

In August of 1959, my husband dedicated this book to me.

"This book belongs to Ann, my wife . . . ," he wrote, and it seems now those words were prophetic.

On Christmas Eve, four months later, I faced the formidable challenge of completing the manuscript for him. I have done so in all humility, always aware of my husband's intentions and of his consuming devotion to the task.

And so I rededicate this book, which lived with us during the last two and a half years of our married life, to my husband's memory.

ANN M. LINGG LESSNER

PRELUDE

The pudgy little boy stood in the grove, which looked like a landscaped clearing in the mass of dark pines that held the hills in an evergreen grip. From the ground, cushioned with moss, leaves, and tired needles, emerged huge drops of water like myriads of splinters of rock crystal that had been waiting in the depth for the call to light. From above came a scintillating drizzle of tiny particles of sun rays that played with the water a game of seek-and-shine.

The boy stared in awkward wonder.

So this was the source of the Danube: the brook called Brigach, which was said to join, a short distance away, with its identical twin, the Brege.

> *"Die Brigach und die Brege*
> *Bringen die Donau zuwege."*

"The Brigach and the Brege together create the Danube," his nurse had taught him.

He had always relished the nursery jingle, but now that he stood in the Black Forest and saw the brook, doubts crept into his mind. This did not look like the source of the Danube to him, not like a budding river, not even a rivulet. This could not possibly create the Danube which last spring, three hundred miles away, had swept houses away like tinder boxes, drowned cattle, and marooned the iron ferry boat so that he and his family had been virtually isolated. This could not be the sturdy, domineering, huge band of brownish-green water sweeping through a countryside that meekly acknowledged its rule.

On the spur of the moment the boy decided to make an irrefutable test of his own to establish the truth. He bent down, stretched out his fat little paws, gravely pressed them against the fissure in the ground from where the water emerged, and remained in this position until his cheeks grew red and puffy. The water chuckled, then seemed to be subdued.

His parents took him back to their house in Upper Austria and told him that he should be pleased to have seen the source of the Danube. The boy obediently said yes, and kept wondering.

Then he asked his friend the gardener whether he remembered what had happened to the Danube last Wednesday, at noon. The gardener, gulping a glass of homemade apple cider, asserted that nothing had happened. "But didn't the river stop flowing suddenly?" The man was adamant. The Danube had kept flowing as it had always done, as it always would.

The boy was crestfallen. He had pressed his fists so solidly to the ground! For the first time he conceived the gnawing notion of futility.

It required more than the imagination of a five-year-old to visualize the crystal streamlet straying beyond its gentle habitat into a strange world of dramatic settings to unite and to rule many more waters, to meet, live with, inspire, carry, and destroy men, and to gather a flotsam of souvenirs.

And now, more than half a century later, saturated with doubts, familiar with futility in an endless variety of manifestations, the man who had been the pudgy boy has set out to write this book, to tell, as best as the Lord gave him the power to do, what happened along the Danube and in its basin, and of the people who made, enjoyed, and suffered its history in the course of recorded or explored events.

CHAPTER ONE

The mountains labored and the Danube was born.

Eons ago the grounds of the prehistoric Central German Mountain Masses lowered, hollowed out by unfathomable forces, and formed a depression which established a link with the lowlands that spread along the spurs of the foothills of the Alps. Thus the bed of the upper Danube was created. It extended east and southeast as other ranges lowered, moved, and carved plains and valleys where the northeastern Alps nod to the southwestern Carpathians, beyond the gap into the vast flatlands of what would become Hungary. Further away the bed of the Danube grew into a mighty moat that extended along the fringe of the rugged Balkans, as a boundary of the Mediterranean rampart. It knocked at the Iron Gate of the Transylvanian Alps, and in a struggle that dwarfed in violence all men's battles broke through toward the inhospitable Black Sea, where it buried itself in immense masses of mire.

According to statistics, the Danube sweeps an annual average of more than 62,000,000 long tons of mud into the Black Sea. And 6700 long tons of water per second spill into the river's terminal.

The Brigach and the Brege, in their cradle 3200 feet up in the Black Forest, contribute only an infinitesimal fraction of the water and none of the mud that hits the ocean. The Danube is, in fact, an agglomeration of diversified fluvial elements from many parts of the continent, just as the people along its banks are the blend of innumerable races.

In its uppermost part the river seems doomed to trickle away. Near Donaueschingen the joint brooks are almost exhausted as they reach the site where a princely castle now stands; the gush from the castle's well, the first tributary which the Danube receives, is only a trifling addition to its power, which is challenged by the obstacles of the Swabian Jura hills. The hills drain the frail watercourse so that, as the boy who wanted to stop the Danube did not yet know, the river often oozes out in various places, disappearing into the calcareous soil for periods of up to three months, then re-emerging after strong precipitation, and still too thin to carry on without powerful assistance. This assistance comes seven and a half tortuous miles further to the west, from a most unexpected quarter: a tributary that comes underground from Lake Constance, the realm of the already vigorous Rhine. The water of this tributary could be claimed by the river gods of the Rhine as their rightful property. But the gods of the Rhine are less covetous than the mundane rulers of the lands along that river often have been. Through this tributary, the Radolfzeller Aach, the reservoir of the lake keeps the Danube alive and helps it to grow longer and bigger than the Rhine. A German legend says that the Lord shed one single tear after completing His creation, and that this tear—whether of joy, or weariness, or remorse—dropped on the earth and formed Lake Constance. The Lord's tear rescued the Danube.

From the discharge of the Radolfzeller Aach on, the river is here to stay, come drought or deluge.

Near Donauried it meets the vanguard of the Alps on swampy ground. Adorned with colorful vegetation, the foothills are signposts waving the river on through a broadening bed toward Ingolstadt.

Ingolstadt and all settlements along its course are late-comers to the Danube as the river's life span goes, but they all have designs inseparably interwoven with the very nature of the Danube. There is not one town, nor even a village, from source to delta, without a permanent purpose, a *raison d'être,* that ties it to the river in a logical, natural manner.

Near Ingolstadt with its cozy, pastoral surroundings the Danube slows down for a brief leisurely course; its previously rather steep fall flattens. But a short distance away, however, elevations of the Franconian Juras hem the river into a picturesque jacket, make it press on with verve and vigor, and hollow its shallow bottom to greater depth. Roman river navigators, Roman military engineers, and Roman traders knew how to utilize the river's approaching maturity. They built Ratisbon (Regensburg, as German-speaking people later called it) and made it a port for their flotilla.

Near Ratisbon the number of tributaries has already reached seven, including the Iller, Lech, Naab, and Regen. Ratisbon has remained the starting point of major navigation ever since the Romans founded it.

On and on the river flows, close to the orbit of mountains that build its roadbed, through land that it parts and links, land that smiles and whose ripening fields are as golden as the hair of fairies of indigenous tales. The primary mountains of Bohemia shudder with mysterious ponds and woods and give the onrushing Danube a new mood and texture. Cutting through rocks thrown in its way by playful titans of nature, it reaches Passau. From Passau to the "Kachlet" (Tiles) of Aschach less than twoscore miles downstream, the Danube bursts through a lane formed by wooded hills where cyclamen grows near granite rocks and succulent moss has the moist scent of mushrooms and fading dog roses. The Tiles of Aschach are steep, lowering banks. Skippers claim that they tax their navigating skill yet are lovely and harmonious in shape and look rather unheroic.

The course down to Linz is dominated by the distant view of the Alps with the domineering Traunstein, a block of dark rock that looks well over ten thousand feet high, though it is not half that tall.

Below Linz and its twin city of Urfahr the Danube has a rendezvous with a host of evil genii. Local fishermen will say that these ghosts have been haunting the stretch from time immemorial, that they have taken a huge toll of human victims, and that they can never be appeased. The evil genii are said to appear at night, with sinister signal lights leading boatmen to destruction, with alluring calls and fiery will-o'-the-wisps, all ushering in death in the roaring waters of rapids, swells, rocks, and shallows. The "Struden," the "Wirbel," and the "Schwall" have long become romantic attractions for sight-seers. They are less formidable than many a vortex or cataract in streams and rivers with lesser lore, but the Danube is graced with a benign theatricalism not easily matched elsewhere.

"Struden," "Wirbel," and "Schwall" are heralds of the Wachau, where the Danube triumphantly parades through another twin array of mountains that bend edgy slopes in proud salute.

These mountains are the outposts of the region where wines can be grown. They were waiting for the sower and cultivator when Biblical gourmets were not yet born and Danubian men were barbaric nomads. The beginning of winegrowing in the Danube basin was prompted by demand and practicality, but there must also have been a call of nature that the suppliers of Roman garrisons and administrators' families could hardly have understood. For wherever wine is grown along the Danube, music is born, more intoxicating even than the elixir of grapes. This music is alive in the wineries from the Wachau down to the Vienna Woods, in Vienna itself, and on the plains of Hungary, where Gypsies fiddle lusciously rhythmic tales which not even the most daring poets could fittingly put into words.

After a leisurely run through the Tullner Field the Danube hems the undulating rim of the Alps—the Vienna Woods—and majestically swings on to the Hainburg Gap, where the Hungarian course opens, whatever crisscross political boundary lines busy map makers draw. The Carpathians shimmer through the haze of those humid regions; they look less sedate than their vis-à-vis, the Vienna Woods, almost like yokels roaming near the villa of city slickers.

There the waters of the Danube are already highly diversified. The Isar, the Inn, the Traun, the Enns, the Ilz, Mühl, and March, have carried flows from the high Alps, from the Sudeten Plateau, and from countless springs and brooks, toward the maturing river.

The lean whitefish, the sharp-toothed pikes, the carps which sparsely populate the upper Danube, are joined by huge sheatfish from the March which occasionally hit the scales at two hundred pounds, but which sporting-minded fishermen disdain for their sluggishness and gourmets for the dull taste of their meat. The sheatfish are, according to standard dictionaries, the longest fresh-water fish to be found in Central and Eastern Europe. But chroniclers of the Danube insist that, once upon a time, giant sturgeons, the size of overgrown tiger sharks, have shot through the waters, its long shallow stretches notwithstanding. There is no conclusive evidence to this claim; along the Danube as elsewhere, fishermen like tales of tall fish.

The Danube turns unruly in the wide Hungarian plains. It forks out into many arms, forms small islets and islands as big as districts, and in spots spreads its waters so thin that a great deal of regulation was required to keep it navigable. The Romans must be credited with the first attempts to that effect.

In these plains the Danube has drowned more people and destroyed more property than anywhere else. The unruliness of the river is equaled by the violence of men along its Hungarian banks. Nowhere has there been more bloodshed, more rebellion, more tragedy, than in these lands, which in all seasons look like perfect settings for somnolent peace.

Budapest, the stage on which for a thousand years tragedy, comedy, and parody, and big spectacles, have been performed, often so interwoven that the true nature of the show can be understood only after the curtain falls, is still not quite on the Danube's halfway mark; yet its altitude is a bare three hundred feet. Ninety per cent of the total fall of the river is consumed. The Danube could settle down to a quaint run of placid conducibleness, but instead it girds for drama. It has gathered more tributary-auxiliaries, the Váh, the Nitra, the Leitha, the Hron among them; and it gathers more waters toward the climax of its run. The western tributaries, the Drava and the Sava, swollen by a host of mountain brooks, are in fighting mettle, belligerent mountaineers who would not feel at ease in a broad bed, performing domestic labors. The Drava and the Sava and the green clear Tisza from the undulating North usher the Danube into its course as a moat of the Balkan fortress which has attracted many invaders but has stopped only a few.

Near Báziás the Transylvanian foothills, the southwestern point of the Carpathian crescent, form the picturesque narrows of Klisura. They are the introduction to the crescendo of the river's symphony; its headlong run against the Transylvanian wall, where nature does not grant the right of way as easily as in the Alps and the lower Carpathians. The islets of Kisiljevo and Moldova, the Babakai Rock, and the wild rapids beyond were once the scene of a titanic battle between the land and the river; and the struggle continues even after the Danube has forced its passage through the walls of the land-fortress. There the river can hardly breathe. After gliding along through a bed over a mile wide in spots, waters rush through a channel that narrows to one hundred seventy yards. Procrustes, the legendary Greek robber, must have seen the Danube at Kazán Pass before he devised his limb-stretching, limb-amputating procedure. Procrustes' victims succumbed; but the raging Danube comes out victorious. Struggling, it follows the bottom of its bed to a depth of one hundred sixty-five feet, speeds its current from a leisurely pace to a brisk ten miles per hour, breaks down one rampart after another until it resembles a fissured fiord rather than a river as it forces its way into a mighty caldron, and from there assaults the Iron Gate. The Iron Gate opens. The Danube has asserted itself, a crowning achievement of a long course of action. The most imposing birds of the continent—golden eagles with wing spans of up to seven feet—keep watching the titanic endeavor.

The Danube is weary as it gathers weary tributaries: the Isker, the Argeş, the Lom, all quieter than their immediate predecessors, the Timok, the Olt, and the Jiu. Slowly, furrowing the runes of its own epilogue through smooth ground, it skirts the northern slope of the Bulgarian chalk formation. The arc-shaped formation in which it made its onset against the final bulwark straightens out in the last *étape* of an august march. Grand and strange, floating messengers from steppes that are outposts of Asia, the rivers Siret and Prut tumble into the seabound Danube. From Galatz to the Black Sea the Danube has a fall of only three feet and yet it proceeds with dignified regularity. At Tulcea it enters the Delta, sixteen hundred fifty-one square miles of fever-ridden swampland, a primeval wilderness where the sudden appearance of a dinosaurian would seem less than surprising. Men cannot make a home in the delta area, but men have been fighting there since time immemorial. Hordes from ancient Siberia and warriors from more cultured realms came to the three-pronged sink of the Danube to kill and get killed. All their battles were futile. Never was a war decided in the Danube Delta. This is what, during World War I, Bulgarians and Germans, Russians and Rumanians, learned again, at the price of staggering casualties.

The delta's three arms are called the Kiliya, the Sulina, and the St. George. The Sulina is now navigable, having been regulated to a depth of twenty-four feet, and its course shortened by thirteen miles. A lighthouse on the spot where the Sulina reaches the sea looks odd in the brooding wilderness.

The lighthouse marks journey's end.

The journey is 1765 miles long, according to some sources. Others say it is only 1725. This makes the Danube rank twenty-third (or twenty-fourth, respectively) among the world's big rivers, and second of its kind in Europe, over 500 miles shorter than the Volga. Three of the world's biggest rivers, the Nile, the Amazon, and the Mississippi-Missouri, are over twice as long as the Danube. The total area of the Danube Basin, estimated at 315,000 square miles, a scant 50,000 square miles bigger than Texas, is small compared with the basins of the giants from Africa and America; and yet the Danube and its basin have witnessed the rise and fall of more empires, cultures, and social forms than the basins of larger rivers have seen. Central Europe is a congested area. Rivers, like people, cannot expand in space, yet they can compress events into a thimble.

CHAPTER TWO

When did man first appear on the Danubian scene? Whence did he come? What were his looks, his ways?

It is sometimes claimed that members of the family Hominidae roamed the Danube Basin during the interglacial period. Adherents to another theory insist that the basin was still uninhabitable during that period and that man came only afterward. But all agree that the oldest calling card left by humans in the Danube Basin was found in the Croatian section. It is a jawbone which enthusiastic archaeologists excavated from thick layers of sand and described as evidence of a prehistoric culture.

Some believe that the earliest human arrivals in the Danube region came from southwestern Asia, possibly even from the site of Paradise. But the fossil jaw cannot establish either the origin of the species or the fact that its defunct owner had anything that could be called culture. Still others contend that the first men to arrive in the Danube Basin were fugitives from wide areas spreading over much of the continent, refugees from the most fantastic invasion of all times: the march of giant forests. In the early Neolithic period the previously cold climate had turned warm and humid. Valleys and hills had become heavily timbered. Forests overgrew steppes and fields. They grew ever thicker until not even the heaviest stone axes could cut paths through the murderous wilderness in which nothing else could grow, nothing breathe. Creatures that had not fled the forest in time were doomed to extinction.

Instinct must have told many to flee for survival, and with the panicky humans a host of beasts must have fled, mammoths, woolly rhinoceroses, and lions among them. Their flesh provided food, their bones the material for weapons with which men hunted their mighty prey after reaching open spaces. Such spaces were found in the Danube Basin. There, thanks to large formations of loess, the retreating glaciers were not completely superseded by timber. Loess is a fine-grained soil generated by wind-borne dust. Grass pushing its shoots through the soil makes it so porous that it does not allow water to stand on, or close underneath, the surface, and even though it is cultivable it does not favor the excessive growth of forests.

On the Danubian loess fugitive creatures could roam and dwell without fear of aggressive vegetation. They were isolated in their havens during the lifetime of many a generation. Then the climate changed again; the Atlantic period was superseded by the subboreal epoch. Precipitation decreased; winters grew cold; summer temperatures, though well above the present average, became bearable; forests thinned; large new areas became inhabitable. It was as if another Great Flood had been receding. Previously isolated creatures began to roam again and apparently to communicate with one another. Danubian dwellers moved across the Alps and the Balkans and established contact with the people of Middle Eastern lands. These wanderings and meetings are not recorded in a manner that would permit flowery accounts or learned computations. Yet there must have been some kind of barter that preceded conquest by a long time.

Some of those Danubian trader-explorers seem to have come from the region in which, tens of thousands of years later, Vienna was built. About thirty miles southeast of the site of that city, near Winden in Burgenland province, human bones were found in caves which also must have had a population of bears. The bones date back to the Paleozoic period, between 50,000 and 20,000 B.C.

During the 10,000 years that followed the Paleozoic, man turned artistic. His earliest preserved work of art was named the Venus of Willendorf after the village of Willendorf on the Danube, a scant sixty miles from Vienna, where it was found. There exists yet another Willendorf, fifty-odd miles south of the river. Its luminaries insist that the Venus is theirs, but there is no substance to their claim to the small figure of clay, which is infinitely older than the cult of the goddess, much older than the earliest figurines excavated in Asia.

The Willendorf figurine shows crude hands clasping sacklike breasts, towering above a ball-shaped belly and fat buttocks. The females of the Danube Valley, vintage 10,000 B.C. or thereabouts, may have been hefty, uncouth specimens, but there are indications that they did not quite resemble the Willendorf monster. An ancient burial place was discovered two hundred miles downstream. Skulls show a tendency to brachycephalism (short-headedness), eyebrow ridges protrude heavily; but chins, ears, noses, and throats must have been well developed. Crude Neanderthal features are relatively few, and skeletons indicate that the people had been rather tall and reasonably well proportioned. Learned anthropologists found them to be a crossbreed of Neanderthal and Cro-Magnon stock. The same anthropologists noted that the crossbreeds were cannibals, to judge from charred human bones that were found north of the central river valley; and that they must have been fearless, since they did not dwell only in caves, but also in open, unprotected settlements.

After 10,000 B.C. man-made disaster visited the Danube Valley. It must have been preceded by a wave of fear spread by means of communication that defy the imagination. Men left the open settlements, retreated to caves or lake dwellings, but evidently could not find adequate protection. Eventually they vanished without leaving a trace.

The vacuum defies historians' attempts to find an explanation. Novelists have ignored the topic. But the French scientist Salomon Reinach advances the theory of a destructive invasion of the continent from the east and of a campaign of extinction in which an Aurignacian type of

Homo sapiens annihilated its counterparts. The means of destruction they seem to have used must appear ridiculously ineffective as compared with later weapons. But they achieved what not even prophets of gloom and doom through radiation visualized as the result of atomic warfare: for about seven thousand years Danubian men were practically extinct, and as if by an act of sublime justice the invaders too perished almost at once.

The vanquished had found no place to hide, not even in the caves of the Bükk Mountains north of the Hungarian Danube, which they had turned into the strongest of their kind anywhere: several stories high and, by modern standards, bombproof. The defeated cave dwellers of the Bükk Mountains were skillful in more than one respect. They also manufactured thin-shelled pottery, highly artistic in design.

When under mysterious circumstances men resurged to the Danube Basin, some built solid homes in which they lived together with their cattle, sheep, hogs, and dogs. They were farmers, miners, and craftsmen.

Teutsch, László, and Dólgozok tell of an ancient village rediscovered in the Transylvanian section of the river basin:

"The site was protected by deep ditches dug into friable soil. The biggest ditch formed a moat, surrounding an area of approximately two acres. The settlement was also protected by a double line of earthworks, reinforced by stakes. Oval pits excavated in the soil may have served as silos. The dwellings were rectangular two-room houses. One room constituted a porch with an open front; the other had no aperture and its ceiling was about nine inches higher than that of the porch. Floors were made of clay stamped on the bare ground, into which no foundations were dug. Roofs seem to have been gabled. Stout posts of timber supported the construction, which had a base of about four hundred square feet.

"[It] consisted of three rows of seven houses each. The villagers apparently loved finery, to judge from bracelets and necklaces of copper and trifles made of bears' and stags' teeth that were found; and they did some weaving, as shown by the discovery of humps of baked clay and clay disks that must have been used as loom weights and spindle whorls. Also, their aesthetic inclinations found outlets not only in making artistic pottery but also, as archaeologists presume, in tattooing their bodies."

Modern Hungarians, though evidently not ethnically related to the tattooed villagers, are proud of this indigenous culture which flourished nearly four thousand years ago. But objectors to such retrospective local patriotism call this architecture an import from the high civilizations which originated in Mesopotamia, where somewhat similar finds have been made.

A legend, built around these discoveries, has it that highly civilized men from Asia Minor went to the lower Danube: fugitives from Troy!

Homer says nothing about the Danube, nothing about any distant big river. The Danube did not bear that name when Helen enchanted and divided her world. But fable has it that, after the Greeks entered the city by deceit, most of its population perished by sword and fire, but that remnants fled. Aeneas, a son of Aphrodite, saved his idol, his father, and his son, and together with a band of Trojans, fled. After adventure and romance galore Aeneas reached Latium on the Tyrrhenian Sea, where he married King Latinus' daughter Lavinia. Eventually his offspring founded the city of Rome.

Latium is far away from the Danube Valley. How could fugitive Trojans have reached the Danube?

Apparently not all of Aeneas' men had stayed with him. One group at least must have left him before he did his heroic-romantic sight-seeing. They wandered north, through the Balkan mountains and valleys, to reach the Ister—the earliest recorded name of the lower Danube. The time of their arrival should have been the thirteenth or fourteenth century B.C. The conquest and the sacking of the ancient city of palaces and temples that was Troy by a Prince of Mycenae, which is the factual background of Homer's epic poem, occurred during that period; the locale of the fugitives' settlement could have been what is now the Yugoslavian part of the Danube Basin.

There idols were found: women's figures with birds' heads made of clay, as Heinrich Schliemann, the German-born American-naturalized discoverer and student of Homeric sites, attributes to Athena Glaucopis, and also strange "carrousels" of clay like the ones that were excavated in the vicinity of the ruins of Troy.

However, there also are reasons to doubt that Trojans who deserted Aeneas actually reached the Danube. The figures of clay may have gotten there from Greece in a most trivial way: as merchandise or souvenirs acquired by roving traders.

Even before Helen's time Thracian and Thraco-Illyrians from the Balkans and the Alps bartered copper from their wealthy mines for products of western Asiatic and Greek handicraft. Yet lovers of Danubian lore prefer to dream of homeless Trojans gazing into the waters of the river, hoping to see a nymph with the features and limbs of Helen rise to the surface.

Thracians and Thraco-Illyrians were people of relatively high culture. They would not have found the Venus of Willendorf to their liking. They hailed from the Balkans but were in no way related to the Slavic Balkanians, who were not yet in existence when the ancient residents of their lands admired, if not adored, the likenesses of Greek goddesses.

Illyrians exploited copper mines and used tin, antimony, and salt. They even used gold that was found north of the lower Danube. Their language was but incompletely transmitted; its vocabulary may have been scant, but it contained one key word, the extended use of which indicates that their land was vast: *hal*, meaning "salt." *Hall* stood for "salt" also in the faraway northwestern Danube Valley, in the present province of Upper Austria, where salt was, and has remained, a most important item of local production.

The little town of Hallstatt, after which a cultural period is named, is a site on which salt is found. Hallstatt is a few score miles south of the Danube. The Hallstatt period, which marks a period of human life near the Danube, dawned around 1000 B.C., when iron came into use and bronze was relegated to the manufacture of ornaments and jewelry. The early bearers of the Hallstatt culture were Thraco-Illyrians, even though local saga has it that their ethnic origin was Celtic.

A naïve mural and an inscription two miles west of Hallstatt, both of recent origin, tell of an alleged Celtic Prince, Ra Ingo, who had his residence there around 2800 B.C. and whose bones are said to be in the Hallstatt museum. If this is true Ra Ingo would have been the earliest royalty in the Danube Basin. The mural shows him as a muscular savage rather than a prince of the blood. But the story of Ra Ingo is highly unbelievable, as the Celts did not bow on the stage of history until two thousand years later.

The Hallstatt period was one of opulence, mercantilism, and industry —the golden age of the ancient Danube Basin. Amber, probably imported from the Baltic, and sea shells typical of the Mediterranean area were found in tombs together with objects of art and finery. And, most significant for a truly golden era, almost no weapons were found. The mining of salt, copper, iron, and gold in this sequence of economic importance was carried out on a scale which must have been prodigious considering the number of people who lived there and the simple tools they used.

Did the miners of prosperous Hallstatt and the regions beyond have a social system, a hierarchy, castes of rulers and priests? No traces of castles are left, no paraphernalia of grandeur. Was theirs a co-operative society? In mining there must be organized co-operation. But the prosperous people left no inscriptions to tell of their social achievements.

Hallstatt prosperity lasted for over five centuries and its foundation was peace.

Then came the Celts. Their culture was characterized by warriordom. With them war returned to the Danube Basin and has stayed there, with brief intermissions, ever since.

After establishing themselves in westernmost Europe the undaunted Celts entered the Swiss Alps, turned up near the present town of La Tène, after which their culture was named, proceeded into the South German plains, then went along the Danube down to the Balkans and also across the Alps well into Italy. They were a nation on the march and the number of their elite fighting men is estimated at one hundred thousand.

The writings of Herodotus, "the Father of History," tell of a river, Istrols, running through the lands of the Celts. This was the Danube. Herodotus also mentions Prene, a city on the river, without, however, elaborating on its location. These writings cover the period around 425 B.C. Celts from the Danube successively served as mercenaries in the forces of Macedonia, Rome, and even western Asia. Their Princes and Kings were army commanders in war and figureheads between campaigns. They were chosen by their men and could be deposed if they did not perform to their electorate's satisfaction. A Roman ambassador quoted a Celtic King as saying: "The masses hold as much power over me as I hold over them." This sounded distasteful to the Roman *Imperatores*, who refused to consider such rulers as either *Imperator* or *Rex*. Later Julius Caesar found what he considered a fitting name for them: *Principatus*.

The Thraco-Illyrians of the Danube Valley did not wage open battle against the Celts. This would have been hopeless. Instead they withdrew into the deep valleys of the Alps.

For a few centuries Celts and the Celtic social order dominated practically the entire Danube Valley.

Even though the "masses" held power over the *Principatus,* the tribal Celtic system was oligarchical in nature: a rule by the privileged few.

The highest-ranking of these few were magistrates (*equites*), who could hale anybody into their courts and mete out Draconian punishment at their discretion.

The next social stratum was the nobles, men of wealth who did not hold office but controlled groups of commoners, who were freemen yet subject to their masters' orders.

Slaves, of which there were many, were practically outlaws. They were traded like cattle and whenever their owner died several of them served as fuel at the funeral pyre of the defunct. The Romans later purchased Celtic slaves because they were industrious and inexpensive: half a gallon of wine for one able-bodied youth.

Above the mundane Celtic dignitaries towered the Druids, the caste of the all-powerful, arrogant priests who often scorned the decisions taken by popular assemblies and defied the military.

Women played a weighty role in Celtic public life. They accompanied their men into war and intervened in their quarrels. A French historian tells of a Celtic lady who engaged in fisticuffs with her husband's opponent and mauled him rather badly. Women were appointed arbiters in litigation between Celtic men and their allies. Women's decisions even affected matters of soldierly discipline. But influential as the women were, the fathers wielded all power over their offspring. A father could have his children burned or drowned if they incurred his displeasure, and he did not have to give a reason. Children had to respect him as a superior being. It was a damnable offense for any boy of pre-military age to appear in public without his father and a capital crime to speak without his father's permission.

All along the Danube the Celtic newborn were dipped into the always cold, and occasionally icy, waters. This was neither a purge nor a form of baptism, but a means of making sure that only the strong would survive.

Men killed in battle were not buried. They were cremated only in periods of epidemics. Otherwise vultures, of which there were many in most parts of Europe, feasted on the corpses of Celtic soldiers.

However, non-military funerals of nobles were most elaborate. The bodies were burned on pyres until the charred remnants had shrunk to the size of the dead man's sword, and with them was burned whatever he had considered his most prized possessions: weapons, household utensils, jewelry—and faithful slaves.

"Tumuli," Celtic sepulchral mounds, are found in all parts of the Danube Valley down to the Balkans. Early conquerors left them untouched. Only later archaeologists removed their contents.

Though the Celts ruled a large part of Europe, they could not organize a single empire, but remained divided into several kingdoms. One of them was known as Noricum, its capital was Noreja, and its original boundaries included what is now Lower Austria and practically all of Styria province. The capital city, said to have had a population of nearly one hundred thousand, was located about a hundred miles south of the Danube.

Danubian Celts from Noricum may have played a part in the near conquest of Rome by the Celtic Gauls, in 387–86 B.C., when only the Capitol remained in Roman hands.

The painful contact established between the Romans and their neighbors eventually led to the Roman march into Gaul, Germany, and the Danubian lands.

The Celts left a biological trace of their Roman campaign in parts of the Italian peninsula, where the population has retained some distinct Celtic features. The Romans, in turn, not only left an imprint upon Celtic features but also influenced the Celts' religious cult and eventually established themselves in Celtic lands. All this turned the Danube into an object of adoration and the background of many Celtic sagas, traces of which are left in runic inscriptions. Celtic gods were said to have risen from the sea and reached the lands of their worshipers by way of great rivers. The Danube was the greatest of them.

One hero of Celtic saga was Dithpater ("Dith" standing for death and destruction). Dithpater was unconquerable, could destroy or spare all creatures as he chose. Death was unconquerable. The Celts measured elapsed time in nights, not in days. Elapsed time was dark and dead, and belonged to Dithpater, who lived above and beyond time.

The Celts did believe in life after death. Sacrifices of human beings, therefore, were considered a fair price the victims had to pay for another life. Later, when the Romans came to rule along the Danube, they were anxious to interfere as little as possible with the local religious practices. Yet they looked askance at the brutish cults. In 97 B.C. a Roman law forbade religious human sacrifices. But twenty-two years later Cicero decried the continuation of the murderous customs in Celtic territory, and more than one century after Cicero, Cornelius Tacitus, antiquity's roving reporter, deplored the neighbors' habit of flooding altars with human blood.

There were exceptions to the barbaric rule of cultic procedure, when a potential victim could afford to bribe the priests. Instead of cutting the victim's throat, the Druids would inflict a minor injury upon him, just enough to stain the altar with some blood, and instead of him they burned a carved log, presuming that the flame was bright enough to please the gods. The victim looked on, as hired bards sang the praises of his devotion and steadfastness.

The Celtic bards were on good terms with the Druids, who appreciated their influence on public opinion. Those bards were the spiritual ancestors of the minnesingers in the Danube Basin. They not only edified and entertained the people, but also were the distributors of news and of praise and censure. They could create and bolster, shake and destroy, beliefs or reputations. The Druids were mindful of their personal reputations so that they might be called in on legal deals among important personalities, including financial transactions. It was one of the Druids' tricks to make debts payable after the creditor's demise, provided, of course, their own fat fee was paid promptly.

The bards eulogized everybody whom they found it otherwise profitable to cajole in a pompous singsong to the accompaniment of the lyre. Bards accompanied the armies to tell of their victories; they praised the Druids for their alleged achievements in the fields of strategy and tactics. The Druids watched the flight of birds to determine the direction of the marching column; they scrutinized the intestines of sacrificial humans and animals to learn what was essential to win battles. Praise of the Druids involved certain risks, however. Although they were exempt from military service, bards who acclaimed wrong prophecies often were drafted and fared badly in the ranks.

As Celtic power slackened, the mighty Romans flocked into the vacuum. In 16 B.C. Noricum became Roman. The Roman eagle spread its wings over what is now Tyrol, Salzburg, Upper and Lower Austria, Styria, and Carinthia. From Noricum the legions marched into the future Hungarian plains, a region of what they called Pannonia. Within a single decade Rome controlled most of Central Europe and its eastern outposts.

Romans were the harbingers of law and culture, though they still retained a refined and glorified paganism. But around 32 A.D. into that world of idolatry, superstition, and corruption came a message of pure faith, a lone spark that did not kindle the light, yet was the first seed of the gospel.

It came through a message from Claudia Procula, wife of Pontius Pilate, to Livia, her former companion, who had married an officer stationed in Carnuntum, on the Danube.

In this message the distressed Claudia disclosed the essence of a strange dream: "The Kingdom of Heaven is like unto a certain King who made a marriage for his son. . . . Then shall the Kingdom of Heaven be likened unto ten virgins who took their lamps and went forth to meet the bridegroom. . . . For the Kingdom of Heaven is a man traveling into a far country who called his own servants and delivered unto them his goods. . . . And the King shall answer and say unto them: Inasmuch as ye have done it unto one of the least of these my brethren ye have done it unto me. . . . And call no man your father upon earth, for one is your father who is in heaven . . ."

But what Claudia had said to Pontius Pilate had been in vain. The just man was crucified, but Claudia Procula could find no rest, no consolation henceforth.

Livia did not understand the meaning of the dream, nor the many things her former mistress had suffered because of Jesus Christ. She could not spread the gospel of the Redeemer. She was a typical proud Roman of her day who believed in the Empire and its institutions. Like many Roman matrons, she had a longing taste for oriental mysticism; but it is one of the many sublime mysteries of faith that the earliest manifestation of Christendom in the Danubian lands, almost unnoticed when it came, was never quite forgotten.

CHAPTER THREE

Carnuntum, where Livia lived, was the first purely Roman city along the Danube, the early point of gravity of a strategic administrative and communications system as that part of the world had not previously known.

The Roman Republic, which had built Rome into a super power, was superseded by Imperial rule. In 26 B.C. Carnuntum came into existence. Never was a strategic location more competently selected.

The site of the new town dominated the gap between the Alps and the northwestern Carpathians. It was a springboard for invasion in two main directions and also a bulwark against aggression. From Carnuntum, Roman administrators could centrally govern the many scattered nations which had come, and kept coming, under Roman sway. The Romans gave the foreigners good government, better government than they had ever had before, and they exploited their skills and economic resources in a manner profitable to both sides.

Carnuntum became the preferred headquarters of Roman military commanders, the center of inland navigation, and a show place where startled visitors from primitive lands had ample opportunity to see Roman might, architecture, and entertainment at its most impressive.

The town, twenty-six miles east of the present site of Vienna, was built entirely of stone. Its fortifications were as solid as the walls of the Roman capital, its circus could accommodate several thousand spectators, its baths were voluptuous, its temples imposing. In Carnuntum, Roman soldiers, officials, and traders lived—as only the Romans could live—with leisurely magnificence and sensuous pomp that struck their neighbors with awe.

The Romans had conceived the plan of establishing themselves in the Danube Valley long before the Republic came to an end, at a time when Celtic soldiery still roamed the Po Valley. Methodical as they were, the first step in a grandiose program of Roman expansion was road construction.

The art of Roman road construction remained unequaled until the advent of the automobile. The roads led over mountain passes, some of them mile-high. They not only linked settlements but also established them. There was one antique superhighway which on its last lap connected the Alpine foothills with Carnuntum. The builders called it Via Vindomina. Shortly before reaching its terminal it passed near dilapidated shacks forming a Celtic settlement, a place without distinction, without established tradition: a region in which various peoples may have been from time immemorial, but in which only a few clans vegetated when the road was built. The Romans first called the spot after the road: Vindomina. A Roman auxiliary garrison which later set up camp there mangled the name into Vindobona, and eventually Vindobona became Wien—Vienna.

The Danube Valley bristled with Roman garrisons. Noricum, Upper and Lower Moesia (which roughly extended from the present Yugoslav banks down to the delta region), Dacia (on the Rumanian side), and Pannonia constituted the main military districts.

A total of six legions guarded the lower Danube; four legions were stationed roughly between present Budapest and Vienna, but garrisons upstream, including the Bavarian course of the river, were relatively small—a total of thirteen cohorts, seventy-eight hundred men. However, the unreliability of Germanic neighbors and the restlessness of many other tribes caused the Roman command to keep strong mobile units close at hand in thinly garrisoned areas.

Roman legions numbered from forty-six hundred to six thousand men. They included all services: infantry, cavalry, and artillery, the last's equipment consisting of siege machines, like battering-rams, as well as ballistae that could be used in open battle.

Encamped Roman units were residents of villages or towns, according to their size. They had their own laws, which were Rome's, their own solidly built houses, their sanitary installations; they also had stadiums and places of worship.

Roman soldiers, a goodly percentage of whom were well-trained enlisted foreigners, did not usually live with their families. The government frowned upon military family life as detrimental to fighting trim, and even legion commanders found it difficult to take their wives to their garrison towns. But civil servants assigned to outlying provinces would receive permission to have their families join them.

Soldiers and officials were free to associate with the local populace, and since the Romans were often good-looking and always had money to spare for presents which native women coveted, nobody had to lead a life of chastity. Native women swarmed around the Roman settlements, and if ethnologists were to search the genealogical tree of later "Nordic-minded" *homines Danubienses,* they would often find a Roman military root amidst other roots of bewildering variety from all parts of the world, from wherever military men came to the Danube Basin.

The local males probably did not relish the affection of their women for the Romans. There must have been brawls, but no Danubian Helen ever sent the armies of a Pannonian Agamemnon rolling toward Rome. The local people of the higher strata did profitable business with the Romans, which may have compensated husbands for the infidelity of their wives. The soldiers were no agriculturists, but heavy consumers of food. Suppliers grew prosperous. And, under the protection of the garrisons, traders from wide and far flocked into the Danube Valley. Wares were attractive; business was brisk. As long as the Romans controlled the Danube Basin commercial relations between tribes and nations were close, and even when the great avalanche of the Migration of Peoples and the southward rush of the barbarians almost drowned ancient culture, commercial traditions survived and economic relations were eventually resumed.

Prior to the Romans' arrival the natives had little knowledge of navigation. Hollowed-out tree trunks were about the only river craft they used. But Rome, at the peak of its might, built a mighty river flotilla on the Danube.

The capital Roman river boats were the so-called *liturni,* with crews of about seventy-five. They were solid craft, essentially like smaller warships used in the coastal waters of the Mediterranean: two deckers rowed by chained slaves, manned by infantry, armed with bows, arrows, javelins, spears, and short swords, and by a few catapults to hurl glowing balls at the enemy. The men carried protective armor, the ships were covered with thick sheets of hide and woolen cloth soaked in vinegar to make them fireproof.

The Roman Danube navy totaled one hundred twenty-five *liturni* and one hundred auxiliary vessels. Forty *liturni* patrolled the Black Sea coast near the delta.

River bases not only included solid harbors, of which Carnuntum was the foremost, but also castle–strong points built in pairs—*castrum* and *anticastrum*—to block the passage if necessary.

The costs of this formidable establishment were high. Special levies kept it powerful, but the taxes were a good investment for everyone concerned, since Danubian commerce and fishing were based on safe Roman control of the waters. The Roman Danube flotilla was not allowed to become obsolete. Ships were automatically replaced after seven years of service.

Only toward the end of the fourth century A.D., when Rome itself seemed doomed, was the river armada abandoned. Ships were left to rot. Crews were hopelessly demoralized; they deserted in numbers, taking along whatever they could carry.

Ostrogoths, Alani, Gepidae, Huns, and Avars entered the Danube Basin. They crossed the river on the backs of their swimming horses or on inflated sacks of hide or on small craft built by slaves and Romanized prisoners of war. Nobody interfered with their river crossings.

Much later Charlemagne had another fleet built, but his power and that of his realm did not last long enough to turn the Danube again into a secure shipping lane. Never again, not even in the days of the Austro-Hungarian Empire, was the big river so securely protected as it had been in antiquity.

Cornelius Tacitus credits the Germans with shipbuilding skills, but there is no evidence of early German boat construction along the Danube.

In fact, Tacitus indicates that the Germans of whom he writes exerted their naval talents far up north, in Scandinavia. Germanic nations, tribes, and hordes were not among the earliest arrivals in the Danube Basin. They originated in Denmark, Sweden, Norway, and possibly also in the vicinity of the Black Sea. They penetrated into Central Europe. They deposed, expropriated, and enslaved less militant men. Many a Celtic group, faced with the pressure of invasion, again retreated into the Alps and into the Bavarian forelands.

When the Romans fortified the Danube line, Germanic Marcomanni and Quadi reached the Austrian and Hungarian parts of the river. Further to the west their kin had already met the Romans: they had parleyed with officers and administrators from Rome. They made pacts which gave them comfortable living space, and alliances which they did not always keep, but which were advantageous to them.

The Romans, confident in their own superiority in the fields of state-craft and soldierdom, felt that no harm could befall them from such arrangements and that the newcomers would eventually turn into a valuable asset.

Rome needed men. It controlled an immense territory. People of Roman stock numbered no more than about six million, and some one hundred twenty million were needed as the lifeblood of the Empire. The Germans seemed to be a welcome addition to human resources.

When the Marcomanni and Quadi requested an allotment of land, authorities from Carnuntum responded favorably, but asked that bondsmen should not be put to hard work and even suggested that they be freed. The question of slavery became an apple of discord between the Romans and the Germans.

When they were on the move the Germans often formed groups of a thousand soldiers accompanied by their families and, for fighting purposes, subdivided into well-disciplined units of one hundred each. In times of war family life was completely neglected. When the fighting subsided, military rule gradually became less rigid; when people settled, the clan superseded the military unit and family life assumed a normal pattern.

The land on which they settled was common property, subject to administration by district leaders, who allotted plots to clans. Agriculture was primitive; cattle breeding and hunting were the main sources of livelihood. As herds grew, allotted pasture lands became insufficient and, forced with the choice of either improving their farming or moving on to vaster pastures, the ancient Germans usually preferred to move. Moving usually led to tribal warfare.

Their society was divided into four classes: nobles, freemen, bondsmen, and serfs.

The serfs were mostly prisoners of war, used for hard menial work; if needed for the army they were "promoted" to bondsmen, who, in times of peace, were made to till their masters' lands and had to pay taxes out of their meager wages. The freemen constituted the bulk of the people and the rank and file of the army; from their ranks came the National Assembly, which nominally held supreme power of government, even under royal rule. The nobles were a hereditary aristocracy—district leaders, generals, priests—who held all offices; the Council of Princes was a major policy-shaping body.

The National Assembly was convened only when King or nobles deemed it advisable, and it voted as told. To defy a directive would have been both mutiny and heresy. The agenda could include the impeachment of a prince or even a King, which was tantamount to his dispossession and execution. Motions did not originate with the rank and file; they were preceded by feuds among the mighty, and when one clique felt strong enough to attain its objective it had the Assembly convoked and stirred up violent passions which turned the session into a show. Priests and princes harangued the crowd until it was intoxicated with enthusiasm, wrath, devotion, and vengefulness, which produced the sort of guided *furor Teutonicus* which has surged up intermittently through the ages.

When the Germanic warriors encountered peoples with advanced farming methods, they remained unimpressed by plows. They considered walking behind them below the dignity of a freeman. They did not think that cattle should be put to work in the fields either. This was a task reserved for inferior humans: women, slaves, and men unfit for military service, who had to work the soil with hooks of stone, while able-bodied men brawled, hunted, idled, or caroused.

The Romans first found Germanic troops to be poorly equipped. Armor and helmets were scarce. The common soldiers wore hoods of fur or leather. The early principal weapon was a javelin. Swords were introduced only later, as were the *bardas,* battle-axes. Yet the warriors were extremely proud of their modernized armament and they occasionally called themselves after the arms. *Sahs,* the term for "sword," gave the Saxons their name, and the *barda* gave the Langobards theirs.

The Marcomanni and Quadi were the largest Germanic nation the Romans had yet encountered. Usually, Germanic tribes kept apart. They preferred to live within natural borders, such as mountains, densely wooded areas, and great rivers. When such boundaries did not exist they would even devastate entire regions to put a desert zone between themselves and their neighbors. Kings and princes often tried to expand their rule over other people and tribes, but the people themselves had no use for unification.

The Germanic nation that first arrived at the Roman outposts when Carnuntum was new and the Danube fleet was growing with imposing strength, had formed during a long trek from the region of the Main, in central Germany, into Bohemia and Moravia, then due south into Upper and Lower Austria, and beyond into the Hungarian lands. Fighting and pillaging as they moved, the roving tribes had been welded by ambitious leaders into the nation of the Marcomanni, who, in turn, absorbed the Quadi. No chronicler has recorded the details of this strange, cumbersome process. It must have been based on perverted laws of gravity and accompanied by numerous intrigues, conspiracies, and acts of violence. The growth of the marching nation did not take Roman legion and river-fleet commanders by surprise, however. They had been watching it through an intricate intelligence service for several years. They knew that King Katwalda, the supreme leader, who had had only two thousand soldiers when he first became the object of Roman attention, had a force of forty thousand as he closed in on the Danube.

Katwalda must have heard of Carnuntum before he actually laid eyes upon the stronghold on the river, but the sight probably defied his power of imagination. The vast buildings seemed like rocks tamed by men, unscrutable machines like tools of titans, stronger than Germanic deities. His urge to destruction was paralyzed by fear and admiration.

Roman generals met the bewildered King with patronizing friendliness; they seemed to know all about him and his princes and priests; they were critical about the abuse of slaves but seemed inclined to want to live in peace with the newcomers. Katwalda was pleased. He did not realize that he was a doomed man.

The Roman dignitaries had studied reports on the Germanic hierarchy and found that Prince Marbod was a more adaptable tool than the King. Marbod had the makings of a glorified playboy, a German who could be shaped into a Roman patrician. Marbod was invited to a gala performance in the stadium of Carnuntum; as he witnessed the spectacle he was asked to come to Rome as a guest of the government. The German was so anxious to visit the fabulous city which, as he had been told, was a thousand times more spectacular than Carnuntum that he did not even return to his camp but traveled right on, along a highway such as he had never seen before, to the heart of the Empire, the center of a world whose vastness and splendor he could hardly grasp.

The Romans were not only builders, soldiers, and statesmen; they also were superb propagandists. Marbod witnessed a constant display of might, splendor, and marvels of organization. It convinced him that fulfillment of a nobleman's wishes could be found only in Rome, and that Rome would last forever.

In Rome, he became familiar with the delights and refinements of superior culture, and he fully conceived the lust of power that went with refinement. The crude prince from the Far North was intoxicated by the voluptuousness of Rome, by its wines, women, and shows, long before his hosts considered him ready for political and military indoctrination.

Marbod was not the only Germanic Prince who was the guest of the city of marvels. Also present were Arminius and Flavius, both Cherusci, both already commissioned generals in the Roman army, both emphasizing their everlasting fealty to Rome. But while Flavius never broke his pledge and stayed in Rome until his death, Arminius went home and turned traitor to the Romans in the legendary ambush battle in the Teutoburg forests.

Marbod was not supposed to stay in Rome forever. After a period of unrestrained indulgence, he was subjected to a thorough training in the military and political fields, trained for a royal career under the wings of the Roman eagle. He was made to proclaim an alliance between his people and Rome before Imperial authorities and deities; and he made the pledge with such enthusiasm that most attending functionaries were convinced of his reliability.

One man was not convinced however: Tiberius, the up-and-coming man of the Empire, the later *Imperator,* then still an army commander. To Tiberius, Marbod was a barbarian and, like all barbarians, a faithless, corrupt debaucher. He would have preferred to teach the Marcomanni and Quadi a harsh military lesson rather than turn them into allies by intrigue and diplomacy. Political responsibility in the Empire, however, still rested with the civilians in the capital, and the army commander's aversion did not stop Marbod's career.

The indoctrinated, sworn-in Prince was politely coaxed into returning home to the banks of the Danube, where the stage had been set for his supreme promotion. Experts from Carnuntum had staged a plot against Katwalda, which materialized as soon as Marbod arrived. Bribed princes and priests enforced the convocation of a National Assembly.

Katwalda was impeached on trumped-up, ill-defined charges. The furor of the voting plebs hit the boiling point and in the general hubbub Katwalda disappeared. The wirepullers were satisfied that he had been thrown into the river.

Marbod raised his people's army to a full seventy thousand—roughly the numerical equivalent of all Roman forces in the Danube Valley. Tiberius, in charge of the Roman garrisons there, put his legions on the alert. Marbod did not turn traitor and showed no inclination to mutiny.

The alert of the Roman legions, however, turned into a blessing. A furious revolt broke out in the Danube region from east of Carnuntum down to the Sava, the first recorded great popular uprising against a controlling foreign power that occurred in the land that was to be Hungary. The peoples and tribes who thrust themselves into the teeth of the Roman high-precision war machine were a blend of Illyrians of Balkanic origin, of Greeks, of Celtic groups, and possibly of people from Middle Eastern nations.

Only sketchy Roman accounts of the rebellion are available. The number of hostile natives must have been quite large. A few Roman outposts were overrun, their occupants cut to pieces, their equipment captured; but the captors could not operate the artillery and abandoned part of their booty. The rebels obviously planned to form massive armies, but their organization was inadequate and Roman alertness paid high dividends. The legions rallied after the impact of the first shock. No major Roman strong point was lost.

The Danube, lazily flowing through the fertile plains, with an occasional idyllic mirage shining on the eastern horizon, from where other conquerors would later emerge, turned into the natives' worst enemy. The Imperial flotilla barred the passage of the rebels, and its missiles destroyed their settlements along the river and kept them away from their fishing grounds. Starvation and fire raged and the help which the natives may have expected from Germans in the West and Dacians in the East did not come. The revolt died, smothered in blood and despair.

A few years went by. Arminius' treachery triumphed in the Teutoburg forests. Rome, still celebrating the restoration of peace in the Danube Basin, which was attributed to Tiberius, received the news of the disaster in Germany with alarm, if not panic. The Emperor's bodyguards, recruited from the finest physical specimens of Germanic auxiliaries, were replaced by men of more reliable origin. Rumors told of a Germanic invasion across the Alps. Actually, Arminius did not once throw his forces against the natural barrier. Tiberius regained the initiative, assem-

bled eight legions, and restored Roman rule in the crucial areas. The
threat of invasion faded, and one year after the disaster the Empire
could breathe again.

Arminius did not even attempt to make peace with the Empire; Rome
could never forget or forgive a betrayal that could have had contagious
effects on other subject nations. *Imperator* Tiberius sought his revenge.
He ordered his nephew Germanicus to pursue the Cherusci deep into
their wild land of origin, and to destroy their power of aggression forever. The campaign lasted from 11 A.D. to 16 A.D. For almost four years
Arminius evaded a major battle. Temporarily he succeeded in inciting
other Germanic tribes to raid Roman supply lines, but eventually Germanicus forced him to fight. Arminius was defeated and fled.

Imperator Tiberius had a score to settle. The civilians had made
Marbod a King against his will. Now that he wielded absolute power
he wanted to avenge the slur. He had known all the time that Katwalda
had not been drowned, but had fled, and lived in the land of the Goths
as a man of means and prestige. Tiberius had political agents in Gothic
territory who reported that Katwalda was ready to go to every extreme
of gratitude if Rome would help him regain his kingdom. This help was
granted and money was sent to hire Gothic mercenaries. Roman intriguers incited Marcomanni nobles to plot against Marbod. In 18 A.D.
Katwalda's men crossed the border and Marbod's Princes rose. Still, the
admirer of Rome could not believe that he was forsaken. He sent an
urgent call for help to Tiberius. Tiberius' reply was scathing: Had not
Marbod defaulted on his own obligations by not actively fighting Arminius? He should no longer consider himself Rome's ally.

In 19 A.D. Katwalda was again master of the Marcomanni and Quadi.
A hapless Marbod presented himself and a small band of bewildered
adherents at a Roman outpost on the Danube in quest of asylum. He was
admitted and so were his faithful. But Marbod was not allowed to stay
with them. Tiberius had him confined to Ravenna, where the ex-King
lived on, for a full eighteen years, in comfort and bewilderment, as an
Imperial pensioner.

His followers were settled on the Roman (right) bank of the Danube,
where they soon were joined by King Katwalda's faithful.

Rome acted toward Katwalda according to the Empire's golden maxim,
"Divide and rule." It did not want the restored King to become too
strong, so it fanned the blaze of feuds and rivalries among the Germanic
Princes who began to build palaces along the left bank of the Danube.
Roman officials and officers from Carnuntum and from budding Vienna

hinted that Marbod might be returned from retirement and be restored to the throne. Factions formed. Civil war broke out. The Romans proclaimed a policy of non-interference. Katwalda lost all but his life. He, too, asked for asylum. The Romans sent him to distant Forum Julii (the present Fréjus) and assigned small enough plots of land to his men on the left bank of the Danube.

Vannius, a semi-Romanized Marcoman, became Katwalda's successor. He ruled over a buffer state established to protect the Danubian lands against barbaric raiders from the north and east. Vannius became the first native nabob in these parts of the continent. He concentrated on amassing riches. Instead of having his soldiers keep barbaric invaders away, he staged raids beyond his country's borders to rob and to steal whatever valuables he could find. And he imposed staggering taxes upon his subjects, who had no share in the loot.

The riches Vannius gathered had a strange effect on him. Had he lived in Rome he might have become a connoisseur of artistic, culinary, and sensual refinement. But in the lands north of the Danube he became a crude parvenu who lived in an architectural monstrosity, a colossal grange rather than a castle; who gorged like a barbarian; and whose orgies were so primitive they disgusted his visitors. His treasury was crowded with objects of expensive material in repulsive shapes.

From their cities beyond the great river, Romans watched Vannius. They reported to the capital that the nabob's value as an ally was steadily declining. His overtaxed people grew increasingly resentful, his looted neighbors increasingly infuriated.

And in 50 A.D., when the neighbors, the Hermunduri and the Rugii, broke into Vannius' territory, Rome adopted an official hands-off policy and Vannius' own subjects did not want to fight. Vannius had many carts loaded with treasures and drove off, as fast as his horses could run, to Roman territory. He made good his escape, and even though Roman dealers drove a contemptfully hard bargain for the things he had to sell, Vannius was still wealthy when he took up a non-royal residence in Pannonia province. Roman authorities tolerated him there. Two of his nephews, both hostile, succeeded him in his realm, which disintegrated soon thereafter.

Many a buffer state beyond the river, many a makeshift empire, emerged and vanished into nought. Princes, princelings, impostors, would-be empire builders, tried their luck, with or without Roman assistance. Rome looked on, mindful of its own security. The ambitious barbarians had accomplices, supporters, henchmen, and favorites galore, but they did not hire chroniclers to present their own idealized version of local history. Greek and Roman historians took scant notice of what went on in the Empire's Danubian forefield, unless Roman legions were engaged in battle there. Later explorations of the wide field of ancient events were essentially confined to excavations, which told of a variety of material cultures and occasional mass butcheries but did not always reveal who was responsible and what sort of an individual he may have been.

CHAPTER FOUR

When Roman vanguards first scouted the lowest section of the Danube Valley, they found a people settled on the left bank of the river whom they called Dacians and whom they described as expansion-minded merchants.

The ancestors of the Dacians had lived there long before Rome was built, even before the era of recorded Olympiads in Greece (776 B.C.). They had had contact with the Celts; they had been hit by raiders from the nebulous East, some probably from the unexplored expanses of Siberia.

Herodotus mentions the Dacians (he called them Daërs) as being of Thracian origin, which is somewhat doubtful, and he does not say that their land was remarkable for size.

Not before the last century B.C. did the Dacians make history.

In 60 B.C. a venturesome King became ruler of Dacia. His name was Burbista and his holdings extended from the foothills of the Transylvanian Alps to the Black Sea. Advancing into the lands north and east of the Iron Gate, the King found a number of decaying fortresses, which he adapted as trade posts, and remnants of forges and rich mines, which he seized and operated most profitably.

It can be assumed that Burbista maintained a primitive merchant fleet on the Danube to ship the products of his new industries to whoever wanted to buy them. The Dacian monarch had gone into the business of manufacturing arms: scythe-shaped swords and curved daggers, the designs of which were related to Thracian and Persian armament.

Burbista's agents skirted Roman outposts across the Danube to solicit business with the mighty Empire. Findings in Transylvania, Moldavia, and Walachia indicate that Roman wares began to pour into the markets of Burbista's land, that Roman coins circulated there and constituted the legal tender. The efficient King's wealth grew as he sat in his squatty capital and monopolized lucrative businesses from the northern rim of the Balkan Peninsula all the way to the Dniester River and beyond. He styled himself the protector of peoples who lived within his realm of trade.

Did he become a real threat to the Romans? Roman history does not say so. He could not operate a military establishment as efficiently as he could handle a business, and he had grown too rich to let his presumptive heirs wait patiently until their heritage fell due through natural reasons. His relatives became restive, and the power of their cohorts was deadlier than that of Burbista's hoard of precious metals and jewels. In 45 B.C. he died under a hail of dagger blows. For more than a century his successors and their progeny kept annoying Rome while much of their own heritage was squandered.

Modern Rumanian historians tell proudly of parleys between Dacian and Roman royalty and claim that even family ties were being considered. However, no high-level deal materialized between mighty Rome and impertinent Dacia, and when Dacian raids in the Balkan Peninsula continued, the Romans consolidated their grip on the peninsula. The early operations of the Danube flotilla expanded to the vicinity of Burbista's former capital of Argedava, and Roman seizure of the lands down to the Black Sea was stepped up.

In 89 A.D., an angry Emperor Domitian opened two wars: retaliation against the resurgent Marcomanni and Quadi, and aggression against the Western Dacians. Along the Danube everything went reasonably well, thanks to the flotilla, but Roman land forces were badly mauled.

Roman Emperor Domitian tried negotiation and appeasement. He dispatched a splendidly garbed embassy to the West Dacian King, Decebalus, to offer peace and friendship. The embassy faced stiff and unusual demands: Decebalus wanted permanent Roman subsidies, and assistance by Roman technicians to raise the country to the economic and military level of Rome. He did not ask for more land at Rome's expense, but left no doubt that he intended to expand in various directions once Roman assistance would have made him the most potent ruler north of the Danube.

The Romans first agreed in principle, then stalled. A few architects and engineers went to Dacia and started operations but proceeded at a rate at which it would have taken several generations to turn Dacia into a modern country.

The engineers and architects found the Dacian people indifferent to their King's and Princes' annexionism but hoping for higher living standards, such as existed across the Danube, in the Balkan Peninsula.

The Romanized Balkans were the Dacians' Promised Land. There Roman legion commanders had established a degree of security which did not exist in the neighboring territories. Roman law, administered by Roman magistrates, regulated human relations. Roman industry and commerce accounted for a degree of prosperity the Dacians had not known even in the days of Burbista's opulence, and Roman settlers lived high.

Dacian commoners doubted that they would ever receive their share and made it plain that they would welcome a Roman administration to bridle their quarrelsome, tyrannical rulers.

When Decebalus collected the first Roman subsidy—he called it "tribute"—a young Roman magistrate officiated in Syria province, Marcus Ulpius Trajanus, who became Emperor Trajan on January 27, 98 A.D.

Trajan did not believe in security by appeasement. Three years after he ascended the throne he led an army against the aging, vain Decebalus. The "tribute"-collecting King of the Dacians scoffed when he learned that Roman land forces were lining up to attack his new capital north of Argedava, the approaches to which were protected by the Carpathian ranges and by the Danube's Iron Gate.

Since time immemorial few people had tried to cross the wild narrows of the Danube. Men usually avoided the whirls and rapids of the river as it rushes on against the titanic rocks in its path. In raging torrents it hurls itself against the stone, plows a furrow one hundred seventy feet deep as it bursts into a caldron between mountains, then dashes through yet another defile. The Danube flotilla usually avoided the fearsome passage, leaving patrol and combat duty on the lowest part of the river to the squadron stationed beyond the Gate.

Emperor Trajan was determined to tame the fighting forces of nature as he would tame the forces of hostile kings. He decided to build a double artery of traffic, on land and on the river, that should last forever.

He summoned his top army engineers, men of superior skill, and told them to conquer both river and mountains. The engineers met the unprecedented challenge head on.

Remnants of a comfortably navigable canal, almost two miles long, still give proof of Roman ingenuity. Through the calm waters of the channel ships of all sizes could row or sail, bypassing the most dangerous section of the defile, and along the canal led an all-weather, all-season artery of land traffic, a paved military highway built like the Roman Alpine roads.

Roman technique of 100 A.D. achieved what no other technicians could have equaled prior to modern times. Superstitious people like Decebalus could not conceive of the workings of superior human minds. He believed that the ghosts of the Iron Gate had joined the Romans to destroy him. In 102, Trajan and his host reached the new Dacian capital. Dacian resistance was spotty.

The Emperor's terms for peace were mild: the lands along the left Danube bank as far down as the Alutus (Olt) River, and Decebalus' solemn renunciation of a sovereign policy. This meant that the King could no longer prepare for war against Rome, but that he would be granted Roman protection in case of attack or insurrection.

Decebalus signed meekly. Trajan returned to Rome for his triumph and was awarded the byname Dacicus. But Decebalus did not believe in the sanctity of treaties he did not like; he resumed an anti-Roman policy, and in 105 Trajan paid his second call to the region near the Iron Gate. Decebalus suffered a complete defeat. Within two years the Romans ruled all the lands upon which Dacian soldiers and mercenaries had ever set foot. A perplexed Decebalus committed suicide.

Dacia was turned into a Roman province and divided into three districts. As a startling innovation in those regions, the people received local self-government.

The lower Danube now was a Roman river, even without the constant vigilance of the flotilla. The *Tabula Trajana* hewn in a rock of the Iron Gate tells of the Emperor's brilliant achievement. In Rome, the hundred-foot high Column of Trajan shows picture reliefs from the Dacian wars. And Trajan's Wall, a bastion up to twenty feet high and thirty-six miles long, was built between the Danube Delta and the present Black Sea port of Constantsa.

Roman administrators proceeded to settle parts of Dacia with people whom they hoped to keep under effective control. Rumanian nationalists proudly contend that these settlers were distinguished ex-soldiers, civil servants in semi-retirement, outstanding pioneers in industry and agriculture, several nobles among them; and that modern Rumanians are their almost undiluted offspring, more Roman than the people of Italy. But the Roman Empire of post-Trajan days did not have members of its elite to spare to go to the lower banks of the Danube, to the Transylvanian forests and mountains, to the Walachian plains, to the fever-ridden delta beyond.

On the other hand, it has been said that Dacia became ancient Rome's Siberia, the ash can for the Empire's human refuse. This acerb antithesis of the Rumanian boast is, in fact, no sounder than the tale of surviving Roman splendor.

The migrants to Dacia undoubtedly were not the pride of their former communities, but administrators were careful not to stage a migration of malefactors who would bring crime rather than peace to the new colony. The average level of intelligence, skill, and orderliness was, probably, mediocre.

Newcomers were rather easily manageable when they arrived in the new land after a long journey over Roman roads along the Danube and over wild lands. They settled down on assigned plots or built their own towns. It was a hard life but they did not suffer privation. As they established themselves they did not grumble or quarrel, but once established they became overbearing toward the natives, tricky toward the Roman authorities, and the unsavory reputation they acquired was not undeserved. The settlers' overbearingness toward the Dacians did not prevent them from begetting hosts of children with Dacian women. Mixed legal marriages were infrequent during the lifetime of the first generation, but in the next, ties were often legalized. The customs and mores of these families would have shocked Roman patricians and astonished Roman plebeians. Rome knew no prudishness, but Dacian Romans were savage libertines who practiced every vice in the book.

One century after Decebalus had met his doom the Roman settlers in Dacia were Romans in name only. Ethnic elements from many parts of Eastern Europe and from the vastness yonder were prevalent among the new country squires and city slickers. Their language was still Latin, but it had become diluted by nouns of foreign tongues. Only the scantiness of foreign vocabularies accounted for the conservation of Latin roots.

Rome never considered Dacia an outpost of its culture, but as a forefield of the Empire. A few territories were promoted to municipalities, a few towns extended and fortified, a few strong points built on the eastern and northeastern fringes of the land from which to watch the movements of roving barbarians. For a few centuries the barbarians constituted no immediate danger. But then waves of them, low and high tides of the Migration of Peoples and the subsequent march of conquest of Asiatic marauders, burst over Dacia, sweeping away most of what was essentially Roman. They turned the lands along the lower Danube into a whirlpool of men of colorful and undefinable origin, and into a perennial theater of tyranny that made wars and of wars that made tyrannies.

CHAPTER FIVE

Pliny's *Natural History,* published in 77 A.D., carries an entry about Vianiomina, a city on the Danube. It was the garrison of the crack 13th Legion, which had been visited sixty-eight years before by Tiberius Claudius Nero.

Pliny's Vianiomina was Vienna. Tiberius had been there first as a general when his army prepared to cross the Danube on a pontoon bridge near Carnuntum to chastise unruly Germans beyond the river, and again six years later, in 15 A.D., as an Emperor returning to consolidate his conquests. Neither Pliny nor court historian Velleius Paterculus recorded what Tiberius had seen on the site of Vienna. Apparently there was little to impress a distinguished, widely traveled Roman.

Legend, charming godmother of history, does not tell of the beginning of Vienna, or of the rebirth of an ancient settled place that probably existed there. It is tempting to assume that it started with the wine— Roman newcomers to the Danube Valley found its wine to be a gift of God, a joy of man.

The legionnaires' rations included a hearty quantity of wine; carts loaded with casks traveled many hundreds of miles from Italy to the banks of the distant river until some blessed year someone got the idea that the Danube Valley was a good place to grow grapes. Was he a Roman commissary officer who thought that his cohort did not get enough imported drink? Was he an efficient Roman bureaucrat who wor-

ried about transportation expenses? Was he a supplier of the army who
expected to triple his profits if the wine were grown where it was consumed? Or did a native girl, tipsy with wine poured for her from a
soldier's flask, conceive the plan to plant grapes?

But whoever it was, this person might have done more to shape the
faces and fates of the people from Danubian lands than the conquerors
and their itinerant mercenaries.

Natives learned to grow wine, and since horticulture required a
higher degree of stability than almost any other type of productivity, the
winegrowers eventually became a special breed with their own traditions,
lore, and manner. The city in the early years of our time probably was a
blending of a military encampment and a winegrowers' bustling village,
spreading on the right bank of the Danube and south along the slopes
of the Alps, over foothills lit up by the rising sun and sprinkled by rains
caused by currents stirred up in an atmosphere in which moist Atlantic
air clashes with the dry air from eastern steppes. The battle of opposite
climes does not generate really devastating storms. There is a great deal
of thunder and lightning; it rarely inundates the land, but it always fe-
cundates it.

And the old-established dwellers of the land are, in turn, grumbling
and frolicking, and in their changing moods world-wise cheer eventually
prevails over martial grimness. At times, the weeds of a dull alien furor
overgrow the basic character; the Viennese and their neighbors are de-
praved into fools and knaves. But after the fool's cap and the knave's
helmet have fallen, a brief hang-over dims into a grouchy smile and the
sons and daughters of the wineland dance back to their true ways.

The Roman wine attracted the Danubian growers, the Danubian wine
the Roman colonizers. It may have been, it should have been so, even
though the true refinement of Danubian horticulture occurred only much
later, between 276 and 282 A.D., when Emperor Probus championed
the growing of wines along the Danube and also along the Rhine. Probus
was not born in Rome, but in Sirmium, Pannonia. He was a son of the
Danube Valley; his soldiers proclaimed him *Imperator* after he came out
victorious in Gaul and Illyricum; and eventually killed him in a mad,
drunken mutiny. A street in modern Vienna is named after him. Hardly
one out of a hundred residents of the Probusgasse know who the bearer
of the name was.

Vienna is a nymph sprung from a flood of wine. Vienna attracted the
dignified officials from Carnuntum. Carnuntum had all the facilities of a

Roman stronghold but it lacked the feminine element that is the prerequisite of gaiety. Roman authorities wanted to keep their spectacular fortress a place of earnestness, but they had no objection about turning Vienna, one day away as the legions marched, into a happy place for officers and administrators who moved in growing numbers to the site of undulating hills nudging the river. The families of officials moved in, prosperous winegrowers came; so did merchants, entertainers and their families, and other human accessories of a community, the development of which was almost vertiginous by the standards of antiquity.

Half a century after Tiberius had set foot on the sightly spot the Romans turned it into a town with a population in excess of thirty thousand, the garrison of a crack legion, a spa, and the site of pompous buildings. The inhabitants of Vienna belonged to many nationalities: Noricans, domesticated Marcomanni and Quadi, Pannonians, Romans, and a bewildering variety of people from Roman colonies, such as Syrians, Egyptians, and Jews, who usually went everywhere that business prospects went.

The legionnaires of the 13th devoted much of their time to construction work, and when toward the end of the first century A.D. one thousand Britannic cavalrymen and a cohort of Syrian archers joined the garrison, they too helped build Vienna into its earliest glory.

Another river port sprang up on the outskirts. The center of the town turned into a military city, with walls thicker even than those of Carnuntum, with towers, redoubts, and gates of strength and awe-inspiring splendor. The inner city was not only to halt aggression but also to attract and to welcome grandees of the Empire, its consuls, even Caesars.

The military city occupied a substantial part of modern Vienna's first district. The Castle stood where the High Market now stands, and on the Castle grounds were the offices of the commanders, the Praetorium, and administrative buildings. The Praetorium was a splendid palace; from it the city's main thoroughfare ran to a great temple near the redoubt where the church of St. Peter now stands. The street, lined with buildings as could have been found in any good-sized Italian provincial town, led to the present Kohlmarkt, where many soldiers' wives and children lived, closer to the military cemetery than to the barracks; and from there it ran to the banks of the Danube, past a smaller temple, upon the ruins of which medieval Viennese fishermen would build their modest church Maria-am-Gestade (Mary by the Waterside), where they would pray to the Virgin to bless their nets. The military city ended at the riverbank,* and to the south, beyond the mighty walls and the colossal moat, was the civilian city. The military section was not usually grim, but rather calm, and the cadence of life within the walls had a touch of the rhythm of marching steps. Outside the walls it was all gaiety.

The system of military highways into which the early Roman road had been expanded crossed and skirted the civilian section.

Hot springs, undoubtedly well known to distant predecessors of the legionnaires, were rediscovered in the suburbs where the district of Meidling later sprang up. The soldiers took the waters in their garrison town, a convenience they could hardly have found anywhere else between the Nile and the Rhine, the Persian Gulf and the Atlantic. Many were cured of aches and diseases, among them Centurio Titus Vettius Rufus, who built an altar in honor of the kindly maidens of the springs.

The Centurion's Altar is still preserved and it is but one of many memorials of Roman Vienna. Tablets record names of Viennese citizens of Roman nationality: Titus Flavius Verecundus, Titus Flavius Bardus, Titus Flavius Dracens; the last-named, so we learn, was born in Gaul, served in the Britannic cavalry, and after twenty-two years in the army died in Vienna at the age of forty-five, under the glorious rule of Emperor Domitian.

The tablets are of weather-beaten stone and the inscriptions are hard to decipher; they do not seem to have any affinity with life, but, looking up, the viewer sees the sights that the various Titus Flaviuses have seen. He breathes the same air, senses the pulse of a procreative nature that inspired them as it stimulated their most distant forerunners and that will keep inspiring men even in an age in which inspiration is scorned as a primitive substitute for efficiency.

Emperor Domitian probably came to Vienna. Chroniclers of his troubles with undomesticated Marcomanni and Quadi consider this a distinct possibility. No inscription sustains the supposition, but already in Domitian's day the castle of Vienna was fit to lodge the supreme lord of the Empire.

Emperor Trajan, the fighting globe-trotter, did not come to Vienna, but he had the 13th Legion relieved by the 10th Legion, his favorite fighting outfit.

The 10th Legion stayed in Vienna until the end of Roman rule. It became as Viennese as the Viennese themselves, more Viennese in character than any unit prior to the introduction of compulsory military serv-

* In modern time regulations transferred the bed of the Danube from its site in Roman days to a region a little further to the north.

ice in the Habsburg monarchy. Imperial in its banners, bearing, and splendor, cosmopolitan in its spirit, soldiers from all parts of the Empire represented virtually every element of the civilized Western world. They were daring and playful, showy and somewhat scornful of all that wasn't 10th Legion.

Emperor Marcus Aurelius called the 10th Legion into battle in the year 171. He himself traveled to Vienna at the head of powerful reinforcements. A battered victory column in Rome immortalizes his Danubian campaign.

Led on by discontented Quadi, twenty-five Germanic tribes and peoples, and other foreigners, all alien to Rome and Vienna in spirit and way of life, had crossed the Danube and swarmed all over the countryside—rapacious, vicious, and destructive. They could neither take nor even beleaguer the fortifications of either Vienna or Carnuntum, but they raided Vienna's easternmost civilian section and did as much damage as hit-and-run assaults could produce. Marcus Aurelius found many a smoldering ruin.

The victory column depicts the Emperor's crossing of the Danube: soldiers, in obviously nonchalant step, loaded rowboats, massive pontoons, one proud horseman, and, three ranks ahead of him, afoot, bareheaded, bearded, with unmistakably majestic bearing, Marcus Aurelius in person. In the background, not too elaborately carved, are buildings which seem to be part of the inner city. At the bottom of the relief Danubius, the burly river-god, watches, imperturbably.

The Imperial army faced a difficult task. The enemy was elusive, often running but also hitting hard, not depending on traffic lanes but perfectly familiar with Roman lines of development. It was a protracted campaign. Supplying the army in the field turned into a major headache for the commissaries in Vienna and Carnuntum. Worried civilians flocked into the fortress section, overcrowding it badly, and, to make things worse, a catastrophic drought hit the farmlands. Brooks and wells dried, soldiers suffered terrible hardship, and the enemy, emerging in closed ranks, attacked the parched Imperials.

Nothing but a miracle could save Marcus Aurelius from disaster, Vienna from destruction, Italy from invasion. The miracle came to pass. Heavy clouds massed as the weary legionnaires rallied for a last stand. Before the hostile masses could charge, the clouds burst and released torrents of refreshing water. The legionnaires drank it and routed the enemy. The victory column shows Pluvius, god of rain, spreading his wings as floods pour down from his hair and outstretched arms.

Christian soldiers who served with the legion said that they had prayed for rain and that the Lord Jesus Christ had heard their prayer. The Lord, whom Roman executioners had nailed to the Cross, saved the Roman legions and made them prevail. Christian soldiers praised the Lord's infinite grace and forgiveness.

Marcus Aurelius did not discourage Christian legends, though he still preferred the tale of Pluvius' assistance. But he must have known the tremendous power of the newer faith which was spreading throughout the realm.

Roman Emperors who had had to take to the field far away from their capital and who defeated the enemy in precarious campaigns were not usually in a lenient mood. They would often take defeated enemies to Rome, and have them dragged in chains in abject humiliation through the Via Triumphalis and executed thereafter, as a warning to all those who defied the Empire.

Marcus Aurelius requested and obtained extradition of Ariogaesus, Prince of the Quadi and leader of the rebellious tribes and peoples. He had him brought into his presence on the stairs of the Praetorium, a solid phalanx of legionnaires standing guard. Everybody expected the Emperor to execute the rebel, but Marcus Aurelius was in a forgiving mood. He decreed that the man who had caused so much destruction be pardoned and exiled.

This was the second miracle of the campaign.

The defeated people also were treated with mildness and consideration. The strip of land they were made to cede was only four and a half miles wide; it ran along the left bank of the Danube, so that more Roman forts could be built to cover the approach to the river. The Germans were directed to muster a modest annual contingent of recruits for the legion, to return all Roman prisoners and deserters, and to submit to Roman market regulations in deals concluded on Roman territory. There was one additional term which characterized the Emperor's gift for psychology: a ban on National Assemblies. Marcus Aurelius understood that mass meetings in which demagogues ranted their followers into fits of furor were latent sources of devastating conflagrations.

The Emperor was in a contemplative mood and the surroundings fitted this state of mind. He started work on a philosophical treatise entitled *To Oneself*. It contained meditations which he considered to be more important than politics, war, and triumphs. *To Oneself* is the first work of literature known to have originated in Vienna.

In 174, one year after the miracle of the rain, the Sarmatian Jazyges, fierce horsemen and archers who had come all the way from the Sea of Azov to the Pannonian Danube Valley, sacked and looted Roman and Roman-protected towns and villages. Marcus Aurelius drew his sword again. It took him another year to defeat the Jazyges in the flatlands around the middle course of the river and to free almost one hundred thousand prisoners and hostages. His son Commodus accompanied him during the war.

Reasons of state and the innate desire for glory caused Marcus Aurelius to accept a Roman triumph and the honorary surname Sarmaticus, but reflections of philosophical humanism kept him from having captives victimized.

Commodus shared triumph and surname. His father hoped that this would endear him to the Romans and secure his succession. But the Prince was a lecher with an outspoken aversion against inconvenience. This the Romans knew well enough, though they acclaimed him during the triumph.

Father and son stayed in Rome until 178. Then a messenger arrived, a feather at the top of his lance, the symbol of evil. The Danube Valley was again in revolt. The Germanic tribes, unappeased by mildness, were on the warpath, claiming that the Romans of Vienna and Carnuntum had violated the peace pact, that legionnaires had violated the privacy of Germanic homesteads, stolen cattle, and helped slaves to escape. Only another major military campaign could restore order.

On August 3, 178, a martial ceremony marked the Emperor and his son's decampment from Rome for the *Expeditio Germanica Secunda.* A small strip of land in front of the temple of the goddess Bellona was proclaimed enemy territory—land across the Danube—and the highest member of the College of *Fetiales,* the twenty-man advisory body on matters of war and peace, threw a lance on that land. The throwing of the lance augured good fortune and soon the augury was borne out by the Quadi's defeat.

The defeated made mien to retire north as a migratory nation, but the psychologist-philosopher-Emperor understood that this could create another problem, another permanent threat to stability in the Danube Valley. They were given to understand that an offer would be forthcoming and so they waited, a score of miles north of Vienna.

The Emperor wondered how he could keep the enemy in the vicinity of his lands and subject him to soothing influences while he himself was preparing to fight. An ailing man in his late fifties, almost constantly beset by premonitions of evil, he held court in Vienna's citadel, deliberated with his advisers, and worked on his philosophical opus. Commodus was present at the deliberations; his father wanted him to understand the issues at stake. The heir to the throne, bored and annoyed at having to stay in the castle instead of enjoying the pleasures of the civilian city and the delights of pastoral life in its surroundings, wondered how he could best manage to leave for Rome.

Deliberations dragged on. The problem facing Marcus Aurelius was, in fact, the perennial problem of the Danube Basin: to deal in a constructive manner with the ever present threat of conquerors from the north and east: barbarians, savage oppressors, greedy impostors, and efficient grabbers; and to deal with this threat in a manner that took heed of the fact that military victory was but a temporary solution.

Imperial political agents, champions of the divide-and-*impera* pattern, worked on plans to set Germanic tribes against the Jazyge remnants, a plan which involved large bribes and sly concessions. The Emperor listened to their reports, but he realized that something entirely new, something beyond stale theories, would have to be devised.

Came the winter of 179–80. The waiting Quadi turned ever more restive. They sneaked or broke through Roman blocks and made a bid for freedom, which, of course, was synonymous with freebooting.

From the walls of Vienna and Carnuntum the Roman guards saw rural homes go up in flames. The Emperor himself, who loved the land in a somewhat sentimental manner, once climbed the tower of the castle to cast a long look at the rolling hills, the fertile plains, and the brownish-green ice-flake-studded river. Then he called his ranking soldiers and issued marching orders to be effective as soon as the drift of ice subsided.

Around March 1, 180, the legions were ready. So was the navy. Generals waited for Marcus Aurelius to take over. Engineers built pontoon bridges. War machines were lined up in a sinister, thrilling array. Viennese civilians, eternally curious, swarmed around as close as they could get to the spectacle, hoping to catch a glimpse of the Emperor in martial regalia. The atmosphere had a theatrical touch, as it always had in the great events in that part of the globe.

The Emperor remained in seclusion. There were no proclamations, but only the Viennese knew that Claudius Pompejanus, governor of Pannonia and a veteran general of Danubian campaigns, was with him, as were several medical men.

Tension was high at the prevailing secrecy.

On March 17 the silence was broken. Marcus Aurelius was dead. Commodus was his successor.

Marcus Aurelius left a magnificent Empire, unfinished plans to consolidate it for all time, and, most cherished by himself, his finished book, a philosophy of stoicism, with himself as the protagonist, in which he presented life as a drama to be enacted by every human being for himself. It was written in Greek, not in Latin, for the intellectual connoisseur and not for the merely curious. It was a sequence of words that no longer seemed animated after the exalted protagonist had departed.

Claudius Pompejanus led the legions across the pontoon bridge. Danubius was invisible but large Viennese crowds cheered men, horses, and machines. The general was under orders to work quickly; Commodus did not wish to delay his return to Rome. He made a fast peace, negotiating with delegates from the enemy camp, despite objections by his generals and the exhortations of his father's advisers.

Rome renounced annexations beyond the four-and-a-half-mile zone on the left bank of the Danube. No provisions were made for keeping peace with and refraining from attacks on Roman troops, civilians, and settlers under Roman protection. But the crowning stupidity of the pact of Vienna of 180 was the lifting of the ban on National Assemblies. The proviso was that one Roman officer should attend the sessions. Even if that officer happened to understand the language in which business was conducted, he was usually of Germanic origin and inclined to put the interests of his boisterous kinfolk above those of his adopted country.

The regions beyond the left bank of the Danube remained unpacified. Feuds, maladministration, and natural catastrophes, such as failing harvests and pestilence, caused group migrations across the river into Roman-governed land. Rome, forgetful of the dangers involved in such an influx and beset by ever more critical shortages of military and agricultural manpower, accepted the immigrants without screening.

The historian Dion Cassius tells that the immigrants were granted land in Dacia, Pannonia, Moesia, Roman Germania, even in Italy. They were freemen with all the privileges held by Roman citizens, but without Roman culture and restraint. They became an element of unrest throughout the Danube Valley, and they did not assimilate, nor did they yield to, the soothing influences of higher cultures. But they occasionally overgrew.

CHAPTER SIX

The Danube ceased to be a barrier long before the stormy billows from the north laid Rome waste. Across the river surged the tides of invasions, not quite with the regularity, but with the immutable recurrence of high and low waters of the sea. In the open country along the banks the invaders shaped the habits of the population, while in the cities the Roman element refused to adapt itself to the changing influences. A great deal of sporadic fighting went on in the river basin.

Commodus did not return to Vienna. He ruled, caroused, and squandered the assets of the Empire for a dozen years. When, at the age of thirty-one, he exited, angry Claudius Pompejanus had been succeeded by Septimus Severus, a native of Africa, who owed his spectacular rise to a marriage with an influential woman, to the favor of Marcus Aurelius, and to his immense popularity with his soldiers. There must have been a great fascination about this Roman-African, a spell which no chronicler has conclusively described, but which created a personality cult in the garrison so strong that the legions of Carnuntum proclaimed him Emperor in 193, the year after Commodus died.

For Carnuntum this greatest day meant the return of a golden age of supremacy over all other Danubian towns, including upstart Vienna, which had developed superiority complexes since Marcus Aurelius had been there. The Viennese could not elude the spell of the new Emperor, but they grumbled about the locale he had chosen for his assumption of supreme power, and even did some vague plotting that came to an abrupt end when Septimus Severus threatened to castigate the plotters.

As an Emperor, Septimus Severus did not stay on in the Danube Valley long; he had to deal with far more serious rebellions than the one caused by Viennese jealousy. Under his son and successor, Caracalla, so nicknamed after a hooded Gallic tunic which he preferred to Roman garb, the city was elevated to the status of *municipium*, which was as high as any city could rank within the Empire; no other Danubian city had that status. This was Vienna's triumph over Carnuntum. The *municipium* had two mayors—the *duumviri*—who were supposed to check each other, and a municipal council appointed to check both mayors and see that the city be safe, peaceful, reasonably hygienic, and obedient to Imperial command.

On May 28, 249, Vienna received a tutelary goddess: Fortuna Conservatrix. An officer from the 10th Legion made the choice. Soldiers and officials outdid themselves in building altars for the greater glory of the idol with the auspicious-sounding name. And a fitting idol it turned out to be. Vienna's good fortunes almost invariably had a conservative touch; the Viennese were always given to nostalgia; however well they fared, they would contend that nobody ever had or ever again would have it so good as their grandparents.

When Fortuna Conservatrix received her altars, the Viennese had Germanic settlers as neighbors. A Germanic belt reached right into the formerly exclusive suburbs of the *municipium*. Roman generals did nothing to stop the infiltration, but in order to strengthen their armed establishment, a second Viennese harbor was constructed, providing better shelter for the Danube flotilla.

Roman engineers had dams built to create an artificial basin, 230 feet wide and 750 feet long, where vessels could concentrate even when drifting ice made shipping in open waters extremely hazardous. But this remarkable technical feat had little effect upon the security of the city and the adjoining river course.

Legion officers and veterans donated statues and altars of Jupiter, Neptune, Salaria, Danubius, and Agaunus (patron-pagan of a small tributary of the Danube, now called the Wien), and for a host of graceful nymphs. Gods, goddesses, and their accessaries did not keep the rising Germanic waves away from the sites of their temples, however, and Viennese civilians, quite a few of them Christians, viewed paganism with indifference, a characteristic mixture of tolerance and indolence that developed into a staple Viennese feature.

More Germanic tribes made their martial bow on the Viennese scene. The 10th Legion belatedly tried to bar the most unwanted types of settlers from the region, and from Rome arrived yet another Emperor, Aurelian, a man of humble birth and risen from the ranks, who tried to restore the Empire's crumbling world power. Biographers tell of his extraordinary accomplishments along the Danube. In fact, he drove invading Goths a short distance away, but could not consolidate the tottering provinces of Dacia, and the citizenry of Vienna built no memorials in his praise.

Vienna had turned blasé, if not outright skeptical, toward military achievements. The city was doing well. It had plenty of food, a great deal of entertainment, some parades, and a steady stream of stimulating visitors.

After Aurelian came Emperor Probus, the Danube Valley's wine-happy native son, who liked tall soldiers and picked the hugest specimens for his bodyguard. Giant Northerners flocked into the city, among them the Batavi, whose immense physical dimensions had already been noted by Tacitus, brawlers with reddish-brown hair from the regions of the present Netherlands whose behavior was so uncouth that the Viennese found it prudent to avoid them when no civilized legionnaires were around to restrain the "immense bodies." Then there were the Bastarnae, who had already a fighting record with Roman units, people who wore short boots, long-plaited trousers, and long robes; their hair was combed to the right and tied with a knot behind the ears. The Bastarnae were well disciplined when they came, but after tasting the Viennese wines they turned unreformable alcoholics and adopted the habit of threatening and insulting anybody who was not their kin. Roman military authorities were careful to distribute the mobilized giants all over the vast realm, and settled the remainder in the Danube Valley, in Pannonia, and in adjoining provinces. The tall people and their chieftains, whom the Romans accepted as backwood popular leaders, did not always stay within the confines of allotted land, but roamed other parts of the Danube Basin, leaving in their wake loss of property and additions to the local population.

As Probus grew wines and recruited giants, he did not seem concerned with potential destructive invasions; but Diocletian, a native of Dalmatia who had served in the army under Probus and became Emperor in 284, faced a vertiginous variety of troubles on the fringes of the Empire. For seventeen years, he fought, parleyed, issued orders; then somebody told him that the Christians were the cause of his perplexities, and, anxious to find a scapegoat, he issued an edict against the Christians of his Empire, charging them with every possible and impossible misdeed, and exposing them to persecution on an unprecedented scale.

In the year the edict of rabid intolerance was issued, the now-Austrian Danube Basin obtained its first martyr saint: Florianus, or Florian, as the Austrians call him.

Florian's acta are somewhat vague. He was said to have suffered martyrdom in the course of an organized mass persecution; to have defied, all alone, an order to abjure his faith; to have been buried alive, burned at the stake, or drowned. His sacred remains were found some

500 years after his end, close to the spot where the Enns River empties into the Danube, and it took another 380 years before Florian was fully accepted as a saint, for deeds of fortitude unspecified. St. Florian, a small place and a spectacular monastery, was founded at the site where his tomb still stands.

Austrian folklore, usually so prolific, has nothing to say about the saint's martyrdom, but countryfolk invoke his name when threatened by fire or high water, and they still appeal to him in characteristic ditties such as:

> O thou Holy Florian,
> spare our cottage,
> burn the other one.

Diocletian abdicated two years after Florian died, and retired to Dalmatia to peaceful gardening; but the persecution raged for a full ten years.

At last, in 313, Emperor Constantine I promulgated the Edict of Milan, which decreed tolerance throughout the Empire. Christendom's crowning victory over the forces of paganism in Rome came too late to give the shaken realm, its feuding administration, and its mercenary army a unifying moral foundation. Constantine himself felt that the city of Rome was not best suited to become the capital of the Christian Empire. Hardly any ruler since Julius Caesar had had so thorough a knowledge of all Roman provinces. His travels also took him to the Danube Valley, including Vienna and Carnuntum, but he never considered either town as a residence, least of all as an Imperial capital. In 326, his choice fell on Byzantium (later called Constantinople, now Istanbul). On May 11, 330, the dedication of that city to the Blessed Virgin was performed by Christian ecclesiastics.

The people of the still Roman-controlled Danube basin did not gravitate to the new city. To them, Christendom was not a world-embracing creed, hardly a *Weltanschauung*. The urban population had become easygoing and provincial. If the Emperor wanted Christ to be worshiped, they would worship Christ. They adopted the creed, but refused to suffer physical or moral hardship for its sake.

Vienna's pagan temples were gradually converted into churches. But conservatives saw little reason to give up paganism as long as Jupiter made no exacting demands on their time and money, and peaceful sectarians kept practicing the Persian cult of Mithras, which oriental traders recommended as a panacea.

Crowned heads of Rome often visited all parts of the Danube Valley, but most rulers of Byzantium (though they were temporarily titular overlords over most of it) showed but mild interest in the river until it turned into a lane of disaster along which rolled the invaders from the eastern steppes.

CHAPTER SEVEN

In the earlier part of the fourth century only few citizens of Vienna, or of any other city on the Danube north and northwest of the Balkan Peninsula, knew much about the Western Goths—the Visigoths—who lived along the lower course of the Danube. The river basin had become divided into two spheres which showed little interest in each other.

Hardly anybody upstream would have cared to learn that the Goths had settled downstream and had been admitted into the military services of the East Roman Empire, with the status of allies.

No information had reached the upper Danube about an eastern branch of the Goths, who in 375 had been hit by a storm. Its gathering had been ignored by Danubian peoples, yet they sensed it with inscrutable instinct.

The storm came from Asia, from the endless vastness of what would be called Siberia well over a thousand years later, where migrating people strayed, bumped into each other, sometimes with the effect of mutual destruction, sometimes snowballing and melting away again before they could hit settled nations. It also happened that their momentum grew into that of landslides, and that they struck calmer nations like thunder out of the blue. The Hiung-nu of Siberia, soon to be called the Huns by fear-chilled Europeans, hit China time and again. At the time Troy fell, they recoiled westward to batter at the doors of other ancient civilizations, such as Persia's. One splinter group of the Hiung-nu sledge hammer was thrown back into the wild glacis in front of the eastern slopes of the Ural

Mountains. Bumped, overrun, never absorbed, often reinforced, it rolled across the wooded mountain range and arrived in the plains of present Russia, probably at the beginning of the Christian Era, over eight hundred years before Rurik laid the first insecure foundation of the Russian Empire. The Hiung-nu vagabonds, a hundred times defeated and never tamed, to whom aggression was the only way of life they understood, were on their way to becoming a world power, without knowing what the world beyond the Asiatic vastness was like.

Slowly, inexorably, they kept moving, pressed on by never ending tides of Siberian migrations, sucked in by the vacuum of power that existed along the Don.

On the Don, they met the Alani, the first Europeans they ever saw, assailed and defeated them, and forced the survivors into slavery.

Roman intelligence records of the early part of the fourth century do not disclose the presence along the Don of an army of the most uncouth men and the ugliest mounts ever heard of, even in those regions where handsomeness was an almost unknown quality.

The men were short, bowlegged, broad-shouldered, and swarthy. Their eyes were deep-set, small, and jet black, their noses flat. Their hair was black, thick, and greasy. They never washed, and smelled accordingly. As noxious as their smell was the high-pitched shrillness of their voices. They spoke little; their vocabulary had nouns only for primitive objects and equally primitive functions; but they always yelled when meeting their victims. Whomever they met on the steppes of the European Far East became their prey. On the back of their big-headed, edgy-boned, shaggy horses they charged in full gallop, discharging swarms of arrows with devastating accuracy. There seemed to be no hope for survival in combat against them, and only scant hope for a brief, humiliating survival in abject slavery after surrender.

Alani slaves may have informed their Hun masters about the Eastern Goths (Ostrogoths), who lived west of the Don and had many men, beasts, and useful objects. The Alani might have hoped that subjugation of these Goths would put the new victims into the lowest echelon of bondage, and promote them, the Alani, to a slightly higher rung of the chattels' ladder.

The Huns moved west. Ostrogoth King Hermanric (Ermanaric) tried to resist, but in 376 along the Dnieper River his forces were hit by a magic wand of arrows, shrill yells, and nauseating smells. The desperate King committed suicide. Many of his people were killed, or enslaved, or looted, but a great number escaped, as an almost incoherent mass of fugitives that soon formed into a tightly knit body, a battering-ram that could hit any nation but the Huns.

The flight of the Ostrogoths slowed to a march. The nation turned into the vanguard of the European Migration of Peoples, the destructive offshoot of age-old Siberian migrations.

The Ostrogoths marched in the direction of the lowest part of the Danube Valley, often calling prolonged halts, never settling down, with the Huns to their rear and the alluring glamour of the Roman Empire ahead of them. The first gusts of the tempest of terror hit the river lands.

It took quite some time before Rome and Byzantium realized that Ostrogoths were but clouds of dust, heralding the real storm.

The Western Goths had gradually consolidated their settlements along the lower Danube. They had established their rule on the Dacian regions, which, at the time the Huns exerted their fateful pressure upon the West, already had lost the characteristics of a Roman province. From Dacia they moved into Pannonia, Noricum, and as far west as southern Germany and northern Switzerland. They did not enter the new lands along and beyond the Danube with the sanguinary paraphernalia of military conquest, but their insolence left no doubt about their determination to stay and rule.

The man who assumed responsibility was Alaric, newly appointed supreme leader of the Visigoths, a native of either the Danube Delta or one of the Black Sea islands opposite. He enlisted in the Imperial army, and spent over a dozen years loafing in garrisons and watching Visigoth mutineers do a great deal of mischief in the forces of Emperor Theodosius. Later he served under Flavius Stilicho, a semi-barbarian, hard-hitting Vandal, who in 391 set out to put a radical end to the trouble. It took Stilicho almost three years to bring the rebels to a battle, and then an order from Byzantium to let the already encircled mutineers march off, prevented him from inflicting the deathblow upon the foe.

This taught Alaric that mutiny did not necessarily lead to annihilation. By schemes and intrigues, he brought almost ten thousand Visigoths under his control, and early in 395, dismissed from the army, crossed the solidly frozen Danube, proceeding into Dacia.

Winter was unusually rough. The land was in foment. Two parties feuded, one advocating an understanding with Rome, the other the formation of a new empire, Alaric joined the party of dynamism. No true Roman would have considered him a good orator, but to the Visigoths he was a splendid demagogue. Princes elected him their leader; Romans called him *Rex*. (This, however, did not necessarily mean "king," but was a title which Roman chroniclers occasionally used to designate military rulers of splinter nations.)

One year after his discharge, Alaric was *Rex* Alaric of the Visigoths, the man who defied both Romes.

His challenge was immediately followed by aggression. Equipped with Roman material, his armies raced through the Danube Valley, crossed into the Balkans, headed toward the heartlands of Greece. And all the time the clouds on the northeastern horizon thickened.

The threat of the Huns was no longer an inscrutable notion. Hun horses drank from the waters of the lower Danube, Hun stragglers turned up in former Roman provinces and were occasionally seen in Visigothic hordes, demons of a world that civilized nations could view only as an inferno.

The cloud hovered, a bank of horror, in the forefield of Rome, while Roman statesmen wondered how to deal effectively but in a civilized manner with internecine affairs.

Stilicho had not yet returned to Italy when Alaric re-entered Greece. His army had lost none of its marauding skills. Byzantium sued for peace. Alaric asked to be appointed commander of all Roman garrisons between the lower Danube and Greece. His request was at once granted, and as an extra bonus he received the title of Governor of Illyria.

Much as Alaric enjoyed being a Roman field commander, he continued to blackmail Byzantium and to terrorize its nationals. His East Roman garrisons were disorganized and mutinous, while control of the lower Danube passed to the horsemen from Asia.

In the year 399, an anti-barbarian party formed at the court of Honorius, sixteen-year-old Emperor of the West Roman Empire, a native of Byzantium. A spokesman exclaimed: "All Romans must defend their state. They must no longer tolerate that fur-clad savages be put in command of soldiers in Roman garb, or allowed to consult with Roman magistrates in matters of the Empire. The barbarians must be given the choice of either returning beyond the Danube and telling their kin that they are unwanted in Rome and in Byzantium, or to stay here as bondsmen and till the soil for the benefit of their Roman masters."

The words spread over both parts of the Empire. It created terror and confusion, military and civilian upheaval. Gainas, a ranking Visigoth officer who had a record of several murders and insurrection, seized temporary control of Byzantium, engaged in a spree of violence, but eventually fled across the lower Danube. He had no opportunity to tell his kin that they were unwanted south of the river. Smallish, high-smelling, black-haired yelling men on shaggy horses seized him, shot a volley of arrows at his prostrate followers, and kicked, pushed, and dragged him before an equally ungainly but ornately dressed character who produced a few inarticulate sounds that did not have the remotest resemblance to any language, and then motioned one of his men. A blow of a sword severed Gainas' head.

The ornately dressed man was a Hun Prince, Uldin. He had learned about Rome and Roman affairs, including Gainas' insurrection. Uldin was not yet certain how to profit from his knowledge, but to oblige the Emperor by a thoughtful gift he had Gainas' head dispatched to Byzantium.

This was the earliest official contact between the Huns and the Roman Empire.

CHAPTER EIGHT

Ammianus, a Greek-born Roman historian, the last chronicler of classic antiquity, wrote about the Huns in an opus of which only fragments are preserved.

"The Huns are of indomitable savagery. The men have no beards; they make deep incisions in the jaws of their babies; crisscross scars prevent the growth of whiskers and make them look like castrates. They are of solid, powerful build, have fat necks, and look repulsively ugly and weird, like two-legged animals or like certain crudely carved figures as can be found on bridges nowadays. Even though they may seem to be uncouth men, their feeding habits are not entirely human. They neither cook nor season their food, but consume the roots of crude herbs and the raw flesh of animals, which they put between their thighs and the flanks of their horses to warm it up. They do not bury their dead in vaults. They don't even have thatched huts. Aimlessly they roam mountains and forests, and from early childhood become hardened to endure snow and rain, hunger and thirst. Only in the direst of emergencies will they look for shelter; they never feel at ease with anything solid above their heads. They cover their bodies with pieces of linen or pelts of field mice pinned together. Once they have donned their undyed robes they won't take them off again until they fall apart from wear and tear. Their head-gear is a round cap; their hairy legs are covered with lamb skins. Their shoes are not made on lasts, so they cannot walk in a free stride. They are therefore utterly unqualified for battle afoot. They will usually sit straight, as if nailed to the back of their hardened, ungainly horses. Occasionally, however, they will sit sideways and perform various equestrian tricks. Day and night they stay on horseback; they will buy and sell, eat and drink, on their mounts, and even sleep on them, deeply bent over the horses' necks. If there is a matter of importance to decide, they meet on horseback.

"Their lives and actions are not controlled by a central royal authority. Under the arbitrary leadership of tribal Princes, they hurl themselves against anything in their way. When attacked or attacking, they open battle in a wedge-shaped array, with shrill, piercing shouts. Since they carry only light arms, they are able to make extremely fast and unpre-dictable moves; they will suddenly fan out and charge without keeping in battle order, and stage a blood bath in a wide area. Their speed is so startling that you may fail to notice in time that they are assaulting a wall or burst over the enemy camp, looting. What makes them particularly redoubtable as dreaded foes is their use of long-range arrows which, in-stead of the customary metal heads, are armed with artfully applied bones. In close-range combat they use short swords. While their oppo-nent attempts to ward off their blows, they will often throw a rope made of rags to catch and tie him.

"They never use a plow; they won't even touch its handles. They have no fixed abode, no fireplace; they are like people constantly on flight, they always use their wagons. In these wagons, the women make their ungainly apparel, mate with their men, give birth to children, and raise the boys until puberty. No Hun could tell his place of origin. He is con-ceived at one place, born in another, and raised somewhere else.

"The Huns are unreliable and fickle in meeting contractual obliga-tions; they abruptly change their minds whenever they expect this to be profitable. Like beasts devoid of reason, they cannot distinguish between right and wrong. Their words are deceitful and ambiguous. They have no reverence for nobleness; they are not even inhibited by superstition; their lust for gold is insatiable; their irascibility is so uncontrollable that they will break, and make up again, with their comrades several times a day without obvious reason."

The Hun tactics had long before been applied in Siberian wars, and in Europe they were rendered even more effective by the terror that only absolute ugliness can implant in the hearts and minds of civilized men.

Nations under attack sometimes attributed magic powers to the Huns. They believed that not only would the ungainly hordes erupt over their lands as a natural disaster, but they could also produce and unleash storms and earthquakes.

The Romans, who had a long tradition of dealing with barbarians, first trusted that they could handle the Huns, which meant that they could use them for their own purposes. A Roman hierarchy enlisted Hun hordes as auxiliaries and thus molded the tribes into a coherent Roman nation. Traitors, usurpers, and turncoats, who wanted to use the Huns for their own sinister purposes, taught them the lesson of Roman vulnerability and the ignoble art of blackmail and extraction of tributes. It would have been against the Huns' nature to be content with riches gathered without fight and with privileges that did not turn them into unrestricted masters. The Huns wanted battle, and if nobody was ready to fight they would slaughter human hecatombs nonetheless. This urge for violence, and the Huns' intellectual incapacity for putting the wealth they grabbed to diligent and enjoyable use, made them constant attackers whom nothing short of annihilation could stop.

The chronicle of the Huns in civilized Europe covers about fourscore years. One man could have lived to witness their first appearance in the approaches to Byzantium, their rise to a great power, the climax of their awesome might and its extinction. But the life expectancy in the Hun era was short. However, what these humans experienced during the age of the Huns is summed up in the words of St. Eusebius Hieronymus (Jerome), a native of the Pannonian Danube Basin: "The Huns appear where they are least expected; their fastness outpaces even rumors. They do not respect religion, age, or station, they won't even spare helpless children. They put to death infants who have hardly begun to live, and the little ones, unaware of the menace of horrible fate, smile as the murderers grasp them and draw their swords . . . Roman blood is spilled every day . . . lands are overrun and ravaged . . . noble lives are destroyed, bishops taken prisoners, other priests and ecclesiastical dignitaries slain, churches turned into stables. Cruel despair spreads everywhere; terror and death have many variants . . . but I could not tell it all, even if I had a hundred tongues, a hundred throats, and a voice of iron. . . ."

A voice of iron! Hardly could a man who had not witnessed roaring, shrilling, bloodcurdling, and blood-spilling extremities have coined these words. Among those who shuddered, suffered, perished, or survived for even worse suffering were practically all the people of the Danube Valley, a strange blend of nations, or rather layers of nations, piled up in eons and more or less thinly varnished with Roman lacquer.

Germanic layers dodged and yielded more easily than the others. Their leaders tried to negotiate, conceded, and vegetated. The old-established, rooted, and settled layers suffered what not even a voice of iron could have shouted. From the lands below the Iron Gate to the vicinity of tottering Vienna, lands which distant ancestors had reclaimed from the wilderness were deserted, and their inhabitants slain, enslaved, or scattered in a diaspora of no redemption.

Germanic historians, with the notable exception of outstanding professors, have an occasional soft spot for Attila the Hun, who was to rule all the lands along the Danube and exact tributes from both Romes: "Attila was not necessarily a devastator," says one source. "He was on the best of terms with Germanic Kings and peoples. The language of his court was Gothic. And his realm was not entirely devoid of culture. In the German heroic saga, in the *Song of the Nibelungs,* he is kindly remembered as King Etzel. He maintained relations with East and West Rome. King Theodosius II, who died in 450, formally ceded him Pannonia. Ostrogoths, Burgundians, Gepidae, Rugii, Heruli, Langobards, Thuringians, and, in addition to these Germanic nations, Slav and Khazar tribes were included in his empire. His name is Gothic."

In fact, Attila-Etzel destroyed the first Burgundian Empire, as he devastated homesteads of all the civilized peoples of his empire. The *Song of the Nibelungs,* which originated 700 years after the unlamented passing of the King of the Huns, in 453, is a fictionalized story of Holy King Stephen superimposed upon the paling, dehydrated figure of Attila; and the Slavs did not bow on the stage of Europe until well after Attila's final curtain.

Chroniclers of both Romes are somewhat taciturn when it comes to the earlier shameful dealings of their governments with the Huns, and the illiterate Huns did not record events for posterity. But long after the Hun law of the club was broken, Christendom, to which most of the people of the Danube Valley adhered, remained polluted by pagan superstitions; and there seemed to be no man in the wide land to revive the pure spirit of the gospel.

CHAPTER NINE

The Avars reached the eastern and central Danube Valley at the turn of the sixth century. They too hailed from Siberia, but did not resemble the Huns ethnologically; they were of Türküt (Turk) stock. They too had been swept west through the boundless steppes by the tides of nations. But it seems to have taken the Avars only about two centuries to cover the distance from Central Asia to the fringe of Eastern Europe, much less than it took the Huns, yet still not quite one hundred yards a day as the crow flies.

The Avars were uncivilized by Western standards, though they did already cook their food and build primitive round villages. And, though unattractive, they did not mutilate their infants into monsters.

They had an innate aversion toward peaceful occupations and tried to force weaker people to provide for them. Somewhere in the plains of easternmost Europe they subdued small Slav groups and made them toil for them. These Slavs, the first of their kind to reach the Danube Basin, were still in the Avar service when Byzantium learned of their presence.

Byzantium first took little notice of the newcomers. The Danube Valley was considered a *cordon sanitaire* beyond which the dust of upheaval, massacre, and misery never settled. As long as the Avars did not cross the river to raid civilized territory, Byzantium would not interfere.

The Avars had no frightening battle record when they first saw the brackish waters of the Danube Delta, but they were formidable fighters nonetheless, like all migrant Asiatics who survived their long trek.

Avars began to cross the Danube into the Balkans to hit, grab, and run. Their Slav vassals served as auxiliaries in predatory violations of Byzantine territory. These raids gave the Slavs little gain but a bad reputation.

Runaway Slavs established themselves in the remote swamps of the river delta. These Slav groups had once been roving outposts of a larger nation on the Volga River, the Bulgars, who left their land early in the sixth century and slowly pushed on, in the general direction of the Danube. This move may have been caused by the pressure of the great migration, by failure of harvests, or by a desire to find and join lost national outposts. Eastern mankind was in foment, the signpost of gravity pointed west, and the Danube Valley was the road to whatever remained of the West's riches.

The Bulgars eventually invested the Danube Delta, incorporated the runaway Slavs into their roving nation, settled, expanded, and around 680 founded Bulgaria, the oldest organized Slavic state, the cradle of Slav Christendom.

The Avars established their villages in the now Hungarian part of the Danube Valley and did well, to the detriment of weaker neighbors. Like their barbaric predecessors, they seemed to grow like weeds, but unlike Attila's Huns, they made no serious attempt at empire grabbing. Their concept of a state was a powerful base dominated by fortified circular villages from where they could raid neighboring regions. They formed a continental version of pirate clans, who established bases on sheltered islands and profited from other peoples' woes, from the patri-, matri-, and fratricidal battles and intrigues that turned the Danube Valley into a jungle in which the aborigines vegetated in destitution and fear.

The Avars grew in strength and wealth, and they made a strange pact with the Langobards, who planned to leave for more comfortable climates and wealthier regions.

King Baian of the Avars took over Danubian districts over which the Langobards had exercised control, but guaranteed that they would be returned to the Langobards should they claim them within the next 200 years. It was a "lease" which the parties involved could hardly expect to outlive. But the Langobards never returned to the Danube Valley. They departed for Italy on April 2, 568, a long column of carts loaded with all sorts of goods and supplies, and they arrived at the site of Aquileja after one month's journey. Italianized, called "Lombards," they survived for about two centuries. In 774 their duchies succumbed to Charlemagne.

The Avars as a nation did not outlive them long. In 791, Charlemagne, not yet Roman Emperor but already lord and master over Franks and Lombards, victor in Spain, forcible Christianizer of the Saxons, and the key figure in the lands along the upper Danube, decided to chastise the Avars and to secure the regions of the Danube Basin in which they dwelled. Frankish chroniclers called these regions the "Avar Desert."

The desert was man-made desolation, destruction of what non-Avar

men had built. Nature never closed its horn of abundance, and men of
good will who dwelled in peace could always reclaim the desert.

The frightened Avar King offered to have his people converted to
Christendom and to accept Frankish suzerainty. Charlemagne did not
trust him, and had his son Pepin watch the Avars to invade their territory if his suspicions were aroused. In 796 it seemed evident that the
Avars had no intention to live as His Majesty's Christian subjects. The
Frankish army overran the "Avar Desert" and penetrated its citadel,
which was not a "desert" but a circular-shaped bulwark of huge tree
trunks and massive masonry within which there were several villages; the
King's own big, but barbarically artless, abode, and his treasury, a strong
underground chamber. The chamber contained jewels and works of art,
objects of thievery by a succession of brutes of exalted rank. They had
been swapped back and forth between civilization and barbary, as loot,
ransom, tributes, and bribery. Their story was that of endless variations
on the themes of corruption, faithlessness, and cowardice.

The Avar King could not defend his citadel, but he protested that he
would, henceforth, abide by the Christian faith and law, provided the
treasury were left to him. But he was not believed and the hoard was
seized. The location of the Avar citadel has not been established beyond
doubt. But there is reason to believe that it was in the vicinity of the city
of Raab (Györ) on the Danube, about halfway between Vienna and
Budapest.

In 803, Bulgarian Khan (King) Krum, the Terrible, the most powerful and violent ruler whom this nation ever had, undertook a campaign
in the Danube Valley and defeated the already prostrate Avars.

There are cycles in the history of many lands: construction, alternating
with destruction and intervals of desolation. One and the same nation
cannot be both constructive and destructive. The Avars were destructive,
and they went through the usual phases of their mischievous mission:
enrichment through violence, corruption, and downfall through counter-
violence.

The memory of the man who shaped events in the Danube Basin,
Charlemagne, is so completely enshrouded by legend and tainted by emotional partisanship that more than a thousand years after his death in
Aix-la-Chapelle (Aachen) on January 28, 814, his character and the
true motives of his actions seem to have remained forever controversial.

Devout Catholics insist that he was a saint. But after he was canonized,
350 years after his demise, his festival was not observed everywhere, and

still the 1957 edition of the Encyclopaedia Britannica (Vol. V, p. 254) says that "this gave him no real claim to saintship." One version pictures him as a rabid imperialist, another as the champion of a universal Christian Empire which Rome had failed to build in its time of grandeur. A man of profound learning, an exalted patron of the arts and sciences, some say; an illiterate whose principal source of information was a vicious dwarf and court jester, claim others. And there are more inconsistencies, such as that he was a man of the purest moral perceptions, or a profligate debaucher who had four wedded wives whom he deposed at will, in addition to five official and more unofficial mistresses.

But whatever else he may have been, he was one of the most remarkable empire builders of all time. In 768, when he ascended the throne at the age of twenty-six, his realm comprised but a fraction of present metropolitan France. When he died, it reached from present Denmark into Spain, and from the Atlantic to the Raab and Elbe rivers. It was not a "horseback realm," which functioned only within the range of the ruler's cavalry, but a superbly organized empire, with supreme legislative power vested in, or delegated to, the monarch; with a regular court system, an "army constitution," and an Imperial Diet, which had a weighty voice in the appointment of top officials. When he was crowned by Pope Leo III in Rome, on Christmas Eve of the year 800, Charlemagne assumed the dignity of Emperor of the West, and with it title to the realm of the Caesars. However, there was a fatal flaw in the splendid pattern: a law of succession. All legitimate sons were supposed to inherit a share in the realm, as if it were an estate, and thus the Empire survived its controversially glorious builder by a bare twenty-nine years. It was permanently split in 843, under the terms of the Treaty of Verdun.

But Charlemagne's rule had lasting effects upon the upper parts of the Danube Basin, and even though this hardly was the Emperor's intention, it laid the foundations of Austria.

Charlemagne believed in a system of buffer states, which was obviously derived from the Roman pattern of turning outlying provinces into military bulwarks where practically everything was subordinated to the purpose of protecting the central parts of the Empire against invasion. The Emperor turned the eastern fringe of his realm into *Grenzmarken* (frontier districts), semi-autonomous territories whose governors held great powers, even though they had to take Imperial orders and to report to the Diet. Settlements and draft laws of those districts were different from those in the interior sections of the Empire. The regime was military in character. Ennobled lords of manors built their residences into fortresses, usually in strategic locations. Dominant hills in the Danube Valley were crowned by castles. Peasants who worked the nobles' land were subject to draft into their master's military contingent. The governors arranged shifts of populations, and the central government occasionally ordered forcible transfers to the *Grenzmarken* to keep the reservoir of manpower from running dry.

The Emperor spent several of his last years in the Danube Valley. He convoked the Diet to Ratisbon, went to that city after his return from the coronation, and resided there for a short time. In Ratisbon, a Roman-built terminal of Danube shipping, where the young river gaily flows through lush fields and groves, were assembled representatives of more nations than Charlemagne could remember offhand and who had all sworn him allegiance. He bestowed titles and defined duties of the Margraves who ruled the *Grenzmarken,* then proceeded to the former Juvavum (renamed Salzburg), where in 803 he named more frontier princes and officials.

One of the frontier districts was the Ostmark, soon renamed Ostarrichi, the original form of Österreich (Austria). Its hinterland was Bavaria, which had turned from an arena in which barbarians paraded their aggressiveness, into a testing ground of ecclesiastic guardianship. When Charlemagne established his Empire, bishops and abbots ruled like feudal lords, jealous of their mundane prerogatives and opposing administrative directives as interference with local affairs. They would not tolerate outsiders having a say in their petty districts.

CHAPTER TEN

Christendom did not take solid roots in Bavaria until late in the seventh century, after St. Emmeram, Bishop of Poitiers, France, came to the foreign land to teach the faith with fierce zeal and against heavy odds.

The people of Bavaria, which then comprised only the southern part of the present state, were still mostly idolators. Many were ready to accept conversion to please the passionate apostle, but they considered Jesus

Christ just another idol and included worship of the Redeemer in their colorful pagan rites.

Emmeram labored for three years, traveling through the upper Danube Valley, making friends who quite often turned out to be neither devout nor devoted.

Duke Theodo also befriended Emmeram. The zealous bishop spent some time in sightly Ratisbon, planning to proceed to Rome to visit the tombs of St. Peter and St. Paul and gather strength and inspiration for his pious mission. He was a guest at the ducal court, where life was not strictly ascetic. The least ascetic of all was the Duke's daughter, Ota, of whom no portrait exists, but whose behavior chroniclers call "scandalous." Emmeram's fervor was never discouraged by bad reputations, and Ota's frivolity did not keep her from seeking a saintly man's advice. When the bishop prepared for his pilgrimage she was in trouble. Her latest lover was a very important person at court; she was pregnant; and the very important person emphatically refused to marry her. Emmeram's advice in the distressing affair is not known, but he may have told the Princess to confess her offense to the Duke.

Ota waited until Emmeram had left before talking to her father. But instead of telling him the truth, she said that she had had an affair with the friendly bishop.

Furious, Duke Theodo sent his myrmidons after the pilgrim. They caught him a few miles south of Munich, and submitted him to a medieval type of third degree of indescribable bestiality. Whatever breath was still left in him was choked by the executioner, who used most elaborate methods. The final act of the bishop's drama took place near Ascheim, fifteen miles away from the spot where he was seized.

Shortly after Emmeram's death, a Benedictine monastery outside Ratisbon that had vegetated in ineffective obscurity, was named after the martyr, who was also canonized. Duke Theodo lived to regret his credulity in his scandalous daughter's confessions. Emmeram became patron saint of Ratisbon, and the name giver of a great number of chapels. But many Bavarians prefer to consider another saint, Ruprecht (Rupert), the patron of their Christendom, and some have even gone so far as to change that saint's time of birth to make it appear that he actually preceded Emmeram.

In fact, St. Ruprecht followed Emmeram. He was a Benedictine monk from Juvavum, which at that time was part of Bavaria. Monk Ruprecht is said to have had a deep urge for apostolic work; he wanted to revive the remainder of earlier Christendom that was buried under a bewildering variety of heresies and occult demonology. Demons and ghosts of rivers and mountains played an important part in cultic aberrations. The spirits of the Danube and its tributaries, in the guise of phantoms wearing features of barbaric invaders, were believed to be no less violent but less predictable than Attila's warriors.

Ruprecht's place of birth is not established beyond doubt. Even the *Breves notitiae Salzburgenses* are not explicit on the subject. But he must have had a terrific power of fascination. Crowds gathered wherever he went. His fame spread all over Bavaria, until it reached the court of Ratisbon, where turning the populace toward nonviolent objectives was viewed with elation. The Duke met the monk. Ruprecht was invested with the two-square-mile territory of Juvavum, a busy place of commerce that now became an episcopal see. From this tiny ecclesiastic realm, Ruprecht was to carry out apostolic activities within all of Bavaria, and from there to the eastern borders of Pannonia. The Bavarian dukes held no power over Pannonia, but Ruprecht's personality was stronger than the Bavarian army.

Ruprecht built Juvavum's first church, St. Peter's, at the site where, in 426, St. Maximus and his companions had suffered martyrdom. The nunnery on the Nonnberg is another monument of his labors. Pious accounts tend to explain that construction work was done practically without funds, but the first bishop of Juvavum was a materialist in his own right, a pioneer also of industry. He inaugurated salt mining in the region, and salt has remained a local source of income, though no longer of abundance, up to the present day. Income derived from salt helped build Juvavum's convents and churches, and gave it its modern name of Salzburg ("Castle of Salt"); and even though, regrettably, the wording of Ruprecht's sermons and admonitions is nowhere recorded, there is reason to believe that their immense fascination was partly due to the fact that they dealt not only with divinity on a lofty spiritual plane but also with the gifts of God and their practical use for the welfare of His creatures.

The eloquent priest did not aim at expanding his tiny realm, but traveling and preaching in Bavaria, Upper and Lower Austria, and beyond, quite often on rafts on the Danube, he built strong cells of a faith which no vicissitude could ever destroy, and also material strongholds: churches and monasteries where even laymen could find a haven in emergencies.

The first churches near Juvavum which his zeal helped build—Maxglan, Bischofshofen, Altötting—set a pattern for many glorious monasteries to rise through the centuries that followed; mighty bulwarks of the Danube Valley that withstood the elements of nature and the violence of man much better than the citadels of nobility. Rejuvenated Ratisbon, Passau, Wilhering, Melk, Göttweig, Klosterneuburg, Esztergom (Gran), became gems of splendor. Prelates, residing in these monasteries, ruled for many miles in the round. Their spiritual estates closely resembled feudal domains whose material existence was based on the affluence of the land. Ruprecht's genius protected his church against creed-perverting vassalage to mundane sovereigns. Without his organizational talents, there would have been no frame for Charlemagne's *Grenzmarken*.

In the middle period of his activities, chroniclers say, "he repaired home, and returned with a niece, Erindruda, and twelve men." "Home" does not seem to have been Juvavum, and which years this middle period covered has not been established. The niece's name sounds Celtic, which would point at Frankish birth, and his "twelve men" were said to have acted in the manner of Irish monks. Therefore, it is widely believed that Ruprecht was of Irish origin. Erindruda, whose name was Germanized into Ehrentraud, became the first abbess of her uncle's nunnery on the Nonnberg.

Ruprecht's successor was Archbishop Arno, whom Charlemagne instructed to turn Christian institutions into bases of Imperial rule. The reward promised to Arno was one third of all taxes collected from communities where his sermons would help restore apostates to the fold. Ruprecht's financial pattern faded.

Arno traveled through the valleys of the Salzach, Inn, and Danube, telling local dignitaries that manifestations of devoutness in their districts would consolidate their own positions; consecrating churches; and writing glowing reports on repenting apostates. Being a rather lazy man, the archbishop returned to his see, offered the Emperor his special blessings, and had his assignment revised. His share in taxes was not reduced, but his activities were confined to affairs of state.

There were quite a few such affairs to attend. New dioceses formed. Bishops feuded about boundaries with frantic, though non-armed vehemence. The Bishop of Passau, whose splendid, immensely strong see dominated the strategically vital spot in which the Danube enters its Upper Austrian defile, laid claim to regions as far downriver as Györ, while dioceses founded as far south as Carinthia clamored for allotments of souls in the Danube Valley. Three synods, held at Lorch, Mautern (sixty miles upstream of Vienna), and Mistelbach, produced no permanent settlement, but added substantial territories to the domain of Passau.

Peasants, including freemen, were subject to taxation, and since Arno's day, the Church was a beneficiary of collecting internal revenue for the states. A friend once warned Arno against levying the tithe, saying that had it not been for the tithe, or tenth, the Saxons would not have rebelled against Charlemagne. Arno ignored the warning; one third of the tithe was his own revenue.

A petition against taxation is already quoted in ancient archives. One Alkunius, addressing himself to the Emperor, wrote: "We, born and raised in the Catholic creed, can hardly resign ourselves into paying one tenth of our entire property. How could those who are still weak of faith, greedy, and childish of mind, accept such a taxation without revolt?" The petition remained unanswered. To the people, involuntary surrender of property, proceeds of labor as well as unsalaried work, was a sinister phenomenon tied to barbaric invasions and wars. They could not reconcile themselves to the fact that the similar noxious compulsion was applied by the peaceful administration of a protecting Emperor, or a patriarchal Church.

Throughout the Danube Valley, most people believed that the bishops personally kept not only all proceeds of ecclesiastical estates but most of the state taxes as well.

In fact, the bishop personally collected one fourth of the income from his estates; another fourth went to the lower clergy, one third for church construction, the rest for alms. Yet, the enraged taxpayers sulked and shirked. It took 250 years until Gebehard, Archbishop of Salzburg, could proudly report for the first time that there were no tax arrears in his archdiocese, and that even the Slavs had met their obligations.

Slavs then constituted the hard core of anti-taxation individualists. They had become a strong element in the population of the central and even upper parts of the Danube Valley.

Some of the Slavs came from splinter groups that had migrated after a short-lived Greater Moravian realm broke up. The Danube Valley had a strong attraction for these people, who were peaceful as compared with invaders from the Siberian plains, such as the Huns and Avars, and such rabid latecomers as the Petchenegs and Magyars. But they were no shining examples of meek mildness. Being skillful farmers, they wanted to be home during the busy season, and their individual interest in conquest never strayed beyond the lands they could reasonably expect to till.

More militant and violent Slavs, however, the Bulgars, threatened to expand their rule over their ethnic kin, and this caused the Slavic tribes from the more distant regions of the Danube Basin to accept Frankish Imperial protection and domination.

In 815, when Ludwig I, son of Charlemagne, held the Grand Diet of Paderborn, in Westphalia, it was attended by Slav grandees and deputies from the upper Danube. More Slavs, deputies from Pannonia, Dalmatia, and regions that became part of Serbia, attended another Diet three years later.

The records of that Diet tell of Slav protestations of fealty, but also of specific complaints about taxes and administrative encroachments.

An anti-tax rebellion started in the lower Danube Valley in 818.

The Pannonian peasants did not listen to demagogues. They held no meetings, did not indulge in spectacular paraphernalia of revolution. They brought in their harvest so that there would be no hunger among those who stayed behind; they stored all implements that could not serve as weapons; and then they trudged off toward the strongholds of the haughty Margrave Kadolaus, whom they considered responsible for their plight.

Kadolaus could hardly trust his eyes when he saw the peasants march against his bastions, and ordered his armored men to disperse the mob. But the mob fought well, the armored men were dispersed, and the peasants returned to their Danubian homesteads in time for the spring sowing. Their leader, Liudewit, sent a delegation to the Imperial residence to ask for redress and guarantees.

The delegates did not get a complete hearing, and in 819, after the harvest, the peasants again marched against the Margrave, fought, and scored, but they did not secure justice for themselves.

Many an able-bodied man did not return to his family and fields, but the others refused to give in.

In 820, Margrave Kadolaus succumbed to an infectious fever, but not before he had appealed to the Emperor to chastise the peasants, lest their rebellion undermine his realm.

One year later, when the men were still working in the fields, three Imperial army groups swept down the Danube Valley. Liudewit fled across the Danube into the mountains of Serbia to conduct a harassing guerilla-type warfare against the soldiery who sacked his land.

This type of warfare has remained characteristic for the western Balkans through the ages, in Liudewit's time as in that of the Turks, and during world wars. It rarely achieved its aims.

There could be no effective resistance against the Emperor's armies. Desperate and destitute peasants now considered taxes to be the lesser evil; many transferred their landholdings to the Church and stayed on as bondsmen in order to gain protection, even though most Slavs were not yet Christianized.

Such transfers were considered most desirable by government and clergy. The Crown did not ask for a share in the donations. Records of Church acquisitions piled up high, but most of the papers were destroyed during the holocaust of the final phases of the Migration of Peoples. Bishops and abbots later ordered restoration of records. There is no reason to insinuate that dishonest intentions were involved, but it has been claimed by such unimpeachable authority as the *Archiv für Kunde österreichischer Geschichtsquellen* (Vol. X, 1853) that some of the restored documents never were authenticated.

For a long period, the Church was the largest landholder along the Danube. This may provide anticlericals with ammunition, but it had no ill effect upon agricultural development in the basin.

The campaign against the peasants took the Western armies to the Balkans, where they established an uncomfortably close contact with the Bulgars.

Krum the Terrible, who relished using goblets made from the skulls of slaughtered enemies, literally drank himself to death during his campaign against Byzantium in 814. In 817, his successor, "Wild Mortago," made a thirty-year treaty of peace with Byzantium and, turning his aggressive attention to the western Balkans and Pannonia, learned of Liudewit and taxation.

Wild Mortago preferred loot to taxation, and he would never hesitate to slay whoever did not obey him. Yet he posed as a friendly liberator when his warriors moved into districts along the left bank of the Danube as far north as central Hungary. The people there, however, learned soon, and the hard way, that the Bulgar regime was worse than Imperial rule and taxation.

It took the wild Bulgar ruler until 824 to understand the governmental setup in the lands his horsemen had invested. Then he sent a letter to the Emperor of the Franks, expressing desire to establish permanent contact. No reply in writing was given. The Emperor had specialists on Danubian affairs. One of them, a Bavarian named Machelm, accompanied the Bulgar envoys back to their headquarters to find out more about these people and their intentions.

He learned of intrusion and reckless violence, and raced back to suggest that the Bulgars be chased away. But the Emperor wanted to spend a quiet Christmas at Aix-la-Chapelle rather than bother with barbarians.

He did nothing; he did not even receive a Bulgar ambassador who arrived early in 825, and ignored two subsequent messages. In 827 Wild Mortago realized that he was being snubbed, and staged a river-borne invasion of *Grenzmark* territory.

Solidly built Bulgar craft rowed—some say, sailed—up the Danube and Drava. Landing detachments raided villages and installed Bulgar officers as local chieftains.

The indignant Emperor looked for a scapegoat for his own negligence, and found it in the person of one of his margraves, Balderich. Then the Diet ordered Ludwig, youthful King of reorganized Bavaria, to dislodge Bulgar intruders from wherever they had established themselves.

Chroniclers record Ludwig's spectacular departure at the head of a splendid army, but they say nothing about the campaign. The Bulgars kept expanding until in 838 a Slav-Bulgar chieftain was defeated by Bavarians.

The Bulgars turned into peaceful peasants, fishermen, and minor merchants, as their great apostles began to spread a Christian creed: the Eastern Orthodox faith. Cyril, who, together with his older brother Methodius, became the Apostle of the Slavs, was born in 827. The brothers turned their people into a constructive element in medieval society, but as they taught and worked, another human storm shook the Danube Basin.

CHAPTER ELEVEN

Around 819, Greek settlers of the lands near the Danube Delta, who lived under Bulgar control, were hit by raiders on horseback, who staged a blood bath and left the few survivors literally bare, their homesteads looted and burned to the ground. And this was their description of the raiders:

"These men were of sickening ugliness. Their deep-set eyes had an inhuman look; their heads seemed bald, but from their pates sprang three thin pigtails. Their voices were frighteningly shrill, and their language was different from any human tongue. Like wild animals, they devoured raw flesh and drank blood."

This sounded reminiscent of the Huns four centuries earlier, of whom, however, the chroniclers of the Magyars had never heard.

The Magyars (Ungern, Ungarn, Hungarians) had reached the Danube, where they would conquer and be conquered, inflict and suffer injury, and become the outside world's objects of disgust, curiosity, and inspiration, for over a thousand years.

In victory and defeat, in glory and prostration, they remained soldiers.

Historian Ernst Dümmler, a scholar of early Magyar life, wrote in 1853:

"The early Hungarian way of waging war was different from that of all other contemporary nations, with the possible exception of Britons and Bulgars. Its very newness spread terror. They were armed with swords, javelins, bows made of horn; they used the sword sparingly, and essentially relied on their marksmanship with arrows. They constantly trained shooting arrows from horseback. Their horses were protected by armor and they wheeled them round with perfect agility. They preferred long-range combat to close-quarter fighting; their victories were more often due to ruse and fast movement than to massive attack. They frequently staged mock flights to lure the enemy out of a strong position and made him take up pursuit in loose formation, then suddenly turned around to strike a surprise blow. Also, they would sever the enemy's lines of supply and swarm around, harassing him in constant skirmishes until he succumbed to exhaustion. Their extremely mobile array was divided into four groups. Their baggage was left behind a screen, behind which they kept a hard-riding reserve.

"Clever use of reserves often turned the tide of battles which seemed lost. Once victory was won, they kept up pursuit until the enemy was annihilated. The Hungarians gave no quarter; according to their creed, every man they slew in battle would be their slave in the next world.

"They would readily suffer heat, cold, and many more hardships, and, intractable as their tempers were, discipline in their camp was rigorous and infractions were severely punished.

"They combined cunning with ruthless perfidy. They would not hesitate to break pledges, and hardly had they accepted presents when they would scheme treason and fraud. Siege was the only kind of warfare in which they were unskilled. Their only means to take a fortress was starvation."

A contemporary who lived in a monastery south of the upper Danube when the Magyars swarmed into Central Europe had this to say:

"The Magyars are undoubtedly arisen from the Hydra of Lerna, for poisonous is the malice of their hearts. They are cunning, and full of deceit; like a smooth serpent, they will slip out of the grips of pursuers, and when they are defeated they will come back in even larger number like frogs engendered in the swamps."

The cradle of the Magyars stood in Asia, in all likelihood in eastern Siberia, the well from which so many migrating nations have sprung. Were the prehistoric Magyars a nation in the usual meaning of the word? Probably not. They may have been no more than a clan of hunters, which ages of shiftlessness and struggle made grow in strength and number.

The Magyars' appearance on the European scene, long before they burst upon the Greek settlers on the Danube, was anything but glorious. They were under strong pressure and in almost constant flight from a stronger Asiatic nation, the Petchenegs, who then roamed the steppes of eastern European Russia.

At the turn of the ninth century, seven Magyar tribes reached the Don, then moved on to a land they called Atelkusu. Atel was an early name of the Volga, but it also meant simply "water." Atelkusu sounds like a region between waters; rivers that may have been northeasternmost tributaries of the Danube.

At the time they reached Atelkusu the Magyars' cult had features of Zoroastrianism, apparently picked up somewhere near the Persian border on the long road west. They worshiped demons who accounted for happy and unlucky events and who, in turn, were being ruled by Isten, a surpreme being. *Isten* has remained the Hungarian word for God.

While the bulk of the Magyars reveled in Atelkusu, tribal chieftains who had reached the Danube Delta established contact with Byzantine military, who hired groups of the hard-riding bowmen and used them at random all over the Balkan Peninsula. Magyars clashed with Bulgars, and must have trespassed the lands which would later be theirs, long before the official date of their entry, which is set at around 875.

After Byzantium had hired them as mercenaries, Arnulf, later King of the Germans, took them into his service. They stormed through the Danube Valley, looting, almost unresisted.

Shortly before 875, while Magyar fighters were engaged in foreign battles, the Petchenegs hit Atelkusu, where mostly women, children, and old people had stayed behind. Smoldering destruction was left in the Petcheneg wake. Many survivors were captured; the rest fled west to what became Galicia province, and across the Carpathian Mountains into Hungary. Through coincidence rather than planning they met scouts of their mercenary army, to whom they told that Atelkusu was lost and that they would have to find a new home, preferably near some fresh and healthy water.

To the cattle-breeding and fishing Magyars, the quality of water was of prime importance. They sampled water wherever they went. They are said to have filled two bottles with water from the Danube, and to have found it much to their liking. So they looked for the Danube, not knowing that the brackish river north of Byzantium and the invigorating waters south and east of the Carpathians came from one and the same source.

Where the valleys of the northern Carpathian Mountains widened they set up camp and called the place Munka ("toil") in memory of their toilsome trek. The army stayed with their people, to keep the way to the Danube open.

Commander of the army was Prince Árpád, their first supreme leader, whose power rested upon a pact between himself and 110 chieftains and elders. He led the Magyars down into the plains. They found the land populated by Slavs, who offered no resistance to the fugitive invaders. Slav nobles surrendered meekly; only one, whose castle stood a short distance south of Munka, fled. The Magyars seized and hanged him.

They found fertile land. Nature's own storehouse seemed inexhaustible: there was plenty of game and the rivers teemed with fish. The people, too, surrendered to the grim-looking newcomers.

The Magyars had no tradition of "buying" property from non-Magyars. They grabbed what they could, and when they sold objects to the nations whom they served, they preferred to be paid in horses. White horses attracted them irresistibly.

When Árpád and his hosts scouted the land, it occurred to them that this would be their home forever. The Prince felt that a home should be acquired in a legal way; in short, he wished to "buy" what was about to become Hungary.

He dispatched delegations to the three chieftains who ruled large regions.

Maroth, who ruled over the territory between the Someş and Nyir rivers, refused to sell on Árpád's terms. On a prearranged signal, Magyar cavalrymen, one day's march behind the delegates, appeared on the scene. The rest was butchery.

Gelo, chieftain over Transylvanian tribes, had a very valuable domain, with rivers containing gold, with salt mines, with an industrious, peaceable people. Gelo did not object to a "deal," but he was nonetheless attacked and killed because, as the Magyars said, he was altogether "contemptible."

Zalan, the third chieftain, was asked to "sell" territory which included the region of Tokaj, and fertile plains between the Danube and the Tisza. Zalan knew what had happened to the two other chieftains. Trembling, he expressed readiness to "sell." The Magyars offered a price: twelve white horses.

Zalan survived. And the Magyars acquired their homeland, roughly 100,000 square miles, for twelve horses.

Postscript to history: Chances are that they had stolen the horses from Byzantine owners.

Árpád loved the water of the Danube: he wanted to be surrounded by it and therefore established his residence on an island in the river, close to the site of Budapest; he called the place Csepel, after one of his favorite servants.

Árpád's residence was an architectural monstrosity, but it was big, which was probably all he wanted. He celebrated his moving into Csepel Island with uninhibited carousing, and whatever affection he had for good water, it was not usually his preferred beverage. The story goes that when he received pleasing news he drank himself into stupors which lasted from three to seven days.

The Magyars could have lived in peaceful abundance for a long time, but peace was not their way of life.

Magyar campaigns were hardly different from those of earlier Asiatic invaders; contacts with one foreign nation usually offered leads toward other countries where looting was supposed to be good. Not only did they consider themselves invincible soldiers, but after acquiring primitive navigating skills on the Danube, they believed themselves to be equally efficient as sailors.

In 900, they invaded Italy. The idea originated with Slav prisoners of war, who also acted as guides. Franks, Bavarians, and the nobles from the Ostmark felt almost secure in the belief that the horsemen would find the South a better and easier hunting ground. But prisoners of war and professional informers told Magyar grandees that a German King had died and a child become his successor. Árpád was positive that a land ruled by a child should be easy prey. While his main forces were still in Italy and a secondary force penetrated Carinthia, a band of horsemen rode up the Danube Valley, into Lower Austria. Another mark of fire and death led to the Upper Austrian border. St. Florian Monastery was practically destroyed.

But the Bavarians and the men from the Ostmark rallied to fight. Under the command of Margrave Luitpold and of Richarius, Bishop of Passau (who was a better soldier than the Margrave), they struck the Magyars where the Enns River empties into the Danube, and killed 1200 at little loss to themselves.

Bavarians boasted of having thanked the Lord for their victory by screaming loudly enough to be heard in the skies. They built a fortress near Lorch on the Enns River, and in 901 their ranking officers presented themselves at the Diet of Ratisbon to render homage to the child King, Ludwig III, who, prompted by his tutor, prattled that the new fortress was being awarded to St. Florian in compensation for damages suffered.

Upper and Lower Austria recovered comparatively quickly. In order to survive, people in the Danube Valley had to be resilient.

Bishops and margraves promoted trade as the best means of keeping out of mischief and overcoming sterile fear. Their reports to the Diet of Ratisbon tell more about customs duties than about preparations for defense. According to one of these reports, ships coming down the Danube past Passau had to pay half a drachma; craft going as far down as Linz had to pay an extra tax for salt, but no extra tax for "slaves and other merchandise." Owners of derelict ships were liable to confiscation of their boats and cargo. There were additional taxes for goods carried beyond Linz. Bavarian subjects could obtain tax exemption for such commodities as food, horses, and slaves. Otherwise, duties levied for a female slave or a stallion were four denarii apiece, and one denarius for male slaves and mares. Jews had to pay a moderate additional tax for slaves and other objects.

In 907 the Magyars were ready for another massive drive up the Danube Valley. At that time, Bavarian nobles, prelates and margraves, met at Raffelstetten, near the mouth of the Enns, to discuss current affairs of trade and taxation. It was resolved that tariff reductions be granted for salt ships that went to special markets. The way of some salt led through Magyar-controlled parts of the river valley.

When the first reports of Magyar aggression reached the dignitaries, their liege lords and vassals expected to annihilate every aggressor. Theirs was a feudal, professional army. Fighters and mounts were heavily armored. There were no foot soldiers. The impact of a frontal mass charge was tremendous. However, if it failed, the maneuverability of the army was practically nil.

Bavarian vanguards soon learned this in the vicinity of Pressburg (now Bratislava), where they ran into a Magyar troop that turned to mock flight and then swarmed over the hapless mass of human and horse flesh in armor. Soon thereafter the victors were in Raffelstetten. The assembly had dissolved, its members fled, and nothing but ruins remained. The Magyars entered Bavaria.

As often when record-keeping peoples are defeated by illiterates, there are no complete accounts of the battle with the Magyars in 907. It obviously took place near Passau, and it ended in disaster for the Bavarians. The flower of Bavarian nobility was wiped out, Margrave Luitpold died in action, and so did Archbishop Theotmar of Salzburg and Bishop Udo von Freisingen; and with them perished their kin and vassals.

The Ostmark turned into a Magyar hunting ground. Bavaria as far up as Ratisbon was under Magyar control. King Ludwig and his tutors fled, towns were overcrowded with refugees, crazed mayors filed anguished applications to higher authorities for permission to build stronger walls, only to see their communities razed before a reply was received.

The chronicle of the Magyars in the Danube Valley—and also in many regions of Western Europe—reads like a second installment of the Hun story, until, in 933, they appeared before the German King to collect more tribute. But Henry I, the Fowler, offered the Magyars nothing but a scabby mongrel whose tail and ears had been cut off.

The Magyars were in no mood to take insult. With their main armies engaged in other theaters, a makeshift force of almost fifty thousand rode into Germany. This time, luck was against them. Thirty-six thousand Magyars perished in a battle near the Lech River that marked their first real defeat since the day of the Petchenegs, and became a grim omen of even greater disaster a score of years later.

In the tenth century, the Magyar type that had disgusted and frightened earlier civilized Europeans had substantially changed. When the Petchenegs captured Atelkusu, the Magyars lost a considerable part of their womenfolk. In their new Hungarian home grounds, Magyar males appropriated to themselves Slav women, and during their campaigns they collected women from Germany, Italy, Burgundy, and Greece. The new Magyar breed, even though it retained certain Mongoloid features, was far more attractive than members of the original tribes had been. Only the warriors' hairdo remained unchanged until their Christianization.

CHAPTER TWELVE

The pagan Magyars fought their Armageddon on August 10, 955, near the Bavarian-Swabian border, close to the fields in which they had been defeated twenty-two years before.

The King of Germany then was Otto I, who seven years later would be crowned Holy Roman Emperor. No diplomatic exchanges between Otto and the Magyar sovereign, Taksony, preceded the new campaign. A state of war with the Magyars had become a permanent institution in the Danubian lands, though war did not preclude trade; salt-loaded ships and barges with other merchandise often crossed battle lines.

As usual, the Magyars opened hostilities. The attack came as no surprise to Otto I, but he did not expect its colossal impact.

They assembled in Lower Austria, which was under Magyar domination as far west as Melk. The Magyars also controlled Vienna and the approaches to that city, which in the mid-tenth century was of much lesser importance than Ratisbon.

After crossing into Bavaria, the Magyar army divided into two groups. One pushed in the direction of Fulda; the rest encircled Augsburg, about twenty-five miles south of the upper Danube.

Bishop Ulrich, the highest authority in the city, stood among the soldiers, in ecclesiastical garb, unarmed, without either helmet or armor, undaunted by a rain of arrows, and delivered encouraging addresses. In the hours of darkness, as the bishop supervised construction of additional bulwarks and defenders rested and regrouped, processions of women toured the city, reciting prayers.

At dawn on the second day of siege, Ulrich, atop a wall, said Mass.

The attack reopened as the sun rose. The assailants raged like a storm. But suddenly it abated and the Magyars rode away.

The besieged believed in a miracle; but in fact a Bavarian traitor had informed the Magyar generals that King Otto was approaching.

He arrived with his forces before the day was over, wielding his sacred lance. Its point was said to be made of the nails from the Cross of Christ.

The gates of Augsburg opened, and the garrison marched out to meet their sovereign. Germans and Magyars girded for a showdown a short distance away from the liberated city. After a long and murderous struggle, the Magyars were put to flight.

The Lech, swollen by recent rains, swallowed many fugitives; others, who tried to hide in nearby farmhouses, were burned to death. Slaughter and pursuit continued for two days. Not only the soldiers were in action; townspeople and peasants rose against the defeated remnants. Magyars who attempted resistance were massacred, but those who offered surrender were not spared either. They were cruelly executed, often buried alive in heaps. Half a century of iniquity was avenged. Their generals were taken to Ratisbon and hanged at the city's Gate of Easter, on the Danube bank.

On learning of his army's catastrophe, Taksony showed remarkable coolheadedness. As the victors celebrated their triumph, he put his land in a state of defense. The defense system was based on the Danube and its tributaries. From Melk to Vienna abatis blocked roads, trails, and defiles; iron chains barred rivers; even shipping of salt and slaves had to stop.

The Magyars were desperately short of manpower; all able-bodied men were drafted and trained to put their tools aside and take up arms should they be attacked.

The attack did not come. The Germans were content with having annihilated the invading army.

Lion-maned Taksony—he had abandoned the traditional three-pigtail hairdo—was a handsome man, and more civilized than his predecessors. He made no attempt again to trespass his country's western boundaries. The bitter taste of defeat remained strong on his palate, and he understood that conquest was not the only way of national ascent.

He tried colonization, offering land in Hungary to skilled and industrious settlers. It was not all too easy for him to communicate with foreigners, and skilled and industrious people familiar with the bad old Magyar way were not eager to join their community. However, a number of families came from Germany, Bohemia, Moravia, the Balkans, Walachia, even Russia, and—an oddity in Central Europe—from the Orient came Ishmaelites. The Ishmaelites went to the site of Budapest near Csepel Island, built houses there, and became an important element in the country's trade.

The Ishmaelites were a northern Arabian tribe, allegedly descendants of Ishmael, son of Abraham and Hagar, who married an Egyptian woman and went to live in the desert. Present Budapest could thus trace its ethnographic origin to the biblical patriarchs, but the city's chroniclers put greater pride in Magyardom.

The settlers did not help restore Magyar military formidableness, but they stimulated the country's economy. The window to Christianity was opened wider, and from Christendom came, if not always salvation, at least survival. Christendom had paid previous calls on the Magyars, the arsonists and pillagers of hundreds of churches and monasteries, the killers of hundreds of thousands of Christian men and women. A few gallant monks from Germany had gone to the lands of the Magyars to preach the gospel. They did not become martyrs, but their endeavors were not successful. As long as the Magyars prospered they did not see why the Lord should be superior to pagan Isten, or Christ to their demons.

The disaster of 955 brought it home to Taksony that the God of the Christians was stronger than Isten. He did not accept conversion after the battle, but he did not object to his son and heir being taught the tenets of Christian faith. The son's name, Géza (also Geisa), was derived from gyözö, meaning "victor," but the triumphal name was no longer quite fitting for the head of a nation that had to exert discretion in its ventures.

Eventually Géza was baptized and married to Sarolta, daughter of a converted Magyar officer.

Sarolta was a woman of striking beauty; through her beauty and her iron will she dominated Géza. She was the real power of the realm. Besides, she was a drunkard, irascible and violent. Once, in a fit of anger, she seized a sword and ran it through the body of a man who had aroused her ire; the courtiers, however, resented such murder less than her habit of sitting on horseback like a man. Géza, too, had spells of violence which accounted for several killed, as his subjects were not supposed to defend themselves against their overlords.

Sarolta ordered her husband to display religious fervor, and, equally afraid of his wife's violence and of the wrath of Isten, Géza gave a grand display of Christian fervor in the presence of Sarolta and her confidants, and staged immolations to Isten when he expected not to be watched by the Christian faction of the court.

The court of Csepel was a hotbed of intrigue. Magyar nobles loathed matriarchal rule, but they coveted their ruler's wife, who granted her favors without much restraint.

Sarolta was involved in many a scheme. She was instrumental in the distribution of sinecures and promotions. She was the cause of many internecine feuds. Cowardly Géza would have preferred overt war to the tenseness of the court atmosphere, but Sarolta enforced a ban on raids by small hordes. Raiding had been the people's main source of prosperity. Far beyond Csepel, common men grumbled about this woman who imposed her will upon males and deprived them of a source of wealth.

Sarolta had learned about Byzantine economic methods; so she insisted that her husband order the Magyars to develop agriculture and mining, and that he bring in more craftsmen and traders from abroad to make the land prosperous.

She was also instrumental in having the doors of Hungary flung ever wider open to Christian missionaries so that the Church would give the ruling family sorely needed support.

Craftsmen came and traders, Italians and Germans. They prospered, though the average Magyar did not profit from their activities. Missionaries also came, but for every convert they made several enemies, who called them foreign agents, imported by a vicious woman.

Around 975, a secret ambassador from Csepel visited the court of Otto II, Holy Roman Emperor and son of the victor of 955. Neither the ambassador's name nor the exact nature of his mission is recorded; however, there is reason to believe that the power behind the diplomatic action was Sarolta, who had just given birth to a son. (The year of birth is not recorded either. Some sources claim that it may have been as late as 976 or 977.)

Otto conferred with the ambassador, and then dispatched one of his most respected diplomat-prelates, Bruno, Bishop of Verdun, to Csepel. Bruno offered to establish friendly relations between Germans and Magyars, and to have Rome take care of the Magyars' spiritual welfare. Géza received him enthusiastically. Permanent embassies were exchanged, and it was agreed that the infant, Vaik, would receive a Roman Catholic tutor.

Vaik's tutor was an Italian, Count Theodate, from San Severino. The Count told Vaik of Christian culture and might, and the little boy, frightened by the shadow of violence that hovered over the Magyar court, probably felt that deliverance could come only from Christian might. In 994, he was baptized and renamed Stephen; he was to become the canonized first King of Hungary, the protagonist of many a legend, of fiction and eulogy—in fact, the titular founder of Hungary, as it has sailed through stormy seas for almost 1000 years.

Pagan Magyar nobles resented the baptism; they considered, more than ever, Christendom to be an instrument of foreign domination. They refused to call Vaik, Stephen, and they even thought of eliminating him from the succession to the throne.

The candidate of the angry faction was Koppán (also Kupa), a member of the ruling House of Árpád, a man of colossal ambition; his men told Sarolta, whom they expected to play a major part in their plot, that Koppán was a vigorous man, while Géza was declining in strength. The plan was that Géza should die, Koppán be installed in his place and marry Géza's widow, who was still a woman of provocative beauty.

But Sarolta had no use for a husband, however virile, whom she could not completely dominate, and Koppán would not be a tool in her hands. She did not expect Géza to live long, but she trusted that she could always pull the wires of the new ruler if he were her son. She prevailed upon Géza to make their son his co-ruler.

In 995, Stephen joined his father on the throne, and in that same year he was betrothed to a German Princess, Gisela, sister of the Emperor Otto III of Germany.

The betrothal was brief. Bride and groom had never laid eyes upon each other, but mutual attraction was the least of the matchmakers' concerns. No busts or portraits exist of the Princess, and chroniclers, usually not averse to flattering descriptions, avoid the term "lovely" when writing of her. The many existing pictures of Stephen, all dating from his mature years, show him as a stereotype of a medieval monarch; imposingly average, a typical stenciler's model.

The marriage contract was one of the most elaborate documents of its kind ever drawn up, and became in part the foundation of Hungary's social system for almost 1000 years.

Stephen would be crowned King by the grace of the Pope, if not by the Pope himself; he would call into Hungary, German and Burgundian nobles who should rank above the Magyar aristocracy and obtain the crucial assignments. The King's patrimonial possessions would be enlarged to turn him into one of the wealthiest monarchs on the continent, and by implication, Gisela one of the wealthiest of all Queens. (Her own dowry seems to have been modest.)

Géza's estate of well over 1000 square miles of fine fertile lands around Csepel was enlarged, so that Stephen personally owned most of the land between the Danube and Lake Balaton, and upstream to the Austrian border. Surveyors did not note the exact measurements, but the domain probably exceeded 15,000 square miles, roughly one seventh of the entire kingdom.

Gisela's bridal expedition embarked in Ratisbon on the most elaborate array of ships to gather in the waters of the Danube since the day of the Romans.

It took many hours before all the Princess' horses and men, with armor, bag, and baggage, all the Princess' attendants and servants, and the boat's crew were aboard the gaily decorated craft. Gisela herself was the last to board her ship, which carried the standard of the German Emperor and the rather strange-looking insignia of a Hungarian kingdom not yet in actual existence. The bride's ship was a huge, flat-bottomed salt boat, which carpenters had rebuilt into a floating apartment house with all commodities but for sanitary ones.

All of Ratisbon was on its toes to watch the embarkment near the site where, some forty years before, Magyar generals had dangled from gibbets.

Tales of the trip and its splendor, adorned by individual reveries and fantasia, circulated throughout Bavaria, and all along the Austrian course of the river. The tales survived bride and groom. Almost two centuries later, Austrian minnesingers and poets brought the saga into a form which fit the tastes of contemporary aristocracy. It told of a Burgundian Princess, the sister of a King, betrothed and eventually wed to King Etzel (Attila), who lived in Hungary, of the bridal trip, of nobles dwelling along the Austrian Danube, of "marvels of nuptial joy, of weeping, and lament, of struggles among valiant heroes. . . ." Actually, the *Song of the Nibelungs* owes its existence to Gisela and Stephen, or rather to the matchmakers.

The voyage led through the smiling lands of Bavaria, which looked like a head of blond hair adorned by a wreath of pine twigs, past Passau and its monastery, which no stranger could dominate, through the narrows and whirls of the river on Ostmarkian (Austrian) grounds, where the sight of almost every bend reminded one of Magyar horsemen roaming, looting, and fighting victorious battles, and where ruins remained to tell of Magyar predatory grandeur.

Gisela was born long after the battle of 955, and even the oldest among her escorts was still too young to have fought on the Lechfeld, but they had all heard gruesome accounts of slaughter and incendiarism. The bride may have trusted that her future people were chastened, but German knights aboard the ships may have wondered about dangerous moods of freemen on their future estates. They had not felt like usurpers when they joined Gisela; they had considered themselves pillars of faith, harbingers of culture, and bringers of lawful order, but as they watched mementos of Magyar might glide past, they may have feared that they were exponents of an alien way of life to be imposed upon a strange and violent nation-to-be.

In Melk they reached a section of the river that only a short time ago had been Magyar, and now was Ostmark territory. An ancient fort, battered but proud, rose on a rock almost two hundred feet above the water level. On that rock, a splendid Benedictine abbey would rise. The town of Melk looked rickety and improvised, though people had lived there from time immemorial. But before abandoning Melk, the Magyars had ravaged it thoroughly, and inhabitants still doubted that conditions warranted the construction of permanent homes.

Vienna: man-made walls, in the settings of God's splendor, every stone bearing marks of man's destructiveness. Spectacle-loving Viennese lined the riverbanks, waving, wondering. They did not quite understand the German-Magyar match.

The Hungarian border was barely ten miles away from Vienna's eastern walls; and only about ten miles downstream of the city were the westernmost boundaries of newly allotted Hungarian estates. There, four prominent German nobles received property expanding from the influx of the small river Fischa to Neusiedler Lake, the reed-studded expanse of shallow water where, according to prevailing winds, men can either fish or hunt, swim or walk.

Hungarian nobles and freemen waited near the mouth of the Fischa to meet, though not to greet, the new feudal lords from the West. The meeting was highly uncomfortable. The presence of many interpreters did not promote personal contacts. Also present were messengers from Géza. The father of the groom suggested that the guests stay together until their absolute security could be guaranteed.

The new feudal lords donned their armor, buckled on their swords, and planted themselves on the deck of their river craft, living allegories of defiance.

Twenty-four hours later, they arrived in Csepel.

German and Italian prelates attended the wedding of Stephen and Gisela; German knights dominated the secular attendance. Glum and grim in their colorful attire, Hungarian clan leaders and nobles thronged in the background, as if trying to block exits and trap the assembly. But when the sagging Géza called upon them to pledge loyalty to Stephen, they took the oath.

Koppán was present at the wedding, and he stayed throughout the banquet that lasted for a full week, with incredible amounts of food and drink consumed. Nobody could tell whether the newlyweds stayed on all the time; they were not among the most conspicuous members of the party. Koppán, however, was conspicuous; and nobody could overlook his wooing of Sarolta and his fraternizing with obviously disgruntled Magyars.

Géza survived his son's wedding only for a short time. He died in 997. His last admonitions to his son and co-regent concerned the survival of the House of Árpád with German assistance, and in his will he stipulated that all pagan members of the ruling house be henceforth excluded from succession.

Koppán dispatched messengers all over the land: he contended that the sacred law of the House of Árpád had been violated, and that Stephen was not their legal sovereign. Koppán claimed title to the realm and to Sarolta. No word came from the stately widow, and the Magyars did not seem to care to learn about her wishes.

Koppán's call to arms fell on fertile grounds. The Magyars developed a fanatical nationalism. They now wanted to be pagans, to keep their lands from new overlords, and to live according to their own traditions. Clan leaders and clansmen, free peasants and bondsmen, even descendants from prisoners of war, rallied against the foreigners. For decades the clans' arsenals had not been replenished. The men were no longer trained in the tactics that once had brought victories, but never had the Magyar fighting spirit been more ardent than it was in the year 997, when the nation battled against foreign control.

In Csepel, Sarolta waited, grim and tense. Her son had always asked her advice, but now Stephen relied only on the foreigners. With the exception of a horde of sullen domestic servants, there were practically no Hungarians left at court. Magyar dignitaries had either asked for leaves of absence or just vanished. A nation mobilized against its sovereign, and that sovereign depended on foreign assistance for survival.

The foreigners, too, mobilized. Feudal lords left their new estates, and together with their foreign vassals and mercenaries rode to Esztergom on the Danube and to Veszprém near Lake Balaton, to protect the Hungarian ruler and their own domains. Wenzellin of Wasserburg, a Bavarian nobleman, assumed command of the foreign army.

Koppán had eyes and ears everywhere; everybody seemed ready to spy for him. Runners and horsemen reported that Wenzellin had established a fortified camp near Esztergom. Koppán struck at Veszprém, knowing that the enemies were weaker there than on the Danube.

Stephen went to Esztergom. His sword was buckled on him in the German fashion. The ruler of Hungary should not fight his own people armed according to this people's tradition.

Wenzellin crossed the Danube and advanced against Veszprém in forced marches. Ahead of him raced informers to warn Koppán. Koppán's rebels were in the process of regrouping when the Germans arrived. Koppán fought in the first line, and Wenzellin, too, did not look for cover. If Stephen distinguished himself in action, chroniclers failed to record his exploits.

The battle of Veszprém culminated in a duel between the two army commanders. Two men cut, hit, and thrust for a prize that was a nation. Wenzellin, the younger of the two, won.

Two armies saw Koppán stagger in the saddle and fall to the ground. The rebel leader was dead, and with him rebellion collapsed. The Magyars fled.

Had Koppán still lived, he would have been tortured and quartered. Death in combat spared him, but his corpse was quartered and the parts carried to every quarter of the land as "symbols of peace." Koppán's family was outlawed, their lands reverted to Stephen. "Civilization prevailed over barbarism," as a later historian put it.

The year was still 997.

Sarolta disappeared from the political scene. The foreigners, who would not have wielded power in Hungary had it not been for this formidable woman, now distrusted her.

Stephen was surrounded by a team of counselors, all faithful champions of a universal Holy Roman Empire, which the Germans hoped to dominate.

The year 1000 was approaching. In the year of the millennium Stephen should be crowned.

The people of Hungary, sulking and licking its wounds, did not believe in the millennium, but Stephen was fascinated by the thought, and so were the new feudal lords, who were building castles as symbols and bulwarks of their power.

Diplomatic exchanges about Stephen's coronation were under way when, on February 18, 999, Pope Gregory V died. Youthful German Emperor Otto III, who then lived in Rome, used his political influence to put his venerated mentor on the Throne Petri. Archbishop Gerbert became Pope Sylvester II.

Pope Sylvester II is said to have introduced the use of Arabic figures and to have invented the pendulum clock. The Catholic Encyclopedia (ed. 1913, Vol. XIV) states: "The common people regarded him as a magician in league with the devil." But, mistrusted as he was by the Romans throughout his brief reign until 1003, Sylvester II accomplished German designs in Hungary.

During his first year in office, he established an ecclesiastic metropolitan for Hungary, with the seat at Esztergom. On March 27, 1000, he appointed Stephen papal vicar to his country, and in a most uncommon gesture granted him the title of King. Yet there was no immediate coronation.

The reason was that Hungary did not have a crown!

Traditional pagan insignia of supreme power could not substitute for the exalted symbol of Christian royalty. One of Stephen's advisers proceeded to Rome "to beg" the Pope for a royal crown and an apostolic cross. Sylvester II, aware of the Hungarian problem, had already ordered a crown.

Roman jewelers produced a hood of finely plated gold, a headband with ornaments in enamel, and precious stones capped by two hoops and with trefoils suspended on small chains. The Pope also ordered an apostolic cross to be carried before Stephen as a symbol of his work of conversion.

Otto III, equally aware of the problem of insignia, offered a symbolic present: the holy lance, adorned with the relic of St. Maurice.

Stephen's emissary had not yet returned to Csepel when an embassy from Byzantium arrived there. Byzantium, hopelessly outdistanced by Rome in the race for supremacy in a Christian Hungary, tried to recover lost ground by offering the young King a headgear worthy of a mighty Emperor. Byzantine jewelers had made a crown studded with precious stones, a diadem with high prongs.

Refusal to accept the gift would have been an extreme insult; so German craftsmen who had settled in Hungary welded both crowns together.

The result was the crown of St. Stephen, which became and remained legendary. (The cross atop the diadem, as it is known from illustrations, is a later addition. It became bent when the crown was temporarily buried in 1848.)

The commercial value of the crown cannot be estimated in present-day monetary terms, but when its two parts were donated they probably represented the value of the patrimony of an average European duke. The Holy Crown became the symbol of legal rule of the Kingdom; its holder was the rightful King by the grace of God and the will of the nation. As this is written, the whereabouts of the crown are not known. The Communist government of Hungary hardly ever had possession of the jewels. Vague rumors have it that it is kept safe in the vaults of the Vatican, to be returned only to a rightful King.

Stephen also is said to have received an autographed letter from the Pope, in which Sylvester II vested him with the right to organize the Church and appoint its dignitaries. It is claimed that according to the letter feudal relationship was established between the Hungarian Kings and the Holy See. In the early nineteenth century, interpretation of this relationship led to a controversy. One faction of legal experts insisted that the papal letter, as it was preserved, was the work of a brazen forger who lived one hundred years after Stephen; the other insisted that the document was genuine.

The legend of St. Stephen, who was canonized in 1083, forty-five years after his death, has it that his coronation took place on Christmas Day of the year 1000. Chroniclers contend that the date was August 15. But both legend and chronicler agree that the place was Esztergom.

In Esztergom, Stephen built a monastery which became the center of an archbishopric, seat of the Hungarian Catholic primates.

No report on the ceremony is preserved, no painter put it on canvas. But to the devout and nationalist Hungarians, who soon forgot that the coronation was the climax of the seizure of their land by conquering conversion, it became a revelation, the source of law.

CHAPTER THIRTEEN

Under King Stephen's rule, many services were held to implore the Lord to keep Hungary at peace. But with the country's military power the number of civil feuds and foreign wars arose; and with economy developing, Hungary became a tempting object for conquerors. Peace ruled only for brief and deceptive periods. There is no stretch on the Hungarian Danube where the waters were never reddened by human blood; no acre of Hungarian soil that would not be an unmarked grave-yard where remains of soldiers have fertilized the eternal earth.

In 1002, two years after his coronation, Stephen took to the field against Gyula, rebellious Duke of Transylvania. One year later he turned against the Bulgarians, who had supported Gyula. In 1021 he repelled Eastern invaders. Stephen prided himself on being a fighter against hea-thens, a guardian of the road on which Western pilgrims journeyed to the Holy Land. Many Westerners traveled along the Danube to Byzantium, and from there to their sacred goal.

Stephen was an absolute monarch. His person was identical with the state in legal, financial, and military matters, but he always was under the influence of foreign advisers and never exerted the arbitrary powers of a modern dictator.

However, religious and social reforms carried out under Stephen's rule were the weightiest in Hungarian history.

The church built its organization: eleven bishoprics and archbishop-rics. Militant Benedictine monks, shock troops of conversion, ranged the country from the Danube Valley to the Carpathians.

The Church founded the first schools of the kingdom. Most teachers were Germans, and they taught in their own native tongue.

The King promulgated decrees for the laity: Work on Sundays was prohibited. Parish elders had to enforce attendance of religious services; only fire wardens were permitted to stay at home. Needless talking in church or lack of attention was prohibited. Violators were tied up in the yard, shorn, and publicly flogged.

Violation of the law of fasting was punishable with one week in jail on Lenten fare.

Persons who refused to accept the last rites forfeited title to a church funeral and prayers for their souls. A master who did not carry the body of his dead servant to the churchyard was punished with twelve days in jail on a diet of water and bread.

Transgressions against Christian law, ranging from refusal to accept baptism to trifling neglect of ritual, were subject to "canonical castiga-tion." Seven-time offenders were turned over to mundane courts, which dealt with them in the manner exemplified by the case of "the obdurate pagan Thomizoba." Thomizoba and his wife had been buried alive. However, this was not the most cruel manner of execution. In one re-corded instance, the doomed man's eyes were torn out, and hot lead poured into his ears.

The scope of marriage laws was extended. No girl should marry without the consent of the relatives "in whose custody" she lived. Marriage without consent was considered rape; rapists were fined the equivalent of the blood money for a killed woman (fifty oxen for a noblewoman, ten oxen for a commoner).

No legal divorce existed, but a couple could separate. If the husband deserted his wife, she was considered a widow, free to remarry even without her relatives' consent. When her husband returned after her second marriage, he could remarry also. A husband could request that his marriage be annulled if he voluntarily accepted bondage or made a vow of pilgrimage to the Holy Land.

The people was divided into classes:

On the lowest stratum were the *"servi,"* who were occupied in agriculture, cattle breeding, handicraft, fishing, and hunting; they had either to perform statute labor for the lord of the mansion or to pay him a portion of their produce.

On the next rung of the social ladder were the "landless guests," or domiciled peasants, who had to pay in kind or money, and to render certain services, in return for the use of land.

Inhabitants of privileged communities were exempt from services for the lords of the estate but duty-bound to serve the King. There was, for instance, a privileged village whose boys had to "take care of the King's dogs," another that supplied "royal jesters," and yet another one whose inhabitants had to serve as coachmen should His Majesty move. (The King owned several castles, and moving from one to another with bag and baggage was a major carting job.)

Miners formed privileged communities. Hungarians were averse to mining, and even under compulsion performed only in an unsatisfactory manner. German miners went to Transylvania to work in the King's mines for considerable wages and grants of free land.

The liegemen ranked above the people of privileged communities. The King bestowed some of his own land on them for a predetermined period, under the provision that they join the army in case of war.

The highest stratum was the nobles. Ownership of land provided title to nobility. Stephen recognized 108 leaders of clans or tribes as nobles. It was a petty nobility, though, as compared with the wealth and grandeur of Gisela's knights and other ranking foreigners. Many members of clans laid claim to titles of nobility. Had all their claims been granted, the Hungarians would have turned into the bluest-blooded nation on earth. However, most claims were ignored.

Arms, food, mounts, and conveyances were stored in castles and abbeys. A permanent defense tax was levied to meet the costs of the military establishment. The King was not exempt from this tax. Hungarian Kings loved their army. Its ranking officers were superbly mounted, well armored and equipped. The rank and file had good horses —Magyar ponies interbred with captured stallions and mares—and they wore the finest-embroidered, brightest-colored coats and high caps the womenfolk of the villages could produce. Apart from paying defense tax, the Kings lavished some of their huge income on martial splendor.

High as the combined taxes were, they were not oppressive by the standards of taxation in most parts of the post-World War II world. And the King, main beneficiary of revenue, usually kept no more than two thirds of it for his personal purposes and spent the rest on building projects and for charity.

Stephen's legal experts drafted a reformed code of law and the administration of law.

The highest official of the land was the Palatinus, the King's deputy, his appointed mediator in disputes among members of nobility, and Supreme Justice in cases which did not fall under the jurisdiction of the Church.

Three times a year the King ordered the Palatinus to administer justice. Civil cases held priority on the court calendar. Procedures were brief, and penalties for non-capital crimes drastic. Killers paid "blood money," in cash or oxen. Arson was a very frequent crime, occurring mostly on Sundays, when people were supposed to attend services. Arsonists had to restore destroyed buildings and to pay for all other damages in addition to a fine of sixteen head of cattle.

Burglary and breach of peace were capital crimes; offenders could be slain without penalty.

Perjurers forfeited the hand they had raised to swear the oath, but they could pay a ransom of twelve oxen. Calumniators and scandalmongers lost their tongues, but they, too, could pay ransom: twenty-four oxen. No ransom could be granted if the King's name had been involved in connection with perjury or calumny.

Hungarian criminologists listed witches, called *striges,* among malefactors. According to the popular belief, *striges* assumed the shape of owls to suck the blood of infants. However, threescore years after Stephen's death, King Koloman of Hungary decreed: *"Striges* shall not be tried, as there exist no *striges."*

The law controlled every social and ethnic group in Hungary, with one exception: the Gypsies. Nobody could tell exactly whence they had come, or when they had first entered the lands along the lower Danube, but they had been roaming the eastern parts of Hungary long before Árpád became ruler, possibly even before the earlier invaders from the eastern infinity had hit the land. However, Roman reports on Dacia did not mention the presence of the perennial wanderers, who never became assimilated, never conformed with the laws of the land.

Lords of the mansions did not register Gypsies as their property. They were not listed as tradesmen or drafted into the army. The Gypsies were just there; "They have always been," as a chronicler summed up.

They were illiterate, but they had a great deal of tradition in such diversified fields as art, music, stealing, handicraft, commerce as a subsidiary of thievery, and prostitution. Their music inspired Hungarian and Rumanian national tunes; in fact, it begot them. Their tales were sometimes plagiarized and purified. Forever unmitigated and purified, however, remained the Gypsies' curses.

Even though no language other than the Gypsy's own idiom can fully convey the gist of Gypsy swearing, here are some of their curses:

"Thy head shall turn into an anvil." "Loose thy bones at thy wedding." "Thy tongue shall turn into a dumpling." "May thy fleas be crayfish." "The devil's grandmother may chew your elbow." "Thy tummy shall serve as a pincushion." "May thy teeth melt." "Timber shall grow in thy nose." "Get blind at the dance." "The devil's own salt may burn thy nostrils."

The Gypsies had proverbs and sayings, some quite philosophical and obviously dating from Hungary's Christian period. (The Gypsies did not seek conversion, and not even the apostolic Kings were anxious to Christianize them.)

"Fever is an old hag's fervor." "Only death builds a house for a poor man." "The minister's wife preached more than the minister." "Wind is the devil's sneeze." "Whether it comes from a clear well or a muddy pool, water extinguishes the blaze." "Better a lame donkey than a dead horse." "The fool's tongue is a mill with no corn to grind." "A household without a wife is a violin without strings." "An old man and a young woman are like a bald head and a comb." "He who kisses an old woman saddles a dead horse."

The Gypsies did not build houses along the Danube. They were itinerant by tradition, and they wanted to stay away from people whom they had cheated or who might denounce them as fortunetellers if events foretold failed to materialize.

Only late in the nineteenth century did some groups of Gypsies settle on the lower Danube, mostly along the Bulgarian riverbank.

The exact number of Gypsies is unascertained, but estimates are that about one fourth of the total roamed the Danubian Basin from the western Hungarian border down to the Black Sea. Their vanguards reached the German section of the river sometime in the fifteenth century.

Hitler's mania accounted for the death of an unestablished number of Gypsies, but did not extinguish them. Subsequent Communist forced-labor policies had no permanent effect upon their outlaw freedom. The Gypsies remain a standing feature of the Danube Valley, indestructible and unalterable in their tattered multicolored garb and their occupations which never grew beyond tinkering and shoeshining and otherwise concentrate on thievery, pandering, and merrymaking. Social upheavals pass them by. They keep rolling, in nag-drawn house carts, through historical places as if they were ditches along an endless road.

CHAPTER FOURTEEN

Christmas celebrations were being prepared in Buda (Ofen) when news arrived that on December 26, 1240, an embassy would call at King Béla IV's castle—delegates from the Lord of the World, the Khan of Khans, the Emperor of all Emperors and Kings.

The Mongol monster cast its shadow over Hungary.

Béla, haughty and showy, asked his nobles how he should deal with the intruders. Some opined that they should be made to cool their heels until the holiday season was over, and then be sent home; others said that they ought to be admitted to court as objects of curiosity and be put in their place if they tried to be insolent. But beneath the surface of braggadocio and scorn was concern. Eventually the King decided that the delegates should not be received like ambassadors, but given a hearing.

During the forty-eight hours that followed, hair-raising reports from

Russia flooded the Hungarian court: The Mongols were sacking, stabbing, burning. Moscow was in flames, Kiev in ruins. Captured Russian princes were stirrup holders and "beard cleansers" of Mongolian generals.

Fugitives from Russia professed to believe every word of it but could not explain how the evil tidings could have reached Buda simultaneously. Skippers of Danube river craft, just in from the lower course of the river, had seen no Mongolians but noticed panic among the people living along the banks.

December 26 dawned—hazy, with snow in the air. The gates of Buda opened. Amidst peasant carts, entered a troop of horsemen such as the gatekeeper had never seen before. The strange riders fell into a brisk trot as they turned in the direction of the royal castle that towered high above the Danube in the murky overcast. Pedestrians scrambled for safety.

At noon sharp, the "delegates" were admitted to the throne room. Béla sat on the "chair of state"; members of his council stood on both sides. The Hungarians looked at the uninvited guests with a mixture of curiosity, overbearingness, and anxiety. The strangers were smallish, bowlegged, black-haired, almost ridiculously overdressed—all except one, who was tall, fair, and garbed in unusually discreet oriental finery.

The tall man explained in fluent Latin, which all Hungarian grandees understood, that he was a native of Scotland but a subject of the Great Khan, and that he wished to talk to the King of Hungary on the Great Khan's behalf. The subject of his call was a complaint:

Hungary, he said, had violated the rules of international behavior and insulted the Great Khan, to whom all nations under the Blue Sky owed allegiance, by harboring notorious criminals who had treacherously assaulted and assassinated Mongol envoys. Also, Hungary was conspiring with refugees from Mongolian control who were preparing for war against the rightful overlords of their countries. Hungary was involved in plots against peace and law and order. The King should desist, submit, and extradite all criminals.

The strange Scotsman did not specify his charges. The members of the council roared angry defiance; the King silently shook his head; the bowlegged, overdressed Mongolians uttered shrill unintelligible shouts.

The Scotsman changed his provocative tune. He pleaded with King, magnates, and prelates not to bring disaster upon themselves and their land by challenging the Mongolians, whose army could destroy all other hosts of the world combined.

There were whispered deliberations as the Scotsman waited, flushed and uneasy. Then Béla spoke up: Hungary was a sovereign Christian state that owed no respect to pagans, and would not pay tribute to any one.

The strangers left, the Scotsman swearing profusely.

In the early spring of 1241, the Mongolians reached the Carpathian passes, then burst into the plains on the shortest route to Buda. Their leaders seemed familiar with every valley, road, and track. Their cavalry covered close to 300 miles in 72 hours, a feat of lightning warfare never before achieved and not nearly equaled in the German motorized blitz-krieg 698 years later.

Buda had walls and battlements. Drawbridges were raised, chains drawn across the Danube. The Mongolians, however, did not usually make water-borne assaults.

Inside Buda, watching the enemy through the windows of his chilly throne room, Béla accepted reports on the deployment of his main army. A number of nobles were standing by with their contingents, and Arch-bishops Mathias of Esztergom and Ugolino (Ugrin) of Kalocsa were ready with soldiers of their archdioceses.

Ugolino was reputedly the greatest military leader Hungary ever had, and certainly was the most handsome man ever to lead the faithful and the soldiers. Tall, erect, with silken curls and iron muscles, he looked like a classic statue and was not only the soldiers' idol, but also that of the ladies of the court.

The handsome prelate wanted to give battle at once. The King stalled, hoping that the solidity of his bastions would induce the aggressors to leave without a fight.

Enemy cavalry circled Buda, putting every hut in nearby villages to the torch, and staging massacres so close to the capital that the victims' shouts were faintly audible.

Béla entertained his warriors. From well-appointed banquet tables guests would rise, step out, look, listen, shudder, and then return to drown their dull shame in goblets of fiery wine.

Two days of massacre and feasting went by; at last, Ugolino pro-claimed that since the King did not want to fight, he, the archbishop, would do so.

As cupbearers continued to pour wine, as drunken grandees belched and stammered, and the King was far from sober, the tall prelate dashed out, alerted his men, forced a guardian to open a gate, and marched down a drawbridge. Inside the castle the party dragged on; outside, the troops from Kalocsa, their leader far out in front, charged a Mongolian squadron.

The Mongolians turned around and fled. It was a sham flight, an ancient Asiatic trick which the Magyars had often used. The Hungarians followed in hot pursuit. The chase led toward the swamps, the fringes of which were patrolled by Mongolian light units. The Mongolian squadron suddenly turned around; the patrols outflanked the Hungarians. It all went so fast that the Hungarians could not understand what happened.

Of six hundred Hungarians, five survived, one of them Ugolino, whose immense physical strength and fencing skill helped him to break out of the lethal circle.

This happened on Palm Sunday, Easter being early that year. Also on Palm Sunday, Mongolian troops entered Vác (Waitzen), found this town on the Danube north of Buda crowded with fugitives, and gleefully set the place afire, watching the fugitives roast in the streets.

In the Hungarian Northeast, hard-riding General Subotai prepared for the deathblow.

The heath of Mohi is not far from Tokaj, where on sun-soaked slopes grows the king of wines. It is as beautiful a place as the Almighty has ever created: wreathed with vineyards to the east, bounded by dark, luscious forests to the west, sheltered against icy north winds by a distant 10,000-foot-high peak, adjoined to the south by a florid plain.

Three rivers water the region: the Tisza, the Sajó, and the Hernád, rushing to a distant rendezvous with the Danube.

When the Hungarians reached the heath of Mohi, they saw in the distance Mongolian tents, an entire city of them in smart rows. Their number seemed to indicate that Subotai's men did not outnumber the Hungarians.

The perimeter of the Mongolian camp was protected by the three rivers: the center by the Sajó, the left by the Tisza, the right by the Hernád. A ford in the Sajó was right in front of the Mongolian encampment. The Hungarians, less familiar than the enemy with their own land, were not aware of the ford. They set up their own camp in the open heath and staged drinking bouts to celebrate the victory they considered certain. As their leaders feasted, Hungarian scouts lolled about on the bank of the Sajó, found the Mongolian camp perfectly quiet, and paid little attention to odd-looking objects of iron which stood on the opposite riverbank. The army and the scouts should have a good night's rest.

As the Hungarians enjoyed the delusive peace, the Mongolians rose to arms, took to horse, and without a sound and with no fires lit, passed over the ford, three shaggy ponies abreast.

The first Mongolian volley of heavy arrows hit the Hungarian camp at dawn. It was followed by shrill, savage battle cries, as the horsemen fell into trot and gallop. Guards and scouts, drowsy and puzzled, made a disorganized stand. King Béla rested comfortably. Ugolino took a calculated risk: he made straight for the Sajó to rout the bulk of the Mongolians.

But as Ugolino advanced, something happened which the militant prelate would have been at a loss to explain had he lived to tell. Thunder and lightning poured out of the odd-looking objects of iron which the Hungarian scouts had disregarded: the first cannon ever to appear on Hungarian soil were in action. Their fire was slow, their range short, the toll they took was not nearly as high as the one taken by arrows; yet the terrifying sounds and flashes, the whiz of the stone balls and pieces of metal, the dull thud of missiles hitting flesh and bone, had a devastating effect upon the Hungarians' tottering morale.

More Mongolians poured across the ford, drawing a tightening vise around the Hungarians. The only barricades in their way were heaps of dead men and horses. Nothing resembling an army remained of King Béla's host.

For two days the Mongolians kept up the pursuit of the small remainder. Mongolian rear guards cut noses and ears from the dead, put them in sacks, and handed them to their commander as trophies and as evidence of the number of enemy casualties.

Archbishop Ugolino was among the mutilated dead; so was Mathias, Archbishop of Esztergom; so was the flower of Hungarian nobility. Thirty-eight members of one single titled family, the Szirmai, had been in action; three survived.

King Béla did survive. His tent was taken over by General Subotai, who is said to have presented it to Batu Khan. The King's inglorious part of the battle was later conveniently palliated by colorful accounts of episodes in which Béla was said to have displayed soldierly virtues and personal generosity. Yet all grants the King made on the occasion went to knights who offered their chargers so that he might flee. Eventually he reached Austria.

It took the Mongolians a few days to reach Buda again. They could have been there even sooner had they not waited for covered wagons with wives and children of ranking officers.

The people of Buda improvised a pathetic defense, which collapsed almost at once. Nearly 100,000 died. The rest were rounded up and driven to the left bank of the Danube. They were divided into groups— men, women, and children—and lined up in three rows. Mongolian soldiers walked along the men's row, stabbing the victims as they went.

Mongolian officers' wives raged against Hungarian women, knifing the attractive ones, cutting off the noses of others, and retaining many as slaves. Mongolian boys were taught to crack the skulls of Hungarian children by strokes of swords. The corpses of the adults were thrown into the Danube; those of the children were impaled, and the poles carried around in triumph.

Buda burned, and so did other towns and castles in the round.

Béla appealed to the German Emperor (Friedrich II) for assistance. The Emperor asked for a pledge of Hungarian tributes after liberation, but after receiving the pledge did nothing to liberate the land. Béla appealed to the Pope. The Pope sent letters of encouragement and promised to organize a crusade, which did not materialize.

Béla took refuge in Spalato (Split), in Dalmatia, where two of his daughters died. The Queen was pregnant and she vowed to dedicate the unborn child to priesthood, should it live.

The child was born—a girl. She was to become St. Margaretha, after whom Margaretha Island in the Danube at Budapest is named.

In Karakorum, 6000 miles east of the Hungarian scene, Great Khan Ogadai, son of the fabulous Genghis Khan, had died. The law required that after the death of a Great Kahn a *kuriltai* (council) be convoked to nominate a successor. All princes of the blood were duty-bound to attend the *kuriltai;* several served in the conquering army of the West. The army should accompany its distinguished members to Central Asia.

The law had to be obeyed, even though Subotai would have wished to continue the campaign to conquer the rest of Europe.

Ogadai passed away on December 11, 1241. In March 1242, no Mongolian horseman was left on Hungarian soil. Not until 1956, when the Hungarians revolted against Soviet Russia, did Mongolian soldiers turn up in Buda again; the Soviet Russians used Mongolian units wherever they wanted to spread extreme terror.

Thirteenth-century Hungary did not know the institution of the census, although it had been introduced in China long before. The exact number of casualties during the Mongolian invasion is not known, but in all likelihood more than one half of the population perished.

A weary Béla returned to Hungary. One knight in his retinue wrote:

"In several days of journey we rarely encountered human beings. But wild animals were numerous and extremely bold. Wolves invaded populated settlements in broad daylight. The beasts tore children from their mothers' arms and even assailed armored men. Fields were fallow, famine rampant, epidemics raged."

The indomitable Danubian land helped raise its dwellers from the depth of decimation and desperation. Yet it would have taken the lifetimes of several generations to start the people back on the road to numerical recovery had not Béla tried everything within his power to attract immigrants.

The natural resources of the land were unimpaired. Farmers could prosper from the first new harvest on, salt and gold mines offered rich returns, hunting and fishing were good, and, with Hungary stripped of many commodities, merchants could sell practically everything on credit. Jews and Orientals were most likely to do that kind of business. The "Diploma" for Jews was given wide publicity. Many came, imported badly needed goods, and took pledges and domestic produce as payment. Slavs also came; Béla favored such hard-working, peaceful people. Walachians and Moldavians were welcome. From the Balkans arrived a blend of various nationalities, some remarkably smart.

Even had Hungary of 1240 been an ethnically homogeneous country, it would have been a land of hard-to-define nationality in 1244. But never could the King and his nobles have conceived the idea that these welcome immigrations would, 674 years later, become the cause of the dismemberment of Hungary, based on the principle of nationalities.

CHAPTER FIFTEEN

In 1246, Austria ceased to exist as a realm. It had been the Babenbergs' domain since 976 A.D., under an act of investiture by the German Emperors. Now the male line became extinct, and women were expressly barred from succession.

The Babenbergs, like all other ruling houses who ever wielded power over Austrian lands, did not originate in Austria proper.

It is widely assumed that they were direct descendants of the Franconian Count Adalbert of Bamberg, who was beheaded for disloyalty to the Emperor, but eminent historians have expressed doubts about this theory. However, no theory has been introduced to substitute for another version that Luitpold (Leopold), Count of Bamberg, had supported another German Emperor's struggle against Bavarian insurrection and was rewarded with hereditary tenure of the Ostmark (then a strip of land along the Danube between Passau and Mautern) and adjoining regions, adding up to a total area of 5000 square miles, part of which was occasionally occupied by rival potentates.

When Stephen was crowned in Hungary, the Counts of Bamberg called themselves Babenberg. Their Ostarrichi was a busy little land. The Danube was a good source of income, not only from trade, transportation, and fishery but also from the washing of gold-bearing sand. Gold was also washed in the Inn, a tributary; Krems was a center of trade before Vienna was solidly incorporated into the Babenbergs' realm.

In 1137, the Babenbergs had Vienna's decaying fortifications rebuilt and granted the city special commercial privileges; shortly thereafter, Heinrich Jasomirgott promoted himself from margrave to duke and moved his residence into a new palace in the center of the city, to a square that was called Am Hof.

The Duchy received a charter, which made it less dependent on the German Empire; it became the Austria that weathered many a storm in medieval and modern history.

The Babenbergs were builders and lawmakers. Under their rule Vienna became a mighty city, and the monasteries of Kremsmünster, Melk, Göttweig, Klosterneuburg, Heiligenkreuz, St. Peter-Seitenstetten, Zwettl, and Lilienfeld were among the most glorious edifices in that part of the continent.

Some Babenberg dukes and margraves married into the families of foreign royalty; two became sons-in-law of Emperors of Byzantium. They ruled with the vacillating support of a colorful variety of German Kings and Emperors, through brief periods of leisure and prolonged spells of calamity turned routine.

During three centuries of Babenberg rule, the Austrians developed ever more characteristic features of an easygoing, devil-may-care philosophy. Abroad, however, the Babenbergs were soon all but forgotten, and not many legends have survived in their own realm.

One Babenberg, Leopold V, second duke of the house, gained a niche in the international hall of fame and saga, not so much because of his general achievements, which included the aggrandizement of his land to about 9000 square miles, but because he allegedly had Richard Coeur de Lion, arrogant King of England, apprehended and thrown, chained, into the dungeon of Dürnstein Castle at the Danube, about seventy miles upstream of Vienna. There, so the favorite version of the melodramatic saga goes, the Lion-Hearted King might have rotted, had it not been for his faithful minstrel Blondel, who, after a long search, discovered his master's whereabouts and helped obtain his release.

There are several versions of the actual misadventures of the English King, son of Henry II and Eleanor of Aquitaine; but in one respect they all agree: if there ever lived a minstrel named Blondel, which is doubtful, he played no part whatever in Richard's release from captivity.

And the Lion-Hearted was neither chained nor kept in a dungeon. He was confined to a small suite of rooms, with hatchlike windows and uncomfortable furniture (all furniture in medieval castles was extremely uncomfortable), and guarded by soldiers with drawn swords.

The hatchlike windows afforded a charming view of the Danube, some two hundred feet below, as it emerged from the Wachau with its many castles, properties of robber barons and honorable aristocrats, and of the monastery of Göttweig to the southeast.

The ruins of the castle of Dürnstein still stand; idyllically crumbling, slightly reddish-brown granite, overgrown with a variety of plants of which the hills and mountains of this part of the Danube Valley abound. From the jagged heap of stone that had been the formidable stronghold of a formidable, long-since extinct clan, the almost droll relic of a wall stretches down to the left bank of the Danube, like a skeletonized crumbling arm. Once upon a time, rebellious clans could block the center of the Austrian Danube Valley by manning that wall and stretching heavy chains across the river; had Richard tried to escape, he could hardly have scaled the once forbidding structure. Today, children find it too low and too shaky to be of much use in a game of hide-and-seek.

The only stately building to stand there now is Richard Löwenherz Inn, an excursion spot little over an hour's drive from Vienna. Each year comes blossom time for the many fruit trees which line the Wachau, tourists throng the place, sip the delightful slightly sparkling white wine which grows right on the castle hill, and homemade apricot brandy, and enjoy the peaceful sight of the eternal land; from time to time they cast a glance of awe to the ruin above and exchange romantic remarks about the poignant tragedy of the emaciated King who had languished there, in rusty chains, in a filthy dungeon, for many years, until he was found and freed through the unflinching loyalty of his servant. And from the heap of stones, nesting birds twitter songs which should make men forget the loyal minstrel who never was there.

With the extinction of the Babenbergs, a *vacuum regis* formed in the center of Europe. As Austria turned into a no-ruler's land, the central Danube Valley became the focus of ambitions that could have rocked the continent.

The first to claim vacated Austria was German Emperor Friedrich II, who under the terms of the investiture held title to the lands along the central Danube and in the central and eastern Alps. Friedrich II was in the most serious of troubles. Banished by the Pope after a prolonged conflict with the Holy See, faced with rebellion in Germany, and engaged in warfare in Italy, the fifty-six-year-old Emperor appointed Count Otto von Eberstein as caretaker of Austria and Styria, and designated his own grandson as the future ruler. But the little boy died before he could ascend the ducal throne, and upon his arrival in Austria, Count Eberstein found nobody ready to take his orders.

Austrian Estates, assembled at Triebensee, debated the election of a ruler who would be wealthy and willing to hand out lavish rewards to those who had nominated him. Two candidates were principally considered: German Duke Heinrich of Meissen, by marriage a relative of the Babenbergs, and Ottokar (Přemysl Ottokar), Crown Prince of Bohemia.

The Estates kept debating for five years in one of the longest political conventions on record. In 1250, German Emperor Friedrich II died, and with him the House of Hohenstaufen died out; Count Eberstein returned to Germany, where he found nobody ready to accept his resignation as a caretaker.

Styrian Estates, not represented at Triebensee, proclaimed secession, which was contested. Hungary cast expansionistic glances across the Austrian border. And Meissen and Bohemia decided to settle their own rivalry: in return for a wealthy Bohemian city, the Duke of Meissen ceded to Ottokar the not legally existing title to Austria.

On November 21, 1251, the Estates at Triebensee recognized the transaction. Ottokar became Duke of a realm whose boundaries were in doubt and which he could not legally bequest upon his heirs, since meantime it had been decided that the Pope should be the ultimate arbiter in the matter of Austrian succession.

CHAPTER SIXTEEN

The tale of Richard was not yet born when, in December 1251, Ottokar proceeded to Vienna. He was enthusiastically received. The populace relished spectacles, in particular if the protagonists were as young and handsome as this Bohemian Prince. Also, ecclesiastic authorities which wielded great influence favored and sponsored Ottokar's triumphant entry; and Hungarian raids against Vienna during the so-called *interregnum,* Austria's rulerless period, had created hard feelings against Hungary, and the Viennese relished Béla's Bohemian rival arriving first.

Ottokar of the House of Přemysl is occasionally called a Czech King, the great medieval standard bearer of the Czech nation, who laid the foundation of Czech claims to territories larger than the ones ever inhabited by a Czech majority.

Actually, the future King Ottokar II could hardly be called a Czech by ethnical or cultural standards. Most European cultures of his time were a blending of achievements from various lands, almost all of them based on ancient Roman law, art, and science. And since European royalty kept intermarrying, it would have required a novel science to analyze consanguinities. Ottokar, grandson of a German Emperor, spoke German. His code of law was drafted in German instead of the traditional Latin. There is no evidence that he knew Czech or any other Slavic language. German settlers, already numerous in Bohemia and Moravia, were called in during his regime in ever increasing numbers, as miners, farmers, and merchants. At home, Czechs were virtually discriminated against. They enjoyed fewer liberties and privileges and paid more taxes than the immigrants, who grew ever more arrogant in their dealings with the natives. Bohemian nobles, dissatisfied with the performance of their own Czech bondsmen, offered free land to German settlers, and like the Counts of Rosenberg, even adopted German names.

Not before the mid-1270s, when Ottokar was engaged in a life-or-death struggle for hegemony in Central Europe, did this onetime champion of Germanism change his national attitude. Wooing for support by Polish and Silesian princes, he then spoke of common Slavic interests and insatiable German covetousness. He never referred to the Austrians as a nation, but for some time Austrian warriors were the core of Ottokar's army, and Vienna remained his home in the years between his meteoric rise and his crushing fall.

Ottokar lived in the ancient town palace of the Babenbergs, on a square in mid-town Vienna, a stately building with large, sumptuous halls, studiously uncomfortable furniture, and no sanitary installations whatever.*

Vienna teemed with minstrels and vagrant storytellers, who recited tales set to primitive but melodious music. They performed on streets, markets, and in back yards; they were the common man's minnesingers, less stilted and courteous than these noble troubadours, but occasionally endowed with a superb natural gift of presentation. They had no sponsors, and their means of support—coppers haphazardly thrown at them—were unbelievably scanty; yet they created much hilarity; and if they ever shed a tear, they never did so in public, and they never made sadness the leitmotif of their performances.

A minstrel who visited Ottokar's Vienna raved: "It is sheer delight to be here in Vienna. If you have got plenty of gold and silver, this is the place to spend it, to make merry, sing, revel. There is nothing you wouldn't find in Vienna—beauty, and mischief too."

Ottokar hardly listened to vagrants' songs, but he patronized minnesingers. Tannhäuser, who was not a fictitious Wagnerian character, but a real native of Salzburg and a prominent bard, is full of praise for the King. Ulrich von dem Türlin, Friedrich von Sonnenburg, Meister Sigeher, are among those who sang for, and of, Ottokar. Ottokar had a favorite, Ulrich von Liechtenstein, a relative of the nobleman who fought in the battle in which the last Babenberg died. The "Liechtensteiner" was a minnesinger, a militant knight, the lord of a manor, member of the Estates, and a prominent politician. He did not only *sing* of Ottokar's rise; he *contributed* a great deal to it. But the friendship did not last.

---

* Much later, the Court War Council and the Austrian Ministry of War were established at the site, to be replaced early in this century by a bank building.

Ottokar came to suspect prominent members of the Estates, and in 1268, had many arrested and their castles "broken."

Ulrich was among the suspects. Only after several years in prison were the men taken before the King to answer the charges. They were disheveled, limping, in rags, trembling shadows of their former proud selves. Only Ulrich was composed, erect, and somehow even managed to look tidy. Ottokar wanted reconciliation; the politician-minnesinger professed not to harbor ill feelings and emphasized his loyalty. But in 1274, when disgruntled nobles gathered in Leoben, one hundred miles south of Vienna, Ulrich von Liechtenstein joined their plot against Ottokar.

The city of Vienna remained loyal to Ottokar to the last. Ottokar had wooed its affection with gold, granted it a number of new privileges, and extended its charter. Orators assured the populace that this would bring better justice, greater security, and higher prosperity to everybody.

Ottokar considered charters a panacea; various Austrian cities got them for the asking. Where charters did not suffice to reward pledges of fealty, Ottokar used more substantial means.

There was a substantial amount of cash in the Babenberg treasury, to which the last duke's widowed sister Margaretha held the key. Margaretha was also heir to the rich allodial estates of her family.

Ottokar needed more treasuries and estates to defray the high cost of his new dignity. Margaretha seemed determined to hold on to her property, and counted on popular sympathy should anyone attempt to rob her.

Bishop Berthold of Passau suggested matrimony as an easy solution to the problem.

Ottokar was a dashing, ebullient man of twenty-three; Margaretha was a dispassionate woman of forty-six, who, as it was in accordance with her standing, had made a monastic vow after her husband's death. Bishop Berthold did not consider this an obstacle to remarriage, and Ottokar, who did not find Margaretha's physique to his taste, might have considered the vow of chastity a relief. Whatever Margaretha might have felt, she eagerly accepted Ottokar's sober proposal.

The ceremony was performed on March 11, 1252, at Hainburg. It was a splendid affair, highlighted by the surrender of the title to allodial estates to the groom. Before the couple left the church, the bride was handed a receipt by the Bishop of Passau on behalf of the Pope. It released and absolved her from all her vows.

Ottokar did not stay at home for a honeymoon. Dowry matters settled to his satisfaction and the papal document no enticement to tarry, he went to Styria province, to expel his Hungarian rival. Before the thaws came to the Styrian mountains, Ottokar occupied the northern parts of the province.

King Béla of Hungary took up the challenge to his own imperialistic designs. One decade earlier he had been a desperate fugitive, but he wanted to be the most powerful monarch of the world. He aspired at successorship to the throne of the German–Holy Roman Empire, which was about to be vacated; and he also wanted to enlarge the Árpádian family realm.

Béla planned a three-pronged attack on Ottokar's sprawling realm.

But none of the Christian military men had the skills of the Mongolian Subotai, who still lived, thousands of miles away. They wasted time occupying a few hamlets, rode for a bloody nose against Upper Austrian castles which they could have bypassed, and sacked Moravia, but their siege of Olmütz (Olomouc) came to an inglorious end.

Intervention by Pope Innocent IV, who himself was involved in struggles against German Emperors, put a temporary end to warfare in the Danube Valley.

On April 3, 1254, preliminaries of peace were signed in Buda. Ottokar kept Austria; Béla and his family, Styria.

Two months after the preliminaries were signed, Béla and Ottokar met near Pressburg, in the castle on the hill. The castle affords a magnificent view: to the west the bluish outlines of the musically undulating Vienna Woods; north, the broad-based Carpathians; south and east, the flatlands over which blow the dry winds from the distant mysterious steppes, with the shining ribbon of the Danube running from horizon to horizon.

Prodigal masses of meat, legions of sweet dishes, countless barrels of noble wine, were consumed. Béla relinquished his hold on Styria, and, unknown by many guests, yet another little document was signed; a family document: Ottokar would marry Béla's attractive granddaughter, Kunigunde von Machow, as soon as an annulment of his marriage with Margaretha could be obtained.

This took until 1261. In that year, a friendly bishop issued a decree to the effect that, whereas Margaretha had made a vow of chastity and lived as a nun for a full year prior to her marriage to Ottokar, the bond was null and void. Margaretha's release from her vow was not mentioned, and the claim that she had been a nun was not substantiated.

The aging woman, fat and bloated, made no objection. She did not even ask for compensation.

On October 12, 1262, one week after Margaretha left for a modest country house, Ottokar married Kunigunde.

The new marriage did not find the Viennese in a joyous frame of mind. The ruins of a great fire of 1258 were still standing when another conflagration hit the city. Ottokar tried his best to help the burghers; he donated a huge forest from his domains to the city, issued a new, favorable marketing charter, deferred tolls and taxes for five years, and sponsored reconstruction work.

The Viennese accepted all this as their due. They spent some of the revenue for construction, some for palatable comfort, and went scapegoat hunting. Jews made loans at interest rates averaging 200 per cent per annum. There were no laws against high interests, but vagrant storytellers gratified their audiences with ditties about people who committed arson to promote their usurious designs.

In 1267, a Provincial Council was convoked to Vienna. Its resolutions forbade priests to lend money at interest and to accumulate prebends, and it introduced measures to "reduce friction between Christians and Jews."

Jews had to wear special garb and were barred from Christian inns and bathhouses. Christians should not attend Jewish weddings; nor should they consult Jewish physicians. Christians and Jews should never debate matters of faith. Jews should neither act as collectors of dues nor hold public office. Indications are that the decree was not rigidly enforced, but antagonism was kept alive.

Central European royalty was faced with a serious problem. The nobles, pillars of thrones, shields and swords of their sovereigns, had long grown too strong and ambitious to be reliable. They built their castles into fortresses that dominated strategic arteries of traffic, the farm districts from where Kings, armies, and cities drew supplies. The nobles were hardly ever united against their sovereigns, but even isolated counts and barons could obstruct national economy and the King's military establishment.

Ottokar aspired at a tightly knit, centralized realm. He got increasingly irritated by the network of castles, each of them evidence of a self-styled petty sovereign. He had tried to rely on cities and burghers rather than on landed estates, but cities, too, formed a network; they, too, were strong, and burghers were almost as proud, and certainly more numerous, than the knights. Local autonomies augured evil for Ottokar's designs.

The King tried to back up centralism by a central law. His *Landfrieden* (Peace of the Land) stipulated that private feuds and vengeance were outlawed, and all litigating parties should settle their cases in court. Judges were directed to take drastic steps if cases of robber barons came up.

The *Landfrieden* interfered with the construction of new fortresses. Venturesome speculators, who presented doubtful diplomas of nobility and were backed by anonymous financiers, built castles which were formidable roadblocks—centers of highway robbery in peace, strategic obstacles in war.

The *Landfrieden* stipulated that nobody should build a castle unless he owned land with an annual revenue of no less than thirty pounds. (Financiers would hardly be willing to advance money needed for a purchase of so big an estate.) Nobody should draft laborers except his own tenant farmers into construction work. Fortifications built during campaigns, and churches converted into fortresses, should be torn down as soon as the war was over.

Wars were hardly ever over; the *Landfrieden* prevented some extension of highway robbery, yet Ottokar's Austrian realm was a mosaic and not a block, and the knights were as defiant as ever.

Ottokar began to destroy many Austrian castles. They were "broken" by wrecking squads, armed to the teeth and equipped with everything medieval demolition techniques could provide. Not all the ruins which modern tourists admire in the Danube Valley and other parts of the Austrian countryside are decaying remains of former grandeur. Quite a few of them had been "broken."

Ottokar did not get the Church's effective support in his attempts at centralized rule; it objected to his violations of religious law by manifold acts of violence. Religious authorities presented Ottokar with demands of their own, and found him grudgingly pliable.

He restored to the Church all landed property it claimed to have lost in periods of upheaval, and granted the clergy unconditional protection against any encroachment upon their rights by the nobility.

The Church emerged stronger and more independent than before, and so did the cities, whose magistrates and burghers bartered loyalty against more privileges; they presented Babenberg charts of dubious authenticity. Ottokar legalized them all and granted more, turning towns into almost sovereign domains. Since he preferred the cities to estates, he founded more cities, such as Marchegg, at the confluence of the Danube and the

March, in sight of Pressburg, and Bruck, eighty-five miles south of Vienna.

New cities meant new fortifications.

Ottokar tried to consolidate his power by making more personal appointments of his own choice. He distrusted Styrians and never appointed a man from Styria to an important office. But whomever else he selected —Austrians, Bohemians, Moravians, soldiers, prelates, jurists—though incorruptible officials, as they often were—he never believed them capable of limitless reliability, which he considered the basic requirement for his grandiose plans.

Ottokar had little opportunity to talk about these plans, lest they be destroyed and nipped in the bud.

He felt that nothing short of total power vested in his own person could assure the realization of his concept as it emerged during the last decade of his forty-eight-year-long life. He would have relished being called a dictator, but he never established personal dictatorship as it emerged in our time. He did not lack the vision, or the ruthless energy, the personal hypnotism, the indomitable stubbornness, that was ever ascribed to modern dictators' heydays at the climax of their violent careers. Maybe he lacked only the mass media to become a medieval super-*condottiere*.

Ottokar's master concept was the abolition of the Holy Roman Empire as the leading world power, and its replacement by a combination of the strongest European powers, in which he would hold uncontested leadership. Ottokar considered the German imperial idea outmoded, doomed, if not already dead.

CHAPTER SEVENTEEN

Friedrich II, last of the violent Hohenstaufen Emperors of the Holy Roman Reich, had died in 1250—a heretic, broken in spirit. His son Konrad, a shadowy figure, was sidetracked to Messina, Italy, and passed away four years later. Another two years and William of Holland, pathetic rival King, breathed his last.

Count Richard of Cornwall, who in 1257 was crowned German King (not Emperor) by corrupt prelates, was a powerless man, almost constantly absent from "his" kingdom. He died in mine-rich Cornwall in 1272.

The Electors of Germany hesitated to elect another Emperor. They remembered how often their princely prerogatives had been violated by the Hohenstaufens; they did not want another powerful ruler whose obtrusive will might prevail. They did not care for a shadow monarch either. If there had to be an Emperor at all, he should be a man without troublesome ambitions, yet not unpleasantly inert: an administrator, a conservator. There was no such candidate in sight.

The Electors continued in session and between banquets drafted discouraging replies to eager aspirants to the throne.

Pope Gregory X too looked for a suitable candidate. He longed for a great crusade to drive the infidels out of all biblical lands forever, and only a strong Holy Roman Emperor could stage such a sacred venture. He considered Alfons X of Castile, Philip III of France, Carl of Anjou; but the Electors wanted none of them.

Ottokar watched events across his western borders with an interest close to anxiety. A restoration of the practically defunct Holy Roman Empire, short-lived as it might be, would scatter his own imperialistic designs. A German kingdom, which would be no more than a shaky superstructure over a house divided by rivalries, would serve his purposes better. Best, however, would be an end to all appearances of German unity, despite the prospect of constant warfare. The convention had the characteristics of modern political-party wrangles, but for the absence of smoke-filled rooms (tobacco was not yet known in Europe) and the complete indifference of the people at large, who neither knew nor really cared what went on.

In September 1273, when the session seemed hopelessly stalemated, Archbishop Werner of Mayence introduced a potential candidate of whom nobody had thought before: one Rudolf, Count of Habsburg. The Count, he explained, was a fine man, a sound administrator, whom he had met in Rome thirteen years before, and who was well liked there. Friedrich, Burgrave of Nuremberg, who happened to be present, called Rudolf his dearest relative and truest friend. Suddenly the convention seemed to turn into a matrimonial agency. Friendly Rudolf had several marriageable daughters, and many Electors were eligible. The Count

Palatine and the Elector of Saxony declared themselves suitors, sight unseen.

On October 1, 1273, Rudolf von Habsburg was unanimously elected German King. On the following day he entered Frankfurt in state, and on October 24 was crowned at Aachen.

The new King was already in his fifty-sixth year, distinguished but not spectacular in any way.

In the history of Europe, of the world, a leaf had been turned.

The people of the Danube Valley stood on the threshold of a 645-year-long era marked by many more battles, upheavals, disasters, but also by periods of grandeur, and finally by a short time of happy contentment.

The Habsburgs were not an old family; nor did they control large areas. Their earliest ancestor was mentioned in the tenth-century records of the monastery of Muri (Aargau, Switzerland). He is referred to as Guntram the Wealthy, and he had helped found the monastery, but he was not a man of really imposing means. His castle, the Habichtsburg (Hawk's Burgh), from which his family name is derived,* was a fortress and not particularly suitable as a home.

Guntram used his unhospitable fortress for purposes which did not meet with the approval of Emperor Otto I, and Otto had him sentenced for high treason.

Guntram's grandson Werner, who died in 1096, was the first to carry the title of Count of Habsburg. Count Werner's offspring served in the armies of German Emperors, married more or less attractive daughters of Princes, and from 1135 on, collected fiefs. In 1232, the Habsburg brothers split their estates, and Albrecht, Rudolf's father, got the lion's share: Aargau, upper Alsace, and a county near Zurich.

Rudolf served with zeal in the forces of the last Hohenstaufen Emperor; so zealous, in fact, that the Emperor called him his godchild.

Rudolf was a good administrator, who knew how to manage and enlarge his holdings by invoking titles to succession, to make bargain purchases, and to acquire more fiefs. When elected King, he owned and controlled much of the left bank of the Rhine from the Vosges Mountains to Lake Constance, in addition to possessions in Switzerland and Swabia.

King Rudolf pledged himself never to restore the German monarchy as it had existed under the Hohenstaufens. This pledge was meant to

* The spelling "Hapsburg" is wrong and should never be used.

win the particular approval of Pope Gregory X, who received assurances that Rudolf would always comply with papal decrees concerning elections of bishops.

Gregory recognized Rudolf on September 26, 1274. The fact that almost one full year went by between election and recognition was due to frantic protests and intrigues by Ottokar, who had a foreboding of calamity.

Ottokar wrote the Pope that he would never recognize as a King "that count who ought to carry a beggar's pouch and is hardly fit for any office." His ranking diplomatic adviser, Bruno, Bishop of Olmütz, drafted a memorandum for the Council of Lyon, which the Pope had convoked for 1274. "Germany," it stated, "divided in herself, torn by conflicting princely interests, is no longer fit to defend the Christian Church in the Occident, let alone across the seas. The Christian creed can rest its hopes only on Bohemia." The memo made war between Rudolf and Ottokar unavoidable.

Even though a beggar's pouch would hardly have fitted the former Count of Habsburg, he was not Ottokar's equal in property and had no army to match Ottokar's forces. Yet, as a King, he refused to acknowledge Ottokar's title to Austria, unless the Pope wanted him to do so. The Pope was reluctant, and suggested an intricate procedure of arbitration to which Ottokar would not agree.

The next diplomatic move was Rudolf's. When the Royal Diet sat at Nuremberg, on November 19, 1274, he asked: "Who shall be the judge if the King has a complaint against a prince of the Holy Roman Empire?" The assembly responded that, according to tradition, judgeship should be exercised by the Count Palatine from the Rhine.

The Count Palatine, an implacable foe of Ottokar, sat down in the judge's chair.

Rudolf stepped forward as a complainant.

Heralds with brassy trumpets, somberly garbed scribes, and colorful throngs of nobles provided the background of supreme medieval justice.

The judge could only win if Ottokar lost—only lose if Ottokar won. And this was his verdict: King Rudolf is entitled to all the lands and domains which the late Emperor Friedrich II had held; he shall take possession of them by force if necessary. King Ottokar has forfeited title to those possessions since he failed to apply for investment by the new King of Germany. Ottokar is summoned to appear before the judge on January 23, 1275.

Ottokar ignored verdict and summons.

Rudolf could not yet go to war. The odds all seemed against him. You cannot conquer lands by verdict; he could not hope to retain his royal title unless Ottokar was subdued.

The Habsburg King invited the Archbishop of Salzburg and the Bishops of Passau and Ratisbon to Hagenau in Alsace, and offered them a long bill of privileges should they assist him in his endeavors. They promised support should Rudolf muster enough strength to execute the verdict.

Rudolf, who could not mobilize a German army, tried to enlist disgruntled Austrian nobles; quite a few of them were only too ready to defect from Ottokar.

Ottokar's informers notified him of the imminent danger. He took hostages, noblemen's children among them, and had them paraded in front of the castles, together with executioners.

Nobles surrendered, hostages were spared; more castles were broken, estates confiscated, owners banished. The regime of terror in the Danube Basin also turned against the clergy, whose incomes were sharply reduced.

Ottokar no longer felt secure in Vienna, and he spent most of his time in Prague. The Viennese had liked the King and resented his distrust, his prolonged absence, and the acts of terrorism committed in his name.

The Bohemian nobles, too, turned unreliable. They coated hostility with the sugar of "advice," advising their King not to waste his resources in a struggle that might involve a host of foreign enemies. Ottokar had spells of violent rage. He would have wanted to "break" their castles too, but he could not struggle on several interior fronts. The host of foreign enemies of which they spoke kept growing. Hungary, in the grip of internecine feud, would unite against him should Rudolf enter Austria.

Already, members of the Hungarian rump government were in contact with Rudolf, who offered personal bribes and the return of several towns and districts once conquered by Ottokar. Ottokar entered the bidding. Through suitable mediators, he offered treasures, estates, titles, assurances, which ranged from eternal peace to effective assistance in war; he made down payments, signed promissory notes, and made arrangements for a congress of Hainburg to tighten bonds of friendship between him and Hungarian grandees. But the Hungarians, who had once attended his Hainburg wedding in a gala that included jewels woven into their beards, stayed away.

The Pope requested that he submit to arbitration. Irate Ottokar lodged a complaint with the Consistorium. The reaction was a double ban.

Still Rudolf's royal prerogatives did not include the draft of his German subjects, but he could enlist the support of various Electors, of most South German bishops, of several counts and knights. The size of his army was anywhere between 5000 and 12,000, but it would grow by the influx of auxiliaries, while Ottokar's would shrink through desertions.

On June 24, 1276, Rudolf declared war. He proclaimed the ban of the Reich against Ottokar; and Friedrich, Archbishop of Salzburg, released "all subjects of the Bohemian King" of their oaths of fealty.

Rudolf's army marched down the Danube Valley; its heavy equipment and supplies were shipped, on flat-bottomed barges, from Ratisbon. Knights along the river would not interfere with the trip, and robber barons, some of whose forts still nestled atop steep hills, would not span chains across the Danube down below; they hated Ottokar.

Rudolf had never before made an extensive trip along the Danube. It had not been his river; it was not his home; but now he spent every hour of daylight gazing at the river landscape.

On September 15 he reached the mouth of the Isar. Two weeks later he camped in Passau, and on October 10 he entered Linz, without ever having had to draw his sword.

Rudolf continued to advance almost leisurely. Ottokar had hoped that Konrad von Summerau, a squire upon whom he had lavished many favors, would defend Enns, on the border of Lower Austria. But Konrad opened the gates of the city, and Rudolf marched in, five days after the capture of Linz.

Many nobles from Styria were on the march to join Rudolf, investing cities loyal to Ottokar as they went. Ottokar's southern realm collapsed before the opposing main forces had laid eyes upon each other.

When, at last, Ottokar understood that the enemy was heading straight toward Vienna, he hurried toward the Upper Austrian Danube; but river passages were blocked and he had to make a tortuous detour through the rugged hills of northern Lower Austria to reach the Marchfeld, the traditional focus of deployment near Vienna.

The dice were not yet cast for Rudolf, but they were heavily loaded against Ottokar. The dragon seeds of his feud with the Bohemian nobles burst into devastating bloom. Many left their King to return home. No promises or privileges could now incite a man to side with him.

But the fickle, mocking Viennese did not forsake Ottokar. They closed the gates of their city, manned its walls, defied Rudolf and his followers.

Rudolf was reluctant to open the assault. Ottokar slowly marched upstream, as his army was reduced in number through desertions with every mile it advanced.

Fires broke out in Vienna. Conflagration had a demoralizing effect. People began to climb over the wall to join Rudolf's camp in the hills of the Vienna Woods and in the rolling vineyards. Among the deserters were entertainers, the minstrels from back yards and taverns. Their gay, mischievous songs contrasted strangely with the recitals of minnesingers from Rudolf's retinue. There was neither music nor gaiety inside the city.

Soon winter would come and Vienna might starve. So far it had been an almost bloodless war, a battle of nerve attrition, a contest of determination.

Rudolf seemed unshakable, Ottokar desperate.

Bruno, Bishop of Olmütz, arbitrated:

Ottokar was to resign all title to Austria, Styria, Carinthia, Carniola, and even the district of Eger, newly incorporated into Bohemia. He would be invested with his hereditary realm of Bohemia and Moravia as Rudolf's vassal. Hostages and prisoners would be exchanged, a general amnesty proclaimed; confiscated property restored to its owners, the rights and privileges of Vienna upheld, and no reprisals taken against the burghers of the city. There should be peace between Bohemia and Hungary; Hungarian territory occupied by Ottokar was to be evacuated at once.

This meant surrender, made slightly palatable by Rudolf's routine of making friends. Ottokar's daughter became engaged to one of Rudolf's sons, and one of Rudolf's daughters to Ottokar's son. Dowries were set at 40,000 marks per match. The King who "ought to wear a beggar's pouch" offered to pay cash. Ottokar was permitted to give land instead.

On November 25, 1276, a glum day, with a cool mist rising from the Danube, the signature of the document took place on a dew-drenched meadow just outside the city walls.

Viennese crowds thronged the enclosure; they saw the two Kings step to a table upon which lay the instrument that changed their destiny; Rudolf first, then Ottokar. It looked almost like a deal among equals until Ottokar—his expression indistinguishable in the dim light—knelt down. Anybody had to kneel to receive an investiture, but by this prostration the King had become a feudal tenant to the Viennese. They watched in silence, while acclaim burst from the knights in Rudolf's retinue.

Deserter bards and minstrels returned to Vienna to poke fun at the victim of humiliation. Back-yard listeners and tavern patrons did not respond.

Then Rudolf entered the city. He was stared at in mute wonder.

Ottokar went to Prague, to scheme a comeback.

In Vienna, Rudolf planned the organization of a powerful hereditary realm. Austria would have to be turned into a recruiting reservoir. The barons of the Danube Valley were tricky, greedy, constantly asking for something. The country people stuck to their feudal masters, even if they did not love them, and the townspeople showed no affection for Rudolf, who restored all Jews to their former privileges so that they would reorganize trade.

Ottokar did not proclaim the general amnesty, but outlawed and despoiled the men who had deserted him on his doleful march to Vienna. Rudolf lodged a sharply worded protest. Ottokar replied that the German King was not entitled to interfere in the internal affairs of Bohemia and Moravia.

Rudolf resorted to protests instead of arms, and Ottokar's reactions were not reminiscent of his prostration. Ottokar's stock with the Austrian nobles began to rise.

Rudolf's stock with Austrian burghers kept falling, as he imposed high taxes on houses, vineyards, and mills. He did not keep his promise of amnesty either. Few hostages and prisoners were exchanged. The contractual parties exchanged curt notes instead, bidding for time in which to prepare for war.

The winter of 1276–77 went by, spring came, and summer. On the Danube, fishermen threw their nets, trade barges floated to markets, robber barons spanned chains, and soldiers set up strongholds.

On July 13, Rudolf scored on the diplomatic front. Another of his flock of daughters, Clementine, was affianced to Ladislas, the new King of Hungary, and four months later Rudolf adopted him as his son.

The crucial postscript to the story of Rudolf's election was written in 1278.

Ottokar had 30,000 men ready.

On June 27, he left Prague for Brünn (Brno), in Moravia. From there he wrote his wife: "King Rudolf is in Vienna; no support can reach him there. I am confident that our wishes will be fulfilled, that we shall not only prevail upon him but also upon our foes and rivals. We trust that, as soon as we arrive, all Austrian towns will voluntarily submit to our control."

The letter was dated July 15. Brünn is eighty-five miles from Vienna. Ottokar's host should have covered the distance in no more than one week. Had it arrived around July 22, Vienna might have submitted to Ottokar's control, and Rudolf might have been either a fugitive or forced to kneel down on the meadow on which Ottokar had knelt to ask for quarter.

But Ottokar did not march on to Vienna without delay, as he could have done. He was irked by the hostile attitude of several small but heavily fortified towns, and he spent irretrievable weeks besieging places like Laa, where he had little to gain, but a crown and life to lose.

Rudolf dispatched urgent appeals to friends whom he expected to trust in his lucky star, and he admonished Ladislas of Hungary not to tarry. On August 22, about 35,000 Hungarians arrived at the March River, a few miles north of the Danube. Ottokar lifted the unavailing siege of Laa and proceeded to the Marchfeld. On August 25, the two armies were only three and a half miles apart.

Rudolf, his face like a bleached wood carving, was with his heavy cavalry, facing north along the western bank of the March.

Ottokar, too, was with his men; he looked tired, but more fit than his aging opponent. Youthful Ladislas watched both armies from atop a low hill beyond the March, well beyond the range of arrows.

Action opened on August 26, 1278, at 9 A.M.

For several hours it was a standing battle; ironclad mounted men hitting at one another without noticeable gain or loss of ground, and no more damage done than edges of swords and points of lances dulled.

Early in the afternoon the weight of Bohemian armor became telling. Rudolf's right wing was pressed back to the village of Dürnkrut. Rudolf tried to stem the tide, but his mount was killed, and he lay, covered by his heavy shield, under the hoofs of charging horses. A Swiss knight rescued the King. Casualties mounted rapidly.

Styrian Ulrich von Kappel, a man of unusual height, threw a force of last resort into battle, to open an avenue of escape for Rudolf. The effect of the charge of the fifty armored horsemen was perplexing. Bewildered Bohemians staggered, a gap opened in their array, and into it poured present-minded, hard-riding Hungarians.

Within minutes victors turned routed, and raced toward the March, many drowning in the lazy muddy river, many more trampled asunder by the pursuers' horses.

Ottokar did not yield. Together with a small bodyguard he stood, a stumbling rock in the flood of his own routed men and the onrushing enemies. A hit by an enemy lance threw him out of the saddle, a blow tore his sword from his hand. He was a prisoner according to the law of chivalry, but cupbearer Berthold von Emerberg, one of Rudolf's men and Ottokar's personal foe, inflicted the deathblow upon the unfortunate King.

The unchivalrous cupbearer's sword may have saved Ottokar humiliations that would have paled his prostration before Rudolf, and a disgraceful execution.

Legend, and the superb drama written by Austria's *poeta laureatus* Franz Grillparzer, who was born more than five centuries after Ottokar's death, tells of Rudolf's homage to the remains of his slain foe. Actually, the body received no salute. Rudolf's and Ladislas' forces raced on in pursuit of the Bohemians, all the way to the border of Moravia. The number of Bohemians killed was estimated at between 10,000 and 14,000.

News of Ottokar's end reached Vienna during the night that followed the disaster. There were no demonstrations.

The Hungarians did not distinguish between allied and enemy territory. They ravaged Lower Austria with grim thoroughness. King Rudolf, anxious to rid himself of his outrageous helpers, prevailed upon Ladislas to return home with his troops, with whatever loot they held.

The victor and his remaining forces entered Ottokar's realm. The late King's nobles quarreled. Some thought that Rudolf would be a hard taskmaster and that it was better to fight than accept his domination; others wanted peace under the best obtainable terms. Cities prepared to render homage to the German King, whom they considered to be their co-national; Czech peasants were frightened.

Bishop Bruno of Olmütz was among the first to heed Rudolf's call for collaboration. His statecraft established peace for the time being.

A twin marriage was arranged at once. Rudolf's son and namesake was married to Ottokar's daughter Agnes, and Ottokar's seven-year-old son Wenceslaus to Guta of Habsburg, who, however, did not receive one mark of the dowry her father had previously promised.

King Rudolf established his residence in Vienna for a full five years. In Vienna, his Queen, Gertrud (also called Anna) of Hohenberg, died. In Vienna, the first Habsburg King first visualized a family realm that would eventually become the core of the Western world, in which the sun never set. In Vienna, the Habsburg foreigners would, in the course of six centuries, grow into the most genuinely Austrian family of all, the symbol of cultured, traditional Viennese-ness.

And yet, in the metropolis of the Danube, so richly studded with memorials of every pattern, Rudolf von Habsburg never had a monument. Shortly before the outbreak of World War I, somebody discovered this bewildering fact. A Rudolf of Habsburg Monument Committee formed, fund-raising festivities attracted the cream of society. Archduke Franz Ferdinand, heir to the throne, attended a garden party, "A Night in the Vienna Woods," in June 1914. But shortly thereafter he was assassinated; war came, and disaster. Rudolf von Habsburg's monument remained confined to the drawing board.

CHAPTER EIGHTEEN

The people of Vienna accepted Rudolf as a crowned resident—no more, no less. Not even the famous *Reimchronik,* the Austrian chronicle in verse, with all its fanciful detail on what happened in the land, mentions roaring manifestations of sentiments in streets and on squares.

Whatever happened on battlefields close to the walls, whoever resided on Am Hof, thousands of carts loaded with grapes rolled into town; wine presses were busy, and so were tavernists and musicians. Everybody who had a penny to spend and no glum story to tell could have a good time, whether under Babenberg or Přemysl or Habsburg.

Street singers did not lampoon fallen Ottokar; nor did they extoll Rudolf and his clan. But they teased craftsmen who did not like any interference with the franchises of their guild, and they sang a rollicking ballad of belligerent cobblers who threatened to storm the town after filling up the moat with lasts.

The cobblers resented the parody. They brawled in taverns and staged protest rallies, which patrician burghers derided.

Rudolf had left Vienna when, in 1284, a storm broke. It was a storm in a wineglass. Albrecht, Rudolf's oldest son, who had been invested with Austria, knew little about Viennese mentality—so little, in fact, that when the cobblers bickered, the patricians jeered, and the street singers bantered, he believed that a serious revolt was afoot.

With bag and baggage, and a guard of knights, he moved to the strategically located castle on the Leopoldsberg, which a munificent Babenberg had built, 700 feet above the Danube, and from there blockaded the city. Chains were spanned across the river by order of the highest authority.

Some supplies got through from the east and south, others from nearby vineyards.

Wine stimulated pugnacity. The craftsmen, who disliked having to tighten their wide belts, charged the patricians with fomenting trouble and asked for either more edibles or conciliation with the blockading Duke. Patricians assembled at City Hall and did a great deal of talking. Much as they were irritated by the blockade, they were even more annoyed by taking orders from untidy cobblers. When nothing resulted from their talks, a committee of twelve craftsmen threatened to take City Hall by storm and extradite as many well-born aldermen as the Duke would care to accept as scapegoats.

Duke Albrecht might have resorted to drastic measures, yet no delivery had to be made by the craftsmen's committee. Instead, the abbot of the Schotten convent, Vienna's wittiest and most popular clergyman, took to horse, visited the Duke, and arranged for a Viennese delegation to call at Leopoldsberg under a safe conduct.

The delegation included only patricians. They carried a huge bundle of documents—all the privileges that could be found in the fire-ravaged city archives—and offered the Duke to preserve those he considered proper and to destroy the rest.

A seasoned Austrian ruler would have destroyed none and added some dealing with wine consumption. But Albrecht had no sense of humor. He ordered a great deal of privilege burning and decreed that the walls of Vienna be breached so that the sovereign could always enter the town at his pleasure. He also made the delegates sign a pompous instrument by which all city officials, magistrates, burghers, and whoever else dwelled within the breached walls promised never to rebel again. Prominent burghers not included in the delegation had to sign personal pledges. Their names read like a late-thirteenth-century Who's Who in Vienna, from repentant masters of the mint and landlords on Vienna's main streets to one Reinhard der Sohlenschneider (sole cutter), who supplied plebeian cobblers with material.

Albrecht returned to his town castle. He did not wish to have details of the burlesque insurrection recorded, but street singers celebrated the affair in their peculiar ways; and their ditties became a source of information for later chroniclers.

But contemporary chroniclers told of what happened to the breached walls of the city. In 1289 and 1291, aggressive Hungarians and later a new hostile German ruler, who held the crown for a few years following the death of Rudolf in 1291, invested Vienna. The Duke found it prudent to close the breach again.

Rudolf had visualized the Kingdom of Germany becoming hereditary in his family and Habsburg marriages bringing crowns of many more lands into a family orbit that would keep expanding through matrimony.

But matrimony was not always a panacea, as Rudolf may have realized one year before his death, when the throne of Hungary became vacant and his endeavor to invest Albrecht with the parent realm was as unsuccessful as his efforts to secure the crown of Germany and of the Holy Roman Empire to his house, independent of Electors and statutes.

However, Albrecht recovered the crown of Germany in 1298. He never went to Rome for a coronation as Emperor, though he had many adherents in Italy, one of them the Florentine Durante Alighieri—the immortal Dante—who urged him:

> O German Albrecht,
> Doest thou quite forget
> To press thy thighs firmly
> On the flanks of the wild nag Italy.

But Albrecht obviously did not think that Italy could be governed from the banks of the Danube.

A tale goes that Dante, the ardent patriot, traveled to Vienna to make "German Albrecht" change his mind. The only vague evidence of such a trip can be found in his *Divina Commedia* (*Inferno*, 32d song, verse 26), which tells of the frozen Danube in Austria.

The central Danube rarely freezes, but in 1300 it did freeze; Dante may have seen the icebound water, and his unique flair for tragedy should have been inspired by the awesome sight of the torpid river rather than by drolleries of tavern gabble he could hardly have understood.

Had cartography been a regular profession in the medieval Danube Basin, it would have flourished in the thirteenth and fourteenth centuries, when boundary lines kept changing in kaleidoscopic fashion. But cartographers were few, and whatever they produced delineated orographical and hydrographical features rather than man-made limits, which were altered again and again as dynasties changed; regicide throve; empires boomed and busted; Kings, Princes, and their kin argued and litigated;

ecclesiastic authorities mediated to little avail; and rulers and pretenders, royalty and republicans, faithful and apostates, mustered armies, river flotillas, and navies, and hired the oddest of mercenaries to conquer what could never be held.

The Árpádian dynasty vanished in 1301. For the next four years a Bohemian King ruled Hungary, then for two years a Bavarian, to be succeeded by members of the Neapolitan branch of the House of Anjou. Hungary lost Dalmatian towns to Venice, recovered them again, fought with Serbia, Bosnia, and Bulgaria, expanded through all of Walachia to the Danube Delta, got a strangle hold on Poland, lost it again, gained and lost as if in a wild gamble, moving from Buda to Venice, from Kraków to Naples.

Bohemian King Wenceslaus II, whom his Habsburg wife dreaded, styled himself King of Poland. Albrecht of Habsburg and his son Rudolf controlled a family empire that reached from the lower Rhine to the central Danube. Luxemburg rulers established themselves on the throne of Bohemia. A Bohemian King of the House of Luxemburg got Upper Silesia and acquired the Italian town of Brescia.

Crowns were bought and sold. German Electors set high marks of corruptibility. Disputes reached a new pitch. Cruelty of execution almost defied wild imagination. Once a noble culprit was tied to the tail of a horse and dragged to the place of execution in three stages: first his right hand was chopped off; next one eye was put out, and then the other; and what remained of the victim was broken on the wheel.

The people survived the orgies of blood and confusion, though all men saw and dreamed blood, and visions of blood begot more bloodshed.

Nobody could have told exactly how it had started, who had said the awful word first; but it happened in the Lower Austrian Danube region near the town of Pulkau.

Somebody was said to have said that, in a church near by, the Host had been found desecrated, the wafer besmeared with coagulated blood. Nobody had seen the Host, but everybody took the story for granted, and everybody trusted another rumor saying that a similar gruesome discovery had been made near Wolfsberg, in Carinthia province. Then, blow by blow, bloodstained Hosts were said to have been found wherever Austrian churches stood. Out of nowhere rose the cry: "The Jews did it!"

No Jews lived in or around Pulkau or Wolfsberg. In all of Austria, Jews were not known ever to have entered a church. But popular phantasm, weaned on blood and fire, did not ask for evidence; the Jews had used blood to desecrate the Eucharistic Host, and nothing but blood and fire could expiate the sacrilege. The phantasm had distinct features of ritual murder. The term was not used in Austria of 1338, but the fable of the Host unleashed a violent pogrom.

The Habsburg Duke and his liegemen rose to prevent arson and murder. In many instances irate crowds were kept in check. A few nobles who granted residential permits on their estates to Jews and did business with them, offered precarious havens in their burghs, but in various towns and many market places Jews were slain, or corralled in their own dwellings and burned alive. The massacre lasted for several days. Few Jews survived outside the protected communities. Survivors mostly left Austria for various destinations.

Hardly had the emigrants left, hardly had the crazed people of Austria shaken off the spell, when another plague came.

The new invaders hailed from Asia, from the endless steppes that had expectorated the Huns, the Avars, and similar hordes upon the milder regions of Central Europe. But the invaders of June 1338 did not ride on horseback; they did not have the bow legs and slit eyes of their predecessors; and they were not human creatures at all; they were migratory locusts.

They came in swarms like clouds, ten to fifteen miles in diameter. They darkened the sun, settled on fields on which the grain already stood high, and they destroyed the harvest to the last blade and stalk. Only the vineyards resisted the Asiatic pests. The peasants' larders remained almost bare. Community and estate storehouses soon emptied. Monasteries opened their reserve granaries. Knights, counts, and the Duke drew on whatever stores they had to alleviate the growing need. In late summer, fall, and winter frightening bread lines formed, and in the lines were many violent drunkards, since there was still wine, and on an empty stomach wine easily goes to the head.

In the spring of 1339, when new grain sprouted on the fields, the locusts returned. Desperate peasants kindled enormous bonfires to destroy the destroyers of their harvest. They fought a savage battle against the persistent invaders, killed many swarms, but suffered a total loss of food that turned to near catastrophes as the season progressed.

The winter of 1340 cost many more human casualties than the war between Ottokar and Rudolf.

In the spring of 1340 the Asiatic invasion petered out. But then came another disaster: an inundation that to the people of the Danube Valley appeared like the biblical Flood.

The preceding winter had been hard. The river carried veritable blocks of ice—the blocks dammed up, forming high rocks that encased enormous masses of water in towering, solid vaults. When the thaws came the valley was inundated to a level never considered possible. Houses that had been standing high above the river were washed away, many men and numerous cattle drowned, whirls and rapids formed where they had never existed. Fishermen who ventured out on the raging river in quest of food and floating objects that could be used, disappeared, and neither their remains nor those of their craft were ever recovered.

The Wachau, with its steep, narrow banks was hardest hit. The churning floods isolated castles on hillsides and washed all villages away. Survivors talked of demons resurrected from oblivion through men's misdeeds. The manes of demons and the ghosts of the drowned have inspired local folklore ever after.

The year 1341 passed without major disaster, but in the following spring the floods returned and destroyed whatever the demon- and ghost-ridden people of the Danube Valley had rebuilt. Ugly, brownish sediments formed all along the banks, covering soft turf and edgy rocks. The people did not dare clear away the sandy mess, lest they antagonize the evil spirits even further. The rains at last cleaned the valley.

A brooding silence, wrought with fears of more and still worse to come, settled over the Austrian Danube Valley. Whatever its people learned of war and internecine feud in neighboring lands seemed trifling by comparison with their premonitions of catastrophe. Men apparently could do no worse than provide a vicious intermission in the drama of nature, the outburst of God's wrath against a kind He had apparently forsaken—thrown before the pagan spirits.

Almost six years had passed since the last deluge, and people still waited, in the grip of superstitious fear. The street minstrels from Vienna sang no scoffing ballads, but innocuous trifles of yesteryear, and jittery popular audiences offered neither encouragement nor acclaim.

On January 25, 1348, came an earthquake, a phenomenon practically unknown to that generation of Austrians. In the Danube Valley the earth shook, ramshackle homes collapsed, and many people claimed to have heard unearthly sounds, the demons' battle cry. The southern provinces of the Habsburg realm were hardest hit. The town of Villach, two hundred miles from Vienna, was completely destroyed; many villages were leveled; several castles which had withstood siege collapsed under the shock. Many thousands died under the debris.

The quake was a ghastly knock at man's door, and without man's doings, the door flung open and a somber, murderous monster crossed the threshold.

The monster came from somewhere in Central Asia—nobody could tell exactly whence. It had traveled across plains and mountains, killing whomever it encountered, leaving behind hecatombs of primitive nomads as it emerged into the cultured sites of the Middle East, mute and murderous.

The Bubonic Plague was on the march.

Late in 1347, merchants fled the Orient by ship to return to Italy, France, and Dalmatia. With them traveled the germs of murder. Crews were decimated. In home ports, the plague disembarked and walked on, leaving destruction in its wake.

The first registered case of the "Black Death" in Europe occurred on Christmas Day of 1347, in Spalato, Dalmatia. The first casualty in the Austrian Tyrol was registered on June 2, 1348, in Trient. The march of the disease was not fast, but apparently irresistible. Physicians were helpless. Only gravediggers were of use.

Carinthia and Styria were hit in the fall of 1348, in the wake of the earthquake.

Churches stayed almost empty. Austrians did penance in their own way, trying to soothe evil spirits in a manner pleasing to demons: flagellation.

From New Year's Day 1349 on, flocks of men and women stripped to the waist went from settlement to settlement. The men formed groups on open squares, the women entered houses, into which they were willingly admitted, and whipped each other with prickly scourges until the blood gushed out of broad weals. The lashing was accompanied by weird invocations; some fell by the wayside, but many a convert to flagellantism joined the howling hordes. The flagellants' processions marched all over Austria and beyond into Germany. Their invocations were outright blasphemous, and the Church tried frantically to stop them.

Flagellantism continued for some time after the plague had run its course. The end of this course was marked by an auto-da-fé which dwarfed all executions by the Inquisition and eventually turned against the Jews.

Actually it started in France, in Provence, in the disastrous year of 1348. Local Jews were usurers, who charged interests of 10 per cent per month; this incited the hatred of the populace, who believed a tale that the Jews had poisoned the wells and who were ready to burn them in their own homes. All Jews from the town where the cry "Burn them" first burst, perished in the flames. Soon the cry resounded all over southern and central France; everywhere, houses and their Jewish inhabitants were consumed by fire.

The Pope issued an ordinance making murder and spoliation of Jews punishable by excommunication, but the mania defied laws and ordinances, and with Black Death lurking everywhere, nobody feared the rope.

From France the craze spread to Germany, where hundreds of Jews were burned alive.

The pogrom finally hit the Danube Valley in the latter part of 1349. The Bubonic Plague was at its climax. Vienna recorded an average of 500 dead per day. Fifty-four clergymen of St. Stephen's succumbed. Suburban communities were wiped out. Beasts of prey devoured corpses in houses and on the streets.

Survivors roared: "The Jews have poisoned the wells. Burn the Jews!"

Among the victims of pestilence were many Jews, but maddened crowds do not care for factual logic.

Duke Albrecht tried to protect the victims. He had 300 Jews marched away under heavy guard to Kyburg Castle in Switzerland, where he thought that they would be safe. But the Swiss authorities insisted that unless the Duke had the Jews burned, they would do so themselves. Albrecht was powerless, and the city magistrates did as they had announced.

On September 28, 1349, the citizens of the plague-ridden towns of Krems, Stein, and Mautern, on the Lower Austrian Danube, resolved to chastise the Jewish families of Krems. Chastisement turned into ingenious torture; subsequent death in burning houses seemed merciful by comparison.

The Duke had the main culprits executed and the townships fined, but the Jews, who had played a vital part in the local business, were all dead.

A full decade after the Bubonic Plague subsided, several villages in the Austrian Danube Valley still remained entirely depopulated.

Yet Vienna was gay again. Past disaster was but vaguely alluded to in mocking songs. Vienna did not know that new clouds were massing on the southeastern tip of the European continent.

CHAPTER NINETEEN

Small splinter tribes of the once powerful Central Asiatic Türküt, dispersed, disdained, and shiftless, had reached the regions of Asia Minor and the approaches to the Holy Land. They vegetated as hordes of mercenaries, in the meager pay of anybody who would hire and equip light-cavalrymen whose tactics were primitive but who were not afraid of death.

By the mid-fourteenth century they had advanced to the approaches of the Balkans. Sultan Orchan, their leader, probably the greatest military organizer of the Middle Ages, learned a great deal about the topography of the peninsula and about the great river skirting its northern approaches. He decided to conquer it all after reorganizing his forces, which by then were called Osmans.

Osman light riders were forged into superbly disciplined cavalry, the *sipāhī*, or spahis; young Christians captured in previous Balkan campaigns became a new infantry corps, the *yenīcheri* ("new troops"), or Janizaries, a mangled version of the original.

The Turkish menace became a terrifying fact. Within a few score years they had grown from a band of nomad mercenaries into a nation with an expanding land of its own, from disdained servants into dreaded masters.

Byzantium appealed to Hungary to help drive the Turks from the European continent. The King of Hungary promised to muster a great army, a Danube flotilla, and a seagoing fleet, but changed his mind. But in 1371 King Vukashin of Serbia, who had won the throne of his small country through assassination, set out to conquer whatever territory the Turks still held between the Danube and the Sea of Marmara.

The decision for assault was taken on September 13, 1371, and celebrated with a boisterous drinking bout. King Vukashin, his nobles, their peasant-vassals, the lowliest camp followers, were all drunk to the point of unconsciousness. There were neither guards nor sentinels; and even had there been a few, and had they stayed sober, they could not have hoped to alert the mob of snoring drunkards. The only spahi squadron left on the Balkans scouted the forefield of the poorly defended capital and staged a raid which turned into mass slaughter. At dawn, few of the conquering boozers were left.

The Occident hardly took notice of the ignominious end of King Vukashin and his army, and when Sultan Murad returned from a successful Asia Minor campaign, he found his European provinces safe, his banners floating on river craft on the Danube, and Byzantium in a tight vise, ripening for his grandiose designs.

In 1388, Murad's fighters descended upon Bulgaria and forced insurgents to surrender. In 1389, they penetrated into Serbia, and on June 15 or 28 (there is some confusion about the date), and even though Murad was assassinated by a young Serbian nobleman who sneaked into his tent, the Serbs and their allies were defeated and the last vestiges of Serbian independence destroyed. Serbian tradition accepts June 28 as the day of disaster; it is St. Vitus' Day, or *Vidov Dan,* which became a day of national mourning, contemplation, and promise.

Sigismund of Brandenburg, who, through intricate crisscross marriages, court intrigues, and ecclesiastic politics, became King of Hungary on March 31, 1387, not only continued his predecessor's indifference toward the Balkans but also had financial worries and hoped that exploitation of Hungarian-Neapolitan imbroglios would be more lucrative.

Young Ladislas of Naples was an aspirant to the throne of Hungary, and his supporters conceived a plan that should have shocked all faithful Christians: the new Sultan, Bayezid, the man who wanted Mohammedanism to prevail over Christendom, should help the Neapolitan boy-King to ascend the Hungarian throne and bring Hungary within Islam's sphere. It was agreed that he would marry one of the Sultan's more or less legitimate daughters as soon as the Turks were in Buda.

The Neapolitan emissary must have been a traitor, for Sigismund heard of the deal almost immediately after it was made. In the summer of 1393, as the Turks began to assemble on the right Danube bank, his makeshift army forced the river crossings. This was the prelude to many battles near Belgrade, in the region in which the Danube, swelled by tributaries, rolls past the bastion of the Balkan foothills, majestically contemptuous of man's frantic destructiveness.

Sigismund gave the Turks time to withdraw and consolidate. Months went by. Shipping was impeded by drifting ice and the Hungarians had supply trouble. The reorganized Turkish army crossed the river far downstream into Walachia, where collaborationists offered services on easy terms.

Early in 1394 Bulgaria was officially annexed by the Turks, who also controlled Little Nikopol (now Turnu-Severin) and most of the Walachian hinterland. Throughout the year, Sigismund did not launch a major drive against the Turks, but indulged in erratic retaliation against those who had betrayed him. In May 1395, he crossed into Walachia and caught Bayezid ill prepared. The badly mauled Turks swam across the Danube and prepared for a last-ditch stand, but they were not pursued: Sigismund's young wife had just died in Buda and his title to Hungary was essentially based on this marriage. He raced back and found things in good control. Many towns and squires tolerated his continued rule and the Archbishop of Esztergom had prevented an invasion by the King of Poland.

War against the Turks could resume; this time it should, at long last, be a crusade with full support from the West and active participation of Byzantium.

In April the contingents of France, Burgundy, and England started their long march southeastward. As they proceeded across the Rhine and entered the Danube Valley, they were joined by Ruprecht of the Palatinate, Burgrave Johann of Nuremberg, and various South German notables. To judge from the brilliant names, the number of Western forces should have been extremely strong. But hardly more than 10,000 men were on their way to battle a Turkish army which might number about 100,000.

The crusaders were supposed to join Sigismund's levies early in May, on Hungarian territory. However, their vanguards did not reach Vienna until May 21, and there they had to wait for the main forces. Waiting turned into a picnic with lavish entertainment.

The people of Vienna, no longer remindful of floods, quakes, pestilence, and pogroms, greeted the romantic-looking crusaders as an innkeeper would welcome prosperous customers. The street singers were out in strength, fair and easy women swarmed around the soldiers' quarters, and the wines of Vienna, thoroughly tasted by the cross-bearing visitors from the West, seem to have compared favorably with whatever the Rhine and the Moselle had to offer.

The main forces arrived and joined the merrymakers in their enjoyable vacation. Hardly ever had business in Vienna been better than in June 1396, never had there been more fun. The Turks, cause and objective of the mass excursion, were all but forgotten.

Only on June 24, after various inquiries had arrived from Hungary, did the crusaders leave the hospitable town, and while from the battlements of Byzantium sentries looked out for the arrival of the Christian army, seedy Westerners trudged into Hungary to join Sigismund's army of 50,000. Down the Danube Valley they marched, rode, and drove, at an accelerating pace. Near Vidin, they crossed the river into Bulgaria; a short distance away they encountered a small Turkish garrison, which surrendered abjectly. On September 12, they arrived under the walls of Nikopol; from there they intended to veer off from the Danube Valley, straight south to Byzantium. But on September 28, a veritable forest of Turkish standards, banners, and field badges seemed to grow out of a blank horizon; some sources put the number of Turks at 100,000, others at twice that number.

With the Byzantine Emperor far away, Sigismund was the Christians' commander in chief. However, German, French, and English soldiers were reluctant to accept his orders, and when he ordered that his own cavalry hold the first line of the array, near mutiny broke out. The French and English crusaders insisted on launching the opening assault; the Hungarians were merely to mop up. Sigismund yielded uneasily.

Bayezid watched the enemy moves from a nearby hill. His word was his army's law.

The French and English attacked with colossal vigor. The Janizaries were overrun, but the sulking Hungarians stayed behind and did not exploit the advantage.

On the southern slope of the hill on which the Sultan had his command post, the elite of the spahi stood, ready to strike. Their blow fell as the French and English caught their breath.

A few minutes later, all was confusion. The French and English had dismounted. Their horses, frightened by the Turkish charge, shied, raced back, and crashed into Sigismund's grumbling, slow-moving, second array. Disorder broke its ranks, while the French and English were either slain or captured.

To the north lay the broad waters of the Danube, with the flotilla of Christian supply ships. King Sigismund, his back to the river, fought hard. As night fell, the battle deteriorated into a mad scramble for evacuation by boat. The Danube flotilla could carry only a fraction of the fugitives, many of whom perished in the silent waters that looked dark as death. On the opposite bank of the Danube, Walachian highwaymen, the vultures of Danubian wars, gathered to despoil fugitives.

Turkey was in Europe to stay, and to have a powerful influence on the continent's destiny. Christianity had lost more than a battle; it had squandered an irretrievable opportunity. Had the crusaders not reveled in Vienna, the Turks might have been doomed.

The Hungarian King survived. He made a bark of his Danube flotilla, and since he did not dare land anywhere on the riverbanks, he set sail for the Black Sea, reached Byzantium one month after the debacle, and returned to Hungary via Dalmatia early in 1397. He interfered in petty strifes in Bosnia and Serbia, traded shares in Balkan mines against unkept promises to fight Bayezid's successors, and was occasionally accused of selling Europe out to tottering Sultans for pledges unspecified. And yet, in 1411, the fugitive from Vidin became King of Germany; in 1413, Holy Roman Emperor of the House of Luxemburg, and King of Bohemia in 1419; he considered himself secular ruler of the Church since he was instrumental in ending the great schism that had lasted thirty-nine years. He was ten years old when he had become the ruler of Brandenburg, fourteen when he had ascended the Hungarian throne, and he lived to be almost seventy. A bewildering maze of events was crowded into that life span, yet his most lasting achievement was not the restoration of peace within the Church, not the personal union of Hungary, Bohemia, and part of Germany, but the ill-fated foundation of the Kingdom of Prussia. It was Sigismund who invested the Hohenzollerns with Brandenburg, which became the focus of the kingdom that carried the torch of war in every direction.

CHAPTER TWENTY

A man who had laid eyes on the Danube only once, though he had never lived far away, accounted for many upheavals in the Austrian part of the valley. He was Jan Hus, magister-reformer from Husinec in Bohemia, who called himself a disciple of John Wyclif, who taught at Oxford.

Hus had been cited before the Council of Constance, where he arrived on November 3, 1414, with a letter of free conduct issued by Sigismund,

King of Germany. Nevertheless, he was arrested on November 28, thrown into the dripping, high-smelling, rat-infested dungeon of the Dominican convent at Lake Constance, and later transferred to a hardly better place of confinement in the episcopal palace of Gottlieben. The magister languished, ailing, praying, stubbornly determined to vindicate himself against all charges of heresy. A few Bohemian nobles stood by him, but their powers were vastly inferior to those of the men bent on destroying the sincere but bothersome reformer.

A commission was appointed to hear the captive. No minutes were kept. All the examiners would say was that Hus was "callous."

Between June 3 and 5, 1415, Hus was given three public hearings before high ecclesiastic authorities. He was charged with disobedience to the Archbishop of Prague, the city where he had lived, taught, preached, and acted as the Queen's father-confessor; he was also accused of disregard of anathema and interdicts, and with heresy committed by championing certain theses from his own writings.

Hus had no defense counsel, but among his accusers were the trickiest legal minds of the Church. He denied ever having taught or written anything untrue. His passionate oratory, which would have carried away popular audiences, only aroused the wrath of learned prosecutors.

At last, on July 6, he was led before the plenary Council, in session in the Cathedral of Constance. Among those present were many prelates, primates, and members of the consistory, King Sigismund and several Princes of his realm, Hus' Bohemian escorts, and, far to the rear but visible from the spot on which the accused stood, an otherwise nondescript man in untidy garb: the executioner.

That morning the Bohemians had bribed the executioner so that he would hang a sack of gunpowder around the victim's neck and make him die instantly from suffocation rather than being slowly fried at the stake.

That morning, too, Hus had suffered from agonizing toothache; his face had been so swollen that he could not talk; he had prayed for the power to speak up for the last time, to say that he had not been proven wrong and had nothing to recant. And, as it is told, the swelling vanished and Hus was almost cheerful when he entered the cathedral.

The procedure was short. Asked to abjure, Hus refused; and when trying to explain, he was interrupted. The Council stripped him of his ecclesiastic rank, pronounced him an unreformed, incorrigible heretic, and surrendered him to the secular authorities. According to the laws

of the land, there would be no other trial. Surrender of a heretic was tantamount to his immediate burning at the stake.

Hus died singing. His end was neither quick nor merciful. The hang-
man was a cheat. The sack he fastened around Hus' neck did not contain gunpowder, but sand from the lake shore, which dragged out the
dying man's agony.

The flame of Constance kindled a far greater fire, which seared large
regions of Central Europe. Yet it took more than five years before it
burst into a devastating holocaust.

In these five years, Hus' spiritual companion, Hieronymus of Prague,
recanted, revoked his recantation, and eventually suffered Hus' fate. A
Bohemian-Moravian convention of nobles sent a letter with 452 seals
attached to the Council of Constance, saying that Hus had been unjustly
executed and that everybody who claimed the existence of heresy in Bohemia was a liar, a traitor, a son of the devil. The signatories pledged
themselves to have the word of the Lord freely preached on their estates,
to resist unrighteous excommunication, to comply with orders from the
Pope or Bohemian bishops only if they were found to be in accordance
with the Scriptures, and to recognize none but the University of Prague
as supreme authority in matters of dogma. Against the 452, only 16
rose to assert their unquestioning obedience to Church, Council, and
King.

The Council continued in session until 1418, solving the *causa unionis,*
the reunification of the Church, by instituting a single pontiff. Baldas-
sare Cossa was deposed as Pope John XXIII; Benedict XIII and
Gregory XII had to resign; and Martin V was elected.

Restive Bohemians did not feel reunified with the Church. Their sacred
cause was their martyr, Jan Hus. Sects formed, all claiming to stand for
the pure creed, dissenting on various issues, but united on one point:
the communion in both kinds. This gave them a common name: the
Utraquists; and a common symbol: the chalice.

One radical sect held gatherings on a plateau near Bechyně, to which
people gave the biblical name of Tabor. The "Taborite" leaders were
Margrave Nikolaus von Pistna (also called Nikolaus Hus, though no
relation to Jan) and Jan Žižka of Tročnov, a noble lansquenet who had
seen Hus at the stake. Members were petty nobles, Czech craftsmen and
peasants, who were anti-royal, anti-German, anti-Rome, and practiced
early utopias with common property and personal equality. They admitted laymen to officiate at divine services, even allowed women to
preach; they did not keep Church holydays, forbade finery and luxuries,

and argued against science as leading to nothing but arrogance and deadly sin.

Pope Martin warned King Wenceslaus against the danger of Taborite propaganda, and in February 1419 the King ordered that Taborites in public office be replaced by devout Catholics.

The first violent explosion came a few months later. Harangued by a former monk and by Jan Žižka, a fanaticized mob stormed the town hall of Prague and threw the chief magistrate, the mayor, and several aldermen out of the windows; down below, other mobsters waited with raised pikes.

When Wenceslaus heard of the outrage, he suffered a cerebral hemorrhage; he died on August 14, 1419. His successor, Sigismund of Germany and Hungary, was in Hungary when it happened.

All over Prague, churches and monasteries were looted. Well-to-do burghers, most of them Germans, sought a sanctuary in royal Hradčany Castle. There were savage riots in Písek, Pilsen, Königgrätz, Saaz, Laun. The old feud between Germans and Czechs revived under a new motto: Catholicism versus Utraquism.

King Sigismund's enthronement resulted in a brief, uneasy lull. After he was deposed by the Taborites, smoldering Prague became a radical stronghold. German hostages were taken, German burghers terrorized, and an army from Germany invaded Bohemia. Žižka, proud and defiant, claimed that Sigismund wanted to extirpate all Czechs and recolonize the country with Germans. He called his Taborites to arms, "not only for the sake of truth and Divine Law but also for the deliverance of the Bohemians and all Slav nations."

Jan Žižka, a one-eyed man who soon would lose his remaining eye in action, had many fanatics under his command, but few trained soldiers. Volunteers flocked to his banner, mostly peasants and craftsmen who had never handled weapons.

Žižka taught the craftsmen how to cast cannon and work them skillfully; he designed a new pattern of laagers: barricades of several rows of wagons, made virtually attack-proof by chaining the carts together, suspending thick boards from the sides, and having cannon fire through breaches. Žižka devised new maneuvers: sections of wagons could drive into the enemy force, cut off and encircle parts of it, and have the men flailed to death by the peasants.

Žižka's Czechs felt that there was no survival but in victory. Sigismund's mercenaries were ready to desert if pay was not forthcoming.

Žižka's men, carts, and cannon, from inside Prague, repulsed the first royal attack.

King Sigismund never went beyond Hradčany Castle, which then was not inside the city. Four hundred families of German fugitives sought shelter there. After Sigismund lifted the inglorious siege, they fled to Vyšehrad and were eventually captured by the Czechs, who gave no quarter.

Later in 1420, Žižka carried the war south, subduing the most ardent Catholics and the wealthiest of Bohemian nobles. For the first time his soldiery entered Austria.

There were no Utraquists in Austria; hardly anybody understood the term. But terror spread to the Danube Valley. Towns strengthened their walls, peasants gathered arms, manors and monasteries girded for an emergency, the nature of which seemed inscrutable. No reports from authoritative sources told of what went on north of the river, but the chill of deadly peril was more impressive than eloquent accounts could have been.

At last, ragged travelers arrived from Bohemia. They said that "Hussites" (as Taborites and Utraquists were often called) had stormed the town of Prachatice and burned its inhabitants and that Czechs from Prague had overpowered other all-German towns and committed untold atrocities. Fear-crazed Austrians expected doomsday to be at hand.

From Hungary, Sigismund tried appeasement, but a Czech Diet called him deposed as a "mortal enemy of the Czech nation" and established a provisional government of twenty men, among them Žižka.

Sectarianism split wild radicals from opportunists, the lunatic fringe from rationals. The lunatic fringe included visionaries who claimed that Christ had left heaven for Bohemia, that He would take care of the land, remove all authorities, abolish all title to property, and create a paradise. There also were the Adamites, who denounced marriage as sinful, preached that lewdness was the duty of every adult, and ran around unwashed and stark naked.

The Hussites were more intolerant than the most bigoted Catholics had ever been. Disgusted, Žižka had members of the lunatic fringe massacred wholesale. Learning of the Czech internecine feud, three German Electors invaded Bohemia with an army of 100,000; but Žižka, discontinuing his blood purge, marched north to meet the invaders, who were indiscriminately slaughtering Czechs. On October 12, 1421, the German soldiers caught their first glimpse of the dreaded laagers and fled in panic.

Sigismund, unaware of the disaster, was just signing a treaty with

Albrecht V, Habsburg Duke of Austria and later German Emperor, who, feeling that events in Bohemia were a matter of life and death for his Danubian lands, pledged himself to raise money for war in return for the hand of Sigismund's daughter Elisabeth, heiress presumptive to Bohemia and Hungary. The two partners hired the greatest theoretician of strategy, Florentine General Pippo Ozera, as a chief of staff of their combined operations. Four days before Christmas, Ozera trapped the bulk of Žižka's troops near Kutná Hora, but Žižka, already completely blind, broke out of the encirclement, using battering-ram tactics against enemy sectors which his guiding-eye aides called the weakest.

A breakout, according to the Florentine chief of staff, was but glorified escape, and escape was synonymous with flight. He permitted his troops to engage in an orgy of looting and on the eve of Epiphany 1422, when sightless Žižka returned with peasant reinforcements, they were caught off guard. Sigismund's men ran, Ozera was unable to stop them; his subsequent dismissal did not improve the Catholic military position.

Albrecht returned to Austria. The Danube Valley girded in horror, and waited. But the Hussites did not come.

Fratricidal feud raged in Bohemia and Moravia. New wild extremists battled moderates; mobs ruled in big cities, including Prague. Daily, countless victims died in what modern ideology might call class struggle. Plebeian ire raged against teachers, aldermen, Utraquist ministers, and everybody who owned, or temporarily held, property.

Žižka's sympathies were essentially with the propertied group, but when its members looked for alliances with Poland and Lithuania, he charged them with plotting against Utraquism and he swore an oath to destroy the cities where alleged plotters were active.

On June 7, 1424, Žižka won a major victory over his domestic antagonists and turned against the Austrians. But before his guiding-eye aides could brief him on the enemy array near the Moravian border, he was stricken by disease and died on October 11, 1424, an undefeated, famous pauper. For Žižka, as it turned out, to everybody's amazement, had spent whatever he had owned to supply his soldiers and had never accepted a share in the booty.

The army continued into Austria. Near Retz, it engaged Austrian troops and won another victory. Vienna was within striking distance.

A new military leader emerged in the camp of the invaders: a former monk, an extremist by origin and ruthlessness. His name was Prokop. Later he was dubbed Prokop the Tall, or Prokop Holy (which stood not for "saint," but for "shaven"). Prokop had burned Retz and wanted to burn Vienna, to which all factions of his army agreed. But then a new faction arose, the "Orphans," who claimed to be the only ones able to continue in Žižka's soldierly path and propagated a new dogma of "transubstantiation" and worship of saints.

It took Prokop until March 1426 to settle controversies with the Orphans. Burning and ravaging Lower Austria, he reached the Danube near Stockerau, twenty-five miles northwest of Vienna. The Austrian people could not distinguish between Orphans and the rest of the Czech host. To them, the flail-swinging invaders with their wagons and fire barrels were the reincarnation of the cavalcade of devastators who had visited their land for a thousand years, the symbols of ravaging elements that had shaken, inundated, scarred, and infected their river valley. Even had they understood that human madness was self-consuming by nature, they would not have drawn comfort from such perception, for they were convinced that they would perish first.

Vienna's gates were locked. From the battlements guards looked out for wagons driving westward along the bumpy dirt track that led to Stockerau. No wagons came. Prokop Holy had been recalled to northern Bohemia, some two hundred miles away, where Saxonian and Thuringian invaders battled Taborites and Orphans.

Vienna had another respite. In northern Bohemia, Prokop and his next-in-command, Prokop Little, won another victory. Tall, shaven Prokop became the Czech's dictator and proclaimed total war.

Years of devastation had drained the country's resources. It faced starvation and total lack of military supplies. Whatever was needed had to be obtained from abroad through invasion and pillage. Prokop wanted the Czechs to strike in every direction, defeat one neighbor after another, until no King or Prince would dare resist.

Austria raised a militia. The clergy was taxed 50 per cent of its revenue, cities were made to pay huge sums, soldiers were made the best-salaried men of their profession anywhere, at six schillings a month. Every fifth man was trained to use heavy ironbound flails, to fight the enemy with his own weapon.

Early in 1427, the Austrian militia engaged a band of Orphans that had been burning a convent. The Orphans fled, the militiamen ransacked their laager for valuables, but then the enemy returned and 9000 Austrian corpses littered the battlefield.

Lower Austria was devastated over and over again. The Czechs reached Stockerau, then marched and drove down the Danube past the walls of Vienna, to the Marchfeld, where Ottokar and Rudolf had fought, and beyond, into Hungary.

Flail-wielding Czech peasants had long become professional soldiers, a power that made Prokop feel uneasy and meditative. In this state of mind, he had a strange caller: a messenger with a letter bearing the royal seal. King Sigismund invited him to Pressburg, to discuss reconciliation.

Early in April 1429, they met at the castle atop the hill overlooking the Danube and distant mountain ranges. Tall and shaven Prokop looked glum and lost in thought as he sat before the aging, bearded, affable King. Behind Prokop stood Utraquist militant nobles, who were embarrassed to see their commander break fundamental rules of etiquette, such as sitting in His Majesty's presence, and clergymen who had been ordained as Catholics and wished to assert their right to deviationism. Sigismund's retinue consisted of ranking officers who glared at their opposite numbers and wondered how to behave toward fellow noblemen who had sided with mobsters, and of zealous prelates who would have wanted to restage the session of Constance on June 6, 1415.

After a claptrap of words the ecclesiastic opponents took the floor. The Catholics requested that the Utraquists return to the Catholic creed; the Utraquists insisted on keeping control of church affairs in their land forever. The soldiers first listened to the repetitious splash of words that grew ever louder and angrier as time wore on, but they did not change its futile course; then they looked out of windows and never even broached the subject of cessation of hostilities. The meeting of Pressburg broke up. Sigismund and Prokop never met again.

Five more years of tumult went by, until, on May 30, 1434, the two Prokops were killed in battle. Thirteen thousand Utraquists were captured, locked in barns, and burned alive.

Hussitism, the Bohemian preamble to the Reformation, had run its course. Bohemia was again predominantly Catholic, but the memory of the Hussite wars survived and fanned the smoldering blaze of Czech-German antagonism. Hitler's misnamed "Sudeten Germans" of 1938 were, in fact, Taborites of different denomination, and some of what they did to the Czechs in the seven years that followed, and some of the subsequent Czech retaliation, can be found, with different names, dates, and details, on the dark pages of the chronicle of the Hussite wars.

CHAPTER TWENTY-ONE

The Danube Valley never had long periods of leisure to gird for future upheavals. Its inhabitants had come to consider the vicissitudes of politics as unavoidable as those of the elements. So why ponder over what seemed to be beyond control? Better forget and enjoy whatever moments of respite you had.

Soon after the Prokops died, Vienna was again in a festive mood. Aeneas Sylvius, a contemporary who was to become Pope, calls Vienna one of the most beautiful and populous German cities—"German" referring to the language spoken there. Its population was approximately 75,000; life was gay, frivolous, opulent, carefree. The Viennese spent on Sunday most of what they had earned during the week. Merrymaking was their foremost concern, winegrowing and trade with sheer oriental delight in circumstantiality were their favorite professions. Street singers serenaded the noble art of free spending.

Among the most popular affairs were the races of the loose girls (called "lovelies" or "girls of joy"), held on a street. The prettiest of their profession, clad in light, extremely revealing garments, sprinted over a few score yards to win a large piece of scarlet cloth. Sidewalks were crowded, windows jammed, roof tops occupied beyond capacity.

The pfennigs, Vienna's small coin, circulated freely; so rapidly, in fact, that everybody could lay hands on some pfennigs and feel prosperous. The coins rotated fast, but they got less valuable all the time and, for a while, the Viennese tried not to notice it.

Public expenses rose; public revenue declined. The government turned to licentious financing methods.

With the introduction of new firearms, costs of army equipment skyrocketed. As the European armament race of 1450 continued without home stretch, revenues from domains and regalia were depleted through sales, pawnings, and unavoidable donations. New taxes were hard to impose and even harder to collect. Popular discontent rose, and to enforce order voracious armies had to be enlarged.

Friedrich III, the Habsburg Emperor of Germany, was plagued by the spiral of rising expenses and declining revenue. So was his brother, Archduke Albrecht VI, who ruled Austria. Often, when two men are beset by similar trouble, they turn against each other.

Austria needed soldiers to protect itself against German intrusion. Germany needed mercenaries, horses, and artillery to protect itself against Austria. Bavaria wanted armies in order not to be squeezed in between the hostile brothers. Hungary needed men to guard against trouble from the West. Southeast, a magnificently unrestrained Turkey was again on the march.

Discharged Taborites roamed the Danube Valley, joined by highwaymen; and robber barons, scenting a new prosperity, descended from their strongholds to intercept whatever craft moved on the Danube and whatever wagon jolted over rough dirt roads.

Certain robbers gained fame for their ruthless splendor. Mladwanek and Ladwinko, who called themselves Taborites of the old school, established their headquarters at the mouth of the March River; they built forts, which they called "tabors," and between looting and arsoning, threw gala parties in which entertainers from Vienna and Pressburg participated at high fees and under safe conduct.

On March 29, 1458, Albrecht VI and his Viennese militia raided a tabor near the Danube where an orgy was held, with many women dressed à la Adamite, and hordes of singers. Five hundred intoxicated robbers were seized and carted off to Vienna, where another party was arranged, this one for the benefit of the burghers. The robbers were hanged in public, while peddlers sold food and drink, and the crowd made merry.

It took another year until the tabors were mopped up and security between the March and the Danube improved, but by then disaster had struck from different quarters. In 1459, severe May frost destroyed most of the crop of wine, and continued inclemency of the weather all but wiped out the harvest of grain. Most food had to be imported and prices went out of control.

The fast-circulating pfennig had scant purchasing power. At the turn of the century, the rate of exchange had been 96 pfennigs for 1 ducat; during the Hussite war, the ratio reached 150; in 1459, it was 240 to 1. Princes used minting privileges to cover the boundless deficit by issuing bad money.

In Bavaria, the proportion of fine metal in copper coins was reduced without warning. Pfennigs with silver content near zero were shipped by the ton on Danube barges to Austria. But already, before 1459, the minting of depreciated pfennigs had been taken up in Linz, Wiener Neustadt, and other towns. The Archduke farmed out privileges to unscrupulous operators who paid him fees in gold but reduced the proportion of silver in a pfennig from the already low 0.25 gram (1 gram = 15.43 grains) to a bare 0.012 gram. Those who wished to obtain wares from abroad had to pay in ducats. The ducat jumped from 240 pfennigs to 500, 1200, 2000, 2500. . . . Ever fewer money-changers were ready to part with their gold for any number of copper coins. Regular commerce came to a virtual standstill. Wheat rose seventyfold; a chicken cost as much as did formerly a fat calf; a hare sold for a price that would have fetched a horse two years before.

Desperate people gathered in the city streets. In 1460, several days passed without a crumb of bread on sale. The Copy Book of the City of Vienna records: "People did not only cry; they scolded and cursed Princes and councilors. General misery reached terrible proportions. Some men ground the bark of trees to get flour; others died of hunger; one widow from the suburb of Nussdorf killed her two children since she could not feed them. Parents offered their children for sale or chased them into the streets or locked them into their apartments and left, so that they would not have to see them starve. The finances of the city were chaotic. Public debt ran into many millions. Intake from taxes [one third of Vienna's real estate belonged to tax-exempt nobles and clergy] stopped, as nobody wanted to pay for anything that was not edible. The city council stopped paying wages. Not only city workers were left penniless; university professors received no salaries either. Emperor and Duke quickly adopted the procedure to pay only for what to them seemed essential: the armed forces."

One Gamaret Fronauer, a petty noble, laid unsubstantiated claim to the castle of Orth, on the left bank of the Danube, a score of miles east of Vienna. When this was denied to him, he assembled 2000 Bohemian and Hungarian bandits, hired a few Taborite "brothers," and opened a predatory war against everybody who still had a chicken left. Soldiers, the best-fed men in the inflation-ridden realm, campaigned against Fronauer's hordes without much gusto, but they were as reckless as the bandits toward the stricken people.

Emperor Friedrich III and Archduke Albrecht blamed each other for the calamity. A meeting, with Bohemian delegates as arbitrators, was called to Vienna in 1460. The Viennese had to tighten their belts even further to keep the participants fed. But no agreement was reached except on urgent monetary issues.

New pfennigs were minted; the ducat fell to 180, but soon was back at 300. The next harvest did not fail, the vintage improved, people ate and drank again, but the gay mood did not return. Profiteers from inflation, Jacks-of-all-morbid-trades as only calamity can beget, spread rumors that the new pfennigs would soon be exchanged against groschen containing not a grain of silver, that wages would be cut in half, and that the government would suspend payments altogether. Fronauer reopened hostilities against the forces of order. The Imperial prestige was still at a low ebb, and the man who did not get the castle of Orth made a bid for most of the Austrian Danube Valley.

Fronauer, who had plenty of ready cash, enlisted stranded mercenaries and got them expensive equipment gratis. Early in 1461, his private army occupied Triebensee, and from there blocked all traffic on the Danube, subjecting ships and cargoes to fantastically high illegal dues. In the spring he established more "check points" along the river and roads leading through its valley. As his ruffians ransacked buildings, Fronauer had people lined up at public places to receive their homage. Robber barons disliked the intrusion, but they were not rich enough to challenge him. In Vienna, market prices rose because of the taxes Fronauer imposed on merchants on their way to town.

And as Fronauer collected dues and homage, Archduke Albrecht went to Innsbruck to sever all existing ties between himself and his Imperial brother and to set up an empire of his own. Emperor Friedrich, who had gone to Vienna, vainly appealed to the Pope, to the Estates of Austria, to the cities of the Reich. Then he mobilized, scraping the bottom of his treasury to hire a strong army, but when the last pfennig was spent, 1000 of his force of 1300 were shiftless outcasts.

The Emperor called a Diet to Korneuburg, ten miles upstream of Vienna, to request support from nobles and estates. The session, on June 15, 1461, was virtually unattended. He sat in the empty hall of the local castle, waiting for four agonizing days, while, outside, bystanders cracked jokes. On the fifth day some callers came. The first was a messenger from Vienna with a formal declaration of war. Next came delegates from the Austrian provinces, from Bohemia and Moravia, all carrying challenges. It looked like a war of succession and for the privileges of Gamaret Fronauer. Actually, it was all the aftermath of the great monetary fraud.

On June 30, Albrecht arrived on the Lower Austrian border, on his way down the Danube to the capital. Local nobles hailed and joined him. Fronauer, at the head of his thieves, received a special reception.

One month later, Archduke, nobles, soldiers, and thieves camped under the walls of Vienna, where Schönbrunn Castle now stands. The Imperial family was in the city castle. Vienna was encircled. Albrecht received reinforcements from Hungary and from disgruntled and greedy German Princes. The King of Bohemia styled himself mediator. Hostilities were suspended on September 6, 1461. Not much had been accomplished on either side.

Emperor Friedrich, blissfully unconcerned about the future, went to Styria to arrange special honors for Apostolic Nuncio John of Capistrano, his adviser, who had recently died. From Styria, he discharged his miniature army without severance pay. The 1300 rioted and looted. And Fronauer's thieves, whose spectacular march to Vienna had been so unrewarding, were on the loose again. Some of the nobles' soldiers also looted, and the Viennese footed the bill.

City Hall imposed new taxes that hit wage earners and craftsmen. Salaries were paid irregularly, if at all. A Viennese Diet was called for July 21, 1462. Normally there would have been a great deal of merrymaking, but the Viennese persisted in their nasty mood and the assembly, supposed to restore peace and prosperity, was hit by a *Putsch*.

One Hans Ödenacker, son of an attendant at a public bath, and one Dr. Hans Kirchheim, a physician, neither one a native of Vienna, formed a team to seize the reins of the Diet and the municipal government. The doctor donned harness, Ödenacker hired sixty roving veterans; they arrested the Mayor of Vienna and all the aldermen, and had themselves appointed caretakers of city affairs by the frightened Diet. As they knew nothing about city affairs, they assigned an expert to run the business: one Wolfgang Holzer, a former livestock man and later master of the mint, whose sarcastic oratory was of the type the Viennese liked best.

Emperor Friedrich was still eighty miles away when the trio took over. With him were 6000 men, greenhorns from the backwoods, who knew nothing about His Majesty's practice of defaulting on wages. The fickle Viennese kept them cooling their heels in the suburbs for three days before opening the gates. The Emperor had to promise full amnesty for every violation on the book of statutes.

He received Holzer in special audience and graciously asked for money to pay his army; Holzer turned him down in scathing terms. The greenhorns were discharged without pay, and they looted. Simultaneously, Albrecht's mercenaries were out in quest of cash, and they looted. Fronauer's host continued to loot.

The fall of 1462 was clear and balmy. Grape pickers went to the vineyards; wagons were ready to roll into the city with last year's wine. But somebody, probably one of Fronauer's men, devised a scheme to hit the Viennese where it would hurt most: they separated them from the new grapes and young wine by drawing a blockade between the city walls and the vineyards. An irate Holzer led an irate deputation to the Imperial castle. On October 5 they notified Friedrich that, unless all abuses were remedied at once, people would pay no taxes and would consider themselves released from all pledges of loyalty. Eleven days later, sixty-six pieces of artillery (four of them capable of throwing 300-pound missiles) pointed at the castle's walls.

Archduke Albrecht rushed to the scene to witness his brother's shame. Friedrich sent frantic messages for help to the King of Bohemia and Mr. Fronauer. The cannon fired a few shots, but there was no storm and Friedrich was rescued. Vienna had its grapes and wine; Holzer received a full pardon and a bribe of 6000 ducats to use his oratorical talent against the Archduke. The Emperor had to pawn many cities and call on usurers to raise the cash.

But before the citizenry could rise against Albrecht, Holzer met an unhappy end. He and five of his cronies were caught by the Archduke's men in a winery in the suburb of Nussdorf; Holzer was quartered, the others beheaded.

The partisans of the two brothers kept fighting, but when, on December 2, 1463, Albrecht died of typhoid fever, as his doctors claimed, or of poisoning, as others said, the Estates of Austria joined the Emperor, and so did the Viennese. Fronauer, and the pastime of looting, vanished into oblivion. A strange war had come to an end. It received no official name, but some people called it the "battle of the flayers' pfennigs."

CHAPTER TWENTY-TWO

Three years before Austria's pfennig troubles reached their climax, a man died in Hungary who was one of that country's national heroes and whose legend has survived through the centuries: John Corvinus Hunyadi, the White Knight.

Modern textbooks call him an innate leader of men. Those who feel that lofty morals, forceful ethical and logical conceptions, and an ideal personal conduct make a leader, will find that Hunyadi does not quite fit that pattern; but those who believe that forceful appeal to fellow men can turn even a ruffian into a leader will find that Hunyadi was indeed a natural idol of the masses, a symbol of the popular taste of the outgoing Middle Ages, which actually was not much different from the tastes of allegedly more enlightened periods.

Hunyadi was very tall, strikingly handsome, obsessed by the urge to steal any show. His stentorian voice, theatrical gestures and mimics, would have commanded general attention even if he had been less concerned with his unique attire. This ancestor of the Counts of Hunyadi would never don anything that other people might also wear. In peacetime his clothes were multicolored, spectacularly embroidered, and extravagantly cut, though never effeminate in design; in war, he wore all-sterling-silver armor. His thunderous oratory could enthrall the crowds. He had a gift of using plain language to express crude feelings that mirrored the audience's own. He never attempted to rise above his listeners' intellectual level. He never urged them to do something gentle and softhearted, but he would ragingly call upon them to do what they secretly longed to do: to kill and dominate. He addressed his soldiers before going into battle even if this meant loss of precious time, and he would do his utmost to avoid battling in the darkness or on a cloudy day, since he wanted the rays of the sun to turn his silver armor into a beacon of white light.

Hunyadi is not mentioned in factual reports on the various campaigns of the 1420s and early 1430s in which Turks, Serbs, Walachians, and Hungarians grappled among themselves with results that can better be expressed in figures of human and material loss than in achievements. Later legends have it that Hunyadi won decisive victories and crushed the Turks.

The Turks controlled most of Serbia and Bosnia, raided Walachia and Transylvania; nothing but the fortifications of Belgrade blocked their road into the Hungarian lowlands. The people of Hungary longed for a national hero as a bulwark against the dreaded invaders. Hunyadi's verbose glamour catapulted him into the limelight when he was already past fifty, but still at the peak of his popular appeal.

As the snows melted in 1440, Turkey was on the offensive. Sultan Murad II made a determined bid to wrest Belgrade from the Hungarians. The Turks had heavy siege artillery, but the fortifications were extremely strong and the defenders used a new weapon: heavy-caliber cannon, firing between five and ten small balls with one shot. After a six-month siege, which cost the Sultan an average of 2000 casualties per month, Turkish engineers of Greek stock filled moats and trenches with logs to allow the infantry to use storming ladders with great effect. But under cover of darkness the Hungarians sprinkled the logs with gunpowder, and next morning, when the attack started, they kindled the explosive, and more than 5000 Turks perished in the blast.

One year after the affair of Belgrade, Hunyadi, in silver armor, crossed the Danube near Smederevo, routed a Turkish covering force, penetrated deep into Serbia, dispatched many messages of victory, and eventually returned to Hungary, leaving the Turkish main army intact and ready for action.

In June 1443, a Hungarian Diet, meeting in Buda, resolved to resume war against Turkey. On July 22, the soldiers left. Cardinal Cesarini was with them, and the King was in command. Hunyadi was slated to join the forces near Belgrade.

The army was nothing to boast about—25,000 in all. Hunyadi waited for the King's host. He outshone and towered high above royalty, magnates, voivodes, and prelates. He delivered an address which the rank and file loved and the dignitaries did not fully understand, yet admired. He was the toast of the welcome banquet.

Ten thousand volunteers arrived. Hunyadi was told to undertake a reconnaissance into Serbia. The oldest man in the army and in splendid fighting mettle, he dashed south, not to scout but to destroy whatever the Turks would put in his way. With indomitable verve he defeated three Turkish groups near Niš, took the city by storm, and kept on in the direction of Thrace. When he learned that the Turks he had defeated were reinforced by reserves from Bulgaria and set to attack the Hungarian main body, he turned around and defeated them again, killing 2000 and capturing 6000, together with nine standards. King Wladyslaw received the trophies. The prisoners were never seen or heard from again.

A howling, chilly Balkan winter closed in. Hunyadi, a live firebrand, wanted to reach the Sea of Marmara by land. The Hungarian host ravaged Balkan land and people indiscriminately, and put Sofia to the torch. From Sofia, the way led through the Balkan passes, which were defended by Turkish regulars, in the direction of Byzantium. Hunyadi reached the passes at Christmas. Throughout the afternoon he led one charge after the other. The glowing winter sun set; his silver armor shone red rather than white; the Turks held their position; Hunyadi kept attacking; dimness set in and darkness. The armor no longer shone, but through the night Hunyadi's roaring voice resounded. The Turks were well fed, warmly clothed, and rested. The attackers were hungry and tired; their clothes were the same they had worn marching through the sun-scorched plains of faraway Hungary. The attack failed. A silent Hunyadi led his men back, through Bulgaria into Serbia, and the Turks followed like wolves tracking a weakening prey.

Near Niš, Hunyadi made a surprise attack. The pursuers were thrown back; among the prisoners was a brother-in-law of the Sultan, a valuable hostage. But the Hungarian retreat had to continue. What remained of the army could not be whipped into shape for another offensive. In February 1444, they were back in Buda.

Hunyadi, whose tempestuousness had thrown the campaign off balance, received a triumph, Roman style; in defeat more even than in victory, the people wanted a national hero. Hunyadi was the nation's idol more than ever.

Ladislas, Emperor Albrecht II's posthumously born son, was Hungary's next monarch, but on Whitsuntide of 1446 the Diet appointed Hunyadi interim "gubernator," regent, with only slightly curtailed regal powers.

But Hunyadi could not rule by peaceful means. The Austrian Archduke made several rather insignificant requests. Hunyadi answered by invading Austria and burning down all settlements within a belt of thirty miles from the border.

In the east, Princes and Voivodes quarreled over control of Moldavia and Walachia. Hunyadi interfered with a maximum of vehemence and a minimum of tact. King Ladislas Posthumus meanwhile snoozed in his cradle.

The White Knight planned another Balkan campaign, which could but provoke another Turkish intervention. He had lost whatever sense of proportion he had ever had. In the summer of 1448, some 20,000 Hungarians and a few thousand mercenaries marched out of Buda, with some field artillery and war chariots resembling the Hussites' carts.

In September, Hunyadi crossed the Danube, this time at Kubin. He wore his silver armor as the soldiers marched, rode, and drove past his reviewing stand and cheered him with hoarse enthusiasm.

Their enthusiasm still ran high when, on October 18, they ran into a Turkish army of allegedly 150,000, and a defiant Hunyadi ordered all-out attack. For three days the Sultan's men could not vanquish the madly charging foe; but then the weight of numbers brought the inevitable result. More than two thirds of Hunyadi's men littered the battlefield. He fled, and after gruesome adventures, which included capture by Serbs and a high ransom, he recrossed the Danube, virtually alone.

He would have wanted to raise another army and keep on fighting, but the magnates, who had already heard so much Hunyadi oratory that they had developed an allergy against its bravado, wanted no more foreign wars. Even the Pope admonished Hunyadi to stay on the defensive. Teeth gnashing, the White Knight chose to negotiate with Turkey and signed a three year's armistice with Sultan Murad's son and successor, Mahomet II.

But in 1452 he agreed to resign as regent in return for the hereditary title of Count, the immensely remunerative assignment as Administrator of Royal Finances, and several other offices, which, combined, gave him the highest income and the greatest executive power in Hungary. His son, Count Ladislas Hunyadi, became governor of Croatia.

The White Knight had little leisure to bask in dignity and wealth.

Byzantium's hour struck. Hunyadi would not stand idly by after the triumphant Turks, on May 19, 1453, planted the Star and Crescent at the crossroads and gateway to the Western world.

Not one single Hungarian soldier was in the city in its hour of despair. Instead, Hunyadi's men skirmished in Serbia and threatened Turkish strongholds on the lower Danube. The Sultan sent a deputy commander to repel them, but before the man could arrive, Hunyadi defeated a small Turkish force and pursued it up the Morava Valley. Well satisfied with himself, he returned to Hungary, eulogized by poets as the avenger of the Cross.

In 1456, an enormously armed Turkish host camped under the walls of Belgrade. The Turks also had a powerful Danube flotilla to block water-borne supplies and Hungarian relief forces.

Michael Szimaghi, the fortress commander, was a courageous man and a sound tactician, but the impact of Turkish artillery seemed overpowering. Huge stone balls, thrown by powerful charges and with remarkable accuracy, opened wide breaches in the walls.

Hunyadi appealed for volunteers. Once his very name had been an asset worth many thousands of men, but the magic spell was no longer effective. To many Hungarian nobles, it was an annoying reminder that their familes had been outshone by an upstart. They did not want the upstart to further increase his stature, and they also felt that, nearing seventy, he was too old. They refused mobilization of their contingents; young King Ladislas was told to fight the German Emperor over some petty claims and was sent to Vienna to gather troops.

Time was running short. Hunyadi could not hope to reach Belgrade by land in time for a relief operation, so he traveled on the Danube. It was his first engagement on water.

He wanted to break the Turkish strangle hold on the river. The Turkish armada included several big ships, captured from Byzantium; it was amazing that they could have been brought to the spot through the sandy river mouth and the Iron Gate. All units were tied together by massive chains, forming a raft that reached from bank to bank.

Near Slankamen, Hunyadi assembled two hundred craft—all more or less rickety, all loaded beyond capacity with men and supplies—and let them drift with the current against the Turkish fleet. A short distance away, forty canoes manned by the best archers from Belgrade prepared to join the great river battle.

On July 14, 1456, the ramshackle fleet attacked. It was like David challenging Goliath, with less than a slingshot. Hunyadi wore his armor and, according to some reports, mounted his horse on his barge. His mighty voice, like Roland's horn, admonished his men. The collapsible craft drifted against the massive chains. From aboard the Turkish galleys muscular arms wielded axes to destroy the attackers, but they could not quite hit the flat boats; a few cannon balls from siege guns whizzed past, the targets too small to be hit. Archers aboard the forty canoes sent carefully aimed volleys into the Turks' floating fortress.

From the battlements of Belgrade and the walls and roof tops of the city of Zemun (Semlin) on the opposite bank, soldiers and citizens watched their stolid old river foaming under the convulsion of battle.

After five hours of struggle, the chains were broken, the Turkish galleys sunk or captured. Hunyadi controlled the river crossing.

The Sultan began to wonder whether old Hunyadi was not actually a demon. The full power of his artillery was brought to bear to pulverize Belgrade. From July 15 to July 21 the big cannon boomed incessantly; heavy stone balls hit targets with terrific impact.

Hunyadi had only little rest. He stood at an outpost, in one hand a cross, in the other a banner with the picture of St. Bernard—both gifts recently received from the Pope. Soldiers and civilians murmured that the White Knight had become an apostle. At his side stood John of Capistrano, the monk who had become a greater crusader than Kings and Princes, cardinals and bishops.

In the small hours of July 21, when a pink-colored dawn rose downstream and the dark pines of the small island which the Turks would call Ada Kaleh assumed a tender luster, the Turks opened the final storm.

Janizaries formed groups of 600, each capable of squeezing through one of the many breaches. They pressed on with perfect skill and discipline. Hunyadi and Capistrano waited for them with their men. They had little discipline and even less skill, but a world of faith and the wonderful determination which only faith can beget.

The fortress cannon could hardly slow down the march of the Turkish elite, but the unskilled faithful were more effective than artillery. Three times the Turks entered Belgrade, over heaps of corpses and rubble; once they planted the Crescent inside the city and set out to storm the outer castle, but the defenders kept fighting and their fanatical devotion prevailed. The Turks were forced back to their points of departure.

But Hunyadi knew that the attack could always resume unless the Turks lost their devastating siege artillery. He led his men in a wild sortie, overran the Turkish positions, continued the charge, and hit the Sultan, who looked like the image of an oriental god of war, in the thigh with an arrow. Six thousand spahis returning from reconnaissance, stemmed the tide and almost turned it into disaster, but the wounded Sultan lifted the siege. He had suffered a setback, but he trusted that Hunyadi could not last forever.

In fact, the White Knight, whose hair was now as light as his armor, survived victory only by a few weeks. The foe that struck him down was the plague, rampant in that region for over a year. On August 11, 1456, Hunyadi died.

His older son, Count Ladislas Hunyadi, resembled his father temperamentally. The King's advisers did not want him to become a power, and one of these advisers, Count Ulrich of Cilli, was either killed by Ladislas Hunyadi in a duel or murdered outright.

The killer was arrested on March 14, 1457, and ten days later tried on charges of conspiracy. He was pronounced guilty and beheaded on a public square in Buda as huge masses watched. The executioner's hands trembled; three blows of the sword mangled the doomed man, but only at the fourth blow did the head part with the body. The crowds were irate. The frightened teen-age King barricaded himself in his castle and forbade, under penalty of death, anyone ever to mention the name of Hunyadi again. When the executed man's widow hired mercenaries who staged a revolt, he fled to Prague, where he died suddenly, probably of poison.

Matthias Hunyadi, the second son, became King of Hungary in 1458 under the name of Matthias I Corvinus and won the crown of Bohemia in 1469. He did not succeed in becoming Emperor of Germany, but he conquered Vienna in 1485.

Matthias Corvinus is often referred to as one of the first Renaissance Princes because of his sponsorship of the arts and sciences. But he did not originate a dynasty. He could not secure the Crown of St. Stephen for his natural son.

The Counts of Hunyadi, however, continued their line into our time. Hungarian folklore kept glorifying their ancestor. In 1896, a victory column was erected in his memory above the whirling rapids of the Iron Gate, near the Column of Trajan. One Count Hunyadi was among the Hungarian nobles who remained faithful to the last King of the land, the unfortunate Charles IV of Habsburg-Lorraine, who died in exile in 1922.

No monument was erected in memory of the army which the first Hunyadi led at Belgrade. The last chapter of its story is sad. The leaderless volunteers turned into a real mob and looted the countryside. Peasants and burghers rallied against their erstwhile liberators, who did not even fight. They had lost faith. The men who had pierced the array of Turks and captured the Sultan's cannon were chased away like cowardly vagabonds, while Turkey marched on.

CHAPTER TWENTY-THREE

In the mid-fifteenth century, when Friedrich, of the Styrian line of the Habsburgs, adopted the vowels of the alphabet A.E.I.O.U. as his motto, few kings could have had more than a scornful smile for its interpolated meaning: *Austria Est Imperare Orbi Universo,* or *Austria Erit In Orbe Ultima,* which said in Latin that Austria shall dominate the world and last until its end.

Late-medieval Austria repeatedly split, reformed, reorganized, but, still essentially a reed shaken by the storms of feuds and wars, did not seem capable of holding together as a realm, let alone of dominating a world the full size of which was not even approximately known when Friedrich's predecessor Rudolf first conceived the game of initials. Rudolf's hobby was gardening, and he made of the vowels centerpieces of flower beds, which he kept much better than his patrimonial dominions. When Friedrich's son Maximilian was born in flayer-pfennig-ridden Wiener Neustadt on March 22, 1459, there were no auguries that he would be instrumental in making the flower-bed oracle come true.

The little boy was exposed to the educational methods of one Peter Engelbrecht, a learned but not yet high-ranking clergyman who believed in knocking and whipping wisdom into a pupil rather than teaching with mildness and patience. Maximilian looked like the boy who would always take the beatings and forever remain on the receiving end.

His growth was slow, his features remained unattractive. His face was dominated by a huge aquiline nose and an almost grotesquely bulging, dripping-wet lower lip. These features appear greatly mitigated in an incomparable etching by the genius Albrecht Dürer, who immortalized the embellished appearance of the ugly man who would be Roman King in 1486, German Emperor from 1493 to 1519, sovereign over many more lands, father-in-law of the heir of the Spain that established itself in a rediscovered New World, and the founder of a loosely knit patrimony between the Danube and the Caribbean, on which the sun never set.

Lashing him with whip and tongue, assiduous Peter Engelbrecht, who eventually became Bishop of Wiener Neustadt, taught his disciple seven languages besides his native German: Latin, French, Italian, Spanish, English, Flemish, and Wendish. Maximilian's mental capacity must have been extraordinary, for he also mastered matters of political science, became an expert in the intricate field of German statutes, and not only read avidly but also wrote several works, including *Theuerdank* and *Weisskunig,* and treatises on warfare, construction, gardening, and hunting.

In 1477, at eighteen, Maximilian married Maria, daughter of Charles the Bold (Le Téméraire), Duke of Burgundy, who in the same year died in action near Nancy, France. As Maria's husband, youthful Maximilian became successor to all Burgundian possessions in France and the Low Countries.

When this happened, the future Emperor was no longer frail. He had overcome his early infirmity by energetic physical training. He was of average stature, a passionate hunter, mountaineer, and jouster. In tournaments he would challenge the most formidable fighters and invariably win.

People who lived near the royal hunting grounds and in the mountains loved their outdoor-minded sovereign and invited him to folk festivals, dances, target practice. His Majesty had a flair for popularity. He not only joined his humble subjects' entertainment but recommended to his successors that they go hunting and mountaineering, to be in touch with the people. One historian noted that Maximilian moved as freely among peasants and artisans as among courtiers and gentlewomen. He also contended that Maximilian was a bold, death-defying fighter, but a charging knight rather than a strategist, an impromptu organizer rather than a long-range planner.

Maximilian I is called the "Last of the Knights." In fact, he is the author of the military reform of 1486 which all but eliminated the heavily armored cavalry in its medieval form and made infantry the hard core of German and Austrian armies. His infantrymen were mostly lansquenets hired by recruiters for four gulden a month, eight gulden if the recruit owned an arquebus. They were organized into banners of thirty men each; between ten and sixteen banners formed a regiment. (One century after the military reform, uniform garb became compulsory.) Maximilian put major emphasis on firepower. He hired specialists to build siege and field artillery, and even though he never found experts equal to the men who served the Sultans, artillery progress in Central and Western Europe was stepped up. Hand firearms, long neglected as impractical, would become standard equipment. But small arms were expensive, and only long after Maximilian's death were half of the lansquenets equipped with guns of various types. Maximilian never had a military budget equal to that of the Turkish Empire or France.

France, still strong after the wars with England, could afford to hire the best soldiers for the royal army. The best soldiers anywhere were the Swiss. Maximilian had to content himself with Germans and the riffraff of multi-national mercenaries that remained in the upper Danube Valley as jetsam and flotsam of endless wars.

But in his earliest clashes with France, Maximilian emerged victorious. In 1479 he defeated King Louis XI at Guinegate, which preserved his Burgundian wife's estate. Maria died young, in 1482. The Burgundian nobles had no love for widower Maximilian and sided with the French King, and he had to cede temporarily Burgundy, Artois, and Picardy.

Maximilian believed in aggrandizement through marriage and inheritance, in realm building by matrimony, according to the first Habsburg King's patterns. His second wife was Anne of Brittany, the idol of French aristocrats, and he expected to be proclaimed King of France. But the aristocrats did not want a Habsburg monarch, and Anne, whose marriage was not consummated because of her husband's apparently more urgent business of state, obtained an annulment and became the lawful bride of Charles VIII, King of France, a somewhat degenerate young gentleman whose memory is linked with that of the so-called Mad War. But eventually Maximilian recovered Artois and parts of Burgundy.

Inheritance brought him Alsace, the Breisgau, and all Austrian domains; but his claim to the Crown of St. Stephen after the death of Matthias Corvinus in 1490 could not be enforced. Ladislas of Bohemia succeeded the Hungarian King.

Budgetary limitations curtailed acquisitions by violent means. Critics blame Maximilian for his inability to economize; they insist that he considered thrift incompatible with Imperial dignity and that his generosity toward artists and scientists was unwarranted by the hard facts of economy. But no amount of thrift could have turned pfennigs into ducats. An ambassador from Venice, who spent several years at Maximilian's court, said that the Emperor had a wealth of good ideas which followed one another so quickly that none was systematically carried out.

The problems facing Maximilian were bewilderingly manifold, but his basic plans remained unalloyed: aggrandizement.

The German Empire was in dire need of administrative reform, lest it became ungovernable. Electors wanted more prerogatives and governmental control; the rising middle class, and the politically vocal people of the lower strata, wanted the Emperor to bridle arrogant Princes, nobles, and prelates; humanists dreamed of a resurrection of the ancient Roman Empire and ranted of an all-powerful Emperor at the helm of the mightiest of all nations—a Germanic nation that would rule the world.

If there was such a thing as public opinion, it favored Maximilian as a symbol of popular ambitions and desires, but the real issues were hardly of a nature which artisans from Nuremberg, and winegrowers from the Vienna Woods, and boatmen from the Rhine and Danube would have understood. On mutual agreement of the major parties concerned, a reform of the Reich was initiated. The aim was Eternal Public Peace, no more, no less.

Violators of peace were subject to ban. A Supreme Court was appointed, a new general tax levied from everyone, regardless of title and status. A Diet, elected by the Estates, should decide on important matters in annual sessions, without, however, curtailing the sovereign's powers.

Eternal Public Peace was not meant to be tantamount to peace on earth. In 1496 Maximilian fought, not all too successfully, in Tuscany. Between 1507 and 1509 he battled Venice, temporarily gained Verona, but was driven out of Udine and Trieste; from 1513 to 1515 he was engaged in a war with France, in which England was his ally. This war brought him one notable victory, but it had sinister consequences which did not become obvious during his lifetime: it made France and Turkey start on a long road of collaboration.

Maximilian got involved in Italian affairs through his third wife, Bianca Maria Sforza of Milan. By marrying his son Philip to Juana, second daughter of Ferdinand of Aragon and Isabella of Castile, he had already laid the foundations for Habsburg rule in Spain; his grandson Charles V was King of Castile in 1504, and would be King of Aragon, Sicily, and Naples in 1515.

In that same year, 1515, the Treaty of Vienna was signed; the most grandiose, the most consequential matrimonial pact on record: Maximilian's grandson Ferdinand was married to Anna of Hungary and Bohemia, and his granddaughter Maria to Ludwig, heir apparent to the Hungarian throne. The four children were between nine and twelve years old. The Treaty of Vienna laid the permanent legal foundation of a union of the heartlands of the Danube Basin—Austria, Hungary, and Bohemia—under Habsburg rule.

The subsequent marriages had been under consideration for over one decade. Oddly enough, preparations started before all parties affected were actually born.

The city of Vienna had its greatest day on July 22, 1515, when the momentous marriages took place.

Again Vienna was at its most glorious. A short time before, Antonio Bonfini, an Italian visitor, had this to say:

"The center of the town lies, like a regal palatinate, amidst the blossoming suburbs. Some suburbs are the center's rivals in size and splendor. Entering the city, you feel like wandering amidst the buildings of a gigantic imperial burgh; each house is most elaborately built and vies with its neighbor in splendor. The sight-seer's eyes are delighted, wherever they turn. The houses of distinguished citizens look like palaces. Almost all houses have not only a fine front but also a solid rear tract, with wide covered or open colonnades protecting dwellers against cold winds blowing in from the nearby hills. Dining halls are often splendidly paneled and equipped with big stoves. Many windows are partly beautifully painted and protected by iron bars. The houses have bathtubs, storerooms, and bedrooms for rent. Outside there are shops and market halls. You find cellars everywhere to store wine and other valuable commodities. The Viennese keep so many songbirds that, strolling through the streets, you believe you are in an enchanted forest. Everything is pleasant: squares, streets, and corners. Churches and monasteries stand in glorious grandeur. The most magnificent of them are St. Stephen's Cathedral and the Church of Maria-zu-den-Schotten [Mary of the Scots]. From St. Stephen's you enjoy an admirable sight of the entire town and its surroundings well beyond the Danube. The architecture of the Cathedral is highly artistic and original; its pictures of saints and lofty sculptures are hardly excelled anywhere in the world. Houses of priests, the University building, and great nunneries add to the glamour of the city. The sight of the abbey and church of the Schotten make you think that the magnificence of Rome has passed on to this people of the North. Some of the most distinguished families have moved from Italy to Vienna, where the Carraras and the Scaligers now reside. You can see their coats of arms on palaces, side by side with those of nobles whose ancestors went to Rome with Friedrich Barbarossa.

"The entire area of Vienna is like an enormous, splendidly kept park crowned by lovely vineyards and orchards. The spurs of the hills are adorned with charming villas, hunting lodges, fishponds, and gardens. Many castles and manors look down from the nearby mountains. The countryside is studded with many flourishing settlements. The better you come to know this land, the more you prefer it to any other region, and if peace were truly established there, you would rather live in Vienna than anywhere in Italy."

The Italian vocabulary abounds with sonorous epithets, and Italian temper prefers superlatives to soberly descriptive nouns, but Vienna was, indeed, blessed by nature and art, though not by peace.

Vienna had had too many vexatious experiences with Bohemian and Hungarian invaders to consider a territorial merger an occasion for rejoicing. But for the Viennese it was a big show; and everybody, from alderman to innkeeper, relished a great display.

The festivities opened with a Princes' Congress, originally invoked to Pressburg. Princes entertained lavishly, and Vienna had more to offer to lavish entertainers than any other city in Central Europe. In 1496 it entered a classical period of music, when Maximilian created the outstanding Hofmusikkapelle. Its first conductor was George of Slatkonia, a former student of the University of Vienna and later a bishop. Three of the period's outstanding musicians: Heinrich Isaak, Ludwig Senfl, and Paulus von Hofhaimer maintained close relations to the Hofmusikkapelle. Popular-music groups, including street singers, actually profited from classical performances, since those who attended the noble affairs usually wanted light fare as a dessert. They got all kinds of fare also in the field of literature. The noblest spirits were represented at the University, where all trends of thought and creed flourished, from the archconservative German knight Ulrich von Hutten to Huldreich Zwingli, reformer from Zurich, Switzerland. In Vienna worked Marcus Treitz-Sauerwein, the Emperor's favorite writer and secret secretary; and Celtes, born into a poverty-stricken German family as Konrad Pickel, was crowned King of Poets.

In this gathering of the literati, a roving cobbler from Nuremberg made an unspectacular and brief appearance. He was Hans Sachs, who, at Wels, 130 miles west of Vienna, had been "ordained a poet by the muses" when he wrote his first poem. The itinerant journeyman had to visit Vienna, the muses' favorite town.

When the Princes' Congress opened, ranking foreign visitors included the Kings of Poland, Bohemia, and Hungary, the Princes and Counts of Brandenburg-Bayreuth, Henneberg, Bavaria, Mecklenburg, and Württemberg, the Cardinal Primate of Esztergom, the Papal Nuncio, the papal legates, and the Archbishop of Bremen.

The children's marriages took place at high noon, at St. Stephen's

Cathedral in the center of the town, its steeple towering high above the roof tops of forts and palaces.

King Ladislas watched over bride Anna, aged twelve, and groom Ludwig, aged nine, as if to protect them from lurking dangers. Emperor Maximilian shepherded his two grandchildren with equal care. The splendidly dressed, playful, though slightly scared boys and girls who had been coached to behave like royalty were the center of the attention of the gaudiest officials and most curious popular crowd ever assembled in the ancient city.

Maximilian's retinue of knights wore high-polished armor that was no longer quite useful in battle, but still magnificent on parade. Ladislas' Polish attendants were all dressed in bright blue; the Hungarians wore red coats, trimmed with lace and gold cords. Tatars, imported from the Crimean Peninsula for the occasion, paraded savage finery.

Town councilors and secretaries wore black, with heavy golden chains brightening the attire. Fifteen hundred burghers and burghers' sons, all distinguished by affluence, wore scarlet frock coats. Their march to the Cathedral was led by six aldermen on horseback, squeezed into harnesses almost as silvery as that of the late White Knight had been.

The Cathedral was crowded to capacity; the air was excitingly heavy with incense, the organ music seemed to make the scene float to and above the cirrus clouds.

Zealous prelates assisted the ceremony, careful lest Hungarians assume priority over Austrians or Bohemians, all trying to impress the children who one day would hold the most exalted titles of the Christian world. Linguist Maximilian was about the only member of the wedding who understood most of the Latin words declaimed by priests to the sounds of the Hofmusikkapelle.

That day the Emperor was the proudest of all men. His dream had come true; he would leave the world a memorial to *"erit in orbe ultima."*

Outside the Cathedral thronged the countless curious of the eternally curious city, hemmed in between minor officials in gala and colorful foreign warriors, joined by six hundred of the Emperor's tallest lansquenets in fantastically gaudy attire, with long spikes and heavy-barreled matchlock arquebuses. The University had sent a numerous delegation; school children waved flags with the embroidered coats of arms of Austria, Bohemia, Hungary, and Poland. Guilds and corporations were all represented. The field music of four nations struck up and was joined by two hundred trumpeters and kettledrummers from the Emperor's German forces.

The noise was deafening, the glitter blinding.

The celebrations that followed were equal in splendor to the wedding. Two hundred youths of noble birth were dubbed knights. A tournament was held on a mid-town square, Neuer Markt (New Market), a few minutes' walk from the Cathedral.

A banquet table was set for three hundred. Sixteen Princes, three dukes, two cardinals, fifteen bishops, shared the meal with many counts, knights, and squires. The Emperor was in an exuberant mood. His "Merry Councilor," Kunz von der Rosen, set the tune of entertainment. It had been Kunz's idea to arrange as a side show a consummatable marriage between the Emperor's young friend Dietrichstein and Barbara von Rottal, the most beautiful woman of the realm.

It was all pleasure and edification. Nobody seemed to care that hardly one hundred miles away angry Austrian peasants battled tax collectors.

Maximilian did not often stay in Vienna. When in Austria he preferred to reside in Innsbruck. But in the summer of 1515, he was the darling of the Viennese, not only because he had arranged the wedding but also because he attended Vienna's horse races, of which the citizenry was immensely proud.

Boy Ludwig's marriage to Anna was pronounced consummated in 1521, when the groom was fifteen; in the same year, Ferdinand became a husband in the full meaning of the word, and since Ludwig eventually left no children, Ferdinand inherited the crowns of Hungary and Bohemia.

After the wedding, Maximilian left Vienna, never to return. His main concern now was to assure to his grandson Charles V of Spain the succession to the Imperial throne, in the face of strong opposition by François I of France, who cajoled and bribed Electors to cast ballots in his favor. In the following summer, at the Diet of Augsburg, Maximilian mustered all his persuasive eloquence to obtain a majority for Charles, but bribes being more powerful than words, he had to outbid the French rival. Roughly 550,000 gulden in cash and 40,000 gulden in annual pensions were promised in addition to dignities and prebends for Electors' relatives. But prospective recipients wanted cash; Maximilian had little, and even less coming. From Spain came word that the country's resources were heavily taxed and that it would take time to raise the funds. Pope Leo X, who was anxious to provide for his beloved nephew Lorenzo de' Medici, would grant no loan. Money seemed to be more powerful than marriage, tradition, and compacts.

From Augsburg, Maximilian left for Innsbruck. The innkeepers of the

city refused to accommodate the Imperial retinue. They presented unpaid bills totaling 24,000 gulden. The Emperor could not pay even that
amount. Annoyed by the innkeepers' disrespectful insistence, he suffered
what contemporaries called "a serious indisposition," and what actually
must have been a stroke. With the bills unpaid, he could not even stay
in Innsbruck for treatment. He had to travel on by sedan chair, in the
direction of Vienna, three hundred miles away. His condition worsened
steadily. At Wels, he suffered another attack and passed away on January 12, 1519.

But Charles V eventually raised the money which had haunted Maximilian and the lack of which had felled him. On October 22, 1520, he
was crowned German Emperor in Aix-la-Chapelle.

CHAPTER TWENTY-FOUR

Money could buy everything also in the Orient, where the Turks, the
lords of an empire that extended from the Danube to the Nile and the
Euphrates, used cash with contemptuous lavishness to corrupt those
whose ilk they wished to conquer. The many who craved for putrid gold
waited, cringingly, for their handout and saw no depravation in render-
ing services that would ruin their brothers, whose keepers they did not
care to be.

Without the help of renegades, the Turkish Empire could not have
lasted long. Without cannon makers, like Master Urban, a German,
they would hardly have conquered Byzantium; and the stronger Turkey
grew, the more it seemed to depend on renegades. "Renegade" was a
term which the Turks themselves used to characterize their foreign helpers. They paid collaborationists in money, titles, even power—but they
never showed them any respect. However, respect was not what the renegades expected from their masters; they could always satisfy their egos
with a substitute: the fear they instilled in the hearts of their own people.

Foreigners, particularly shrewd Greeks, could climb highest on the
ladder of Turkish officialdom. They could become governors, tax col-

lectors, even generals and viziers. Mahmud Pasha, who served as vizier under Sultan Mahomet I, was a Greek. A Sicilian was Turkey's expert in anti-crusade action, an Italian was the Sultan's chief interpreter, and after Master Urban died, another German, one Jörg from Saxony, became Turkey's foremost cannon maker. He was the pioneer of the mortar, which, deeply dug into the ground, could throw stone balls and fire bombs.

When Mahomet died in 1481, at fifty-one, he was the first Sultan to be buried at Byzantium. The next Sultan, Mahomet's oldest son, Bayezid II, was no conqueror by Turkish standards, but he made Turkey enormously wealthy. His son Selim, who succeeded him in 1512, used his inherited riches for the benefit of his soldiers: a Janizary private got twice the pay of a colonel in Emperor Maximilian's army. Backed by the army, Selim terrorized his family and his officials.

Persia was the first victim of Selim's pattern of conquest. Then, in 1516, came Syria and Egypt. He acquired much of Arabia, including Mecca and Medina, and proclaimed himself Caliph and Protector of the Holy Places, which made him the spiritual leader of all Mohammedans.

Came 1518, Sultan Selim moved into his palace of Istanbul to prepare for yet another campaign. He did not tell his advisers what the goal of his next move was, but he ordered that the Turkish fleet be at once enlarged beyond the size of any imaginable combination of hostile navies. Such a production goal would have startled modern shipyard engineers, but in sixteenth-century Turkey, the choice was between breakneck speed and the executioner's rope.

The Turkish navy grew at a prodigious rate. The year 1519 passed, 1520 began. Still the Sultan had not said where he would use his men-of-war. Then he died as suddenly as Sultans do, and with him the secret war plan passed away.

Selim had but one son, Solyman, whose surname "the Magnificent" was well deserved by the splendor with which he surrounded himself. As the only son, Solyman did not have to dispose of potential rivals when he ascended the throne at the age of twenty-six. By the standards of his father, he was a mild monarch; only two great viziers were executed in forty-six years of reign. But when he was well past the halfway mark of his reign, Solyman had his oldest son, Mustapha, strangled, and, in due course, all but one of his male offspring met similar deaths.

These murders were attributed to the insistence of the Sultan's Russian-born favorite concubine, Roxelana, who had an Asiatic despot's violent and unscrupulous mind and maintained her pernicious influence long after her attractions faded. For thirteen years she had to share it with another foreigner, however: Great Vizier Ibrahim. Ibrahim's original name was hardly known to himself. He had been an infant Greek boy when roving slave hunters caught and sold him to a woman in Magnesia, who raised him as a Mohammedan and gave him a musical education. Ibrahim's musicianship attracted the Sultan's attention when he traveled through Magnesia in 1522. One year later, Ibrahim was Great Vizier, the Sultan's brother-in-law, his constant companion, his most trusted adviser.

Ibrahim was one of the champions of Turkish conquest of Hungary, but he had not originated the idea. Already in 1521, when the later Great Vizier still practiced music rather than government, Solyman had led an army of 100,000 against Belgrade held by a garrison of 700.

The Turks had 300 cannon, the defenders of Belgrade had almost none. What had happened to the strong fortress artillery that was there in the previous wars? Could it have been sold to renegades?

After seven days of bombardments of Belgrade and entreaties by the population, the garrison evacuated residential sections and withdrew into the castle. Solyman spared the civilians and waited six more weeks before the castle was destroyed by a mine.

Subterranean engineering was a new feather on the Turk's military cap. The people of Belgrade thought that it was pagan sorcery. Actually, French sappers had trained Turkish personnel to mine fortifications. Military collaboration between France and Turkey showed its first results.

The Turks crossed the Danube, added scores of miles of the Danube Valley to the territory they controlled, but did not continue toward Buda. Solyman interrupted his Hungarian project to capture the fabulous island of Rhodes on a sea-borne operation that was a technical achievement of the first magnitude.

In Istanbul, meantime, Great Vizier Ibrahim planned further campaigns. He urged the Sultan to attack Hungary as soon as possible.

In Buda eighteen-year-old King Ludwig and his Queen Maria tried to have the best time of their young lives. Maria was much more vivacious and brilliant than her husband. She laughed off troubles and worries, loved banquets, dances, and tournaments. Had she lived in Vienna, the citizenry would have adored so gay and gracious a young Queen, but in Buda stingy burghers grumbled about her spending habits. Maria was unpopular, and her unpopularity grew as she kept enlarging her retinue with Germans.

In Buda, people reminisced about the horrible things that had happened just before the children's marriage. A crusade planned against the Turks had deteriorated into civil war. Peasants, nobles, and fanatical monks had turned mob leaders and committed hair-raising acts of savagery. Castles had been stormed, lords impaled, wives and daughters raped. George Dózsa, a soldier of fortune who styled himself "Prince and Supreme Captain of the Blessed People of the Crusaders," had a blood-encrusted pale carried to every community, threatening everybody with death and confiscation of belongings who would not join the impalers and rapists. Sixty thousand had joined in terror. Dózsa threatened Buda and ravaged the countryside wide and far. Some four hundred nobles and tens of thousands of commoners had died in an aimless holocaust.

Among the men who had helped put down the revolt was John Zápolya. He devised the method of execution for Dózsa, who had been wounded and captured. It was the most barbaric in recorded history.

Dózsa was chained to an iron chair, which had been turned red hot in a furnace; he was pinched with red-hot tongs, crowned with a red-hot iron crown, and while he still breathed, some of his followers, who had been famished for several days, were handed knives and made to cut pieces of roasting flesh from their leader's body.

It was in the wake of these outrages that Ludwig had become King. The gruesome occurrence was considered a portentous omen.

Now the Turkish shadow loomed large over the land, but some people felt that they had little to lose, while turncoats and fortune hunters felt that they had much to win. Turkish agents were generous with down payments and promises.

Ludwig was afraid of the Turks. With his kingdom threatened by bankruptcy and sneaking rebellion, he could not hope to raise an army to stop Solyman if he came up the Danube Valley. He wrote letters and traveled to Germany, Austria, and Bohemia. Maria accompanied him, for entertainment's sake. Germany first pledged an expeditionary force of 24,000, but immediately reduced it to 3000 because of the war with France. Austria promised 2000 and defaulted. The Bohemian Diet voted 6000 men, but when Hungarian nobles made disparaging remarks about Bohemian military prowess, the vote was reversed.

Hungary needed an army of 100,000, but nobody could tell when it would be ready. Little money came in. Only a fraction of taxes was collected, and most of it vanished in the collectors' pockets.

Traffic on the Hungarian Danube increased. Turkish craft abounded.

Their skippers were allegedly merchants, actually spies. They saw only few and greatly neglected fortifications along the riverbanks, no troop concentrations; and they found people pessimistic or indifferent.

France urged the Turks to attack immediately. On February 24, 1525, King François I had been captured near Pavia, and once France was prostrate, all the Habsburg resources would face the Turks. In Turkey proper, the Janizaries, who wanted another lucrative war, rebelled and pillaged Ibrahim's mansion. Turkey scheduled the Hungarian campaign for the following summer, 1526.

Meantime, during the fair season, there was more lavish royal entertainment. The King attended a national gathering of nobles; he did not wish to seem poor or stingy. His treasurer borrowed from Jewish moneylenders on the pledge of the royal tableware.

The Queen danced little. She had evil forebodings. She nagged her husband because he did not rise early. Ludwig replied that longer working hours would make issues seem more bewildering. Nobody could simplify matters for him or even tell him who among his nobles had secret dealings with the Turkish government and who was still loyal. The young couple returned to Buda for a winter of penurious entertainment and alarming rumors.

In March 1526, rumors said that the Turkish invasion army was ready. A Hungarian state council assembled and talked. Tax arrears should be collected to buy cannon, river boats, supplies, and men, men, men!

A new treasurer gave a small advance from his private funds, then settled back and waited for debates to produce results.

Debates droned on.

On April 23, 1526, the Turkish army, led by Ibrahim, left Istanbul. It was expected to cross the Danube near Belgrade by mid-May and march on to Buda, which, barring resistance, would be reached three weeks later. But heavy rainstorms slowed the Turkish advance to a crawl. Artillery sank axle-deep into quagmires. The army reached Belgrade only on July 2. Hungarian scouts reported that over 100,000 Turks and an estimated 300 cannon rolled on, slowly but inexorably.

Ibrahim's first strategic performance was poor. Instead of heading straight up the Danube Valley toward Buda, he had a corps of 35,000 attack the fortress of Pétervárad (Peterwardein), whose 1000 men fought a magnificent battle. Only 90 survived, but they held out until July 28.

One week before Pétervárad fell, King Ludwig with a troop of 4000 loyal Hungarians left Buda to march south. Optimistic Hungarian intelligence services kept reporting that the Turkish forces were split; but actually they were already deploying in full power.

A war council was held. Ludwig was bewildered by shortages of men, weapons, and cash. But suddenly the spell of shortages seemed over. Count Schlick arrived from Bohemia with 4000 Polish and Moravian mercenaries hired by the Pope. Stephen Báthory appeared with 3000 soldiers and bags of money from the Cardinal of Esztergom; a handful of Croatians and Slavonians joined the army, and from Vienna arrived nine cannon with ammunition to last through a full day of battle. More Hungarian cavalry came, obsoletely equipped but riding strong horses of fine breed.

Ludwig loved thoroughbred horses. He ordered a parade to lift morale. The parade was somewhat troubled by rainstorms and news of the Turkish army approaching—at least 70,000 elite soldiers and powerful artillery.

It was suggested that Ludwig meet the Turkish attack near the village of Mohács, on a large swampy meadow, close to the Danube and Drava. With both rivers swollen and the grounds soaked, the Turkish army might be immobilized.

The Turkish army was somewhat unwieldy, but moving on steadily toward Mohács. It had not yet left one single cannon behind; and Solyman and Ibrahim knew of every move and every word in the enemy camp. More words were spoken there than moves were made. Commanders bragged. Troops underwent some drill.

It rained hard all of August 27 and 28. Hungarian cavalry officers scouted for firm ground on which they could charge, found little, but still boasted. Rains grew into cloudbursts and visibility was near zero. On August 29, the fogs lifted on a huge camp of Turkish tents.

The Hungarians expected the battle to open on August 30. It had been agreed that Ludwig stay behind the first line of charge, lest care for his safety slow down action. Early in the afternoon positions were occupied. As the Hungarians settled down for a siesta, the Turks began to move. The Hungarians lost many precious minutes before rallying. The battle was on, one day early.

Soaked meadows splashed under the beat of thousands of hoofs, moist air resounded with the Hungarian battle cry: "Jesus!" The Turks seemed to fall back toward the hills. The Hungarian horsemen pressed on. Another clash, another withdrawal. Then, suddenly the spahis moved; it was like a curtain opening. A thunderous hail of balls hit the Hungarians.

The entire Turkish artillery was concentrated; the Hungarians had been led into a deathtrap!

Their ranks broke. The Turks acted like beaters on a hunt, driving their game into the depth of swamps and morasses.

The Battle of Mohács lasted no more than one and a half hours. There were only a few survivors, and these were so numb with terror that after they reached Buda on their mad flight up the Danube, they could say nothing except that God had forsaken Hungary.

Near Mohács the victors sifted the swamps for prominent victims. They found Archbishop Paul Tomory first, and carried his head around in a mock parade. They identified the remains of the Cardinal of Esztergom, of five bishops, and of several hundred nobles. King Ludwig was among the last to be identified; he had suffocated in a mire; apparently his horse had turned a somersault and, exhausted and encumbered by armor, he could not free himself. He had been twenty years and two months old.

The Queen did not wait to learn what had happened to her husband; she had her wardrobe and jewels packed and made off for Vienna, heading an exodus of burghers with their mobile possessions. Panic spread. People who had been talking about Turkish rule as being not too frightening, turned frantic. Fortunes were spent for carts and boats, horses and oarsmen. A long column moved upstream.

Hungarian chroniclers put the number of prisoners at 1500. Sultan Solyman's diaries said 12,000, and also that on August 31 their severed heads were heaped up before him as he was sitting on his golden throne.

It took two more days until all the dead were buried, the squalid village of Mohács put to the torch, its inhabitants killed. Ibrahim wanted terror to paralyze all attempts at resistance.

The only substantial Hungarian force, some 15,000 men under John Zápolya, was far away, and the Great Vizier had reason to believe that the man who had had Dózsa fried would not cross swords with the Turks.

On September 3, the Turks left the scene of their triumph to march to Buda. The grounds were drying; the pace was fast. On September 11, Solyman entered the capital. Ibrahim rode by his side. Janizaries were quartered in the castle. Halls resounded with martial music. Bronze figures adorning courtyards and façades were removed to be recast into cannon.

Solyman wanted a magnificent triumph.

A solid bridge links Buda with its younger sister city of Pest. All streets were deserted. The Magnificent decided to make the wide greenish waters of the Danube the witness of his military splendor. Across the bridge moved the spahis at a light trot; they were followed by horsemen, camel riders, columns of artillery, infantry in full kit, rumbling train columns. On the left riverbank the Sultan and his Great Vizier on horseback, looking like statues of Asiatic gods of war, accepted the army's roaring salute.

Then suddenly, as more than three fourths of the army was already across, the bridge wavered, creaked, cracked. Within seconds, a host of men and beasts drifted in the slow current. The Janizaries' martial music drummed and blared, drowning out the cries of the drowning. Sultan and Great Vizier remained motionless. The Turkish Danube flotilla was at anchor in the waters that turned into a mass grave.

The commander of the Turkish rear guard was a coolheaded, present-minded man who did not want a river to interfere with a Sultan's triumph. He signaled the leader of the flotilla. A short time later, after "only a few thousand men had died," boats ferried the remaining troops across.

The Sultan nodded gravely.

He left the city two weeks later. On November 13 he was in Istanbul. His diary gives a few data on the trip: Unfriendly weather; Hungarian roaming bands a nuisance; a dues collector's check point set up near Pétervárad to deal with slave traders; arrival in Niš on October 18, in Sofia on October 25. No entry discloses the Magnificent's thoughts. Most of the army, including all the elite troops, were with him.

Turkish rear guards set huge fires in Buda and Pest. Turkish reconnaissance cavalry roamed upstream to Györ and across the primeval Bakony forests to Lake Balaton. They found not a single soldier but many civilians, 200,000 of whom they either killed or sold as slaves.

Famine raged throughout the fertile farmlands in central Hungary. The specter of civil war raised its ugly head again. Ibrahim made a token gesture of non-interference; he had already chosen his candidate for the Crown of St. Stephen: John Zápolya.

By virtue of treaties and relationship, Archduke Ferdinand of Austria, the late Ludwig's brother-in-law, was heir to Hungary and Bohemia. After some wrangling with Bohemian nobles, he was crowned in Prague on February 27, 1527. The coronation in Hungary should have followed, but Zápolya, assured of Turkish support, was a fast-acting man and the only Hungarian with the semblance of an army.

The Zápolyas, who hailed from Slavonia, had become wealthy and powerful only during the lifetime of the past two generations. In November 1526 John had already made a bid for the vacant throne. A puppet National Assembly, not legally authorized, crowned him King. Zápolya made friends by championing anti-Germanism and by awarding titles and offices. He obtained recognition from governments which had scores to settle with the Habsburgs, such as France and Venice. England and, to everybody's surprise, even the Pope recognized King Zápolya.

In April 1527, at last, King Ferdinand interfered. He entered Hungary and caught Zápolya off guard. After a few skirmishes, he reached the ruined city of Buda, moved into the castle, and Zápolya withdrew in an easterly direction across the Danube.

On November 3, twenty-five-year-old Ferdinand was crowned.

Zápolya begged for the Sultan's assistance and on February 28, 1528, became officially Turkey's puppet King of Hungary.

The young King Ferdinand was scared by the Sultan's might. He would accept every humiliation short of vassalage to keep the Crown of St. Stephen and to avoid another Turkish march upstream. On May 29, 1528, his embassy offered Turkey a pact of friendship, and meekly suggested that it evacuate Belgrade and certain border spots in the Danube Valley.

Great Vizier Ibrahim scornfully lectured that they might just as well request the evacuation of Istanbul, that all lands upon which the Sultan's horses had trodden were the Sultan's property, and that Ferdinand should at once get out of Hungary to create a promising atmosphere for further parleys.

The ambassadors requested to see the Sultan. Solyman received them on his golden throne, glancing absent-mindedly at his armed palace guards. The ambassadors recited their original suggestions, trying in vain to catch the Magnificent's eyes. At last, the Sultan spoke, in the direction of the ceiling: "I shall visit your master with my entire army, and present him with what he is bidding for. . . ."

On leaving the Sultan's palace the ambassadors were arrested as spies and kept in prison for months.

In the summer of 1528, King Ferdinand toured his realm in search of an army, weapons, and money. In February 1529, he appeared before the German Diet. The German Princes did not want to be involved in foreign wars; reformation feuds were all they could handle. Also, they did not believe in the imminence of the Turkish threat. A princely accountant discovered that in 1521 the German Diet had voted 630,000 gulden to finance an expedition to Rome by Emperor Charles V. Charles had not used the money; and Ferdinand was told that it would hire 20,000 German lansquenets for six months.

Solyman could have paid several such pittances out of every pocket of his magnificent gala coat. He did not have to bicker with Diets when he wanted to mobilize soldiers and collaborators. He had spies wherever King Ferdinand went in quest of means of waging a war which he could not win.

Solyman wanted to wage the decisive campaign in 1529; his goal was Vienna. His will was the country's supreme law, and it would decide the fate of the Old World, which was now being more and more closely linked to the New, the overwhelming panorama of which began to unfold.

On the Danube, under the walls of Vienna, the fate of Habsburg Austria, Germany, Spain, and, through Spain, of America, would be decided.

CHAPTER TWENTY-FIVE

Early in May 1529, the Sultan's army assembled: an amazing 270,000 men and 300 cannon. The men included baggage gangs, camp followers, and the *akindschi,* undisciplined, lightly armed incendiary squads which had no other pay than loot. But at least 100,000 soldiers were superbly trained and officered elite troops. When the Turks broke camp at Istanbul, Ferdinand had less than 10,000 combatants in and around Vienna, and only a pathetically small force in Hungary.

The weather in the Balkans was appalling; rain and heavy fogs turned roads into obstacles rather than lines of communication. The army was soaked, but Solyman, Ibrahim, and the generals spent comfortable nights in waterproof silken tents. The bulk of the troops reached Belgrade on July 17, crossed the Drava on July 31, camped on the fields of Mohács on August 18.

John Zápolya came with a deputation of Hungarian nobles to prostrate themselves before Solyman. Also to Mohács came a wooden case draped in silk, which contained the Crown of St. Stephen, which renegades had taken from a man who had tried to smuggle it out of the country. The greatest Prince of Islam received the symbol of Christian Hungary, and he made John Zápolya wear it by the grace of the Turkish army.

Zápolya, his nobles, and their guards joined the Turks. They were told to march on the left bank of the Danube, while the Turks advanced along the right bank. Soldiers saw little of the waters of the river, which were all but covered by a colossal supply flotilla.

Sultan and Great Vizier refused to see Nikolaus Juričić, whom King Ferdinand dispatched to the invader's camp to offer a ten-year armistice and an annual pension (to avoid the term "tribute") of 100,000 ducats for the Sultan and 6000 for the Great Vizier.

An entry in the Sultan's diary indicates that they were outside Buda on September 3.

On September 21, 30,000 *akindschi* arrived in the suburbs of Vienna.

The suburbs were no longer like gems studding a lovely countryside. The defenders of Vienna had burned down villas, hunting lodges, and idyllic villages, so that the enemy would find no shelter. The *akindschi* razed whatever was not completely in shambles.

On September 26, Vienna was tightly blockaded on the Danube, and on September 27 the siege ring closed on land.

Whoever could find transportation, fled. *Akindschi* swarmed after the fugitives as far up as the Wachau and did a fearful job. The Turkish blockade of the Danube expanded and stopped 8500 Germans, hired from the funds which Charles V had not used, who had embarked in Bavaria. Supplies were less than adequate. Commander in chief was Count Niklas Salm, an aged and sickly man. In Vienna the populace glanced at the Turkish river flotilla and the Turkish tent city, shuddered, and hoped for no more than a respite.

The Viennese saying "Die I must, but I don't want to be rushed" can be traced back to the day when Solyman, Ibrahim, and their generals stared at their prey from a vantage point in Vienna's abandoned vineyards.

The arm of Turkish espionage reached far. The Sultan knew that the city walls were strong, that the moat was wide and deep, and that there had been some last-minute work on bastions and towers that made them more bombardment-resistant than anything the invading armies had ever encountered since the capture of Byzantium. However, there should be nothing which heavy siege artillery could not reduce—or, rather, might have reduced, for the heaviest Turkish pieces did not arrive. They had sunk in a mire one hundred miles east of Vienna and had been abandoned by crews, oxen drivers, and baggage gangs. Solyman's diaries do not tell what happened to the deserters.

The Turks kept walls and bastions under constant fire. Arquebus bullets and arrows rained on the defenders' positions. Where the bastions could not be shaken by missiles, mines were dug to blow them up.

Eiteleck von Reischach, an Austrian sector commander, devised a new system of counter-mining. Through death-defying scouts and clever calculations, he detected the location of subterranean saps and had his own sappers dig mines to meet the Turkish tunnels, wall them off, and fight eerie close-quarter battles underground.

Viennese civilians volunteered to scout Turkish saps. They did so less as a heroic gesture than because it was a thrill, relief from the boredom of waiting for doom, a way of challenging the Grand Old Leveler before he struck.

Reischach, champion of aggressive defense, also led several sorties, but the furor of his men was no match for the Turks' superior firepower. As the leaves turned, it still looked as if every last Viennese would die.

On October 9 the crisis was at hand. Reischach's counter-sappers missed two huge mines driven under the walls on both sides of the Kärtnertor, near the present site of Vienna's Opera House. They missed by a few yards, but the Turkish mines exploded and opened a breach wide enough for twenty-four men abreast. Count Salm rushed to the spot, with whatever soldiers were around. Already the Turks had hurled themselves into the breach, a deep, howling column of murder. The battle lasted for a full hour. Corpses piled up wall-high. The breach was closed by corpses. The attack was repulsed.

People in Vienna ate little. Food rationing was tight. Losses were high. The condition of the wounded was appalling. Tight-lipped, an angry grand seigneur, Count Salm prepared for a last stand that should at least disconcert the Turks.

On October 11 and 12 the Turks returned. The corpses barred their way. Again mines exploded but the defenses did not collapse. The impact of attack was slackening.

Nobody in the city in distress knew that the foe was in trouble. The chilly humidity of autumn caused a high number of violent colds in the Turkish ranks, and, more trivial even, half the Sultan's army suffered from colics. The vineyards around Vienna joined the people in the defense of their city. Mohammedans drink no wine, but the Prophet did not forbid the eating of grapes, and the sweet grapes of the Vienna Woods created veritable gluttony among the Turkish rank and file. On October 13 Solyman held a war council. Infantry commanders reported that morale was low, that the soldiers had to be whipped into advancing. Solyman resolved to try one more storm and to lift the siege if it failed.

At noon of October 14 two more mines exploded. Thirty minutes later, whips and flat swords drove Turkish infantry into the breaches. The defenders stood, fought, died, so that the city might survive. The storm was repulsed. Among the wounded was Count Salm.

During the following night, the Turkish Danube flotilla lifted anchor, the army folded tents, and at dawn the weary Viennese saw huge columns march off. They did not believe that this was the glorious end of an epos. They were too shaken and too hungry.

"October 25—Buda; November 6—Pétervárad," the Sultan entered in his diary. It was a fast journey, yet it might not have been so smooth had King Ferdinand struck.

The garrison of Vienna did not celebrate the event. The lansquenets requested bonuses, and when they were not granted they mutineered. The mutiny was eventually settled by a shabby and disgraceful compromise. The militia asked for jobs; eventually they were used to rebuild the 834 houses that had been destroyed.

Solyman was far away when Count Salm, recovered from his injuries, decided to engage in a campaign of his own. He could not try an invasion of the Turkish Empire with his little band, but the valiant old Count hoped to recover Hungary from Zápolya, who was temporarily deprived of the Sultan's protection.

But not only had Solyman promised his puppet to return next spring; he had also left a force of spahis in Hungary which made Salm retrace his steps after taking Esztergom. In Pressburg he waited for royal orders and reinforcements that never arrived. The Hungarian people, equally terrorized by the soldiers of the "Turkish party," as they called Zápolya's faction, as by those of the "German party," as they called Ferdinand's, suffered agonies.

In his Istanbul palace, Solyman received an embassy from Vienna. They were to notify the Sultan that King Ferdinand was well armed and firmly supported by the Emperor and many Princes; that all Christian monarchs were united; and that only their peaceful intentions made them seek friendly relations with the Turks. The two diplomats should offer the Sultan a financial compensation for the return of all territories wrested from the late King Ludwig, and raise the price if the Sultan drove a hard bargain. Also, they should bribe Great Vizier Ibrahim and look for other Turkish notables ready to peddle influence.

The Sultan did not enjoy driving bargains. He treated the messengers with a minimum of courtesy, limited two audiences to a pompous display of ceremonial, and left business dealings to the insolent Ibrahim, who refused to be bribed. "One cannot acquire countries by letters," he shouted, pointing at the ambassador's credentials. "Lands and nations must be conquered by the sword."

On November 17, 1530, the Great Vizier handed the ambassadors a note which stated that Solyman was the rightful owner not only of Hungary but also of all German lands; that he had gained legal title of possession by visiting them and beholding them with his eyes; that Charles V was the Sultan's enemy and should leave Germany at once.

The ambassadors packed. King Ferdinand, unwilling to risk war, sent another ambassadorial team to ask for an armistice rather than peace, to concede that Zápolya might rule Hungary for his lifetime and that St. Stephen's crown would not have to be returned to Ferdinand or his heirs until after Zápolya's death. Formalities delayed the ambassadors' departure. In June 1532, when they reached Niš, they met, to their dismay, the Sultan, the Great Vizier, and an army of 200,000 on their way to Central Europe and beyond, to Spain.

Ibrahim, more arrogant than ever, said that the Sultan would not deal with Ferdinand at all. To him, Ferdinand was no King, but a poor little squire from Vienna who tried to grab Hungary. He refused to listen to the ambassadors; there should be no strings attached to the recognition of King John Zápolya. Ferdinand was notified that Solyman was marching against the King of Spain.

Solyman's diaries indicate that the army reached Belgrade on June 21, and the small town of Köszeg (Güns) on August 6. The diaries do not explain why their august author concentrated on conquering the little town instead of proceeding to the flatlands south of Vienna.

Köszeg may have offered a personal challenge. Nikolaus Juričić, who had been on the first frustrated ambassadorial team, was feudal lord of the place and its rural environments. The snubbed nobleman closed the gates, mustered all his soldiers and every able-bodied peasant, and raised the standards of King Ferdinand atop his rather thick walls. His soldiers numbered thirty-eight, his peasants less than seven hundred.

The bulk of the Turkish army was hurled against Köszeg. Heavy artillery fired at the small target from emplacements in vineyards; this time, crews were forbidden to touch a grape. Turkish infantry charged, and was repulsed, eleven times. Sappers went to work, sharpshooters kept the town under fire, mines exploded, but Köszeg held out.

Suicidal folly became glory and glamour. Juričić was savagely determined to resist, and his peasants would die rather than disobey a master who never personally mistreated them. On August 28, the peasants numbered about three hundred. No soldiers were left.

Ibrahim, who had insulted "Ambassador" Juričić, sent "General" Juričić a respectfully worded summons to surrender. He promised to spare the town, for a contribution of 2000 ducats.

"I cannot surrender a town that is the King's, and I don't have 2000 ducats" was the reply.

The Sultan himself rode up to the vineyards to witness a general assault.

One hour later, the walls were partly pulverized, partly passed over. Turks threw the royal banner into the moat and raised eight of their own flags. Then, to the beat of the kettledrum, they rushed toward the barricades. One hundred and eighty peasants waited mutely, but behind them their womenfolk and children raised a deafening clamor. The clamor spurred the men's fury. In a melee unequaled in history, a small band of peasants drove back a host of elite soldiers. Seventy survived.

At dusk, a Turkish officer, carrying a flag of truce, invited General Juričić to visit the Great Vizier. An exuberant Ibrahim told the visitor to consider Köszeg his property, a gift from the Sultan. On August 30, all pashas of the Turkish army offered congratulatory homage to Hungarian valor.

Sultan Solyman did not continue toward Spain. He did not try to reach Vienna, where a formidable army assembled while the Turks battered Köszeg. He showed no concern for Zápolya, whose regime tottered as the Turkish army recrossed the Danube and the Drava.

Had there been some unity in the Central European camp, some intelligence and determination, the little town of Köszeg might have turned into a memorial of world history, no less important than Waterloo. But Germans quarreled with Bohemians, Moravians with Austrians, generals feuded with politicians, the economy-minded with the free spenders, and everybody was set against everybody else in the momentous conflict of Reformation versus Catholicism. The stand of Köszeg remained an episode. The Danube and the Nile remained, in part, within one and the same empire, and not even all of Hungary returned to Ferdinand's realm. The Turkish flood was still to ride its crest, and for several generations the so-called peace in the Danube Valley was but a precarious breathing spell between Turkish wars.

Solyman wanted a breathing spell. Conquest on land had been no walkover, and conquest at sea seemed even more difficult, after Charles V's navy under Captain General Andrea Doria defeated the gigantic Turkish fleet near Morea. Also, the Sultan wished to enjoy the embraces and listen to the guileful chatter of "Sultana" Roxelana.

For a full five years the Sultan looked on as Ferdinand's and Zápolya's forces battled; and during this time, in 1536, Ibrahim met violent death on orders of Roxelana, who was jealous of his influence. Allegedly she smothered the Sultan with kisses so that he could not hear the death rattle of his alter ego from the adjoining room.

Hardly one single acre of the good Hungarian soil remained unscathed. There were many plots and counterplots; the oddest, weirdest characters turned up and vanished, leaving no other traces than puddles of blood. Solyman gave "Slave János," as he called Zápolya, no more support than needed to keep the witches' caldron boiling and to drain Ferdinand's strength.

Zápolya was scared: scared of the Hungarians, whom he ruled by taxation and intimidation; scared of Ferdinand, who might win the upper hand and subject him to punishment more gruesome even than Dózsa's; and most scared of the Sultan, who could destroy him at his whim.

In this conflict of fears, he tried deceit. On February 24, 1538, he reported to Solyman that he had signed a one-year armistice with Ferdinand, and waited, trembling, for a message of wrath that did not come. But what "Slave János" had really signed was a peace treaty: both parties would retain whatever sections of Hungary they controlled; Zápolya retained his royal title; and after his death his lands would revert to Ferdinand. Ferdinand pledged himself to marry off Zápolya's daughters as royal Princesses and to grant Zápolya's son—should there be one—a duchy.

On July 21, 1540, Zápolya died, after suffering several strokes. On his deathbed, "Slave János" appointed Brother George, his Bishop of Nagyvárad (Oradea), guardian of his infant son and tutor of his widow, Isabella. He urged the bishop to see that Hungary never be ruled by an Austrian King and that the Sultan's favors always be secure. Peasants and commoners detested Brother George as a ruthless inventor of new taxes, nobles despised him as an upstart, Isabella called him a cheat and a knave.

Solyman awarded Hungary to Zápolya's son, and another war loomed.

On October 31, 1540, another embassy from King Ferdinand arrived in Istanbul. The Sultan did not carry out his initial threat that he would have the ambassador's ears, nose, and lips cut off, but the audience was brief and rough. "It is almost winter now. But soon, summer will come," he interrupted the visitor's circumstantial salutations, dismissed him, and had him detained in the capital.

Summer came, and with it the Turkish army.

By then, King Ferdinand's troops had seized Pest, but Buda was still in Turkish hands.

When the Sultan's army arrived before Buda, the Hungarians crowded into the river boats. The Turkish Danube flotilla attacked. A river battle brought disaster to the King's men.

On August 26, Solyman arrived in a gilded river barge, a replica of the pleasure craft at his residence. The few hundred prisoners remaining of Ferdinand's forces were massacred wholesale.

Two days later, he requested that the infant King, Zápolya's son, be brought before him, since, as he wrote Isabella, the Mohammedan law did not permit him to visit her. He did not deign to look at the child, but exclaimed that he could never leave the country in the care of a woman. But it was not left in the care of a little boy either; it was formally incorporated into the Turkish Empire, and for 145 years Buda was the seat of a pasha-governor. The wealthy people left the city, which degraded into ruins, populated by destitutes.

Until 1547, Ferdinand struggled to recover Hungary. On June 19 of that year the two rulers signed a five-year armistice. Ferdinand retained the Danube Valley west of Komárom, and the adjoining parts of Croatia and Slavonia, but had to pay an annual "gift" of 30,000 ducats. For the first time, Austria paid a tribute to Turkey.

Maximilian's Universal Empire declined.

The Turkish realm rose.

The Danube and the Nile, the Euphrates and the Tigris, flowed through it; the Mediterranean, the Adriatic, the Arabian, the Black, and the Red seas washed its shores; its provinces reached the Caspian Sea and the Persian Gulf. Its northeastern borders cut deep into Russia; its northwestern boundaries were within striking distance of Vienna; its southwesternmost points were well beyond the city of Algiers, across the narrowing Mediterranean from Spain. And while Habsburg Kings and Emperors had to compromise with Princes and Electors, the Sultan was The Ruler.

In 1566, Solyman led his armies in his thirteenth major campaign. The Magnificent was seventy-two years old, plagued by gout, unable to ride a horse or even stand upright, and getting senile. His record on the throne, however, made him still the most redoubtable of men, and even though his concept of current affairs may have been blurred, his memories and his designs were intact: he wanted to be supreme lord of the Danube Valley. Nobody else, least of all Ferdinand, should dare reach out for what he had conquered with his jewel-studded sword.

Ferdinand's son Maximilian II had succeeded his father as German Emperor. He mobilized funds and troops. Among the latter were 3500 horsemen who came from Hungary, which irked the Sultan most. Turkish commanders in Hungary spoke of Austrian aggressive designs in the Danube and Drava valleys.

Preventive wars were not considered damnable. Whoever may have assisted the Sultan in mapping his campaign, the strategy was sound. Not only should Vienna be conquered; all fortifications that interfered with Turkish free movements on the approaches of Austria should be eliminated, the Emperor's men should have no respite.

On June 5, 1566, Arslan, Pasha of Buda, opened the attack against the fortress of Várpalota, west of Székesfehérvár (Stuhlweissenburg); he was forced back, and the Austrian commanders wanted to press on, but the Emperor decided to stay on the defensive.

Solyman still kept his diaries, but the day of his departure from his capital is not recorded. Indications are that it was April 29, 1566. The rate of advance of a unit is usually determined by the speed of its slowest member. The Sultan could travel only in a sedan chair, and this for no more than one hour a day, lest his gout cause him agonies. Only around June 20 did the army reach Belgrade and cross the Danube to Zemun. Solyman had his sedan-chair carriers stop halfway across the bridge, and he looked out of the window.

The countryside was not as graciously tended as his landscaped gardens. The air inside the sedan chair was sticky even though its top was sprinkled with water. But Solyman, oblivious to the heat, gazed at the familiar sight. The Danube unrolled its greenish ribbon from far away into yonder, caressing and fecundating the vastness of fields—rolling on, scorning conquerors, past or present, young or aged. To his left, he saw the waters of the Sava mating with those of the Danube, with many small arms fanning out like little bridesmaids. To his right, he saw the densely wooded island on which a small new mosque shyly looked out from behind succulent pines. The army waited in silence, so that the supreme warlord might not be disturbed. Tiny waves and whirls rippled the river.

They were not bothered by one more host trampling toward bloodshed; they had seen many of them come and go.

At last the Sultan motioned his army on. He did not speak. He did not look back after they reached Zemun, where the puppet governor of Transylvania province prostrated himself before Solyman, who was absent-mindedly condescending.

Solyman ordered the capture of the fortress of Gyula, and moved on toward Szigetvár. It was again a slow march, but the crawl was blamed on swollen rivers rather than his aches and pains.

In Szigetvár, Miklós Zrinyi girded himself to hold town and fortress with 2000 Hungarian regulars and a small band of volunteers untrained in combat but death-defying by tradition.

Zrinyi became a legendary figure. Hungarian and Austrian textbooks have pictured him as a paragon of all virtues championed in the curricula of public schools: kindly, wise, patriotic, and devoutly Catholic. In fact, the defender of Szigetvár was a typical Hungarian product of an age of savagery: violent, greedy, arrogant, placing his personal interest at least at par with those of the King, and a secret Lutheran sympathizer. But he was a fighter the like of which might hardly be seen again in a world in which overage philosophers advocate surrender rather than exposure to fallout. Zrinyi scorned surrender, even in the face of certain death.

The Sultan may have remembered Köszeg as from the entrance to his silken tent he watched his engineers fill ditches, and bridge swamps with logs and sacks full of pressed soil, to permit assault in tight ranks. He listened intently as his entire artillery opened a furious barrage against the outer walls, from where, at long intervals, a few small-caliber Hungarian pieces fired back.

On August 9, the Turkish infantry charged. Before the second assault opened, the defenders set the so-called new city afire and a curtain of flame and smoke covered their withdrawal into the old town.

For ten days and nights they battled, house by house, room by room, cellar by cellar. All the Turks could win at a terrific price was rubble permeated by the stench of death. The Citadel, the castle of Szigetvár, resisted two major Turkish charges and the concentrated fire of hundreds of cannon.

Again, engineers went to work to sap one of the bastions of the castle. On September 5, a mine of powder, straw, and timber opened a gaping breach. Fire and blinding smoke forced Zrinyi and his men to concentrate in the innermost parts of the roomy castle.

The general storm was scheduled for September 7. For several days nobody had seen Solyman sitting at the entrance to his tent. Janizaries murmured that he was ill.

The first infantry wave of assault broke, but the attackers set everything inflammable ablaze. Later in the morning they charged. As they hurled themselves against the stonework of a tower, a door opened and before them stood a tall, bearded man in shining gala: Zrinyi. He lifted his hand, then stepped aside, and a huge mortar that had not fired before, hurled a thunderous blast of pieces of iron at the attackers, who reeled and at once were set upon by Zrinyi and his men.

This was their final stand. The Janizaries rallied; the defenders, hopelessly outnumbered, succumbed to the last man. But as the exhausted victors entered the tower there was an immense blast. The powder magazine blew up, killing every invader inside the castle.

Legend has it that Zrinyi himself kindled the match. However, there is evidence that the raging fire spread to the magazine, and that Zrinyi, fatally wounded by several bullets, was dragged before Great Vizier Mahomet, who had him decapitated and his head sent to Ferdinand.

Solyman did not live to see the fall of the fortress. On the eve of the first great mine explosion, he had had a fit of rage about the various delays, and suddenly collapsed, dead.

Great Vizier Mahomet kept Solyman's death a secret until Crown Prince Selim was notified and ascended the throne.

Zrinyi died unaware of the fact that he had made world history. The struggle for Szigetvár put an end to the Turkish campaign, and the heir to the Turkish throne could not continue in the tradition of the Mohammedan empire builders. Had Solyman not met death in an outburst of mad fury he might have changed the line of succession, which led to Selim, who won the well-deserved epithet "the Sot," and from him to a long line of Sultans who, however violent some of them may have been, were incapable of conceiving a global pattern of domination.

CHAPTER TWENTY-SIX

Astute as Turkish political agents were, however thoroughly they mastered the tricks of interference in the internal affairs of the lands their master wanted to grab, they did not take sides with feuding factions of Christianity, with Catholics, Lutherans, or Calvinists, Baptists, or Anabaptists. Whatever was not based upon the Koran was anathema to conquering Mohammedanism. But Turks well realized that the great and intricate religious struggle that rocked most of Europe could only profit Turkey.

The masses of Austrian and Hungarian peoples, haunted by memories of past disasters and fearful of future misfortunes, longed for a path to God. Hardly ever before had there been so earnest and deep a trust in the Lord, who daily manifested His unfathomable creative splendor in the beauty and fertility of the land. Hardly ever had there been so much misery in such startling settings. This misery was not confined to want and grief; it was a desperate yearning for the Lord's spiritual mercy.

Quacks, brutes, and demagogues offered remedies; saintly and wise men called for betterment through truthfulness. Yearners could hardly distinguish between the righteous and the frauds.

King Ferdinand had tried to struggle against confusion. Already two years before Solyman's armies plowed their way to the gates of Vienna, through lands in foment, he had issued a mandate against "all heresies." The mandate made minor deviations from the teachings of the Catholic Church. Transgression of the Lenten law and omission of the confession were punishable by prison terms; changes of forms of baptism and services were punished by banishment; those who destroyed or desecrated images of the saints should be punished "by fire and sword." Printers and sellers of heretical books should be drowned and their products burned. No book could be printed without the government's consent.

In 1528 the most learned of the Anabaptists, Balthasar Hubmaier, a former professor of divinity, was burned at the stake in Vienna; his wife, who had helped distribute his books, was drowned in the Danube, near the village of Erdberg, where King Richard had been arrested on his return trip from the Holy Land.

This also was the year of the first book burning in the Danube Valley. Seventeen Anabaptists were executed in Lower Austria, seventy in Upper Austria, one hundred and six in the Tyrol, twelve in Styria. Within the next two years, the number of victims of the mandate rose to seven hundred in the Tyrol alone. Yet Anabaptism remained rampant.

The King ordered that "honorable, well-learned, skillful, and intelligent Catholic preachers should prevent the spread of new creeds." He learned that there was not a single minister in the diocese of Vienna who could be called at least average, that conditions in the diocese of Passau were despicable, that the University of Vienna had failed to produce outstanding clerics. The number of students there, which had been well over one thousand in 1515, had declined to one hundred in 1526, and in 1532 there were twelve.

The century-old Vienna University was fundamentally Catholic. Theology was a major subject. Reformation had reduced the attendance at most Catholic universities, but in Vienna many teachers also quit. The only professor of divinity who was a member of the staff in 1532 was not even a theologian, but a humanist.

The King tried to reform the University of Vienna. He abolished its autonomy and subjected it to tight control by a state-appointed superintendent. No professor could be appointed unless he was an obedient member of the Catholic Church. Candidates for teaching assignments were few in number and deficient in scientific qualifications. There were practically no students. New decrees forbade Austrian citizens to study at universities other than those of Vienna. Freiburg and Ingolstadt were all under Catholic control.

No decree, however, could create a rush of students to Vienna.

King Ferdinand put great hopes on the Society of Jesus, Ignatius of Loyola's order, founded in 1538 and recognized by Pope Paul III in 1540.

Father Petrus Canisius, a highly cultured, well-learned, and energetic Jesuit, came to Vienna to teach, but only two students of divinity graduated in twenty years.

A visitation of Lower Austrian parishes in 1543 found a substantial number of vicarages and prebends vacant because of inadequate revenue and encroachment by patrons. Many poor people were compelled to live and die without baptism, confession, and the other sacraments. Many

Viennese were found to know neither the Credo, nor the Lord's Prayer, nor the Ten Commandments.

Anabaptists still increased in number. Some were drowned, some beheaded; one died at the stake. A Protestant journeyman baker, charged with having scorned the procession on Corpus Christi Day, was quartered.

But the Viennese had no taste for martyrdom. In the midst of trouble and violence, they rediscovered their innate taste for entertainment, fine food, and inspiring drink.

Wolfgang Schmelzl, a contemporary teacher and poet, calls the city "a garden of roses, a place of delight, a veritable paradise. Winegrowing flourishes, carloads of grain are sold at Neuer Markt; on the Graben and Lichtensteg seventy butchers have their booths; eggs and poultry are marketed at St. Peter's Cemetery, where you can also buy all sorts of fish: sturgeon, perch, and carp from the Danube. A lot of construction goes on. Fortifications are improved. The Schweizertor of the Imperial Castle is almost finished. The Landhaus, the palace of the Estates of Lower Austria, turns into a splendid building. A variety of works of arts are created: paintings, etchings, sculptures. . . . Art does not die in Vienna, even though souls are starving.

"But mutual distrust and suspicion are rampant. Even many persons at court are said to 'smell of Lutheranism.'

"Austrian nobles often turn reformers in their patrimonial estates to reduce their own dependency on the monarch. They protect Lutherans, secularize and confiscate ecclesiastic foundations. Noblemen even have Lutheran chaplains. Quite a few Catholic ministers have turned Protestants, and their flocks stayed with them."

In Hungary, where the German element still prevailed in cities, the writings of Martin Luther were almost as widely read as in Germany; the books were brought to the country by merchants who visited the Leipzig Fair, which had been founded around 1390. The question of whether or not to accept Reformation was affected by the struggle of nationalities. Hungarian nationalists condemned anything of German origin and distributed pamphlets "against Luther's blasphemous and pestilential dogma."

Already the Diet of 1523, in which partisans of Zápolya held a majority, had resolved that all Lutherans and their sponsors and adherents be executed and their property confiscated. And in 1525 a Convention of Nobility used even more drastic language, and requested that Lutherans be exterminated by fire.

Wealthy burghers from Hungary sent their sons to German universities. By 1560, a total of 442 Hungarian students had gone to study in Luther's Wittenberg. Many towns abolished Catholic institutions and abandoned Catholic customs. In 1549 five "Royal Cities" in Upper Hungary (present Slovakia) established religious institutions of their own, which were not fully identical with those of any established creed, and in 1550 the Saxonians from Transylvania adopted ecclesiastic regulations drafted by a layman burgher.

Ferdinand realized that people needed persuasion. Persuasion was entrusted to the Jesuits. Ignatius of Loyola selected twelve outstanding members of his order to serve in Vienna: Among them were Dutchmen, Spaniards, Italians, and Frenchmen. Their program included education, preaching, and guidance in the confessional. They established themselves on Am Hof, where the Babenberg Palace had stood, and lectured at the University, where the number of students was rising. They founded a gymnasium, an institution of learning for future university students, and —evidence of their adaptability to the Viennese mentality—they arranged public theater performances.

Jesuit societies sprang up in Prague, in Innsbruck, and in Tyrnau (Trnava), Upper Hungary. More Jesuit schools were established. They were monolithic in religious structure, but their teachers were among the best to be found anywhere in Europe.

Reform by educational persuasion was a slow process, and it did not heal a searing wound on the body of Austrian Catholicism. Ferdinand was reluctant to expose this wound to observers who might not keep the secret. In 1561, at last, he unbosomed himself to the Papal Nuncio. The result was a visitation of Austrian convents and monasteries.

Grievous aberrations were found to exist almost everywhere. Neither abbots nor monks observed the rules of their orders. In 36 convents, 135 monks' wives were found, and 223 children; of 436 monks, 55 were married, 199 had concubines. Abbots squandered their monasteries' properties to provide for their women and offspring. "Summoned to redress the nuisances," they replied that the Emperor ought to know that there was hardly a minister in the land who did not live and act like that. Monks asserted that they would rather leave than part with their legitimate or illegitimate families. Holy Communion was generally administered in both species. Clergymen protested that this was what the faithful wanted.

Ferdinand, who felt that his end was approaching and that he would have to answer to the Lord for what he had been doing to uphold his faith, would not yield his title to determine the creed of the land. But to make Catholicism acceptable to all men of good will, he was prepared to introduce some reforms, subject to the Pope's approval. After much soul searching, word juggling, and consultations with the highest luminaries of the Church, he suggested that Rome decree the acceptance of "the layman's chalice," grant dispensation to married clergymen, and permit the ordination of "honorable husbands."

Pope Pius IV granted the "layman's chalice" on April 17, 1564, for Austria, Hungary, Bohemia, and Catholic parts of Germany, but refused to abolish the celibate.

Nuncio Delfino reported from Vienna that the people were pleased with the Pope's conciliatory spirit and that two thirds of "all apostates" had returned to the fold.

The Catholic "reformation" was short-lived. Pius IV died one year later, and Pius V, a former Grand Inquisitor, pronounced his predecessor's decree "expired." Ferdinand did not live to see this happen. However, the usual pomp and fanfare was absent from Pius V's pronunciamento, which was handed down to the episcopates as a secret document. It took most churchgoers a long time to notice the change. The new Emperor-King, Maximilian II, chose to pass over the matter in silence.

The gossipy Viennese had savory stories to tell about scandals in the local nunnery of St. Jacob's, yet their favorite topic was royal weddings.

Widower King Philip II of Spain wed Austrian Archduchess Anna in 1570. Even though the ceremony did not take place in their city, the Viennese were busy admiring the bride's glamorous trousseau and seeing her off on her voyage to meet the groom.

On August 26, 1571, Vienna had a royal wedding of its own. The Emperor's brother, Archduke Charles, married Maria of Bavaria, or, as the official publication put it, "the most worthy Christian princely marriage and nuptials between the serene Right Honorable Lord Carol, Archduke of Austria, Burgundy, Styria, Carinthia, and Carniola; Count in Tyrol, Cilli, and Gorizia; and the Right Honorable Miss Maria, born Duchess of Bavaria, which took place in the Imperial City of Vienna on August 26."

The author of the official publication was one Heinrich Wirrich, who bore the odd title *Oberster Pritschenmeister*. *Pritsche* is a rattle, and the guild of the rattle masters was the successor to the street singers, popular rivals of the meistersingers, the living gossip columns of the "Imperial City."

When *Pritschenmeister* clapped their instruments, everybody from bum to burgher stopped to listen to entertaining news garnished with romance and served hot with quibbles and quips. "Supreme *Pritschenmeister*" Heinrich Wirrich was one of the few members of his guild whose name appeared in print, but his account of the wedding shows him as one of the rare bores of his profession.

Meistersingers in Ferdinand's and the second Maximilian's time did not have much publicity either. The files of their schools are lost; only a list of members is conserved. Names listed—Furrier Lorenz Wessel, "Burgher and Locksmith" Veit Caroler, and Weaver Tobias Schmied—mean nothing to connoisseurs of literature.

But literature was popular among the high and the humble. Archdukes and their spouses wrote poetry, though it is said that they hired ghost writers to bring their works into shape.

The Viennese thronged theaters. They applauded entertaining shows and sat silently through tedious affairs, such as a drama by the Bishop of Gurk, entitled *Spiritual Preparation for War and Christian Sermon against the Turks, the Cruel Archenemies of Christianity*.

The court orchestra flourished. Royalty lacked cash for the army, but funds for music were always available.

The people wanted showmanship—on the stage, in the streets, at church.

The Jesuits produced a priest who suited this Viennese demand to the highest degree. He was Franz Scherer, from Tyrol, one of the best operators of his time, a most successful re-converter to Catholicism by wit rather than earnest persuasion. Hundreds of Lutherans returned to the Catholic fold after listening to Scherer's fascinating harangues, which included but few volcanic threats of a million years in purgatory. Eyes twinkling, his sharply tapered goatee pointing forward, he was never sardonic even in exorcism, and irresistibly funny in satire.

At the turn of the century, Vienna seemed to be a Catholic city again, but its people had a major grievance: they had no court; their city was no Imperial or royal residence! The Viennese did not always agree with royalty, but they considered it part of the game that the sovereign occupy the local castle.

Imperial Governor Archduke Matthias stayed in Linz, where, according to the angry Viennese, stuffy provincials drank apple cider instead of wine.

In 1608 at last, Matthias returned to Vienna, not as a mere governor, but as King of Austria, Bohemia, and rump-Hungary and a prospective

Emperor of the Holy Roman Reich. The Viennese were delighted and gave him a spectacular reception.

"Ten triumphal arcs and four archways were erected," writes one Johann Holzmüller. "Three archways spanned the Tabor Bridge across the Danube. They were resplendent with fir branches, wreathes of flowers, southern fruits, and coats-of-arms. The wealthy burgher Lazarus Henckl had the fourth archway built at his own expense on his landscaped pleasure grounds on the right bank of the river. The royal parade marched, and rode, past the Henckl gardens to a beautiful Virgin Mary. The infant Jesus on her lap gave royalty the benediction and offered a royal crown. Both mother and son were living persons, and so were all the allegoric figures and standard bearers surrounding them. . . .

"Two fountains dispensed wine: Bacchus' fountain red, Neptune's white wine. Near the drawbridge, fishermen engaged in a merry competition of spear fishing; a cripple with a wooden leg performed swimming tricks. Kettledrums boomed, trumpets flourished. At the Rotenturm Gate, the town councilors offered His Majesty the key to all gates, and, under a clear, resplendent summer sky, they escorted him into the city. A lane of gaudy uniforms reached all the way to St. Stephen's Cathedral. The Jews also turned out in fine sacerdotal attire, carrying their Talmud and the Ten Commandments under a beautifully decked canopy. In front of the Cathedral the Bishop of Vienna and eleven abbots greeted royalty.

"After a *Te Deum,* the parade proceeded past the house of Chief City Magistrate Augustin Haffner. In front of that house three beauteous goddesses sat on an artificial rock. One goddess presented His Majesty with a big golden cup. Beside the goddess was a shaggy lion. The beast acted strangely, tearing hats from bystanders' heads and raging frightfully. Next to the lion there was a young lamb, most prettily dyed, velvety smooth and patient, as authorities should be. Astride the Kohlmarkt stood the gate of the court merchants. In front of the castle Court Jeweler Philip Holbain had set up many trees bearing fruits from the South. The last triumphal arc, close to the main gate of the castle, had been built by Jews. The day of rejoicing was terminated by great fireworks.

"The Viennese had had their long missed grand spectacle, a carnival catering to everybody's taste, moving from the shacks beyond the city gates, past the most glorious edifices which artists from many lands had built, to the royal front door.

"It was good to have a mighty monarch in town. There would be more festivities with freely spending visitors attending."

Matthias ranged high in the Viennese' fickle favor, not only because he came in pomp and glamour, or because he had married a Princess whose attractions met the citizens' demands for a true Fairy Queen, but also because his later coronation as Emperor led to the creation of a bakery product that would outlast the monarchy, even though its name, *Kaisersemmel* (Imperial roll), seemed forever tied to that institution. The *Kaisersemmel*, the crisp, dainty roll which a dozen-odd generations of Viennese have consumed in enormous quantities for breakfast and *Jause,* and to sop in coffee, sauces, and gravies, never changed its name, not even during the sordid interlude of Hitler's rule.

This was the time of Shakespeare. He never came to Vienna, yet he used Viennese backgrounds and Austrian, Hungarian, and Bohemian characters and settings in several of his plays. Richard von Kralik, in his *Geschichte der Stadt Wien,* published in 1926, states that the play within the play in *Hamlet* has the settings of the Austrian Court; that the background of *Measure for Measure* is Viennese and that "Ragozine, a most notorious pirate," is none else than the Hungarian rebel Rákóczy. Shakespeare speaks of Bohemia in *The Winter's Tale;* and the hermit in *As You Like It* resembles Emperor Rudolf II. The same Emperor is said to be the prototype of Prospero in *The Tempest.*

English actors visited Austrian lands since 1595, three years after the Bard emerged as a playwright, and were highly acclaimed by the Court.

Matthias, as a middle-aged man, was extroverted and showy, though always rather dumb. Nobody was as prompt as he in signing decrees and ordinances, possibly in full view of his retinue. Nobody ever remembered having seen him read what he signed. What councilors explained to him, he did not try to understand. The director of his secret council once said, conjuringly: ". . . they all trust that Your Majesty won't ask questions, and will let events take their course. . . . Your Majesty ought to learn facts, discuss matters, be careful. . . ." Matthias did not try to understand this admonition either, and it was never repeated.

When Matthias grew old and frail, his extroverted attitude changed. His favorite haunt became a collection of antiques and objects of art, which he kept arranging and rearranging with absurd devotion. Only music and the pranks of his favorite fool could divert him.

The citizenry kept flocking to Jesuit theater performances, and crowded churches. And may the best actor or preacher win the crown of popularity!

CHAPTER TWENTY-SEVEN

Late in 1617, a Body of Governors was appointed in the Habsburg realm to cope with vexatious feuds over religious issues. The Body included seven Catholics and three Protestants, all ranking nobles. Catholic zealots aimed at the radical suppression of the opposition. Protestants nominated Defensors to safeguard the rights of their creeds.

The procedure, at first, aroused little popular interest. An uneventful winter went by.

Came March 5, 1618—a crucial day in world history, a prelude to what all European school children have to remember as the "Prague defenestration." It had momentous effects on life in all of Europe, and in the Danube Valley in particular. Yet like a good many other crucial days, it did not at first appear remarkable to those who lived through its damp coolness in Vienna and Prague.

The Defensors called a meeting in Prague to ask for redress of their grievances and the release of people imprisoned for exposing or denouncing Catholics. Not all Protestant districts sent delegates; quite a few assumed a cautious wait-and-see attitude. Cardinal Melchior Klesel, who had abandoned early ambitions to become a popular orator in favor of a phenomenal official career, issued a harshly worded rescript, threatening to have the Defensors arrested unless they canceled the meeting.

But the meeting was not called off.

On May 23, in the morning, some one hundred participants went to the Castle of Prague, to convey a protest to the Body of Governors. Most of them were nobles. They and their servants carried arms. Actually, the meeting was legal and Klesel had no authority to forbid it. Ill feeling among the participants ran high, even though many of them were, by nature, rather discreet and conservative people.

Only four of the Governors, Burgrave Sternberg, Slawata, Martinitz, and Diepold von Lobkowitz, were present when the angry callers arrived. They answered the question whether they had any personal share in drafting Klesel's rescript with a curt reference to the secrecy of office.

The delegates assumed a threatening attitude. The burgrave was scared and muttered something about not having been consulted. The three other Governors, even more scared, resorted to insults. Tempers flared. A delegate produced a letter and read out loud that Slawata and Martinitz had refused to sign a decree of amnesty in 1609, and asked that these two be declared enemies of the commonweal, violators of an Imperial act, and outlaws.

A wild clamor followed. The delegates' choler had got clear and present objects: Slawata and Martinitz. The other two Governors were pushed into an adjoining room. The objects of fury were seized by their collars, shoved and dragged to an open window, and thrown into a moat sixty-five feet below. As the maddened aggressors recoiled, they detected, in a corner of the big hall, a thin and trembling man, Secretary Fabricius, whom nobody had noticed before. Fabricius just whimpered as he was seized and thrown after the two Governors. He landed in the moat athwart his exalted superiors and recovered sufficiently to apologize, in a profusion of stammering, for having followed Their Excellencies. Their Excellencies too were reasonably whole. Of all three victims of defenestration, only Slawata suffered minor injury, when his head hit a pediment. The moat was cushioned with a soft matter, which dignified chroniclers did not relish to call excrement.

Slawata and Martinitz found a haven in a nearby palace. Some called their escape a miracle; others contended that it was an act of black magic.

Hardly would even the most irascible of dictators go to war over two officials and a secretary hitting the mud, and the Bohemian estates, embarrassed rather than excited, immediately issued an official apology in which they euphemistically called defenestration an ancient custom.

But then a spark hit the powder keg: an appeal by a ranking participant in the act of "ancient custom," Count Heinrich Matthias von Thurn, who wanted to persist in rebellion and lead an army to war.

Guided by Thurn, the Bohemian Protestant Meeting, superseding the Defensors, constituted itself as a national Diet. The legislature swung into action; the Jesuits were banished from Bohemia and their properties confiscated; the directors began to expropriate wealthy individuals who, at some occasion or other, had incurred their individual disfavor. Millions of acres of fine land were taken away from their owners and sold or assigned to new proprietors. Dealing with such lands turned into the most remunerative real estate business in the history of Bohemia, where confiscatory transfers were not novel. Speculators had their golden opportunity.

Thurn did not have trouble forming an army; Bohemia swarmed with veterans of many wars, who all found peace dull and unrewarding. With 4000 of them he captured Budweis (České Budějovice) and Krumau (Krumlov), which were held by Imperial garrisons. This meant civil war, but civil war did not necessarily herald major calamity.

News that reached Vienna was contradictory. Emperor Matthias was declining in mind and body; more important even, the title of King of Bohemia had just passed upon Archduke Ferdinand, who was about to become titular King of Hungary and was also the true head of the Austrian provinces. Ferdinand was a graduate of the Jesuit college, a Protestant hater, who could be ruled out as a settler and compromiser. But he was irresolute, a prey to inhibitions that revealed his hapless mediocrity. He lacked clarity of design; he was neither a soldier nor an administrator. His generals and civilian officials did as they pleased. He could not run his household either. Not even when cash was desperately short could he devise, or agree to, ways of economizing. His interests concentrated on hunting and music, his loyalties on what he considered the quintessence of Catholicism. These loyalties led him to believe that the Lord was well satisfied with him and that, in the end, everything would be all right.

Such was cataclysm's figurehead-protagonist, who as Ferdinand II would be Emperor of Germany from 1619 to 1637.

Matthias died on March 20, 1619, the first Habsburg Emperor to be entombed in the Kapuzinergruft in Vienna, the funeral vault a few hundred yards from St. Stephen's, which he had ordered built and which was completed only ten years after his death. The antique-loving monarch hardly deserved a monument, but the funeral vault turned into a lasting memorial. All Habsburg Emperors, and the lone Empress, Maria Theresa, were buried there, according to the same awe-inspiring ceremonial.

First in the procession came two liveried grooms on horseback carrying black-draped lanterns; then came one squadron of cavalry, and a long fillet of black court carriages with two-and-sixes, in which rode the highest dignitaries and officers. Lantern bearers marched between the conveyances. They were followed by the hearse: a gun carriage draped in black and drawn by four teams of black horses; the coffin was covered with black satin. To the right rode the Lord Chamberlain, at both sides walked valets and pages carrying burning torches, and forty guardsmen.

Infantry and cavalry followed. No sounds came from the multitude that lined the streets. Nothing was heard except walking steps of men and horses and the tolling of church bells all over the mourning capital. After the consecration at St. Stephen's, the six highest dignitaries carried the coffin to the vault, where the honor guards waited, swords drawn, at the top of a few outside steps leading up to the gate. The new Emperor, his family, and a long array of dignitaries walked behind.

The door to the vault remained closed. The Lord Chamberlain stepped forward and knocked at the gate, three times, to the rhythm of the tolling bells.

From within, the muffled voice of the Father Guardian inquired: "Who requests admission?"

"His Apostolic Majesty Matthias the First, by the Grace of God Emperor of Austria . . ."

A long pause followed, then a curt reply: "I know him not."

The Lord Chamberlain knocked again. The same voice asked: "Who requests admission?"

"The repentant sinner Matthias."

A key rattled. The gate opened. The eminent pallbearers placed the coffin on the threshold and stepped back. Four monks emerged and carried the coffin inside. The gate closed. The key rattled. The curtain had fallen on an Emperor's life.

When Ferdinand became Emperor the latent conflict was not yet a "real war," but the infernal machine of international schemes and aspirations was ticking.

The Bohemian army moved into Moravia. Cardinal Dietrichstein, nominally in charge of the defenses, did nothing to stop the advance. The only higher-ranking officer who did not join the invaders was one Albrecht von Waldstein, a colonel of infantry.

A provisional government established itself in Moravia and offered to make an alliance with the rebellious Bohemians.

Count Thurn crossed the Lower Austrian border near Znaim (Znojmo) late in April; Vienna was fifty-five miles away. There he temporized, stunned by the scope of his venture.

Austrian Protestant nobles welcomed Thurn and told him that Ferdinand was still in Vienna and might be captured if it fell.

Reports on Vienna's preparations for a siege were less than perfunctory. The Protestant nobles opined that half of the city's population sympathized with Bohemians and Moravians, and would open the gates.

Otherwise, Thurn had little chance to conquer. On May 31, 1619, he was on his way south to the Danube. He intended to cross the river near Fischamend, in sight of the steeple of St. Stephen's. The weather was fair and the water level low as the Bohemians built a pontoon bridge; lazy waters reflected the azure of the sky. A few fishermen in *Zillen* (flat-bottomed little skiffs) rowed away as the invaders trampled across the bridge. It was always safe to keep away from armed men.

Vienna was ten miles near. Marching infantry could have covered the distance in three hours, but Thurn set up quarters in a cozy local inn whose keeper was duly frightened and did not even remotely understand the implications of the billeting.

In Vienna, people still went about their business as usual. Walls were manned only by sentinels, and gates were locked only during the hours of darkness.

Ferdinand stayed in the capital. Legend, intolerant of triviality, attributes his attitude to a miracle. Praying before his crucifix, Ferdinand is said to have heard a voice, "I shall never forsake you." The ornate crucifix is still kept on the tabernacle of the court chapel.

Viennese Protestants and Catholics talked about co-operation, but nothing resulted. Mayor Daniel Moser told the aldermen that Vienna would have to remain the residence of a monarch, lest it turn provincial and dull. Catholic and Protestant Estates from Lower Austria admonished each other to do their patriotic duty, and parted in noisy disharmony. The Jesuit theater played to capacity audiences. During intermission, Jesuit padres told students and burghers to defend their creed and ruler.

The parting of the Estates fanned the blaze that smoldered under the ashes of prattle. The Catholics sent messages to Krems on the Danube, where reinforcements were said to have arrived, requesting that all reliable troops be at once dispatched to Vienna. The Protestants sent a delegation to sullen Ferdinand, demanding demobilization and the Protestants' title to elect deputies.

Vienna's local patriotic history abounds with tales about the delegates' rudeness and Ferdinand's steadfastness. It is said that spokesman Baron Thonradel seized a button of his sovereign's doublet and asked that he sign at once. In all likelihood, the Imperial button remained untouched and Ferdinand usually signed nothing. Then, from outside, came the sounds of trumpets, marching steps, cheers and plaudits.

The forces from Krems had arrived. It was June 5, 1619, 11:00 A.M. When the Protestants had entered the palace, Danube rafts and barges, carrying soldiers and mounts, had landed near the *Fischertor* (Fishermen's Gate). The curious populace rushed to see them disembark, gather in formation, and proceed, bands playing, through the narrow streets, past St. Stephen's toward the castle. Streets were jammed wtih spectators, many of whom cheerfully marched along. Nobody cared about the implications of the parade; the only element which interfered with its orderliness was popular enthusiasm. When the trumpets sounded outside the castle, 400 soldiers with readied muskets lined up on the grounds. The delegates were too afraid to leave and to walk past musket muzzles, and Ferdinand was too benumbed with terror to order their arrest. So Thonradel and the rest stayed in the palace for a full two hours, muttering apologies and disclaiming personal responsibility; it took Ferdinand quite as long to recover his dignity and pronounce the audience terminated.

The Viennese watched gleefully as soldiers installed fortress-cannon emplacements, destroyed one bridge, and manned ramparts, while recruiters set up tents to enlist men from the town and suburbs.

It took Thurn until June 8 to set his forces in motion. When he reached the city walls, he found Vienna in a state of defense. The siege lasted five days, then it was all over. To the people of Austria, it still seemed inconsequential. Yet the greatest war in Central European history had already been under way for a full year: the Thirty Years' War, the scourge that destroyed two thirds of the people whom it engulfed!

On August 28, 1619, in Frankfurt, Ferdinand was elected Emperor of Germany. There was no dissenting ballot.

As Emperor Ferdinand wined and dined Electors and Princes, couriers arrived from Prague. His Majesty did not see their reports and they did not seem to matter to his ministers.

The Bohemian Directory seemed to be in trouble. The new constitution it had promulgated was in the ministers' opinion a mere farce. This constitution, the "Confederation Acts," proclaimed Bohemia an Elective Kingdom and stipulated that all important public offices be filled by Protestants. Royal powers would be nominal; the Estates would make all important decisions. Actually the Confederation Acts had been adopted by a minority; Catholics had not been present and moderate Protestants had abstained from voting.

To be a shadow King by the grace of a minority was not an attractive proposition, but Palatine Friedrich was not choosy and he wanted a crown for his beauteous spouse. As he seemed the best man available, 150 out of 153 voting members elected him King of Bohemia. Electors and Protestant Princes vainly warned him that his coronation would cause religious struggle, war, and tumult, and that history would blame him for terrible bloodshed, destruction, and corruption. He and his wife had already crossed the Bohemian border when a courier brought a letter from his father-in-law, James I, King of England, who disapproved of his ambitions. Friedrich studied the letter, then proceeded to Prague.

On November 4, 1619, he was crowned in a ceremony that lacked all pomp and splendor. There were neither signs nor miracles, but there were indications that the somber prophecies would come true.

Emperor Ferdinand had to make a detour to reach his capital. The Protestant Estates of Upper and Lower Austria pronounced themselves in favor of Friedrich, and the prevailing mood was portentous; from rump-Hungary came disastrous news.

In Transylvania, Gábor Bethlen made a bid for the throne of Hungary, by the grace of the Sultan and with the cautious support of the Great Vizier. Ferdinand would have needed time and an army of 100,-000 to gird for an attack from the East. His realm had far more than one million able-bodied men; but his treasury lacked the millions of gulden needed to set them afoot. Gábor Bethlen had more forces than Ferdinand had inside his little strip of Hungary and all along the border.

On September 21, 1619, a convention of Hungarian nobles and municipalities appointed Bethlen Leader and Regent of Hungary (*Vorgeher und Verweser,* a title which, 300 years later, would be adopted by Miklós von Horthy). He left Transylvania, hit the Danube Valley west of Esztergom, and continued toward Vienna. Garrison after garrison surrendered. Pay arrears and petty quarrels among local officers accounted for the absence of resistance. Early in October, Bethlen reached Pressburg; 1200 German lansquenets had been dispatched to defend the castle, where the Crown of St. Stephen was held in less than safekeeping. The lansquenets did not have enough time to put the castle in a state of defense. On October 14, Bethlen had city, castle, and crown.

When this happened, Ferdinand was still making detours on the road to the insecurity of Vienna.

On October 25, a dense fog rose from the river as from a boiling caldron; under its cover, the Imperial army rumbled into Pressburg.

Only on November 21 did the Bohemians, who had moved in behind the Imperial army, deploy outside Vienna; on November 27, Bethlen camped at Ebersdorf, on the Schwechat rivulet a few miles away.

To believe Austrian chroniclers, the Hungarian soldiers behaved worse than the Turks. But all soldiers, regardless of their flags, were rapacious, utterly contemptful of human lives, completely unaware of the conception of human dignity, but ingenious in devising new means of torture and abasement. One mercenary would often cause scores of civilian casualties before engaging in actual combat. This fact, and also the appalling state of health and nutrition in the afflicted land, accounted for an almost incredible reduction of population figures.

As Bohemians, Moravians, and Hungarians camped on the eastern approaches to Vienna, a small but ferocious troop came down the Danube Valley from the opposite direction: 2500 Upper Austrians under rebellious Count Gotthart Starhemberg. They seized Persenbeug Castle, one of the most romantic spots of the river; they invested Ybbs, looted Pöchlarn (of Nibelungen fame), cannonaded Melk, attacked Krems. They blocked the river, robber baron style, to starve Vienna. Starhemberg already visualized himself as the lord of the Imperial castle.

But Vienna was neither starved nor captured.

Destiny shunned a climax that might have been charitable in view of things to come, and men violent in action but vacillating of conception began to stall. Leaders parleyed, negotiated, called conventions, and signed covenants which would have settled no basic issue, even if their signatories had intended to honor them.

A personal foe of Gábor Bethlen, Drugeth of Hommonay, used his antagonist's absence from Hungary to stage an uprising of his own. Supported by Poland, he hired the cheapest mercenaries available—Cossacks, the highwaymen from the Ukraine and pirates of Russian rivers. Of 7000 Cossacks who enlisted, 2000 deserted to go into their own predatory business in the Danube region, but the rest fought well enough to cause Bethlen to abandon his position on the Schwechat rivulet and return. From Pressburg, he called a Diet of nobility, had himself elected "Prince of the Kingdom of Hungary," and concluded alliances with Friedrich of Bohemia and rebellious Austrian Estates.

Ferdinand was back in Vienna, signing every paper that grave-faced advisers put on his desk. The papers left him titular King of only part of his hereditary realm, but his tenure of the Imperial throne did not seem threatened, and auxiliaries from various Catholic lands were expected.

The palace of Vienna was a somber place in the winter of 1619–20. The people of the city, awakening to a notion of true peril, hoarded food.

The Sultan's good will was in rising demand. Gábor Bethlen's ambassadors brought costly presents, Friedrich of Bohemia offered annual gifts. Seekers of Turkish favor were summoned to sign a form, committing them to send at least every five years donations worthy of a Sultan. To please him, ruinous taxes were levied, properties seized. Christian

people in the Danube Valley were despoiled so that the Mohammedan
monarch could build even more sumptuous gardens and kiosks.

All through the winter of 1619–20, German Catholic Princes chipped
into a pool of lansquenets that should protect them against Protestant
aggression. Maximilian of Bavaria was titular commander; actual commander was Baron Johan Tserclaes von Tilly, a Dutchman who then
held the title of lieutenant general. Tilly, a gnomelike man past sixty, who
rode the hugest horse royal stables could provide, was a living encyclopedia of war.

Early in June, Catholics and Protestants agreed to a policy of non-
intervention in their respective affairs. The Catholics received a free hand
to deal with Bohemia and the still rebellious Austrian province.

Late in October, the Catholics turned north toward Prague, meeting
only token resistance. Hardly ever had two opposing armies been so little
bent on action as the Catholics and Protestants were in the early days of
November 1620. The war might have petered out then and there.

However, there was one man with the Catholics, a Carmelite White
Friar, Pater Dominicus, who did not want to see the campaign come to
so ignominious an end. Dominicus was from Aragon, Spain, and had a
reputation of saintliness. His sponsor was the Duke of Bavaria. The
White Friar stormed into a peasant's hut where a frustrating war council
was being held; with fiery eloquence he told the officers to rely on the
Lord's guidance, since they apparently did not trust their own gift of
leadership. Tilly dropped his thin, scornful grin and agreed. Italians and
Spaniards engaged in pious braggadocio. War would not be allowed to
peter out. A saintly man's persuasion sealed the fate of one generation.

On November 8, Catholics and Protestants faced each other on the
slopes of the White Mountain, a fortified hill dominating the old section
of Prague. King Friedrich was not an early riser, and by 10 A.M., when
not a single shot had been fired, he surmised that nothing was going to
happen. He was just holding an abundant repast when he heard a sudden roar of cannon. But artillery duels were not always followed by big
battles; the windows of the dining hall afforded no view of the White
Mountain, and it would have been a breach of etiquette had anybody
talked about fighting. Unperturbed, Friedrich went through every course
of the meal, and then rose to ride out to lead a morale-boosting parade.

He did not have to ride all the way to the hill. He had hardly reached
the city gates when the remnants of the Protestant army surged against
the walls, in desperate quest of safety. There had been a big battle; it
had lasted for one hour and led to complete Protestant disaster.

On November 13, a dejected Prague vowed allegiance to Ferdinand, but the Emperor was urged not to show undue mercy, to cancel Bohemian privileges, and to have the leaders of the rebellion executed.

Bohemian nobles fled, valuable belongings packed on carts and wagons. Imperials seized the vehicles with their precious loads; they entered castles, took whatever they could cart and carry, sacked villages and hamlets, staged "billetings," levied contributions, sat in kangaroo courts. Brutish, dull, and dumb, they destroyed immense values without much profit to themselves.

News of the Battle of the White Mountain took one week to reach Vienna. Ferdinand's cabinet staged a special celebration, the Emperor participating. All documents on privileges once granted to the city of Prague had been brought to Vienna, and in the presence of a select inner circle the Emperor tore off Imperial seals and used a pair of sharp scissors to cut the parchments. Friends and admirers applauded the performance. This was a time to cajole authority.

Protestant ministers were banished from the Minoriten Church and the Landhaus; a suburban castle owned by a prominent Protestant was turned over to the Cathedral chapter; the University of Vienna came under more stringent Jesuit control. Nobles were granted nominal religious freedom, but those who aspired to high public office and top military commissions understood well enough that practicing Protestantism would be detrimental to their ambitions. Untitled burghers had to attend Catholic services. Those who wanted to persevere in Protestantism had no choice but to leave town.

A law was promulgated giving Catholic burghers the right to acquire houses and properties of migrants at their "assessed value," which was but a fraction of regular market quotations.

The third year of the Thirty Years' War saw little military action in the Danube Valley. However, the land was plagued by the billeting of mercenaries of various origins, by mutual denunciations, by contributions. The cost of living skyrocketed as minting privileges were farmed out to favorites who ruthlessly produced bad coins. Disease raged beyond control; hospitals closed because of lack of funds. The fishermen on the Danube still went about their trade, but commerce on the river was near a standstill. Merchants could not do regular business where no stable currency existed, river piracy was rampant, and robbery was practically everywhere in the seething land.

The Imperial government was hit by inflation. Though devaluation reduced former obligations to next to nothing, it was well-nigh impossible to lay hands upon a substantial amount of cash to keep armaments going. In early 1622, the government signed a deal with one De Witte from Prague, who obtained a minting monopoly that canceled all existing privileges. He and his syndicate were committed to pay the government, in installments, a due of six million gulden. Six million were more than Ferdinand had ever seen, more than his cabinet had spent for the war. The son of a Serbian butcher acted as front man for various dignitaries in the Imperial Chancellery. Cardinal Prince Liechtenstein had a share in the new minting business; so had the ubiquitous Colonel Waldstein. Waldstein supplied the syndicate with silver at rates which rose rapidly from 2.25 to 10 gulden per ounce.

The devaluation of the syndicate's coins immensely enriched the partners, and it reduced the actual value of the installments payable to the government. The government had to finance some of its operations by assessment of fines, which, however, were reduced by inflation before they were collected. The Emperor listened sympathetically when corrupt minions lamented about losing their savings. After not quite two years, the deal with the syndicate was canceled and the bad money exchanged against new currency, at the rate of 6 to 1.

On New Year's Eve 1621, another treaty was signed at Nikolsburg, near the border of Lower Austria and Moravia. After much haggling and intriguing, Gábor Bethlen resigned as ruler, leader, and Prince of Hungary, but was created Prince of the Empire and retained control of seven districts. He pledged himself to return the Crown of St. Stephen and the crown jewels to Ferdinand. Like all other treaties of peace in a sphere in which war seemed to be the only stable element, it was hardly meant to be kept. In 1623 Bethlen reopened unavailing hostilities. In 1624 he signed another treaty, this time in Vienna, the terms of which differed but little from the Nikolsburg covenant. In 1626 he tried war again, failed again, and prepared for another war in 1629, when death erased him from the rolls of belligerents.

On January 29, 1621, Emperor Ferdinand pronounced Friedrich of Bohemia an arch rebel, a traitor and usurper, a violator of Imperial prerogatives, a disturber of public peace. Friedrich was solemnly outlawed and pronounced stripped of all titles and possessions. He survived the banishment for more than twelve years, most of them comfortably spent in Holland.

Four hundred and ninety-one huge estates, covering almost 75 per cent of the area of Bohemia, were seized, worth, in terms of United States currency of 1960, close to $300,000,000. Whatever could not be sold was given away, or left ownerless and unattended.

When Friedrich had come to Prague, Bohemia's public debt was 4,300,000 gulden. When he left, it was 8,200,000. Creditors never collected. The officers of the Imperial forces did splendidly by themselves; Tilly, the incorruptible, got a bonus of 120,000 gulden. However, nobody fared better than the strange Albrecht Waldstein, who managed to have immense estates worth 5,000,000 gulden assessed at 970,000 and acquired at 686,000.

CHAPTER TWENTY-EIGHT

War profiteers viewed the spell of relative peace with dismay and alarm. War was supposed to beget more and more remunerative wars, but what went on in Germany and in the Danube Valley after Friedrich became a refugee in Holland was too petty to keep the pot of profits boiling. Several adventurers invested in professional armies to fight local wars, and used them to ransack lands rather than to pursue defined political objectives.

Tilly was promoted to Imperial field marshal and created a count. Curious Viennese saw him for the last time in 1624. They had little admiration for the aging dwarf on the back of a colossal horse. His sober efficiency all but stifled the profiteers' unholy expectations; yet the greatest profiteer of them all eventually saved the day for war.

Albrecht Eusebius Wenzel von Waldstein, popularly known as Wallenstein, was certainly a genius in the general usage of the term. John Dryden's "great wits to madness sure are near allied and thin partitions do their walls divide" may well apply to him. The goals for which the middle-aged Wallenstein reached would have seemed raving mad by the standards of the young Wallenstein, even though, in the last phase of his fantastic career, they were almost within his grasp. Wallenstein's incredible instinct for shock opportunities bridged the gap between paltry beginnings and the final drive to infinity.

Wallenstein might have passed generally unnoticed in a world not in foment: a frustrated man, a dilettante in arts and sciences, a more or less successful hunter of wealthy women ready to buy virile company. In the world he lived in, Wallenstein displayed the gifts of a man who could dig for treasures in the crater of a volcano and come out unscathed and enriched, to keep fortune hunting in holocausts ever after.

Poet Friedrich Schiller chose Wallenstein as the protagonist of an immortal trilogy. When Schiller thus built Wallenstein's monument in 1799, he created the portrait of a soldier of vision, torn by the tragic conflict between duty toward his sovereign and temptation to pursue personal ends, a man who never actually planned treason, though he toyed with it; who was maligned, and who succumbed to assassins before he could escape the net in which fate had ensnared him. Schiller was too high-minded a man to look for the venom in a character's dramatic iridescence.

Historical records indicate that Wallenstein's father died in 1595, when Albrecht was twelve years old. The mother had preceded him in death by two years. The couple left seven children, five of them girls. Somehow, two estates bequeathed among them melted away during legal procedures involved in settling the estate. Albrecht's guardians sent him to the Jesuit school of Olmütz, Moravia, where he was, of course, converted to Catholicism. He never became a religious zealot, and was never opposed to re-conversion, if profitable. From Olmütz, he went to Altdorf near Nuremberg, to continue his studies in the local Protestant academy.

In Altdorf, he had his first opportunity: well-to-do gentlemen occasionally scouted academy grounds for personable and adaptable students; Wallenstein was both. A Bohemian nobleman hired him as a companion and they traveled through western Germany, the Low Countries, England, France, and Italy. Wallenstein enrolled at the Universities of Padua and Bologna to study mathematics, astrology, and military science. He never graduated.

The wealthy Bohemian took the adolescent to Prague and left him there for undisclosed reasons. Albrecht made an unavailing attempt to recover some of his paternal heritage, but found himself scorned as a nonentity without means or connections. He tried to enlist in some noble's fighting forces, but they had no use for an eighteen-year-old who boasted of having attended a course of military science in Italy and expected a commission. Royal recruiters told him that he would either have to serve as a private or invest in an officer's "patent," asserting that this was the soundest of investments: an officer could requisition, expropriate, and otherwise collect, provided he gave his superior a proper share. Albrecht had no money to invest, and how he eventually procured the means to buy his way into the army is open to conjecture, but he emerged as a captain at the age of twenty-one. He did all the requisitioning within the reach of a person of his modest rank, and he outwitted and defrauded less mathematically trained superiors, securing a nest egg to invest in a more brilliant future. Equipped with the nest egg and a credential letter signed by a newly acquired in-law, he went to Vienna and presented himself at court, where he impressed no one and was immediately forgotten.

The only friend Albrecht made in Vienna was Jesuit Padre Pachta, whom he told of his Catholic zeal and his determination to do something useful. Padre Pachta had a useful suggestion: a devout lady owned large estates in Moravia, but the devil of Protestantism was rampant among the peasants and townsfolk there; she was looking for a vigorous person to do effective exorcism, a young and handsome man preferred.

The year was 1609, and the nest egg was all but gone. The Captain met the requirements of Dame Lucretia Nekesch, a widow at the peak of maturity, and a marriage contract was signed. Groom Wallenstein would inherit the Nekesch land, villages, and townships. The bride obliged by passing away while the Captain was still young. The devil of Protestantism was still rampant, but the new landlord had devised a system of exorcism by spoliation, taxation, and confiscation, making a fortune out of alleged heresy. At the time Lucretia Nekesch died, the means of her Protestants were near exhaustion, and whatever the consolable widower could still hope to grab did not satisfy his growing ambitions.

In his Moravian backwoods, he tried astrology to find the road to grandeur. Was it the stars, or was it nostalgia? The road led back to soldiering. In 1617, the Archduke of Styria was involved in a feud with Venice; Wallenstein recruited mercenaries afoot and on horseback on the Nekesch estates, and joined the Archduke. He was promoted to colonel, but that seemed all that was in the stars for him.

The year 1619 found thirty-six-year-old Colonel Waldstein in seething Olmütz as commander of the local garrison. This was not much to brag about for a man of thirty-six. The citizenry of Olmütz sympathized with the rebels, and many nobles were in favor of seceding from the Habsburg realm. Wallenstein put out feelers, but realized that he could not join them in a truly prominent position. He seemed to have missed that band wagon. Yet there was still another; that of the Habsburgs.

The Colonel had a key to the garrison's war chest. It contained a lot of full-weight gulden. He grabbed the cash, alerted his men, paid arrears out of personal funds, and marched through Moravia straight on to Vienna. At first, his arrival caused no great stir, but soon dignitaries in quest of patriotic deeds began to hail the action as a glorious feat and, after he had delivered the cash, also as an act of sublime honesty. He was introduced to the Emperor. To Ferdinand's bewilderment, the strange colonel offered to lend him funds to take care of a few embarrassing obligations. It was an all-or-nothing speculation. If the Emperor lost, Wallenstein would go down in ruin; if he won, the investment would bring immense returns.

Came Ferdinand's victory on the White Mountain. This was the first round.

Wallenstein was made *Obrist zu Prag,* the equivalent of military commander of Bohemia. This was but a down payment on the part of the Emperor, who urged his faithful officer to name what he wanted and to present an account of what was due him. The ex-student of mathematics drafted accounts; they looked wonderfully accurate compared with the usual reports by exchequers, for they were detailed to the last gulden. He charged 154,059 gulden for cash expenses on His Majesty's account; nobody had ever known that the Emperor had had so many obligations falling into the category of "embarrassing," but everybody was relieved to learn that they had all been taken care of. He charged 554,903 gulden for the maintenance of his Olmütz infantry; this made it by far the most expensive Imperial unit of all, but everybody was full of praise for a colonel who so lavishly supported his regiment. Wallenstein's Moravian estates which rebels had seized were, of course, returned to their owner, and it seemed but fair that he claim compensation for alleged damages: 182,297 gulden. Wallenstein modestly agreed that the damages be credited to his account, from which he began to buy wholesale properties confiscated from rebels. In view of his unusual merits, the *Obrist zu Prag* received top priority as a purchaser of confiscated estates, and assessments made by state estimators turned every purchase into a "steal" in the fullest modern meaning of the term.

Wallenstein kept "purchasing" after the first stealing spree was over. Eventually, his acquired lands reached an assessed value of 2,891,794 gulden, and Moravian nobles of uncertain loyalty were forced into selling land to him for another 1,712,889 gulden, a fraction of their real value. He paid them in promissory notes, knowing that the money would soon be depreciated. As he got his fingers into the minting pie, no syndicate could have refused him partnership, and he learned one fundamental of inflation: the debtor always wins. When redeeming the promissory notes he "saved" five sixths of the nominal value. And all the time, Wallenstein did a thriving business selling, buying, and interchanging real estate, always winning through deceit, blackmail, and, of course, inflation.

His property skyrocketed. Wallenstein, now officially "Commander in Bohemia," kept an army at the disposal of the Emperor, subject to later accounting. Soldiering had been the key to his vertiginous rise; soldiering remained the key to social infinity. And matrimony, which had started him on his financial career, was another profitable element not to be neglected.

On June 9, 1623, Wallenstein married Isabella, daughter of Count Harrach. The Harrachs were not his peers in wealth, but they were related to the families of several Imperial favorites. These favorites had been eying Wallenstein with grudge and might have intrigued against him, but after he became a relative, they bet on him as he had bet on the Emperor.

Among the properties which Wallenstein acquired was the domain of Friedland, which included the town of Reichenberg (purchase price 150,000 dubious gulden). Reporting this acquisition to the Emperor, he asserted that he would be glad to accept it as a fief. Ferdinand made him Lord of Friedland and created him a Count Palatine with the privilege of opening mines, arranging fairs and weekly markets, and acquiring fiefs even from persons above his present station.

Three months after the wedding to Isabella Harrach, the Emperor raised the "Head of the House Wallstein [as a scribe misspelled the name] and Friedland" to the rank of "Prince of the Holy Roman Empire," and the domain of Friedland, into which fifty-eight other domains were incorporated, became a principality. The Emperor retained taxation prerogatives, but Wallenstein exploited his lands to the limit; not only agriculturally and industrially but also by oppressive excises and by awarding himself a brewing monopoly which alone yielded an annual return of 12 per cent of the total capital investment in the principality. Wallenstein was later credited with having promoted the raising of livestock, road construction, and education of youngsters of noble descent. His manorial officials had to write exhaustive reports on such matters as the feeding of suckling pigs, calves, and colts, the treatment of sick fowl, road conditions, and the progress of students in the school of Gitschin.

In the spring of 1624, when war threatened to extinguish, Wallenstein's father-in-law appeared in private audience at the Court of Vienna to convey a message from the Prince: Venice was a thorn in the side of the Empire; it ought to be put in its place by conquering Friuli. Prince Wallenstein was ready to conquer the province on credit.

Ferdinand consulted the Duke of Bavaria, who was outraged at the idea of starting a fight in Italy when Germany was hardly pacified and Hungary still an enigma. The Harrach mission failed, but Wallenstein cleverly insinuated that the Emperor should become independent from the Princes of the Catholic League, by setting afoot a strong army of his own, financed and maintained by his faithful vassal, the Prince of Friedland. The Emperor's advisers were reluctant to suggest acceptance, but the faithful vassal was given to understand that he would receive more powers.

On April 7, 1625, these powers were specified. The center of gravity of international disturbances had moved from the Danube in a northwesterly direction. Ferdinand sent a message to *Obrist Feldwachtmeister Albrecht Eusebius Wenzel, Prince of Friedland, and Ruler of the House of Wallenstein,* appointing him *Capo* over all troops stationed within the Holy Roman Empire and the Netherlands, and all troops still to join them; he should keep in readiness to proceed to field headquarters on short notice. The message did not have to be dispatched; it had hardly been sealed when the addressee arrived in Vienna with a retinue as pompous as only a Sultan or a parvenu could muster. Wallenstein carried a bagful of secret documents, confidential reports received from agents he now maintained all over Europe, which told of impending attack from Denmark and Sweden, of France turning ever more hostile, of Turkey set to kindle another Hungarian explosion. Ambassadorial reports were not quite that alarming, but they bore out some of Wallenstein's information.

The parvenu Prince warned, supplicated, stormed that a strong Imperial army had to be mobilized at once. The Emperor did not have time to consult with his advisers. He assented, dazedly, but he did not want Wallenstein to burden himself with the full expense; he would contribute 25,000 men to Wallenstein's 21,000.

But Wallenstein knew better than Ferdinand that the Imperial exchequer could not afford the number of fighting men promised by the Emperor. He waited gleefully until the exchequer announced that the Emperor had no more than 100,000 gulden in ready cash that he could hand over to Wallenstein, but that the Prince would have to recruit the entire army. Wallenstein expressed his most obedient consent to a blushing Emperor.

On June 27, 1625, Wallenstein was created a duke; on July 25 he was promoted to full general. He was told to keep his soldiers under rigid discipline, to deny unnecessary requests, to punish robbery, arson, and rape, and never unduly to molest friends and neutrals by the passage of troops. He should not ravage townships and districts without explicit Imperial authorization, but he could levy "tolerable contributions" from captured places.

Wallenstein did not even have to invest in recruitment. He offered colonel's commissions for sale; the sales price included bounties, at least one month's pay for recruits, and expenses for weapons, horses, uniforms. But all equipment was also billed to the Imperial government.

Within a matter of weeks, 24,000 men stood ready. In September 1625, Wallenstein's Imperial army was on the march via Bohemia to Magdeburg. From there, it rolled on toward the border of Denmark, whose King Christian IV was engaged in hostilities with the Catholic League. The Danes' mercenaries were plagued by disease and hunger; mass desertions spread. The Catholic League's host under Tilly was not strong either, but it could keep the enemy at bay. Wallenstein might have wiped out Christian's forces, but he did not wish to decide one issue before other issues, even more pregnant with all-out war, had time to ripen.

Hardly ever before had the fate of the world depended so much on one single man. Hardly ever had one of the would-be world conquerors, from Alexander to Genghis Khan, wielded so much power.

On December 19, 1625, Denmark, England, and Holland signed an alliance at The Hague. France, Sweden, Savoy, and Venice were invited to join. Fat bribes were slipped into the hands of the Turkish governor of Buda to make him stage border incidents in Ferdinand's realm.

Christian IV was the centerpiece around which the table of conflagration was set. Wallenstein had reason to be satisfied with himself. Had Denmark been wiped out, a phenomenal opportunity would have been missed forever; he would have withered as a parvenu duke instead of becoming the key figure in what could turn into a war of succession to the Holy Roman Empire, out of which the wealthiest and trickiest would emerge as an Emperor of awesome might. He did not wish to lift a finger against Denmark before a general war was under way.

But an overzealous Danish commander of a Danish re-formed corps attacked Wallenstein's troops on the Elbe River. The attack was repulsed, but, overriding Tilly, Wallenstein prevented victory from being exploited.

In the spring of 1626, the forces of the King of Denmark gathered again. One corps of the Danish army penetrated Silesia and Moravia, unmolested by the Wallensteinians. Another horde of human-looking, but inhumanely acting, scavengers hit the devastated lands, looting, raping, killing.

Another Danish corps roamed the northern parts of Germany. Tilly asked Wallenstein to disperse that small army; Wallenstein asked Tilly to send reinforcements first, and this the old field marshal refused to do, since he did not want to put more men under Wallenstein's command. It is not established what he reported to the Viennese Court, but from Vienna came an anxious query about Wallenstein's next intentions. Wallenstein replied that, since Vienna sent neither money nor ammunition, he could not engage in large-scale operations. Vienna accepted the reply, which was accompanied by statements that showed the Empire in a virtual state of bankruptcy. Wallenstein had scored. An Emperor who did not reprimand his temerity was open to blackmail.

Tilly won a few minor engagements, but the Danish corps marched, unobstructed, through Brandenburg, into Silesia, and proceeded toward the Hungarian border. Rejuvenated war rolled toward the Danube Valley; the Emperor's heartlands were threatened not only from the north but also from the east, where corrupt and aggressive Pasha Murteza of Buda invaded the Habsburg districts of Hungary.

Wallenstein, who had gone to Prague, where he lived in style, bided his time. Only in August did he move, shoving the intruders out of parts of the lands they occupied, keeping the campaign a short distance north of the Emperor's residence and the Danube Valley. He was pleased to learn that King Christian, who had received money and even men from France, England, and Holland, concentrated the bulk of his forces against Tilly, who, hard-pressed, applied for Wallenstein's assistance. Wallenstein sent a few thousand men just to keep the struggle going. Tilly inflicted defeat upon his enemies near Lutter am Barenberge on August 27, 1626. The King of Denmark lost his entire artillery.

At first, Wallenstein showed no inclination to help. Tilly inflicted the deathblow upon the Danes, but when the old field marshal was wounded and temporarily out of action, he suddenly threw the full weight of his superior forces against Denmark proper. In the next year, 1627, the Danish army, for all practical purposes, ceased to exist.

Wallenstein revised his policies; to continue stalling would have left him isolated. If he abandoned the Emperor now, he was bound to lose. Should Ferdinand survive, he would find means of disposing of him, but, should the Emperor fall, the victors would not feel obliged to his stalling general.

Wallenstein marched to Hungary. Vienna breathed relief. The Danish corps was thrown off balance, and the Pasha halted operations before Wallenstein's army had fired a single shot, except against civilians who tried to resist pillaging.

On September 9, an Imperial courier reached Wallenstein in Freistadl

(Hlohovec) on the Váh River: a strong force of loyal Hungarians was about to join him, and he was urged to attack. He had not yet drafted the reply when the loyal Hungarians arrived, 2000 in all, under Palatine Eszterházy.

The Eszterházys were a proud and ancient family. The Palatine first tried his best to be obliging; Wallenstein, the upstart, immediately tried his worst to be insulting. He did not want the Palatine to watch him too closely, so he wrote the Emperor that his army was decimated by forced marches, that food supplies were short, that the treasury owed him a fortune, and that the Palatine's forces impressed him as unreliable; unless he received, at once, supplies, money, and soldiers he could trust, he would resign.

Eszterházy did not see the letter but was outraged by Wallenstein's general attitude; he called him a coward and worse than a real enemy. The Emperor, who could not meet Wallenstein's demands, was frightened at the prospect of seeing him resign and sent Count Trauttmannsdorf to headquarters to parley him into attacking.

Wallenstein had again asserted himself. He was sure to get whatever he asked for. On September 19, he issued marching orders; two days later his troops reached the western Hungarian Danube Valley, yet he did not bring Bethlen or the Pasha of Buda to bay, much as conditions favored him. He parried a light thrust, and did not hit back. Somehow, enigmatic Hungary began to frighten him; the people were hostile and unfathomable, and he came to detest them. He withdrew to the Váh Valley and wrote his father-in-law, "Nobody shall ever again induce me or any of my men to return to that land of scoundrels."

In Vienna, courtiers began to make caustic remarks about Wallenstein, and Count Harrach informed him of a strong movement to relieve him of his command.

In November 1626, Lieutenant Colonel St. Julien, a member of Wallenstein's staff, presented himself at the Court War Council. He carried Wallenstein's offer of resignation and mentioned in passing that the army had not received its pay, and that this was the Imperial government's responsibility. As usual, the government had no money; if Wallenstein's resignation were accepted, the unpaid soldiers might ravage the land and even march to Vienna. Meekly and mildly, war councilors spoke of obvious misunderstandings and asked for an exchange of views.

Wallenstein agreed to meet the government's negotiator, Prince Eggenberg, at a castle some twenty-five miles east of Vienna. No minutes of the parley were kept. Later records are based on hearsay, but the hearsay sounds logical. Allegedly, Wallenstein withdrew his offer of resignation, agreed to satisfy his soldier creditors, but demanded to be free to establish winter quarters in Bohemia, Moravia, or Silesia, and collect, locally, whatever the army needed. Taxes levied in Bohemia should be paid to him instead of to the fiscal authorities, and he would credit them to the account of the Imperial government. He even offered to enlarge his army to a full 70,000, circumstances permitting, if Emperor and government pledged themselves to refund all expenses involved. The Emperor hastened to agree, to pledge, to confirm.

The first stop on the rapacious march to winter quarters was in Moravia. Wallenstein had personal grievances against one of his former partners in the minting business: Cardinal Dietrichstein. Not even an invading army could have robbed the Cardinal's estates more drastically than the General did under the title of collecting taxes.

Silesia was the next victim. Districts were ordered to deliver food and forage to the "Wallensteinians," as they were called; also, they were to meet the payrolls of the garrisons. Payrolls were padded, the number of soldiers given as two, three, four, five times the actual figures, and extra bonuses had to be paid for "soldiers' entertainment." Available cash did not satisfy the extortioners. People surrendered objects of gold and silver, cloth, linen, and garments; and they issued debentures which they had to redeem if they wanted to live. Silesian chroniclers estimate the damage wrought by the billeted Wallensteinians at 5,000,000 gulden.

Wallenstein's officers enriched themselves, and his men had never had it so good. Wallenstein's nominal monthly salary was 2000 gulden. It is impossible to estimate how many times over he made on the side. His way of life was expensive in the extreme, and money being the basis of his power, his lust for money was indomitable.

Wallenstein no longer needed potboiler wars; a great design emerged, which the Emperor hardly understood though he gave his majestic nod: the Empire should switch its point of gravity to the Baltic and the North Sea; an Imperial navy should be created to drive the Dutch out of the lucrative commerce in the area; a German-Spanish trading company should receive a virtual monopoly of trade.

In February 1628, Wallenstein was appointed General of the Oceanic and Baltic Seas. He obtained naval craft and control of large land areas, but suddenly his ardor slackened and he suggested peace with Denmark.

On May 22, 1629, a treaty was signed at Lübeck. Christian IV pledged himself never again to interfere in the affairs of the Empire; he relinquished his small holdings in Germany, but kept his patrimony.

Wallenstein, the genius of war, posed as a peacemaker. In fact, *his* war seemed certain: the conflict between the Empire and expansionist, aggressive Sweden.

Axel Oxenstierna, Sweden's leading statesman and Chancellor to King Gustavus II Adolphus, reminisced fifteen years later: "Pomerania and the Baltic Sea shore are the bastions of the Swedish crown, protecting it against the Emperor. They were the main reasons for His Majesty's taking up arms."

Actually, the King of Sweden was in arms ever since he ascended the throne, and he was more aggression- than protection-minded.

At thirty-five, the King had ruled eighteen years. Gustavus II Adolphus was extremely ambitious, a bold, outstanding soldier, and intelligent enough to let himself be guided, politically, by his wizard Chancellor, who visualized the foundation of a Great Baltic Empire which would, in due course, spread its tentacles over most of Central Europe.

However, early in 1629, the Swedish army was still heavily engaged in Poland; but France, fence sitter in its neighbors' struggles, wanted more Central European fighting. Cardinal Richelieu, chief minister of Louis XIII, mediated a six-year armistice between Poland and Sweden. This gave the Swedes a free hand against the Emperor.

The Empire smarted under the billeting of Wallenstein's host. All forces under Wallenstein's command were stationed in the Emperor's domains; only Wallenstein could commission officers up to the rank of colonel; generals whom the Emperor commissioned had to be confirmed by Wallenstein. He determined wages, rations, and controlled supplies.

This so-called Imperial army was neither German or Austrian, nor Catholic. German and Austrian soldiers were in the minority. Many were Walloons, Croats, Italians; Italians held most of the higher commissions, and there were also other nationals among the officers, including Irishmen. Wallenstein's recruiters hired both Catholics and Protestants. Several colonels were of Protestant nobility. George von Arnim, a Protestant, became one of Wallenstein's trusted advisers.

The army lived high, and many lansquenets had their women and children stay in the camp. All camps swarmed with prostitutes, who participated in the men's raids, robbing with no less fierceness than the most rapacious of their bedfellows.

Wallenstein himself wrote the Emperor that theaters of war were practically ruined, that "misery and desperation caused peasants to drown themselves in the sea," and that, but for his untiring efforts, the soldiers would have starved. The "untiring efforts" meant that Wallenstein had become the army's chief supplier. From his estates, grain and cattle were shipped to the soldiers; tenant farmers were drafted into shops to manufacture footwear and uniforms; Wallenstein built industries from which a steady stream of arms and ammunition went to the army.

And all the time, a steady stream of fantastic bills poured into the Emperor's chancellery. According to these bills, the army should have numbered close to 100,000, whereas the actual figure was not always in excess of 20,000. Wallenstein offered to accept payment in land. The Spanish ambassador to Vienna advised that the Emperor should rather pawn his jewels, even his wardrobe; but Ferdinand did not have many jewels left, and he had no intention of parting with what he wore. Wallenstein collected estates and Imperial domains and confiscated properties. Even in 1627, when he owned more land in Bohemia than all other ranking nobles combined, Sagan in Silesia was added to his sprawling domain. Sagan was worth at least 1,000,000 gulden; corrupt appraisers assessed it at 150,850. Princes of the blood ruled lands, but Wallenstein owned them. His claims to the treasury kept snowballing.

Wallenstein never put personal ambitions on paper. Tall, wiry, his clear-cut, enigmatic features always under control, his clipped voice rarely rising above *sotto voce,* he talked only to his confidants and his astrologer. His headquarters were a hotbed of rumors, the origins of which could never be ascertained.

The Emperor sent a member of the Court War Council, Questenberg, to Wallenstein's headquarters, requesting partial demobilization: the army's excessive strength ruined the civilian population; there was a clear danger of revolt; it was beyond the Emperor's power to provide for the army; pay arrears had reached an alarming level; and the Emperor had no design to stabilize his rule by means not embodied in the Constitution of the Reich.

Hardly ever had a monarch so pleaded with his general. Wallenstein seemed to stand at the parting of the roads. Had he discharged most of his men and kept only about 6000, as Questenberg now suggested, he would have lost much of his power, and what he had acquired would be nibbled away. If he defied the Emperor, he would throw the realm into a turmoil that would most likely destroy the Habsburgs, but might destroy him too, since the enemy forces he had helped to set in motion were inscrutable or, at least, not yet ready for a deal on his terms. Wallenstein authorized Collalto, president of the Court War Council, to discharge half of his cavalry which camped west of the Elbe River. Of 24,156 horsemen, 12,556 were discharged. The men staged a minor mutiny, which was quelled by sixty executions.

The people, plagued by billeting, noticed only that the scavenging soldiery remained on their land, and that those discharged were more savage even than those on the padded payroll. Already, the uppermost part of the Danube Valley was visited by uniformed bandits speaking foreign tongues; but violence needs no articulation.

Europe swarmed with political agents, high-placed intriguers, and scheming careerists. At the Court of Vienna, dignitaries maintained more contacts than they would ever care to acknowledge; in Vienna's smelly taverns, suspicious characters offered to arrange secret deals with important persons anywhere. The Swedish Chancellor did not need suspicious characters to contact Wallenstein; feelers must have been put out early in 1630, but not before the end of that year did Wallenstein engage in concrete negotiations with his Emperor's most powerful foe. By that time, something momentous had happened: Wallenstein was no longer the Emperor's general!

The Catholic League and loyal Protestant Estates had pressed for his dismissal. Maximilian of Bavaria called a convention of Electors, which opened in Regensburg on June 19, 1630. Ferdinand, his wife, their son, and an immense retinue were present. The ancient city on the Danube was crowded and business was thriving; yet, what filtered out from the convention hall sounded ominous, and people longed for peace.

On July 3, the Emperor requested the Electors' advice on what to do if peace could not be established, and how to wage war in an orderly fashion.

Three days later, after a bombardment of the island of Usedom, off the coast of Pomerania, King Gustavus II Adolphus landed with an army of 13,000; 6000 Swedish soldiers were already concentrated at Stralsund, more than 20,000 massed in Sweden proper, in the Baltic provinces, and along the border of Russia. War with Sweden was on.

The Swedish army was also a typical lansquenet force, a medley of several nationalities outnumbering the Swedes. Its Finnish riders were among the most savage fighters anywhere. But three weeks later, the conferees at the upper Danube still discussed who should replace Wallenstein.

Wallenstein, strangely inactive, waited in his new headquarters of Memmingen in Swabia. At long last, on August 26, two members of the Imperial retinue proceeded there to notify the General that he had been

discharged "with indulgence, and without injury to his personal honor."
It was as if a rabbit would try to banish a lion from his hunting grounds.

Strangely, the lion took the rabbit's orders. Wallenstein only asked
that the Emperor remember his "faithful and profitable" services and
pay the soldiers. Then he left for his Bohemian duchy.

The Catholic Electors set a ceiling of 39,000 men for the Imperial
army and pledged themselves to maintain a League army of 21,000.
Tilly was placed in charge of both.

In Bohemia, Wallenstein studied the feeding of piglets and did not
even send the customary balance sheets to the Imperial government.
Only his valet saw his few visitors, but did not always know who they
were. In November 1630, the King of Sweden stretched out feelers.

Tilly found himself with more trouble on his hands than he had expected. Several Imperial regiments refused to leave their garrison towns,
for fear the burghers would keep them from returning. Fortifications
that had been reported built, and were billed to the government, did not
exist. Pestilence and desertion decimated units in the field. Discipline was
lower than ever.

One by one, Imperial outposts fell to the Swedes. At Christmas 1630,
they held all of Pomerania and Stettin, while far away, in Transylvania,
George Rákóczy threatened rebellion. The Swedes were beset by money
troubles, but, on January 23, 1631, France offered an annual subsidy to
support an army of 36,000. Gustavus Adolphus' recruiters enlisted many
discharged "Wallensteinians."

Wallenstein threw a regal New Year's party in Prague, where he then
lived.

The Saxonian city of Magdeburg proclaimed its secession from the
Empire; Swedes occupied the strategic town dominating the Elbe Valley,
and Gustavus Adolphus took his main forces south, toward Bohemia,
Moravia, and Vienna.

Emperor Ferdinand turned to Wallenstein for advice. Wallenstein may
have expected this move. His reply got lost in the Imperial archives, but
what it contained can be guessed from a remark he made to the Swedes'
Count Thurn: "I am disgusted with the Emperor and would do anything
for your King."

Tilly laid siege to Magdeburg and, supported by General Pappenheim's soldiers, destroyed it almost completely. The maddened Elector
of Saxony hired one of Wallenstein's former generals and joined the
Swedes, whose army was equipped with a new and lighter type of rifle
with improved firing velocity. The Imperials were attacked near Breiten-

feld and put to flight; Tilly had no more than 12,000 men left and lost all his cannon.

Two months later, the Saxonians were in Prague, the Swedes veered off toward the Rhineland, the Catholic League broke up. Tilly fell back to Bavaria. The upper Danube Valley was threatened by invasion, and Tilly reported that he could not offer serious resistance: "My men are ill fed, ill clad, and melt away like snow."

To the people of the Danube Valley, the presence of Imperial troops was most oppressive. The worse the soldiers were clad and fed, the more rapacious they became.

After Breitenfeld, there was some correspondence between the King of Sweden and Wallenstein. Wallenstein asked for 12,000 to 14,000 men to wipe out Imperial forces in Silesia, Bohemia, and Moravia, and to establish a bridgehead at the Danube near Vienna.

The King replied that he could put no more than 1500 men under Wallenstein's command and that further requests should be addressed to the Elector of Saxony.

Wallenstein could, apparently, no longer effectively play both ends against the middle. The Emperor was losing the war, but Wallenstein might still help him turn the tide.

There was a letter, dated May 5, 1631, in a secret drawer of Wallenstein's desk. It entreated him to come to Vienna or some place near by, to be available for consultation. Wallenstein had not reacted to the Imperial plea. Ferdinand must have been hurt, but Wallenstein was positive that he would bridle his pride. And he knew that former Leaguists blamed Tilly's defeat on the Dutch-born field marshal's age and asked that a younger commander be appointed, a man of pure German blood, who owned land in the Reich. Wallenstein was not of "pure German blood."

Ferdinand III, the Emperor's son, was not of "pure German blood" either. He was twenty-four, and certainly not Gustavus Adolphus' equal in military prowess; but he wanted the appointment badly. He was appointed with the proviso that he share his command with Wallenstein if the latter were available. Wallenstein had the answer ready when a discreet inquiry reached him. He regretted: gout prevented him from campaigning.

Soon he had another Imperial letter: "I hope, my dear Duke, that you will keep in touch with me and not forsake me in my distress."

Wallenstein considered more stalling, until he learned that one of his letters to Gustavus Adolphus had been intercepted and that the elderly

mother of one of his confidants had done some sinister gossiping. He
had to act promptly.

The intermission was over. On December 8, 1631, Wallenstein was in
Znaim, close enough to Vienna to be in constant touch with the Court,
still far enough to make his way back to Bohemia should his enemies
make a dangerous move.

Early in 1632, Wallenstein was in command. He had agreed to accept
an assignment for a three-month test period. His Imperial force spread
rapacious wings over Bohemia and Moravia. However, mischief had
run its course. In February the Swedes turned south. Tilly fell back; the
invaders took Nuremberg, whose populace hailed the victors. On April 7,
they were in Donauwörth, crossed the Danube unopposed, and raced
toward the Lech River, where Tilly made a stand. On April 15, he was
defeated and fatally wounded.

With the exception of Ingolstadt and Regensburg, all of Bavaria was
conquered by the Swedish army. The upper Danube Valley experienced
a novel visitation of wild cruelty. Gustavus Adolphus' soldiers distinguished themselves for an ingenious sadism that became legendary, and
even increased the vocabulary. The term *Schwedentrunk* (Swedes' drink)
has survived. It stood for liquid manure, which the brutes forced down
their victims' throats for the sheer pleasure of watching their convulsions.
The King's soldiers virtually made the people laugh themselves to death
by tying them, rubbing their bare soles with salt, and having a goat lick
them. In his headquarters at Munich, Gustavus Adolphus issued no restraining orders. He drafted a plan for a campaign to Vienna. Terror was
part and parcel of his soldierdom, and he apparently did not believe that
Wallenstein, the gambling multiple dealer, would stake everything on
one card and block his advance. But Wallenstein had a strong force,
steadily increased by desperadoes and ready for action. Angrily, the King
of Sweden turned north and left only small garrisons in the Danube
Valley. Wallenstein's agents did not seek contact with the King.

Wallenstein, the master of intrigue and blackmail, had rumors spread
to the effect that he would not prolong his generalship beyond the test
period. The Emperor asked Prince Eggenberg to persuade him to stay.
Eggenberg was ill and sent a letter to the General imploring him to keep
his command until they could meet. The Bishop of Vienna made a pilgrimage to his headquarters, appealing to the General to wait for Eggenberg. No one dared summon him to Vienna.

On April 23, the feeble Emperor's cringing and crouching Chancellor appeared at headquarters, and the haughty General agreed to accept a permanent assignment. He became Supreme Commander of all forces in the Austrian lands and the Holy Roman Empire, with unlimited powers. All commissions without exception were granted only by him; he would receive taxes from the Imperial patrimony, and all confiscated rebel property from the Reich and Bohemia, as a contribution toward the upkeep of his army. Whatever Wallenstein owed from purchases of estates was remitted.

This capitulation signed, Ferdinand hoped that his general would sweep the Swedes out of the realm. Wallenstein had enough men, yet he temporized; so did the King of Sweden, who was busy drafting "peace terms," according to which Sweden would control all territories between northern Scandinavia and the approaches to the upper Danube Basin.

These unrealistic terms infuriated Wallenstein, who learned of them through his agents. Some of the territories which Gustavus Adolphus claimed were Wallenstein's own!

The Imperial army swung into action, cleared all of Bohemia, entered Germany in forced marches, was joined by marauding remnants of the soldiers of the Catholic League, and, on July 16, stood outside Nuremberg. The Swedes along the upper Danube were isolated, and behaved like packs of vicious wolves, raiding whatever farms were left standing. Gustavus Adolphus concentrated his men and auxiliaries outside Nuremberg.

For over six weeks the two armies faced each other, the King and the General each waiting for the other to open new secret negotiations. On September 3, the King attacked, but was repulsed. The effect on the Swedish army's morale seemed dangerous, and disease plagued the King's men. The camp had to be evacuated, though a garrison was left inside Nuremberg.

Wallenstein had a visit from a Bohemian emigrant in Swedish employ. Wallenstein replied that he would not negotiate unless the Emperor appointed him his political plenipotentiary.

The Emperor was not informed of the exchange, but he received a message that the enemy was vanquished since he did not win a victory.

There was little rejoicing. Austria faced yet another threat. Some one hundred and twenty miles from Vienna, near Linz, the peasants revolted; they controlled a number of hamlets and castles, fanned out in all directions, burned and ravaged. Already the King of Sweden was preparing to return to the Danube Valley and to co-operate with the peasantry. And Wallenstein made no move to help, but marched to Saxony, where his generals acted more systematically, though no less barbarically, than the peasants from Upper Austria.

But Gustavus Adolphus did not return to the Danube Valley, and the rebellion burned down to the ashes of paralyzing despair.

Gustavus Adolphus had little more than 20,000 men and he raced to Saxony to merge with whatever Saxonian troops still existed. Wallenstein, believing the Swedes far away, had split his army, so that his main force consisted of less than 15,000. However, the rest, under Pappenheim, was not far away.

On November 16, 1632, the King and the General faced each other again, this time near Lützen, in Saxony. There was no waiting for messages, no strategic temporizing. A crucial engagement was at hand, one of the greatest battles in the world, yet no more than a total of 40,000 soldiers were in action.

Gustavus Adolphus, wearing a leather doublet with a solid-gold chain and an ornate iron hood, was at the right wing of his array; Wallenstein, clad in a heavy coat, kept at a short distance behind the scrimmage.

First the King's men advanced, pressing Wallenstein back. The Swedish center overran enemy artillery emplacements. Then the Wallensteinians recaptured their cannon and, around 3 P.M., a gap opened in the Swedish ranks. A slight drizzle had been falling; visibility was poor. Unnoticed, Pappenheim's cavalry had reached the battlefield. It charged, hit the Swedish right wing, but the charge got out of gear when the leader was struck by no less than six bullets. Piccolomini took over and resumed the attack; the Swedish King, fighting with great courage and tactical efficiency, threw his best regiments, the "blue" and the "yellow," into the gap. Losses were heavy on both sides. Fighting in the ranks, like a private, he shared the fate of many a private: he was killed.

It seemed as if the clock of history had come to a stop.

News of Gustavus Adolphus' death spread with incredible swiftness. The Swedish lines staggered, the Wallensteinians gained ground. Someone stripped the dead King of doublet and chain and carried them to Wallenstein, who later sent them to the Emperor. But the Swedes rallied before Wallenstein could take up pursuit. General Kniphausen, a professional soldier whose name appears only in very few textbooks, took charge of the orphaned Swedish army, threw in the last reserves, and carried the day.

Wallenstein retreated slowly, but the very fact that Lützen did not result in the Swedes' annihilation was of tremendous importance. Searching historians and military scientists have tried to establish whether

Wallenstein had not deliberately given victory away, but no conclusive evidence to this effect has been found.

The war still had a long way to go. Wallenstein's gamble was far from won.

CHAPTER TWENTY-NINE

Gustavus Adolphus' only child was a daughter, six-year-old Christina; the Swedish Diet granted Chancellor Axel Oxenstierna unlimited powers to conduct "German affairs," and the course of history resumed its crooked, blood-drenched course.

In the spring of 1633, the Swedes held all of Franconia, part of the Rhineland, and much of Swabia and Bavaria, including the sources of the Danube. They needed vast foraging areas to supply their army. Land which had once easily supported between two and three million inhabitants could hardly satisfy the need and greed of forty thousand soldiers.

Wallenstein's army licked its wounds suffered at Lützen. A court-martial sent one colonel, two lieutenant colonels, and eight other officers to the gallows. Others, also found derelict of their duties in the last battle, were sentenced in absentia and proscribed. Sheets bearing their names were nailed to gibbets. General Piccolomini and soldiers who had given a noble account of themselves received lavish rewards.

The Emperor, shuddering at the thought of Wallenstein becoming forever the decisive force in Europe, talked about an armistice. Wallenstein called it impossible. With the enemy still on Imperial territory, this would be tantamount to surrender. He and his chief astrologer, Seni, gazed at the stars.

A new Swedish agent, General Bubna, came to Wallenstein's camp, then returned to Frankfurt, where Chancellor Oxenstierna spent most of the summer of 1633. After listening to Bubna's report, the Chancellor mused: "A general peace is impossible. More estates and lands of the Reich will have to be ruined before serious negotiations can begin." Then he added quickly, "If Wallenstein wants the crown of Bohemia and the provinces attached to it, we shall recognize him as King and assist him against his enemies, provided he supports our Queen Christina."

King of Bohemia! To Wallenstein this was inadequate, but the offer could provide a basis for further negotiations.

In Vienna, the president of the War Council, Count Schlick, expressed misgivings about Wallenstein's inertia. He proceeded to the headquarters in Silesia to request that the General take action in Bavaria, open the road to the Netherlands, free the Austrian Danube Valley from the threat of invasion, and never again billet his army in the Emperor's patrimony.

Wallenstein called Schlick's demands an affront. Schlick denied unfriendly intentions and, apparently assuaged, Wallenstein promised to open the road into the Netherlands and spare the Imperial patrimony from future billetings.

On August 21, 1633, a bomb burst. It was learned that Wallenstein and Oxenstierna had signed a four-week armistice. Neither side would send reinforcements to the Danube.

Schlick could do no more than accept the facts and listen to the honeyed phrases by which Wallenstein reaffirmed his loyalty to the Emperor. He could not know that, a short time before, the General told an enemy plenipotentiary that he had never forgotten the affronts to which he had been exposed, that he was determined to avenge himself and would accept Protestant support for that purpose; that he would get rid of unreliable officers and march against Austria; that a coalition, including France, should be formed to destroy Habsburg rule in Germany and "chase the Emperor to Spain."

The plenipotentiary who had conveyed these utterances to Oxenstierna added this comment: "The General is a knave; it remains to be seen whom he will betray first, his master, ourselves, or the Elector of Saxony."

Wallenstein, in fact, had not yet arrived at a treacherous decision. He wanted his astronomer to read in the stars how loyal his army was to him, but the stars seemed undecipherable.

The armistice was prolonged until October. The Swedes exploited it to the limit, while Wallenstein lost time and advantages he had held. Swedish agents who saw him shortly before the armistice expired learned that there would be no peace unless "all foreigners were thrown out"; that Sweden would get nothing. After finishing this harangue, however, the General mused that he did not want to break up all bridges, but to keep a "seesaw."

In October, Wallenstein attacked near Steinau in the Oder basin. Five thousand Swedes surrendered, most of whom he enlisted. The men did not mind who hired them; soldiers changed jobs. Yet Wallenstein got more than he bargained for. The plague, already rampant in various parts of the stricken continent, raged among the new enlistees. The stricken army ran, trying to outpace the disease, leaving the dying and dead behind. The army eventually survived, though ever larger regions became infested.

On the upper Danube, the furies of disaster raged most violently. Colorful bands of mercenaries, arrayed to protect Bavaria and the Imperial heartlands, moved toward the French border, baring the river valley; into the vacuum poured 10,000 enemies under Duke Bernhard of Weimar. On October 29, 1633, they seized Neuburg on the Danube, where twenty-five marauders formed the "garrison," and dashed on toward Regensburg. Fifteen hundred soldiers lived in the town, most of them deserters whose defensive performance was limited to the raising of a soiled white flag.

By mid-November, Bernhard was on the way to Upper Austria. Couriers from Vienna galloped to Wallenstein's headquarters with orders, requests, supplications, to parry the threat against the capital. Wallenstein contended that Bernhard's drive was foolhardy, but he consented to dispatch some cavalry to the northernmost part of Upper Austria, across the Bohemian border.

In the wake of the cavalrymen rode the resurgent plague, the army's cataclysmic rear guard. The populace was mum. War, the embodiment of all visitations, turned into the essence of their lives.

The Duke of Weimar proclaimed that only the Emperor and Catholic zealots wanted war, and that he and the Protestants wanted peace. Popular hopes, buried under the ashes of disillusionment, flared into passionate enthusiasm; but the Duke brought no peace, and his host was no less demanding than other soldiers. Enthusiasm subsided after many a frenzied peasant had paid with his life for attempts at rebellion against remaining Catholic outposts.

Along the wooded slopes of the Danubian hills, between Passau and Neuhaus, in the fertile meadows between Aschach and Linz, beasts of prey feasted on human remains. Wallenstein, who had moved his headquarters to Pilsen, near the Upper Austrian border, did not attack the Duke of Weimar.

From Vienna, Councilor Questenberg arrived to tell the General to deal with the invasion and then to move away from the Imperial patrimony. Wallenstein wined and dined the Councilor but did nothing else.

The Emperor signed a paper and had it dispatched to Pilsen. It told

Wallenstein to march to Passau and to drive Bernhard of Weimar from all places he had conquered: "The threat in the Danube Valley is most dangerous to the Imperial House." This statement was followed by a passage which caused the General to assemble his ranking officers and have it read to them: "Should you not be in a position to undertake this operation, you ought to appoint a well-qualified and able *Capo* to carry out the task."

The officers' reaction sounded spontaneous: Wallenstein was the only man to undertake any operations; there should be no winter campaign against the Duke, and the army should stay where it was.

Wallenstein believed that he had won another test of strength, yet he had signed his own death warrant. The Emperor's camarilla felt ever more strongly that only his removal could save them; and Wallenstein's own officers gradually came to wonder whether an "able *Capo*" would not be preferable. Their oath of loyalty read: "I do solemnly swear to be faithful and loyal to the Duke of Friedland [Wallenstein] as long as His Highness will stay in His Majesty's service, not to part with him, nor let anything interfere between him and me . . ." But when, at a banquet, the oath was read out to the half-drunk officers, the words "as long as His Highness will stay in His Majesty's service" were omitted.

Wallenstein told Questenberg that the men would rest and recuperate and that the Emperor should trust him; later events would bear out the soundness of his strategy.

There was a brief period of vacillation and procrastination. Many dignitaries played possum. But, by the end of 1633, the anti-Wallensteinians gathered courage and said that Wallenstein should be rendered harmless, one way or other.

Some appeasers contended that Wallenstein was not really a traitor, that the omission of the crucial line in the oath had been due to intoxication. A Spanish diplomat called him a wildly ambitious man, a fool indulging in astrological reveries, but an able general, a pillar of Catholicism and of Habsburg rule.

But attitudes stiffened; assassination was in the air. Even had Wallenstein wished to compromise, he could no longer have settled for the crown of Bohemia, not even for a German realm. He had to be the supreme power or be doomed.

He had his army, but he was the debtor of many regimental commanders. The most grandiose economic scheme in an age in which immeasurable fortunes were changing hands, had been too smart. He had bestowed colonelcies upon men who recruited and equipped regiments at their own expense, with the understanding that expenses would be refunded later, and that the colonels would also take care of the maintenance of their men under similar terms. Nothing was refunded; none of the colonels could keep advancing cash. Hordes of usurers pooled resources to finance the army. The bills which Wallenstein would have to pay were absurdly high; he could expect nothing from the Emperor, and his creditors accepted depreciated money at face value.

Wallenstein, the symbol of power, who believed that only the stars determined his fortune, was a virtual prisoner of moneylenders.

Four colonels exhorted him never to accept a limitation of his powers, never to relinquish the hold on anything he held; but more colonels wondered whether it would not be better to see him disposed of, and his fabulous estates sold for the benefit of creditors.

France offered a subsidy of one million livres per annum should Wallenstein openly turn against the Emperor. One million livres could buy an average duchy, but it was only a drop in the bucket for the man whose creditors charged several million for annual interests.

The anti-Wallenstein party presented the Emperor with a memorandum saying that "Wallenstein wants to drive you from Germany. He intends to build his own good fortune and grandeur upon the ruin of Your Majesty and the humiliation of the House of Austria."

There was a lull in the fighting in the Danube Valley, but Vienna hummed with excitement. Moneylenders established their offices and kept high-smelling "army accounts," nurturing rumors to the effect that Wallenstein plotted to make the Danube a foreign river. Demagogues in taverns ranted about cabals and countercabals.

The Viennese had not laid eyes on Wallenstein in a long time and resented his absence. They gossiped about explosive developments.

On January 24, 1634, the Emperor issued a patent releasing all officers and men from their duties toward Wallenstein and directing them to accept orders henceforth only from Lieutenant General Gallas. Amnesty was promised to those who had transgressed their obligations toward the Emperor.

The Emperor was panicky when he signed the decree in the presence of Prince Eggenberg, Count Trauttmansdorff, and the Bishop of Vienna, immediately afterward locking himself up with his father-confessor.

Three generals were entrusted with enforcement of the patent: the new commander in chief, Gallas; General Aldringen, whose corps was stationed in eastern Bavaria; and General Piccolomini, titular commander in the Upper Austrian theater.

They were ordered to seize Wallenstein, but they had little more than a scrap of paper. Ferdinand was crazed with fear, and fear begot the decision that Wallenstein be murdered—murdered, not executed. The Emperor suffered from insomnia; he yearned for sleep, and it would hardly come to him unless Wallenstein had gone. As he issued the order for murder, he trembled with fear that Wallenstein might turn the tables and dispatch his own henchmen to Vienna.

Wallenstein had no illusions of security, but in the supreme emergency his courage failed him, and he was bewildered by a constellation of the stars which astrologer Seni called ghastly. He pleaded, granted promotions left and right, and made unconvincing protestations of loyalty to the Emperor. The remaining faithful wavered. They did not trust a man who no longer trusted his own power.

On February 18, 1634, Ferdinand issued another patent addressed to his army, which was, technically, still Wallenstein's. The Emperor charged "the former Field Captain von Friedland" with conspiracy, sedition, defamation of the Imperial person, and attempts at dispossessing the Emperor and at usurping his crown and scepter, and he admonished the soldiers "to obey only loyal generals," such as Gallas, Aldringen, and Piccolomini.

Wallenstein appealed to regiments he still expected to stand by him. He concocted a story about a conflict between the Emperor and his son that had split the army. He asked that those who were faithful to the Emperor be faithful to him. The story was little believed. The commander added a sequel, telling of the Emperor's intention to make the army "independent." The gathering point of his independent army should be Eger (Cheb), in the strategic northwestern corner of Bohemia.

The garrison of Eger consisted of one regiment under Lieutenant Colonel Gordon, a Protestant Scotsman. On February 24, 4 P.M., Wallenstein arrived with a regiment of dragoons commanded by a noble Catholic Irishman, Walter Butler. Unknown to Wallenstein, Butler had been in contact with Gallas and Piccolomini through the good offices of an army chaplain who said that the Irishman was ready to perform a heroic deed. Also, Gordon and his assistant commander, Leslie, another Scotsman, were anxious to cast their lot with Wallenstein's enemies and, in turn, to perform heroic deeds. Deeds—heroic, ambitious, or egotistical —all had a common denominator: murder.

On February 25, Wallenstein rested in a private home on Eger's Ring. His hostess, the widow of burgher Pachelbel, was a drab person, indifferent to events beyond her nervous comprehension.

Wallenstein did not want to attend a banquet which Walter Butler had arranged for that evening in the Castle of Eger. But Gordon and Leslie would be there, and so would Wallenstein's close associates, Illo, Terzky, and Count Kinsky. Only after the other guests had arrived did Butler learn that Wallenstein would not come. He had intended to commit the deed right at the banquet and had to revise his scheme.

The party opened as if nothing had happened. There was plenty of food, and even more wine. There were confused and hypocritical toasts. When the sweetmeats were served, one hundred Irish dragoons from Butler's force entered the hall with several of Butler's officers. Illo, Terzky, and Kinsky were slain before they knew what had hit them.

Leslie, taking charge of a number of dragoons, rushed to the main guardhouse of Eger to assume control of the city against a possible uprising of forces loyal to Wallenstein. Gordon, together with other dragoons under Captain Devereux, raced to the widow Pachelbel's house, where they found Wallenstein in his bedroom. His last words are not authentically recorded. The closing paragraph of his incredible tale remains vague and fragmentary. Wallenstein died, pierced by Captain Devereux' halberd. The life of a titan is as easily extinguished as that of the humblest and weakest of men.

Control of Eger remained in the hands of Wallenstein's murderers. Most of his troops accepted his violent death without a sign of emotion; a small rebellion of one regiment was put down almost leisurely.

Rewards were paid to the participants in the murder, but their total amounted to but a fraction of the proceeds of the assassination. Wallenstein's coffers are said to have contained 9,285,589.20 gulden, Terzky's almost 4,000,000. The dead men's properties were confiscated, and accountants, used to underassessing values, arrived at a figure of 15,007,-703.50 gulden. But Wallenstein's usurer-creditors went empty-handed.

The puzzling cycle of a fantastic career, which had opened with a crooked game of figures, closed fittingly with a crooked report on assets.

The sufferings of human objects of conquest were not alleviated by the event. Disaster, perpetually in motion, trampled on.

CHAPTER THIRTY

In the upper Danube Valley, mothers still sing the old lullaby:

> *Pray, children, pray.*
> *Tomorrow comes the Swede.*
> *Tomorrow then comes Oxenstern,*
> *Who'll teach the children to pray . . .*

Today's children have heard of many a bugbear that came since, and the fervor of children of the Thirty Years' War concentrated on their rumbling tummies. To them and their parents, every "comer" was an ogre against whom prayers offered no protection. Rarely in the history of human ordeals had faith been at so low an ebb. God seemed to have forsaken His men and to be sublimely unconcerned with the wickedness of two-legged creatures.

No earthquakes, no floods, not even severe storms, are recorded. Settlements and their inhabitants rotted through man-wrought destruction, and nature covered ruin with a luxuriant growth more eloquent than the construction of places of worship. Practically no new churches were built. The highest ecclesiastical authorities used their funds to keep the war going.

In late May 1634, an Imperial army of 15,000 infantry and 10,000 cavalry marched from Bohemia toward the Bavarian Danube. On June 3, they opened a cannonade against the fortifications of Regensburg. On July 9, the bridge of stone, which had resisted demolition charges, was in the attackers' hands. Walls were breached in various places, gunpowder magazines empty. The commander, Lars Kagge, asked for terms. Parleys dragged on for three weeks. Eventually, Kagge was granted safe conduct for the garrison, free exercise of religion for the citizenry; actually, the garrison was reduced to a small band of stragglers, and the citizenry did not practice religion.

The furies of war continued their *danse macabre* along the Bavarian

Danube, no matter which flag waved from the battlements of Regensburg.

The Emperor's son Ferdinand and Gallas conquered Donauwörth, where the mighty Danube is still a precocious rivulet, and from there went to Nördlingen, for more than four centuries a free city of the Reich; with its picturesque towers and battlements, its gables and balconies, it looked like a giant's toy box. Nördlingen closed its ornate doors to the Imperial army. Gallas received reinforcements, and on September 2, the Imperial artillery hurled its first balls against the city; on September 6, fifteen Swedish mass assaults collapsed. Retreat turned into a rout.

Swabia, Franconia, all of the uppermost part of the Danube Valley, came under Imperial control. But Ferdinand and Gallas did not exploit victory. War begot and sustained but did not smother war.

In 1635, two months of deliberations produced a mock peace: The Peace of Prague, which stipulated in detail restitutions, confiscations, amnesties, pensions, transfers, and retransfers. The Emperor reserved for himself the right to decree changes of religion; those who refused could migrate and take their possessions along.

Already millions had died, objects of immense value had been destroyed, but nobody who read the clumsily worded document could have understood either meaning or objective of the sacrifices. Seventeen years after the defenestration, peace paid a call on Prague, a travesty of peace, of which most mercenaries remained unaware.

Emperor Ferdinand suffered from dropsy. En route to Regensburg he lost consciousness and was expected to die, but he recovered sufficiently to be carried aboard a boat to Vienna, where he concerned himself with his estate. Four children laid claim to his allegedly indivisible Austrian realm. Bloated, suffering, he hoped that peace would solve his problems. The Pope made an attempt to bring it about, but France raised insoluble problems and Sweden refused to accept papal mediation.

Ferdinand devoted his sinking powers to settling the income of his youngest son, who, without being ordained, held four war-scarred bishoprics.

On February 15, 1637, Ferdinand II passed away, not yet fifty-nine years old but looking one hundred. Ferdinand III, who succeeded him, was twenty-nine, frail, affable, a gifted musician, but otherwise undistinguished.

The Emperor convoked a Diet to Regensburg for the first time in twenty-seven years. Viewed from the distance, the city looked its traditional, proud, artistic self. But visitors found the ancient jewel of the upper Danube Valley neglected, decaying, demoralized. Sessions were scheduled to open on July 26, 1640, but not until September 23 was a quorum assembled. Participants talked peace and war credits. They were bored; Regensburg smelled. The Swedish general, Count Banér, drafted a bold and dramatic plan to seize Regensburg, and capture the talkers and the supreme member of the house-divided, the Emperor. He was reinforced by troops under another Swedish general, who called himself Stålhandske (Hand of Steel). On January 12, 1641, they approached Bavaria. The winter was unusually severe; drifting ice on the Danube coagulated into a solid cover. Eight days later, Swedish vanguards reached the river. However, from the opposite direction came Imperial regiments headed for Regensburg through meadows silvery with hoar-frost. They entered the city, and on January 22, when Banér came in sight, he found it in an unexpected state of preparedness.

The general waited five days. A sudden thaw set in; the ice cracking open sounded like cannon booms. Banér made one attempt to cross the rebellious river near Deggendorf, but eventually abandoned his plan and made for Bohemia, leaving desolation in his wake. Hotly pursued by Piccolomini, he could not stay in Bohemia either and continued through Saxony to Halberstadt, where he died on May 20, 1641. It is said that his powers of resistance were "consumed by excesses."

The general's demise produced a few minor mutinies: regimental commanders made violent attempts to collect what was due to them from Banér's war chest. But Piccolomini missed his opportunities; there was only minor action.

From Sweden, a new commander in chief was on his way to Central Europe, cautiously carried in a sedan chair by specially trained attendants; Field Marshal Lennart Torstensson suffered from a gout that turned a minor shock into insufferable torture. He could neither ride on horseback nor walk. But his very ordeal made him eager to see other people suffer. In him, the satanism of war had another worthy priest.

The Regensburg Diet continued in session for almost another year, achieving what could be expected: absolutely nothing.

Another crisis, the worst in years, was at hand. In July and August 1643, Torstensson camped in southern Moravia; his cavalry patrolled Lower Austria down to the Danube and the vicinity of Vienna.

"Tomorrow comes the Swede." The Swedes came with torch and tricks—the drink of liquid manure, and goats licking people to death.

And further east, in the Danube Valley, George Rákóczy, who for more than a decade had schemed and plotted to enlarge his Hungarian-Transylvanian domain, was on the warpath. It had taken much diplo-

matic skill to get into position again after he had once exited from the
scene at a time when Gustavus Adolphus had hoped for his continued
collaboration. Rákóczy respectfully asked Oxenstierna for men, weapons, and subsidies; he humbly applied for a political free hand from
Turkey and tried to placate the Bethlen family. He first found the Swede
unresponsive, Turkey aggressive, the Bethlens defiant. His ambassadors
roamed from Stockholm to Constantinople in quest of a formula. Eventually, Torstensson dispatched to Rákóczy's Transylvanian residence two
German Protestant colonels, who told him to attack the Emperor at once.
Their host threw lavish parties, bragged about his army of 40,000, nay
50,000, and all the means to engage in a large-scale campaign; but when
the fog of wine lifted, he wanted reinforcements, artillery, subsidies, and
some extra cash to bribe Turkish officials into thwarting ratification of
another treaty which the Imperial government and that of Turkey had
recently signed, and into giving him their blessing to join the Swedes and
the French.

This time, Oxenstierna was agreeable, but the French government
asked that compacts be drafted in a manner that left nothing to chance.
Many months went by. Rákóczy stepped up his demands for men and
money, and even asked for some reinsurance in case the venture went
awry, an annual pension of 40,000 thaler for his family.

His demands were granted, compacts drafted, redrafted, and signed.
When the Swedes patrolled the Austrian Danube Valley, Rákóczy opened
up with a resounding manifesto to the Hungarian nation, appealing to
his countrymen to fight for their freedom.

The Hungarians, of course, were not to be freed from the Turkish
yoke and did not collect pensions, but the manifesto entered the pages
of glorified history, and it asserted that general response was elating.

On February 2, 1644, Rákóczy was poised to strike a massive blow in
the Danube Valley, but, by then, Torstensson's army had moved away,
toward distant Denmark, whose King had turned against Sweden.

Twelve thousand Imperials under Palatine Eszterházy pressed Rákóczy's host back all the way from Pressburg, beyond the Danube to the
Tisza Valley. Both parties were anxious to avoid trespassing on Turkish-
held territory. Rákóczy turned into a liability on the Franco-Swedish
balance sheet.

The tide of war again turned in the direction of the upper Danube.

In the fall of 1644, General Gallas, whom an official report called
"sick, decaying, lost," could no longer evade an engagement. His army
was badly mauled. By the end of January 1645, Swedish vanguards in-

vested the martyrized land again, and a few weeks later, Torstensson, suffering cruelly in the rough weather, arrived with the bulk of his army. The wretched Gallas was superseded by Field Marshal Hatzfeldt.

On March 24, Torstensson cowered in his sedan chair before the rickety walls of Krems. A stream of burghers and peasants cluttered the Danube bridge of nearby Stein and the rough roads to Vienna. Only a few could make the voyage by boat, as almost no river craft was left. Those few reached Vienna; the others were overtaken by Swedish cavalrymen, who robbed and butchered to their hearts' delight.

Krems fell, Stein fell, but the bridge was shaky and the sweeping hill beyond, crowned by the fortresslike monastery of Göttweig, made a forced river crossing against gathering defenders inadvisable.

Torstensson left only a screen of marauding cavalry on the right bank, kept his main forces on the left, and, in April, moved on to invest Vienna.

The Emperor had been in Prague when Gallas was defeated. He returned to his capital on a detour via Regensburg. All Austrian provinces were ordered to mobilize and to make contributions.

Torstensson established headquarters in Stammersdorf, virtually a suburb of Vienna. Klosterneuburg, on the Danube bank, in sight of the city walls, was in Swedish hands. Villages and farms smoldered; Torstensson appealed to the destitute peasants to join his army, but they did not heed the appeal. He called on Rákóczy to march to Vienna, but Rákócyz did not budge.

The Swedish army was not equipped for a prolonged siege, and not strong enough numerically for one great, reckless assault. Its commander turned away to southern Moravia, where there were still spoils to grab, but remained within a distance of eighty miles from the Danube Valley.

A small memorial was built in a tiny village near Stammersdorf. The inscription reads: "Thus far and no further came the Swedish horsemen." The memorial still stands. Oddly enough, a subsequent Swedish thrust also got just so far and no further than the previous one.

In May of 1645, Rákóczy's cavalry strayed to within thirty miles east of Vienna. Camping in the vicinity of the battlefield on which the first Habsburg Emperor had won his crown, he negotiated simultaneously with Ferdinand III, with France, with Turkey. In Turkey, his ambassador was outbribed by the Emperor's plenipotentiary, so Rákóczy made peace with the Emperor, who gave him a number of castles and estates in return for a pledge to sever alliances with Sweden and France.

The gout hit Torstensson harder than the enemy, and by the end of 1645, he surrendered his command to General Karl Gustav Wrangel.

Protagonists—or rather, names—changed, and numbers. Ferdinand III was not essentially different from the second Ferdinand; Gustavus Adolphus' remains fell to dust, but ubiquitous Oxenstierna directed Swedish policies even after the adolescent Queen of Sweden came to dislike him intensely. Richelieu breathed his last on December 4, 1642, but his powerful position was occupied by another cardinal, Jules Mazarin, who continued where his predecessor left off. Generals changed in kaleidoscopic procession; brutes and blockheads, sophisticated strategists and primitive improvisers, daring soldiers, and frustrated temporizers; none of them obtained a decision, all just fed the Moloch of war.

Ever since the dull Diet of Regensburg, international busybodies racked sterile brains to organize conferences between belligerents; party lines defied definition—today's allies could be tomorrow's enemies and vice versa—diplomatic bureaucrats dreamed up formalistic obstacles to peace talks. Imperial agents claimed that nobody but the Emperor should be addressed "Your Majesty"; their French counterparts insisted that their King was "His Majesty"; circumstantial haggling developed over the opening formula of credentials, and it took almost four years for the credentials to be drafted in the conventional manner. Not before June 1645 were French and Swedes ready to present preliminary terms. They included the restoration of conditions as they had existed prior to 1618 (which, however, did not mean the territorial *status quo ante bellum*, since the proponents asked for cessions of territory to themselves) and what amounted to the breaking up of the Empire into many sovereign states all represented in the Diet, every single one of which had the power to veto every resolution. Sweden added vaguely worded demands for religious reforms; Cardinal Mazarin could not very well endorse requests that were detrimental to the Catholic Church, but he did not oppose them.

The Emperor's reply dwelt upon formalities; it circumscribed essentials, but did not accept the basic claims.

Fires kept burning, guns firing; jocose lansquenets forced "drink" down gasping throats; neither the torturers nor their victims knew of the high-level exchange of notes and political incivilities.

The barter for peace did not subside after the exchanges of 1645, and the game of intrigue reached a climax when Bavaria and France came to unofficial terms at the Emperor's expense.

On September 13, 1646, still two years prior to the war's official end, the Emperor ceded Alsace to France against an indemnity of 3,000,-000 livres—1,200,000 thaler. One year later, Sweden received territorial grants in Pomerania and the Baltic region. Negotiations continued in Münster and in Osnabrück.

Chances of an early peace were impaired by meddling prelates and generals, princes and princelings, and by diplomatic misunderstandings, some of them not involuntary. But, as the year of 1648 drew to a close, the treaties of Münster and Osnabrück were signed. The clock of history struck "peace."

Provinces changed hands, but provinces were in ruins. Millions were paid in cash and in bonds of dubious value, but high as nominal figures were, the rate was less than one thaler per human life destroyed. Religious privileges were granted, restored, withdrawn; they did not benefit the humble faithful, but were devices of mastery for the mighty, means to divide and to conquer.

Scores of millions of words have been written about the senselessly tragic episode called the Thirty Years' War and the compacts of Münster and Osnabrück that were called Peace.

The uprooted peasants, the shiftless soldiery, all the jetsam and flotsam of nightmarish decades continued uprooted and shiftless; they could not adapt themselves to an orderly life, which, in itself, carries the germs of evolution. A few aristocrats, ground in the mills of disaster, reached the point of no return to splendor, and turned hirelings and initiators of rebellion, bent at keeping the forges of destruction blazing; burghers, whose life expectancy was suddenly prolonged from hours or days to years, reveled and had no other objective than frolicking for its own sake.

Records of destruction during the Thirty Years' War in Bavaria and Upper and Lower Austria are far from complete, but figures from Bohemia are indicative of what the war did to lands and people.

In 1618, Bohemia had 782 towns, 36,000 villages and hamlets, a population of 2,500,000, and 150,000 peasant families lived on their own land.

In 1648, only 230 towns and 6000 villages and hamlets were left, less than 30,000 peasant families still had farms; the population figure was down to 700,000—a total human loss of over 70 per cent.

The percentage of human loss all over the German Empire was but slightly lower. Close to 10,000,000 had died there.

Compared with these figures, combat casualties were negligible. The rate of human devastation of the Thirty Years' War can be compared only with that of the conquest of China by the Mongolians.

Embattled but surviving townships were left in a condition of ruin that matched that of bombed cities after World War II.

CHAPTER THIRTY-ONE

Pleasure-seeking townspeople and aristocrats who had not irrevocably bet on wrong horses recuperated, partly in licentiousness, partly by sponsoring the noble arts. The Imperial Court, like lesser households, accepted unsinking debt as an economic *Weltanschauung,* putting splendor and pleasure above budgeting. They built new castles while fortress walls decayed, and they indulged in entertainment with little concern about tomorrow's essentials.

Events showed that creative talent was not eliminated, not even adversely affected by torture, starvation, and permanent instability. There were poets, musicians, and builders to satisfy every demand. Mankind's potentials are a tough vegetation. It takes more than a long, devastating war to extirpate it.

The poet laureate of the war was Hans Jakob von Grimmelshausen, a chronicler less eloquent and imaginative than any other narrator of conflagration from Julius Caesar to Romain Rolland. His *Adventurous Simplicissimus* is a soldier's story, so vivid and exciting that many modern war correspondents seem dull by comparison.

Johann Scheffler, the Emperor's personal physician, wrote the *Cherubic Wanderer* under his immortal pen name of Angelus Silesius.

The Jesuit theater flourished as never before. The people's craving for music was satisfied from a variety of sources, ranging from itinerant bards to distinguished composers of oratorios. Emperor Ferdinand III sponsored Italian grand opera, which was performed in the most lavish style, and he concentrated on musical composition, which was his pride and comfort, rather than on matters of state.

A rich harvest of art and science was reaped as early as the first decade that followed Münster and Osnabrück, while destruction threatened the Empire from the east.

Ferdinand III died in 1657, aged forty-nine, leaving behind many pieces of music, dubious military commitments in Italy, and an alliance with Poland which he had signed without giving it much thought.

In 1667, a brilliant theatrical event took place in Vienna: Ferdinand's heir, Emperor Leopold I, married Princess Margareta of Spain. A coronation opera was performed, *Il Pomo d'Oro* (*The Golden Apple*), a masterpiece of art and stagecraft, set to music by the most famous opera composer of the period, Marc'Antonio Cesti. The topical apple of Paris did not go to the goddesses, but to the Imperial bride, who was said to embody the best qualities of Venus, Minerva, and Juno. This sounded servile; in fact it was a political innovation to propagandize the ruler's superiority in all fields. The opera was performed three times a week with "admission to everybody." In every performance, settings were changed twenty-four times, and the most elaborate machinery was used for the pompous spectacle, including "flying machines," more than a century before the Montgolfier balloon first took to the air.

The skeptical Viennese did not believe unquestioningly in royalty's embodiment of might, beauty, and wisdom, but they relished the spectacle nonetheless.

The Imperial marriage was a brilliant affair; moneylenders from Italy to the Rhine and Danube worried about its implications.

On the Burgplatz, the glorious square outside the Imperial castle, ballets on horseback were arranged; the most elegant cavaliers on mounts of the finest breed paraded before a large and brilliant audience.

The Emperor's mother arranged intimate music festivals in her private apartments. To be admitted meant to be established at the top rung of the social ladder. Italians and Germans vied for the theatrical palm.

Leopold I was crowned at the age of eighteen. He was the product of Jesuit education that had developed his mediocre talents as far as circumstances permitted, and cleverly directed him toward conservatism, preservation, and extension of the powers of the Church. The marriage with Margareta, second daughter of King Philip of Spain, was based on reasons of state. It had been conceived when the bride-to-be was aged nine and the future groom not yet twenty. Ambassadors, prelates, statesmen, busily drafted compacts, all the bywork of matrimony, establishing Margareta's title to Spanish succession despite the priority of firstborn Infanta Maria Theresa, wife of Louis XIV of France. The result of their diplomatic maneuvers was the War of Spanish Succession, a longlasting enmity between Austria and France, and a further *rapprochement* between France and Turkey.

The sanguinary seventeenth century hardly knew the word "nationalism"; it adopted slogans of religious dominance to justify butchery; regimes dealt with lands and people as if they were objects to be acquired

by due process of unlawfulness. The people fared ill, but later generations fared little better as motives for war got social or national mis-
nomers.

The gay Viennese did not believe in "peace in our time." They had
no political philosophy, but they enjoyed glamour. Romantically inclined dignitaries thought that things were better; so did burghers with
bulging purses; and even the lower strata in the Imperial city found life
more livable and less precarious than before.

Leopold, who relied on Jewish moneylenders, invited Jews to settle in
his capital. Christian bankers and merchants resented the competition
and asked that the Jews be expelled. The Emperor tried to placate the
Christians by issuing orders of removal, but he saw to it that they were
not properly carried out. After some angry wrangling, the banishment
was really put into effect in 1670. Five years later, the Jews were back.
They found their synagogue near the bank of the Danube torn down, and
a new church, the Leopoldskirche, standing in its place. The Jews settled around the church, and the district in which they lived was called
Leopoldstadt. Leopoldstadt retained a considerable percentage of Jewish inhabitants until Hitler's day, when the smaller part of its proscribed
people escaped into exile, while the majority was shipped to the gas
chambers.

But while it was better in Vienna than before, one day's ride down the
Danube by boat or raft the "peaceful" 1660s were more sanguinary than
most periods between 1618 and 1648 had been. Bands from Transylvania, Turkish marauders, and freebooters without distinguishable marks
of origin roamed Hungary and border regions.

Turkish bands alone had burned down 428 settlements, killed over
2000 people, stole 20,000 head of cattle, and collected several hundred
thousand gulden in ransoms.

In 1658 a Turkish army assembled near Adrianople for a major campaign in the Danube Valley.

The Emperor waited for some time before he ordered ten regiments,
under the command of Margrave Hannibal of Gonzaga, to take up
positions near Komárom, but with orders not to trespass on Turkish
territory, lest Turkey feel provoked into attack.

The Turks crossed the Danube, poured across the southern and eastern
Carpathian passes, destroying every settlement on their way. The Hun-
garians could not stop the hard-hitting, fast-killing invaders. In 1660,
George Rákóczy, who could no longer play the game of diplomacy and

intrigue, made a desperate stand against the Sultan whom he dreaded, but lost battle and life near Kolozsvár (Cluj).

Three hundred miles away in Pressburg, a Hungarian Diet discussed defensive measures; the magnates wanted to be defended, but they had neither the spirit to defend themselves nor the desire to be protected by German soldiers. As eastern Hungary bled, Rákóczy died, and the Turks massed for a push west, the Emperor's Prime Minister reasoned that Turkey should be contained by every means short of war.

On April 18, 1663, Turkey declared war "against the Germans." Seven weeks later, the main army entered Belgrade. Anguished messages to Vienna put its strength at 121,000. Actually, 24,000 servants and female accessories and some 60,000 auxiliaries were included in the figure. Most auxiliaries came from Walachia and Moldavia; they were a mere rabble that could hardly be kept in formation. Only 10,000 of the regulars were elite troops. The rest were second- if not third-rate; among them were Asiatic horsemen who could not handle firearms and overage infantrymen.

They crossed the Danube in driving rain. The rain continued as soldiers waded through mud and pools. Only in July did they reach Buda, where they joined the troops of the local pasha.

The Emperor wrote from Vienna: "Daily the Turkish threat increases, and we can expect the enemy any time."

The people of Vienna turned emergency into a carnival. Owners of conveyances did a thriving business, and when Empress-mother Eleonore, accompanied by one archduke and two princesses, left for Linz, flight became the preferred topic of conversation and ditties. From churches chimed "Turk bells," and daily sheets told of thrilling horrors committed by "Turkish bloodhounds" and of how to cope with the danger.

The citizens hired carriages for escape, but usually stayed on, staged drills and parades, and, in the evening, went to the theater.

The weather in Hungary continued foul. The Great Vizier's host trudged on at a snail's pace along the right bank of the Danube toward Neuhäusel (Nové Zámky).

The commander of the fortress, Count Adam Forgach, a hot-tempered daredevil to whom battle was the true sport of a gentleman, had scouts watch the enemy advance. On the night of August 6–7, he attacked and, to his surprise, his men ran into resistance, indicating that there were more Turks than had met the scouts' eyes. At dawn, it became apparent that Forgach was facing the entire Turkish army. The rest was carnage.

A few hundred prisoners were brought before the Great Vizier, who ordered that they be "slaughtered with knives like calves or hogs." A handful of Hungarians, Count Forgach among them, escaped to Neu-häusel.

It took the Turks a full week to forge a siege ring around the poorly fortified place. Four thousand citizens took up arms in defense; a few Turkish assaults were repulsed, but when gun crews were decimated and powder stores about empty, the citizens forced Forgach and his chief of staff, Marchese Pio, to capitulate. On September 26, 1663, 2472 survivors laid down their arms.

In Hungary, meantime, Count Miklós Zrinyi engaged in lightning guerrilla warfare with the assistance of Catholic magnates, Hajdúk, and Hussar volunteers. Battles without strategic patterns were fought against impossible odds; exploits were legion; and the Great Vizier, who had no stomach for that sort of campaign, returned to Belgrade to spend the winter beyond range of Zrinyi's raids. In Belgrade, he had a super-heavy siege gun cast for future use against Vienna.

Emperor Leopold, dressed in somber Spanish gala, in which he felt more comfortable than in any other garments, traveled to Regensburg and obtained authorization from a reassembled Diet to treble the Empire's army and to use it against the Turks. German Princes contributed a few auxiliaries at a stunning per capita price, and from France came a strange offer of support, conceived in such urgent terms that the Emperor could not refuse to have 5000 French soldiers join his army; King Louis XIV staked a token force to have a foot in the door of the Imperial fortress, and to teach the Turkish government never to take French collaboration for granted. Money came from Spain and the Holy See.

Zrinyi, fierce and impetuous, scorned methodical planning. In January 1664, when Imperials and Turks drowsed in winter quarters, he took off with a motley army of 20,000, wrested a number of small fortresses from napping Turkish defenders, and stormed toward the left bank of the Hungarian Danube, inflicting heavy devastation as he raced on. It was land of the Holy Crown of St. Stephen which Zrinyi laid waste; scores of Hungarian people perished for every single Turkish soldier killed, but he did not care what sacrifices glory impelled.

The drive lasted for three weeks, then bogged down under the walls of Pécs (Fünfkirchen). Zrinyi destroyed one strategic bridge across the Danube, but Turkish engineers rebuilt it in a matter of weeks. He had captured multifarious booty, but his men were exhausted.

The "real war" of 1664 opened on April 15. Field Marshal Montecuccoli took Nitra, north of the Danube, while the Turkish army moved upstream spreading desolation and devastation in the direction of the Austrian border. The Great Vizier had twice as many combatants as the field marshal.

On July 31, they met on the banks of the river Raab, a southern tributary of the Danube. The Raab is nowhere more than twenty yards wide but its banks are steep and loamy. On August 1, a downpour swelled it into a raging torrent; no Turkish reinforcements could cross to bolster their sagging cavalry, which was pressed back right into the river. Ten thousand drowned in the muddy waters.

Victory, however, was only the beginning of trouble. The battle of St. Gotthard, as it was called, produced a disappointing peace.

Zrinyi wanted to become Palatine; when the Emperor did not grant his wish, he plotted with the Turks and got his name on the French political payroll. Another ranking magnate, Count Ferencz Nádasdy, who had offered to stage a Hungarian national demonstration of loyalty at a price which Leopold could not pay, called upon the Hungarian nation to rise against the Emperor, who, "instead of protecting the fatherland, sold it to the Turks."

On September 13, Nádasdy was arrested and taken to Vienna; Zrinyi and his relative Count Frangepan were incarcerated in Wiener Neustadt.

An extraordinary tribunal of twelve members selected from Court Council, War Council, and the local government of Lower Austria convened in Vienna. The verdict of guilty was a foregone conclusion.

Nádasdy's head fell in Vienna's city hall, Zrinyi's and Frangepan's on Wiener Neustadt's open square.

There were no issues that could have been settled. Diplomats looked for topics that would at least seem to warrant treaties. Nominal topics were formulated early in 1681. Emperor Leopold appeared before a Hungarian Diet at Sopron (Ödenburg). Papal Nuncio Buonvisi came; so did deputies of districts and townships, representatives of estates. A Palatine was elected, complaints were aired, personal animosities provided themes for acrimonious debates; messages to Turkey were discussed; candidates for appointments paraded. Clerics raised faded banners of militancy; anarchist longings found outlets in heated requests that the government relinquish many of its prerogatives. The Emperor and his government lost ground, even though the apparent profiteers' gains were no better than ephemeral.

The Turkish government could not fail to presume that the days of the Empire were numbered, that now or never was the time to plant the

Crescent in the heart of Central Europe. Turkey had a war on its hands at the mouth of the Danube, and beyond, in the Russian plains; it went well for the Turks, but settling scores with Russia could apparently wait. The weather vane of war pointed toward Vienna.

CHAPTER THIRTY-TWO

Vienna, the fancy cork tumbler of a world laboring in unavailing change, was prospering when, one day's march away, Count Thököly bickered for Imperial consent to his romance and, another day's march further to the east, death in all species mowed the Danubian fields.

Merrymakers dominated the Viennese scene; song, play, and drink were the people's major concern. Piety and restraint were left to odd characters and ludicrous nonconformists. But the Viennese loved parody, and they did not mind a tongue lashing by moralizers, provided they had a ready sharp wit, a colorful vocabulary, and a gift for play acting.

The most popular person in town, the immortal chronicler of Viennese habits and mores, was a priest, Ulrich Megerle, later known as Abraham a Santa Clara. Born in 1644 in a Swabian village, son of an impecunious innkeeper, he received his education in Austrian Jesuit and Benedictine schools, was ordained, rose to the ministry of the Augustine Church in Vienna, and became court chaplain with the unique privilege of appearing before the Emperor unannounced. Abraham was as fanatical a local patriot as only people born outside the capital could be. "Our customs may be called clumsy, rude, and old-fashioned," he would say, "but they are the most honest and straightforward of all. We send our youngsters to Italy and France to shop for wit and courtesy, but they acquire only shoddy goods." He loved the Viennese, but he castigated them in his sermons. The Augustine Church near the Imperial castle was crowded to capacity when the minister preached, in a manner unequaled even by star actors on the Jesuit stage.

The Viennese raved at his "salutary hodgepodge," his most worldly eulogy of the city's patron saint, whose virtues were not embodied in his followers, his scorn of alleged witches, his scathing dictum "Prayer is not always the answer."

Emperor Leopold relished the presence of the ascetic-looking court chaplain with the hardly concealed smirk, who told the unvarnished truth to the high and mighty. Despite his Spanish grandeur, the Emperor was enough of a Viennese to appreciate sparkling dialectics.

Abraham was a prolific writer. Some of his works crossed the Atlantic and are preserved in libraries here; they make splendid reading in their original German, but his puns and jingles, his parables and seventeenth-century allegories, defy adequate translation.

He became the chronicler of the great plague of 1679.

The plague, bred in the absurd Hungarian wars, skirted Vienna for some time. The Viennese chose to ignore it even when the Black Death sneaked into the suburbs and began to infiltrate the heart of the city. The people did not wish to look into the grim face of the Black Death. But death does not permit anybody to ignore him permanently.

In his "Take heed, Vienna," Abraham a Santa Clara relates the beginning: "The Emperor's residence in Austria, his archstronghold, that town full of honor, erudition, and power, is called Wien, with a capital W. Yet I have to remind you, with tears in my eyes, and with an aching heart, that everybody who wishes to write the name should do so with the biggest of Ws, standing for Woe, Woeful, and Wailing, Woe to Wien, Woeful Wien, people wailing for Wien.

"In the year of 1679, in early July, this famous city was at the peak of its glory. In the beautiful castle dwelled the Roman Emperor and his large retinue. The nobility, almost innumerable and of priceless magnificence, visited the castle on duty and for gala occasions; hurried couriers came and went from and to everywhere. Everything in town was prosperous, and nothing was lacking to satisfy all tastes and lusts. There was not a single pebble in Wien's more than one hundred streets which men's feet did not tread in merry and busy stride. The sound of trumpets from the courtyards of nobility, and of music from almost anywhere, produced a din that seemed to pierce the sky, and through the hole in the sky, joy descended right into Wien.

"But, oh fickleness of fortune! In mid-July, the abominable pestilence which, for quite some time, had been rampant, but was ignored by unscrupulous people as just some fever, suddenly exploded into a general virulent contagion. Suddenly, to everyone's dismay, dead bodies littered every street; dismal tragedy became manifest.

"No pen could fittingly describe the general flight that followed. It seemed as if a new Moses had arisen to guide people from Egypt to the Promised Land. By day and by night, you heard doleful farewells, and 'God protect you.' People were spurred on their hasty flight by the sordid sight of bodies lying in odd postures all around.

". . . The first breath of human life is already wrought with the sigh of death. From its first moment on, human life is under the sway of Reaper Death; the first sip from the mother's breast is a drink to the assailant of the universe; the rocking cradle is a reminder of the inconstancy of life.

"Behold, oh men! Shout it, write it down: die you must, not possibly, but certainly. You don't know when, where, and how you shall die, but death is certain. Men's life is less permanent than that of a leaf on a tree, a shadow on a wall, a house built of sand. . . .

"Death is a thunderbolt that hits not only the frail hut of straw but also the monarch's stately mansion. To death, a crown of gold and a shabby cap, a scepter and an ax, a purple cloak and a crude jacket, all look the same, and carry the same weight.

"Death was, indeed, the supreme ruler of Vienna. It first began to flare up in Leopoldstadt. For quite some time, it devoured people in a rather thrifty manner. Then, pestilence crept across the Danube, into other suburbs. However, it seemed at first as if death did not dare to invade the heart of the city, and would satisfy its murderous lust in the outskirts.

"There was a great deal of devastation. Filthy alleys were hardest hit, and the most affected were the vulgar mob, the kind of vagabonds that could be found in every town. Respectable people trusted that only the rabble would succumb to the scythe of death; that death took only the chaff, searched beggars' bags, quenched its hunger from paupers' crumbs, and that mansions and fine houses were sanctuaries.

"But death spoke up: 'Hey, you, you ought to realize that no fortress is so strong that I cannot carry it by assault, be its ramparts and bastions as high as the highest mountain, and surrounded by a moat that could lend water to the ocean. I shall conquer this city despite everything.' At the time of Dictator Caesar, an ox talked in Rome; at Prophet Balsam's time, a jenny ass spoke; at Bede's time, the stones spoke. In Vienna, when sick men cower on one corner and dying men sigh on the other, when a few steps away corpses lie right in the way of carts, streets and rows seem to talk, to exhort people to repent and do penance.

"Who stayed in Vienna in the month of September 1679 must bear

witness that no painter could depict the misery; that death has so raged
that it seemed an epilogue with the world's end at hand. . . .

"There is not a single street or row in Vienna and its suburbs over
which raging death does not roam. . . ."

Thus far the chronicler.

Many fled, the Emperor and most of his family among them. Horses
and carriages were at a premium; Danube boats were little in demand,
since salvation lay upstream and oarsmen were almost impossible to get.

Pestilence caught the careless authorities unprepared, but even had the
authorities been keenly aware of the danger, preventive measures would
have been too primitive to cope with, or to substantially reduce, the
threat.

A contemporary etching shows an improvised "plague hospital," several of which were established in barracklike structures. Over crude,
ladderlike stairways, "sick wardens" carried the stricken like potato bags,
depositing their loads on rickety cots, from where orderlies removed them
after they had breathed their last, to drop them through chutes to the
ground below. The etching does not show any physicians in attendance.

The Viennese medical faculty of 1679 was not inferior to its counterparts elsewhere in the civilized world, and Vienna's physicians did the
best they could. It was not their fault that the best was not nearly good
enough.

From the ground to which they were dropped, the dead were taken to
deep ditches dug by militia and sick wardens and thrown into these cess-
pools of pestilence. Lime was applied as a sterilizer.

The sick wardens—their official designation was *Krankenknechte*—
were untrained, medically unskilled, and dedicated to nothing but earn-
ings as they could be grabbed. Most of these men were, in fact, the scum
of filthy alleys and rows. They were hired by city officials who had stayed
in town, and paid paltry wages, but they made more money by taking
valuables from the stricken and selling dead men's clothes. Quite a few
murders were committed and the victims handed over to the sick wardens,
who looted and deposited them in the sordid ditches. The identity of
corpses and the causes of their demise were never checked.

As murder and pillage got out of control, military commanders staged
some hangings, mostly of sick wardens.

Nobody interfered with excesses of a different nature. The Viennese
who remained, and whom death seemed to ignore temporarily, reveled
as never before. They crowded inns and, while trumpets no longer
flourished in the courtyards of nobility, music from pubs frolicked with-

out letup. Popular minstrels made resounding appearances, mocking death, and, more often than not, succumbed to it. The most popular of minstrels was one Augustin, whose song *"Oh, du lieber Augustin, alles ist hin"* ("Oh my dear Augustin, everything's gone . . .") was the rave of a moribund city. The minstrel is said to have been a sick warden before he struck it rich. The inn to which he attracted the crowd was almost two hundred years old, and it has survived to the present day. Its name is Griechenbeisel (Greek Pub), and the beverages they served since the outgoing Middle Ages had a well-deserved reputation of stimulative effect. Augustin was a heavy drinker and an accomplished dancer. His staggering motions derided disaster and inspired merrymakers in the face of death. Augustin's authentic biography was never written, but the man who danced to the lyrics "everything's gone" was a symbol of the town.

The scythe of pestilence missed him by a hairbreadth. Strolling through the nocturnal streets, loaded to capacity with the Griechenbeisel's potent drinks, he fell, or was pushed, into a ditch full of corpses. There he slept soundly until he was awakened by a corpse thrown on top of him. No one, least of all Augustin, could have told how long he had been snoring atop the pestilence-exuding pile, but it was high noon when the seedy minstrel crawled out of the pit, whole, uninfected, and not even divested of his bagpipe. In the evening he was back at the Griechenbeisel.

All houses in which more than three persons had been stricken were ordered closed under penalty of death, but a check disclosed that only twenty houses were unaffected, and so the ordinance was not carried out. In the largest house in town, the number of dead exceeded three hundred. Official statistics were all contradictory, one giving the number of dead at 49,486, another at 122,849.

The cold season brought the calamity to an end. By Christmas most fugitives had returned; on Christmas Eve, ninety-five couples were wed in St. Stephen's Cathedral. New settlers flocked into the city. A memorial to the plague was completed in 1693, the Trinity Column on the Graben, a highly artistic combination of realism and allegory. The Viennese call it *Pestsäule* (Plague Column).

The survivors of 1679 had reason to anticipate another affliction, but Augustin, singing, belching, dancing, and staggering, had nothing to sing or mimic about Turkey and war.

Activities in the city's fortified zone could not be conveniently overlooked by the merry townspeople, yet they were not scared. The Viennese liked spectacular constructions, be it churches, palaces, columns, theaters, or fortresses.

A new military commander, Count Ernst Rüdiger von Starhemberg, who was appointed shortly after the end of the plague, cracked the whip over slack working parties. The people applauded him. Why should their town not have the finest fortress? Pressing the rabble into construction labor kept them out of violent mischief. Vienna became the most modern bulwark, built according to the latest designs by Italian, Dutch, and French fortress engineers.

It had twelve projecting, and reciprocally covering, bastions, and an equal number of *curtines* (ramparts), which were, in turn, protected by peaked bulwarks (ravelins). A wide moat surrounded the defenses; the outer part of the moat was enclosed by a covered gangway, reinforced by embankments of soil and palisades. Many gun emplacements were built, most of them mounted with cannon.

The Viennese liked to picnic in the fortified zone and proudly took visitors from abroad sight-seeing through ramparts, ravelins, and palisades. Among the visitors were gentlemen from France, Hungary, and the Orient, who voiced admiration of the stronghold and made sketches to serve as souvenirs. In this manner, the Emperor's enemies learned every detail of the defenses of the capital!

Leopold considered Louis XIV the most aggressive of his foes; Imperial and French armies had, of late, fought a series of engagements in which the Emperor's men fared rather badly; a French spearhead pointed toward the Rhine to the sources of the Danube. Yet a French assault on Vienna seemed unlikely. Diplomats who knew their way around the labyrinth of Turkish statecraft warned of Great Vizier Kara Mustapha's hostile designs, but the government relied upon compacts which assured peace with Turkey at least until 1684 and probably could be prolonged at a bargain price. Emperor Leopold did everything to humor Turkey, and otherwise believed that spectacular fortifications were a deterrent to war.

The greatest statesman of the late seventeenth century was Pope Innocent XI, Benedetto Odescalchi, who was sixty-five when he ascended the throne of Peter in 1676. As a cardinal, he had struggled against the immorality of the clergy and had tried to combat Louis XIV's cabals. He now wanted the evil in the East to be stamped out by a crusade that would unify the faithful against the infidels. If the vast resources of the huge Christian territories could be united, the West would dominate the world. Protestants were welcome.

Francesco Buonvisi, Papal Nuncio to Vienna, championed the crusade with noble eloquence but little resonance. The Court saw no point in lofty designs, but the Emperor's hereditary predilection for matchmaking resulted in a *rapprochement* with Poland. Leopold offered an Imperial Princess as a bride for King John Sobieski's son, and a vacant duchy in Silesia as a premium for a defensive alliance.

Great Vizier Kara Mustapha, whatever his personal pitfalls, was a man of immense ambitions, the guiding one of which was to conquer Vienna and to follow Attila's path to the Occident. The French ambassador to Turkey used skill and charm to goad him and keep him from diverting forces toward secondary enemies.

On September 30, 1681, the French armies seized Strasbourg. Emperor Leopold shouted that he would rather lose a town to the Turks than unguard his western border. You could always recover what you had lost to Turkey, but not what you had had to cede to France.

In the fall of 1682, most of northern Hungary was in the hands of the Emperor's eastern enemies; flying columns fanned out in the Danube Valley.

French military engineers, superbly trained sappers among them, enlisted in the Turkish army. They had detailed plans of the fortifications of Vienna and prepared drafts of trenches to be dug to invest strong points without heavy loss.

In October, Sultan Mahomet IV and Great Vizier Kara Mustapha left for Adrianople, the traditional gathering place for Turkish mass armies. All accredited envoys had to accompany the Sultan. Emperor Leopold received a note saying that there was no choice; he had to stand and fight. Yet another note implored him to mobilize every available man and gun, and to meet the invaders in Hungary.

By the year's end, the Emperor did not have his men and guns mobilized; nor had his court resigned itself to the fact that all-out war was on its way from the southeast.

King John Sobieski, however, was in a fighting mood. He had learned of a French scheme to overthrow him in favor of a ruler more amenable to Louis' designs, and he now wanted to support the Emperor, come what may.

On March 31, 1683, their great alliance was signed. It provided that the Emperor put 60,000 and the King 40,000 men into the field. These forces would operate jointly only if either Vienna or Kraków should be attacked.

Also on March 31, 1683, Sultan and Great Vizier decamped from Adrianople. The army slowly rolled toward Belgrade, where it arrived on May 3. The town could not hold even a major part of the army and baggage. Outside Belgrade, all along the Danube and Sava rivers, tents sprang up; campfires were lit; riverbanks looked like a martial country fair.

From Asia had come mounted men who became the bugbears of every district through which they rode; and from what would, two hundred years later, be Rumania, came mercenaries, the scum of a destitute peasantry.

Three weeks later, the army rambled on, over pontoon bridges, in the direction of Osijek (Esseg).

Soldiers, merchants, gamblers, quacks, whores, homosexual boys, fortunetellers, vendors of every imaginable and quite a few unimaginable services, long processions of pack animals, including thousands of camels and hundreds of artillery pieces of the latest design, stretched out for miles on end.

Kara Mustapha was the army's chief commander in the field. His personal baggage included a tent of the finest heaviest painted silk, the size of a small modern city block. The tent contained several ultra-luxurious apartments with bathing installations with water running through tubs for the benefit of the Great Vizier's well-stocked harem. The ladies had maids, lap dogs, and a wardrobe and cosmetics that held transportation priority over cannon balls.

Had a reasonably mobile force attacked the Turks on the march, disaster would have been inevitable. But as Kara Mustapha well knew through his informers, the enemy was not ready.

The Sultan returned to his residence. Before leaving Belgrade, he issued a proclamation to Emperor Leopold and King John Sobieski, which was his way of declaring war. It read:

"We, Mola Mahomet, by the grace of the God who rules and commands the heavens, glorious and all-powerful Emperor of Babylon and Juda, of the Orient and the Occident, King of all earthly and heavenly Kings, Great-King of Holy Arabia and Mesopotamia, by birth resplendent King of Jerusalem, ruler and lord of the grave of the crucified god of the infidels, we pledge to you, Caesar of Rome, and you, King of Poland, our most sacred word, and be it known to all your followers, that We are about to invade your puny countries and that We have with Us thirteen Kings with 1,300,000 soldiers, infantry, and cavalry, and with that host, the very existence of which defies your imagination, We shall tread your puny countries under horseshoes, and put them to fire and sword without mercy or compassion. We hereby command you to wait for Us in your residential city of Vienna so that We may have you beheaded there, and the same goes for you, petty King of Poland. We shall exterminate you and all your followers, and make the *giaours* [Christians], the lowliest of God's creatures, perish from this earth. Adults and children alike will be subjected to the most cruel of tortures before I shall make them suffer the most shameful of deaths. I shall take away from you your puny realms, and clear them of their entire population. But I shall let live both of you, Caesar and King of Poland, long enough to convince yourselves that We have fulfilled all parts of Our pledge. This shall serve as your guidance."

CHAPTER THIRTY-THREE

On June 26, 1683, Kara Mustapha arrived in Székesfehérvár, not far from the Austrian border. There the Khan of the Tatars joined him with his savage horsemen, and the Pasha of Buda came with his regular troops.

Three days later, the advance resumed toward Györ. Nothing had stood in the Turks' way thus far; nothing prevented them from bursting into Imperial territory.

The Imperial Court War Council later claimed that it had intended to strike before the Turks reached the border, but that the unexpected speed of the enemy advance had foiled its intentions.

In fact, the Turks covered an average of five miles per day. But the Imperial army, instead of the contractual 60,000, numbered 32,000. Despite the imminent threat to Vienna, not a single man or gun had yet arrived from Poland. And there is reason to assume that Kara Mustapha's fighting men numbered almost 275,000.

Commander of the Imperial army was Duke Charles of Lorraine, husband of the Emperor's stepsister and governor of the Tyrol. The Duke was a scholarly strategist, but critics contend that he was bolder in defense than in attack, and always prepared to trade ground for time.

On July 2, he staged a strategic withdrawal. He ordered infantry and artillery to march along Great Schütt Isle in the Danube, in the direction of Vienna, while cavalry covered the passage over the Leitha River. But swarms of Tatars forded the Leitha and roamed the approaches to the Vienna Woods. On July 6, Kara Mustapha headed for Vienna.

Cavalry officers raced to Vienna, where the Court and part of the citizenry blinded themselves to the last against the mortal threat.

The estafettes of disaster reached the city gates on July 7, at 4 P.M. Heedless of strollers and vehicles, they galloped through the streets right to the Imperial castle, leaving injury and panic in their wake. They delivered an oral message: "There is not a single moment to lose. The Imperial family must leave at once."

Four hours passed before Leopold, his Empress, their kin, and cumbersome luggage were ready and the first Imperial carriages, coachmen furiously whipping thoroughbred horses, rattled away. It was a large convoy; hundreds of servants accompanied their Imperial masters. Soon, all streets were jam-packed with less illustrious though still ponderous fugitives. Members of the nobility and foreign diplomats clamored for the right of way, their servants recklessly fighting to break through walls of wailing people. Rumors had it that the army of Duke Charles had been annihilated. The exodus was more turbulent than it had been four years before when the plague struck. Taverns stayed almost empty that night; people would rather listen to rumor mongers, however sordid, than to minstrels, however popular.

The Imperial family headed for Linz, which seemed safe as long as Vienna did not fall; and if Vienna fell, the days of the Empire would be numbered.

By midnight of July 7, it seemed as if Vienna could not be defended, but when July 8 dawned, panic subsided. Garrison commander Count Starhemberg co-operated with a newly established civilian authority, headed by seventy-two-year-old Count Kaplirs. The mayor of Vienna, Johann Andreas von Liebenberg, proclaimed that citizens would stake their lives and property in defense of their town.

All able-bodied men were ordered to work on palisades, fieldworks, and gun emplacements. Nobody disobeyed the order. The mayor led the citizens, pushing a cartload of earth and stones. Work, not always the Viennese' forte, created an almost happy frame of mind. Wits coined puns directed against Turks and fugitives alike.

Gunpowder and cannon balls arrived from Krems by boat on the Danube. Traffic on the river still moved freely from the west.

In the afternoon of July 8, fortification workers spotted cavalry heading from Fischamend for the suburbs of Tabor and Leopoldstadt. They were no foes, but Imperial soldiers; with them was the Duke of Lorraine.

Rumors about the annihilation of the Imperial army were superseded by fictitious accounts of Turkish defeats.

On July 13, Imperial infantry reached Vienna. Burghers formed eight companies, university students another; merchants and guilds did the same, and court servants who had missed the convoy to Linz also enlisted. The Emperor's chief ranger, Baron Kielmansegg, came with a group of sharpshooters. All reinforcements combined brought the number of defenders to 16,000.

The Bishop of Wiener Neustadt, Count Kolonitsch, rushed to Vienna to organize hospitals. Kolonitsch, who had once fought as a Maltese Knight on the island of Crete, was an expert in various essential fields and, even better, he carried several hundred thousand gulden for medical purposes.

It was dusk when the bishop arrived. Nobody in Vienna slept that night of July 14. Military and civilian authorities had ordered that all suburbs be put to the torch. A belt of fire ringed the fortifications. In the small hours, a brisk wind sprang up, carrying a hail of sparks across the walls. The Schottenhof caught fire; one arsenal, in which most of the city's gunpowder was stored, was a very short distance away.

The Schottenhof still burned when the first Turkish spahis came within sight of the walls; still on July 14, a tight row of enemy troops clamped a siege crescent around Vienna, leaving the waterfront unblocked.

The Duke's troops, trading vital space for dubious time, fell back in good order. Hindsighted chroniclers praised the retreat as a superb preparation for relief of the capital, a clearly calculated risk. But in July 1683, it was a meek gamble to avoid a bold move; an outflanking attack on the clumsy Turkish columns as they pushed on over tortuous dirt tracks south of the Danube, would have been better strategy.

The citizens of Vienna did not talk strategy; war had come to roost; this was their home battle. Nothing mattered but their bastions, their cannon, their banners, and their bodies. Turkish soldiers set up tents, built artillery emplacements, began to sap trenches, while oriental merchants set up booths.

In the beleaguered city, the inns flourished; minstrels offered boisterous entertainment and patrons indulged in a braggadocio that was less barbarous but fully as magniloquent as the Sultan's declaration of war.

On July 16, the rear guards of the Imperial army vanished out of sight and Kara Mustapha's men occupied Leopoldstadt. The siege crescent shaped into a ring and, as night fell again, the still smoldering remains of suburbs along the left bank of the Danube provided ghastly light for the construction of Turkish siege batteries.

From the southern sector, the first Turkish cannon balls whizzed toward the city, aimed at scaring the defenders rather than destroying the solid bulwarks. A few missiles hit houses. Burghers tore down shingle roofs to reduce fire hazards. They did it in a mocking frame of mind, saying that Kara Mustapha would have to put every shingle back in place, after his army had been destroyed.

Kara Mustapha's tent was installed by a working crew big enough to build a dozen battery emplacements. Female occupants of luxury compartments moved in with shouts, chatter, and barking lap dogs.

Defenders of the western sector could see the besieger's headquarters, which were located near the present site of the Deutsches Volkstheater, less than half a mile from the deserted Imperial castle.

The head of the Turkish intelligence services, who had once drawn a fine sketch of the fortifications, held the floor throughout most of the Turkish war council's first session. Swarthy Achmed Bey, who looked more oriental than both the Great Vizier and the Pasha of Buda, was, in fact, Italian-born, a former Capuchin monk who had dropped the cowl. The master spy introduced his own sketches and reports by French, Italian, and Hungarian engineers to emphasize that the main attack should be directed against the strongest points, the Löwel and the Burg bastions. He also opined that sappers should lay out their multi-angular trenchwork right from the site of headquarters to the ravelins of the main bastions, and that mines be used to spring breaches wide enough to permit penetration by a score of men abreast.

The ex-Capuchin's suggestions were accepted in principle, but Kara Mustapha grew impatient and made an attempt to take Vienna by lightning attack.

On July 23, 25, and 27, heavy infantry assaults surged against the palisades, but were all repulsed. A written summons to surrender was shot into the bastion on a big arrow. In reply, a chorus of defenders accompanied by a brass band, and with minstrels acting as cheer leaders, chanted scornful defiance.

Kara Mustapha was given to occasional spells of hypochondria. The mineral springs of Baden, ten miles south of Vienna, had the reputation of a cure-all. To Baden the Great Vizier went, but the waters did not heal his affliction. He returned to his tent, determined to avoid further fatiguing travel until the city was seized.

Turkish cavalrymen did not think that traveling was fatiguing. They ranged through the defiles and valleys of the Vienna Woods, to the plains of the Tullner Field on the Danube, and to the foothills of the higher Alpine ranges. Many people fled at their approach, hiding in woods and under cliffs, vegetating like hunted animals; others tried to placate the foe by staging elaborate surrender formalities. The horsemen butchered them wholesale or dragged them away for sale to camp-following slave traders.

Statistics, drafted in 1689, put civilian losses at 500,000, including 88,-000 sold into slavery, and the number of settlements and farms destroyed at almost 15,000. These figures are probably exaggerated, and they are, in part, due to domestic incendiaries. Peasants from the district of Krems, from the Styrian domain of Admont, and iron-ore miners from Eisenerz, staged plundering raids against their own countrymen.

On August 3, the Turks penetrated the counterscarp near the Burg Bastion. The breach was sealed, counterattacks were launched, but the defenders became aware of the seriousness of their plight. No band played on the walls; minstrels joined the ranks.

Count Starhemberg directed operations from the Imperial castle. He suffered from attacks of dysentery, which had reached almost epidemic proportions and took a higher toll than Turkish artillery fire. Turkish cannon blasted away at all bastions, but damage was still rather light, and counterbattery was busily kept up. Close-quarter fighting near the Burg Bastion continued until August 12; then the attackers exploded a colossal mine and established themselves in the moat.

Count Starhemberg had his own master spy, who knew his way around enemy headquarters. He was a Pole, Franz Kolschitzky, who, with his fez, drooping mustache, slightly slit black eyes, and the flawless Turkish of an ex-interpreter, could have passed for an Asiatic Turk. He was assisted by his manservant, Georg Mihailovitsch, a daredevil who walked through Turkish rows of tents and returned on rather mysterious paths. Kolschitzky and Mihailovitsch had a collaborator, one Kunitz, whom the Great Vizier detained in his camp, where he gathered information on casualties suffered by the Turks and on their next plans. Through Kolschitzky and Mihailovitsch, Count Starhemberg sent and received messages to and from the Duke of Lorraine, who controlled much of Lower Austria north of the Danube. The Duke was not yet ready for relief operations when the first big Turkish mine hit the Burg Bastion.

The Emperor and his cabinet, who began to feel unsafe in Linz, moved further upstream to Passau.

More devastating than artillery, more dangerous even than Janizary charges, were the sappers' operations.

Deep angular trenches covered the forefield of Burg and Löwel bastions like a dense network of arteries. The defenders suffered heavy casualties in close-quarter fighting, and unusually damp and hot weather caused a great deal of food spoilage. Rations were shortened.

By mid-August, Starhemberg learned that Kara Mustapha was worried about the religious implications of a prolonged siege. Oriental wisdom and soldierly experience knew the detrimental effect of long sieges upon the attackers' health and morale; also, the Koran set a time limit on such operations and Mohammedan soldiers might stage a mutiny if the time limit was not kept. He wanted to conquer Vienna within no more than two weeks.

The defenders concentrated the bulk of their strength between the two crucial bastions. Kara Mustapha wanted to hit them with all he had. Pasha Ibrahim of Buda cautiously suggested that a surprise attack be directed against a different sector. The Great Vizier was adamant. He would take the Burg Bastion, which he called the "magic rock." Count Starhemberg had no illusions; the "magic rock" would soon be reduced to a heap of rubble, as would the adjoining wall.

On August 19 and 27, and again on September 1, messages reached Duke Charles, who had stayed on the Tullner Field; they were variations on the theme: "The danger is greater than we can confide to paper. Not a single moment must be lost."

Trenches dug by superbly efficient sappers almost choked the fortifications; skillfully placed powerful charges demolished bastions and breached walls.

During the night of September 3, the defenders abandoned the "magic rock." On September 4, the biggest mine ever used until then blasted the adjoining walls. Janizaries stormed and were repulsed, and stormed again, without, however, penetrating the city. The number of defenders within the crumbling walls was reduced to 8000, that of citizen soldiers to 3000. Ammunition and food grew desperately short. Civilian casualties through artillery fire and disease were high. But the Viennese, bewildered but determined, did not advocate surrender. Minstrels and tavernists carried weapons; they would die rather than cater to the enemy.

King John Sobieski neared the Tullner Field in forced marches. His army numbered no more than 15,000, but he could not wait for reinforcements. The Duke of Lorraine rode to meet him. Their first interview posed diplomatic problems which, to the participants, seemed more serious than the plight of Vienna. Tension was lessened by elaborate tact, but Sobieski requested that he be awarded supreme command of all Imperial forces and auxiliaries. And while the walls of the Emperor's capital collapsed, two men bickered over questions of military etiquette.

Marco d'Aviano, a Capuchin monk, the Pope's personal envoy to the roving Imperial Court, came down from Passau. His diplomatic skill prevented a disastrous crisis.

Marco d'Aviano's first report to the Emperor evaded the topic of command. Leopold, aboard a river barge, waited until September 8 and then continued his trip. At Dürnstein, he had another letter from Marco d'Aviano, suggesting that King John Sobieski, influenced by his ambitious wife, insisted on being put in command, and that it would be risky to antagonize him now that every man and every minute counted.

Emperor Leopold, vacillating between angry unrest and stiff decorousness, eventually continued toward the Tullner Field, not in a single lap—the barge could have covered the distance in eight hours—but in small installments. By September 13, as he pondered about his bothersome Polish ally, portentous news reached him a short distance upstream of Tulln.

On September 8 and 9, 70,000 Imperials, Poles, Bavarians, and Saxonians had joined and crossed the Danube near Tulln on a pontoon bridge. Still on September 9, John Sobieski assumed the title of commander in chief.

The soldiers of the relief army were in better fighting trim than the Turks, but numerical odds were heavily against the Christians. The Turks knew it well enough. On September 10, Turkish cavalry commanders reported that the enemy was pushing through the Vienna Woods, toward the rolling crest of the range which overlooked the city in distress. Another council of war was held in the silken tent. Kara Mustapha wanted to continue the assault with utmost vigor; Pasha Ibrahim asserted with ceremonious submissiveness that the Great Vizier's strategic concept was grandiose, but that it might also be considered to move the bulk of the siege army to the crest of the hills and repulse the brazen Christian assault before it got within range of the city.

John Sobieski left staff work to Duke Charles and his officers. Among them was a volunteer, a rather sickly-looking teen-ager who would later become the greatest military leader ever to serve any German or Austrian Emperor: Prince Eugene of Savoy.

Trails through the Vienna Woods proved impassable for artillery; but for its left wing, which marched along the bank of the Danube, the relief army remained practically without cannon.

During the night of September 11, the vanguard reached the top of the 1580-foot-high Kahlenberg, 1000 feet above the center of the city. The vanguard planted a huge red flag with a white cross, which the defenders could see after daybreak. Several rockets were fired to tell the Viennese that their ordeal was coming to an end, one way or another.

Flag and rockets were also watched in the Turkish camp but, incredibly enough, the besiegers made no attempt to drive the relief forces back. Kara Mustapha did not live to write explanatory memoirs.

September 11 went by; the relief army took up positions. The left wing, under the personal command of the Duke of Lorraine, should open the assault down the slopes of the Kahlenberg and Leopoldsberg. The center should drive down the slopes of the wine-blessed hills of Grinzing. The right wing was to push through the defile between Hermannskogel and Sophienalpe into the ruins of Dornbach and the suburb of Hernals.

The Duke of Lorraine had a long look at the city. What he saw caused him to insist that the drive open on September 12 instead of September 14, as it had been originally intended.

Sobieski raised no objections. He was busy planning his own solemn entry into the freed city and some elaborate celebration on the eve of the battle, involving the knighting of his young son.

Marco d'Aviano wrote another letter to the Emperor, knowing full well that it would reach Leopold only after the fighting was over: "From the top of this mountain [Kahlenberg], we can look down upon our goal. All our generals are in perfect harmony. A sudden arrival of Your Majesty, without previous agreement on matters of ceremony, might possibly trouble this concord. The Duke of Lorraine neither eats nor sleeps; he personally inspects every sentinel; his prudence is admirable; he does everything a perfect general can do. Tomorrow, God willing, the battle will take place."

When the letter was written, clouds blanketed the area, but in the small hours of Sunday, September 12, the weather cleared. At 4 A.M., Marco d'Aviano said Mass in the half-destroyed church of the convent atop the Kahlenberg. King John Sobieski officiated, and his son was knighted.

The Turks had improvised a line to cover the lower slopes of the Vienna Woods, but their positions had several weak spots. The elite troops kept up the siege, charging the breaches to take Vienna in view of the relief army. Kara Mustapha had gone into the extraordinary inconvenience of walking a solid fifteen minutes to inspect trenches that led to the fallen "magic rock." Turkish artillery kept up a furious bombardment of the town; only a few guns pointed at the attackers from the west.

The left wing under Duke Charles opened the downhill drive shortly after Marco d'Aviano said *missa est. Allons, marchons* was the Duke's battle cry; when excited, he reverted to his native French. His men hardly understood the words, but they understood their meaning, and attacked lustily, pushing down the slopes toward the embattled inferno that was Vienna. When they reached Nussdorf, a spirited counterblow threw them off balance. From the city walls, desperate scouts watched the apparent setback, but Franconian infantry restored the lines and occupied the Nussberg. The fine vineyards of that hill became emplacements for the scant artillery.

By noon, the city was swept by scathing fire and furious attacks.

The King of Poland, a spectator rather than a leader, suggested that the fighting be halted until the following day. The Duke of Lorraine did not wish to give the enemy time to regroup, counterattack, and drive the relief army back into the hills.

The fateful Sunday was radiant; only smelly layers of gun smoke dimmed the gorgeous view. The shrunken band of the city's defenders stood by in close ranks for sorties should the Turks waver, for a last-ditch stand should the relief host be repulsed. A rain of destruction hit Vienna. Count Starhemberg waited to lead either the first sortie or the last stand with the back to no wall.

In the early afternoon, the Christians' right wing was not in action. The Polish King's men were late. They were mostly mounted and had trouble passing narrow, heavily wooded defiles. By 2 P.M. the center was dangerously far ahead of the slow wing. The gap widened as observers in the embattled city noticed, with horror. From the silken tent, the gap should have been noticed, but Kara Mustapha was again in the trenches, savagely determined to overrun the tottering defenses before the field battle was over. Massive formations of Janizaries hurled themselves against breaches, men climbing over the bodies of fallen file leaders, roaring with rage that was directed against both the stubborn Viennese and Turkish commanders who forced them to keep up the assault against the Koran's military law.

Shortly after 2 P.M., a passionate outcry burst from the parapets; far out on the western hills, a glittering array debouched; the right wing moved into position, the rays of the sun were reflected by a sea of lances.

Two squadrons of Polish cavalry charged, but broke as the Turks met them with military fire and a spirited countercharge. Had not German infantry come to the Polish cavalry's assistance, the Turkish success might have assumed dangerous proportions.

For a full hour, the fate of the world hung in the balance. Then the Turkish right wing was outflanked; from the bank of the Danube, the Imperials wheeled toward the enemy's main encampment.

By 4 P.M. the first Turkish units broke into flight. The Great Vizier had the green banner of the Prophet unfurled and ordered an all-out counterattack, but the green banner did not arouse religious passions; the attack failed.

The Turks were overcome by general panic. The army turned into running rabble. Kara Mustapha, who did not wish to ride up to the crest of the Vienna Woods, mounted the fastest of his Arabian stallions. His mighty beard fluttering, his embroidered turban oblique on his head, he galloped toward the deceptive security of Hungary. His harem did not follow: the Great Vizier's executioners strangled the ladies lest they disgrace their owner by abandoning themselves to the victors' lust.

At 5 P.M. vanguards of the Duke of Lorraine reached the city walls near the Schottentor, from where Count Starhemberg had just begun the final sortie.

The Turkish army had lost 12,000 dead, five times the figure of Christians killed, but still not too high a percentage of its effectives. "A miracle," King Louis XIV grudgingly called the sudden disaster. The battle of Vienna was also hailed as a miracle in parts of the Christian world that, unlike the King of France, had not made common cause with Turkish aggression.

The Poles collected the lion's share of the immense booty as bewildered crowds of hollow-cheeked Viennese flocked to Abraham a Santa Clara's Augustinerkirche, where the *Te Deum* was sung.

Polish ranking officers attended the services; the others stayed away in protest against what was called King John Sobieski's importunate tactlessness. Church bells did not toll.

But they tolled on September 14, when the Emperor, who had spent the previous night in Klosterneuburg monastery, arrived in Vienna. Leopold, in dark Spanish gala, and his retinue, in equally somber attire, circled the city on horseback before entering at the Stubentor, where the Emperor was welcomed by all ranking soldiers with the exception of the Polish King. Through half-ruined streets, lined by cheering throngs, the Emperor and his retinue proceeded to St. Stephen's Cathedral, where Bishop Kolonitsch officiated High Mass. From there, Leopold went to his castle. He burst into tears at the sight of the devastation. Sentimental chroniclers noted that accommodations for the lord of the castle were not available, and he was compelled to establish quarters at the Stallburg.

What remained of the Turkish booty was given to the people and to non-Polish soldiers. Turkish cannons were cast into a church bell the like of which the world had never seen, so big in size that it seemed impossible to hoist it up to any steeple, least of all on the spire of St. Stephen's, almost 450 feet above the ground. However, engineers accomplished the apparently impossible. When it was found that the bell's tolling might damage the tall structure, the Viennese did not mind. They liked their *Pummerin,* as they dubbed the cannon-bell, even if it had to be mute forever. The mute *Pummerin* remained in its lofty place until 1945, when an aerial bombardment sent it crashing to the ground. The Viennese heirs of 1945 at once resolved to restore the *Pummerin* to its historical place, even though this still posed difficult problems.

The most spectacular selection of booty was made by Bishop Count Kolonitsch and by master spy Kolschitzky.

The bishop, who was a man of great wealth, chose 500 orphans, widows, and infirms as his permanent wards. His deed was highly praised, but far less remembered than Kolschitzky's choice. As the popular story goes, Kolschitzky chose a few canvas bags containing small pale-green objects for which nobody else had any use: coffee beans! The Viennese did not know coffee, but the master spy was familiar with it from previous trips east. Soon the efficient man opened the first Viennese coffeehouse, initiating a new, but lasting, fashion, an essential tradition in the Viennese way of life.

The story was handed down to posterity and readily believed. In fact, Kolschitzky was not the first to bring coffee to Vienna, but he was the first to be allowed to sell it without restriction. Well over a century prior to the battle of Vienna, the Coffee Council of Mecca had banned coffee as harmful; the ban was soon relaxed and eventually reached Islamic countries, but in Europe churches and governments fought coffee as a stimulant to a "rebellious state of mind." Not before the mid-seventeenth century did a few venturesome men dare to open coffeehouses in major cities, but they were harassed by authorities and sparingly patronized by a citizenry that did not find the beverage to their taste. Kolschitzky was never harassed and his coffee must have been tasty, since the Viennese passionately took to it.

Some of the captured Turkish equipment was preserved in the Imperial arsenal, including the silken shell of Kara Mustapha's tent.

On September 16, four days after disaster struck, Kara Mustapha was in Györ gathering the remnants of his army together. The Great Vizier held a court-martial against his generals and found Pasha Ibrahim guilty of neglect of duty. The old man was strangled.

On September 17, Kara Mustapha was on his way again, this time to Székesfehérvár. Ahead of him traveled rumors of disaster which some Hungarian nobles found hard to believe. In Székesfehérvár, the Great Vizier drafted a circumstantial report to the Sultan, which caused Mola Mahomet to send him the silken cord, the tool of execution of the highest dignitaries of the realm. The silken cord caught up with traveling Kara Mustapha in Belgrade, where it was put to proper use on December 25, 1683.

CHAPTER THIRTY-FOUR

The Emperor and his cabinet did not have the courage to exploit the fruits of victory: the citizenry, so steadfast under siege, now was more anxious to mock the frustrated would-be conquerors than to see pursuit pressed to the limits of the continent, and the allies wanted to go home. Saxonians, Franconians, and Württembergers marched back through the Danube Valley; Bavarians were set to follow them.

Emperor Leopold spent a few uncomfortable nights at the drafty Stallburg and then returned to Linz, where accommodations were more cozy, and there was no threat of infectious disease.

In Vienna, printing trades flourished. The output of siege diaries, technical essays, historical works, and, last but not least, poetry was prodigal. One epic set a mark with 12,000 Alexandrines; its title was *The Eagle's Power, or the Essence of European Heroism.*

Minstrels deplored ruined buildings, praised burghers and craftsmen who had carried arms, mocked Turkey as "the sick man of Europe" and Louis XIV as "the Gallic cock with the crooked face."

Poles and Imperials invaded Hungary; they took the city of Esztergom on October 27, 1683, bringing the Cathedral of the Primate of Hungary back into the fold of the realm.

The Emperor acknowledged the conquest with remarkable lack of enthusiasm. He wanted peace rather than laurels. But there could be no peace along the Danube; either the Emperor or the Sultan had to yield.

Duke Charles of Lorraine was again commander in chief of the Emperor's main forces. A river flotilla of over one hundred flat-bottomed barges was built to carry supplies and siege artillery down the Danube to their next goals, the "water fortresses" of Visegrád and Buda.

Visegrád fell after a three-day siege.

On June 30, 1684, the Imperials were in Pest, Buda's twin on the left bank of the Danube. For several generations, Pest had been an undisputed Turkish domain. Few of its inhabitants had ever laid eyes upon any of the Emperor's men, and none of them had ever given much thought to the possibility of becoming the Emperor's subjects. They had all accepted Turkish rule unquestioningly and submissively.

Ancient Buda remained in Turkish hands, its gates closed; hundreds of gun muzzles defied the attackers.

Leopold I tried his talent on the music to a German-language comedy, and all the ladies of the Court were delighted with the results. A new ballet, *The Restoration of Fortuna's Wheel,* was conceived in the spirit of general rehabilitation. There were many diplomatic activities, promoting peace and precluding war. The Emperor's daughter was married to the Elector of Bavaria.

A new Pasha of Buda sent well-groomed agents to Vienna to talk mutual understanding, and to bribe corruptible officials. In March 1685, a representative of the Great Vizier arrived: glib, smug, enigmatical; Hungarians of undefined allegiance added color to the confusing picture. Diplomats mingled with highborn young men from abroad, who came to volunteer in the army.

Vienna attracted students of soldiering, not because the greatest generals could be found there, but because there was always war near by.

Along the Danube, down to the Iron Gate, the political situation was in flux. Great powers engaged in the game of "first grabbed, first legitimately established" were joined by Russia, a clumsy, greedy, fumbling giant that tried to gobble up whatever came within reach.

Russia was not yet Turkey's military peer, a fact which the campaigns of 1677–81 amply evidenced. But when Turkey was otherwise engaged, the Tsars could cut their pounds of flesh out of the body of the Sultan's patrimony.

Since 1682, a woman had ruled in the Kremlin: Tsarina Sophia, guardian of her minor brothers Ivan and Peter. Sophia combined recklessness with a longing for melodramatic inspiration. To her, the Catholic Church was a romantic riddle. Wishing that Rome would perform miracles in Moscow, she welcomed Jesuits to her capital. They became Sophia's most confidential advisers and intimated that Russia could join the Western world spiritually. In 1686, Russia joined the Holy League and pledged itself to support the West's struggle against the Sultan without selfish aims. Russian support was unsatisfactory, but Russia conceived an aim that was never abandoned by either Tsars or Bolsheviks: the conquest of the Straits, the Dardanelles.

In 1687, a Russian embassy arrived in Vienna to cement the professed friendship between the two Empires. It stayed from March 18 through May 12. Pomp and debauchery made it the main topic of local conversation, but otherwise its achievements were not noticeable.

Eleven years later, Tsar Peter, Sophia's brother-successor, visited Vienna "incognito" but with a retinue of several hundred. The Imperial couple arranged a gala performance of a new type of show that became the fashionable rave of the metropolis. Scenes from peasant weddings were performed on stages and improvised in hostelries by members of the Court. The Tsar was also invited to the Favorita, named after an Imperial château; Emperor Leopold and his wife posed as tavernists; Princes and Princesses impersonated patrons, including Jews, chimney sweeps, gatekeepers, and a variety of odd characters. The Emperor-tavernist made a *faux pas* by offering a toast to the Ruler of Russia instead of to "an anonymous caller."

Records have it that Peter and Leopold had a conference or two on matters of politics, but nothing resulted.

The Viennese found Peter of the jolly good type since he was lavish with tips and, apparently, not arrogant. The "incognito" sojourn ended abruptly. News of the revolt of the Streltzi reached Peter, who dashed home and had over 1000 rebels and suspects executed.

The Duke of Lorraine planned another campaign against Buda. "Once that gate on the Danube is opened," he wrote, "other places are bound to fall, and more extensive operations will be facilitated."

The original schedule was already badly upset when, on June 9, 1686, the Imperial Chancellor appeared in the camp of Parkány, the Duke's headquarters, and announced that, in view of the extreme difficulty of the venture, it was His Majesty's "carefully considered wish not to hold anybody responsible for the outcome."

Two days after the declaration of His Majesty's wish, the huge host began to move.

Abdurrahman Pasha, commander of Buda, was a septuagenarian of indomitable spirit; he had only 7000 men, but they were superbly trained, well supplied, and skillfully arrayed.

The besiegers forged their ring. Imperial, Swabian, and Franconian regiments established themselves on the slopes of Schwabenberg; the troops of the Bavarian Elector continued the line in southern and eastern directions. With the Elector was Eugene of Savoy, whom the soldiers considered to be funny-looking and whose rank of colonel was not unusual for a Prince aged twenty-three.

By June 25, the besiegers controlled every approach to Buda and bragged that the fortress was sure to fall within a few days; but many days would pass and the slopes of the hills and the waters of the Danube below would be reddened by streams of blood before it was over.

The Citadel of Buda, the former royal castle, seemed cannon-ball-proof; from its ramparts, Turkish fire raked the besiegers' gun emplacements. But on July 22, a red-hot ball hit the northeastern corner of the castle; the main ammunition dump exploded with a shattering crash, tearing a wide breach and killing 1500 Turks. The Duke asked for immediate surrender; the Pasha haughtily rejected the request.

Late in August the siege army was reinforced by 11,000 men.

On September 2, after a nine-hour bombardment, the general attack opened. Turkish resistance was hopeless, though magnificent. Abdurrahman at the head of the rest of his Janizaries held the so-called Vienna Gate. He and all his soldiers died battling the Brandenburgers. From the north, Imperial infantry and dragoons pressed into the city; Bavarians charged from the west. Savage close-quarter fighting raged for the citadel. Prince Eugene's cavalry reserves occupied Székesfehérvár Gate to block the last route of escape. The massacre continued for two hours.

By 5 P.M., when only a handful of Turkish soldiers were left, 2000 crazed civilians burst into the courtyard of the citadel, wailing, imploring the victors' mercy. The Elector is credited with having taken them into his custody.

The conquering soldiery put Buda to the torch. On September 4, only ruins were left. The thick walls of the citadel withstood the blaze. Inside, in huge cellars, Jews had established their refuge; no Jews were among the civilians in the Elector's custody. The rapists of Buda staged a thorough pogrom.

Marco d'Aviano sent a note to the Emperor that God had granted the return of Buda to its rightful overlord.

The hard-riding messenger covered the distance of 150-odd miles in eighteen hours. The combined efforts of various Christian armies to regain the capital of Hungary had covered one mile per year.

Arson destroyed architectural landmarks of Turkish domination; mosques and bathing establishments. Churches superseded the former; nothing superseded the latter.

Buda and Pest were a deserted spoil bank, junk yard of an era that seemed to have come to an end. Yet the cities recovered without ever gaining a completely Hungarian complexion. Many new settlers were of Austrian and German stock, and quite a few hailed from northern Serbia. The layer of Hungarians that spread over the settlers' families never absorbed them. A thin sprinkle of Gypsies gave the city an exotic touch that thrilled tourists and travelers, regardless of origin.

In 1703, Buda and Pest, as separate cities, received new Imperial privileges; during the eighteenth century, the highest judicial authorities of the land moved to Buda. Empress-Queen Maria Theresa had the castle splendidly rebuilt, but not before 1848 were the Hungarian Diet and the country's new government transferred to the city, and not before 1872 was the twin city legally united as Hungarian capital and royal residence. King of Hungary, by the authority of the Constitution of 1867, then was Franz Joseph I.

The Turkish hold on Hungary crumbled after the fall of Buda. The Imperial army proceeded deep into the southern regions of the country. Hungarian nobles, peasants, and burghers forgot age-old conflicts, collaborated, and joined. They scathingly denounced Turkish rule and pledged loyalty in glowing terms that were rarely trusted, and even more rarely kept.

War along the Danube was indestructible.

CHAPTER THIRTY-FIVE

The Turkish Empire was young, as empires go. There was no sizable traditional nucleus to fall back upon, no large regions which, in the course of slow, orderly processes, had been welded into a national, cultural, and religious entity. In order to continue its existence, Turkey had to hold whatever could be held anywhere. With its huge resources of manpower, it mustered a big new army to stand and fight before the triumphant foes could reach Belgrade and cross the Danube into the Balkan Peninsula, in the direction of the Sultan's capital.

Great Vizier Solyman's soldiers of 1687 were by no means the equals of the defenders of Buda. They were a colorful medley, reminiscent of Kara Mustapha's troops, but they were well equipped, and French officers, who acted as master technicians as well as strategic advisers, added to their fighting power.

The Turks assembled near Belgrade, the Imperials south of Buda. Duke Charles commanded not quite 40,000 men, the Bavarian Elector some 20,000. The divided command was the result of a compromise.

Summer had just begun, warm and bright, when the Duke's army crossed a pontoon bridge over the Danube near Mohács. The army was still crossing the bridge when rains began to fall which grew into a veritable deluge. The river rose, the bridge was damaged, passage proceeded at a snail's pace. More than two precious weeks were lost. The Turkish army left Belgrade and arrived at Osijek, where French engineers established a strongly fortified camp.

In Vienna, the Court War Council deliberated. The wigged members of that proud body of blunderers at long last realized that the Danube was a useful artery of communications, and that big flat-bottomed barges were useful craft; but how to build them and put them into operation on short notice remained a problem never satisfactorily solved.

Food and forage grew short. Hungry horses were of little use in carting and cavalry action, and human hunger did not boost discipline.

However, discipline also slackened in the Turkish camp. The soldiers wanted to loot, and pillage around Osijek was not lucrative. The Great Vizier expected action to be a panacea and marched out to meet the enemy.

Back in Vienna, the stalemate near Mohács was considered boring. The Emperor commissioned Saxonian-born philosopher Gottfried Wilhelm von Leibniz to write essays against France, a constitution of war, a paper on matters of currency, and yet another on the Jewry of Frankfurt.

As Leibniz probed into Imperial prerogatives in the Jewish district of Frankfurt, the two armies clashed near Harkány, a hill not far from Mohács.

Terrain conditions favored the Turks, and so did jumping-off positions, but the Great Vizier's timidity caused him to lose his big chance. By midday, the odds were even. In the afternoon, the Christians launched an all-out attack, their soldiers, anticipating the end to shortages, fought with gusto; even horses showed some spirit. The Elector of Bavaria charged with telling effect. He wore blue battle regalia and terrified Turks dubbed him the "Blue King." But a better fighter and tactician even than the Blue King was Prince Eugene. At the head of a group of infantry and artillery, he assaulted Turkish entrenchments, broke clean through, and created havoc.

The Great Vizier tried to rally his battered army near Pétervárad, but mutiny broke out. The Great Vizier knew of no better expedient than to return to the capital, and mutiny followed him all the way through the devastated lands north of the Danube, and beyond, into the Balkans.

Arrived in Constantinople the Turkish mob staged wild outbreaks. The Great Vizier was assassinated, Sultan Mahomet dethroned, his brother Solyman released from prison and established on a throne that seemed more dangerous than a prison cell.

Turkey was very sick.

The Hungarian territory held by the Emperor's men at the end of 1687 reached deep into the south; Croatia and Slovenia were cleared of Turkish occupation. The stage was set for an attack on Belgrade and the establishment of Habsburg rule over most of the Danube basin. In May 1688, the province of Transylvania returned to the Emperor's fold. "The three nations" of that land solemnly renounced all ties with Turkey, but petitioned for privileges, including freedom of Protestant worship, which was granted. Transylvania was well worth many masses of a reformed creed.

War on the Danube swept regions which, as long as anyone could remember, had seen the display of ruthless Turkish power but had never seen it challenged. Pashas and other officials came and went like spells of bad weather. People took shelter when they raged at their worst, but they did not defy them. People who lived south and east of Hungary, less emotional and more stoical than their neighbors, took the Turks for granted. Greeks who occupied high civilian offices in the Sultan's land, Jews who dominated business and finance, were, if not ethnically, functionally integrated in the fabric of Turkey, which was as ornamental and colorful as its finest rugs. Integrated aliens were profitably loyal to their rulers and frightened by any change.

In Belgrade, Greeks, Jews, and the few prosperous Serbs began to pack. Grapevine told of an avalanche of men, horses, and cannon coming down the Danube, about to burst upon the Sultan's inner fortress.

There were many treasured objects and real treasures in Belgrade which had to be carried to whatever safety could be found. Boats on the river piers would not suffice to meet the hectic demand. Shrewd entrepreneurs rented nonexistent cargo space but ultimately managed to provide it. Eventually, four hundred craft were loaded on the wharves of Belgrade with a cargo of treasures, their owners, kin, and friends, and a few stubborn stowaways, for a trip to the Iron Gate and beyond. The Imperial army that could have prevented the exodus had not yet arrived.

On July 29, 45,000 Imperials closed in on Belgrade. By August 9 they had crossed the Danube near Zemun and stood under the walls of the city, on which no reliable intelligence reports were available. The citadel crowned the hills; on the northern slope was the "water town," on the opposite side the "fortress town," ringed by a double wall. Defense artillery was formidable. The attackers were outgunned and the city was well supplied with essentials.

The heaviest siege guns arrived only on August 25, after the attackers had suffered substantial casualties without crossing the moat. A few days later, the southeastern-corner tower was destroyed and two breaches opened. Still, the defenders held out. Among the wounded attackers was Prince Eugene.

The general assault opened on September 6; it was supported by cannon emplaced on boats on the Danube. Within four hours all resistance had ceased. The unconditional surrender of the citadel yielded a small batch of prisoners, some of whom were subsequently massacred.

The seizure of Belgrade was not exploited, first because of wrangling, personal feuds, and strange delusions; later, because the great wars between the Empire and France had begun and the Emperor had no big army to spare for a Balkan expedition, not even enough soldiers to hold and consolidate fringe gains, of which Belgrade was the most important. Two years after their defeat, the Turks returned to the city. Belgrade remained embattled for generations to come.

CHAPTER THIRTY-SIX

The Emperor had two major creditors: the Pope and one Samuel Oppenheimer. But while the Pope financed His Majesty's ventures with the often hard-strained funds of the Catholic Church and left repayment largely to Providence, Oppenheimer relied essentially on deposits made in his establishment by trusting and interest-hungry people of all walks of life, depending on the Emperor's will and ability to reimburse them all.

Samuel Oppenheimer was a learned, cultured, and refined Jew whose mansion contained almost as many objects of art as that of a ranking nobleman, and whose library contained more books than those of all the aristocrats combined. He tried to develop banking into a science; commerce, crafts, transportation, and construction became increasingly dependent upon his bank. Popular income was boosted by interests received, and it all rested on Imperial solvency.

His Majesty's solvency depended on imponderables that invariably turned against him and his creditors. The treasury was drained by wars. A Jew, even if, like Oppenheimer, he carried the proud title of Court Banker, could not sue the Emperor or claim publicly that the Emperor was a defaulter. However, when his Court Bank could not collect, Oppenheimer was bankrupt.

This happened in 1703; the effect was hardly less staggering than Kara Mustapha's approach twenty years before. At first people were stunned; they simply failed to understand how such a thing could have happened; then panic broke out, a panic that could not find vent in flight. You cannot flee from loss. The entire city burst into a mad rage. Rock-throwing, knife-wielding crowds gathered in front of the Oppenheimer mansion; and even if the owner and his family had been present to have their throats cut, this would hardly have sufficed to satisfy the demonstrators, depositors, thrill seekers, thugs, and pickpockets. Demagogues had a field day. They harangued the populace with stories about the Jew Oppenheimer cupping the Christians and about alleged other Jewish wrongdoing crowned by an unprecedented act of thievery.

Many Jews had come to Vienna since 1683; most of them had gone into business and, more often than not, indulged in sharp practices. The demagogues' harangues fell on fertile soil. Pogroms ensued.

The embarrassed authorities did not wish to take harsh measures to quell the disorders. On the other hand, they knew well what had really caused the bank's failure, and they also considered Jews to be a useful commodity.

The pogroms cost lives and property, and were eventually halted with kid-gloved prudence. Oppenheimer returned to his mansion and was given to understand that if he were able to mobilize new funds, his exalted debtor might continue to do business with him. Somehow, Oppenheimer produced funds, and the dubious Imperial promise was kept. The banker became instrumental in organizing supplies and transportation for campaigns that, thanks to him and Prince Eugene, became the glory of the House of Habsburg.

But no promise could placate despoiled depositors; nor could mere promises keep people in business who relied on credits from the Court Bank.

The Municipal Council of Vienna established a City Bank, which was run by dull town clerks. Businessmen, dissatisfied with its operation, remonstrated that malicious Jews either sabotaged the venture or were its malevolent wirepullers. Vienna seethed, demagogues and entertainers had another rewarding topic. Craftsmen again threatened Oppenheimer's home; students who never had financial dealings with anyone except their landladies joined them. The Academic Senate made no move to curb the boys. Oppenheimer again left town; from his mansion, demonstrators went straight to the Imperial castle and threw rocks at the lanterns outside. The city guard opened fire, but the survivors gathered again in the suburbs for a brief peripheral pogrom.

To please the populace, the government tightened restrictive control of Jews, subjected them to strict settling regulations and licensing of business. The restrictions mostly affected latecomers and people of modest means. Also, the authorities went into another line of business which had been a Jewish stronghold: pawnbroking and auctioneering. The

Versatz- und Fragamt (Pawning and Interrogating Office), founded in 1707, was not a pawner's paradise, but it was welcomed by many and has survived to the present day.

When rioters attacked the lanterns, Leopold I no longer resided in the Vienna castle. The Emperor who had lived through a period of sixty-five years—from the Thirty Years' War, through the Turkish conflagration, into the Spanish War of Succession—who had three times married heiresses of princely blood, and had found time for music, dramatics, and other hobbies, died on May 5, 1705.

He was succeeded by his oldest son, Joseph I, then twenty-seven, who was born in Vienna and already wore two royal crowns when his father passed away: that of Hungary since he was nine, that of Rome since he was eleven.

Joseph I lived to be only thirty-three. He did not have the makings of a great ruler. His achievements were not outstanding, but he was fortunate to have Prince Eugene of Savoy as his principal soldier, and sensible enough to understand that in a world torn by apparently self-perpetuating wars, a perspicacious military genius is the best statesman. During Joseph's brief rule, the Prince and Reichsmarschall was established as the most influential man of the realm.

The new Emperor's first official act had nothing to do with either war or politics: it was the inauguration of the new Academy of Creative Arts.

The creative arts flourished. The family of one of the greatest Baroque architect-sculptors graced the Imperial capital with monumental creations. Johann Bernhard Fischer von Erlach, a native of Graz, in Styria province, built the Karlskirche, the south wing of the Imperial castle, and new Imperial stables; he also drafted the first plans of Schönbrunn Castle. For his great patron, Prince Eugene, Fischer von Erlach built a town castle and also a gem of a seigneurial country seat at Schlosshof on the lower March River. Salzburg, Prague, even distant Breslau, were ennobled by his rich talent. His son, Joseph Emanuel, completed most of what his father left unfinished. Much of the Fischer von Erlachs' architecture survived the splendid, troubled, humiliating, and undeified years that followed, and it still stands, a symphony of magnificently shaped stone and copper patina begotten in an era which, along with greatness, contained many elements of cruelty, foolishness, and triviality.

Joseph I inherited his father's love for music and drama and had a laudable aversion to dilettantism. He had two court theaters built, one for grand opera, the other for Italian spectacles. Both houses, which stood where the Redoutensäle would later stand, were the work of Galli da Bibiena, an Italian architect.

An Italian poet, Francesco Ballerini, suggested that Joseph I build a municipal theater rather than a court theater. He explained that the latter was extremely expensive; that it had to close in periods of court mourning, which were rather frequent; and that royalty would enhance its popularity by establishing a theater that was accessible to the public.

The suggestion was turned down; the city already had its theater, which had opened in 1708, near the Kärntnertor. An Italian troupe performed there until 1710, and was superseded by the company of the immortal Austrian comedian, Josef Anton Stranitzky, and his actress-wife, Monica.

Hanns Wurst, the Austrian punchinello, was a comedy figure of firmly established ancient standing, a buffoon in Alpine costume, who made simpletons laugh and children marvel, whom most people knew but few really appreciated.

Garbed as a yokel from Salzburg, and with some of the paraphernalia of a historic *Pritschenmeister,* Stranitzky created a novel Hanns Wurst (Hanswurst), a philosopher-comedian-interloper. He was then still an itinerant performer in market squares, where vendors, customers, idlers, and urchins watched him. In Vienna he struck popular fancy when he first appeared in a market stall. Carriages stopped so that the gentry could see him act, hear him wisecrack—a new minstrel whose wit did not respect social and political taboos.

By 1710 he was the toast of the town, the darling of the mighty and the humble, the most popular actor, not only in Vienna but wide and far in the Austrian lands. The government, not usually in favor of freedom of expression, did not mind Hanswurst saying whatever Stranitzky meant, and Stranitzky meant quite a few things that were not strictly respectful of authority. Even the Emperor, breaking with the established custom of visiting only the court theater, went to see Stranitzky.

Hanswurst assumed many parts in Stranitzky's plays. He was, in turn, a comic ambassador of love, a confused mail carrier, a stupid assassin, a sly sycophant, a fake blind man, a doctor-favorite of King Wenceslaus the Lazy, a braggart-dueler, a fumbling spy, and, the highest achievement and climax of his career, the funny antagonist of the tragic character in the drama *The Life and Death of Doctor Faustus.* In Stranitzky's *Faust,* which preceded Goethe's sublime tragedy by about one century, tragic thirst for knowledge vies with naïveté, and naïveté prevails over the demons of ambitions but cannot vanquish an evil woman.

Today, only a few connoisseurs know Stranitzky's *Faust,* even though some of his minor plays were reprinted between 1908 and 1933. These minor plays are not very impressive, but the forgotten *Faust* is considered an outstanding work of poetry showing typical Viennese philosophy, aesthetics, wit, and mood better than any other work of literature, even though dated.

Much as the Emperor appreciated Stranitzky as an entertainer, he did not deem the impersonator of Hanswurst fit for the office of Court Poet. In the Emperor's opinion, a poet laureate should not entertain, but edify, and he appointed Carl Gustav Herseus, a Stockholm-born German, who sported an Olympic smile, wore the curliest head of hair wigmakers could produce, was well versed in numismatics, and wrote ponderously tedious poetry. Stranitzky, however, made a fortune without being Court Poet and, oddly enough, wound up with the appointment of Court Dentist and Mouth Surgeon.

Various travelers tell of Vienna in the years 1715–17.

A Swiss monk, Georg König, who came to the city as a chaplain to French ambassador Count Luc, opens his account with the praise of Stranitzky's *Faust,* which he saw at a matinee. The next thing to arrest his attention was the *Stock im Eisen* (trunk in iron) across the square from St. Stephen's. He relates the legend of the trunk:

Once upon a time, a journeyman locksmith put an iron ring around a tree that grew in the center of the budding city, and fastened it with the most complicated lock people had ever seen. He left no key to the lock when he departed and, hard as many tried, nobody could make a key to fit. The honorable guild of locksmiths promised that a journeyman who could solve the riddle would be named master craftsman. Many years and many unsuccessful attempts later, a young fellow made the fitting key. Full of joy, he threw his masterwork high up into the air—but it never returned to the ground and the young journeyman could not duplicate it. The maker of the lock was Satan incarnate, and Satan had snatched the flying key. The dejected young journeyman would never become master and, in a gesture of renunciation, he drove an iron nail into the trunk. Ever after, journeyman locksmiths who either came to or left Vienna followed his example, and an armor of nails encased the trunk.

In September 1716, the English ambassador to Constantinople and his wife, Lady Mary Worthley, arrived in Vienna. In her letters to Alexander Pope, the poet and translator of Homer, Lady Mary tells what she saw on her trip and in the capital.

They had traveled down the Danube all the way from Regensburg on a boat that was as comfortably furnished as a house. A team of twelve oarsmen rowed the boat at formidable speed. Sights along the river were charming; towns with splendid palaces, romantic secluded landscapes, forests, rocks, mountains, vineyards, and ruins of ancient castles.

In Vienna, Lady Mary admired tall white palaces in narrow streets, various six-story structures, and apartments with furniture worthy of Princes. She was infatuated with landscaped suburbs and villas: "The very air of this papistic country has an intoxicating, converting effect." She praised the garb of the nuns of St. Laurenz, who showed her a relic: a wooden head of Christ said to have talked during the siege of 1683.

The Worthleys attended the court opera at Fortuna Garden. Settings were of bewildering splendor; stage machinery was of incredible efficiency. A naval battle was performed. The opera cost the Emperor 30,-000 pounds. The Worthleys also witnessed an Italian comedy with female parts enacted by men. They were amazed at the custom of keeping court dwarfs, men and women, some of them not mere jesters, but persons of considerable standing. The Lady also claims that more alchemists than scientists lived in the capital, and she tells of a party in the house of Jean-Baptiste Rousseau, the lyrical poet, where she met Prince Eugene. Nobody could fail to be thrilled by meeting the already legendary marshal, and the Worthleys could soon report from Constantinople that Prince Eugene's latest triumph at Belgrade caused a panic in the Turkish capital.

The Lady's letters do not mention love life in Vienna, but the famous Charles de Montesquieu, who called Austria "the land in which the subjects are better housed than their ruler," wrote about the delicate subject: "The ancient Greeks used to say that life was beautiful only in Sparta, and this now applies to Vienna. In Vienna, not only the young women but even those of sixty have lovers; even the plain are loved. You may die of old age in Vienna, but you never feel old there."

Prince Eugene, whose influence continued under Joseph I's successor, Charles VI, called the leading spirits of poetry, architecture, and philosophy to Vienna and, being a generous man of great opulence, he patronized them lavishly. Quite a few, including Montesquieu and Jean-Baptiste Rousseau, were French, members of the nation against which the Prince had fought and won many a great battle and which was the realm's most dangerous but most congenial enemy.

In Eugene of Savoy's time, a strange and admirable new spirit pervaded relations, however hostile, between countries. It was an aristocratic, truly chivalrous spirit that created cultural ties above and beyond political animosities. In fact, it created respectful affections. Vienna and Paris battled, but they believed that their opposite number was the one and only worthy rival for hegemony in the world and, as such, well deserved admiration. Thousands of soldiers died in action while men of arts, science, and refinement knotted ties unaffected by brutish vicissitudes of belligerency. Prince Eugene, a Frenchman by descent, an Austrian by chance and choice, was the guiding spirit of this development.

CHAPTER THIRTY-SEVEN

"He was of medium height, but well built. His face was rather long, his cheeks were slightly hollow, his complexion was swarthy, well becoming a soldier. His eyes were black, lively, and full of fire; his mouth, which he usually kept half open, was neither large nor small; his nose was somewhat long but well shaped. He had black hair, which he wore naturally until it turned gray; then he covered it with a wig. He usually had a grave and serious expression, but he could look hilarious on proper occasions." Thus describes the Prince of Ligne his friend Prince Eugene of Savoy, in a sequel to the latter's memoirs.

The author was habitually courteous and an enthusiastic admirer of his great friend. But even though Eugene's portraits lead us to assume that his nose was far more than "somewhat" long, that "medium height" stands for short and "slightly hollow" cheeks for ghostly cavernous, the greatest soldier of his time still emerges as an able-bodied man whose lack of handsomeness was compensated for by "an air of greatness and majesty that emanated from his person when he showed himself to his troops and which impressed everybody, from highest general to lowliest soldier."

Much of the literature about Prince Eugene, who was born in 1663, is not overly enlightening, because of a lack of fundamental source material. His memoirs were apparently lost for over half a century and the hundred-odd pages in small print which were published in early-nineteenth-century England have become a rare oddity, even in France, Eugene's native country, and Austria, the land of his choice. However, a copy exists in New York.

The volume contains none of the bombastic entries that can be found in diaries, memoirs, and proclamations of dictatorial mediocrities, no exclamations about "missions," "inspiration," "intuition," etc. The Prince emerges as a keen human being, often sarcastic, sometimes pitiless.

Had Louis XIV, at whose court he was introduced in the late 1670s as François-Eugène de Savoie-Carignan, granted his fervent wish to be commissioned a colonel in his late teens, Eugene might have become just another of several marshals of France, an habitué of Versailles parties, a connoisseur of many things, hardly different from other grandseigneurs as they came, acted, and went, more or less graciously, their records paling like withering plants. His fellow marshals would have seen to it that his military genius never was permitted to shine above their own mediocrity. But his transplantation to Vienna, where he was needed to fill a gap, turned him into a phenomenon.

What caused this transplantation? One story tells of a frail, hunchbacked youth who longed for a commission, however modest, and miserably stalked the slippery parquet floors of Versailles; who was snubbed by everybody, excluded from all pleasures, cruelly derided by the King, who called him "the little abbé," while he dreaded being relegated to obscure priesthood. The pathetic misfit, so the story has it, began to hate the merciless Louis XIV, his arrogant and reveling courtiers, the very kingdom that was his ancestral home, and he ran away to become the military leader against France.

But this is not what Eugene writes in his memoirs: "Never was the Court as dull as in [1683]. This was the period of Louis XIV's devotion, occasioned by the loss of two sons, Colbert, and the Queen. . . . [I was] weary of being called the little abbé of Louis XIV. He was very fond of me. . . . I was perfectly satisfied with my reception in society, but I wished to distinguish myself in war. Accordingly, at twenty, I was in the service of Leopold I."

The banishment of his mother from court, which occasionally is considered another reason for Eugene's departure, is not mentioned in this connection. He was just one of the young Princes, the students of war, who went east.

He received his baptism of fire in the battle of Vienna. "The Turks, not knowing which way to front, . . . behaved like idiots," he noted. In 1684, he was with the Duke of Lorraine when the siege of Buda was raised. He spent the following winter in Vienna and about that time the

Margrave of Baden introduced him to the Emperor, saying: "Here, Sire, is a young Savoyard whom I have the honor to present to Your Imperial Majesty and who bids fair to equal in time the greatest generals that have ever lived."

Eugene was never flippant about war and disapproved of the young seigneurs who joined armies in "elaborate gala, with a prodigal amount of luggage, incredible numbers of caretakers, and to whom it was a gentlemanly hazardous sport." But he also understood the older generals' concern for the lives of these youngsters.

He never had much trouble understanding the people with whom he had to deal. His judgment was to the point, without confusing speculation. This was also the foundation of his unerring strategy and politics. His personal policy was based on the conviction that *noblesse oblige*. He did not preach generosity, but unobtrusively used some of his opulent means to patronize scientists in various fields. Once, when Vienna was visited by dearth, disease, and unemployment, he hired 1500 men to work on the embellishment of his palace, three times as many as he needed, and for twice the usual wages.

Even in his twenties, Eugene had no illusions, no delusions, no frustrations. He was not an object of seduction either. He usually treated the fair sex with polite attention as long as they did not lavish their charms all too obtrusively upon him. His only "affair" on record, with the attractive Countess Batthyány, occurred in his advanced years and was platonic. Once a gentleman told her that it was rumored she had married Prince Eugene. "I love him much too well for that," she replied. "I would rather have a bad reputation than take away his, and thus abuse his age of seventy-two." Eugene went to her home practically every day; they talked and played piquet. The last time he saw her was on April 20, 1736, a few hours before he died in his sleep.

During the last three years of his life, Prince Eugene, whose advice the Emperor had previously sought on every occasion, was never consulted. For the better part of the last decade, his influence had dwindled. The greatest soldier-statesman the Empire ever had was considered an odd, saber-rattling *bon vivant* who could not understand the ingenious subtleties of statecraft by compact, legal captiousness, and superior sophistication.

Before Eugene's crowning achievements brought the machine of Turkish expansion to a prolonged standstill, the Balkans had been seething with trouble untold.

Already in 1690, when Belgrade was little more than a fortified pole for the Imperial flag, a city without civilian population, Serbian families from the vicinity left their rickety homesteads after a bombastic decree assured them of the Emperor's protection. It also was explained to them that they would be safer in his realm than in a land which the wrathful Turks might retake. This led to a mass exodus such as the Danube Valley had not witnessed since the Migration of Peoples.

The government reluctantly granted land for new settlers in Danubian districts as far upstream as Györ. Thirty-nine thousand Serbian families, with animals, carts, and baggage, gathered at crossings and bridges over the Danube and the Sava, a praying, prattling, mooing, bleating, barking, screeching host that was as colorful as anything that had ever wandered along that exotic path. Their march lasted through most of 1690. Some fell by the wayside, but nobody looked back in nostalgia. Families and clans stayed together, settled, toiled, and eventually fought together, and their immigration strengthened the already considerable Serbian element in Hungary.*

One generation later, the Imperial government used the migrants' children to secure and expand the *Militärgrenze* (military border region), one of the strangest districts on the continent. Its population was molded into a military cadre. Able-bodied men were professional soldiers who worked the land on prolonged furloughs. The womenfolk adopted the men's military jargon, a guttural sort of German without regular syntax, and became army servants, breeders of soldiers, and, if necessary, formidable fighters. The people of the *Militärgrenze* were total soldiers; discipline was their nature, defiance of violent death their dominant impulse. Like their peasant ancestors, they accepted their humble station without objection. The men first did not aspire at commissions; it took some generations before a few of them were promoted lieutenants at the threshold of old age. But regardless of rank, nobody could be more loyal to the Emperor, more determined to serve him and his realm, than those people.

A new Great Vizier, Mustapha Kuprili, learned from his informers that, after the elation about the Turkish defeat had subsided, the Balkan people began to resent the brutishness of the occupation forces and the Imperial manifestoes read on public squares, which promised free elections and other rights but were mere sound and jugglery. Imperial outposts began to crumble. Vidin, on the lower Danube, farthest point of

* This became another factor in the disastrous operation of 1918, by which the Austro-Hungarian monarchy was vivisected along undefinable national lines, and the Danube Basin lay prostrate to foreign tyranny.

Imperial penetration, surrendered to a small Turkish force. Other towns in southeastern Serbia fell. On August 28, Turkish vanguards again sighted Belgrade.

Eight thousand lansquenets under the defeatist Count Aspremont held the city when 30,000 Turks struck. Field Marshal Duke of Croy was sent from Vienna to assume command. He found the glacis along the Danube already in Turkish hands. He used a clever stratagem to enter the fortress, where he found Aspremont dejectedly drafting an offer to surrender. While the two of them argued and exchanged discourtesies, the Turkish artillery opened up. A fireball hit the so-called lead tower of the citadel. A huge flame started up; the three main powder magazines exploded. The blast tore the citadel asunder, destroyed rows of houses, killed many soldiers. A fourth magazine, half a mile away, blew up, causing further casualties.

Croy and Aspremont ran for their lives. Their ceremonial gala torn and soiled, they jumped into a skiff and rowed across the Danube to inglorious safety as yelling Turks triumphantly burst into Belgrade to butcher the dazed remnants of the garrison. Aspremont was court-martialed, but acquitted; incompetence and overindulgence were not punishable under the military code.

Early in 1717, Prince Eugene prepared the most ambitious campaign of his career. He wanted to recover not only Belgrade but all of the lower Danube Valley. His itinerary called for the opening of operations early in the season, but Emperor Charles VI asked him to stay in Vienna a little longer. The Empress was expecting a child and he would rather see the Turks complete their military preparations than be deprived of his mentor during the critical period. The Imperial couple was childless; their only son had died in infancy. They prayed that the new baby would be another boy, a Crown Prince, a future Habsburg Emperor of Austria and Germany.

The child born on May 13, 1717, was a girl. No woman could ascend the German throne, and according to the old family statutes, possession of even the Habsburg realm by a woman was a tricky problem. Already on April 12, 1713, when Charles VI was only twenty-seven years old, he followed the advice of legal experts to assure his progeny's succession in the Habsburg patrimony by an immensely intricate document, the Pragmatic Sanction (the term adopted from Roman Law). Legal mountains labored to give birth to a momentous convolute that was signed, sealed, and filed at the top of the Imperial archives. After a girl became heiress to the throne, it had to be further enlarged and amended, guaranteed by foreign powers, solemnly confirmed by oath by the Estates of all king-doms, principalities, and provinces of the realm. The not too happy fa-ther had food for thoughts that would have overtaxed a much keener mind, and he asked Prince Eugene to postpone his campaign even fur-ther to help him solve the problems of succession. But Eugene insisted that a large, well-equipped, and competently generaled army was the safest protection for the future Empress, Maria Theresa.

On May 14, 1717, Eugene left Vienna. One week later he arrived in Futak, Hungary, on the left Danube bank. Forty-two gentlemen of princely blood waited there to witness the campaign as if it were a gala performance. Many noble volunteers attended to learn the superior art of virtuoso warfare. The Prince, according to his own words, "felt some-what embarrassed."

He had an army of almost 100,000, and a flotilla of some fifty armed river craft furnished by army factors, the most prominent of them one of the indestructible Oppenheimers. The craft were oversized, so they could be used only on the Danube, while Eugene had wanted to use them also on the Sava. The factors were not to blame; nobody had told them that the Sava was a smaller river.

On June 15 and 16, the army crossed the Danube near Pančevo. It went with clockwork precision. Students of war witnessed a masterwork of organization.

The Turkish army, almost 200,000 strong, was not yet ready to strike. Eugene's forces massed near Visnica, east of Belgrade. His engineers, whose skills had improved in decades of practice, built a massive semi-circle of contravallation and circumvallation earthworks that clinched Belgrade in a vise ranging from the banks of the Danube to those of the Sava. The position was called *Eugenische Linie* (Eugene Line) and was the ancestor of twentieth-century lines of fortifications, including the ill-fated Maginot. New pontoon bridges were built across both rivers. Ze-mun, across the Danube from Belgrade, turned into an armed camp and an emplacement for siege artillery that had not yet arrived.

Construction work lasted from June 20 to July 9, an incredibly short period. By July 22, the heavy guns had come, and bombardment of the fortress and the "water city" opened at once. The garrison numbered 30,000.

Slowly the main Turkish army pushed north through the Morava Valley. Small and splendidly maneuverable Turkish river craft raided the big Imperial boats.

Great Vizier Chalil took up positions circling Eugene's semicircle.

"Prince Eugene's advantageous line dominated the fortress, but was in turn dominated by the Great Vizier's position," Imperial war archives recorded. Belgrade was under constant artillery fire. Two ammunition dumps exploded, but the garrison was well supplied with essentials.

Diseases plagued the Imperial camp. Turkish outposts pushed close to headquarters. Prince Eugene sent the inquisitive Princes and noble volunteers to Zemun.

No eyewitness account, no war archive, tells of his embarrassment in the hour of trial. On August 15, he assembled his generals and told them in his typical campaign lingo—French interspersed with German army terms—that he would stage the decisive attack in the small hours. Nobody dared object that their position was precarious. The Turks outnumbered their shock troops three to one.

At midnight, the first Imperial cavalrymen rode out of the circumvallation. Infantry followed. One corps of 10,000 was left behind to block the approaches to the fortress.

The deployment proceeded with swift precision, but dense fog reduced visibility to zero. The Imperial right wing ran into a network of new Turkish trenches. The men fought a murderous close-quarter battle in fog and darkness. General Maffei, a Bavarian, reported that he could not distinguish friend from foe. Every general was on his own, taking mad chances and trusting that Prince Eugene would solve all riddles somehow.

A wide gap opened in the center of the Imperial array. To the rear the fortress of Belgrade was silent. Since artillery did not fire in the fog, the fortress commander did not even know that an all-out battle was raging outside. Had he known and ordered a sortie, the Imperial army might have been annihilated. At daybreak the fog thinned to a translucent haze. Turks infiltrated the gap and began to envelop the split army.

At 8 A.M., the haze lifted as if on cue. Prince Eugene saw the danger. Coolheaded, a superior mathematician of battle, he concentrated all his reserves in the center and, by a hairbreadth, and a minute's time, averted the threat. Imperial ranks closed. The Turks recoiled, fumbled. Prince Eugene saw their lines in confusion. At the head of Bavarian infantry he led a savage onslaught on the enemy key position. He accomplished what the Turks had failed to accomplish two critical hours before—rolling up the enemy lines with devastating effect.

The Great Vizier tried desperately to restore order and regroup, but his soldiers were on the run. It was not yet 11 A.M. when the Imperial standard was planted on the high hill where the Crescent had stood minutes before.

On August 17, Prince Eugene asked for surrender of the fortress. Forty-two Princes and many more students of war watched as a cavalry officer carried the flag of truce to the walls to convey the request. Belgrade was still strong and its 30,000 men could have held out, but the white flag went up.

The Turkish soldiers' main concern was the fate of their women and children. They asked for safe conduct for families and property, and Prince Eugene was amenable. Surrender terms, signed on August 18, included free departure for the soldiers, their kin, and their belongings. Followed a circumstantial exodus; Christian nobles and commoners, generals and privates, sutlers and canteen women, gleefully watched the show.

It was probably in this mood that one of Austria's greatest martial songs was conceived: *"Prinz Eugenius, der edle Ritter . . . ,"* it began.

> *Prince Eugene, the noble knight,*
> *Wanted to recover for the Emp'ror*
> *Town and fortress of Belgrade . . .*

For two centuries Austrian school children have smarted under the necessity of memorizing the bewildering dates, locations, and alleged results of the battles of the period, but they sang this song with an enthusiasm oblivious of the carnage involved. The author is unknown, but whoever it was, possessed an unusual gift for clear-cut presentation and well-cadenced melody.

Once Prince Eugene said bluntly that he liked war. The Emperor's peace negotiators, who a few months later met Turkish negotiators at Požarevac (Passarowitz), remembered this statement and "forgot" to consult him before drafting a peace treaty which gave the Emperor much less than Prince Eugene had wanted to conquer and less also than the military situation warranted.

On learning of the terms, Prince Eugene remarked acidly: "For us, this is only a truce."

CHAPTER THIRTY-EIGHT

A second melody linked with events on the Danube in Prince Eugene's day has survived. It is more popular internationally than the song on the conquest of Belgrade, and the name it glorifies became known to people of many lands who know little else about its bearer and his achievements.

The composer of the original *Rákóczy March* is not known, though he probably hailed from the Hungarian Danube Valley, and there is no evidence that he ever composed anything else.

It is said that the march was the favorite tune of Franz II Rákóczy, the magnificent rebel scion of a family of rebels, to many Hungarians a symbol of their country's struggle for freedom.

The march was first adapted by one Wenzel Ružižka, who died in 1823. The original version was published by G. Matray, twenty-one years prior to Hector Berlioz's use of the motive in *The Damnation of Faust*.

The Duke of St. Simon, who met Rákóczy as a young man, speaks of him as a person of dignity, tact, and common sense, but of no outstanding capacity, so that he could not help wondering "how such a person could create so much unrest in the world, and play so big a part in it altogether."

Baron Hengelmüller, who painted a portrait of Rákóczy, who was born in 1676, tells of his marriage to a German Princess at eighteen, and calls it "only a minor episode." The portrait shows the self-styled champion of Hungarian independence and martyr for Hungary's freedom, in dark polished harness, with long black hair, a carefully groomed mustache, dark round eyes, and a thick lower lip. His features do not indicate any outstanding capacities. By the standards of his time he was a handsome man, even though his looks had a coarse touch.

The fame of the name he carried, his wealth, and his popular appeal made him well suited as a tool of ambitious wirepullers. In 1697, Rákóczy had been the Emperor's unflinchingly loyal subject. A few years later he plotted with Turkey and France, and incited Hungarians to rebellion. His appeals were, at first, not effective, but a salt tax angered the

Hungarians, who were also plagued by bands of demobilized soldiers. In April 1703, unruly elements, including petty nobles, gathered in the hills near Munkács and wrote Rákóczy to lead them to freedom.

Six weeks after his arrival he had 8000 armed followers. The uprising spread like wildfire. The population of the Upper Hungarian mining towns were mostly German Protestants who had religious scores to settle with the Emperor. They joined Rákóczy. Encouraged, he appealed to the people of Moravia and Silesia to rise for freedom's and Protestantism's sake.

The rebel host burst all over Hungarian lands north of the Danube, burning, looting, recruiting. The raiders called themselves Kuruczu and behaved like Turks; from this period dates a Viennese curse: *Krutzitürken!*

War again hit the eastern gates of Vienna. Prince Eugene had fortifications built around the suburbs. The government wanted to have Palatine Paul Eszterházy talk with Rákóczy, but Rákóczy's advisers told him to ask for guarantees and concessions before the parleys opened, and Prince Eugene refused to negotiate with rebels. Archbishop Paul Széchényi gave no hope that the conflict could be settled by religious means.

England and Holland offered to mediate. In Vienna, Prince Eugene hit the conference table with a mailed fist, calling for energy and determination.

During the winter of 1703–4, Rákóczy reveled, celebrating his own rise. The magnificence of his stormy banquets became almost proverbial, and his own elation gave him a mysterious power over the masses. His very appearance led to emotional outbursts.

While Prince Eugene prepared the western campaign, Viennese courtiers implored Archbishop Eszterházy to find out what terms Rákóczy would consider.

Rákóczy asked that a Hungarian Diet be called, not by the Emperor, "from whom the entire nation had defected," but by himself, "whom all Hungarians acclaim." The Diet would state the terms to be negotiated in the presence of delegates from Sweden, Prussia, Poland, and Venice, who should bear witness to Hungary's regained freedom and guarantee any agreement that might be reached.

A postscript to Rákóczy's answer confirmed this assumption. It requested the title of "Prince" and a solemn annulment of his banishment.

Another Rákóczy proclamation followed, summing up charges against the House of Habsburg and its rule in Hungary. It was in Latin, but it did not matter that people did not understand the words; whatever Rákóczy signed turned them into raving fanatics.

Appeasers in Vienna insisted that Rákóczy's reaction be studied most thoroughly and used as a basis for continued negotiations.

Archbishop Széchényi offered mediation by the Emperor's heir, Joseph I, crowned King of Hungary. Rákóczy thundered that Joseph's coronation was invalid; that he should try his luck in a free election, which alone could establish a legal King. Negotiations stalled.

Prince Eugene took a firmer hand on Hungarian affairs. The Emperor himself was all out for drastic action, not only because of dynastic considerations but also because Hungarian raiders had just burned down his beautiful castle of Kaiser-Ebersdorf near Vienna.

Field Marshal Count Siegbert Heister was put in command of Imperial forces in the provinces adjoining the Hungarian border. The arsonists were caught and badly mauled. This was the first setback Rákóczy had suffered. His adherents wanted to hush it over, but grapevine carried the news downstream. The hypnotic spell began to lift. There were dissidents who had to be forced into submission.

The struggle for Hungary turned into a dreadful free-for-all.

Rákóczy was with his army when it laid siege to several strongholds. The men hailed him wildly, but their determination to scale walls under fire was less than stormy. The rebel leader hoped that the armies of Louis XIV, which were massed in the Bavarian Danube Valley, would march down all the way to meet him. He wrote the French King asking for cash and soldiers; the King dispatched Marshal Marsin to Rákóczy's headquarters. Rákóczy was far less haughty in his dealings with the French marshal than he had been in his exchanges with Archbishop Széchényi; he did not even protest too strongly when offering the Crown of St. Stephen to the turncoat Bavarian Elector was suggested.

The French-Bavarian defeat at Blenheim interrupted the negotiations.

Meantime, Transylvanian nobles, assembled in a rump Diet in Weissenburg, proclaimed Rákóczy Prince of Transylvania. Other nobles, officers, and popular representatives of Saxonian stock called the proclamation null and void, but Rákóczy considered himself a legal sovereign, and his pride knew no bounds.

In the spring of 1705, the new Emperor, Joseph I, faced demands by Rákóczy which were actually a repetition of former claims. *"Horrenda execranta,"* the Emperor stormed, and urged Count Herbeville, who had replaced Heister, to hurry to Transylvania.

Herbeville forced Rákóczy to give battle, defeated him, marched on, but his small army was driftwood in the stormy sea of Hungary. When it reached Transylvania the rebellion was far from being quelled.

Rákóczy came to fancy that not even defeat could stop him. He wanted the nation to solemnly sanction his supreme authority. He wanted to stage a princely spectacle.

A National Assembly was convoked to Szécsény, north of Vác.

Representatives of all groups and communities were called upon to elect a leader and agree on a system of government. Rákóczy proclaimed that he would participate as a "simple noble" and put all power into the hands of the Estates. This was the prize idea of his guiding spirit, Count Nicholas Berczény: a display of self-renunciation that had to lead to self-aggrandizement.

The Estates camped in medieval tents as bellicose barons and knights had once done when they gathered to curb and to direct their kings. The general mood was one of dramatic determination and infinite expectation. The Estates had prepared the first word of their program. It was *freedom*. Beyond that word, their views were blurred.

As a "simple noble," Rákóczy, the proudest man around the tent city, was the symbol of freedom, but whither he and it should lead was a riddle.

A reddish sun ball rose over a silvery belt of fog in the morning hours of September 18, 1705. The previous night had been spent with banquets at which everybody was inebriated by golden wines from Tokaj and glittering words from wild-eyed orators.

The session of the Assembly opened with an attendant reading out a federal statute: "The House of Austria, striving for unbounded domination, perjuriously transgressing royal diplomacy, disregarding, nay, trampling asunder, all our laws, having despoiled our nation of its freedom and persecuted it with every conceivable cruelty, . . . Prince Rákóczy, together with all of us, has taken up arms against the House of Austria that wants to destroy our Fatherland and thirsts for our innocent blood. . . ."

The Estates roared and raved, in hate-stimulated exuberance. They hailed Rákóczy as no grandee of this exuberant nation had ever been hailed before. Had he demanded that they rush all the hundred-odd miles to Vienna to wipe out all members of the House of Austria, and carry on to conquer all western lands and seas in the name of the Fatherland and his own, they would have been off like lightning. However, Rákóczy, proud as a peacock, just stood up quietly, radiating magic.

The Estates stormed that he should be their King, and that he was their leader. But Rákóczy, much as he wished to take the helm of a hundred-masted ship, spoke up to say that he would be their Prince if they so insisted, but that they should also appoint a body of twenty-four state councilors and a council of financial affairs.

The fire of enthusiasm was dampened. The councilors began to talk religious matters, finances, internal affairs, political ties to Transylvania. The agenda kept the Estates soberly busy and they resolved to negotiate issues with the House of Austria.

Negotiations soon opened at Tyrnau, in northwestern Hungary (now Slovakia), and dragged on well into the early summer of 1706.

Rákóczy signed high-phrased letters to the Queen of England and the Duke of Marlborough which were printed in the English and Dutch press. Public reaction was favorable, but his partisans could see no way to accomplishment.

Rákóczy offered the Crown of St. Stephen to King Augustus of Poland, who was no taker. He offered an alliance with Sweden, France, Turkey, and Prussia. Sweden and Prussia were reluctant; France and Turkey would have been pleased to use the confusion about Rákóczy for their own designs, but they did not want to accept him as a partner of equal standing.

Many Hungarians still idolized Rákóczy, but in a letter dated November 8 and 9, 1706, to French ambassador Feriol in Constantinople, he said, "Despite all the efforts I have made, and all the advantages King Louis has gained through the struggle, I am like a ship without masts, drifting on stormy seas."

The military struggle resumed, a seesaw affair that caused scores of thousands of casualties and millions in damages.

Rákóczy called another Assembly to meet near Ónod, not far from the site of the historic Mongol battle. It was May 24, 1707, when he greeted the Estates, June 1 when the opening celebrations were over and he could deliver a passionate harangue against the Emperor and his rule. A new note crept into the violent oratory; irritability against recalcitrants in his own ranks. Nobles resented high taxation of feudal estates. City representatives wanted to depreciate the currency. A city official spoke of bad coins. Rákóczy heaped invective upon him and threatened to leave. Swords were drawn. The objector was killed. Another man, who had supported him, was put on the rack and beheaded.

The Diet wound up in terror, but continued terror required greater power than Rákóczy could muster.

Ónod was to mark the turning point in Rákóczy's career. Hungarian camp followers began to leave him, and he no longer had a good press anywhere, including England and Holland.

The fortunes of battle that had, lately, seldom smiled on the rebels, took a turn for the worst in August 1708. Rákóczy personally led his "federal army," the best force he ever had, against the Imperials, who were again under the command of Count Heister. They clashed near Trenčín, north of the Danube. Rákóczy wanted to teach the hated Field Marshal Heister an object lesson, but his dilettantism led to his complete defeat.

Winter brought a terrific cold wave that caused desolation and did not suppress an outburst of the plague.

Rákóczy's magic vanished; Hungarians, heroic or mercenary, were not inspired by disaster.

Rákóczy, his back to the wall, wanted to fight on. It would be a desperado's war to save his life and prevent destruction of his dreams. Those who stood by him had almost nothing to lose.

He tried a desperate move. He visited the Tsar and offered him control of Hungary; he would act as Russia's puppet. But the Tsar knew the score and declined.

Emperor Joseph I died and, during a brief interregnum while Charles VI traveled from Spain to Vienna, the regency in the Imperial capital convoked the magnates of Hungary to restore peace in the unhappy country. That peace was essentially a restoration of the old order, highlighted by a mass oath of allegiance.

The oath was enacted on April 29, 1711, in Szatmár. Ten thousand Kurucz horsemen were among the guard of honor. Rákóczy was in Poland when it happened. But he was mentioned in the compact of Szatmár: "Prince Ferenc Rákóczy" was granted a pardon and the possession of all his family estates in Hungary and Transylvania, provided "he makes a pledge of loyalty within three weeks, and surrenders whatever regions his partisans may still hold."

Rákóczy never pledged loyalty, never returned to Hungary. England refused to grant him haven; he journeyed to France with a few companions.

In 1717, he went to Turkey and offered to serve in the war against the Emperor. The Sultan had no use for him and Turkey lost the battle of Belgrade without Rákóczy's assistance. He wound up an exile, in Rodosto, on the shore of the Sea of Marmara, writing memoirs. There he lived, a forgotten man, until 1735. The Rákóczy family is extinct since 1756.

The memory of Franz II Rákóczy became first glorified in the era of the French Revolution, and not until 1848 did it turn into a heroic legend. When, in 1906, the Hungarian cabinet of Franz Joseph I officially permitted the ceremonious return of the rebel's remains, it was widely believed that Hungary would stay loyal to Habsburg forever.

CHAPTER THIRTY-NINE

Prince Eugene was the only statesman who, as early as the 1720s, visualized Prussia as a major threat to the Empire and to Habsburg rule in the Danubian lands.

Other statesmen, who believed in old-established tradition as the essential source of power, did not think that the kingdom of Friedrich Wilhelm I could be a vital piece in the European chessboard, despite some territorial gains at Sweden's expense in 1720.

Prussia was an upstart. Friedrich Wilhelm's father had merged his holdings around Brandenburg into a kingdom. Originally, Prussia was but a Baltic province centered around the city of Königsberg, a land of little culture and low living standards.

When Prince Eugene was aging, Prussia reached from the Baltic to the Silesian border. It had a zealous, incorruptible, spreading bureaucracy, sound finances, and a charmless but extremely disciplined population that provided the ruler with obedient fuel for his military machine. The King did not care for culture; he had appallingly little of it himself; insiders called him illiterate.

The population figure of Prussia was well below 2,000,000, little over 10 per cent of the corresponding figures for France and Austria.

Prussian army regulations provided that only one third of the soldiers in every unit had to be natives; a thousand recruiters traveled all over the continent to hire men for the King's army. Their spectacular promises were not always kept, but ruthless discipline and the threat of monstrous punishment kept most of the enlisted foreigners from running away.

Friedrich Wilhelm I told his oldest son, Fritz: "Whoever has the cash gets an army, whoever gets the army is respected and admired by the world. Always make a plus."

"Making a plus" meant making profits.

Fritz was one of fourteen children. The King, always intent on setting examples, wished his subjects to beget as many offspring "to arms" as possible.

The features of Fritz—the future Frederick the Great—which would spell catastrophe for the Danube lands, were rooted in his upbringing. His military drill started when he was four. He was trained to live on strict schedules and according to rigid rules, which covered every detail, including the use of soap for washing his hands and face (the latter only at lengthy intervals). Any infraction of rules was severely punished. His father used a stick and slapped Fritz's face rather freely. Fritz's mother, a Princess of Hannover, felt humiliated by her coarse husband, in particular after her brother became King of England. She was a reasonably sly woman, but she found no way of relieving the hardships imposed upon the boy. Exertions made him look aged when he was still a youngster. He walked stiffly and was a poor horseman; his movements were awkward, and he suffered spells of exhaustion. At fourteen, a fever had left him "thin as a hot pole" and when, at fifteen, he had an attack of jaundice, his condition deteriorated to an alarming extent. His mother wept; his father attributed his heir's debilities to his teachers' inefficiency and to the boy's obstinacy, all ills against which the stick was a panacea.

According to the Saxonian ambassador, he forced his son to follow him everywhere and thwarted all his inclinations and desires. "He has only to realize what might please his son, and he refuses it to him."

Friedrich Wilhelm was heavy-set, red-faced, and deplorably unhygienic. Later in life, he was plagued by headaches; his sleep was troubled by nightmares; he had violent attacks of gout, and was turning deaf. In his last years, he was swollen by dropsy to the shape of a barrel, his legs were the size of an elephant's, and he measured eight feet six inches around the belly.

The old King's physical ordeal made him even more eager to inflict ordeal upon his son. The abasement to which Fritz was subjected evoked in him a tendency to masochism; and his military training promoted a distinct touch of homosexuality.

A touch of homosexuality pervaded the gatherings of the old King's evening company: generals, ministers, an occasional ambassador, the army's supreme drillmaster, Prince Anhalt-Dessau, and Professor Grundling, president of the Academy of Berlin, who could drink heavier, smoke more, and tell dirtier jokes than anybody else. When everyone was duly tight, the men danced together, Fritz looking on quizzically. Once the King learned that Fritz had visited Dorothea Elisabeth Ritter, sixteen-year-old daughter of a Potsdam parson. He had performed music with her and given her a few trifles. Friedrich Wilhelm had a surgeon and a midwife examine the girl. Her virginity was found intact, yet the King ordered her arrested and whipped—first in front of the town hall, then in front of her father's house, then in every corner of the town, before sending her to Spandau Prison for a life term at hard labor. (She was pardoned three years later.)

Fritz made no attempt to allay his father's brutality, but in 1730, at eighteen, he tried to run away and was caught.

The raging father called him a scoundrel, a good-for-nothing, a guttersnipe, and a rogue, had him court-martialed and imprisoned, and one of his friends executed. He behaved in such a manner that the Dutch ambassador noted, "If the King of Prussia continues in this state of mind, we shall witness the bloodiest scenes of all times."

The King's state of mind continued, but Fritz humiliated himself with perverted eagerness, and accepted his demotion and discharge from the army and an assignment as a minor clerk in the Chamber of Domains. Then his father decided to marry him off.

Fritz was shocked and frightened. He was not quite twenty when he wrote Baron Grumbkov: "As long as I am permitted to remain a bachelor, I will thank God, but if I have to marry, I shall certainly make a very poor husband. I feel neither constant enough nor sufficiently attracted to the fair sex. The very thought of a wife makes me feel uneasy. . . ."

And to Lieutenant General von Schulenburg, who had presided over the court-martial, he said: "If the King is irrevocably determined to make me marry, I shall obey. But after that, I shall leave my wife and live as I please. I shall grant her all the liberties I shall take myself."

At midnight of February 4, 1732, a royal messenger rushed into Fritz's bedroom, which he usually shared with a male friend, and handed him a letter announcing his father's choice: Elisabeth Christine, Princess of Bevern, a descendant of the House of Brunswick. The King had found her "well brought up, modest, and sensible as a woman should be. You must write to me at once and tell me how you feel about it . . . I will give you a regiment in April . . . The Princess is not remarkable for either good or bad looks . . . You are not supposed to discuss this with anyone, but you must write your mother what I have told you . . . The marriage will not take place until next winter . . . She will be a bearable creature for you . . . May God bless you and your successors."

Fritz replied at once that, "in all submission, I shall not fail to obey orders."

The obedient Prince went into a writing spree, notifying friends, calling his bride-to-be the Corpus Delecti or the Merchandise, and confessed: "If I could be married by proxy, and the proxy could stay on as husband, how happy I would be! I would rather be a cuckold than live with a monster that maddens me with her stupidities."

Three weeks after receiving the royal midnight message, he met Elisabeth Christine. His first impression was expressed in a letter to his sister: "She is an animal quite without charm. She is neither beautiful nor ugly; fair, with a fresh complexion, a pleasing neck, deep-set eyes, an ugly mouth, a silly laugh which reveals blackened teeth, poorly dressed, ill-mannered, not daring to raise her eyes, waddling like a duck, her belly sticking out, always embarrassed in conversation . . ."

The Queen's opinion of her future daughter-in-law was expressed in these words: "Fritz is rightly desperate at having to marry her. She really is stupid. She responds to every remark with a dull Yes or No, accompanied by a silly laugh that makes me sick."

A historian described Elisabeth Christine as having "eyes of periwinkle blue, ash-blond hair, a dainty mouth, a childish charm, ready to blossom forth. She was brought up strictly by parents who frightened her, but when she felt at ease, she talked with wit and gaiety."

The engagement was announced on March 10, 1732. Fritz received a regiment on April 4, and on June 27, he and Elisabeth Christine made their gala entry into Berlin. One week later, the groom left for the garrison town of Ruppin, without the bride.

The old King, who had begotten so many offspring without either love or lust, wanted his son to procreate. Stingy though he was, he invested considerable amounts of money in a seigneurial nest for the young couple at Rheinsberg, not far from Ruppin, and he even tolerated Fritz's having it furnished and decorated in the fancy French manner.

After the marriage, he "animated" the young couple "to make children". He appointed eavesdroppers and keyhole watchers to report on goings on in the princely bedroom which Fritz was ordered to share with his wife. He even promised his son to let him travel abroad after he had produced an heir. General von Manteuffel was assigned to remind the Prince of his duties, and give practical advice, if needed.

The marriage was no mean ordeal for Fritz, and had poor Elisabeth Christine left a diary, it would have had a great deal to tell about her agonies. Fritz felt harried by reproaches and unfriendly glances and told the watchful general that his wife's body might be beautiful, but it did not incite his passion. "Passion is unnecessary," the general lectured.

The tormenting toil continued. In the fall of 1736, Fritz jubilated: "I feel like a stag which is, right now, in rut. In nine months, what they all want will happen." Manteuffel replied dryly: "May God grant that the country air produces its effects," and Baron Grumbkov grumbled that one must "keep trying to do one's duty."

But neither Fritz's staglike feeling nor the country air did their duty. Fritz tried to evade his father's disparagement. At Rheinsberg, which was beyond the sick King's traveling range, he surrounded himself with French artists, philosophers, and refined wits; at Rheinsberg began his friendship with Voltaire; at Rheinsberg he arranged sumptuous banquets which were the very antithesis of his father's parties, where beer or inexpensive Hungarian wine was the basic beverage. In a single delivery, Fritz would receive 800 bottles of champagne, 100 bottles of Volney, 100 of Pommard. The King raised his son's meager allowance, but it was far short of his expenses. Trying to "make a plus," he got involved in shady deals. Creditors closed in on him.

Most of the last period of the King's life was spent in the company of Fritz, who was twenty-eight when the old man died. He had dreaded him as a child, he had knuckled under when in his teens, and he had tried to outwit him when in his early twenties, but he remained fascinated to the end.

The dying King pondered about hell; he dreaded punishment, even though, when in bad humor, he still talked about "making men's heads fly like carrots." He once asked his pastor: "Would it be fair if God, after having loved me sufficiently to let me rule so many men in His place and at my own whim, would, one day, treat me like one of my subjects, and judge me with the same severity?" When the pastor fearlessly replied that God was more severe on Kings than on humble people, he was, at once, discharged.

For several months Fritz waited, writing stories such as "False Prognostic" and "The Miracle that Failed"; occasionally he sneaked out of the palace.

In the small hours of May 31, 1740, Friedrich Wilhelm had Fritz, the ministers, generals, and regimental commanders summoned into his presence. Then he had himself wheeled into the Queen's apartments and ordered her, "Get up, I am about to die." After ordering his wife out of bed, he instructed that all the royal horses be taken out of their stables. Looking out through the window at dawn, he saw grooms putting a blue saddle on a yellow saddlecloth, and told the general to have the grooms beaten with a solid stick. More than twelve hours went by before he breathed his last. Everybody had long thoughts and spoke of him as "the old King." Actually he was not quite fifty-two.

Fritz was now King Friedrich (Frederick) II. Mustached Marshal Leopold of Anhalt-Dessau, more than ten years the old King's senior, chief organizer of the Prussian army, deviser of the goose step, threw himself at his feet and begged him to let him retain his rank and the authority vested in him. "I will leave you in your position," was Fritz's first utterance as a King, "but I don't know what authority you have in mind. It is my intention to retain all prerogatives, and to be the sole authority in the realm."

Elisabeth Christine was in Potsdam. Frederick did not stay with her, but moved to his grandmother's castle at Charlottenburg. May his peasants beget soldiers; his officials, clerks. He, the King, was sex-deferred. He now ruled many people "in the place of God" and he intended to bully many more people, whom he did not yet rule, into submission.

The target of his aggression was Austria: Emperor Charles VI had died, the Pragmatic Sanction was but a wall of paper behind which a once glorious army decayed in noble splendor. France threatened the Habsburg possessions; the Elector of Bavaria coveted the crown of the Holy Roman Empire.

The very fact that Austria was now ruled by a woman aroused Frederick's spiteful ire. Maria Theresa was very feminine, living in wedlock with a full-blooded man whose virility brought results even without the benefits of country air and sense of duty. She was twenty-three, an age that made females embarrassingly lustful. Frederick detested her.

He sent diplomatic agents to France and England to stir up hostility against Austria and readied his army to march into Silesia, which was Austrian and almost without troops. He planned to strike first and then offer Maria Theresa Prussian protection against aggression from other quarters for a price: the "plus" he was trying to make was all of Silesia.

Frederick did not bother with formalities such as a declaration of war. His army marched up along the Silesian border. The provincial capital of Breslau had an autonomous status; the burghers' consent was required to station soldiers in town. The Austrian commander, Count Maximilian von Browne, wearily applied for permission to send half of one battalion and waited for a reply, as the Prussians goose-stepped up the Oder River, invested Glogau on December 22, 1740, and continued toward Breslau. Frederick drafted a proclamation saying that he had come to assist the Protestants of Silesia against Catholic conceit. Some Silesian Protestants welcomed him; many more were lukewarm. Frederick applied subversion. He had stooges and agents planted in many places to organize pro-Prussian riots and frighten loyal Austrians into submission.

Pompously dressed, and at the head of a large martial retinue, Frederick made his entry into Breslau. He ordered all Protestant ministers to base their sermons on I Maccabees, XV, 33: "We have neither taken other men's land, nor holden what appertaineth to others, but the inheritance of our fathers, which our enemies had wrongfully in possession for a certain time."

After the display, he returned to his capital in a triumphant mood, though haunted by secret fears. His Prime Minister, Otto von Podewils, did nothing to allay them: Austria, he explained, had spells of weakness before; it might rally and strike back. Frederick made secret overtures in Vienna: he offered "protection" at a reduced price, Lower Silesia, which did not include Breslau, and he also offered to lend Maria Theresa 2,000,000 thaler for defenses against her "real" enemies.

The answer was a disdainful no.

But France was out to reduce Austria to a second-rate power. The Elector of Bavaria was on his way to being elected German Emperor, thus frustrating the candidacy of Maria Theresa's husband. Even Spain was in the anti-Austrian camp, since a grandson of Louis XIV ruled there. England and Holland were friendly, but this meant little in terms of combat troops.

Frederick opened negotiations on all sides, frantically trying to make the greatest possible "plus," without bringing them to a conclusion. "Levity, presumption, and pride are the main features of his character," wrote the French ambassador.

Poland, displeased at Prussian expansion along her borders, took a strong stand for Austria. A palace revolution in St. Petersburg seemed to herald evil for Prussia. Podewils warned that Pandora's box was opening and all its evils pouring out.

In a gesture of panicky heroism, Frederick decided to deliver a stunning blow. He reinforced his Silesian army to 45,000 men and, on February 19, 1741, left for the theater of war.

Maria Theresa's General Neipperg was about to enter Silesia with less than 20,000 soldiers. Frederick's agents reported on every Austrian move, on every man, horse, and cannon. Prussian Field Marshal Schwerin advocated a massive blow; Frederick's intuition produced no plan of action. There were awkward marches and countermarches, and not until April 10 did the weary and footsore armies meet in the vicinity of the village of Mollwitz.

The battle opened around noon. The Prussians outnumbered the Austrians, but the Austrian cavalry by far excelled the Prussian. By mid-afternoon, Frederick was in despair; Schwerin talked retreat and expressed concern about the King's security. The King, anxious to save himself, rode off in the direction of Glogau, accompanied by only four men. For once, his intelligence services functioned badly. They did not report that the Austrians were back in Glogau, and that the city gates were closed. Austrian sentinels did not notice the approach of the small royal party, and the fivesome fled. Sheer exhaustion made them stop near Löwen. Frederick was a picture of fear of God's corporal stick: "O Lord," he moaned, "this is too much, don't punish me too hard."

At dawn, a courier from Schwerin arrived. The rapid fire of the Prussian infantry had broken the Austrian attack, Neipperg was in retreat, the Prussians had won the battle.

Frederick returned to Mollwitz and received Field Marshal Count Belle-Isle, who had come all the way from Paris to form an anti-Austrian coalition. After some haggling, the Prusso-French alliance was signed on June 3. An army of 40,000 Frenchmen was scheduled to cross the Rhine within two months.

Cardinal André Fleury, who had refused to accept the title of Prime Minister but was, in fact, France's leading statesman, wrote to Marshal Belle-Isle: "Good faith and sincerity are not his [Frederick's] principal virtues. He is false in every respect . . . all of Europe detests him. . . . If he were offered an attractive bribe, he would leave our alliance under some unscrupulous pretext." In fact, Frederick had already entered secret negotiations with Francophobe Lord Hyndford.

By August 22, two French armies, of 60,000 and 50,000, respectively, were across the Rhine, converging into the upper Danube Valley. They were joined by the Bavarians of Elector Carl Albrecht.

Two months earlier, King George II of England had committed himself to support the bid of Maria Theresa's husband, Franz of Lorraine, for the German throne; and he had also pledged to defend the Pragmatic Sanction. England was engaged in war against Spain, and all Parliament could do was to vote subsidies for hard-pressed Austria. The Dutch, also, helped financially.

Sympathy and subsidies, however, could not substitute for the strong army which Prince Eugene had considered essential.

The French and Bavarians encountered no resistance. On September 14, they were in Linz; the road to Vienna, along and parallel to the Danube Valley, was open; Vienna could have been reached within one week. The Habsburg Empire was on the verge of collapse, but it was temporarily saved by Frederick's falsehood and Carl Albrecht's eagerness to secure all votes for his election to the Imperial throne.

The Elector told French generals that they should conquer Bohemia first, that its electoral vote would be cast in his favor. After his coronation they would mop up the Danube Valley.

Frederick concluded his negotiations with Lord Hyndford: the strange Anglo-Prussian pact of Klein Schellendorf stipulated that Austria should evacuate Silesia until a general peace had been signed which would give Prussia Lower Silesia up to the Neisse River. The King of Prussia would undertake no further aggression against Maria Theresa or any of her allies. General Neipperg would be free to turn against the French. The treaty would be kept secret while "on both sides small bodies of troops will continue *pro forma* hostilities."

Maria Theresa could but approve of the pact, though she had to abandon a fundamental principle, the indivisibility of the patrimony, as stipulated by the Pragmatic Sanction.

Frederick had betrayed France, hoping that the double deal would bring him a greater "plus." The day he signed the pact of Klein Schellendorf, he sent Marshal Belle-Isle a letter overflowing with protestations, such as: "To be the arbiter among Kings is the privilege of Louis XV, to be the arm of his power and wisdom is that of Monsieur Belle-Isle."

However, the situation continued grim for Maria Theresa. Saxony joined the ranks of her adversaries, Poland made an about-face, Sardinia laid claims to Austrian possessions in Lombardy. In Linz, the Bavarian Elector proclaimed himself ruler of Upper and Lower Austria. Maria Theresa still had no other forces to face her opponents than Neipperg's small army.

Maria Theresa had left Vienna four weeks before the Anglo-Prussian deal. Already on March 13, 1741, when she gave birth to her first son, who would later become Emperor Joseph II, frightened courtiers agreed that Vienna was no longer a safe place and, as the season advanced and more clouds massed, it was certainly not a safe place to nurse the boy through his infancy.

Hungary, the traditional rebel country, turned into a haven.

Maria Theresa's majestic femininity, which shocked Frederick, aroused the chivalrous feelings of a nobility that had so often defied the Habsburgs, and they now came to the rescue of their first ruling Queen.

Count Johann Palffy, seventy-seven-year-old Palatine—Maria Theresa called him "Papa Palffy"—convoked a Diet to Pressburg and she promised to appear before the assembled grandees and present her case.

The session took place on September 11, 1741. It was one of the noblest spectacles the ancient palace near the Danube had ever witnessed. The Hungarians were in splendid regalia, wearing the most elaborate finery of European and Asiatic, modern and ancient, fashion. Their mood was one of dedication, of almost violent resolve to noble deeds. They rose to pay homage to their sovereign, who came to appeal and to entreat, not to exact or to summon. Carrying her infant son in her arms, in the glorious bloom of her youth, her blond hair radiating, her blue eyes shining, she appealed to the magnates' conscience and chivalry. Whoever may have helped in drafting her address, it was delivered with an emotional power that enthralled her audience.

She spoke of the infamy of Prussian aggression, of the faithlessness of some rulers who had once called themselves her friends, of her own helplessness, but also of her trust in the Estates assembled and in their determination to preserve her patrimony, to protect her from indignity.

The reaction was instant and overwhelming: *"Moriamini pro rege nostro Maria Theresa* [Let us die for the rule of our Maria Theresa]!" Jewel-studded swords were drawn, gloved hands raised to solemn oaths.

The Prussian agent in Hungary, Count Marwitz, made frantic efforts to quell the contagious enthusiasm, but bribes and cabals were to no avail. Hosts of volunteers from all regions and all social groups flocked to the Queen's banners.

Still, the French and Bavarians could have reached Vienna and crossed into Hungary to frustrate the mobilization, but after trudging through the Danube Valley to within thirty-five miles of the capital, they veered north into Moravia, Bohemia, and on to Prague, the Elector's goal. On November 20, the French were in Prague, the Elector was proclaimed King of Bohemia by a rump body of impostors, and on February 12, 1742, he was crowned German Emperor by his own brother, the Elector of Aix-la-Chapelle. As Charles VII, he was supposed to control the upper Danube Valley, among many other districts. But by then he had lost control not only of all of Upper and Lower Austria but even of his own Bavaria.

The regular army had arrived from Silesia, and the greatest Hungarian force since the day of the pagan Magyars was on the rampage. It was a ramshackle force, inadequately supplied with artillery, but the soldiers were determined to fight for their Queen.

On December 31, 1741, all of the Austrian Danube Valley was cleared of the invaders; on New Year's Day of 1742, Austrians and Hungarians crossed into Bavaria, capturing Braunau, Schärding, Straubing, Landshut, Munich, and Ingolstadt in rapid succession. Charles VII, an Emperor without patrimony, took up residence in Frankfurt am Main, dazed by his own simultaneous rise and fall.

Frederick felt that the pact of Klein Schellendorf might become unprofitable, and he resumed the offensive early in 1742. Since Neipperg's army had left, nothing stood between the Prussians and Moravia province and the lands beyond.

Frederick's hussars dashed as far as Stockerau, where they were harassed by light Hungarian cavalry.

In Vienna, a short distance away, Field Marshal Count Ludwig Khevenhüller improvised the rickety defenses; the small garrison was strengthened through mobilization of craftsmen, burgher volunteers, and student corps, and even by Hungarian militia, whom elderly Viennese remembered with vivid horror from Rákóczy's campaign. Maria Theresa, back in Vienna, permitted herself not only to be scared but to admit it quite openly. When Frederick's hussars at last veered off, she called Khevenhüller the savior of her capital.

Charles of Lorraine, Maria Theresa's brother-in-law, drove the Prussians back into Silesia. Field Marshal Khevenhüller took part of the Vienna garrison to Bavaria, to foil an attempt by Charles VII to regain his land.

The fortunes of Maria Theresa and her loyal friends improved in all parts of the war-torn continent. In London, the cautious cabinet of Sir Robert Walpole was defeated in the House of Commons. England pursued war against France and Spain with increased energy; George II even forced the King of Naples to stop fanning further trouble in northern Italy.

What had looked easy to Frederick in January, looked bewildering to him in April. He blamed everybody but himself. The French ambassador reported home: "He is in a dreadful state of mind. His remarks are rough, his laughter is forced and sardonic, his jokes are bitter. Everything arouses his angry suspicion." He did not know of Frederick's entry in his diary: "The welfare of the state demands that I make peace; let us swallow affronts to reach our goal. . . . It is bad to break one's promise without a reason, but I have no good complaint to make against France."

Young Charles of Lorraine was anxious to force Frederick to give battle; he did not know that fresh troops from Prussia, drilled by the much wronged old Anhalt-Dessau, had just reached the King's camp.

On May 17, 1742, the two armies joined battle near Chotusitz, fifty miles from Prague, and the superbly trained Prussians forced their green opponents back as far as Budweis in southwesternmost Bohemia, a short distance north of the Danube.

French advisers urged Frederick to exploit the victory and bring relief to the battered French forces, but he replied: "No French army exists. Your affairs are beyond repair. I am working for my own peace. . . ."

Maria Theresa did not relish the thought of Frederick's "own peace." She loathed the Prussian, and the idea of having him make one of his "plusses" at her expense sickened her; but she needed a breathing spell. George II now wanted her to end the struggle with Prussia, so that England could concentrate on its French and Italian wars. He brought pressure to bear upon both Maria Theresa and Frederick, and a peace of Berlin was signed on July 28, 1742, which gave Prussia all of Lower and most of Upper Silesia, including the county of Glatz.

Charles VII briefly returned to Bavaria. His field marshal, Count Seckendorff, recovered most of the territory lost. Bavarians welcomed their legitimate ruler with cautious enthusiasm, wondering how long his regime would last. It lasted from April to May 1743. Then, reinforced Austrians inflicted staggering defeat upon Seckendorff; Charles VII ran for cover at Frankfurt. An Austrian government was established at Munich, and on September 17, Maria Theresa received the homage of her new subjects.

But an extremely formidable French army under the Duke of Noailles was in the field. The Bavarians now wondered how long the Austrian government would remain in office.

The French King's own guards were among the new forces; they were not supposed to be unduly strained by forced marches. The army was accompanied by many carriageloads of stylish ladies, who took several hours every morning to have their coiffures arranged. The host hardly ever broke camp before noon.

Had the French been early risers they would have overrun the Austrians, who were engaged in time-consuming palavers with German Electors and in diversionary moves.

George II wanted to defeat the French wherever they could be brought to battle. Together with his son, the Duke of Cumberland, he assumed command of the Austro-Hungarian-English forces, and began to move late in June 1743. The comradeship in arms between Prince Eugene and Marlborough was briefly revived.

In the opposite camp, the Duke of Noailles, who had been reprimanded for his dilatory campaigning, also looked for action.

The two armies met near Dettingen in the Main Valley on June 27. The French King's pampered guards were decimated, his soldiers forced back across the Rhine.

Eight months later, a French-Spanish fleet was defeated by the English navy. Louis XV was ready to negotiate peace, but Maria Theresa, flushed with victory, wished to keep whatever her armies held.

The general mood in Vienna spurred Maria Theresa's boldness. Forgotten were the gloomy days when Khevenhüller improvised the capital's defenses, when curious burghers ventured to Stockerau for a glance at the Prussian hussars. The "great hubbub," as the citizenry called it, seemed to be over.

CHAPTER FORTY

The "great hubbub" was superseded by festivities, opening with a thanksgiving for the averted siege of Vienna.

Maria Theresa participated in the affair that drew crowds of dignitaries and immense masses of commoners. At Pressburg she had discovered the appeal of her oratory and personality, and now she wanted to try them on the Austrian Estates and masses.

The Austrians loved lofty showmanship and found their young sovereign very much to their liking.

The liberation of Prague from the French was celebrated in Vienna by a "Ladies' Carrousel." Maria Theresa participated on horseback and gave a remarkable account of her riding skills. The audience raved about their gracious Empress and their marvelous horses; the splendid white *Lippizaner* looked different from the crude Prussian horses that had grazed on the Danubian meadows near Stockerau. The Viennese were positive that they had absolutely nothing to fear from those Prussians.

Maria Theresa's public appearances on horseback were limited by her many pregnancies. She gave birth to sixteen children, ten of whom survived her.

The carnival of 1743 was the gayest that even the old people in Vienna remembered, and certainly the most patriotic. Colorful Bohemian and Hungarian costumes abounded at masked balls; there were parades and dances in national garb; a Bohemian peasant company, organized by Count Schlick, presented Maria with a "patriotic composition as a token of joy." In 1743, Maria Theresa went to masked balls. She and her suite appeared in peasant costumes and danced the rustic *Ländler* at a masquerade in the Ballhaus.

Still there was war, but there had almost always been war, and few common people cared about it as long as it did not directly affect them.

Frederick confided to his diary: "My age, the fire of my passions, my craving for glory, and my secret instinct have torn me away from sweet peace . . . the satisfaction of seeing my name in the gazettes, and later in the annals of history, carries me away . . ."

Maria Theresa had no secret instincts to push her toward war; it gave her no satisfaction to see her name printed; she dreaded defeat, but she relished the homage of handsome armed gentlemen and festivities celebrating victory.

A victory won over the Spaniards near Camposanto came in handy. Eight horn-blowing postilions announced the glorious event to the Viennese, who had had no idea where Camposanto was but who flocked to a splendid *Te Deum* celebrating the event.

In May 1743, Maria Theresa traveled to Prague to receive the royal crown of Bohemia. From Prague she proceeded to Linz. When the French and Bavarians occupied the twin city on the Danube, there had been instances of outright disloyalty which the official lingo called: "rebellious misdemeanor and illegality." But Maria Theresa received a thunderous ovation and everything was forgiven and forgotten.

In July 1743, she boarded a big Danube boat, a floating palace, which experienced skippers and diligent oarsmen took safely through the shoals and whirls along the route to Vienna. Hardly ever before had Maria Theresa seen so much of her country in its radiant summer best, never so much of its rural population. The banks of the river were lined by rows of men, women, and children. Crowds were densest in the last lap of the voyage, from Klosterneuburg to the *Schänzel Ufer* ("bank of the little bulwark"), where Maria Theresa disembarked to ride to her castle.

Official orders were to avoid "reception compliments," but the people went wild with enthusiasm and she enjoyed it immensely.

Austria raved as Austrian armies still battled, and another storm, a replica of the latest holocaust and a forerunner of more evil to come, gathered on the northern horizon.

The Viennese were not efficient political weathermen; they often ignored approaching tempests.

Maria Theresa arranged a shooting match at the town's rifle range, and the Archbishop arranged a vintage festival in his own vineyards in the suburb of St. Veith, which the court society attended in stylized vintagers' costumes.

The carnival of 1744 was less exultant than its predecessor, but ballroom owners, tavernists, and the huge lot of entertainers and their accessaries did well enough. Maria Theresa again took part in the fun. She and thirty-two ladies of the Court masqueraded as Columbines; thirty-three dignitaries, dressed up as Harlequins, had to select their masked Columbine and take her to the ball. The Harlequin who chose the royal Columbine was her own husband.

A few hundred miles away, Frederick prepared for another aggression. Realizing that Maria Theresa had ceded Silesia only under duress and would hardly reconcile herself to the loss, he wanted to fight a preventive war. Worried about the attitude of Russia's Tsarina Elizabeth Petrovna, he wanted to appease the ruler of Russia by selecting a fitting bride for her nephew and heir, Grand Duke Peter.

Frederick seemed successful in his matrimonial endeavors: the Russian Crown Prince was married off to Princess Sophie of Anhalt-Zerbst, niece of a Prussian field marshal. The Princess was not yet sixteen, but, according to Frederick, she combined "the talents of mind and the virtues of heart with the liveliness and gaiety of her youth."

Tsarina Elizabeth did not interfere in Austro-Prussian wars until 1756, when she joined Prussia's enemies, and Frederick's kingdom came within a hairbreadth of destruction. But the former Princess of Anhalt-Zerbst, who was to become Catherine II (the Great), saved Prussia in 1762, when her "virtues of heart" did not keep her from having her husband assassinated and becoming the pro-Prussian mistress of a formidable array of favorites.

Frederick's diplomatic preparations in 1744 were no less careful than his military preliminaries. It was easy enough for him to make agreements with itinerant Charles VII, and with Electors who liked to fish in troubled waters; but France still distrusted Prussia.

Louis XV, however, had another ax to grind with Austria, because Maria Theresa and the King of Sardinia had come to terms that seemed unacceptable to him. On April 27, France declared war on Austria; it was preceded by a declaration of war on England.

Early in May 1744, grave heralds with kettledrums and trumpets announced to the people of Vienna that there was again war with France.

On May 22, at Frankfurt, Frederick signed a union between Prussia, Bavaria, Hesse, and the Palatinate. Two weeks later France joined.

Another "great hubbub" was in the offing.

Under the terms of the compact, Charles VII would be restored to his possessions, Bohemia partitioned between him and Frederick, and France would receive a big slice of Belgium.

Early in July, lucky postilions told the Viennese that King Louis XV's army had been trounced near Germersheim in the Palatinate, and the Viennese celebrated.

But as the Viennese celebrated, Frederick proclaimed that Austria's attitude forced him to safeguard the Empire. The proclamation made little sense morally, but militarily its meaning was unmistakable.

Austria was not prepared to fight a major war along its northern borders. Its main forces were on the Rhine; they had to be disengaged and switched toward Bohemia to protect the Austrian heartlands.

On August 7, the Prussian high-precision fighting machine, the infantry trained to keep up rifle fire much faster than any opponent, burst into Saxony. On August 10, the blue-uniformed Prussian columns trod upon Bohemian soil. On September 2, they were in sight of Prague; two weeks later they entered the city. Its people were summoned to do homage to Charles VII again, which they did in a fatalistic attitude. Frederick continued in the direction of Upper Austria.

But the terrain over which the Prussians marched was difficult; the Bohemian peasants buried their cereals and fled into the deep forests to hide their cattle. Weather was dismal.

Morale deteriorated. By November 18, the number of deserters was estimated at 17,000.

A high Prussian official noted that even a minor defeat in the field would result in mutiny.

On November 19, the Austrian main forces entered Bohemia. The Prussians fled. By Christmas, the Austrians had retaken not only all of Bohemia but also Upper Silesia and Glatz.

Vienna applauded, but the horn-blowing postilions did not tell the full story. The army was getting tired; it had to recoup instead of continuing into Prussia; the mauled French had staged a comeback against virtually no opposition and were established in Bavaria. Jittery on-and-off Emperor Charles VII again lived in his Munich palace. On January 20, 1745, he died.

His demise was celebrated by the Viennese almost simultaneously with the birth of Maria Theresa's second son. The city was illuminated and the childbirth celebrated in super-patriotic epigrams.

Frederick meantime wrote bombastic letters to his Prime Minister: "I would rather perish with honor than live on without either glory or fame. . . . I have crossed the Rubicon; either I must keep my power or else let everything be destroyed, and the name of Prussia go down to oblivion together with my own."

The bottom of Prussia's manpower was scraped, discipline restored. In Lower Silesia, drained by ruthless requisitions, a Prussian army of 90,000 was ready to keep the King's power.

But before the army could strike, the son of Charles VII, Maximilian Joseph, who was averse to perishing, made it known that he would renounce his claims and Prussian sponsorship if Austria would restore Bavaria to him.

Maria Theresa was amenable. She was most anxious to see her husband installed on the German throne, and, on April 22, 1745, some stability returned to the upper Danube Valley as Bavaria was restored to Maximilian Joseph, who, in return, pledged his electoral vote to the consort.

The Viennese hailed the future Emperor and did not pay too much attention to troublesome war reports. In February, the Prussians won a battle at Habelschwerdt; Glatz was evacuated; a dashing Hungarian cavalry raid into occupied Silesia produced no worthwhile results.

But Vienna celebrated diplomatic achievements which actually were restatements of already existing alliances with England and Holland and the consolidation of ties with Saxony and Poland.

On June 4, an Austrian army attempted to trap a weak Prussian detachment near Hohenfriedberg in Silesia. It turned out to be a bait. Frederick with 65,000 men was waiting in a nearby ambush. Hohenfriedberg turned into a major Prussian victory. The Prussians re-entered Bohemia.

Maria Theresa was momentarily stunned, but on learning that her forces had not been annihilated, she resumed elaborate preparations for her husband's coronation, and shrugged off Frederick's victory message to Berlin: "*Te Deum* is suitable for the occasion."

Frederick's civilian advisers dreaded the aspect of continued war with manpower reserves exhausted, but the King wanted his "plus." Summer went by. Austria made no lucrative peace offer. Frederick waited and corresponded with his sisters, the Queen of Sweden and the Duchess of Brunswick, who idolized him blasphemously. "You are my deity," the Queen extolled him; "You are my saint," the Duchess wrote.

Frederick was indignant when somebody showed him an Austrian gazette in which his name was mentioned in a most disparaging manner. He blamed it on Maria Theresa and felt morally justified for every iniquity he had already inflicted upon her, and all the iniquities still to follow.

On September 14, Maria Theresa triumphed in the long struggle for her husband's Imperial crown: on that day the Electors, with seven votes out of nine, made him Emperor Franz I of the Holy Roman Empire.

On October 4, he was solemnly crowned at Frankfurt. Maria Theresa sat in an ornate box amidst other guests of honor and hailed Franz I with an enthusiasm bordering on hysteria. Until then, hostile statesmen and sovereigns had referred to her as the Queen of Bohemia and Hungary. Now that Franz was Emperor, she was his Empress. She had no prerogatives in the Holy Roman Empire, however, just as Franz could not rule the Austrian, Bohemian, and Hungarian patrimonies.

The Empress' subjects were urged to rejoice, and they did so with their traditional gusto. Their city was an Imperial capital again!

The Duke of Lorraine made another attempt to defeat Frederick but was repulsed in Saxony.

On December 25, a peace signed in Dresden confirmed Prussia's possession of Silesia, guaranteed by England, Holland, and, supreme irony, by the Holy Roman Empire. Frederick made a "plus" by collecting an indemnity from Saxony. He had been worried by the drain on his father's treasure chest of seventy million.

"The future is beyond my grasp," Frederick told Monsieur Darget, one of his French readers. "I have acquired, let others preserve. I shall henceforth not even attack a cat, except in self-defense."

One hundred and ninety-three years later, Adolf Hitler, whose main object of cult was Frederick of Prussia, exulted that all of his claims were settled after he had been awarded, with an English guarantee, districts in Bohemia and Moravia, to which he held no legal title whatever. The world had believed Frederick in 1745; it seemed to believe Hitler in 1938; but while Frederick waited a decade before resuming his attack, Hitler's settlement lasted for less than a year.

In 1745, the people of the Danube Valley were not aware of the continued threat. The Viennese merrily felt that everything was being rejuvenated. The Emperor looked younger than his thirty-seven years, the Prince of Lorraine was a very youthful commander in chief; new faces appeared on the stage, a new smart set bowed gracefully. Everybody talked about the end of the old system.

The most obvious changes occurred in the world of the theater. The expensive pompous court opera was temporarily discontinued. The venerable Ballhaus was rented to a private entrepreneur who arranged glittering balls as well as performances of opera, mostly Italian, and of drama, mostly French. Whoever could afford a ticket could dress up and see opera at the Ballhaus, which was soon renamed "Royal [later Imperial] Privileged Theater Near the Burg," and it became the ancestor of the Burgtheater, one of the leading German-language stages.

On festive occasions, the Court rented the former Ballhaus for one single performance—the fee usually was 200 ducats—and invited the nobility and ranking burghers to attend as guests.

On May 14, 1748, Gluck's *La Semiramide Riconosciuta* (*Recognized Semiramis*), libretto by Court Poet Metastasio, was first performed at the Royal Privileged Theater Near the Burg.

The former Court Opera House was transformed into the Redoutensäle, where masked balls were arranged between walls hung with priceless tapestries. The brothers Lopresi managed the Redoutensäle. The code of behavior in which they believed was far too liberal for the Empress' taste, which took a sharp turn toward austerity as she reached thirty.

Continued pregnancies prematurely turned Maria Theresa into an overweight matron. The radiancy of her youth vanished. Emperor Franz I was still dashingly handsome, and his wife did not wish to see him pay attention to anybody but herself and their sprawling family.

When Franz embraced Freemasonry, as quite a few ranking grandees did, his Empress joined the foes of this institution and had her police raid lodges, including the one to which Franz maintained close relations. A hushed tale of Imperial adventure circulated in Vienna. Franz was said to have visited the Redoutensäle as an incognito masquerader and a masked pretty lady had kept him stimulating company for the rest of the night. Maria Theresa decreed that masked persons who violated strict rules of decency should be ordered to leave the Redoutensäle; severe infringements should lead to arrest. Henceforth, mutually attracted masqueraders left the Redoutensäle for the untroubled privacy of small rooms rented by complaisant tavernists or plain procurers. Franz I could and would never have indulged in such licentiousness, but Maria Theresa did not want even her subjects to indulge in lechery. She issued orders *in puncto sexty* and established a special commission to see that all clandestine trysts be prevented or, at least, disturbed. This caused a scornful stir in the foreign press. French newspapers coined the term *Commissions de Chasteté* (Chastity Commissions), which became the object of much satire.

France had not conquered Austria, but a dainty intruder from Versailles, Rococo,* took the place of the proud hymns in stone that characterized Baroque. Rococo was as playful as Baroque was forbidding, and Austria wanted to play.

Border lines between social strata were no longer as rigid as before. Noble parents asked poor people to attend the baptism of their infants. Commoners of means and merit were titled; the Court participated in popular festivities, provided they could pass as religious. The Emperor undertook a short pilgrimage on foot, to the horror of his courtiers, who were not in the habit of hiking.

The Austrians liked their army, its mounts, brass, and banners. The Empress also liked martial display. In a great spectacle arranged in December 1748, seven-year-old Crown Prince Joseph led a parade of his own cavalry regiment before his parents. He had had his first riding lesson three weeks before the occasion, and the parade was not yet over when he parted abruptly with his gentle mount. People found this very charming, and it made Joseph even more popular than he had become a short time before, when he had cried bitterly at a rustic passion play.

Much as the Empress liked display, the expenses involved frightened her. Her urge to keep expenses under control was almost as strong as her desire to recover Silesia. But in order to recover Silesia, she would need a formidable army of 100,000 men as a standing force, in addition to huge levies during campaigns.

The Empress studied the accounts of her provinces like a good housewife studying her housekeeping record, and found them alarmingly unpleasant. Governors and Estates complained about ruinous military contributions, but in a report of 1747, Carinthia listed military contributions as 2,800,000 gulden, while the provincial debt had risen by 4,000,000. The army's commissariat proved that no more than 100,000 gulden had reached its coffers. This smelled like mismanagement and called for an investigation.

* The name is derived from *rocailles,* the artificial grottoes and rock gardens of Versailles.

Maria Theresa learned that an investigation of Carinthian affairs had been under way for forty-seven years and that, four Emperors and two generations of investigators later, the matter was still pending. However, it was now established that more than half of the disputed 2,800,000 gulden had gone down a secret drain into the pockets of the Estates, and that the members of the investigation commission drew fees and bribes for stalling.

The realm's very foundations seemed to be rotten; Estates were corrupt, and it was remembered that they had also been subversive. Maria Theresa's younger advisers insisted that the power of the Estates should be curtailed and that a clean, centralized government should supersede old-fashioned provincialism. But Count Friedrich Harrach, First Chancellor of Austria and Bohemia, called the estate system the ideal safeguard against centralized absolutism. Count Harrach was a man of learning and experience, and his affluence made him immune to bribery. Other members of the government also said that the Estates would eventually weed out corruption and carry the monarchy over whatever crisis could arise.

With a housewife's view of the affairs of the land, Maria Theresa failed to see how corruption could be weeded out through greater power vested in the corrupt.

The young advisers, who advocated centralized government, did not have the prestige to draft reformers. But Maria Theresa knew of a man who might meet every requirement: Count Wilhelm Haugwitz, son of a Saxonian general, who in 1725 had become a member of the administration of Silesia. His career had been slow for a person of his standing, but he had had plenty of opportunities to study the pitfalls of regional administrations and the noxious system of contributions. His superiors called him a grumbler. When the Prussians invaded Silesia in 1741, their civil administrator, Baron Fürst, had called him a moron.

Haugwitz had left for Vienna, his most cherished possession being a credential letter to Maria Theresa's husband. Franz passed Haugwitz on to some courtier who had not much use for him and got some countess interested in the poor but patriotic refugee from Silesia. The countess knew that Maria Theresa had a soft spot for victims of Prussian invasion but hesitated to introduce him to the sovereign because he had a constant nervous tic in his eyes that might irritate her. Eventually, however, Haugwitz was granted an audience. Eyes nervously twinkling, he told a story of loyalty which fitted Maria Theresa's mood, and she appointed him *Capo,* chief of the provincial administration of whatever would be left of Silesia. Haugwitz tried hard to turn leftovers into a going concern and a showcase of good administration, and almost immediately found himself involved in a bitter feud with the Estates. He did not enforce his will, but he made *notates* (notices) which eventually became the basis of administrative reform.

According to the notices, the sovereign should have complete power to decide in all financial and administrative matters. This was absolutism —not objectionable in the mid-eighteenth century—but Haugwitz wanted to amend it into a representative system through delegation of powers and broadening of advisory influences. In 1747, the author of the notices edited his learned words into a pattern to meet the wishes of the Empress.

A Crown Council was called for January 29, 1748. The Imperial couple was present, Franz acting as an observer. Present also was the entire cabinet, of which Haugwitz was a member, and other top dignitaries of the realm. The Empress and Haugwitz stood alone against all the other participants. Haugwitz presented his program. Ulfeld, Kinsky, Colloredo, Sallsburg, and even Harrach courteously voiced scathing objections. Maria Theresa's representation did not have the smooth sophistication of her minister's oratory, but she ordered that the Haugwitz reform be put into effect forthwith.

This is what the Empress wrote under her signature of the minutes of the meeting: "Placet, and this settles the matter. In fifty years from now, one will be at a loss to believe that these were my own ministers, whom I have appointed."

On May 2, 1749, the new central authorities were installed; "deputations" from the provinces had to consult with them on local issues. The reform ran into much sabotage, and a keen observer, Prussian Prime Minister von Podewils, predicted that the new system would fizzle out.

But centralization gradually became an established fact, and Haugwitz, though later sidetracked by the omnipotent Chancellor Prince Kaunitz, always kept his cabinet rank and retained the Empress' unflinching favor until his death in September 1765.

CHAPTER FORTY-ONE

Count Wenzel Anton von Kaunitz (later Prince von Kaunitz-Riet-berg) was the architect of Vienna's foreign policy from 1749 to the end of Maria Theresa's regime; he continued in office through the successive regimes of two of her sons, and resigned only in 1792, at eighty-one, when an unappreciative grandson ascended the throne.

March 7, 1749, was a crucial date in Kaunitz's career; he received an Imperial summons to outline his opinion on "what our policies toward France, England, and the Reich should be, now that peace is restored." Similar summonses went to all members of the Imperial cabinet, but when the opinions came in, Maria Theresa paid attention to no one but Kaunitz.

He wrote: "We must consider the King of Prussia to be our worst and most dangerous enemy. We shall never forget, never accept, the loss of Silesia. We must set our minds upon weakening said King and recover the lost province. Co-operation with naval powers [meaning England and Holland], good as their intentions may be, is of doubtful value; the naval powers hardly have the means to achieve Austria's objectives. Therefore, understanding with France should be brought about. . . . A generous price should be offered to achieve this purpose; it could consist of the sacrifice of a province in the Netherlands or Italy."

Maria Theresa appointed Kaunitz ambassador to Versailles. The su-perbly dressed and mannered gentleman, the Vienna-born scion of wealthy Moravian aristocracy, had already held two ambassadorships. The refined charm of Versailles pleased him immensely; it made him feel even more that France and Austria were a fitting match, both politically and socially.

Louis XV saw Kaunitz quite often, and the royal mistress, Madame de Pompadour, found him very much to her liking. Kaunitz repeated, time and again, that past quarrels should be forgotten, that the French and Austrian courts should be allies, while Prussia . . . He did not imme-diately elaborate on this point.

Louis XV spoke of Maria Theresa in terms of gentlemanly admiration; however, he said that France was not in the habit of changing allies.

Kaunitz became ever more insistent. He said that France had changed allies before, and so had Austria. He spoke of the sympathies of the Protestant English merchants for Frederick of Prussia, of King George II's troubles, of the feebleness of the French navy, which, a short time before, had had only one capital ship in European waters. Kaunitz predicted that England would drive France from her overseas possessions, that Prussia would supersede her on the continent, unless she became Austria's ally. Louis XV listened and said niceties.

For three years Kaunitz wrote vaguely worded reports to Vienna, where the State Chancellery professed enthusiasm to please the Empress, and secretly hoped that he would fail and vanish from the international stage.

In the spring of 1753, an angry Maria Theresa recalled Kaunitz, appointed him Chancellor, and replaced him in Versailles by Prince Starhemberg, who continued to play his predecessor's game.

A new political era began. The Danubian lands became the pivot of world events. World events began to usher in world wars.

Frederick of Prussia had had a premonition of war since 1753. In 1755 he wrote: ". . . armament will invariably lead to more armament, and eventually to diplomatic ruptures in a manner unplanned and unforeseen."

Kaunitz established a new foreign affairs division at the Chancellery and staffed it with men whose intelligence and integrity he trusted. The veil of secrecy that covered its operations was not easy to penetrate. A Prussian official complained: "In the past, there were many ways of learning secrets, but Count Kaunitz and his staff are incorruptible, and too prudent to give anything away."

In 1754, when global disputes between England and France seemed to defy solution, Kaunitz played both sides against Prussia. King George II of England wished to maintain friendship with Austria, but did not want to commit himself to go to war against Prussia.

Frederick, who once had not wanted to "attack a cat," pondered another preventive war. He requested that France join him against Austria, regardless of who opened hostilities, that it keep the "schemer of Hannover" (the King of England) from intervening, that its minister to St. Petersburg pressure the Russians into remaining at least neutral, and that Turkey be invited to join action against Austria. Louis XV's reaction bordered on impatience, which Austrian ambassador Starhemberg exploited with a clever intriguing hand.

In Vienna, Kaunitz said: "Prussia must go down so that the Imperial House may be preserved."

The shower of sparks grew ever denser.

Austrian generals grumbled about the lack of men and supplies, but Vienna society talked mostly about a new Chinese ballet and the collection of rarities in the Imperial castle.

Early in 1755, in Versailles, orders were signed to assemble a huge convoy of merchantmen, troopships, and men-of-war to sail to Canada.

On April 16, 1755, English admiral Edward ("Old Dreadnought") Boscawen, commander of His Majesty's American squadron, was instructed to station a cruiser in the St. Lawrence estuary and attack without warning the French convoy due to leave Brest at the end of the month.

England's machine of European alliances was out of gear. England would have to get more continental support, or at least establish a balance of power in the Danube Basin, so that she might have a free hand on the St. Lawrence. Austria, tit for tat, refused to be drawn into a war brought about by "piracy beyond the seas"; and the only offer for the support of England came from Hesse-Cassel, whose landgrave had 8000 auxiliaries for sale. So England tried Prussia. The Duke of Brunswick, a relative of Frederick in desperate need of money, was the go-between.

Frederick played hard to get. In turn abusive and amenable, he drafted instructions, bickered with England and France, and mobilized. His army was the most formidable and best organized anywhere.

England also negotiated with Russia, and on September 30, 1755, they guaranteed each other's territorial possessions. Russia agreed to station 55,000 soldiers in Lithuania to enforce the guarantee, and charged 600,000 pounds for it.

The Austrian ambassador to Versailles emphasized that now or never was the time for France to become Austria's ally; he warned of an impending Prusso-English deal.

Early in December 1755, the Prussian King protested that he had made no arrangement with England, and that reports to the contrary were "malicious insinuations." Technically, the first part of the protestation was correct. He decided to make the disputed arrangements only five days after he issued the demento.

The Treaty of Whitehall was drawn up on January 1, 1756, and ratified in Berlin and London on January 16. It stipulated that the Kings of

Prussia and England undertook, "whatsoever foreign power upon whatsoever pretext desired to march its forces into Germany, to unite their forces to prevent the entry or passage of the troops aforesaid."

The Tsarina was so furious that she even refused to accept the first installment of the 600,000 pounds.

France was ready to join Austria, but it took until May 1, 1756, before the Treaty of Versailles was signed. France renounced her Prussian ties, Austria her English alliance; both exchanged territorial guarantees. Maria Theresa asserted that she had never put her name under a paper with so much satisfaction.

The Tsarina received the news of the Treaty of Versailles with elation; she offered her "sister Maria Theresa" an army of 80,000 and promised not to lay down arms as long as Frederick held Silesia and Glatz. France was ready to foot the bill for the Russian army. Austria promised France Luxemburg, Ostende, Nieuport, and more of Belgium, "after victory." Sweden talked with France about Stettin and Pomeranian duchies to be snatched from Frederick. Europe was a coat-turning madhouse. In America, the French and Indian War was about to start.

The Austrian army was concentrated near Vienna, many days' march away from the theater of operations; orders were issued to "refrain from unnecessary display that could lead to a premature outbreak of hostilities."

In May, June, and July, arms were silent in Europe, though high-ranking tongues kept wagging.

The English ambassador warned Frederick not to let himself be provoked into aggression. The King replied furiously: "Do you think that my nose is made to be pulled? By God, I won't stand for it." And, pointing at a portrait of Maria Theresa on the wall of his study, he shouted: "This lady wants war, and she shall have it soon enough."

Late in July, the Prussian ambassador to Vienna requested an explanation for Austrian military preparations. No satisfactory reply was forthcoming. He asked for an audience with the Empress and told her that Frederick found it hard to believe that she wanted to attack him. "Circumstances being rather critical," he learned, the Empress wanted to take every precaution to safeguard the security of her country and its allies.

Troops marched through Vienna. From suburban camps, regiment after regiment moved toward Bohemia and Moravia.

While troops still at peace crossed the Danube bridges, troops already at war battled for control of the strategic Ohio Valley. The American fighters included one not widely known officer whose name was George Washington.

On August 25, 1756, Frederick received Maria Theresa's cryptical and challenging reply to his ambassador's *démarche*. He decided to move at once, figuring that the Empress, pregnant again, would wait another three or four months, until after the childbirth, before taking action. Prussia had a population of nearly four million, still a small fraction of the combined populations of Austria, Hungary, France, Russia, and Sweden; but the Prussian army of 100,000 was not too much outnumbered by its opponents, and Frederick counted on poor co-operation among his foes.

On August 28, at 4 P.M., Frederick left his capital and later that day his vanguards crossed into neutral Saxony. He had always wanted to incorporate it into a Greater Prussia, and he also hoped to find proof in the Dresden state archives that Maria Theresa and Louis XV had tried to lure Saxony to join their policies of "encirclement" and "dismemberment of Prussia."

But when he entered Dresden without meeting resistance and had the state archives ransacked, he did not find a single paper that fitted his scheme. He entered the royal palace and ordered that the secret files be opened. King Augustus III had not yet returned from a hunting trip, but the valiant Queen and her daughter refused to comply. Frederick called his grenadiers and from their ranks selected professional burglars to break into the archives. The ladies tried to block their path. The grenadiers pushed them away as Frederick looked on. The private correspondence of Saxonian royalty was spread out before him. But much as he searched, he did not find anything he could hope to exploit.

Augustus returned from his trip, and found his capital seized, his family abused and terrorized. He assembled a handful of soldiers, hoping to hold out until Frederick should be engaged by Austrian troops. But by October he had to surrender and "withdraw to Poland," while his soldiers were inducted into the Prussian army. They did not strengthen Frederick's forces, however, which had long ceased to be desertion-proof, and the Saxonians set a mark with 90 per cent turning deserters.

Maria Theresa reacted to Frederick's Dresden performance with emotional indignation. She sent the Saxonian Queen comforting letters, and, at last, on September 21, issued a war manifesto. Three of Vienna's principal churches arranged public prayers for victory, and on September 25, the Prussian ambassador was asked to leave. Chancellor Kaunitz issued a scathing denunciation of Frederick's violation of Saxonian neutrality.

Near Lovosice in Bohemia, the Austrian army, again under Count Browne, waited for marching orders. Frederick invaded Bohemia and the two armies joined battle. Both suffered heavy losses, both claimed victory; but when Frederick veered off to finish his business in Saxony, Browne was in no position to interfere.

After Frederick's troops set up winter quarters along the border, he engaged in violent psychological warfare. He had a pamphlet mass-distributed by secret agents all over the Reich and the Austrian provinces, showering readers with maliciously false, but impressive, claims that war had been forced on Prussia. Austrian authorities countered with a "manifesto," exposing Prussia; Prussia published yet another pamphlet; Austria called it "more, ever more indecent and scurrilous effusions," and had a "general refutation" printed, which the Viennese read with less interest than the announcement of the birth of Archduke Maximilian and the unusually moving story of the late Privy Court Paymaster Karl von Dier.

Faithful Karl von Dier, through a life devoted to dealing with the Imperial accounts, had managed to "put aside" the fabulous sum of 400,-000 ducats and had willed it all to the Empress.

Had it not been for Dier's nest egg Austrian soldiers might have gone without pay in the fall of 1756. The state balance sheet showed a deficit of 19,000,000 gulden. The Empress pressed for strict economy and forbade all masquerades during the carnival.

The people of Vienna did not expect the war to last long. On January 25, 1757, the German Empire pronounced the great ban (anathema) upon Frederick, and decreed mobilization of the Reich's army. The Tsarina assembled 80,000 men, and Louis XV promised—a promise confirmed by the Second Treaty of Versailles, May 1, 1757—to join the Austrians with 105,000 regulars and 24,000 auxiliaries.

But as spring approached, Prussian forces held Russians and French in check, while inflicting heavy blows upon the Austrians. Kaunitz wondered whether unstable Frederick was not a military genius, or whether Austrian generals were plain incompetent.

In April, the Chancellor left for Bohemia, accompanied by a small staff of experts. From the opposite side Prussian columns moved in the direction of Prague. The Austrian army closest to the Bohemian capital was under the command of Charles of Lorraine, and expected another Austrian force, under Field Marshal Count Leopold Daun, to arrive in time to help defend Prague.

Kaunitz proceeded to Daun's headquarters at Böhmisch-Brod (Český-Brod). The fifty-two-year-old field marshal rated highest among Austrian top commanders as a calculating, shrewd man who never procrastinated. In his youth he had been with Prince Eugene, but his attitude in the early spring of 1757 did not indicate that he had learned a lesson from the great master. First, Kaunitz thought that Daun was a dull, stuffy courtier, with a rather stupid face. But after they had several lengthy talks, he came to feel that Daun was more intelligent than he looked, and he was impressed by his determination to reach Prague without further delay and give a battle that would seal Frederick's doom.

As Chancellor and field marshal talked victory, hordes of fleeing soldiers reached Böhmisch-Brod. They had a grim story to tell. The battle of Prague had been fought and lost. Charles of Lorraine had an upset stomach; his cavalry charge collapsed; Field Marshal Browne, who rallied the wavering Austrians, had his right leg smashed by a cannon ball, and the leaderless army succumbed to a concentrated Prussian assault.

Kaunitz started to write to the Empress. He opened with the phrase that he would tremble at the thought of endangering the lives of Emperor and Empress by a crushing shock if he were not convinced of their admirable fortitude. At that point, he reconsidered, implored Daun to turn defeat into victory, and drove off to Vienna.

He hoped that a hard-riding courier with happy tidings would overtake him on the bumpy road. But no harbinger of victory overtook him, and he appeared in travel clothes before Their Majesties to tell what he had not brought himself to write. But his speech faltered and he asked one of his companions, General O'Donnel, to explain. O'Donnel said that the cavalry had given a despicable account of itself, and broke into sobs.

Maria Theresa, thunderstruck, retired to her fancy castle of Laxenburg, ten miles south of the capital, and from there toured churches, made short pilgrimages, and had local people and her courtiers assemble every evening at the Nepomuk Column to sing litanies and say prayers.

Yet, even though the battle of Prague on May 6 was a Prussian victory, the panicky soldiers at Böhmisch-Brod had presented a wildly exaggerated version of what had actually happened. Austrian losses totaled a little over 13,000, as against 12,500 Prussian casualties. Forty thousand Austrians and most of their cannon had reached Prague, where from his sickbed Browne directed the operations. Prague was under Prussian artillery fire, at an average of 4600 balls daily, but it would hold out until relief came.

Relief came from Daun; a glorious charge of Austrian cavalry decided the day at Kolín on June 18, 1757. The Prussians lost one third of their effectives and much of their artillery. Prague was relieved three days after the battle. Count Browne lived to see the entry of the Empress' troops, but succumbed to his wounds a few days later.

Frederick was defeated, Bohemia free. French, Russian, and Swedish columns closed in on Prussia.

Kolín would have been a decisive battle had not subsequent lack of co-ordination, energy, and intelligence in the anti-Prussian camp destroyed a chance that might have altered the course of world history. And whenever, between 1757 and 1763, Prussia was again threatened with destruction, similar shortcomings made the theme of Kolín repeat itself with tedious variations.

In Austria few battles created a multitude of legends comparable to Kolín. The affair was turned into an endless sequence of individual heroic deeds. The legends were preambled by the Empress' thanksgiving letter to Daun, in which she called June 18, 1757, the birthday of the monarchy.

When the report of Kolín arrived by mail coach four days after the battle, Maria Theresa dashed back from Laxenburg to Schönbrunn; the galleries and halls of the huge castle turned into one reception room for whoever ranked high enough in society, newly knighted war profiteers rubbing shoulders with peers of the realm, while outside the castle commoners cheered wildly and quick-witted peddlers sold refreshments.

Celebrations continued for five days, during which more couriers reached the capital with more elating details of the battle and a few captured Prussian banners; sixteen postilions and three postmasters did an incredible amount of trumpeting.

On June 22, the Empress expressed her thanks "to all My military" by creating a new decoration, the *Militär Maria Theresien Orden*. Its first Grand Cross went to Count Leopold Daun. This decoration remained the highest any Austrian or Hungarian officer could gain in action, until the end of the monarchy in 1918. It was bestowed in three classes: the Grand Cross, the Commander's Cross, and the Knight's Cross. Unspectacular as the small white cross looked, the *Militär Maria Theresien Orden* carried a hereditary barony and a generous lifetime pension. Regulations provided that neither high birth, nor rank, nor seniority should be considered when the award was made, and that the number of candidates should never be curtailed. The more heroic deeds were performed, the more decorations would be awarded.

But the lure of glory and opulence exemplified by that decoration resulted in much calamity, because of a strange proviso that was added soon after Daun received the Grand Cross. It was an amendment which a male monarch would hardly have dreamed up but which fitted the emotionality of the Empress.

The idea was born after the heroic prank of General (later Field Marshal) Count Andreas Hadik, who, on October 16, 1757, raided Berlin at the head of 3500 Austrian cavalry. The Prussian garrison of more than twice that number fled ignominiously and Berlin was in Austrian hands for twenty-four hours, after which Hadik learned that a Prussian army was approaching at forced marches, and left, not without collecting a contribution and destroying the cannon foundry of Spandau.

Jubilantly, Maria Theresa said that Frederick would never recover morally from the humiliation, and she considered it extremely funny that part of the contribution, sixty pairs of leather gloves for Her Majesty, were all left ones. The Empress thought that Daun had masterminded the raid, but on learning that Hadik had acted against Daun's orders to cover the approaches to Dresden, she decreed that, beginning with Hadik, officers who, defying orders, performed an important feat of arms should apply for the *Militär Maria Theresien Orden*.

Many foolhardy, silly, tempestuous actions were carried out by Austrian and Hungarian officers stimulated by the maniacal urge for knighthood.

But, crowned steward as the Empress was, she economized on her military establishment. When told that a standing army of 200,000 should be maintained, she sighed that she could not afford to pay for more than half that number; when generals insisted that fortresses be built, she agreed, but did not want any of the fancy elaborate constructions as French luminaries drafted them, but something solid, simple, and inexpensive. She also wanted transportation to be economical, baggage trains and artillery to share horses, provisioning to be less expensive. She did not wish officers to take their women along on campaigns at public expense; if these gentlemen could not do without tender company, they should pay for it.

The Empress spent weeks and months calculating a per capita budget for the provisioning of enlisted men and non-coms; she was satisfied that it would suffice to purchase all the victuals a healthy country cousin could eat, but refused to take into account that the army was moving, that supplies would often stay behind, that reserve stores had to be on hand, and that spoilage was greater in the field than in an orderly household.

Most remarkable for a woman, she even tried to economize on uniforms. Everybody liked them gaudy; the more gold and silver trimming the better—even buttonholes were trimmed with glittering stuff. But this was another drain on the tight budget. So, no more trimmings for officers below field rank, and Maria Theresa was proud to see junior officers soberly garbed. Whenever she attended parades on horseback, she wore a simple white-and-purple riding dress, barely trimmed.

Much as she liked horseback riding when her condition permitted, she was a poor sailor. Even during her spectacular boat ride down the Danube, she had spells of uneasiness.

Her father had once planned to have two powerful navies, one on the Adriatic, the other on the Danube. But as time went by and Prince Eugene, a champion of shipping, retired, Charles VI's ambitions dwindled, and when he died he left his daughter fifteen men-of-war, mostly of modest size, at Trieste, and one lone frigate on the Danube. Economy-minded Maria Theresa had no desire to add more craft to her cut-rate navies, and eventually decreed that they be disposed of in a sensible manner.

It took eighteen years to sell the bigger men-of-war and the Adriatic equipment to some private operators. Small naval units remained as coast-guard vessels, and were eventually abandoned to rot. Trieste, once the center of a lively maritime commerce, the major outlet to the sea of a great power, declined; the Austrian naval standard vanished from the oceans and Austrian merchant ships had to take care of their own protection.

No bid could be found for the Danube frigate. It is not recorded when and under what circumstances it went to the sandy bottom of the river. With the frigate gone, one infantry battalion was assigned to safeguard all Austrian rivers, including the Danube, which was but in sections a border river. This meant one guardsman for every two miles of watercourse.

However, trade along the Danube was little impaired by lack of protection, and business-minded authorities even established an "official wharf" at Klosterneuburg. In 1768, a venturesome "ship architect," Mr. Ernst Achsberg, undertook to launch a new frigate of his own design. Chroniclers paid no attention to the venture, though. But there was yet another slight of the Danube by the Imperial family. When the bottom of the Danube at a place where a so-called warship arsenal once stood began to be choked up with sand, Maria Theresa's son Joseph decreed that the section of the river just outside Vienna be drained and a military bakery built there.

However, from the maze of droll, cumbersome, and sometimes stupid regulations stand out a few badly needed effective reforms.

Army medical services were improved: Medics were trained, and only trained medics were permitted to treat and operate on patients. The Crown Prince had been present at a bloodletting at which the surgeon manipulated the lancet so ineptly that the victim was seriously injured. It turned out that this "surgeon" was a tailor, to whom his superiors had given the assignment because he was supposed to be skillful with sharp and pointed objects.

Austrian military schools were reorganized. Officers of the post-Prince Eugenian period were excellent horsemen, daredevils in action, cavaliers in ballrooms, but otherwise ignoramuses. Maria Theresa founded the Cadet School and the Military Settlement School of Wiener Neustadt, and appointed Field Marshal Daun as *Oberdirektor* (General Manager) of both institutes. The curriculum included: fortifications; arithmetic; geography; German, French, Italian, and "Bohemian" (Czech); drill, fencing, horseback riding, and dancing.

The Cadet School of Wiener Neustadt is only half a century older than the U. S. Military Academy of West Point; and the Militärakademie of Wiener Neustadt, which originated through a fusion of the two earlier schools, is but thirty-three years West Point's senior.

Despite those reforms and her thrifty solicitude for the army, Maria Theresa never saw her wish to settle scores with Frederick fulfilled.

After the Seven Years' War had ended in seedy disappointment, she wrote her oldest son that stringent economizing had prevented her from sufficiently building up the army; yet she still admonished him to economize, economize, economize! Joseph, who would soon be Emperor Joseph II, was not given to penury but, frustrated by his domineering mother, he turned almost pro-Prussian, and became, though not directly an admirer, at least an appreciator of his mother's lifelong foe.

CHAPTER FORTY-TWO

Vienna's thirst for heroes was insatiable. The Viennese cheered Daun, Hadik, and, most enthusiastically, another ranking soldier, Baron Gideon Ernst von Laudon, the latter not so much because of his true soldierly excellence, but because of his exotic shyness.

The Laudons were an impoverished clan of petty Scottish nobility who had gone to the Baltic. Gideon Ernst enlisted in the Russian army at sixteen; seven years later, in 1739, he was discharged as first lieutenant and went to Berlin. King Frederick refused to grant him a commission because he did not like his face.

Laudon's face was ascetic, almost skeletal; it was crowned by a reddish head of hair and always looked somehow reproachful, which annoyed some people.

The discharged Russian officer went to Vienna. Somebody helped him enlist as a lieutenant with the Pandours. It took him more than a decade of drudgery and humiliation to become a lieutenant colonel. The Pandours were an auxiliary group of dubious repute; exasperated, Laudon once called them robbers and was promptly discharged. For several years the shy and vexed man vegetated as a part-time clerk and teacher of mathematics. Then he somehow came to the attention of Count Kaunitz, who was just about to leave for Versailles; Kaunitz helped him to obtain another commission, this time as a captain, in a "frontier regiment." Frontier troops were the first to bear the brunt of raids, the last to settle down to routine, the least spectacular, the least respected of regulars. In six years of service with the frontier regiment, Laudon regained his former rank, but had few furloughs and never went to Vienna, where ugly-duckling officers with lean purses were not in demand.

Frontier service taught Laudon a lesson in hit-and-run fighting, ambushes and raids that did not form part of the curriculum of training. When the Seven Years' War began, he surprised friend and foe by an aggressiveness that reminded scholars of war of ancient Mongolian tactics. His soldiers loved him, different as he was from them by origin and bearing. In the second year of the war, he was promoted to major general for his exploits as "leader of light troops."

The Empress was not annoyed by Laudon's looks; she did not think that he had a disagreeable physiognomy. She studied his expression, smiled, and was keenly interested in his exploits.

Laudon never quite fitted into life at court. He ate and drank, dressed and spoke, as unwritten rules required, he even danced with the slightly awkward grace of a lightweight outdoor man, but the hustle and bustle made him visibly uneasy.

The Empress wanted her ranking officers to attend all major festivities, unless they were actively campaigning. Once, at a great gala affair, she did not see Laudon, and asked what had happened to him. "He is here, Your Majesty," she learned, "standing in the shadow of a door, bashful as usual." Courtiers called this a "lack of social instinct," but Laudon did not change.

Even as a field marshal he never moved into a mansion close to Schönbrunn, as befitted his rank and income; and he did not settle in the swank section of the Inner City either, where the crowds embarrassed him by their temperamental hero worship. So, between wars he moved into a small castle in Weidlingau, almost ten miles west of the city walls, and in his will stipulated that he be buried in the charming solitude of a meadow near his home, since St. Stephen's was getting crowded.

He was the only officer ever to receive the Maria Theresa Order twice; the first time soon after its foundation, the second time three decades later, when Maria Theresa was already dead and Joseph II bestowed upon old but still intrepid Laudon the Grand Cross and had it set in diamonds. The field marshal, who had never known Prince Eugene, had again conquered Belgrade.

King Frederick of Prussia told Joseph in 1769 that Laudon's fast maneuvers had sometimes startled him.

Certainly it startled Frederick after Kolín, when his brother Wilhelm led a corps to Bautzen, Silesia, to join the remnants of the King's army. Wilhelm, harassed by fast enemy moves, was never able to make a stand, and during zigzag marches lost baggage train and artillery.

In the summer of 1757, the Tsarina's armies invaded East Prussia and penetrated deep into Frederick's kingdom, a host of well-drilled savages who frightened the population. Troops from Sweden, France, the Reich, closed in on him. The Austrians advanced in Silesia and were about to recover it. Frederick admitted that he was desperate.

Postilions on Vienna's thoroughfares trumpeted victories. The Empress bestowed promotions and decorations. On November 22, Prussia's Prince Bevern was defeated outside Breslau. On November 24, Breslau was in Austrian hands, and Bevern a prisoner.

Silesia would have been back in the Empress' fold of provinces, much of the Oder Valley would have been ruled from the banks of the Danube, the destiny of North America would have been different—had it not been for a few "ifs."

If the Russians had carried on, they would have seized all of Frederick's resources. But the Russian generals played a double game: their Tsarina wanted victory; but their Crown Prince, influenced by his wife, did not wish to see Frederick crushed, and so the victorious Russians suddenly halted and waited.

If the Swedes had veered west-southwest, they would have turned the Prussian flank. But they began to fall back faintheartedly toward potential embarkation points.

If the French and the Reich's forces had joined, Frederick, who had no more than 24,000 men ready, would have met disaster. But there were changes in the French high command, and the French army did not move.

Despair, to the frustrated, can be an incentive to act against the weak. Desperate Frederick watched the procrastinating French, and decided to attack.

The bulk of the French army camped west of the Saale River, near the village of Rossbach. The others were too widely scattered to join action on short notice. When the Prussian ranks came in sight, the French commanders, Soubise and Richelieu, wanted to take the initiative, but could not decide how and when. Their appeal to the Reich's forces to join them was heeded in a slow, slovenly manner that increased the confusion.

On a memorable November morning in 1757, Prince Soubise discovered a polished wooden tub. He took a leisurely bath, requesting not to be disturbed. And as the French field marshal enjoyed the long-missed cleaning operation, Frederick struck.

Prussian hussars charged into a desperate mob which wanted to surrender, but the Prussian cavalry leader wanted his men to practice sabering. They killed 8000. Frederick called Rossbach a "genteel engagement." He lost only 165 dead and 376 wounded.

The "genteel engagement" stirred him into fervid activity. He went "to look for new dangers in Silesia," where the Austrians were on the loose.

The marching prowess of Prussian infantry, and the strict organization of its supply services, enabled them to move with smooth celerity; yet the road to Silesia seemed dangerous indeed.

Hardly could Frederick have known that the fateful luster of the *Maria Theresien Orden* was beginning to lead his opponents astray.

Prince Charles of Lorraine was jealous. In terms of seniority, he was still Count Daun's superior. When news of Rossbach arrived, Daun suggested that they wait near Breslau, but Charles overruled him, and the Austrian army, tired and undersupplied, marched west to engage Frederick wherever he would turn up.

The battle took place on December 5, 1757, near the village of Leuthen. The Prussians were prepared; the Austrians did not deploy properly and were set upon piecemeal. One Austrian regiment was decimated to one officer and eight men. There were many instances of disgraceful surrender. Breslau was back in Prussian hands on December 21; Liegnitz, eight days later.

Christmas was gloomy in Vienna. A contemporary chronicler recorded: "The Empress was disconsolate; she kept crying; crying, she said prayers in her chapel, and spent the rest of the day lamenting her affliction. The Emperor simulated steadfastness. 'We suffered only a single defeat,' he would say, 'this is no more than an incident.'" *The Magic Garland,* a festival play celebrating Austrian victories, which had attracted huge crowds, no longer made sense. The people were outraged; and some of their wrath turned against the autocratic Kaunitz, who did not even request the counsel of ministers but wanted to direct everything personally.

The Prince of Lorraine was not reprimanded, but his resignation in February 1758 caused no stir.

Daun spent most of the winter in Vienna attending many religious ceremonies; on March 9, 1758, he left for headquarters again.

The Viennese said Daun's trip back would be very short, that the Prussians were closing in on the Danube Valley, that nothing but Saxonian deserters and auxiliaries from Tuscany were on hand to defend them.

In fact, the Prussians were inside Moravia, attacking Olmütz.

Vienna was still waiting for the conquerors when, early in July 1758, gaudily clad postilions came to town, blowing, tooting, and shouting an epic of Laudon.

His exploit was most unusual: a raid worth far more than a victory. King Frederick had a huge convoy moved into Moravia; its safe arrival would have tremendously increased his army's fighting power. But Laudon, with a small cavalry force, attacked it with lightning speed and took thousands of prisoners, loaded carts, horses, cattle, and even thirteen cannon. It happened near Domstädl, on June 30, 1758. Vienna's urchins made Laudon their chief idol and played convoy capturing all summer long.

The postilions of Domstädl were followed by other heralds of glory; but the story they told bored the audiences: the Prussians were retreating, that was all. Daun turned toward Dresden.

The leaves were turning when Austrian columns reached quaint Hochkirch, a lively rural community amidst lovely rolling hills and picturesque groves. Daun decided to let his men rest and establish a strong position. Frederick had lost track of his adversaries. Looking for them in the direction of Bohemia and Moravia, he groped his way through Saxony, approached Hochkirch, and detected Daun's army only when it was within artillery range.

The Austrian position was screened by nature's own camouflage. Only a gambler, or a general who believed in intuition, would lead his men headlong into the throng. Frederick, between spells of depression, believed his intuition. He trusted that Daun would stay on the defensive. From October 10 to 13, he watched Austrian campfires and found that everything pointed at defensive routine. In the small hours of October 14, when Frederick had long retired, Austrian patrols closed in on Prussian outposts, and by 5 P.M. Daun's surprise attack opened.

The Prussians rallied after the initial shock. Frederick led a counterblow. Prussian drill had almost restored the line when the ubiquitous Laudon hit but did not run—hammering away at the enemy front, flank, and rear. By 10 A.M. the battle was over.

But Daun did not press his advantage. His instructions were to restore the Saxonian ruling family to its Dresden castle. His troubles began at the gates of the city. The Saxonian King would be distressed to find beautiful Dresden damaged. Therefore, artillery must not be used. But Dresden was held by a strong Prussian garrison, under General Count Schmettau, who was not instructed to struggle in kid gloves and who would neither surrender nor leave. The Austrians moved into Dresden without firing a shot, but fought at close quarters for every square of street. On November 9, they were near the center of town, and Count Schmettau threatened that all the houses along their path would be put to the torch. Daun did not wish to see the Saxonians chagrined by vandalism, and discontinued the attack. On November 10, the army moved out of Dresden, toward winter quarters in Bohemia.

Thousands of lives, an entire campaign, a victory that could have been decisive, had been wasted.

Viennese government offices hummed with activity. It was decided that the war should be won in 1759. Statisticians compiled data of forces available and submitted them to the Court War Councilors, who calculated that Austria and its allies would have 412,000 men in the field. Reports to the effect that Frederick would have 150,000 were discounted as propaganda.

In fact, the allied contingents never exceeded 260,000. Co-ordination was poor, fighting prowess uneven; and never was as much as one third of the allied armies concentrated on a single battlefield. The Prussian army also suffered from concentration difficulties, but in the summer of 1759 it had 205,000 men under arms.

The people of Vienna paid more attention to the personalities attending the martial parleys in their city than to the scant news that filtered out from palatial conference rooms. The most interesting of the gentlemen was French general Montazet. He had been at Hochkirch as an observer; in the thick of the battle an Austrian cavalryman mistook him for a Prussian and by a stroke of his saber almost cut off the general's aquiline nose. It dangled by a thread of skin; a skillful surgeon sewed it on again and it healed so beautifully that the general then had a nose as straight as that of a Greek statue. The Viennese talked a great deal about this first instance of plastic surgery.

They also talked a great deal about "Hänsel," the Right Honorable Baron Hans Klein, who was sinking rapidly. He had lived through the great plague, had known Augustin, had witnessed the Turkish siege. At ninety-four, he could tell from personal experience what to young people was ancient history. He had not only known but had been the favorite of quite a few Emperors, for Baron Klein ("Baron Little"), as he had been created in accordance with his size, was a court dwarf, the dean of that noble profession, the prototype of a court jester turned confidential adviser to the Court. He was a widely traveled little man; Charles VI even had had him come to Spain for company. He was an aging man when the Empress was born. She, too, called him Hänsel, though he preferred to be called Baron. Now that he was fading away, everybody affectionately called him by his nickname. He was the symbol of good old days which, as Hänsel could have testified, had not been really good and which, with slightly changed settings, kept repeating themselves in an unfathomable cycle. As the year 1759 grew into adolescence, Hänsel could no longer testify. He passed away, intensely mourned, rapidly forgotten.

Not before late July did the "year of decision, 1759," bring major battles.

On July 24, a new Russian commander, General Count Peter Simon Soltikov, who arrived away behind schedule, was thrown back in the direction of Kunersdorf. On July 31, the French were shamefully defeated near Minden in Westphalia by a numerically inferior Prussian army.

Frederick moved toward Kunersdorf, where the Russians regrouped. When news of the new move reached Austrian headquarters, Laudon alerted a corps of 18,000 and, his skull-like head covered by a huge black gold-trimmed hat, wearing an embroidered long white tunic and stylish riding boots, he galloped out in front of his army. The corps arrived at its destination on August 12, at high noon. The battle was already on and no time was left to fit the Austrian corps into the Russian army. But Laudon was at his best as an improviser in an emergency. While his corps still deployed behind the Russian center, the Prussians turned Soltikov's left flank; Russian ranks faltered, fell back in confusion, abandoned ninety cannon. Without Laudon, Kunersdorf would have been the graveyard of the Russian army; his spontaneous intervention turned the tide. The Austrians provided cover for the still powerful Russian batteries. Austrians assisted the Russian infantry to re-form and halted a Prussian cavalry charge. Laudon gathered fourteen squadrons of dragoons and mounted grenadiers for a surprise blow. Visibility was reduced by dense clouds of smoke; King Frederick did not notice the enemy concentration until it thunderously burst through his lines. The weary Prussians retreated, deaf to orders. Retreat turned into flight, flight into chaos. Frederick lost two horses to enemy bullets, and he is said to owe his life to a golden case in his breast pocket, which kept a bullet from piercing his chest. "Never before had a Prussian army been in such a condition," a Prussian general reported. Frederick spoke of suicide, but he had said similar things before.

At nightfall of August 12, 1759, all that was left of the Prussian army were 3000 soldiers. However, many units were only dispersed, and gradually more men returned to the embattled ranks.

Laudon's corps and the Russian units were interspersed; Laudon asked that they destroy the remaining Prussians at once. Soltikov said that his men were tired and had to rest. Laudon's couriers galloped to Daun's headquarters to ask that Daun make Soltikov co-operate. Daun replied that no Austrian commander could give orders to a Russian, but that he would "suggest" to His Excellency Count Soltikov to take up pursuit. Soltikov was not open to suggestions, and a foaming and cursing Laudon extricated his dispersed soldiers from the Russian ranks and attempted to make for Berlin. He had lost two irretrievable days, during which the Prussians had set up a formidable roadblock near Lebus.

Laudon, joined by Hadik, lacked artillery. They could not attack the roadblock.

Five days after Kunersdorf, the Russians left the site of the battle, roamed Silesia, and approached the Polish border. Austrian liaison officers asked for explanations, but received no answer. At last, from St. Petersburg came orders: Tsarina Elizabeth asked that the Prussians be finished off. The Tsarina's star was setting. At fifty, she was an aging debaucher, alleged to be a tool of her strange favorite lover, Field Marshal Rasumovsky, whom she had once picked up as a tattered shepherd's boy and promoted to the highest military rank; some said that she had even secretly married him. It was again remembered at court that Elizabeth was of illegitimate birth, born prior to the wedding of her father, Peter the Great, to Catherine I. Insiders said the Tsarina would die soon, of sickness or "otherwise!" Soltikov trusted that her daughter-in-law would see that she died very soon. The courier from St. Petersburg carried various letters in his pouch. The general read them all, then crossed into Poland, and waited.

Still, Daun could have joined Laudon and driven on to Berlin. Yet he did not feel free to base his decisions on military expediency, but had to consider the Empress' determination to lead the Saxonian royal family back to its castle for Christmas. And since Maria Theresa's husband was German Emperor, he would have to let the Reich's army enter Dresden first.

The war again turned into a social event. The Duke of Zweibrücken, with his Reich's outfit, accepted the surrender of Dresden, Daun standing by with the Austrians to do the fighting if it were required. Dresden suffered no more scars.

Relieved, King Frederick made an attempt to wind up 1759 with a success in the field. He delegated General Friedrich August von Finck to ambush the Austrians as they trudged back to winter quarters through sleet and rain. But on November 21, near Maxen, Finck was forced to surrender. In a verbose fit of despair, Frederick claimed to have lost 15,000 men, while Viennese postmasters and postilions said 12,000. He fretted about not keeping control of his own people, about his personal finances, and, last but not least, about the army.

The Prussians, raised by corporals' sticks and ordinanced into blind regimentation, now plotted as the youth Frederick would never have dared to plot against his stick-wielding father. Deserters instigated Berliners to rebellion and arson. The police made over 300 arrests, court-martials and executioners got busy, but Frederick was afraid that insurrection was not easily weeded out.

Also, he could no longer "make a plus." Treasury accounts sounded alarming. He would have to continue war on his principal and the idea scared him almost as much as the reports from his military staff. He had lost 134 generals. His best field-ranking officers were gone. All units were depleted. Soldiers were needed. But most of the goose-steppers, fast sharpshooters, obedient cannon fodder, were dead or crippled. Recruits were not up to par, and when it was suggested to do more recruiting outside Prussia, Frederick snapped that all they would find were "scamps, thieves, bootblacks, and chimney sweeps."

Frederick pondered about a panacea, and eventually wrote a letter to the Turkish Great Vizier, suggesting a pincers attack on Maria Theresa's patrimony. Only his secretary knew the contents of the letter. But not even his secretary ever learned the contents of the Turkish reply. Frederick read it in seclusion, and it was never seen again.

He had still another iron in the fire: enigmatic Russia. The Tsarina's heir presumptive was said to play with dolls, to get drunk in the company of his menservants, and to have rats caught, which he hanged on crossbeams. Catherine would soon occupy the throne. Frederick thought that she would reverse tables and make an alliance with Prussia.

When spring came, Frederick had 90,000 men, not all of them scamps and thieves, not even members of lowly professions, but many of them green. Yet, in action soldiers ripen quickly.

The anti-Prussian coalition had 200,000 veterans and recruits, including Russians. Russian general Fermor, now in command, vaguely promised to fight.

Laudon should concentrate on Silesia, Daun watch Saxony; Vienna hoped the other generals would make some contribution.

Again, armies clashed, triumphed or were routed, casualties ran high, and after another winter intermission, another fair-season tragedy produced no result.

However, in America, a small fraction of the forces engaged in Europe fought a meaningful, determined war. By September 8, 1760, Montreal had surrendered. All of Canada, a single province of which was larger than all embattled European regions combined, was about to pass from French to English domination. France and England were members of the cast of the Seven Years' War, but in Europe they remained as sterile in the conflict as all the other partners were.

In July 1760, Laudon captured Glatz. There was a great deal of trumpet blowing on Vienna's thoroughfares, countless cheers for the shy field marshal, a new song, "La-la-la Laudon," and a great deal of temperamental merrymaking.

July 31 saw Laudon at the gate of Breslau, whose Prussian commander, General Friedrich Boguslaw von Tauentzien, refused to surrender. Meanwhile, Daun had been so concerned with keeping the Prussian King from marching into Silesia that he had not prevented him from turning west toward Dresden. A Prussian bombardment of the Saxonian capital destroyed four hundred houses and five churches before Daun could drive the attackers away.

Laudon again wanted to seize Berlin. Daun did not consider it practical and forbade Laudon to make the move, but Russian general Count Fermor unexpectedly offered co-operation. On October 6, 1760, Austro-Russian forces arrived in the outskirts of Berlin. From a huge windmill, their commanders got their first glance at Berlin; from there they dispatched a summons to surrender. Berlin surrendered on October 9; its garrison of 6000 was granted safe conduct. The city paid a contribution of 1,500,000 thaler plus 20,000 thaler in occupation costs. The practical Russians pocketed the lion's share; the Austrian commander, who wanted to show his refinement, took King Frederick's portrait and his flute and sent them to Vienna as a souvenir for the Empress.

When King Frederick headed for his capital, the occupiers left without a fight. The episode was over, and not before November 3 was a major battle fought, near Torgau in Saxony. Again, the Order of Maria Theresa cast its evil spell. In the afternoon, the Prussians were in retreat. Daun, who had been wounded, left the field to undergo treatment in Torgau and assigned General Count O'Donnel to take charge. The operation seemed mere routine, but O'Donnel wanted to do something spectacular and ordered a general regroupment, abandoning the Austrian key position. The Prussians rushed to the spot, and unexpectedly found themselves masters of the battlefield. The farcical incident reversed the outcome of the battle. The Prussians could record Torgau as their victory.

An armistice that would expire in April 1761 brought down the curtain over another "year of victory."

When the curtain rose again, the numerical superiority of the anti-Prussian coalition seemed as formidable as ever, but the French did little marching and even less fighting, and the Russians had yet another commanding general, whose name was Buturlin and whose intentions seemed unfathomable.

Austrian information services reported that the Prussians had a master agent in St. Petersburg, the secretary of the heir to the throne, who snatched Austrian communications to the Russian Court and sent them right on to Berlin. The secretary ingratiated himself with the heir to the throne by procuring for him the only kind of women who stirred his virility: one-eyed, hunchbacked specimens.

Buturlin suddenly agreed to join Laudon. It would have taken them no more than two weeks to reach the Prussian positions near Schweidnitz; but Buturlin reneged on the agreement, then changed his mind again, and joined Laudon in mid-August. But much as Laudon urged him, he did not wish to attack. On October 9, tired of being pressed, and irritated by the fact that the Tsarina kept on living, he announced that he would march off to Poland.

The ring around Schweidnitz was broken. Frederick escaped the deathtrap. Laudon entered the city and captured rear guards, 4000 men in all.

Vienna did not celebrate the affair, yet was gay. October saw the triumphal arrival of Princess Isabella of Parma, the lovely fiancée of Crown Prince Joseph, and the Viennese relished the pageantry.

At last, on January 5, 1762, Tsarina Elizabeth died.

King Frederick sent an ambassador to St. Petersburg to make peace. On May 5, 1762, the Russians agreed to evacuate all Prussian territory; on June 19, an offensive and defensive Prusso-Russian alliance was signed; Russia pledged to contribute a corps of 20,000 to help Frederick recapture all of Silesia.

The Austro-Russian treaty had not yet expired, however. Vienna received no formal notice, but the Prussian ambassador quoted the Tsar as having said: "If your King orders me to do so, I will wage war against hell itself."

Frederick knew of Peter III's state of mind and of his repulsive perversions, and he expected him to be removed, soon; but this did not keep him from writing repulsively adulating letters, which Peter hardly ever saw. Peter was deposed three weeks after the alliance was made, and assassinated on July 17. His wife was in full control of Russia.

Sweden withdrew from the war posthaste.

Frederick could not afford to snub England and avenge past humiliations. But in 1762, when the war overseas was decided and England entered negotiations with France, he ordered his two ambassadors to London to try to overthrow the Prime Minister, and used language unprecedented in Western diplomatic history. Foul language could not oust the English cabinet, but in November 1762 England and France signed a preliminary peace. It was soon followed by the final treaty, which deprived Frederick of further subsidies but also resulted in the withdrawal of the French army from all operations.

Frederick dreamed of 100,000 Tatars and Turks swarming into Hungary, of a glorious campaign in the Danube Valley, and of a requiem for Maria Theresa, which he would attend in either Vienna or Budapest.

The war fizzled out. Austria still had reserves, but Austria had lost all faith; Frederick could fight against a single adversary, and he was positive of Russian support. But as the Turks and Tatars did not come, he asked the new Tsarina to mediate, and on February 15, 1763, peace was signed at Hubertusburg, a small castle near Dresden. Frederick kept Silesia. He did not keep Saxony, however, which soothed Maria Theresa's grief for seven wasted years of war and a thousand frustrated hopes.

CHAPTER FORTY-THREE

The popular song "La-la-la Laudon" was quickly forgotten, superseded by one that called Maria Theresa the Empress of Peace.

The melody of the peace *Lied* was not inspiring, but peace was an attractive novelty.

Despite constant bloodshed, the capital had remained an island of culture, romance, even prosperity. It was the site of a glorious merger of remnants of traditional pomp and nascent artistic and social refinement that, in Vienna, as in Paris, never quite reached a blooming climax but withered on the tree.

As the Seven Years' War drew to a close, a musical child prodigy was the rave of the town. Johannes Chrysostomus Wolfgangus Theophilus

Mozart, aged six, had been brought by his father, Leopold, from Salzburg to the Imperial Court, where he was received with affectionate wonder.

To the Empress, the little boy was like a cute gem from the huge human treasure chest that was her realm. To Vienna society, he and his sister "Nannerl" were musical dolls to present at parties. In front of the house where the Mozarts had put up, carriages with liveried coachmen and gaudily uniformed footmen waited to take the prodigies to the most elaborate affairs, such as galas arranged by the Prince of Saxe-Hildburghausen, by Bishop Count Eszterházy, and by Countess Kinsky, who entertained Count Daun. The Mozarts also were guests in the mansions of lesser-born but immensely prosperous people. They collected beautiful trinkets rather than cash, according to the custom of the times; otherwise, the boy might have been provided with a nest egg for the deplorably short remainder of his life.

Still, the Vienna of the 1760s was a jolly place for many who contributed to its entertainment. However, seven hours downstream by raft or boat from Vienna began a land that Maria Theresa came to know better only after her elating experience with the Diet of Pressburg: the Hungary of cavaliers turned out to be bewildering and distressing the more the Empress familiarized herself with its facts.

It seemed to be a country of forlorn hopes, where capricious powers, using slogans of national freedom, acted according to their whims, often rebelled against the bearer of the crown, occasionally gave theatrical display of seigneurial loyalty, and always bludgeoned faceless chattels into submission.

Hungarian royal powers were limited. Many prerogatives of the Hungarian Court Chancellery and the Palatine were delegated to district administrations in which members of magnate families ruled supreme and absolute.

These magnates took joint decisions on matters that not only concerned all of Hungary but affected the entire realm. District tyrants collected all the local revenue and determined, highhandedly, how much of it would go to the central government. Also, they would not tolerate interference with their autocratic treatment of the local peasanty. Hungarian authorities met an ever smaller fraction of the Empress' financial demands and she could not fail to notice deplorable social conditions in that kingdom, which was immensely rich in natural resources but maladministered almost beyond belief, and with a population dispirited by bloodshed and oppression.

A Court Council, investigating the state of Hungarian affairs, reported that the peasants who worked on the huge domains of mundane and ecclesiastic lords were slaves in everything but name. The lord of the mansion imposed taxes at will: parts of the harvest and livestock, cash tributes under the title of land tax, were collected with deliberate brutality by guards who were the scum of destitute peasantry. There were prolonged periods of unlawful socage.

The outraged Empress refused to call another Diet, saying that Diets had proven useless. A Court Deputation was established "in Transylvania, Banaticis, and Illyricis," to govern these parts of Hungary as her sole organ, and in 1765 she undertook to reform the status of the Hungarian peasantry.

Court Councilor von Raab, a well-meaning, cinder-dry-minded magistrate, drafted a new statute for the *jobbagyen*, as the peasants were called.

The *jobbagyen* were granted the right to migrate and to choose new professions for their children. Dues collected by the lords of the mansion were limited to one ninth of the crop and small cattle, and the land tax to no more than one gulden per annum. Socage periods should not exceed fifty-two days of "hand robot" and fifty-two days of "draught robot" (transportation service) a year.

Still, no less than half the peasant's toil went into dues. But the reform already was a vast improvement of their dismal situation, and even where local administrators tried to make a travesty of it, few peasants emigrated. Many of their sons looked for new professions, soldiering preferred, but few were accepted by the recruiters. The offspring of a once sturdy breed were found to be frail, mentally retarded, and sickly.

Making a travesty of a royal reform was comparatively easy. The peasants were too scared, and often too dull, to go to court. Administration of justice was extremely intricate. The Supreme Court (*Curia Regis*) was divided into two *curiae,* and lower instances were even triple-tracked: patrimonial courts, courts of nobility, and community courts, operating without clear co-ordination. There also were episcopal and archiepiscopal courts. Any lawsuit was a venture in which peasants could hardly engage.

But whatever the actual effects of the reform, it did not increase the rural population. The Court Deputation records disclose that certain parts of Hungary, in particular along the southern Danube, were sadly depopulated wastelands of fat earth, blooming deserts that did not bear fruit.

As often before, Hungary had to be colonized. And as often before, the most-wooed settlers were Germans.

A Colonial Commission for Hungary was set up in 1768. Its first president was Count Lamberg, an Austrian of German origin. Districts that had become virtually no man's land were offered to settlers, but lords of the mansion who were in short supply of peasants competed with the authorities, offering big slices of land to foreigners, who would not have to perform socage services and who would pay lower taxes than the natives. The Germans attributed this preferred treatment to their superior qualifications, if not their supermanhood.

Imported supermen were disliked in Hungary, and old antagonisms revived. Just the same, immigration commissars recruited settlers in Ulm, Regensburg, Cologne, Frankfurt am Main, and Schweinfurt. Families who signed up received "settler passports," which entitled them to buy cattle and agricultural implements on a long-term, low-interest installment plan, and to loans in cash. They were allotted land in preassigned districts, moved into villages, or founded villages of their own, which looked seigneurial as compared with the cluster of hovels in which the natives lived.

Between 1768 and 1771, 4878 families, totaling 16,989 persons, arrived in Hungary. Most of them settled in the southern Danubian regions of Bácska and Banat. Sanitary and schooling conditions were despicable when they arrived, but soon every settlers' village had a school, every two villages a surgeon; and there was even canalization, something previously unheard of in these parts of the land.

Colonization gradually decreased until 1782, two years after the death of Maria Theresa, then grew again, when immigrants were granted transportation from Vienna to every point in Hungary; long neglected shipping on the Danube was again encouraged. Another decree granted newcomer families a dwelling house with garden, cattle, and ten years' tax exemption. The oldest sons of immigrant families were draft-deferred. New hospitals were built for newcomers. Craftsmen got sufficient cash to buy the finest tools of their trade. Between 1784 and 1790, Austria spent four million gulden to encourage migration to Hungary.

Alarmed German Princes issued anti-migration regulations after 30,-000 of their subjects had left for the subsidized Lubberland. Yet some colonization continued until the climax of the Napoleonic Wars, and it included not only Germans but also Tyroleans and even French. Travelers on the Danube who had come all the way from civilized Bavaria and aristocratic Austria to visit Hungary and had found that, but for a few proud castles, it looked like an Asiatic vastness, returned after a short time to find new villages that reminded them of the smiling neatness along the upper course of the river.

Maria Theresa's colonization of Hungary, her reforms, and the restriction of abuses did not make her beloved throughout the kingdom, however. The peasants were resentful, the nobles in revolt. At Pressburg, they had shown chivalrous loyalty to their ruling lady, but now they resented what they called her ill-advised concern for the plebs of their estates. They began to draw unflattering comparisons between the Empress' personal appearance at the historic Pressburg Diet and in the years of her reforms. Then she had been a majestic beauty, golden-haired, fiery-eyed; now she was heavy, her eyes were dim, her hair had paled, her face was pock-marked (she had contracted smallpox at the sickbed of a daughter-in-law). And her gait, once so proud, was impaired by fractures suffered in a carriage accident. Aristocratic tastes despised ungainliness. Had war again knocked at the gates of Maria Theresa's capital many a Hungarian aristocrat would have turned a deaf ear to her plea.

And the Hungarian peasants? They blamed their ruler for the German influx; otherwise, she was as remote to them as a star, and much less visible. The only authorities they knew were parish priests, beadles, collectors, and, more remote yet still perceptible, the lords of the mansion. Whatever relief the peasants obtained through the reform, they attributed to the authorities they knew rather than to their monarch's motherly concern.

This is how an eminent contemporary described her: "When she was young, she had a sprightly way of speaking, underlined by sweeping gestures. Her anxiety and bitterness exploded in fits of anger, and her words bubbled over. She became emotional whenever she encountered resistance, when her ideas did not swiftly materialize, when she saw that wrong was being committed. She was subject to emotions, but she never knew destructive passion. She was easily aroused, and easily soothed, and almost timidly anxious to do the right thing. Once convinced that something was illegitimate, she would drop it at once, important and advantageous as the matter seemed to be."

She remained emotional as she grew older, but became more patient. She tried to learn to compromise, even in matters such as the partition of Poland, which she had originally called iniquitous.

The Empress always viewed mercantile and industrial ventures with amazement; but since her husband had engaged in several of them and done quite well, she considered economics worthy of respect and created a Universal Board of Commerce (*Universal Kommerzdirektorium*) as the highest authority on commerce, with subsidiaries in various parts of the Empire. Bohemia became the center of an expanding industry.

Efficient Emperor Franz owned textile plants and bleacheries there. Local labor supply met a growing demand. In Vienna, nobles and burghers did not wish to see crude and vulgar laborers invade the city and ugly structures spring up amidst their proud buildings. Loving fancy objects, however, they did not raise objections against china plants and a silk weavery owned by the Court. The Empress was fond of Viennese chinaware, and after her husband's death, she asked that the business be continued in regal style.

Great painters of miniatures were commissioned to design artistic patterns: skillful master craftsmen from Meissen, Saxony, were called to Vienna to bring manufacture to the highest level. Porcelain clay from Engelhardtszell on the Upper Austrian Danube was carefully cleansed and shipped to the Vienna factory. As long as the Empress lived, the china business prospered; later it suffered from the competition of less artistic, but more efficient, Bohemian industries. In 1865, it was temporarily discontinued, but eventually resumed.

Another typical Viennese industry, in which Maria Theresa had no share but which aroused her keen interest, was the production of synthetic diamonds, which originated in 1765.

Goldsmith and jeweler Joseph Strasser found a chemical process to produce glittering stones. It seemed controversial whether or not a lady should wear make-believe jewels, and while Viennese socialities kept debating, Strasser took his stones to Paris, where *Pierres de Strass* were unquestioningly accepted and bought in a volume that made costume jewelry a thriving industry.

The Empress promulgated decrees concerning customs duties; she never quite understood them, but since Franz had told her that they helped protect business, she signed them anyway.

Most imports of goods that were also produced locally were prohibited. Provinces and districts levied bewildering excises; one and the same merchandise was taxed several times without ever leaving the confines of the realm; imported merchandise was occasionally seized and on one instance even publicly burned; a full-scale war of duties broke out between Austria and Prussia, just as their armies happened not to fight.

Paper money was introduced shortly before the end of the Seven Years' War. The state-owned Vienna Municipal Bank issued twelve million gulden in bills called *Bankozettel*. They were redeemable in gold or silver; the public accepted them in perfect faith, and the bank kept its promise until 1793, when the chronic financial troubles worsened. The government, trying to replenish its bullion, seized gold and silver owned by miners, and even treasures of churches and convents; but none of it was used for the benefit of the holders of *Bankozettel,* and a constant flood of new bills poured into circulation. Coins all but vanished. In 1809, one gulden in silver rated seventeen in bills, and by the end of 1810, circulation of *Bankozettel* hit an astronomic 1060 million. The president of the Court Chamber wanted to stem the tide of inflation by converting *Bankozettel* into new bills at the rate of three to one, redeemable in silver, but no silver was available. People tried frantically to convert *Bankozettel* into goods, ranging from a small piece of bread to a big piece of real estate. Turnover was rapid, giving an erroneous impression of prosperity. Old-fashioned thrift became a signpost on the road to ruin, careless spending led to profit. He who was indebted became a profiteer, as inflation made debts melt away; he who had savings saw them wiped out for similar reasons. On March 15, 1811, it was decreed that the nominal value of the *Bankozettel* be reduced to 20 per cent and that new paper money be the only legal tender to be amortized in the process of the sale of church estates, a pledge that was never kept. Next, a fraudulent financial administration decreed that taxes due in old *Bankozettel* were payable at full face value in new bills. The arithmetics were crushing. A person who owned 50,000 gulden in *Bankozettel* but owed 15,000 in taxes, received 10,000 gulden in new bills, and still owed 15,000. Liabilities were high; everybody had withheld payment of taxes to profit through devaluation.

The Viennese took it with sheer fatalistic stupor; in Hungary, provincial assemblies raged and contested the validity of the decree. But it was virtually self-enforcing. There was no legal tender except the new bills.

Later generations of Austrians and Hungarians did not benefit from their elders' sordid experience. The facts of inflation were never taught in the schools of the land which had seen so much of it. In 1921, when the Austrian paper krone hit a low of 1/14,400 of its rate at the outbreak of World War I, and the Hungarian currency dropped to almost the same level, people never fully understood the cause of their loss and of the profiteers' gain.

During Maria Theresa's regime, the government paid little attention to the nation's rivers. But enterprising foreigners planned to expand Austria's and Hungary's trade on waterways by linking them with an ingenious system of canals.

One canal would link the Danube with the Moldau (Vltava) River. The Upper Austrian rapids would undergo regulation to facilitate shipping on that section of the river; another canal was supposed to link Trieste with the Sava and, through that tributary, the Danube with the Adriatic Sea. The Danube would also be linked with Lake Balaton; and the Tisza would become a part of a net of Hungarian waterways. But the people who came 1700 years after Emperor Trajan were not as efficient as the Roman engineers of antiquity. They worked on several projects simultaneously, in a haphazard manner, and achieved little.

New types of ships were tried out on the Danube. Their designs might have been sensational, though what is handed down to posterity is not fully conclusive.

It is said that, in 1772, a ship from Budapest arrived in Pressburg. It had been driven upstream by "machines moved by twelve men," and carried a load of fifty long tons; the distance was covered in eighteen hours, instead of thirty, as on a conventional boat. The inventor intended to have convicts work on the ship. Nothing more was ever learned of the odd craft.

One report of 1777 tells of what may have been the grandfather of the steamboat: "In Vienna there is a little ship model. A certain legation secretary had it built at his own expense. It has two wheels, and between them is a stove. When that stove is heated, it is expected to propel the ship even against the current. The inventor claims that its pull will be powerful enough to tug several boats tied to it. . . ." The report was never amplified, but chances are that no steam-driven tugboat traveled on the Danube in 1777 or thereabouts.

There were, however, several recorded experiments with full-scale steamships on the Danube even before April 1828, when the English shipbuilders John Andrews and Joseph Pritchard obtained an "Imperial-Royal Privilege" for the exclusive shipping privilege on the Danube with "steamships of an improved constructional design." This privilege became the basis for the *Erste Kaiserlich Königlich Privilegierte Donau-Dampfschiffahrts-Gesellschaft,* the Danube Steamship Company, which was founded in 1829 and continued in business through fundamental political and economic changes.

While Austria's and Hungary's waterways were still the government's stepchildren, many foreign and domestic suggestions were made to build them up to a splendid net of communications. A Belgian engineer named

Maire prepared a super plan to link all Austrian and Hungarian naviga-ble rivers with one another, with the Adriatic, and even with the North Sea. It seemed likely that this plan, like its lesser predecessors, would be filed and would gather dust, but somehow, in 1786, it came to the cog-nizance of Emperor Joseph II, who, to everybody's surprise, ordered that it be acted on. Eight years and two Emperors later, the Maire plan again reached the Imperial desk, and quick action was taken. A general was dispatched to England to study canal construction. The general studied the subject with cheerful slowness and missed a great deal of irksome fighting in the Napoleonic Wars. The upshot was a diminutive canal link-ing Wiener Neustadt and Vienna, passing just outside the Imperial sum-mer castle of Laxenburg. Imperial children and grandchildren played along its banks, but otherwise it served few useful purposes. The age of the railroad dawned, and, in 1879, at long last, the Wiener Neustädter Kanal closed its rusty gates.

The Danube-Moldau canal, another part of the project, was eventually superseded by a railroad inaugurated in 1832, linking Budweis and Linz. Many Austrians have since fancied that theirs was the oldest railroad in the world, but in fact the early Budweis–Linz run was made by horse-drawn carts on tracks. Not until 1871 did engines supersede propulsion by horse.

In Hungary, it took until 1801 to finish the Franzenskanal between the Danube and the Tisza, and until 1827 to complete the Kapos and the Zichy canals, which contributed little to general transportation.

During Maria Theresa's regime, the history of wine was a major topic of writers, who frequently started their accounts with events of the four-teenth century.

In fourteenth-century Austria, the convents were major wine produc-ers. Abbots took great pride in their product and had it cultivated with the best available scientific care. Peasants, who worked their own vine-yards, were less scientific, but as the demand for Austrian wines grew, and buyers came from abroad, rural growers learned that better wines fetched better prices, and tried to improve their methods.

In 1313, one carload of average peasant wine (about one long ton's weight) fetched one gulden on Lower Austrian markets; nine years later, a drought resulted in a price rise to ten gulden. In 1352, the harvest was bountiful and the wine sweet and strong; it fetched four gulden. The year 1499 brought a "wine crisis." There were not enough casks to hold all the new wine; much of it was poured out right from the presses.

Hardly ever did the quality of wines grown on the idyllic hills along the Lower Austrian Danube and its small northern tributaries match that of the noble drink that hailed from Vienna and its outskirts. The vineyards in the rural areas were caressed by gentle moist winds, but the eastern foothills of the Alps near Vienna were occasionally benefited by brisk gusts from the wide eastern lowlands. Briskness proved to be a better fecundator than gentleness.

Viennese vineyards extended from the walls of the Inner City to what became the districts of Alsergrund, Landstrasse, Wieden, and Gumpendorf to the rim of the great forests beyond. Aeneas Sylvius wrote: "Every house in Vienna has its own wine cellar; it could be said that the city is built below ground as well as above. The vintage lasts for forty days; carts loaded with mash and cider make two or three daily round trips between the city and vineyards; 1200 horses pull the carts. Apart from the local produce, wine is imported to Vienna in incalculable quantity. Some of it is consumed on the spot, the rest is laboriously shipped on the Danube to other countries. Ten per cent of the proceeds from the sale of wine goes into the treasury; this nets 12,000 gulden a year." (When this was written, one gulden was the equivalent of ten days wages of a mason, or the price of one pair of shoes.)

Viennese winegrowers and dealers were exempt from *Strand und Grundruhr*. These ancient laws stipulated that "creatures and objects" that had drifted to the banks of a river were the property of the owner of that bank, and also that lords of the manor could claim whatever objects fell upon their land. This accounted for deplorable road conditions. No lord of the manor would invest in road repairs that would keep carts and wagons from breaking axles and their cargoes falling by the wayside. It took several centuries before the laws were repealed.

Ever since the fourteenth century, burghers of Vienna were entitled to retail the wines they grew. If they wished, they could hire *Weinmeister* (wine masters) for the purpose. They were appointed by the City Council; they provided tables, chairs, crockery, and advertising. Hawkers, carrying poles adorned with green foliage, walked through the streets shouting at the top of their lungs the places where wines were being poured.

The sale of new wine by its grower in his own house and garden was the origin of the Viennese wineries, the *Heurigen,* the settings of countless happy or melancholy, tedious or inspired, solitary or companionable, mild or wild, drinking bouts that survived all vicissitudes, that stimulated good writers and bad ones, and in modern times, movie makers.

The *Heurigen* is occasionally said to have dated from Maria Theresa's time. But the Empress only encouraged a custom that originated well over a century before Columbus was born. And after the *Weinmeister* and their hawkers went down to oblivion, winegrowers adopted the custom of displaying a wreath of branches at their front door to advertise the sale of their produce. The wreath is called the Lord's finger, which shows the way to the Lord's gifts.

Maria Theresa's government issued licenses to favored applicants, entitling them not only to sell their wines but to engage in a large variety of professional and commercial activities, and *Maria Theresien Konzessionen,* which had no time limit, became coveted high-priced privileges.

In Maria Theresa's time, an ancient book on wines by Johannes Rasch, a servant in the Schotten Convent in Vienna, was rediscovered. Published in 1583, the *Weinbuch* tells not only of the production of the noble beverage, its connoisseurs, and bards, but also of regrettable machinations. The wines of the fifteenth century were often sweetened and heavily spiced; some of the spices were outrightly dangerous, and one of the artificial sweetenings, called Roccheta powder, was pure poison. Its use was prohibited in 1478, a decree that became the forerunner of the *Codex Alimentarius.*

Maria Theresa enjoyed an occasional cup of wine, but she was never a connoisseur, and she never visited a *Heurigen.*

CHAPTER FORTY-FOUR

After the death of her husband in 1765, Maria Theresa abandoned herself to despair. She considered abdication and retirement to a religious institution. Her deep grief was far above and beyond the ritual that was supposed to regulate a monarch's mourning. Her subjects, who had thought of her husband in terms of a friendly gentleman rather than the wearer of the most exalted crown of the world, sympathized.

Maria Theresa's son, Crown Prince Joseph, already held the title of Roman King since March 27, 1764. This automatically put him in line for the German throne, as the first Emperor of the House of Habsburg-Lorraine.

The mother had no illusions about his eccentricities, and his tendency to be guided by ideas that he had picked up from various sources and which he believed to be his own; but at forty-eight she felt too weary to struggle, too old to understand the modernists and reformers who influenced her son.

Chancellor Kaunitz dissuaded the Empress from resigning, assisted by a mystery man who played an important part in most decisions the Empress made.

Kaunitz did not overlook Joseph's disposition. "Ideas should not be mistaken for facts," he wrote in one of his reports to the Empress. But he expected her to gradually assign responsibilities to her son that would teach him proper evaluation.

The Chancellor's circumstantial dialectics never failed to impress the Empress. He called politics "algebra," "not an art based on innate genius, but a science based on a factual system"; to which Maria Theresa admiringly replied: "Nobody could sum up facts and classify them according to a system better than you do."

Kaunitz counseled that the new Emperor, Joseph II, be made his mother's co-ruler in charge of military affairs. On September 23, 1765, Maria Theresa, abandoning all thoughts of resignation, accepted Kaunitz's counsel.

The Chancellor began to teach Joseph the algebra of politics, but Joseph was an unsteady, irascible pupil who did not always hide his impatience. He even criticized Kaunitz for organizing his own working day as he deemed fit rather than to adapt it to the Imperial wishes. Three months after he became co-ruler, Joseph drafted three voluminous memoranda calling the governmental system inefficient, defective, if not rotten. He presented critical ideas as adverse facts, and his exasperated moods as personal intuition. Kaunitz was at his diplomatic best. His retort sounded like a flattering approval of the memoranda, yet amounted to a scathing repudiation of their contents.

The breach seemed difficult to heal. Kaunitz doubted that it could be healed at all. In June 1766, when Joseph left for maneuvers in Bohemia, Kaunitz tendered his resignation. Immediately after placing the fateful letter in Maria Theresa's trembling hands, he left for his Moravian estates.

One day later, the Empress sent him her reply: "You made me spend twenty-four bitter hours. My heart was heavy, I did not wish to follow my first impulse, but bide my time and let reason come to my assistance. After mature consideration, as your sovereign and as your friend, I return your letter to you and I wish never again to hear of its content. You owe it to me. Never has my confidence in you been more complete. You know that even in the dreadful condition in which I have found myself, it has been my foremost concern to establish my son's faith in you as solidly as my own. In this I hope to have succeeded, even though I must admit that, in the beginning, he was not all too favorably disposed toward you. And now you wish to leave me? Has your heart changed, or has your loyalty . . . ? Is jealousy or suspicion involved—false rumors, poisonous tongues? Or is it all my own fault? If I have made mistakes, why didn't you tell me? I couldn't possibly have wronged you so grievously that you would leave me without even listening to what I have to say. Whatever I may have done, could only have been caused by my depression, and by my decline, but never by a change of character. How often have I asked you to tell me about my faults? Should I complain about your not telling me often enough? Could it really be that Kaunitz's heart is affected by abject jealousy, could Kaunitz doubt in my own heart, suspect a change, listen to insipid gossip? You may judge yourself how deeply hurt and humiliated my soul was by the very thought that you consider me capable of failing you! How unfortunate we are not to be permitted to keep a true friend! I thought that I would keep you and this made me feel tranquil and content. . . . Now, as in the past, I offer you my full friendship, my unshakable faith. . . . This is all I have to say. I am not angry. But it still hurts. . . ."

Poor as Maria Theresa's grammar was, literarily inadmissible as her helter-skelter blending of German, French, and Italian words was, this letter, which she wrote herself, without a secretary's assistance, was a gem of female persuasion, of statesmanship through humble grandeur, outshining many a shortcoming of her administration, and it should silence many a voice of hindsighted criticism.

She requested by express courier that Joseph join her in trying to persuade the Chancellor to stay on. Joseph obediently wrote at once, and Kaunitz received the message shortly after the Empress'. Joseph's letter was better in spelling and grammar, but without Maria Theresa's it could not have induced the wealthy and independent Kaunitz to change his mind. "Get rid of all routine work, my dear Prince," it said. "Concentrate on the welfare of the state, on the service of its rulers who love you and to whom you would not want to deny your gifts in the future. I know you well enough to trust that you will stay on, and you know me well enough to be positive that I mean what I say: that I hold you in the highest esteem, that I honor, and sincerely love you . . ."

The "dear Prince" knew the co-monarch well indeed, and even though his letter of resignation may have included the standard phrase "for reasons of health," the suggestion that he dispense with routine work caused a flare of anger.

Kaunitz did not confide his anger to the Empress. He wrote Maria Theresa that he would continue "for a year or two."

The "year or two" lasted for twenty-nine years. After Maria Theresa was gone, he was so strongly under the spell of his office that he became its captive, even though his position of immense authority was gradually undermined. After his resignation, he lived on for a short while, a hypochondriac grand seigneur, in the shadow of his own legendary past.

The mystery man who contributed to Maria Theresa's decision not to resign was a puny and all but handsome scion of an impoverished family of Portuguese aristocrats who had turned diplomat and soldier to make a living. His full name was Dom Manoel Téllez de Menezes e Castro, Duke of Sylva, Count of Tarouca. He entered the Imperial service at the age of twenty-eight, when Maria Theresa was a child of nine, in the administration of the Netherlands. From time to time he visited Vienna, where his father was ambassador, and there he met an all-powerful lady, Countess Maria Karoline Fuchs. Despite his long name, Sylva Tarouca was not a ranking personality, but the Countess thought that he could be useful and introduced him to Emperor Charles VI, who was impressed by his intelligence and modesty, had him promoted Senior Councilor to the Netherland Offices, and gave him 15,000 gulden as a down payment to a grant of 100,000. But Emperor Charles VI forgot about further promotion, and also about the balance of the grant.

Austrian state archives contain various papers on Sylva Tarouca, but they do not disclose what caused Maria Theresa to call him to Vienna immediately after her coronation, and to appoint him to high, though purely representative, office, such as president of the Italian Council and Director of Court Buildings. His true functions were those of a tutor in matters of everyday life.

The Empress tried to stick to regulations drafted by Sylva Tarouca: Rise at 8 A.M.; take one hour for dressing, breakfast, and first Mass; "never let your coffee get cold, it upsets the stomach; see the children for one half hour every morning, attend to business from 9:30 to 12:30, have your midday meal after a fifteen-minute pause—always remember to eat your food and to drink your coffee while it is still hot. After the meal, relax for one hour in the company of your children. Then concentrate on serious work until 8:30 P.M. Afterward have supper, and after supper, dance and play." Maria Theresa was an enthusiastic dancer, but even though dancing at court was sedate, the Empress' combined total of 144 months of pregnancy made it necessary to restrain her. Sylva Tarouca preached wise restraint in dancing, horseback riding—and gambling.

"Keep on exhorting me," Maria Theresa would say. "I may not immediately heed your words, but I shall remember them a little later." The Empress' gambling habits exasperated the exhorter. Thrifty as she was in state and household matters, the very sight of a pack of cards changed her from a penny pincher to a wastrel. He was afraid that some of her children might inherit her habit. He did not live to see Marie Antoinette's passion for "pharaoh," but he warned the Empress that national anti-gambling laws could hardly be enforced when everybody talked about the Court's card games at fantastic stakes. In order to show her that money should never be a dominant impulse, he had his annual salary cut from 26,000 to 10,000 gulden. She was impressed, but it took her a long time to change from the dangerous "pharaoh" to the more modest "lansquenet" and to reduce the stakes.

Sylva Tarouca had been among the first to warn Maria Theresa about the character of some of her children, in particular Joseph, the most problematical of them. She tried to guide him, but soon realized that this only stimulated his rebellious fantasies and frustrations. Sylva Tarouca urged her to be firm, but she was afraid to alienate her oldest son even further. She craved love. "Love, as confidence," Sylva Tarouca lectured, "must be mutual. Stubbornness must not be allowed to antagonize feelings. . . ." But she did not understand him, and her worries did not abate.

After Emperor Franz died, Sylva Tarouca, then past seventy, resigned his titular offices, but remained the Empress' confidant. Answering his New Year's greetings for 1766, she lamented: "I live like a beast, without reason. I can hardly think. I forget everything. I rise at five, and I retire late, but I get nothing done. It is terrible. I feel a little better only when I see a good old friend." Ailing Sylva Tarouca rushed to the castle and pleaded that loyalty to the country required the Empress not to abandon herself to her misery and Austria to its fate.

That fate seemed personified by Joseph.

Austrian state archives contain a letter in which Maria Theresa thanked Sylva Tarouca for his congratulations on the occasion of Joseph's birthday in 1769: "Who could have thought, 28 years ago, that you and me would live to see this day and spend it as we do now . . . It is humiliating, sad, inexplicable . . . I look forward to my death with impatience rather than fear."

Twenty-eight years before, on March 13, 1741, when the Empress was in her birth pangs, news came that the Prussians had captured Glogau, that enemy vanguards were across the Bohemian border. Maria Theresa hoped that her first son—after she had had three girls—would be the avenger of her iniquities, the stanch preserver of tradition.

The future stanch preserver of tradition was frail. "He looks like a squirrel," a visiting grandee quipped. Normally, Princes were entrusted to the care of men as soon as possible; however, Joseph was almost exclusively in female company throughout the first seven years of his life. A few foreign diplomats who watched him like a cub in a gilded cage differed in their judgment: "He is highly gifted," said one. "He will never be a genius," said the other. "He is vanitied and obstinate," said a third.

Joseph's first civilian tutor, Baron Johann Christian Bartenstein, voiced hope that the boy might have "better qualities than meets the eye, and that by the grace of God, all troubles may vanish." Joseph's first military teacher, Field Marshal Count Károly Batthyány tried to make the prospective Emperor a good prospective soldier. But Joseph disliked the field marshal, who, in turn, found him misanthropic and confused. Jesuit teachers took care of the Prince's primary tuition. They were assiduous flatterers and reported that Joseph, though "unindustrious," had a splendid memory and was mentally very alert. Yet the Prince resented being taught and examined. He resented the Jesuits, and would later expand this resentment to the entire clergy without distinction. He blamed everybody for not recognizing him as a fabulous genius.

Resentment begot inhibitions, inhibitions begot frustrations, and frustrations a frantic desire for retaliation and reform, for changes that would make him appear to be the benefactor of mankind. Maria Theresa tried to keep the lid on Pandora's box until experience as a co-ruler would have produced its soothing effect upon her son. Joseph, meantime, irritated her friends, and favored her antagonists, such as Frederick of Prussia.

After Joseph became friendly with Frederick, the Prussian Prime Minister called him "very well built and perfectly handsome," while lesser sycophants admired his "regular features and bright-blue radiant eyes." Portraits do not quite bear out the glorification. Joseph had a prominent nose and a less than prominent forehead. He seems to have been reasonably handsome, but neither as fair as his flatterers said nor as staggering as he wished the mirror on the wall to tell him.

All his frustrations and his rebelliousness might have been overcome by the panacea of true love, but in this respect fate was cruel to Joseph. Maria Theresa married him off when he was not yet twenty to Isabella of Parma, a granddaughter of Louis XV. Isabella was hardly glamorous, but intelligent, warmhearted, and tender. Gradually Joseph's frustrations lessened; even his letters to his mother sounded relaxed, almost happy and grateful. When their first daughter was born the young couple called her Maria Theresa. The happy event occurred during the last year of the Seven Years' War, in which Joseph did not even try to distinguish himself. Strange changes occurred with Isabella after childbirth. She turned into a bluestocking, and wrote dissertations on ethics, morality, and commerce, and also philosophical meditations. She was no longer her husband's devoted young mate, but the rapturous friend of his sister Archduchess Maria Christine. Even though they met almost daily, the sisters-in-law engaged in an intimate correspondence, and Isabella's letters give little evidence of tender feelings for Joseph. Nevertheless, she became pregnant again, and while pregnant contracted smallpox, the constant scourge of Austrians, high and low. On November 20, 1763, she gave birth to another girl. The infant lived for only two hours; the mother survived for six excruciating days.

"I have lost everything . . . my adored wife, the object of all my affections, my only friend," Joseph lamented. He had apparently never noticed the complete estrangement that preceded her death. His frustrations hardened again, his resentments turned violent. Joseph became bitter, sarcastic, an atheist in the cloak of a Christian monarch, who would do everything in his power to harm the Church, but who idolized his country, of which he dreamed to be an incarnation, while desperately trying to be idolized by his people.

The people pitied him when he was widowed at twenty-two; pity is both root and shoot of love. They were ready to love him in the traditional manner and would have responded to lovable actions. But Joseph's reforms did not endear him to the simple man, and his bids for popularity failed to produce the desired effect. Eighteenth-century Austrians did not eagerly respond to a monarch's stunts that resembled later politicians' baby kissing. The common man's notion of Imperial dignity was incompatible with, say, clumsy attempts at handling a plow or talking to his subjects on the street incognito. The common man's reserve added to Joseph's self-pitying frustrations.

Maria Theresa hoped that his coronation as Roman King would lift his spirits. But from his trip to Frankfurt he wrote her: "Bereaved as I am of my Queen, I am a deeply afflicted King." The teen-age Johann Wolfgang von Goethe witnessed the grandiose spectacle of the coronation on April 3, 1764. "The young King, burdened with colossal pieces of vestment, drags himself as if in a disguise," the future "Prince of Poets" noted.

Maria Theresa made her son remarry, again for reasons of state. This time, the bride was a Bavarian Princess, Maria Josepha of the House of Wittelsbach. Joseph's inhibitions were weaker than his mother's determination. This is how he described his new fiancée to his first father-in-law: "Her short-set fat figure lacks all juvenile charm; she has little blisters and red speckles all over her face, and her teeth are ugly."

On January 23, 1765, the wedding was performed in the court chapel of Schönbrunn. The unfortunate bride could see acid derision in the faces of the ladies and gentlemen of the Court, and what she could see in the groom's face heralded evil. Joseph once called her a woman beyond reproach whom he held in high esteem for her good qualities, but added ominously that reason could not beget affection. His attitude toward his young wife became so intolerable that her chief lady in waiting resigned because she could not bear to witness the young Emperor's mental cruelty. But the hapless young wife loved her husband and struggled for his affection, until she died, also from smallpox, on May 28, 1768. Her husband did not attend her funeral.

Joseph was soon called to another sickbed, that of his daughter Maria Theresa, his adored "alter ego," as he called her. Physicians could not diagnose the nature of her malady and they could not save her. She passed away on the fifth anniversary of Joseph's second wedding. "God return my child—return her to me," he screamed.

Joseph became frantically officious. He had met the Prussian King a short time before tragedy struck him, and he wished to see Frederick again for a heart-to-heart talk. Maria Theresa had a bewildering notion that her son was turning imitator of the King whom she had never ceased to hate; but she consented to the meeting under the condition that Chancellor Kaunitz be present. The affair took place on Austrian territory, in Mährisch-Neustadt (Uničov). Kaunitz rather than Joseph did the talking for Austria, and when Joseph remarked that Austria was no longer concerned about Silesia, Kaunitz's stony silence was a severe motion of censure and Frederick did not quite trust Joseph's remark. Prussia worried about extreme Russian ambitions, and looked askance at the latest *rapprochement* between Austria and France, exemplified by the carefully arranged marriage between Marie Antoinette and Dauphin Louis (later Louis XVI). Kaunitz offered no comfort to Prussia, only dry, glib, noncommittal phrases, and nothing resulted. There was no official announcement in Vienna, but Austrians had a notion that if statesmen traveled, people soon would have to fight.

In fact, peace hung on a thin thread. Joseph's intentions were not all peaceful, though he did not wish to fight Prussia. Russian armies had just crushed a rebellion against Stanislaw Poniatowski, puppet King of Poland by the grace of Tsarina Catherine II; they had pursued the remaining rebels into Turkish territory and defeated Turkish troops who tried to keep them away. Joseph ordered Austrian units to invade southern Poland, allegedly to protect the security of the monarchy, actually to interfere where the risks seemed least and the prospects of gathering personal laurels seemed greatest. Two districts of Poland were seized.

Poland had been sick, politically and socially, for several decades; the serfs, who constituted the bulk of the indigenous peasantry, were brutalized; they were "denied the air to breathe, and there was hardly a difference between them and their beasts." Poland had no national schools, no industry, no trade other than the one controlled by German or Jewish immigrants. Its Diet of Nobility had the sole legislative power, but many nobles were desperately poor and therefore corrupt. To make things worse, Poland had a fantastic institution, called the *liberum veto:* any single member of the Diet could veto any law, and his veto could not be overruled even by the combined vote of all other members. A *liberum veto* could be purchased with no more than 100 ducats, and any piece of legislation could be pushed through the Diet for no more than 2000 ducats. For almost half a century, Russia controlled Poland's military establishment by purchasing vetoes and legislation that kept the army down to a small, ill-armed, ill-fed mob. The *liberum veto* choked the nation. It vanished after Poland was dismembered, but was ingloriously resurrected on Soviet Russia's request 150 years later, minus the word *liberum,* in the statutes of the United Nations.

The Tsarina had installed her Poniatowski as a puppet King to give the once proud realm the status of a Russian province. This, and dismemberment of Turkey, which was another kingpin of Russian expansionism, was supposed to turn the semi-Asiatic empire of the Tsars into the keeper of the keys to Central Europe and the Middle East, and the ruler of the Danube and Nile valleys.

Frederick of Prussia wanted a share in the loot of Poland. Vain Joseph wanted one too. Kaunitz at first did not agree, and in 1771 even signed a treaty with Turkey to the effect that Austria would prevent the Russians from crossing the lower Danube. In return, Turkey offered to cede part of Walachia province to Austria. The Russians postponed their drive across the Danube. They might even have waited in Poland, but Frederick wanted his share at once. Joseph pestered his mother to participate. She objected: "Partitioning is iniquitous by nature, and damaging to our own interests." But Kaunitz, the wizard of algebra, reasoned that the only other alternative would be an aggrandizement of Russia and Prussia. The Empress was stunned to see her Chancellor side with her son. She suggested that Austria should not begrudge Prussia and Russia their ill-gotten gains provided Frederick returned Silesia and Glatz. Neither Joseph nor Kaunitz was surprised to learn that Frederick would not even discuss the suggestion.

In February 1772, Russia and Prussia reached an agreement on a partition of Poland and invited Austria to join. Maria Theresa cried, but finding no support from Kaunitz, she gave in. The tripartite treaty was signed in St. Petersburg on August 2, 1772. Russia got most of Polish territory, Prussia its least backward sections, and Austria the most destitute regions, which, however—as it was not then appreciated—were the only ones that yielded oil.

In January 1773, the grabbing great powers issued hypocritical declarations to justify their action. What remained of rump-Poland was wiped out in two more partitions, in 1793 and 1795, respectively. Austria participated only in the latter.

Joseph, looking for a territorial link between the parts of Poland acquired in 1773 and the eastern lands of the traditional monarchy, seized Bucovina, a distant province held by the Turks, which had strategic importance, fertile soil, good cattle-raising opportunities, and mineral deposits, including gold.

Joseph had further plans of annexation, and he quoted Prince Eugene, who had said that the permanent incorporation of Bavaria would enhance Austria's strategic potential. Joseph wanted as much of Bavaria as he could get. Kaunitz, who viewed all policies from the angle of their effect on Prussia, was in favor of removing Bavaria from the range of its aggression, possibly without war. He felt that a tight Austro-French alliance would discourage Frederick from armed intervention.

Since 1774, Marie Antoinette was Queen of France. A clever and popular French Queen might have achieved Austria's aims, but the frivolous young woman did not create good will for Austria. Maria Theresa was chagrined. She admonished her daughter to behave, and through her ambassador sent candid advice how to arouse King Louis XVI's dormant virility. The Empress' instructions being to little avail, Joseph went to Paris. He traveled incognito, but took good care that Parisians knew who he was and gave a display of simple affability. To his brother-in-law, he suggested surgical remedy for his sexual deficiency, which embarrassed the poor man no end. To his sister, he delivered schoolmasterly harangues, which made her burst out laughing and promise, giggling, to improve. But she said that Bavaria was none of her concern and that he should talk to the cabinet. The ministers were extremely polite and promised political assistance, but refused to make any military gestures; France needed peace and an internationally negotiable currency.

Back in Vienna, Joseph ordered crown jurists to prepare an airtight case for the annexation of Bavaria. The jurists searched archives for documents that would convince everybody, including Maria Theresa, that Austria's westward expansions were legal. Maria Theresa was not convinced, and Kaunitz again tried diplomacy rather than a hairsplitting legalism that would not keep Prussia from moving into a power vacuum along the upper Danube.

On the last day of 1777, the Bavarian Elector passed away. His successor, Karl Theodor, was persuaded to sign a compact which gave Austria large slices of Bavaria, and Vienna trusted that his heir, the Duke of Zweibrücken, would join the compact. But at this point Prussia interfered, saber-rattling, in the novel part of champion of small provinces. Frederick, who had obtained a pledge of neutrality from Russia and a veiled promise to the same effect from the French cabinet, pressured the Duke of Zweibrücken into putting himself, his land, and his claims of inheritance under Prussian protection, and then requested that Austrian troops already moving into Bavaria be removed at once.

"Don't count on me, if there is a war," Maria Theresa warned her son. "I shall flee to the Tyrol and stay there in seclusion to the end of my days."

She did not flee to the Tyrol, however, when Prussia declared war and its armies entered Bohemia. Austria's army of 170,000 was outnumbered, and the startling swiftness of early Prussian operations upset the Austrian advantage of the "inner line." Field Marshal Laudon, aging and grouchy, made no secret of his pessimism. Joseph ranted battle while his mother dispatched a cabinet minister to settle the conflict outside the battlefield and tried to induce the Tsarina to mediate.

The campaign was limited to maneuvers, without shooting. At last, in

March 1799, Austria, Prussia, France, and Russia negotiated in Teschen. On Maria Theresa's birthday a peace without glory was signed to end a war without casualties. Austria renounced the compact with Karl Theodor and all claims to Bavaria, in return for 800 square miles of land, the Innviertel, between the rivers Danube, Inn, and Salzach. Joseph remarked: "The object seems trifling, compared with what we might have obtained otherwise; but the district is lovely and fits well into Upper Austria."

People in both camps spoke disdainfully of "potato war" and "plum row," referring to the main crops of the region. Nobody thought that it would make world history. But in the Innviertel, in the small city of Braunau, Adolf Hitler was born ninety years later; because of the Treaty of Teschen, the Führer of Germany was a native of Austria.

Joseph attributed the "trifling" result to Russia's attitude. He resolved to charm Catherine II into supporting him and had the Austrian ambassador arrange a meeting. Kaunitz had doubts about the effects of Joseph's moderate showmanship upon the Tsarina's reckless shrewdness, and Maria Theresa voiced strong misgivings because of Catherine's notorious immorality. But Joseph boldly went into the aging lioness' den, and in April 1780 met Catherine in Mohilev. They traveled together to St. Petersburg. After a trip to Moscow, where he mingled with boyar society, Joseph returned to St. Petersburg to see her again. The Viennese made caustic remarks about the hazards of Imperial traveling and about the biblical Joseph and Potiphar. It took a full year before the meager results of the trip were summed up in a colorless Austro-Russian pact of friendship.

When Joseph returned to Vienna, his mother's health was failing. Yet they had long debates on the fundamentals of politics. Maria Theresa insisted that most reforms were meaningless in fact, and that virtuous catchwords could do much harm. "Tolerance can be tantamount to indifference; indifference undermines everything, and nothing will be conserved," she told her son.

They had quarreled on that subject before; Joseph had even threatened to resign as a co-ruler of Austria and make public the reasons for his resignation should his mother not revoke certain ordinances which he termed intolerant, such as the draft of religious sectarians in Moravia. But he did not resign when Maria Theresa refused to yield, and she was less than ever in a yielding mood when she felt that her end was approaching. She never believed in the sincerity of the motto "everything for the people, nothing by the people," which Joseph kept repeating, even though he would never let popular representatives interfere with legislative matters. In fact, Maria Theresa actually believed in a division of functions and responsibility in government and even, to some degree, in local autonomy, while Joseph was more of a centralist than she had ever been; he wanted all power to be vested in the state, or rather its symbol, the Emperor, who would exercise it in the best interest of the people, as he saw it. There should be but one basic law, one nationality, no special privileges for any class or group, no powers for the clergy. Society should be reformed. It sounded vague, but dangerous. The land was not uniform in culture, language, prosperity, and tradition. What could suit one province might destroy another. Centralization could turn into a strait jacket.

The Empress realized that her arguments were in vain, that Joseph would insist on his program after her death. "He tortures me, but I still adore him," she had told Sylva Tarouca shortly before the old man died, and she was very much concerned with her soul's salvation.

Shortly before her death, Joseph made a confession of his creed, according to which Providence manifested itself in the laws of nature; God and nature being one, he was entitled to act in accordance with the law of nature, which prevailed over man-made law. It was an Emperor's duty to take care of the happiness "of the greatest number"; to achieve this, the hereditary monarch had unlimited powers. According to this theory, autocracy was not arbitrariness, but the exercise of a divine right.

The confusing confession presented autocracy as democracy, without the consent of the governed. Maria Theresa did not understand it, but she hoped that Kaunitz would prevent disastrous effects of her son's reforms.

On November 8, 1780, the Empress' condition took a turn for the worse and she died three weeks later, at sixty-three. Her last kind words were addressed to Joseph, who was by her bedside, disconcerted and haunted by secret fears.

The Emperor would have wanted to let Kaunitz go, but this would have required more courage than he could muster. Instead, he asked him to be his friend, support, and guide, and assured him of his esteem.

Kaunitz had no delusions, but he was tied to his office by inertia and by the awareness of being the only stanch guardian of Austria's position as a great power, the most effective counterpoise against dilettantism, emotionalism, and frustration. He did not call at the Imperial castle, but, pleading indisposition, had the Emperor visit him in his sumptuous *palais* in the then swank district of Mariahilf.

Kaunitz expressed readiness to serve Emperor and country on his own terms. He wanted to have the final say in foreign affairs, to be consulted in all matters of domestic policy, to act on the Emperor's behalf in the latter's absence; and he would transact official business from his home, at his own convenience. Joseph agreed, pleased to delegate some responsibilities to the Chancellor, whose prestige would cover up his own mistakes.

The court mourning for Maria Theresa was long, pompous, and circumstantial. Joseph ordered that every letter of the ceremonial be respected. The carnival of 1781 was the quietest all Austrians could remember. There were more Masses for one dead than diversion for all the living.

CHAPTER FORTY-FIVE

Joseph's reforms started with an Edict of Tolerance, by which the Emperor expected to endear himself to the religious minorities of his realm and to become the idol of champions of progress everywhere.

The edict granted Protestants the right to "practice their religions" privately. Parishes of no less than 100 non-Catholic families were entitled to establish their own schools and places of worship, provided their temples had neither bells nor belfry and no public street entrances. Many restrictions were lifted. Non-Catholic Christians could own houses and estates, became burghers and master craftsmen, and held academic degrees. Children of mixed marriages no longer had to be raised in the Catholic faith, but boys in the faith of their father and girls in that of their mother.

Protestants were relatively few in Austria and Bohemia, and they did not hail the Emperor as their liberator. But a small band of Bohemian Hussites, who, outwardly, had abided by Catholicism, now asked that they be permitted to secede from that Church and be without confession. A state commission passed the Hussite problem on to local authorities, who agreed that all applicants for secession would be subjected to twenty-four blows with a solid stick. In Hungary, the edict caused no stir either; the provisions it contained had long existed under laws which Joseph had not known.

Emancipation of Jews was discussed in many parts of Western and Central Europe. Nowhere, including in Joseph's Austria, was it strictly carried out. But priests were admonished to preach the equality of the Jews, restrictive regulations were eased, their children were admitted to Christian schools, and occasionally they could become farmers and craftsmen; they no longer had to wear special garb or to pay special duties for entering certain cities.

The Austrian clergy girded for a showdown.

The Emperor struck the first blow.

In Maria Theresa's later days, 2163 convents, with a combined membership of about 45,000 monks and nuns, existed in the realm. An Imperial decree expelled all foreign monks and nuns; and soon seven orders were abolished.

On December 12, 1781, Pope Pius VI lodged a protest against governmental interference in religious matters. The Emperor, who had not previously consulted Kaunitz, now went to his *palais* and asked for advice. The Chancellor drafted a diplomatic masterpiece: a one-sentence reply that should placate the Pontiff and keep Joseph from going too far in his reforms: "Matters of dogma and cure of souls are not involved; everything else is within the province of the state."

The Pope was alarmed; the Emperor was not restrained. Not long thereafter, 738 convents had ceased to exist. Their assets were supposed to go into a "religious fund," but actually were secularized. Little money was needed to set up vicarages in remote communities, which official terminology called new "stations for the cure of souls."

A Court Commission drafted a flood of regulations concerning cult and church administration, and wooed public support. They launched rumors of fantastic riches amassed by mendicant friars, of millions gathered in their treasuries, which should have contained no more than copper coins, and of nunneries keeping costly wines in their cellars. The Emperor was said to consider convents institutions of idleness and harmful to the country's economy, since they did not efficiently cultivate their estates; the clergy's educational activities were severely criticized, and somebody devised the slogan of the clerics' "polyp-like absorption of the laymen's property." Actually, there had been various abuses; some mendicant friars were too well off; Church estates were not always properly operated. But the state was even less efficient than the Church had ever been.

Pope Pius VI, highly alarmed, decided to travel to Austria to restore the traditional cordial relations between Emperor and Church. Joseph did not relish the prospect of the Pontiff's presence; the Austrians were a rather superficial lot, but their emotions were easily aroused; the presence of the Pope might stir feelings which the Emperor secretly dreaded. So he sent a letter to Rome saying, "We are so perfectly convinced of the righteousness of our views that it is impossible to present arguments that could make us desist from our endeavors."

But the Pope did not change his mind. Another Pius, second of this name, had been the last Pope to visit Vienna, almost 350 years before. He then was still Aeneas Sylvius (de Piccolomini); he had tasted, raved, and written about the delicious wines of the Danube Valley; he had to struggle against an unfriendly government. The sixth Pius, who had just solved the problem created by American independence by releasing the American Catholic clergy from jurisdiction of the vicar apostolic of England, was determined to solve the bewildering Austrian problem and replied, sanctimoniously, that he would pay the visit anyway.

On March 22, 1782, after a relatively fast journey through the Austrian Alps, where few people became aware of the presence of the supreme authority of their faith, Pius VI reached Neunkirchen, thirty-five miles south of Vienna. Joseph met him there as a matter of courtesy, and also because he would have preferred to keep his distinguished visitor at some distance from the fickle, irritable capital.

The first interview culminated in the Emperor's emphatic assertion that he was a faithful Catholic and the Pope's solemn acknowledgment of Joseph's *singularis in Deum devotio*. Upon Pius' mild-mannered insistence, they proceeded to Vienna.

In Vienna, the Emperor temporized, the Pope diplomatized, and Kaunitz chose to feel unwell whenever confronted with unmanageable problems.

Chroniclers are not unanimous about the attitude of the Viennese people. But those who describe them as curious but otherwise neutral in the conflict, are in the minority, and their writings conflict with eyewitness accounts. Most contemporaries tell of the people's fascination. Even the Emperor acknowledged the immense popular interest for the visitor in a letter to his sister Maria Christine: "For the last three days, the gathering of crowds outside his [the Pope's] windows was extraordinary. It was a beautiful spectacle the like of which I have never seen before and shall hardly ever see again. It was impossible to ascertain the number of people."

And a distinguished Protestant, Mr. Bourgoing, told of having been moved to tears by the spectacle of 50,000 people (Bourgoing's own estimate) gathered on the square outside the castle and expressing devout enthusiasm. Tightly crowded but oblivious of physical discomfort, they held their breath when the Pope appeared and raised his hands to heaven in the attitude of a man who is deeply convinced of presenting the wishes and longings of an entire nation to God.

Easter came, the people prayed, looked up at the Pope, and wondered about the Emperor, who occasionally stood at his side, torn between stubbornness and fear, but anxious to abide by all commandments of the season.

One month after the meeting at Neunkirchen, the Pope left Vienna and traveled, via Munich and Innsbruck, back to Rome, pondering about a compromise that even the most enlightened mind could hardly have conceived.

The Emperor wanted the state to expand its prerogatives at the expense of the Church and to reduce the Church's power even further. As long as the Pope was still on Austrian soil, the Court Commission did nothing; but as soon as Pius reached Italy, decrees poured out again.

Cardinal Archbishop of Vienna, Count Christoph von Migazzi, whom Maria Theresa had greatly respected, was also Bishop of Vác in Hungary. A decree stipulated that, henceforth, no prelate should hold more than one prebend. Migazzi had to vacate his Hungarian bishopric.

Bureaucrats reduced the number of holidays, regulated the number of candles to be burned in services, standardized the adornments of pictures of saints, drafted rules to be observed on pilgrimages and at obsequies. They meddled in many traditions that were deeply rooted in public usage.

The staff of the Commission grew; its salaries ran higher than the proceeds of secularized Church property. Commission members called the people ignorant and superstitious, and proclaimed that better non-clerical education was needed to enlighten the dull masses.

In 1783, the Emperor suppressed many ecclesiastic educational institutions and established a number of mundane schools. He even substituted priests' seminaries with "general seminaries," to raise a new kind of priest who would be the servant of the state rather than of the Church.

Various prelates opposed the Emperor and his Commission, but some collaborated. The Emperor's bureaucrats promptly introduced *Arrondierung,* redistribution of the holdings of bishoprics, taking land away from objectors and assigning it to collaborators. Two canonical bulls, *In Coena Domini* and *Unigenitus,* which curtailed the rights of mundane rulers, were removed from the books; marriage dispensations should no longer be granted by Rome, but by bishops, who were directed to give them for a nominal fee.

This was reformation, not by a dissenting clergy, but by the state; not a separation of state and church, but an intertwining of both institutions with the state expanding its control.

In 1783, Joseph claimed the right to nominate bishops and archbishops, including the Archbishop of Milan. The Pope renewed his protests. This time Joseph traveled to Rome. In September 1783, he threatened to make himself independent from the Curia. Pius, torn between anger and apprehension, granted him and his successors the right to nominate bishops, abbots, and other prelates in the district of Milan. Thinking in terms of long periods as Pontiffs had learned to do, Pius VI felt that the stormy petrel on the throne would be succeeded by devout and meek rulers, who would wish to please Rome.

The Emperor was acclaimed by various Austrian groups, including the Freemasons, who considered him their natural champion, if only on the grounds that his mother had detested them. Freemasonry had come to Austria from England via Holland. The first lodge, "The Three Cannon," was established in Vienna in 1742; it was followed, seven years later, by the "Three-Crowned Stars and Honesty" in Prague. But Joseph never took to masonry, and he wrote in 1785: "These so-called Freemason societies, whose secrets I fail to envision, and whose buffooneries I have no desire to understand, are now spreading everywhere, even in small communities." The Emperor wanted to confine lodges to Vienna and to provincial capitals, which eventually caused the Freemasons to write him off as their champion.

However, as time went on, some of Joseph's reforms created genuine progress in important fields. He promoted a new and sounder system of taxation. Farmers should never pay more than 30 per cent of their gross product as combined total of all dues. A ceiling on all taxes was a vital innovation. But Austrian peasants did not enthusiastically respond to Joseph's decree. They had been used to paying as much as they could spare and letting the collector worry about the balance.

The Emperor reformed the criminal code. In this field, however, he could not help following in the footsteps of his mother, who had abolished torture. The man who had inspired Maria Theresa to undertake the reform was Joseph Sonnenfels, who also inspired Joseph.

Joseph Sonnenfels, aged forty-seven when the Empress died, was professor of "police and financial science" at the University of Vienna. He had come to the capital from Nikolsburg, Moravia, where his Jewish father, Perlin Lipman, had attained a residential permit and had changed his name and his creed. The son was raised as a Catholic. He became a linguist, a jurist, a soldier, teacher, and a magazine publisher, in which capacity he ran into trouble with the censor. However, it was not lofty idealism that caused his magazine, *Der Vertraute* (*The Confidant*), to be prosecuted. Sonnenfels liked to write inside stories about the private lives of well-known personalities, who brought suit and eventually joined action to have the authorities banish the magazine. Sonnenfels founded another publication, *Der Mann ohne Vorurteil* (*The Man without Prejudice*), in which he crusaded against superstition, shortcomings of education, perversities, legal abuses, the decline of the German language, and the deplorable level of public taste. As a crusader, he gathered a large following, was appointed university professor, and won the Empress' ear. Sonnenfels championed abolition of capital punishment and police censorship.

Joseph did not go along with the former, but he viewed the latter with cautious sympathy, provided, of course, it would not leave him exposed to sarcasm and disrespect.

In 1786 and 1787, civil and penal law was codified.

The General Code of Crimes and Their Punishment no longer mentioned sorcery and black magic. The death penalty was limited to murder and rebellion. New penalties were introduced, such as "pulling ships" on Austrian rivers (a substitute for the galleys) and sweeping streets.

Viennese and even generally less curious provincials gazed at gangs of convicts who pulled heavily loaded ships upstream on the Danube. Shipowners had to pay the authorities for the services, and soon found out that old-fashioned teams of horses were more efficient and cheaper. Shipping on the Danube was not affected by the penal innovation.

The Emperor introduced Sonnenfels' language program in the field of civilian administration; this was justified in the babel of languages that was the Empire. Joseph established German as the official language. To the Court and the aristocracy, French had been the first language, but German was spoken by more people in the realm than any other tongue. In Czech, Slovene, and other non-German-speaking districts, people could still use their native idioms in dealings with the authorities, but interoffice communications and official documents had to be drafted in German. Such papers often sounded hideous to linguistic purists, but they were entirely understandable.

Hungarian authorities were outraged and rebellious. Rebellion in Hungary had been fanned, shortly before, on April 7, 1784, when Joseph had the Holy Crown of St. Stephen transferred to the *Schatzkammer,* the Imperial jewel vault in Vienna. Extreme Hungarian patriots considered this an insult to their nation, and the imposition of the German language let the pot of excitement boil over.

In fact, only peasants and the urban plebs spoke Hungarian; the idiom of the higher strata was German; ranking nobility used French and something they called Latin—but which Julius Caesar would not have understood—which was also used in official correspondence. Officials were ordered to change to German within three years. Members of the Diet would have to debate in German.

Historian Franz Xavier von Krones recorded: "It became a national duty to resist stubbornly, since that language [German] became an intruder, the hated symbol of innovations, of breach of Constitution, and intolerable tyranny . . ."

Yet another Josephian decree, ordering the transfer of the Hungarian Diet from Pressburg to Buda, poured oil into the blaze of rebellion.

The only people in Hungary who hailed the reforms were illiterate rustics of Walachian origin. They believed that the Emperor had done something great for them, and that nobles and clergy would now parcel out their land among the needy. They cheered, and waited—but when the privileges failed to materialize they began to riot. The Emperor had to use military force to quell arson and mass murder.

There was neither murder nor arson in other parts of Hungary, and certainly not in Austria, where many journals debated the issue: reform versus conservation. The Viennese liked controversy, but they preferred a show to printed matter, and fighting animals to opera and tragedy. The Hetzamphitheater unter den Weissgerbern, situated on an arm of the Danube, sold out daily.

This theater, a huge, circular three-story building with a capacity of well over 2000, had been founded in 1755 by a venturesome Frenchman. For decades no human had appeared on its stage. Lions, tigers, leopards, panthers, bears, wolves, even oxen, were set upon by dogs or mangled each other in duels of repulsive ferocity. Only in the later 1780s were fights among beasts occasionally superseded by shows that were a crude blending of horror and sex and which had such titles as: "Minotaurus, the half ox in the labyrinth, or the moving story and *salve venia* gruesome end of the beauteous Princess Ariadne, and the subsequent merry consummation of the nuptials with Mister von Bacchus."

Audiences preferred merry consummation of nuptials to the *Marriage of Figaro.*

The Hetzamphitheater prospered until 1796, when it burned down and Emperor Franz II (Joseph's nephew) decreed that it should never be rebuilt, so that there would be "an end to these disgusting spectacles which are a disgrace to the nation and its capital."

In Joseph's day, the most respected playwright was Kornelius von Ayrendorff, an army general. His tragedies, written after French models, include *Aurelius, Antiope, Cleopatra, Virginia;* his comedies the *Mail Procession* and the *Noble Passions*. They were frequently performed, but their eventual disappearance from the stage constitutes no loss to posterity. Ayrendorff, whose name would be hard to find in modern reference works, also wrote many critical essays. He had a low opinion of Shakespeare and called *Hamlet* silly, immoral, contemptible, "the sort of play that could please wet nurses, children, and the mob of the upper galleries." He censured the Bard for choosing as protagonists "downright morons, lowly porters, and drunkards." He called the Shakespeare mania a literary disgrace. He had no patience with German classical poets either. He derided Goethe, whose *Götz von Berlichingen* he called "Anglicized," meaning that it contained the same crude flaws as Shakespeare's works. He tried his pen at a "sarcastic epigram to Friedrich von Schiller's *Die Jungfrau von Orleans*." An insipid tinkle with words insinuates that Schiller's drama was meant to make the audience cry, but could make no witty person shed a single tear.

Contemporary reports tell of high sales figures of books, which are hard to verify. But it is established that Sonnenfels' brochure about Empress Maria Theresa had an advance sale of two copies, and that, only after her death, some 8000 copies were sold at ten kreuzer (about four cents) apiece, which was not all too impressive for a city of 300,000.

An average of 30,000 visitors from abroad came to Vienna every year. Some chose to stay. Among them was Mozart, who, in March 1781, arrived from Salzburg and lived in Vienna until his death in 1791. Even though the former child prodigy had a hard time establishing himself as an adult musician, he wrote his father: "I can assure you that this is a wonderful place, the best place in the world for any profession. I like it here."

CHAPTER FORTY-SIX

While looking for some great design he could not quite conceive, Joseph got a confidential letter from the Tsarina. Maria Theresa would have called its contents absurd, but the Emperor was enraptured. Catherine II proposed to drive the Turks out of Europe and to restore a Byzantine Empire that would include most of the Balkan Peninsula. Her second grandson, Constantine, would be Emperor of Byzantium, and Austria would receive some land along the lower Danube, if it joined a war against Turkey.

Kaunitz told the Emperor that existing pacts of friendship required that Austria assist Russia if it were attacked, but that there was no commitment to join Russia in a war of aggression; and that what the Tsarina offered as a compensation was a mere pittance. Joseph, in the pose of a resurrector of classical antiquity, resented the Chancellor's attitude, but could not bring himself to assume sole responsibility.

News of Catherine's "Greek project" filtered out and was ill received in other European capitals. Four years went by. Late in 1786, Prussia and England agreed that changes of sovereignty in southeastern Europe were undesirable. Friedrich Wilhelm II then was King of Prussia; Frederick the Great rested in the small crypt beneath the terrace of Sans Souci Castle in Potsdam, where, on March 21, 1933, Adolf Hitler would make his farcical proclamation of the birth of the Third Reich.

Prussia and England urged Turkey to declare war on Russia, and in August 1787, Turkey took the hazardous step.

In the spring Joseph had paid another call on the aging but still fierce Tsarina, but her professions of friendship were noncommittal.

When Turkey went to war, Joseph issued mobilization orders far less enthusiastically than he would have a few years before. At last, on February 2, 1788, Austria declared war on Turkey. Yet the Emperor is quoted as saying: "Turkey's existence in Europe will continue for a long time."

The Austrian army had 245,000 men, 36,000 horses, and 898 cannon, but seasoned generals had aged, and rising commanders were showy mediocrities. Joseph hesitated to call on Laudon, and put Field Marshal Count Moritz Lascy in charge, whom he considered a military reformer and who devised one of the most stupid campaign plans in military history.

A concentrated attack by so huge a force would have overrun the Turkish army, but Lascy scattered the 245,000 over a tremendous line from the Dnieper River to the Adriatic Sea, and decentralized the command by creating six independent groups. Nothing decisive could ever result.

Joseph left gay Vienna to stay with Lascy. Authors of Austrian primers, in quest of heart-warming episodes, later told of the Emperor's gallant generosity during the siege of Šabac, west of Belgrade: Watching the bombardment from an exposed battery, Joseph allegedly noticed that the ailing Lascy could hardly keep on his feet, and personally rolled an empty powder barrel toward the field marshal, so that he might sit down. The whole campaign was about as brilliant as this episode.

After Šabac fell, Lascy took up a defensive position in infection-ridden swamps along the Danube. The summer was hot, drinking water scarce, dysentery rampant. The army melted away, and the field marshal drew heavy reinforcements from less infection-plagued areas.

The district turned into a mill of death; 172,000 Austrian soldiers fell sick; 33,000 died right away, more succumbed later elsewhere. Death hung over the huge camp of misery like a pestilential cloud.

Had it not been for the vanity of Turkish generals the entire Austrian army might have perished without battle. But the Turks sought victory in action; they invaded the zone of stenchy destruction, and in a series of engagements in which the Austrians gave but a sickly account of themselves, pushed the remnants back, upstream along the Danube—to safety.

On November 18, 1788, the Emperor left the army. He, too, had suffered from dysentery; he, too, carried the germ of death. With him went Lascy, a human wreck, but still strong enough to intrigue against Laudon, whom the Emperor wanted to recall, and to suggest Hadik as his successor. Only after Hadik refused on the ground of old age did Laudon, old and grouchy himself, assume command.

Laudon wanted to take Belgrade, the site of Austrian military lore. He promised to capture the town within two weeks, provided he could get reinforcements. Lascy called the promise "somewhat extravagant."

Not before July 9, 1789, could Laudon's advance begin; only on August 28 were the Turks driven across the Danube near Orşova. A strong

Danube flotilla would have been of great help, but Maria Theresa's hydrophobia, which Joseph had inherited, prevented Austria from having solid fighting ships on the great river. Laudon mobilized whatever craft could stay afloat. On September 14, 1789, the ring around Belgrade closed. The Emperor received the news in Vienna, on his sickbed. He felt mortally ill, even though his physicians still voiced hopes for complete recovery, and he sent his young nephew Franz—who would be the last wearer of the ancient German crown and Napoleon's father-in-law—to Laudon's headquarters. As it was his ceremonial duty, Franz fired the first cannon shot against the fortress, and left the rest to the experts.

On October 6, fortress commander Osman Pasha requested an armistice of fifteen days. "Not fifteen hours" was Laudon's curt reply. The Austrian artillery had already wrought fearful damage, and it kept throwing 50,000 missiles per day into the smoldering rubble. The attackers doubted that anybody could survive the holocaust of fire and iron. However, 25,000 of 30,000 Turks did survive, only to surrender on October 7.

The Austrians lost 300 killed and 740 wounded. They captured 351 cannon, 34 mortars, 6000 quintals of gunpowder, and colossal amounts of staples of every kind, from river boats to bags of flour, evaluated at 20 million gulden of dubious currency.

A courier brought the victory message to Vienna, and as in the Seven Years' War, he was escorted by a flock of postilions, who produced more clamor than a siege battery.

Vienna raved, Vienna reveled, Vienna arranged elaborate fireworks. This was, at long last, something worth celebrating, something everybody could understand. The name of Prince Eugene was revived; everybody sang the song of the Noble Knight. Places of entertainment were crowded, bustling with life that celebrated destruction. Beer and wine flowed from fountains.

The Emperor sent Laudon his second Maria Theresa Order, expressing hope that the triumphal march would continue. More couriers came, more postilions flourished, Vienna's festive mood continued for a while, but little enthusiasm was found beyond the capital. In Hungary, disgruntled petty nobles, one of them of Prussian ancestry, plotted with Berlin to have Joseph deposed and a German Prince installed as King of Hungary. The capture of Belgrade did not impress the rebels. Belgrade had changed hands many times before.

The Viennese came to think of this, too. Also, there had been many postilions before, trumpeting victories that heralded reverses. The song of the Noble Knight was superseded by disrespectful ditties. Mock-gold glory had run its course, and the town was dense with rumors that the Emperor was dying. Even grumblers saw fit to display decorous sadness on such an occasion.

Laudon conquered the greater part of little Serbia, but Russian co-operation was scant. The Tsarina seemed to have lost interest in her war, and with the great Russian scheme adjourned, the entire war made no sense whatsoever.

Kaunitz still would rather see the Turks astride the lower Danube than have Russia rule all of the Balkans. Secret messages were exchanged between Vienna and Constantinople. Kaunitz held the reins. He once paid a call on the Emperor. The latter rallied to suggest a *rapprochement* between Austria and Prussia so that Prussia would no longer interfere in Hungarian affairs. The Chancellor replied that it would be better to appease the Hungarians, who still resented Joseph's reforms.

On January 28, 1790, Joseph, aged forty-nine, but looking eighty, signed a document which revoked practically all his innovations in Hungary and pledged to restore the Crown of St. Stephen to the Hungarians.

Then he wrote his brother Leopold, who was next in line for the throne, to come to Vienna without delay. "You may still find me here, a man who looks forward to death as the only happiness. There is no time to lose. The month of March is treacherous for the sick."

Joseph did not live until March. He died on February 20, 1790. Leopold arrived in Vienna on March 20, and he read his brother's self-drafted epitaph: "Here lies Joseph, unfortunate in all he undertook."

Two guardians of the Hungarian crown carried St. Stephen's priceless headgear to Buda. Crowds welcomed it with wild outbursts of enthusiasm; they hailed a national legend and its symbol, and displayed no grief about the passing of a ruler who had been unfortunate in his bid for their love.

Only insiders learned that the dying Joseph had had a few harsh things to say about "the general insanity of peoples"—the French rebelling to achieve freedom and equality, and the Hungarians rioting because he had tried to give them what the French wanted.

Joseph II had shown amazingly little concern about the fate of his sister Marie Antoinette. His subjects did not like what they learned through their newspapers about events in France. A popular song went: "What wild news we get from Paris, high and low are overturned . . . Can this ever bring blessings? Criminal hands cannot build a house of peace." The Queen of France, whom her own subjects disdainfully called "the Austrian," was considered a Frenchwoman by her compatriots.

Her brother Leopold, now Emperor Leopold II, was almost as alien to his Austrians as Marie Antoinette. He had lived in Tuscany for many years, and his Empress, Maria Louisa, daughter of Charles III of Spain, was a perfect stranger who hardly concealed her aversion toward Austrian moods, Austrian music, Austrian culture.

Leopold signed routine manifestoes and proclamations and made an unofficial declaration of his views in a letter to his sister Maria Christine: "I believe that a ruler—even a hereditary ruler—is only a delegate, a functionary of the people, destined to devote to them every effort and thought, even his vigils. It is my opinion that there exists a compact between people and ruler which limits the ruler's prerogatives . . . and that a ruler who does not respect the compact, forfeits his high office . . . if he violates the terms of the compact, nobody is duty-bound to obey him. The ruler represents the executive. Legislature is the duty of the people and its representatives."

Leopold was familiar with the Declaration of Independence. It could be that he borrowed some of his notions from the United States.

The new Emperor liquidated the absurd war with Turkey. The treaty of peace of Giurgevo (Giurgiu, on the later-Rumanian bank of the Danube), signed on August 2, 1790, restored the *status quo* but for two small districts near Orşova that were ceded to Austria. Again, Turkish pashas resided in Belgrade. Again, the people of the tortured fortress city emerged from hideouts; troglodytes for whom peace was never more than reprieve. Their river boats, built at great pain and diligently used for trade and fishing, were lost. Fatalistic Belgraders pushed skiffs into the untroubled waters of the Danube and the Sava and carried on.

Fugitives returned to the swamp regions near Zemun. The wave of epidemics abated, and they had found no better places to live.

Leopold faced revolt in Belgium, which was still an Austrian dominion. After Imperial troops crushed Belgian volunteers, the Emperor restored ancient constitutional rights; England, Prussia, and Holland undertook to guarantee Austrian sovereignty over the Belgian provinces.

The people of the Imperial heartlands read about Belgian events as if they had happened on another continent. But there was unrest in Hungary again. The Diet, again deliberating in their special brand of Latin, requested that royal powers be curtailed. When Leopold refused to comply, the Diet postponed his coronation as King of Hungary, and not until

November 15, 1790, did he receive the well-traveled crown, in a display of glittering loyalty until further notice.

In Austria, Joseph's system of taxation was amended, censorship tightened; curtailed power was restored to local governments, sequestrated property returned to the Church.

The people found this equitable, Diets applauded; political scientists wrote millions of words of legal opinion on how Joseph's anti-Church edicts could best be invalidated.

In September 1790, the King and the Queen of Naples visited Vienna on the occasion of a double marriage between two of their daughters and two of the Emperor's sons. (Leopold had fourteen children, ten of them sons). There was a great and extremely expensive sequence of gala affairs, including premières of operas by Josef Weigl and Antonio Salieri. Young Beethoven, who was about to settle down in Vienna, wrote a coronation cantata, and Mozart composed *La Clemenza di Tito* for the coronation in Prague. The series of coronations was climaxed by the solemn event in Frankfurt, where Leopold gave a display of sedate Imperial showmanship.

A steady trickle of refugees from France reached Vienna, and what the people heard of events in Paris made them disapprove of a revolution which, as they thought, could have no effect on their lives. The rural population of Austria paid no attention to the distant sheet lightning out west.

During the first year of his rule, the Emperor maintained a perfunctory correspondence with Marie Antoinette, and admonished her to be patient. Leopold was visiting in Padua, Italy, when he learned that Louis XVI and Marie Antoinette had tried to flee and had been taken back to Paris on June 21, 1791. On July 6, he dispatched identical notes to all European powers, recommending assistance for King Louis. Returned to Vienna, he learned that Prussia—alarmed by events in France—had offered a pact of mutual territorial guarantees; the pact was signed on July 25, and all European powers were urged to form a coalition against France, but England's refusal frustrated the plan. The King of Prussia and Emperor Leopold met in Pillnitz, Saxony, and signed another pact, but they did not invade France.

The *perpetuum mobile* of revolution kept moving. Louis yielded to the demands of the French National Assembly, which was interpreted to mean that everything was settled by mutual consent. Leopold pronounced the French problem solved.

The new French ambassador to Vienna was a so-called "constitutional diplomat." But courtiers exhorted Leopold not to accept his credentials, but in vain.

Russia now urged war against France; but Russia had been a calamitous partner in the Turkish campaign, and it was quite obvious that the Tsarina merely wanted Austria and Prussia busy elsewhere while Russia gobbled up remnants of rump-Poland.

In 1792 the pact of Pillnitz was supplemented by an Austro-Prussian alliance which was still defensive in nature. But revolutionary France, which had threatened to trespass its borders, did not believe that its neighbors were essentially defensive-minded, and so prepared for war. The Girondists in the National Assembly forced King Louis' powerless hand to sign a dispatch to the effect that unless Austria expressly renounced all undertakings against France, war would be declared by March 1.

Prussian Colonel Bischoffswerder, a cool, dispassionate strategist, went to Vienna to arrange for joint operations. He arrived on the last day of February 1792, but was not admitted to the Emperor. Leopold II was ill with smallpox, and died on the following day.

Revolution had not yet won a single battle, but it had gained infinitely precious time, and it held the initiative.

Franz II, Leopold's oldest son, aged twenty-four, became ruler of the Habsburg patrimony and, on July 5, 1792, German Emperor. He did not understand the seriousness of the French threat; and to him, Marie Antoinette was merely an aunt whom he had never seen. His ministers were in favor of letting the dust in the West settle, and when Kaunitz presented him with a note answering the French ultimatum, he signed it without hesitation. The note said that Austria wanted peace, and that its military preparations were of a purely defensive nature. But when Franz mentioned casually that he relied on Prussia's friendship, the aged Chancellor refused to assume further responsibility, and resigned. The age of Maria Theresa sank below the horizon.

Emperor Franz, relieved of his French worries, called in the mayor of Vienna to discuss details of enthronement celebrations. Since the traditional triumphal arches and processions would not satisfy either man's ambitions, St. Stephen's Square in front of the Cathedral was to be embellished and enlarged for the event.

And as they discussed embellishments of the square, a new note arrived from France, requesting that Austria disarm and relinquish its alliance with Prussia.

The new Chancellor, Count Philipp Cobenzl, was bent on appease-

ment, but in turn requested that France make reparations for the violation of the rights of the Pope and the Alsatian Princes of the Empire.
Thereupon the French National Assembly declared war on "Franz, King
of Hungary and Bohemia." French troops entered Belgium, where they
were well received by the people, who were radically anti-Austrian.

The French declaration was considered a mere bluff by Imperial statesmen, and plebeian impudence by the Viennese.

Almost three months went by without major military operations; then
Franz II and Prussian King Friedrich Wilhelm met in Mainz. Kaunitz
came out of semi-retirement to accompany the Emperor, who had no
use for the old Prince but could not bring himself to tell him to stay
home. Kaunitz's main concern now was Marie Antoinette. The thought
of having arranged the marriage of the little Princess who was now a
graying Queen in the hands of violent demagogues, was a nightmare to
him. He traveled to Mainz to save the Queen, but had to listen to arguments about a barter of Belgium against Bavaria. His angry protests
helped put military matters on the agenda, but neither party wanted to
commit huge forces and to spend much money in the venture.

Duke Ferdinand of Brunswick, appointed supreme commander,
opened action on July 25, 1792, with a manifesto to the French in
which he threatened to destroy Paris and to execute everybody involved
should a hair on the head of any member of the royal family be bent.
But the French, after initial setbacks, could not be stopped. The manifesto, and the new government's appeal to resist foreign invasion, had
whipped their furor into a fighting frenzy. On September 21, 1792, one
day after an anemic "cannonade" near Valmy, the Austro-Prussian
forces, ill and demoralized, began to retreat. In December, all of Belgium
was in French hands.

On January 21, 1793, Louis' head fell on the guillotine; the French
Republic, already at war with Austria, the Reich, and Prussia, was em-
boldened to declare war on England, Holland, and Spain. Russia, Portugal, Naples, and Tuscany joined the enemies of France, and eventually
only Turkey and Denmark remained neutral.

Had the enemies of France taken the war seriously, an armed avalanche of over 500,000 soldiers would have buried the Republic, but
only 140,000 men were ready, only 80,000 went into action, and war
plans called for no more than recovery of lost territory.

Revolution's propaganda arm had a longer range than the French
armies. French agents, some of them posing as émigrés, established themselves in various capitals, including Vienna; they set up clubs and socie-

ties, with a façade of respectability, posing as champions of arts, science, and progressive economy. Clubs and societies were joined by local people of good standing, most of whom did not know that they were used as stooges of subversion.

In France, the Convent Commission, set up to control and spy on pre-Revolutionary officers, established the pattern for French wars of conquest of unprecedented magnitude that led to the rise and fall of countries and rulers that ushered in the period of Napoleon. The member of Convent who became "Organizer of Victory" was Count Lazare Nicolas Carnot, who drafted the decree of the *levée en masse,* turning France into an armed camp and most able-bodied Frenchmen into soldiers.

Intelligence reports called the recruits enthusiastic patriots, but in Vienna, Berlin, and other capitals, enthusiastic patriotism was considered an inadequate substitute for military drill. And yet, the ill-equipped, scantily uniformed, often barefooted battalions became the nucleus of the superb armies that would carry the eagles of France to Vienna, Berlin, Moscow.

Carnot planned the 1796 French offensive against Austria, in which the twenty-eight-year-old General Bonaparte inflicted staggering defeats upon Austro-Sardinian forces under seventy-year-old General Beaulieu.

And as the French girded for unprecedented operations, allied interest in the war of a continent against one nation slackened even further. Robespierre was executed in Paris, and "moderates" took over. Tuscany headed the procession of former enemies who made peace with the Republic. On April 5, 1795, Prussia followed suit.

But treaties of peace were just so many scraps of paper. The Danube Valley turned into an avenue of colossal invasions, but it took its people some time to become aware of this.

CHAPTER FORTY-SEVEN

Marie Antoinette rode to the guillotine on October 16, 1793, her bearing more queenly than she had ever displayed in Versailles and Trianon.

The people of Vienna suddenly changed their attitude. The dead Queen became a major concern in her native city, which had ignored her in her visitation. The Viennese were against regicide, and a faction derisively called "archpatriots" became very popular. The archpatriots were anti-Jacobin, anti-French, and in favor of drastic action. Even the Emperor encouraged them; and when they collected contributions to finance war against France, he donated a set of golden tableware and everybody admired this as a noble deed.

French-sponsored clubs and societies continued their activities; a few local malcontents formed clubs of their own, championing liberty, equality, and fraternity, and asking for "revolutionary reforms." The "archpatriots" called them "Jacobins." French agents were embarrassed, but eventually supported them and Hungarians of the same ilk. The country resounded with denunciations, but authorities were slow to interfere.

The only real changes the French Revolution produced in Austria were, at first, essentially confined to fashion.

Caroline Greiner (later known as Caroline Pichler) relates:

"Our strait-laced, many-plated garments changed to lighter shapes. Belts were no longer tied on the hips, but under the breasts. The garb had a touch of ancient Greek taste, and this resulted in a degree of tightness of dress that did not leave a single crease. It seemed to be the true purpose and glory of this fashion to model physical shapes. Arms and shoulders were bare, or exposed under flesh-colored tights. Women wore laced shoes, fashioned after the cothurns, their hair was either clipped and curled or tucked up in a single knot. Flesh-colored tights dominated the stage, dancers of both sexes appeared practically nude."

As Paris turned drab, Vienna became the swankiest town in a world in foment. Foreigners who still had the means and the courage to travel went to Vienna to relish entertainment, fashions—and inflation, which made it all relatively inexpensive.

But unwanted visitors closed in on Vienna and the Danube regions: the French armies of General Jean-Victor Moreau in the direction of Upper Austria, General Count Jourdan along the Main toward Bohemia, and Napoleon Bonaparte through northern Italy toward the Alps.

Austrian official bulletins magnified inconsequential successes and mentioned events in Italy only in a brief and evasive manner. But people developed a simple method of checking the accuracy of the bulletins through geography, and geography showed that the more setbacks the French were said to have suffered, the closer they moved to the heartlands of the Empire.

Official lore tried to build a new popular hero: Archduke Karl, the

Emperor's younger brother. At twenty-five, he was put in charge of the best Austrian armies in the areas where enemy pressure was lightest, and the borders of the realm farthest away.

Zealous chroniclers regaled the public with anecdotes and quotations: As a child of six, the miniature Archduke had got himself a miniature sword and taken position at the front door of Joseph II's private apartment, telling everybody that he was guarding his Imperial uncle. Later, he was quoted as saying that a good general was a precious crown jewel and, in 1796, when he led armies in the West, he assigned his personal physician to treat a captured French general. When the treatment did not prevent the general's death, Karl had his remains delivered to the French by a guard of honor, which stayed on enemy territory to attend the funeral.

The Viennese listened, looked at maps, and were skeptical.

In fact, Karl was a poor soldier. Napoleon later called him a great general and a virtuous man. But as the eighteenth century roared through its staggering finale, Karl's record justified an earlier entry in Napoleon's journal: "Archduke Karl might have become the best of soldiers had he not faced obstacles which his talents could not overcome."

Early in 1797, the Emperor put Karl in charge of all Austrian forces in every theater of war, including Italy. But by then the troops there had already suffered such heavy defeats through Bonaparte that no general could have welded them into an effective fighting force.

Napoleon's "genius" became proverbial. The Viennese came to dislike the term so intensely that, long after the Napoleonic Wars, "genius" retained a derogatory flavor in Vienna. Various ingenius inventors, including Josef Ressel, who made the first propeller, and Siegfried Marcus, who built the first gasoline engine, died there, unrecognized and poor.

Borrowing a leaf from the French, the Imperial government proclaimed a *levée en masse*.

Recruits were not drafted, however, but expected to volunteer. In Vienna, 6000 reported, most of them scions of wealthy families, who sported gaudy uniforms and proudly insisted on defraying their own expenses except for ammunition. From other Austrian towns came smaller, less elegant contingents. In Hungary, aristocrats, who did not wish to see Revolutionary armies on their estates, combed their labor forces and opened stables and storehouses. Hungary contributed 50,000 men, 10,-000 horses, 20,000 oxen, and great quantities of grain. But too little came too late.

The first volunteers were thrown into battle piecemeal, and there was no time to organize and train later levies when, after capturing Mantua on February 2, 1797, Napoleon entered Carinthia and proceeded into Styria province as far north as Leoben, 100 miles from Vienna.

Napoleon's campaigning was highly unorthodox; no Austrian general had expected the French to invade the mountainous regions before the spring, but the young French commander, who had already disregarded textbook rules in Italy, knew well that the Alpine winter would hardly stop him. "The citizens of Vienna are groaning under the self-deluded despotism of their government," he told his soldiers, "and I shall also bring freedom to the gallant Hungarian nation."

The citizens of Vienna were not vulnerable to psychological warfare. Actually they were annoyed that the demagoguery of some young French general was trying to make them join the ranks of unkempt violent upstarts and abandon their traditional way of life in favor of a demagogue's concept of liberty.

When the French gained control of most of Styria, the Viennese responded with another outburst of theatrical patriotism.

The municipality issued a call to form a "general militia" to strengthen the dilapidated fortifications of their town and to defend it to the last drop of blood. Doctor Quarin, Rector Magnificus of the University, rallied his students under the battle flags of the second Turkish siege. The famous etcher, Jacob Schmutzer, director of the Academy of Graphic Arts, led his pupils to the colors. Estates recruited a corps of their own; merchants vied to outdo everybody else; the carpenters' guild mobilized 1500 and proclaimed that all cowards should be outlawed.

On April 17, 1797, the presentation and blessing of various banners took place on Vienna's glacis, in the presence of the Imperial couple. The Empress distributed colored ribbons, brass music blared, contingents moved into suburban camps to be lavishly entertained. Franz Xaver Süssmayer, Mozart's favorite pupil, who had completed his late master's *Requiem,* composed a march for the militia; and in nearby Klosterneuburg, a long-forgotten poet authored the "War Song of the Austrians" and "Farewell Song to the Citizens of Vienna," which were set to music by Beethoven. Joseph Haydn composed music to a patriotic poem by Professor Haschka, a prolific writer of odes.

Haydn had already suggested that Austria receive a national anthem, as in England, where he had heard "God Save the King." In the patriotic excitement of 1797, his suggestion was accepted, and the "Emperor Song," to words by Haschka, became the Austrians' national hymn.

A preliminary peace was signed in Leoben on April 18, followed, six months later, by the Peace of Campoformio. Austria lost Belgium, Lombardy, and the Breisgau, and, in return, received Istria, Dalmatia, and Venice.

Swapping real estate had nothing to do with the real issue: the conflict between revolution-born expansionism and conservative statics.

Vienna went wild with triumph over the territorial gains, without mentioning the much greater losses. There were parades, reviews, and medals; honorary doctorates were freely distributed among students from the Tyrol, who were credited with having harassed French invaders of their beautiful land.

The Viennese did not fight soldiers in 1797, but on April 13 of the following year, unarmed street crowds fought a spectacular battle against the despised French tricolor less than 1000 yards away from St. Stephen's Cathedral.

The tricolor was the protagonist of the spectacle; its lone bearer was General Jean-Baptiste Bernadotte, once a stableboy from Pau, France, who after a fantastic career as a soldier and diplomat was to become King of Sweden. In 1797, he was French ambassador to Vienna and had established himself in a three-story *palais*.

The members of his staff neither looked nor acted as the Viennese expected diplomats to look or act. They were young, ebulliently intellectual, dressed with flashy sloppiness, and they delivered revolutionary harangues in a mangled German at places where no diplomat was supposed to appear.

Bernadotte's own behavior was bewildering. He bullied his way into society, talked revolution, and tried to enlist artists into the service of subversion.

Emperor Franz II received him in special audience. He was not pleased by the ambassador's attire and offensively defective grooming. But anxious not to provoke an incident before Austria was ready, Franz was painstakingly polite and Bernadotte bristled with pride.

On April 13, 1798, he ordered that a six-foot-long tricolor be hoisted on the second-floor balcony of his *palais*. Darkness was falling, but passers-by could not help noticing the hated flag that almost touched their noses, and, looking up in anger, they saw a bunch of the ambassador's vexatious young men sneering down at them.

This was too much even for the Viennese sense of humor. It was outright provocation, incitement to plebeian rebellion, derision. Within minutes a menacing crowd had gathered, shouted invectives, and asked that the "nasty rag" be removed at once. The vexatious young men shouted abusive wisecracks, and servants appeared at the embassy doors making remarks which the Viennese hardly understood but heartily disliked.

Noisy exchanges continued until the chief of police and the town colonel rushed to the spot. As they tried to placate the crowd, Bernadotte came out, surrounded by servants, yelling insults, making threatening gestures typical of street brawlers. Excitement rose to a fever pitch. The town colonel implored the ambassador to remove the flag and retire into the building. Bernadotte refused.

Pickets of infantry and cavalry were called out. The crowd was already smashing windows and pelting the building with whatever they could find from cobblestones to copper coins. Somebody called the *palais* a "beggar's embassy." A slender young man climbed a rail with apelike agility as the crowd applauded. Bernadotte's vexatious young men withdrew. The climber tore the flag down, the crowd spat and trampled on it, set it on fire, and dragged the flaming tricolor into the courtyard of the *palais,* where it turned to ashes. The ambassador's coach house, kitchen, and living quarters were invaded. His staff fired a few pistol shots, which caused no casualties but poured oil on the fire of public wrath. The invaders pushed battered French carriages out into the street, smashed chinaware and kitchen utensils, but inflicted no bodily harm upon French personnel. Bernadotte fled through a rear door and sought political asylum in the nearby quarters of the Papal Nuncio. After seven hours of rioting the crowd dispersed. Meantime the entire city garrison had been alerted and the gates of the city closed.

In the morning, a French officer drove to the Imperial palace through streets milling with agitated people; he carried an angry letter from Bernadotte asking for his passports.

The Austrian government asserted that it was not to blame for the regrettable incident. Bernadotte offered to stay under condition that the burned flag be replaced and raised on his balcony by Austrian officials. This the government, fearing a popular outburst, termed contrary to international custom. Bernadotte and his young men departed at noon of April 15. The Viennese looked on, in grim silence, as five carriages drove out of the *palais* under the cover of Austrian cavalry. They had carried their day.

Technically at peace, Vienna was an armed camp; however, the Danube Valley turned into the zone of deployment of forces which included allies who had never been to Vienna before. The Russians came as members of a coalition to end all revolutions.

The great coalition now included Austria, Russia, England, Naples, and Turkey, the latter aroused by Napoleon's invasion of Egypt. Austria mobilized 250,000 men. Russia had 100,000; its vanguards crossed into Austria late in 1798, and from there proceeded to Switzerland and Italy. The formal declaration of war with France was made on March 20, 1799.

The Russian commander was Field Marshal Count Alexander Suvorov, of Swedish-Finnish ancestry, the Russian soldiers' idol. Pictures of the field marshal, showing a decorous, well-groomed gentleman, were distributed in Vienna, but when he arrived and established temporary headquarters in the palace of Count Rasumovsky, Beethoven's generous sponsor, the Viennese came to consider him a savage.

He would not tolerate furniture other than a straw mattress, a table, and a rickety chair. He detested mirrors and smashed them whenever he saw one. His wardrobe consisted of one uniform and a sheepskin. He ate the rough food of his soldiers and washed as little as the most uncouth buck private. He had a perfect contempt for everything and everybody non-Russian, in particular for the well-drilled Austrian grenadiers, polite Austrian statesmen, and well-groomed Austrians altogether.

Suvorov was granted supreme command on the southern theater of operations. He wanted Austrian soldiers under his command for the most hazardous fighting, but he invariably ascribed success to Russian gallantry. Suvorov had no use for military science, for excellence in artillery. He had devised a few tricks in close-quarter fighting with the bayonet and considered them the final word in tactics. Austrian officers did not like the Russians, but their superiors insisted that they would have to get along with Suvorov. Austria's Prime Minister, Franz von Thugut, was outraged to learn that the Tsar's field marshal called him "Mister Know-it-all" and the "chief rooster of the Austrian poultry." However, anxious to preserve good feelings, he accepted a statement by Russian diplomats, who called Suvorov "a powerful, faithful, and loyal soul."

The Viennese saw another allied superior officer: Admiral Horatio Nelson, whose victory of Abukir Bay in 1798 had sounded the knell to the French invasion of the Middle East. He arrived early in 1800 and ingratiated himself with the Austrians by his cultured manners and by attending a performance of Haydn's *Nelson Mass*.

On April 14, 1799, Austro-Russian forces crossed the Mincio River in Italy. On April 28, the French were defeated near Cassano d'Adda. One day after the battle, the victors entered Milan. Suvorov rode in the parade in shirt sleeves and brandished a heavy riding whip. The Milanese sang, danced, and shouted *viva*'s for Emperor Franz and in opposition to imposed "freedoms" that were but shackles of tyranny in verbal disguise. Public wrath turned against local Jacobins.

In Vienna, people also cheered, but the brass of the Court War Council shook periwigged heads over the fast campaign. Estafettes raced from Vienna to Milan to warn Suvorov not to proceed too far too hastily. Suvorov shouted that the members of the Court War Council were turtles that ought to be trained as reindeers, and he fought another major battle, beating the French again on August 15.

But afterward, Suvorov trudged on, at a turtle's pace, toward Genoa, and he did not annihilate the French, missing an opportunity that would not recur for many years to come.

Tsar Paul thought that the most urgent task was to restore every ejected Italian petty prince to his throne, but the Austrian cabinet objected. The Italian campaign stalled. "Plans drafted by people who conduct war from conference tables, who know little about the weight and importance of operations, are bound to fail," Archduke Karl complained.

Tsar Paul distrusted Emperor Franz and detested Prime Minister William Pitt the Younger, who did not wish to cede Malta to the Russians; so he attributed Russian reverses in Switzerland to a conspiracy among his allies. In December 1799, Russia seceded from the coalition and made neutrality pacts with Sweden, Denmark, and Prussia.

In Austria, Archduke Karl resigned his command "for reasons of health." The resignation was meant to be a gesture, but the Court War Council accepted it, without formality.

Austrian armies in Germany were put under the command of the romantic-looking twenty-year-old Archduke Johann, and those in Italy under the sickly, old, fuzzy Feldzeugmeister Baron Michael von Melas. Bonaparte, First Consul and head of the Republic since his *coup d'état* of November 9–10, 1799, used the rough season for military preparations, carried by popular enthusiasm and unhampered by periwigged councilors and feuding allies.

June 14, 1800, became a day of military decision: Would war move toward the Seine or the Danube?

French and Austrians fought near the village of Marengo, in the district of Piedmont. By 6 P.M. the battle seemed won by the Austrians. Old Melas, who had suffered a minor injury, wished to rest and ordered his soldiers to camp and repose. As they camped and reposed, scattered French troops rallied and Napoleon decided to stage a night attack. The Austrians were caught by complete surprise, and virtually leaderless. Midnight had not yet struck when they ran. Melas had lost victory.

War moved toward the Danube.

Melas hastened to sign a short-term armistice that surrendered most of Italy to the French. Napoleon sent a letter to Emperor Franz expressing his desire for peace, and winding up: "I beg Your Majesty to read this message with sentiments similar to those which prompted me to write it, and to be convinced that, next to the good fortune and the benefit of the French people, nothing could be closer to my heart than the happiness of your warlike nation whose courage and military virtues I have admired for the past eight years."

The letter arrived two days after Prime Minister Thugut had signed a treaty of subsidy with England, committing Austria to stay in the war for at least another six months!

Prime Minister Thugut was the driving power behind Austrian belligerence. His conservative zeal, however, brought him little more than popular derision. Being a man of humble birth, he was said to be more anti-republican than royalty itself. A learned contemporary called him a man of intellect and talent, but without either ethical or political principles, cynical in his appraisal of the people and in the choice of his means.

In October 1800, Thugut resigned under fire; Count Cobenzl, whose conduct of foreign affairs had been less than successful, assumed his post. But even the greatest of diplomats would not have been able to deal with the military troubles. The Italian armistice had been called off to hold England in line. But England was financially potent, whereas the state of Austria's finances was deplorable and that of its army even worse.

CHAPTER FORTY-EIGHT

Napoleon was well informed about Austrian preparations, but he had more grandiose designs than just another victorious campaign. Even without his personal interference, another victory over Austria seemed certain. Austrian morale became constantly lower, and even though the Viennese would gladly have repeated their performance against Bernadotte and his tricolor, they would not readily fight the French army.

Operations in Italy looked almost like a walkover. General Jean-Victor Moreau, in charge of the French forces poised to strike along the Bavarian and western Austrian border, was the peer of youthful Archduke Johann, who was "fiery, witty, and universally educated," but less than ably advised by two older generals, one a scholar of the Seven Years' War, the other an organizer of supplies.

Austrians were skeptical, the French scornful.

Soon Austrian forces in Bavaria were in full retreat. Philippsburg and Ingolstadt fell; the French pushed on to Munich and marched through Blenheim, past Ulm, through the uppermost part of the Danube Valley. Moreau's avalanche reached the Inn on December 1, 1800, set to invade Upper Austria.

Austrian troops prepared to strike a counterblow. Official bulletins said that all was well on the western front.

French vanguards retreated in a planned move to lead pursuers into a woodland trap. No skillful general would have run, headlong, into a natural obstacle behind which the enemy could concentrate his main forces, especially in the dense snowfall of December 3; but the juvenile Archduke and his advisers carried on, and suffered staggering defeat.

The retreat was disorderly; many deserted; abandoned equipment littered the roads over which the French marched and rode. The victors crossed the Inn and Salzach rivers, poured past Passau into the Austrian Danube Valley; their right wing entered Salzburg. The fortress of Hohensalzburg, reputedly impregnable, was not even defended.

Archduke Karl's "state of health" was no longer considered poor. Recalled, he assumed command of Johann's former army, saw the 30,-000 stragglers, and broke into tears.

Two weeks later the French were in Lambach, Upper Austria. The little town on the Traun River, a tributary of the Danube, was dominated by a massive monastery; but the Benedictines did not wish to see their venerable building with its priceless treasures exposed to artillery fire, and did not permit its use as a military stronghold.

Archduke Karl tried to delay the French advance without the benefit of a stronghold, but the Austrian stragglers were no match for the cocky French.

By December 20 most of Upper Austria was in French hands. A few French cannon balls whizzed at the bridges over the Enns, the gateway to Lower Austria and to Vienna, 100 miles away.

Two roads led to the capital, one through the Danube Valley, the other slightly south. French units used both; Austrian remnants preceded the French as distressing messengers of disaster.

On Christmas Day the two French columns joined at Melk. There could hardly be a more beautiful sight from the west. But the French were not impressed by the Danube, which bends its liquid muscles as impetuous green waters emerge from rapids to press on into the narrow defile of the glorious Wachau hills. They hardly glanced at the wooded crests crowned by castles that looked like plaits of jagged rock, and at the distant plateau to the north with its patches of dark green under a bright, crystal cool and clear sky. To the south, waves of earth rolled against Alpine peaks yonder. And, as a grandiose man-made centerpiece set on nature's miraculous table, stood the Monastery of Melk.

The French advance did not proceed beyond Melk, though Vienna was only sixty miles away. Another armistice was signed: the new demarcation line gave the French armies temporary control of all of southern Germany and the provinces of Tyrol, Upper Austria, Illyria, and Styria.

Archduke Karl gloomily rode into Vienna to prepare for resumption of hostilities at its very gates. On December 28 he proclaimed general enrollment for military and construction duty. But then the Emperor made a disastrous peace: the Peace of Lunéville, of February 9, 1801, was the dragon seed from which seventy years later a new, wildly aggressive German Reich would emerge to put the world out of joint. The crucial terms were the cession of the left bank of the Rhine to France.

German Princes who held land there were compensated at the expense of those who held land east of the river. Clerical principalities disappeared; most of the Reich's free cities lost their status. The constitution of the Holy Roman Empire was virtually destroyed as the fabric of limited sovereignties, which had been its foundation since the Thirty Years' War, disintegrated. France supervised the "compensations," bribed Princes whom it expected to collaborate, ruined potential resisters.

Regensburg, the venerable town on the Bavarian Danube, turned into a market of territories. On October 2, 1801, a Reichs Deputation of four Princes and four Electors was established there to distribute secularized estates.

Austria showed hardly more dignity than aspirants for handouts who pilgrimaged to Paris. Count Cobenzl applied for an audience with Bonaparte and offered an alliance in return for compensations. Napoleon did not wish to buy an alliance with Austria, but suggested that Austria invade Turkey and grab whatever it could; this would have tied down the

Austrian army and annoyed England and Russia. Cobenzl's reaction was a stony smile.

The Prussian ambassador to Paris kowtowed before Napoleon's Foreign Minister, Talleyrand; he professed undying enmity toward Austria and admiration for France, but collected no further bribes. Tsar Alexander I styled himself a champion of progress, made protestations of admiring friendship to Napoleon, and received a voice in the drafting of plans with which the Reichs Deputation could not deal. Even England, stanchest of France's enemies, seemed not inclined to stay at war forever and concluded a peace at Amiens, France.

Late in 1803, Bonaparte notified Vienna of his intention to make France a hereditary monarchy with himself as an Emperor and requested that Austria extend immediate and unconditional recognition of the change. Emperor Franz was badly frightened; a refusal might mean war.

Napoleon was confidentially notified that Austria would grant his monarchy immediate recognition if Emperor Napoleon would recognize Franz as hereditary Emperor of the German Reich. Napoleon's reply was not encouraging: he did not wish to commit himself to grant the vanishing Empire another lease on life. But after hurried ambassadorial bickering, he condescendingly agreed to accept the Habsburg-Lorraine dynasty as an equal with his own up-and-coming one. On May 18, 1804, Napoleon was Emperor.

On August 10, Franz II announced that he had adopted the title of hereditary Emperor of Austria, and asked a State Conference assembled in Vienna to draft a patent organizing the realm. The patent, prepared long in advance and approved by the French government, stated that "all kingdoms, principalities, and provinces shall retain, unchanged, their titles, constitutions, privileges, and statutes."

This was pathetic pettifogging under a cloak of magnificence. Franz I of Austria, certain to lose the Holy Roman throne, retained the title of Emperor by transferring it to a patrimony that his family had ruled for centuries.

But the Viennese had their show. On December 17, 1804, to the sound of trumpets and kettledrums, the Patent of August 10, rechristened "Pragmatic Law," was solemnly proclaimed. Troops and city militia paraded; stands were set up in the center of the town; red-and-white flags fluttered from roof tops and balconies. Everybody was urged to celebrate though few people knew what and why. Eventually it all turned into a local affair. A new mayor was installed on the same occasion, after his predecessor had served for thirty-two years.

The clouds of war thickened; political thunderclaps growled from various corners. The Tsar about-faced from Napoleon, whom he did not want to see Emperor, and negotiated a defensive alliance with Austria. England discontinued its brief state of peace, made a pact with Sweden, and extended feelers for the formation of an Anglo-Russo-Austrian bloc.

Archduke Karl supervised military preparations. The Imperial cabinet disliked him as a stern taskmaster. The Emperor's mother-in-law, Queen Caroline of Naples, found him personally unbearable, a sentiment which the Archduke heartily reciprocated; and the Emperor himself, henpecked by voluble Caroline, found fault with the Archduke's "new methods."

These "new methods" consisted in making regimental commanders train their men rather than do paper work and in seeing that units did not remain understrength, that administration be less negligent, that recruiting be sped up—all that aiming at an Austrian field army of 320,-000 plus reserves by the end of 1806.

The Archduke cautioned against starting hostilities any earlier, but wishful thinkers, who accepted the great army as a fact before it was organized, did not heed his warnings. A new quartermaster general (the equivalent to chief of the general staff) was appointed: Baron Karl Mack, of whom the Archduke said that his "imbecility and conceit prevent him from even seeing difficulties."

Before the end of September 1805, Napoleonic armies moved toward the Bavarian Danube in a formation that expanded like a giant fisherman's net, from which only a quick-thinking and fast-acting opponent could have extricated his forces.

Never before, and hardly ever afterward, was Napoleon's conduct of war so awe-inspiringly brilliant. French political warfare also was at its most effective. Spies and emissaries swarmed all over Austria and transmitted every move of every military unit with bewildering speed. They made Viennese rabble rousers incite bread riots: there was no bread shortage at all, but organized suburban thugs set bakeries afire, the government called out the soldiers, who started to shoot, and at nightfall, when theatergoers arrived at the Theater an der Wien, just outside the city gates, they found themselves on a veritable battlefield. The riots ended abruptly, but the general mood remained gloomy, civilian morale low, and hurriedly trained soldiers bewildered.

Even Emperor Franz, who was not much of a soldier, could see that nothing went according to plan. Thirty-four thousand Russians under General Mikhail Kutuzov were still a long way from joining Mack, who had only 75,000 men and inadequate supplies and whose requisitions embittered the local populace and turned them into French sympathizers. The Emperor decided to cede his nominal command to Ferdinand d'Este, another member of the Imperial family, who remained an indignant figurehead during the disastrous weeks that followed.

In Vienna circulated the story of Mack's earlier career: Emperor Joseph, fascinated by his rhetoric, had made the Bavarian-born officer a colonel and a baron. Later, Franz "lent" him to the King of Naples to lead the Neapolitan army against the French invaders; but despite his vast numerical superiority, Mack was badly beaten by the French, almost lynched by the incensed populace, and forced to seek refuge with the victors. He was taken to Paris and admitted into the presence of General Bonaparte, whose laconic reaction to Mack's eloquence was: "Charlatan." "Charlatan," it sounded through the streets of Vienna in the fall of 1805. "Charlatan," it echoed up the Danube Valley even before Mack ever fought there.

By the end of September, Mack spread his Austrians thinly along the Inn, Iller, and Danube, and kept them in constant aimless motion. Next he slowly began to concentrate near Ulm, the magnificent old town on the Danube at the influx of the Iller. He told Ferdinand d'Este of a major offensive he would undertake jointly with the Russians, who had not yet arrived, of a French frontal attack that would easily be repulsed, and of various other odd-sounding projects.

Around October 1, the Ulm army had 38,000 men in line. Napoleon exulted: "If they keep napping a few more days, while I keep turning their flanks, nothing but debris will escape."

On October 7, the French were established in Donauwörth, and Mack's line of retreat through the Danube Valley was blocked. Later that day, Mack talked at length about retreat to the Inn, but issued no orders. "His tomfooleries could fill an entire book," Ferdinand d'Este shouted. Austrian units coming up from the south floundered into the French dragnet.

Between October 10 and 13, Mack twice issued and countermanded orders to abandon Ulm. On October 14, his last unit was caught. A war council was held in Ulm. Mack indulged in pompous rhetoric, generals listened in dejected silence, Ferdinand d'Este announced that he would try to get out with as many men as he could gather and dared Mack to stop him. After the session, he slipped away from Ulm with 1800 cavalry.

On October 15, the French were at the city gates, but Mack still insisted on waiting for reinforcements. He said no when French marshal Michel Ney requested surrender, but a day later he asked for terms.

Carrying a flag of truce, Prince Moriz Liechtenstein called on Ney and learned that all Austrian officers and men would be taken to France as prisoners of war. Liechtenstein asked to see Napoleon.

The Emperor received the splendidly garbed Prince while wearing a private's overcoat and hat without insignia. Liechtenstein said Mack could hold out until the reinforcements came and asked for free departure of the entire army. Napoleon explained with cool logic why no relief could arrive, and sarcastically declared himself ready to wait five days. If relief came, the Austrians would be free; if not, they would have to surrender.

Mack waited four days, then capitulated. He offered his saber to Napoleon with a deep bow and the well-rehearsed phrase: "Here is the deeply unfortunate Mack."

Napoleon did not take him into custody, however. It was better strategy to return him to the Austrians, who might give him another command.

Mack rode back to the Inn, expecting to be put in charge of the troops assembling there, but found written orders to proceed to Vienna. He was arrested at Hütteldorf, the westernmost suburb, and put before a military tribunal. Archduke Karl wrote that Mack was ripe for confinement in a lunatic's asylum, but that the army's honor and morale required his punishment. The tribunal passed a death sentence; the Emperor mitigated it to two years' confinement in a fortress and demotion. Mack served the sentence under almost comfortable circumstances, and after the war, was restored to his rank and retired with full pension. He survived Napoleon and died at seventy-six, in St. Pölten, forty miles west of Vienna.

Vienna received the news of Ulm with little surprise; the "charlatan" had shown his imcompetence. Gossip had it that the Emperor was packing. Armchair strategists discussed the defenses of the city and usually decided that it should not be held and exposed to bombardments.

Art treasures and valuable state possessions were shipped to Hungary; greedy eyes watched the loading of barges on the Danube. Militiamen, sons of minor nobles, and wealthy burghers protected the embarkation.

Soon traditional messengers of victory sounded their trumpets. Archduke Karl had beaten Masséna near Caldiero, Italy. But nobody believed that a French setback in that secondary theater would stop Napoleon's march east. And messengers did not say that Karl had received orders to return in forced marches. His army had not yet covered half the distance to Vienna when Napoleon was established there.

After Ulm, Napoleon's legions marched toward the Austrian border. Kutuzov waited for them a few miles from Passau; he and his Russians had come from home barracks 2000 miles away, afoot and on horseback. They frightened the civilian population, but they did not frighten the French, who thus far had won their victories by maneuver rather than combat. The Russians were joined by 25,000 Austrians under General Count Maximilian Merveldt, a battle-scarred veteran of several narrow escapes. While Merveldt and Kutuzov argued who should command whom, the French reached the Inn.

The Inn River line was not defended; neither was the crossing of the Traun. Napoleon spent the night of November 7 in Linz, where his compulsory ally, the Elector of Bavaria, arrived to thank him for the "liberation of the fatherland."

On November 8, the French resumed their march. In the Danube Valley they trailed Austrians and Russians, whose generals were still quarreling. Another Austro-Russian column moved back via Enns.

The bulk of the French army crossed the Enns bridge, but two divisions, under careless Adolphe Mortier and boastful Bernadotte, respectively, proceeded along the northern bank of the Danube. They reached the Wachau, and in loose formation trooped through the late autumnal splendor toward Dürnstein. Russian artillery fire caught them by surprise a short distance away from the scenic ruins.

The French fought under the eyes of their Emperor, who happened to be near Göttweig Monastery, a short distance southeast. It was no glorious action for the French, who had become accustomed to conquer. At sunset French supply vessels had to evacuate the mauled divisions to the right Danube bank. One of the craft, carrying 400, was sunk in midstream; another was captured by Austrians in skiffs. Napoleon was furious about the travesty that his "invasion army" had turned riverborne with inglorious results. His losses totaled nearly 7000.

He and his retinue rode into the courtyard of Göttweig. A venerable abbot greeted him with a faint ironic smile on his thin lips. Angrily Napoleon rode on horseback up the flight of broad stairs to the Imperial suite with its priceless French gobelins.

The last monarch to sleep there had been Maria Theresa. The abbot had presented her with a bouquet of flowers from nearby meadows; the Empress had them cast in colored wax and left them in a brass washbasin that was hardly big enough to keep the bouquet. It was still there when Napoleon came, and the monks kept it ever after, a venerable error in taste.

On November 11, Emperor Franz was on his way to Olschau to meet Tsar Alexander. The Emperor was resigned to defeat, the Tsar eager to fight and certain to win. Franz hoped for acceptable terms, Alexander for everlasting glory.

On the same day, Marshal Murat camped in Purkersdorf, barely ten miles west of Vienna.

The Viennese were prepared for everything but battle. Elaborately dressed, they mounted big carriages and drove to Purkersdorf to greet Murat and deliver carefully worded addresses. They asserted that Emperor Franz had decided to spare the city from a siege and that they were authorized to surrender Vienna to Napoleon, trusting his righteousness and his promise to safeguard religious rights and title to property. Murat was curt and noncommittal. The delegation traveled another ten miles to Sieghartskirchen, to call on Napoleon, who was polite and reassuring.

No regular Austrian troops were left inside the city. Militia lined roads and streets through which the French entered the first major European capital to open its gates to the conqueror Napoleon.

The grand entry opened at midday of November 13, over the Maria-hilferstrasse, through which Austrian rulers used to ride from Schönbrunn to the Hofburg. French brass bands blared, crowds stared in mute horror.

Marshal Murat and his gold-braided staff were the vanguard of helmeted guard cavalry; Napoleon, the legendary bugbear, was nowhere to be seen. Murat was in a great hurry; unlike Emperor Franz, he did not think that the decision had already fallen, but believed that the French still might lose the war.

In fact, Kutuzov's divisions, reinforced by new arrivals from Russia, Austrian remnants from the West, and new contingents from Hungary, were expected within a month. Unless the French could cross the Danube at once, and strike, the conquest of Vienna could mark the beginning of the end. Napoleon knew that the fate of France could depend on a few hours' time.

All the French had ready in Vienna were 15,000 men. Austrian general Prince Auersperg with about 13,000 men and strong artillery held the northern end of the great Tabor Bridge; his orders were to burn it rather than let the French across. Murat and Marshal Jean Lannes and their glittering staff continued through the Burgtor, over the Graben, past St. Stephen's, toward the river.

From the opposite end of the bridge, the staff sergeant in charge of the arson squad saw them coming. Everything was ready to kindle the match. But the man, who had been in the army throughout his adult life, was confused. The gold-braided gentlemen who were approaching waved frantically with gloved hands; they could be no ordinary attackers. The sergeant hesitated, motioned his squad to wait. They waited as Murat's magnificent steed pranced onto the bridge. To the rear of the idle squad, Austrian outposts and gun crews looked on.

Murat kept waving; a trumpeter rode up to his side, sounding the bugle. Somewhere fluttered a flag of truce.

Staff sergeant and squad snapped to attention. Murat answered in smart salute, but somehow the squad seemed to block his path. Cannon muzzles pointed at him; a single salvo would have swept the French from the bridge. Murat addressed the staff sergeant, who did not understand French. The situation was odd, and turning odder by the minute. Already the rays of the setting sun were reflected by the murky greenish waters of the Danube. Suddenly there was a flourish of trumpets, a cloud of dust, the beat of hoofs: General Prince Auersperg arrived. He did speak French, more sophisticated French even than Murat, and the two men exchanged martial civilities. Then Murat said that an armistice had just been signed between the Emperors of Austria and France, that the demarcation line ran several miles north of the Danube, and that French troops would take up positions there. Auersperg had not heard of an armistice, but he could not for one minute believe that a marshal, an Emperor's in-law, would tell a barefaced lie. He had his forces withdraw, and even left his artillery behind.

A French division calmly crossed the bridge and established itself on the left Danube bank. The story of the armistice was, of course, humbug —a "stratagem," to use the official term. Prince Auersperg was relieved of his command, but the French had scored a tremendous advantage.

Napoleon put up in the Hofburg for one night. He was never frightened in battle, but the desolate emptiness of the huge building and the weird echoes in its corridors made him shudder. And he could not understand the quizzical expression on the faces he saw gazing from the streets at his windows. He wondered whether the people would attempt an attack, but he did not want to draft too many of his soldiers into a personal bodyguard.

Next morning he moved to Schönbrunn, but the Inner City, with its ghost-ridden magic, attracted him. In the hours of darkness he would occasionally drive there incognito to have a look at nocturnal Vienna, which seemed so strangely different from what he had heard about the city of frivolity. If he had any forebodings that the victims of his aggression would sit in judgment in Vienna after his days of glory were over and that his only son would die there, he did not confide them to anybody.

The only worry he mentioned to his entourage concerned Prussia. Should Prussia turncoat again and join his enemies, even the Tabor Bridge crossing might have been in vain. Napoleon's political machinery was in motion to tie Prussia into a close alliance and pay the price of Hannover out of the pocket of the King of England. Already Prussian delegate Count Haugwitz was on his way to Napoleon's headquarters to sign whatever he would be asked.

On November 18, in Olschau, Moravia, less than one hundred miles away, Austrians and Russians had held joint sessions; the Russians were arrogant, the Austrians irritable. Only 16,000 out of 83,000 soldiers were Austrians, which gave the fat, morose, sixty-year-old General Kutuzov a predominant voice. Kutuzov, an officer of mediocre talent but long experience, wanted to stay on the defensive until more reinforcements would arrive, but Tsar Alexander ordered an immediate attack. Soon travelers told of a grandiose host rolling down from the north.

On December 1, 1805, the main forces faced each other across the Goldbach (Golden Brook). Between their lines lay several villages. Pratzen, on the slope of a chain of hills, was the key point of the terrain.

Dense fog fell during the night; the temperature was well below freezing; soldiers on both sides huddled at campfires. The "golden brook" was covered with an opaque layer of ice. The fog was not expected to lift before midmorning; the hillsides would be clear much earlier. A battle in the fog against the French high-precision war machine, with Austrian and Russian officers unable to understand each other's language, would be sheer madness. Every non-com in his right mind would have kept on high ground until visibility improved, but the Tsar decided to hold Pratzen while simultaneously attacking in the valley of the brook.

Napoleon planned to clear the valley with several co-ordinated moves and, after sunrise, hurl against Pratzen all he had.

The "Three Emperors' Battle," as it came to be called, opened in the early morning of December 2. (It is also known as the Battle of Austerlitz, after the small town near by, but this is a misnomer.) Down in the foggy valley, men fought at close quarters, Austrians and Russians grimly but with little co-ordination, the French smoothly and resiliently. Whatever happened in the valley, whoever held one village or other, would not divert a single man, horse, or cannon from the prize objective: Pratzen and the hills. In midmorning, in a hue of dark red and pale blue, the sun floated through the dissolving haze.

Twenty-four thousand Frenchmen, led by General (later Marshal) Nicolas Soult, a former buck private risen from the ranks, moved into what they expected to become a long murderous struggle; but before their unbelieving eyes the Russians marched out of the village, down the domineering hill slope, onto low ground. Tsar Alexander had ordered the move.

Twelve thousand Russians and Austrians ran headlong into twice their number of French and total defeat. By 11 A.M. the French established themselves in the strategic village.

Napoleon spent the night after his triumph at Austerlitz. There Emperor Franz signed an armistice with him on December 6, without consulting the Tsar.

On December 26, they made peace at Pressburg, while French troops in full kit patrolled the streets. For the first time since Charlemagne had French forces pushed so deep into the Danube Valley.

Austria lost Venetia, Friuli, Istria, and Dalmatia to a Napoleon-ruled Italy; Vorarlberg and the Tyrol to Bavaria; and to Baden and Württemberg, possessions along the upper Danube. As a "compensation," Austria received the archbishopric of Salzburg, which, for all practical purposes, had already been Austrian, and the district of Berchtesgaden. The population of Austria was reduced by 2,800,000, roughly 15 per cent.

It was called a peace, but actually it was an armistice, with prospects of renewed hostilities which could only be destruction for one side. At Pressburg, Napoleon reached the point of no return.

On December 28, the phantom peace was proclaimed in Vienna and celebrated by a *Te Deum* at St. Stephen's. The people showed no dismay at the humiliation; all they wanted was that the occupation forces go home. Had it not been for constantly worsening currency trouble, and heavy taxes and tributes collected by friend and foe, they would have rejoiced.

On January 16, 1806, the Imperial couple returned to Vienna. An honor guard, cavalry, and the mayor in full regalia greeted them near the Praterspitz, in the meadows of the Danube, and escorted them in triumphal procession through the streets through which Murat had ridden two months before. The city was gaily decorated with branches of fir and pine. For almost forty-eight hours the sidewalks were jammed by boisterous crowds. Then came the highlight of the show; the only undefeated army and the only non-discredited general entered Vienna: Archduke Karl and his troops, who had not been in Moravia. The Viennese raved with proud delight, as if they had won the war.

The Emperor issued a proclamation. It omitted the embarrassing topic of war, but promised to strengthen the "interior powers of the state," the spread of true spiritual culture, invigoration of national industry, and restoration of public credit.

It was all words. The people, suddenly sobered, were not beguiled by them after they had seen the facts. But the average man did not know how to deal with calamitous problems, and there were no demagogues and rabble rousers to guide them toward deceitful phantoms.

CHAPTER FORTY-NINE

Archduke Karl talked with members of the Austrian government. "I found a tower of Babel," he recorded. "Everybody gives advice, orders, decrees, but nobody obeys. They do only stupid things, they have inflicted mortal wounds upon the state."

The government was on its way out. Count Cobenzl resigned; Count Philipp Stadion became Prime Minister in January 1806. In February, Archduke Karl was appointed a generalissimo. The Emperor wrote a circumstantial autograph letter in which he said: "In case I am forced into another war, the soldiers serving under your command may remember the laurels they have so often gathered on the battlefield under your leadership."

There could be little doubt that there would be another war, but even the oldest Austrian soldiers could hardly remember gathering laurels.

In the ceded province of Tyrol, the peasantry girded for rebellion against the conquerors, waiting for popular figures to assume leadership; and popular figures, tragic, naïve, wonderfully dedicated simple men, did emerge and succumb, proving, though never understanding, that patriotism becomes unwanted if it is too stormy for the ponderous, rickety ship of state.

Count Stadion found Austria left without a friend. He was a man of education, a patron of the arts, a champion of the traditional culture of all nationalities, and a violent hater of violence as exemplified by the French Revolution and its imperialistic aftermath.

It was Stadion's unhappy duty to preside over the formal dissolution of the Holy Roman Empire. On July 17, 1806, sixteen German Princes, headed by the Kings of Bavaria and Württemberg, formed the Confederation of the Rhine. Their territories included practically all of Germany except Prussia, which quite obviously was next on the French itinerary of subjugation. The German Princes, four Electors among them, claimed that the notion of a common fatherland had become meaningless, that the term "Reich" no longer made sense. The German Reich and the Confederation of the Rhine were, geographically, all but synonymous, and controlled by Napoleon. In addition, the Emperor of the French ruled Italy and Holland, and it seemed as if Spain was about to succumb to his domination.

The French requested that Emperor Franz at once resign all title to the German crown. This was not much more than a formality, yet the Emperor hesitated. In over 500 years, twenty of his ancestors had worn the crown that was now stored in Vienna; they had held on to it amidst the wildest of tempests. Little as it had come to mean, he did not want to sign it away. But Paris sent another note: Resign or fight. Austria could not fight. On August 6, 1806, Franz resigned. The lands of the Rhine and the lands of the Danube parted political company.

A few German nobles left their palaces in Vienna to move into what they believed to be a new Reich. Businessmen bought the abandoned mansions. They had profited from Napoleon's economic war against industrial England, they prospered on inflation; manufacturers did well by themselves with English competition out of the way. New plants sprang up. Industrialists were knighted; their offspring intermarried with military and civil-service nobility.

The population of Vienna and various other cities grew as the demand for labor increased. Wages were low and hours long, but this did not discourage the migrants. Domestic servants were better off. The new rich treated them as pets.

Fashions, too, changed. Rococo was declared obsolete; the new trend was a long step backward in disguise, as new trends often are. Men wore black tail coats, light pantaloons, Hungarian-style footwear, and funny flat hats. Women sported turbans of white crepe with gold ribbons.

An innovation in the field of furniture was enthusiastically accepted: beds in the shape of antique sarcophagi.

Authors, musicians, and scientists from many lands visited Vienna. In 1808 a literary magazine, *Prometheus,* was founded. Friedrich Schlegel was among its contributors; Goethe's *Pandora* was printed on its pages. Ludwig Tieck came from Prussia to establish himself at the Burgtheater, but unsuccessfully. Madame Anne de Staël, exiled by Napoleon, came and wrote a great deal about the Imperial city.

The Viennese police kept secret files on foreigners who were in the local news. The files referred to Madame de Staël as a woman who, through extreme opportunism, managed to rub shoulders with persons of rank.

Madame hardly knew about that description. She had words of admiration for the Cathedral, for the Prater with its herds of deer, and the affability of nobles toward little people. However, she complained about "nobility and genius not sufficiently complementing each other," about the excessive number of foreigners, and a tendency to undermine love, enthusiasm, and religion, which she ascribed to the influence of French superficiality and sarcasm. She became one of many chroniclers of the widowed Emperor's second marriage to Maria Ludovica of Modena, an attractive young Princess with an unrestrained enthusiasm for Austrian militarism and antique German attire.

Renascent Austrian militarism dominated the local picture. After Prussia's defeat in 1806, Napoleon offered an alliance and the return of Silesia to the monarchy. Stadion did not expect to keep Silesia very long, and he knew that Napoleon's allies turned satellites.

The year 1807 witnessed the Congress of Erfurt, with Napoleon, the Tsar, and Archduke Karl attending; it resulted in a division of Europe into two spheres of interest: French and Russian.

The year 1808 went by without war between France and Austria, but in the fall martial emotions in Austria were at a fever pitch, and Paris dispatched mobilization orders to every corner of the inflated Napoleonic Empire.

In February 1809, the French ambassador to Vienna was recalled; on March 27, the French made a sharply worded inquiry about Austrian military preparations. The inquiry drew a reply which was tantamount to a declaration of war.

Vienna was in a mood of melodramatic heroism. The young Empress wound gaily colored ribbons on flagstaffs; militiamen took their oaths; ranking socialites and burghers' wives vied in preparations for the wounded to come; priests bestowed blessings, writers produced patriotic poems; printers' presses clattered, brass bands blared, bells tolled; people up and down the shrunken realm were stirred into frenzy, a furor that might have swept Napoleon away had emotions had the impact of arms.

Archduke Karl had no delusions about the sweeping power of emotions, and he had misgivings about the effectiveness of mass mobilization. On paper, his army was the largest since the day of Persian greatness. (The files listed: from Austria 279,372 infantry, 36,204 cavalry, 791 pieces of artillery; from Hungary 224,000 men; and from all parts of the realm combined another 156 battalions of infantry.) But actual effectives were much lower, and several scores of thousands of men would have to be concentrated in the far northeast to guard against Polish insurrection or Russian invasion; Karl wondered whether his planned invasion of Bavaria could be carried out in sufficient strength to defeat a French army of 140,000 concentrated there.

As Viennese chroniclers reported the unconfirmed sob story of the cobbler who committed suicide after being rejected by the draft board; as poet Heinrich Collin wrote his militia songs; as Schlegel, Gentz, and Hormayer drafted fiery proclamations, theater performances turned into patriotic displays, and processions thronged the streets—Karl's main army crossed the Inn near Schärding, south of the Danube, took Passau, entered Munich, and closed in on Landshut.

In the distant hinterland, delirious crowds shouted: "Austria above everything," when they learned that the Austrian armies swept through Bavaria, that the peasantry in Tyrol had risen, and French eagles had been captured in Italy.

But a series of engagements fought west of the upper Danube brought the Austrian advance to a standstill, after a mere nine days. On April 18, French soldiers heard a proclamation: "I have come like lightning. . . ." Napoleon had arrived. His lightning strategy upset the Austrian plans.

He raced on to Landshut. Without General Joseph Wenzel Radetzky, who was to be the last of the Austrian legendary soldierly figures, the battle of Landshut might have been the end of the campaign. But even so, the French won. Archduke Karl had no choice but to cross the Danube with his badly mauled forces and to try to reach Vienna via Bohemia. They crossed over a wooden bridge at Regensburg. Austrian cavalry kept it open for foot soldiers and carts for three hours, then crossed it swimming, while artillery maintained a slow, steady fire on the pursuers. The town, defended by General Count Kolowrat, suffered heavy losses.

Another Austrian corps, under General Hiller, which had remained on the right riverbank, abandoned Bavaria after some fighting near Linz, and again near Mautern, opposite Göttweig Monastery. On May 9, it reached the western approaches to Vienna, after a long, fast trek back.

Austrian forces from Italy were recalled to unite with Karl's western army. Archduke Johann was in command in Italy, not because of his military record, but because of his popularity with the people there, who put romantic glamour above military science. Nobody knew when Johann would reach the Danube Valley, nor where the French might then be.

A few hours after General Hiller, Marshal Lannes and his corps were in Hütteldorf. Emperor Franz had left for Prague.

This time the Viennese wanted to fight. A capitulation requested by Lannes was answered by a few cannon shot that missed their mark. Marshal Lannes countered with a nocturnal bombardment of the city.

During the same night of May 12, French troops crossed the narrow Danube Canal into the Prater, as other units closed in on the capital in a pincers movement. The Viennese were hapless and furious, but did not rally for heroic defense. The white flag went up on the Burgtor; Napoleon again moved into Schönbrunn and issued a manifesto to the Hungarians: a Diet should convene on the fields of Rákócz to depose the dynasty of Habsburg-Lorraine and elect a national King. He ordered newspapers to report that Prince Eszterházy had been elected, but the Prince reacted by visiting Emperor Franz in his refuge and offering him his services. Also from Schönbrunn, Napoleon decreed the annexation of the Papal States and the arrest of Pope Pius VII.

The Danube became the general line of demarcation between friend and foe. He who controlled the crossings of the river would be the victor. On May 16, Archduke Karl's 80,000 soldiers began to deploy on its left bank between the Bisamberg and the Marchfeld. The crucial battle drew close.

A short distance downstream of the Prater, the Danube splits into several arms, forming small islets and one fairly large one: the Lobau. The arm to the right of the Lobau is broad and deep; that to the left, narrow and shallow. Napoleon chose this spot to throw a strategic bridge across the Danube. On May 19 he left Schönbrunn for the village of Kaiser-Ebersdorf, from where he could supervise construction work.

A contemporary account said: "General Count Bertrand threw three-fold pontoon bridges across the Danube. The waters were still swollen by thaws. Archduke Karl, advancing along the left bank, had fire ships, and huge barges loaded with stones, launched against the bridges, which were severely damaged three times in rapid succession.

"When Napoleon massed his army on an islet between two arms of the treacherous stream, in a season in which the indomitable element usually mocks men's power, even some Frenchmen shook their heads. The success of the ingenious but risky venture depended on various minor contingencies. However, French military scientists are well entitled to call the crossing of the Danube at the Lobau islands one of the greatest military master strokes.

"The boldness and also the levity of the plan can be fully understood only by those who are familiar with the terrain and who realize that all French technical equipment was not yet assembled. To throw bridges across the main river with its rapid current, and with a depth running to thirty-six feet, and to cross the bridges with 80,000 men, 20,000 horses, 200 cannon, and twice as many heavy wagons, in three lanes, was a miracle, but similar miracles had been achieved in the past by Asiatic geniuses. The venture was typical for the character of Napoleon, who had Persian rather than Roman features, who had less of Caesar than of Xerxes."

In the afternoon of May 20 the bridges were ready. A few French battalions and squadrons moved across, but then floodwaters burst against the pontoons and tore several away. Only by superhuman efforts was the damage repaired overnight, and the next morning 30,000 French were deployed on the left bank of the Danube.

Archduke Karl could not lose another day. During the evening of May 20 he issued his order of the day: "Tomorrow there will be battle. The fate of the monarchy depends on its outcome. I shall do my duty, and I expect the army to do the same."

During the night the city of Vienna turned into a grandstand. Grapevine carried the news of the coming battle to all quarters of the town. Tens of thousands climbed on roof tops and steeples to have a view of the battlefield on and near the Danube. The crowds did not brag; they did not sing; they just waited.

At dawn—it was the dawn of Whitsunday—they saw French troops in high-precision motion pour across the river and deploy in agonizing exactness, while a few miles away the Austrian host seemed to stand motionless almost like ghosts. The right flank, under General Hiller's remnants, was based on the Bisamberg. Then came Count Bellegarde's and Prince Hohenzollern's infantry; still further to the left were masses of cavalry under Prince Johann Liechtenstein; the left flank was formed by the corps of Field Marshal Prince Rosenberg. To the rear were reserves under Feldzeugmeister Prince Reuss.

The Viennese were familiar with these names; they knew their bearers by sight. Not long ago they had lived in sumptuous city palaces, sat in theaters, driven through the Prater. Crowds on roof tops and spires wondered why their army stood as though petrified.

Church bells tolled midday. The Austrian array began to move.

One hundred and three battalions, 148 squadrons, 288 cannon, formed a semicircle, both wings trying to anchor themselves on the river.

Napoleon had not expected an Austrian attack before the following day, trusting that his enemies would be late, as usual. Had the Austrians attacked in the morning, the French might have faced annihilation; but even at noon, odds were against them.

French deployment was stepped up. Still, spectators heard no sounds of battle until, shortly before 4 P.M. the vanguards came within range of each other. Like a deep growl, a few shots rang out. Clouds of dust and smoke rose. The Austrian right wing advanced. Applause burst from the distant mass audience. The soldiers could neither see nor hear them; their eyes were glued to their goal, the village of Aspern, with its massive twin row of stone houses straight ahead.

Furor of artillery raked village grounds; smoke rolled in dense white clouds, mingled with dust; through the haze poured a withering counterfire from the defenders, who were protected by thick walls and improvised fortifications.

The picture of the battle for Aspern was blurred. The sight of marching columns a short distance downstream indicated that the Austrians were still on the offensive; but already, the French struck furious blows.

The Viennese looked for fire ships, but none floated down the river. The view of Aspern was still hazy when sounds near by alarmed the spellbound audience. Through the city streets trotted Napoleon's legendary iron riders, a host of heavily armored and helmeted men whose indomitable charges had already battered many a massive enemy formation into dust. Soon they would hurl themselves against the Austrians; it would be dusk by then. The Austrians would be weary. But nobody could warn them; not even the most foolhardy runner could reach them in time.

In Aspern meantime, cursing, yelling, sweating men battled for every house, every hedge and bit of palisade, like crazy dogs whose teeth are locked in a gigantic bite. Every square foot of ground was madly contested; the village changed hands ten times within three hours, but when the iron riders crossed the bridges the French held the ruins.

The Austrian semicircle moved, units shifting for reasons the Viennese could not even surmise. But the flabbergasted spectators could see that contact was loosening, that a gap opened precariously close to the French cavalry. Yet nobody could alert the apparently somnolent Austrian command. Should Napoleon see the gap he would call his horsemen, and this would be the end.

Napoleon, standing in front of a small brick building between Aspern and the village of Essling, had already noticed it; twelve French cavalry regiments, led by the dashing General d'Espagne, massed for a lethal charge that tore through the thin screen of two Austrian regiments and a light battery. D'Espagne on a white horse galloped out in front, brandishing a riding whip instead of a saber.

Napoleon smiled. Far away, from roof tops and steeples, people began to climb down into attics. They did not want to witness the inevitable.

But when the rough-riding armored men thundered into the open, a few Austrian infantry battalions moved up from the rear and fired. The French slowed down; d'Espagne lifted his whip and roared a summons for surrender. The iron riders put into gallop. The Austrians were 100 yards away, 50 yards, 30, 10. A salvo roared. Rows of French horsemen fell, including their general. The field was covered with bodies of mounts and riders; frantic squadrons dashed into piles of dead and dying creatures; Austrian fire continued, volley for volley, rows of soldiers with loaded rifles changing place with others who had just fired and needed a few seconds' time to reload. It was a well-drilled maneuver, carried out with flawless precision.

The gap closed; from left and right, Austrian corps reserves ran and rode to the crucial spot. The French fell back. Three thousand of their comrades littered the field. The Austrians had retaken Aspern.

The sun set behind the crest of the Vienna Woods.

As darkness fell, Napoleon tried another cavalry charge. He had won seventeen battles, each in no more than one day. He wanted to win his eighteenth victory on a similar schedule. But he failed.

The battle died down. Weary soldiers rested. Napoleon dozed on a bivouac on the left bank of the river. Archduke Karl slept in a peasant's house near Breitenee. People in Vienna took cat naps.

During the night, French reserves along the left bank of the river were carried across by ferries, for action on the morrow, May 22.

Roof tops and spires were again crowded at dawn. The French carried

Aspern in the first strike; but the Austrians retook the ruins. Yet they made no headway toward Essling, which had remained in French hands and which Archduke Karl wanted to take at any price. But the village was dominated by a huge massive silo, which the French had converted into a fort armed with cannon, and the attackers could take but a few houses.

The French slightly outnumbered their enemies, but they were still hemmed in in the semicircle, harassed by artillery. In order to win, they had to pierce the enemy center, and it was one of Napoleon's favorite operations. The drive started at midmorning. Austrian lines crumbled, French cavalry infiltrated the shaky array. To the people of Vienna, it was all smoke and roar, rolling north, meaning a French advance.

But in the early afternoon the rolling sight and sound stopped, then slowly moved in the opposite direction. Archduke Karl had seen the ranks of one infantry regiment break, and seized its flag; the men rallied and followed him in an assault that averted disaster.

The Austrians launched another river-borne assault. They set floating mills afire, piled burning timber on rafts. The swimming incendiaries interrupted for several hours communications between the bridgehead and the southern bank. Another setback on the northern bank and Napoleon's army would be annihilated.

But hard as he tried, Archduke Karl could not penetrate beyond Aspern and could not take Essling. His troops were near exhaustion. But so were the French. In the afternoon of May 22, the battle died down to a cannonade.

Napoleon wanted to cede his command to Lannes; but the marshal was dying; a cannon ball had shattered both his legs. Marshal Masséna took over as Napoleon rode back to the Lobau. The French had suffered 40,000 casualties, the Austrians 23,000. Should the Austrians press the pursuit, Napoleon would lose the war, and perhaps the throne.

Crouching on a fallen tree trunk at the Lobau, he watched his defeated soldiers return to the island and he listened silently to their loud derogatory remarks. Later he boarded a small boat and was rowed back across the river. Collectors of quotations claim that he said: "I was defeated by General Danube."

The Austrians did not follow up their victory, however. Archduke Karl did not want to overtax his men and hoped that, with new reinforcements, he would win another battle. He lacked the element of true greatness in generalcy.

In Vienna people read the French bulletin admitting a reverse; but the enemy did not evacuate the city.

In Prague, where Emperor Franz held court, Aspern was brilliantly celebrated. Poets wrote many rhymes, which were dispatched to Archduke Karl, who would have preferred soldiers and cannon.

Haydn and Beethoven had stayed in Vienna. Haydn, on the brink of death, celebrated victory by playing the national anthem three times over. Then he had to be carried from the piano. He died on May 31. Viennese city guards and French grenadiers stood at his bier.

Otherwise, the French soldiery was not strictly considerate, nor were the Viennese easily manageable. A Viennese master craftsman got into an argument with a French officer, broke his sword, and was put before a firing squad. A saddle maker who had been hiding arms was also executed.

The French needed maps of the Danube regions and offered fancy prices; but all maps disappeared and search parties were heckled. The French military governor was publicly derided, and firing squads were no effective answer to what the governor called "the spirit of unrest and disorder."

Napoleon, again residing in Schönbrunn, methodically prepared a battle of revenge. He would have to tame "General Danube" before he could take another chance, 1000 miles away from Paris, in a hostile land.

On July 3, 1809, a French bulletin boasted: "The Danube no longer exists for the enemy. General Count Bertrand has accomplished an amazing and admirable feat. In fourteen days he had a bridge built over the most rapid stream of the world, a span of 2400 feet, resting on sixty vaults, wide enough for three wagons abreast. Another bridge stands, on stakes firm enough for marching infantry. A third bridge on rafts was just added, so that we can cross the Danube in three columns abreast.

"The bridges are protected against all hazards, including fire ships and infernal machines, by palisades rammed in between the islands, 1500 feet from the structures. This enormous construction work gives the impression that it had taken years to complete. . . .

"The bridges are secured by bridgeheads, 10,000 feet in circumference, by redoubts, palisades, and moats. The island of Lobau is now a fortress, supplied with huge stores of food and armed with 100 heavy-caliber cannon and 20 mortars and howitzers. Yesterday the Duke of Rivoli had another bridge thrown across the arm of the Danube which faces Essling. It is protected by the bridgehead set up during the first crossing. Now that the crossings are safe, and our bridges attack-proof, the fate of the Austrian monarchy will be decided in one single battle. . . ."

The Danube was by no means the most rapid stream of the world, but the fortress-bridges stood, and it has never been explained how the work could have been done so quickly and why the Austrians did not interfere.

Archduke Karl had 110,000 men and 450 cannon concentrated near Aspern, another 80,000 men camped, all but immobile, along the left bank of the Danube up to Linz; 70,000 under Archduke Johann were concentrated northeast of Pressburg. The war archives of Vienna throw no light upon the huge army's inaction, and Archduke Karl's memoirs do not clarify the implications of this passage: "A general who receives inappropriate orders interfering with his own concept of operations is not only entitled but even morally obligated to act according to his own judgment. However, should these orders be based upon political considerations of which he does not have advance knowledge, and if their execution affects several generals and their troops, he is duty-bound to obey. To act against one's better judgment, and to put a glorious reputation at stake, is the greatest sacrifice any man could make in the interest of public welfare."

But could the army's inertia be in the interest of public welfare? Could defeat promote interests other than those of the enemy? What did go on at court in Prague? Who devised nefariously stupid schemes, veiled in the term "political considerations"? The author of the schemes must have been sacrosanct in order to escape denunciation for 150 years, and, in all likelihood, forever.

In the evening of July 4, French troops were alerted. Archduke Karl dispatched an estafette to Archduke Johann, asking that he march west as fast as possible.

In the morning of July 5, the French moved into attack positions. Their swift passage across the fortress-bridges was not contested. In the late afternoon Napoleon gave his signal.

An assault on the Austrian center, led by the always inept Bernadotte, collapsed with heavy casualties. The Austrians held their lines.

Next day, as Archduke Karl hoped, Johann's army would envelop the French right wing. Another courier raced east to urge Johann to hurry. Karl grouped his forces for all-out attack, leaving the left wing weakest, as the other army was expected to move in. Even a lesser general than Napoleon would have noticed the strange array.

July 6 dawned; the Austrians pressed the French back toward the old battle lines of Aspern and Essling; their guns were now trained against the Lobau and the bridges. But Napoleon began to gain ground.

There was still no sign of Johann when the Austrian left wing wavered, lost coherence. At 2 P.M., Karl had to order a general retreat toward Moravia. The inconsequential victory of Aspern was more than upset by the disastrous defeat of Wagram. A trifling incident, one underling's wantonness, had caused Johann's fateful delay. The first courier found a bridge across the Váh River torn away by swollen waters, and wasted six hours looking for an intact bridge instead of swimming across on horseback. These six hours made the difference between triumph and disaster. Johann arrived near the battlefield at 5 P.M.

A few days later an armistice was signed. Almost 400 miles of the Danube Valley were under French control.

Archduke Karl resigned. He was only thirty-eight, but his soldiers considered him an old man. He was. He lived yet another thirty-eight years, as a grand seigneur of great wealth and anxious to evade the limelight of politics and soldierdom.

The demarcation line of 1809 was so drawn that Austria's main resources remained in French hands. Emperor Franz, urged on by his wife and several generals, would have wanted to resume fighting, but cool-headed experts warned against any such risk. Napoleon held all the trump cards.

Among these cards was inflation as a weapon of destruction. It occurred to Napoleon that by forging bills he could deal a mortal blow to the Austrian economy. On September 6, 1809, from Schönbrunn, he wrote his police minister Joseph Fouché: "You will receive a complete collection of Austrian bank notes. Have 100 million of all denominations printed at once." What happened to these bills is not reliably recorded. The forgery campaign was discontinued after a disastrous peace was signed in Schönbrunn Castle on October 14.

Bavaria got Salzburg, Berchtesgaden, and parts of Upper Austria. Napoleon grabbed parts of Carinthia, Carniola, Gorizia, Trieste, and the rest of Austria's Adriatic coast for his Italian kingdom. The King of Saxony, who had actively supported the French in the fateful year and would keep supporting them longer than was profitable to him, received a slice of Galicia for his newly established Duchy of Warsaw. The Tsar, Napoleon's friend, got another district of Galicia. Austria had to recognize territorial changes Napoleon had made in Italy and Spain; it joined Napoleon's continental system barring English goods; it had to pay an indemnity of 85 million francs and limit the effectives of its army to 150,000.

While peace negotiations dragged on, Napoleon did a lot of visiting: he went to Györ and held a French troop review; to Brünn and Austerlitz, to Krems and Melk, to Wiener Neustadt and to the Semmering. The Emperor of the French made a bid for popularity in Vienna by lifting certain censorship regulations, but there was no response. On August 15, when the Viennese had been ordered to celebrate Napoleon's fortieth birthday by an illumination, they used tricky transparent inscriptions to deride the occupier.

Count Stadion, unwilling to put his signature under the disgraceful peace treaty, resigned on September 26; his successor became the German-born Prince Klemens Wenzel Metternich, who thus made his bow on the European stage in a less than enviable part.

Napoleon left Vienna on October 16; the French army marched off on November 20, leaving the Viennese wondering whether to rejoice over the evacuation, to mourn the fate of their country, to rebel against their humiliated government, or to worry about inflation.

In this dilemma they decided to prepare a pageant that promised diversion from depressing realities. They arranged a festive welcome for their army and a belated celebration of the Aspern victory.

Parts of the army arrived on November 26, crossing the bridges of Lobau. The chilly city streets were lined with jubilant crowds. Pranksters of "illumination day" were hailed, so were soldiers who had escaped French prisoner-of-war enclosures and burghers who had hidden arms.

Emperor Franz and his Empress returned on November 27, in a big carriage and with a strong desire for incognito. Yet, desirous of another spectacle, burghers unharnessed the Emperor's horses and pulled the carriage to the Hofburg, shouting: "Welcome our father." Vienna was genuinely illuminated, happy despite defeat, inflation, and more clouds massing on the murky horizon.

It was the cabinet's thankless task to deal with the clouds.

The Metternichs had entered Austria's civil service through the good offices of Prince Kaunitz, and like Kaunitz, Metternich tried *rapprochement* with France through matrimony. But when Kaunitz had acted as a royal marriage broker, he could select a groom who was the Princess' equal, and single. Napoleon, however, did not have one royal ancestor, and the law of the House of Habsburg-Lorraine required that there be many of them; worse even, he was a married man. Metternich discussed his diplomatic marriage plans with French diplomats of the old school, and they told him that Napoleon's marriage to Joséphine de Beauharnais was about to be annulled on the grounds of non-consummation, which, according to all evidence, was utterly ridiculous; the real reason was that no progeny could be expected.

Annulment was pronounced on December 15, 1809, and the ancestorless Emperor decided to marry a Princess of ancient exalted rank—Emperor Franz's daughter. Marie Louise was eighteen, not unattractive, and to judge from her august ancestors, hardly lacking in fecundity. Napoleon had not laid eyes on the candidate, but he had seen her portraits on the walls of Schönbrunn and he agreed with Metternich that he should wed her.

Emperor Franz was flabbergasted when Metternich made his report, but to say no under the circumstances would have meant disaster. The Empress, though only Marie Louise's stepmother, called it an outrage. But another French invasion would be catastrophic.

Marie Louise was the last to learn of the project. Her acceptance was a foregone conclusion. In whatever amount of hero worship romantic young girls may have indulged, this girl saw in Napoleon but a vile upstart whom the bloody waves of revolution had swept from the depths to exaltation. She dreaded him.

Early in March 1810, Napoleon sent his delegate to Vienna to ask officially for the Princess' hand. The delegate was Marshal Alexandre Berthier, who had been with Lafayette in America and was now Prince of Wagram, Duke of Neufchâtel, husband of a Bavarian Princess, and Napoleon's chief of staff.

The people of Vienna learned of the impending marriage one month before Berthier's arrival. It had been feared that they would resent the deal, but when financial wizards predicted that this would end all currency troubles, people took gold and silver coins out of their stockings, purchased government bonds, and threw the black market into a crisis as stores of merchandise were openly sold at cut-rate prices. Berthier reported to Paris: "People are deliriously happy. . . . It is hard to imagine their enthusiasm."

The formal wedding ceremony took place on March 11 at St. Stephen's, Archduke Karl acting *per procura* for Napoleon. There were official celebrations and free balls. Berthier appeared as a guest of honor at a performance of Gluck's *Iphigénie en Tauride*.

Empress Marie Louise left for France on March 13 and dutifully gave birth to a son in the following year. Another three years later, when the Austro-Prusso-Russian victors entered Paris and the French Senate deposed Napoleon, she left her husband, returned to Vienna, and, still very young and eager for life, all but forgot the four years in which she had been the weak link between the two Empires, which even in embrace were locked in a struggle for survival.

Their son, Napoleon Franz Joseph, stayed with her, a strangely beautiful boy, who, in the twenty-one years of his life, was the French's l'Aiglon (the Young Eagle), King of Rome, Duke of Reichstadt, and the second Napoleon, who, in Vienna, was never called by that name.

His father vainly asked his estranged wife to return and bring their son to see him. Marie Louise, whom the Congress of Vienna made the ruler of Parma, Piacenza, and Guastalla, remarried without legal trouble. Her second husband was Count Adam von Neipperg, a scion of ancient nobility. The Duke of Reichstadt was tutored by poet Heinrich Collin. He wanted to be a soldier like Prince Eugene of Savoy and was idolized by romantically minded ladies of the Court, but he contracted his fatal illness at a military parade, which he attended with the rank of a colonel.

The sweet, curly Duke, whose portrait by Daffinger fascinated women long beyond his death, became the protagonist of a great many melodramatic fictions. Historian Richard von Kralik fittingly calls him a celebrity without achievements. But he was charming, of unusual birth, and somewhat lost in a world in which he fitted neither into niches nor on pedestals, which might be a good substitute for achievement.

CHAPTER FIFTY

In 1812, Emperor Franz and Empress Maria Ludovica joined Napoleon and Marie Louise in Dresden, where the Emperor of the French held ostentatious court on the eve of his Russian campaign.

Austria and France now were "allies," meaning that Austria had been forced to mobilize troops to join the *Grande Armée*. Their Majesties are said to have been very friendly, but their mutual feelings are better illustrated by a snarling remark of Napoleon that the following October he would be back in Vienna, and by Franz's pondering how his troops and other compulsory allies could manage to run over to the enemy.

War, the inevitable state of European affairs, bade a temporary farewell to the Danube Valley, even though men from the Danube kept dying in various other parts of Europe, as chattels of, and deliverers from, Napoleon.

Sixty thousand Austrians were enrolled in the *Grande Armée,* which was to have conquered Russia and then used it as a base for a march to India, with reckless disregard of casualties. Only one fourth of its 600,000 men were French; the rest were forced soldiers, whose lives were the least of Napoleon's concerns. When a Russian diplomat warned him about the immense human sacrifices of the campaign, he replied: "For every five Russians you may lose, I shall lose one Frenchman and four swine," meaning Austrians, Hungarians, Italians, Bavarians, Poles, Saxonians, Rhinelanders, and Portuguese.

The Austrians who fought the Russians in the former Polish provinces were inadequately equipped for extremely cold weather. In October 1812, Upper Austrian Infantry Regiment No. 14 urgently demanded lamb furs, but the men had to freeze in light overcoats to the bitter end. The lamb furs were eventually delivered five years later, when No. 14 was garrisoned in balmy Naples.

Prince Schwarzenberg, aged forty-one, commanded the Austrians. He had been a captain on Laudon's staff when in his teens, a general at twenty-five; later he had served as ambassador to St. Petersburg and to Paris. On May 8, 1813, after Napoleon's disaster in the Russian winter, when the foundation was laid for the Austro-Prusso-Russo-Anglo-Swedish coalition that would lead to the battle of Leipzig (October 14–18) and Napoleon's downfall, he was selected supreme commander.

Schwarzenberg's chief of staff was a tough cavalry general of Regensburg fame, Count Radetzky. Radetzky lived to be ninety-two; he was an officer for seventy-four years, and served under five Emperors from Joseph II to Franz Joseph I, fighting Turks, Italians, French, and, in their armies, nationals of a score of other lands. He was a dashing horseman when he was young, a sound expert with an amazing memory when he turned middle-aged, and idolized by his soldiers when he was old. To be idolized by the rank and file made him invincible even when he was so shaky that the grooms hardly knew how to make him sit in the saddle. He had every decoration the Emperor could bestow, and had he ever tried to wear them all—which he never did—there would not have been enough space on his tunic. Franz Grillparzer, Austria's greatest poet, dedicated spirited poetry to the field marshal and drafted the diploma by which, on the occasion of the sixtieth anniversary of his commission in the army, Radetzky was made an honorary citizen of Vienna. Johann Strauss, Father, wrote the *Radetzky Marsch* in his honor, but, having no taste for music, Radetzky took almost two years to hear the march that had won the acclaim of an empire.

Radetzky was of Bohemian stock and sported a thick, funny Czech accent. Rising Czech nationalism never disowned this Austrian hero. "Austria is in your camp," Grillparzer wrote, and the Austria of Radetzky, unaffected by provincial boundaries, was tied to the venerable field marshal's personality and his not easily explicable charm.

Schwarzenberg sighed: "I wish I could pass on to somebody else every thread of the tissue I hold in my hands." The commander in chief had the mixed pleasure of explaining everything in every detail to the allied monarchs. The King of Prussia always thought that his own army was being slighted; the Tsar, who still did not understand the fundamentals of strategy but wanted to be the guiding spirit of operations, turned into an abusive hindsight critic; Emperor Franz had a military aide who made a point of disagreeing; and Austrian, Prussian, and Russian secondary figures struggled among themselves, asking the higher-ups to act as arbiters, which meant to decide every argument in every arguer's favor. Last, but not least, there was a "peace party," third-stringers who emphasized that, in a modern world, wars may still be declared but would not have to be fought, that a display of strength would show Napoleon that the tide was running against him.

Napoleon actually did have a chance of victory in 1813, but he relied too much on his paling military star, instead of exploiting the squabbles that plagued the enemy.

On October 17, 1813, when the Battle of Leipzig already shaped up as a French disaster of shattering magnitude, Napoleon sent an emissary, captive Austrian general Count Merveldt, to the headquarters of Emperor Franz. The emissary was not received. Two days later, the French army was in disorderly retreat. It had lost 30 generals, over 60,000 men, 370 cannon, 900 ammunition carts, and 130,000 rifles. German forced auxiliaries deserted.

Had it not been for disunity among the allies Paris would have fallen before the end of the year. But Chancellor Metternich was more frightened by the aspect of an overpowering Russia than by that of a chastened France.

Allied leadership wasted garrulous weeks in Frankfurt while Napoleon went before the French Senate to request 300,000 men and more ammunition. The Senate voted in his favor, but French ammunition makers sabotaged deliveries, fearful that they would not collect.

Materialistic motives, unpatriotic as they were, were at least sensible. But when, after many sterile palavers, the allied armies started moving on December 20, 1813, considerations of a less than sensible nature caused further delay. Tsar Alexander forbade his elite troops to march before January 13, the anniversary of the Russian crossing of the Neman River after Napoleon's disaster in the previous year, claiming that such a celebration would be "wonderfully poetic." This touch of poetry would cost thousands of casualties, and Schwarzenberg had a few irreverent things to say about "puppet shows in war."

Bernadotte, now, through a comedy of errors, Crown Prince of Sweden, could not be reckoned with at all. Emperor Franz asked for so many detailed and calligraphic reports that his generals in the field would have to discontinue operations in favor of paper work.

"I envy Wellington," Schwarzenberg exclaimed. "He hardly tells what he has done, and he would not even tell his sovereign what he intended to do."

Napoleon, encouraged by intelligence from allied headquarters, left Paris on January 25 to stake his crown on one campaign.

In the two preceding years, the military genius seemed to have deserted the Emperor of the French (or the "Emperor of Battles," as even Schwarzenberg called him in a letter to his wife), and he had been little more than a magnificent routinist. When he was cornered, it seemed as if the fire of genius was burning bright again, but he no longer had the resources of many lands at his disposal, and his men no longer blindly trusted his star. He scored various minor victories, which gave their names to so many Napoleonic successes for future textbook use, but actually were grindstones of French attrition.

Diplomatic feelers extended from both sides found no basis for understanding; Napoleon rejected the demand to have France limited to its borders of 1793.

On March 29, 1814, the enemy stood at the gates of Paris. On March 30, 1814, Paris surrendered. March 31 saw the King of Prussia and the Tsar enter the silent capital. The Austrian Emperor did not partake in the triumph. His daughter and grandson were still in the conquered city, and it would have been difficult to work out a ceremonial under which the Empress of the French could fittingly greet her father.

On April 2, the Senate deposed Napoleon and granted him eighty-five square miles of the Mediterranean island of Elba as his future Empire. On May 3, the late King Louis XVI's younger brother, aged fifty-nine, returned to Paris as Louis XVIII. Various deposed Princes returned to their former realms, and the Pope re-established himself in Rome.

On May 30, peace was signed in Paris. France had to evacuate all conquered lands. Yet peace could not really establish the *status quo* within the land mass that had undergone kaleidoscopic changes; it could not determine what structure should stand on the ground of the Germany of yore, nor what should become of the debris of Poland left in foment after Napoleon's intrusion, nor what to do about Saxony, whose King had stayed with Napoleon until after the Battle of Leipzig. There were many claims for reward and reasons for punishment and, unfathomable, but inevitable, mankind's title to an international instrument that would make future holocaust impossible.

All these agenda would have overtaxed the mental capacities of a congress of the most dedicated geniuses, but in 1814, as on many occasions before and after, the task of dealing with such problems fell upon an assembly that was sadly inadequate.

The victors agreed that, within two months after signature of the peace treaty, a congress should convene in Vienna; vanquished France would be invited to attend.

Tsar Alexander and his German-born wife, King Friedrich Wilhelm III of Prussia, King Frederick VI of Denmark, King Karl Friedrich of Württemberg, and King Maximilian I of Bavaria made it known that they would come with their retinues. A host of German Princes and princelings were due. More than 100,000 foreign visitors, including 700 ambassadors were expected.

Vienna would be, if not the capital of Europe, at least the seat of many European governments and the world's center of gravity.

The opening of the Congress was delayed until November 2, 1814, by sheer unpunctuality.

The capital was again a grandstand. Its people, unmindful of recent disaster and current trouble, concentrated on the greatest show with the largest, most colorful, most brilliant cast in recorded history.

The show that was the Congress of Vienna had a bright prelude. In June, Emperor Franz returned to Vienna. The city fathers left reception festivities to the burghers' patriotic fancy.

Conscientious chroniclers tell of the burgher's wife Franziska Klähr, who welcomed the Emperor fifteen miles west of the town with a spirited speech, while her husband, an aging locksmith, at the head of a numerous delegation, threw palm branches. In the suburbs, an arch of triumph was set up; a well-intentioned architectural monstrosity. Poems in print and manuscript showered upon the Imperial carriage. White-clad boys and flower girls waited in Schönbrunn to shout: "Welcome, O dear kindly father," and to present the weary monarch with more samples of poetry. Another triumphal arch stood at the Kärntnertor; many bands struck up, huge crowds staged perilous commotions to greet the august homecomer. Soldiers had to restore order so that flowers could be thrown along the street to the Cathedral, where the *Te Deum* was celebrated.

Merry abandonment was the popular keynote to the events following the capture of Paris. It was fun again to live in Vienna. The high and mighty began to assemble in September 1814; the city burst at the seams with strangers.

The Congress constituted itself in a ponderous procedure whose long-drawn formalities gave the participants time to ponder issues.

As the principals met, constituted, drafted, and parleyed, they found themselves in a mental void. Napoleon was in Elba, France had disgorged its conquests, those who had once cast their lot with Napoleon were frightened. What were the issues they had assembled to solve?

Prince Metternich became president of the Congress; Russia's top representatives were Count Nesselrode and a shrewd Corsican, Pozzo di Borgo. England had Lord Castlereagh and the Duke of Wellington; from France came turncoat Talleyrand; from Prussia, Prince von Hardenberg; from Bavaria, Count Montgelas. Cardinal Consalvi, the Pope's delegate, carried his purple over the shining parquetry of the conference rooms.

An original "acting committee" of representatives of England, Prussia, Russia, and Austria was enlarged by the admission of France, Spain, Portugal, and Sweden.

This committee never arranged joint sessions. Everybody who wanted to be heard was admitted singly to present views, suggestions, and requests. The minutes, entombed in giant archives, have left researchers bewildered by the accumulation of vainglory, greed, sterile puns, and outright stupidity.

Negotiations seemed to be the pretext rather than the purpose of the Congress of Vienna, the greatest social affair of all time.

Short-lived queen of social affairs was Empress Maria Ludovica. She gave the meaningless political rantings the complexion of superlative entertainment. Goethe glorified her in his *Westöstlicher Diwan*. And while statesmen bungled for a political line, she set the tune for flattering lines of fashions—simple, tight-fitting "antique" for 1814; ruffled, puffed, full of drapings and sashes for 1815. To the delight of the millinery trade, everything was topped by immense hats full of lace and feathers.

Festivities kept all of Vienna on its toes. There never was a dearth of ideas for amusements, some highly artistic, some pompous, some just oversized.

On October 1, Handel's *Samson* was performed in the court riding school; it was followed by his *Alexander's Feast,* by a supercolossal carrousel on horseback, and by Beethoven conducting an orchestra of thousands, and in between there was a commemoration of the Battle of Leipzig, during which royalty dined in the *Lusthaus* of the Prater and 14,000 veterans of that battle entertained 4000 survivors of earlier carnages.

Theaters enjoyed the greatest boom on record. It was all pomp and luxury. One act of a since forgotten show played in Paradise, and every night hundreds of bottles of perfume were poured into the auditorium to make the illusion complete.

Distinguished audiences applauded Schiller's *Die Jungfrau von Orleans,* but their favorite author was Adolf Bäuerle, who had eight "patriotic" comedies premièred in 1814 alone. Even foreigners whose German was less than fluent and who were less than enthusiastic about Austrian patriotism, were carried away by the happy mood.

Painters from everywhere portrayed the celebrated beauties gathered in Vienna. The most beautiful of them all was said to be the Tsar's sister, Catherine Pavlovna, widow of Prince Peter of Oldenburg. During the Congress she met the Crown Prince of Württemberg, who divorced his Bavarian wife to marry the statuesque Russian Venus with the classical features. The abandoned wife, however, soon found herself a better than equal substitute: Emperor Franz I in person, who married her after the sudden death of Maria Ludovica. Next to Catherine Pavlovna, chroniclers ranged as leading beauties Dorothy, Duchess of Courland, and the Princess Eszterházy, also called the "Queen of Diamonds." The list of seductresses did not only include members of ancient nobility; there was also "the Incomparable," the wife of banker Baron Arnstein, a black-haired, white-skinned Jewish siren from Berlin, who became the heroine of a duel in which Prince Liechtenstein was killed.

Tsar Alexander worked on a "Spectrum of Beauty" and distributed titles: Countess Zichy was dubbed "Divine Beauty," Countess Széchenyi "Coquettish Beauty," Countess Saurma "Devil's Beauty," Princess Eszterházy "Stunning Beauty," and Princess Auersperg "the Beauty who, alone, inspires sentiment."

Historian George Gervinus wrote: "Private balls and court masquerades, pantomimes, fireworks, carrousels, hunts, parades in carriages and on horseback, troop reviews, and maneuvers kept the visitors busy and entertained. One morning a requiem would be held for Louis XVI, the same evening the crowd would gather at a ball, and the morning after in a gala sleigh *corso*. The background of this grandiose picture was of amazing variety. Within the narrow space of Vienna lived many Princes and their retinues, celebrities of soldiering and politics, the ostentatious nobility of Austria, Hungary, and Bohemia, and its guests, the wanton wits of drawing rooms, together with odd characters, libertines, adventurers, impostors, gamblers, singers, dancers, actors; beauties of high society put themselves up on display and for sale, in competition with prostitutes. Refined Western passions clashed and blended with cruder passions of semi-oriental potentates. Immense sums were spent on women. Frivolous or coquettish jokers told spicy secrets of love. The press did not give too much space to indiscretions that could have set the censor's pencil in motion, but it gave dithyrambic descriptions of official affairs. Not only stern critics of a shallow, jesting, profligate society condemned the immeasurable waste of time, money, and thought at the Congress; even tolerant persons shook their heads in dismay."

The Prince of Ligne's bon mot that the Congress was not "going" but dancing—brilliant when it was coined, but soon hackneyed through over-quotation—was a fitting one, and even though friendly chroniclers interpreted dancing as a sound means to achieve political aims, results remained unsatisfactory.

Metternich made suggestions that another German Empire might fill the vacuum in the center of Europe. Less than a decade had passed since the 1000-year-old creation of Charlemagne had been erased from the political map. Many among the millions who had lived in it were homesick for the decayed historical structure, but the few whose vote could have revived it had no affection for the defunct Reich.

A German commission—Austria, Prussia, Bavaria, Württemberg, and Hannover—engaged in sterile talking. Then Russia and Prussia put political aims on the agenda: Russia wanted the rest of Poland, Prussia all of Saxony. But Austria did not want to part with her own Polish spoils; England and Austria did not want Prussia to become again a leading military power; France, secretly wooed by some of the victors, sided with them.

On January 3, 1815, with a phenomenal New Year's Eve hang-over still unconquered, Austria, France, and England signed a defensive alliance against Prussia and Russia, and soon their strategists began to map a not strictly defensive campaign. They worked in tight seclusion, but news filtered out. Prussia looked to Russia to lead a countermove, but instead the Tsar changed his mind and offered to settle his claim for Warsaw, which softened Prussia's belligerency. Yet there remained enough fire smoldering under the ashes to set the continent ablaze in a conflict among allies whom common adversaries, not common interests, had brought together.

Had Napoleon had the patience to wait in Elba for one more year, he might have sold his support to the highest bidder and re-emerged as the domineering factor in world affairs. But patience had never been Napoleon's forte. He was used to come and strike, lightning style.

On March 7, 1815, the disunited powers assembled in congress learned that Napoleon had landed near Cannes, sweeping France by the sheer magic of his name and by the discontent of his former marshals, whom the stingy and suspicious Louis XVIII had stripped of part of their pay and of most of their privileges.

On March 25, England, Austria, Prussia, and Russia reaffirmed their earlier alliance and pledged themselves not to lay down their arms until Napoleon had become utterly incapable of creating further trouble.

The "hundred days" had begun.

The old war started anew. Napoleon did not stand a chance, whatever legend has since told. His resources were limited to those of a France with a population of twenty million, the male part of which was decimated, and with an industry that was by far outproduced by that of England alone. At best, he could muster an army of 350,000, while his enemies had almost 1,000,000 men under arms, who covered a line from Belgium to Italy. Whatever local successes the French would score eventually, they were bound to succumb to numbers and distances. Actually, only the English and Prussians joined battle with Napoleon. On June 18, 1815, came Waterloo.

July 10 already saw Emperor Franz I and his allies enter Paris in triumph.

Now that Napoleon was definitely prostrate, the Congress could go on—entertaining, intriguing, accomplishing nothing.

Some foreigners adopted Vienna as their home, and Vienna, in turn, adopted them if they were spectacular. Among them was Silesian-born Friedrich von Gentz, who, despite his earlier infatuation with the French Revolution, had entered the Austrian civil service and written several of Emperor Franz's manifestoes. Secretly he also drew another salary from

England, for representing that country's interests. But not even two salaries were sufficient to satisfy his passion for the finest delights that Vienna had to offer. He was the best-dressed man about town, he looked a little like Metternich, he was considered an arbiter of good taste, and even though he fought a steady uphill fight against a host of creditors he was appointed permanent secretary of the Congress.

Gentz knew all about trends and intrigues. Royalty and Princes came to him and granted friendly loans in exchange for inside information.

Only Gentz could have disclosed the sources from which Russia and Prussia had learned of the clandestine alliance of January 3, or of the channels that had linked Vienna and Elba. But nobody suspected him; one rarely suspects spectacular characters.

Gentz remained a favorite of Vienna until his death in 1832. He was a prolific writer on politics, a champion of conservatism, a bulwark against progress and reform which he considered destructive. It was his avowed aim to rid society of mob rule and the preponderance of scientists, students, and journalists. He remained Metternich's most trusted consultant to the end; and various excesses of censorship and police control were his brain children.

France paid dearly for the hundred days. Instead of a peace without reparations, an indemnity of 700 million francs was imposed upon the exhausted land. But even 700 million could not stabilize currencies or compensate small-time losers all over the continent. The money went down the drain abroad, while in France the expenditure caused economic hardships and subsequent rebellions.

In July 1815, the Austrians celebrated the return of Milan, Venetia, Illyria, and Dalmatia, of Salzburg, the Tyrol, and Galicia. Prussia got a savory slice of Saxony, and Russia settled down to digesting its intake of Polish land.

On June 5, 1815, the *Deutsche Bundesakte* (German Federal Act) decided the future of Germany until further notice, replacing the Holy Roman Empire with a synthetic prop without tradition, a German Federation of thirty-nine sovereign states, which included several Austrian provinces. The Emperor of Austria was the permanent president of the *Bundestag* (Diet), *primus inter pares* (equal in rank, though superior in function, to many German Princes), but not a sovereign in the old sense.

The Federation was intended to be permanent, but it was too loosely knit to become a political or military factor. Only a domineering, conquest-minded president could have tried to forge it into an instrument of aggression, and Austrian Emperors were not of the domineering kind.

The Federation was by nature not nationalistic; the Kings of England, Denmark, and Holland, who had possessions on German territory, held seats and votes. Metternich, who scorned pan-Germanism and did not want to see Austria and Prussia at war over nationalistic issues, considered the Federation a safeguard against such a danger. But, for all practical purposes, it was but a wall of paper.

But one document came out of the Congress of Vienna, the highest-principled, least meaningful bombast ever to emerge from a conference room so far: the Holy Alliance between Russia, Prussia, and Austria, the prototype of a supergovernment that could never function. Tsar Alexander I was its godfather, but its actual source of inspiration was a middle-aged lady, a Congress hanger-on. She was Baroness Barbara Juliane Krüdener, nee van Vietinghoff, of Riga, wife of a Russian diplomat twice her age, mother of two children. She was said to be high-strung, irritable, and other synonyms of hysterical, easily enamored out of wedlock, always in quest of "ideals" which her aging husband could not provide. After his death in 1802, she turned to literature, and later to mysticism, which she met in the person of a Moravian cobbler who made people undergo "conversion."

She underwent several with unspecified results. Then, on a trip to East Prussia, she met a peasant quack who prophesied that a man from the North would destroy Napoleon and bring about the millennium. He quoted from the Bible to support his prophecy and agreed with the entranced baroness that this man could be no other than the Tsar. She resolved to notify him of his mission; but the Tsar, who was then Napoleon's ally, was not available to be notified. The baroness toured Switzerland, preaching, and collecting expulsion decrees from several cantons. At last, on June 4, 1815, she saw the Tsar, who had one of his reformer spells but did not quite know what and whom to reform. Barbara Juliane, who by then would have had no place in the "Spectrum of Beauty," started preaching, told Alexander about his millennium mission for a solid three hours, and urged him to join her in the pursuit of other people's happiness. It is said that the two talked about a new cult called chiliasm. She followed him on his trips to Germany, France, and Vienna, during which period the Holy Alliance was born.

"Relations among the powers," it read, "must be based on the sublime truth which the Holy Religion of our Savior teaches . . . precepts of justice, Christian charity, and peace must have a direct influence on the councils of Princes who regard themselves as fathers of their subjects . . . governments and subjects are members of one and the same Christian nation . . . A realm of peace will be established in Europe . . . all sovereigns who adhere by the same principles will be invited to join . . ."

With this document, which he called the pattern of permanent peace and friendship, and for which he could find no more fitting name than "Holy Alliance," Tsar Alexander surprised the rulers of Austria and Prussia when they met in Paris in 1815. He asked that they sign his draft without consulting their statesmen.

Franz of Austria and Friedrich Wilhelm of Prussia felt that it required more courage not to sign the sonorous phrases than to accept them as just another document, and since they did not want to see their ministers' sardonic smiles, they put their names under the draft in almost conspiratorial secrecy.

Only back in Vienna, early in 1816, was the secret revealed as the Tsar tried to enlarge the Holy Alliance. Metternich called the thing loud-sounding nonsense, Castlereagh spoke of "sublime mysticism and nonsense," and Hardenberg shrugged it off; yet the text was forwarded to every European potentate and eventually only the Holy See, England, and Turkey abstained. The high signatories passed the Holy Alliance on to their cabinets, who made uninspired attempts to amend it into something workable. It was expected eventually to become an instrument to safeguard the divine rights of Kings and to put an end to representative government.

Strangely enough, the Holy Alliance had an effect on American politics: its interference with the Spanish revolution of 1820, which had kindled the spark of secession in Chile, Argentina, and Mexico, caused President James Monroe to issue his historical doctrine of December 2, 1823: "We owe it, therefore, to candour and to the amicable relations existing between the U.S. and those powers, to declare that we should consider any attempt on their part to extend their system to any portion of this hemisphere as dangerous to our peace and safety."

Researchers will look in vain for the date of expiration of the Holy Alliance. It dragged on, a lingering shadow, a vague phantom, but it was never officially dissolved. In 1833, Prussia, Austria, and Russia talked Holy Alliance again in Teplitz; and in 1848, Russia's massive intervention to crush rebellion in Hungary was technically based on the vague stipulations of the compact. It is said that the last Tsar, Nicholas II, was inspired by the Holy Alliance in his rescript that led to the unavailing International Peace Conference at The Hague in 1899, and perhaps both the League of Nations and the United Nations contain vague echoes of Baroness Krüdener's preachings.

CHAPTER FIFTY-ONE

By 1816, most of the distinguished visitors had left Vienna, leaving behind hang-over and disillusionment. Back to normal, the currency was worth one third of its already depreciated nominal value; savers again footed the bill, business was slow, unemployment rampant. Yet private initiative made the wheels of industry and commerce turn faster.

Gala parties in the Prater almost ceased, but in the early 1820s the Viennese flocked to the banks of the Danube in quest of a sensational new entertainment: test runs of steamboats. Those who expected infernal catastrophes, explosions with mountains of flames shooting skyward, were disappointed: floating contraptions were at the mercy of the current, their engines not being powerful enough to keep them on an even keel. Safety officials in charge of river traffic eventually forbade further experimentation until improved boats were produced.

Shipbuilding was not Austria's forte. But from England came John Andrews and Joseph Pritchard, and produced steam-powered craft that held their own in the calmer parts of the Danube and rode better and faster than anything previously afloat. People watched, admired, and admitted that those panting mammoths with their odd paddle wheels might be useful innovations. Even the Emperor agreed, but he did not have the stomach to board one of the contraptions.

In April 1828, the two Britishers applied for the exclusive privilege of navigating the Danube with steamships of an improved type. In 1829 the "Imperial-Royal Privileged Steamship Company" was constituted. In 1834 a British globe-trotter, Michael J. Quin, started on one of the longest early steamboat voyages on the Danube, from Pressburg to Galatz, Rumania, and lived to write a book on it, which was widely read in Western Europe.

A motley crowd traveled on the Danube in those days, judging from Mr. Quin's report. The majority of his companions seem to have been Tyrolese, wearing green hats with black-and-white feathers from a cock's tail and bristles of a wild boar. Then there was a party of Hungarian noblemen, playing cards around the clock. Near them lounged a very elegant petite young woman, a countess whose husband had gambled his fortune away and who now went home to mother, with a French maid and a harp, the only vestiges of her short-lived splendor. In Vidin, Bulgaria, he was in a group invited to land and be received by Pasha Hussein.

"We were conducted through an immense crowd to the pasha's palace," he wrote, "which is just at the entrance to the town. Ascending on an open staircase, we were shown, in the first instance, to a large balcony, which commanded a fine view of the river. Here we found the pasha's chief officer sitting in state in the usual Turkish fashion, on a wooden sofa, which was covered with a carpet. He . . . was smoking a long pipe with an ordinary amber mouthpiece, and was surrounded by eight or ten domestics, some of whom were wretchedly attired in the Greek or European dress, barefooted, and wearing on their heads the red Greek cap, which, in fact, is like a red cloth nightcap with a blue silk tassel at the top, and to my mind peculiarly unbecoming. . . .

"The Pasha's chief officer was a fat sickly-looking man, about fifty years of age, and grave even to stupidity. He asked whence we had come, and whither we were going. Having exhausted these topics, he sunk into a sort of Sybarite dreamy torpor, as if the odor of his tobacco were the perfume of paradise. . . .

"At length it was announced that the pasha had returned. Passing through a line of twenty or thirty shabby officers, some of whom were dressed in turbans and covered with silk pelisses, we entered a large plain saloon covered with a blue carpet, and containing no other furniture except a divan or bench hung with yellow damask, which extended all round the room close to the walls. In a dark corner, seated in the usual Turkish attitude, was Hussein, apparently about fifty-five years old, his face deeply marked by the smallpox, swarthy and tremulous, as if he had not been unaccustomed to opium. He wore a dark-olive pelisse, edged with sable fur, and the red Greek cap with its blue silk tassel. He was smoking when we entered, and continued to smoke while we remained.

"On his right was seated, also in the Turkish fashion, his own son by his favorite consort, about ten years old, dressed precisely like his father, beyond all comparison the most beautiful boy I ever beheld.

"Count Széchenyi, who was with our party, stated that he was a nobleman of Hungary appointed by the Emperor of Austria to direct improvements which were necessary to facilitate the navigation on the Danube by steamboats from Pressburg to the Black Sea, whence they might then proceed to Stamboul [Constantinople]. The enterprise, when completed, would be equally advantageous to Turkey as to Hungary, and he availed himself of that opportunity to recommend it to the pasha's protection. Hussein bade the Count welcome, and said that he was very glad to see him, but made no allegation to the enterprise, which he did not appear to comprehend. A pause of one quarter of an hour then ensued, during which we seemed all conscious of being employed in conjecturing how this oppressive silence was next to be broken. At length, the pasha having exhausted his pipe inquired if the Emperor was much liked in Hungary. The Count answered in the affirmative. An effort was then made to prolong the conversation by an allusion to the relations of peace which were now happily established between the Turks and the Hungarians, who had been so long engaged in hostilities; but Hussein cut it short by the maxim that it was always better for men to be at peace with each other than at war. This truism having been pronounced with great self-complacency, a second quarter of an hour elapsed in solemn taciturnity, which was really very embarrassing.

"The assigned period for the generation of another idea having been fully accomplished, the pasha delivered himself of an observation that the Emperor had several officers of distinguished talent in his service. The Count confirmed the justness of this remark, then rose and we took our departure."

Count Stephen Széchenyi was leader of the liberal party in the Hungarian Diet when Quin met him during his trip. In 1847, thirteen years later, Széchenyi came to feel that there was among the candidates for the Diet a man so potentially dangerous that he decided to run for the lower house to keep that demagogue in check.

The demagogue's name was Louis Kossuth. He was born in 1802, in Monok, between the Danube and the Tisza, into an impecunious family of Protestant petty nobility. The Kossuths were of Slovak stock; Slovaks were held in utter contempt in Hungary, yet Kossuth became a fanatical Hungarian nationalist, and eventually a Hungarian national symbol.

He studied law and became the counsel of a wealthy widow. At thirty he was appointed to the Diet as an *absentiist,* that is, personal substitute and reporter to some magnate. Kossuth's magnate was Count Hunyadi.

Kossuth produced exhaustive reports on all sessions of the Diet and verbatim accounts on the most rambling speeches, and sent them not only to Count Hunyadi but also to all the districts of Hungary, where they circulated among the literate minority. Debates in the Diet usually centered around national grievances; Kossuth's "Municipal Accounts" told of "reform parties" which denounced agrarian conditions, of peasants complaining about duties and taxes, of watered-down bills and toothless legislation that benefited nobody, of frustrated attempts to make Hungarian, instead of the archaic Latin, the official language, and of coveted freedoms. The government frowned at such publicity which gave vague popular discontent direction and objective. Kossuth was dismissed and charged with high treason.

His fierce harangues and his defiance of the court catapulted him into the limelight. His defense became the talk of Budapest. Annoyed by his boldness, the court sentenced him to five years in prison, but he did not have to serve in full.

His release from jail—whole, eager, and ambitious—was celebrated by his admirers, who made him their standard bearer of a struggle against every injustice, real or imaginary.

In 1841 the publishers of the newly founded *Pesti Hirlap* (*Pest Newspaper*), looking for a spectacular editor, hired Kossuth, whose editorials turned the newspaper's front page into a periodical beacon which no member of Hungary's intelligentsia could afford to ignore. To keep his popularity, he had always to be one step ahead of other people's reform programs. Since those programs expanded with increasing rapidity, the editorials gained radical momentum with every issue, and when other politicians championed reforms, Kossuth donned the cap and cloak of revolution.

Count Széchenyi wanted betterment of agrarian conditions; Kossuth editorialized about the necessity of changing Hungary's political complexion. Ferencz Deák, the thoughtful, imaginative leader of the opposition, wished to preserve the foundations upon which the Hungarian order rested, but asked for an independent Hungarian cabinet and equality of the law; Kossuth asked secession from Austria and the establishment of a Hungarian republic.

As in the cases of many other men whose names were lit up by the lightning of political storms, it is almost impossible to determine Kossuth's motivation: was it personal ambition or genuine concern with what he considered to be public welfare?

The sultry atmosphere of Hungary was again fraught with riot. Rebellious impulses were as numerous and variegated as were the groups of people in the colorful country. Rebel aristocrats scorned conservative nobles. Catholics feuded with Protestants; intellectuals fought among themselves and jointly aspired at superseding the officials in charge. Serbian, Rumanian, Slavonic, and Ruthenian minorities were against everything Hungarian or German; and Germans and Hungarians were at odds. Demagogues wooed the poor to lead them into a battle in which they had nothing to win. Village feuded with neighboring village, villagers with townspeople.

In September 1847, elections for the Diet were held in Hungary, not popular elections in the true democratic sense, but the most democratic the country had yet known. Count Széchenyi won a seat in the lower chamber, where he hoped to curb Kossuth; Deák was too sick to accept a mandate; Kossuth, in fine health and sonorous voice, scored an overwhelming victory and became leader of the opposition.

The Diet opened on November 7. Emperor Ferdinand, who ruled Austria since 1835, was hailed by all traditionalists and most reformers as King Ferdinand I of Hungary. He delivered the inaugural address, reading from a Hungarian script of which the kindly but simple-minded monarch did not understand one word, and which many deputies could not understand either. Hungarian was proclaimed the official language of the land; and Kossuth, whose Hungarian was flawless, basked in a glory that carried the germs of rebellion.

Came news of another revolution, and proclamation of another republic, in France. In stormy times, opposition leaders usually are afraid of falling behind their counterparts, foreign or domestic, and Kossuth did not wish to fall behind the French. On March 3, 1848, he moved that an "address" to the Emperor be filed (the term "petition" was carefully avoided), requesting a national government for Hungary and a constitution for all other parts of the monarchy. Legally, no member of the Hungarian Diet could make requests concerning other parts of the Empire, but the frightened Palatine of Hungary, Archduke Stephen, hastened to comply and took the document to Vienna.

Everybody in high office was frightened those days; and frightened, with a sprinkle of self-propelling enthusiasm, were also the masses, who felt the ground tremble under trampling feet. Vienna was no less restive than Budapest and other big cities of the Empire. The Emperor could not understand what went on, and his ministers were napping indignantly.

On March 11, 1848, a group of prominent and vocal citizens of Prague gathered in a public bath and drafted a petition to bring the provinces of Bohemia, Moravia, and what remained of Silesia under a common administration.

Polish nationalists ("Polonists") wanted to restore their state within the borders of 1772, and they chose the parts grabbed by Austria as the nucleus of their new country. They were, however, not acclaimed by the peasants, who feared that they would be worse off in a restored Poland; and many ranking nobles, who had been on friendly terms with Vienna, were all but enthusiastic about secession.

The Polonists' southern counterparts were the "Italianissimi," who asked that Venetia, Lombardy, the Tyrol as far north as the Brenner Pass, as well as Trieste and all towns and provinces along the Adriatic, be incorporated into a united Italy, which, in 1848, was an alluring phantom with the nucleus of Sardinia and Piedmont.

Subjects of the Empire, who had lived under the protecting roof of a united realm, suddenly seemed determined to tear it down. Claims, petitions, addresses from outlying provinces flooded into Vienna, which itself seemed to turn into a witches' caldron in which anything but the sensible could happen.

No single individual determined the course of erratic events. Kaleidoscopically changing characters shouted and gesticulated themselves momentarily into the foreground of events. Sensible claims alternated with half-baked emotional demands which their own authors hardly understood, which were hailed and immediately forgotten, but which fanned the general excitement beyond fever pitch. With a strong government any uprising might have been nipped in the bud, but in Vienna of 1848 there was little will, no constructive determination, and only dilettante self-assertion.

The trouble began almost one year before Kossuth made his fateful motion. The Viennese did not like their mayor, one Ignaz Czapka, who did not know how to deal with the latest controversy: retail butchers versus municipal slaughterhouses. Also, the National Bank again printed bank notes on an inflationary scale, and silver coins were scarce. There was unemployment (the number of jobless was under 1000), and soup kitchens and charity balls did not solve the problem. Censorship was the object of many debates; writers objected to the stupid obstinacy of police officials, claiming that they suppressed as subversive whatever they did not understand. All this was annoying, but Vienna had experienced worse without rebellion.

Yet a strange new note pervaded Vienna: nationalism. Nationalism was alien by nature to the capital of a multi-national Empire; it had been imported from Germany. Shiftless elements hailed a nationalist Germany and wanted to join a Reich that its most radical promoters wanted to be a republic. A flare-up of nationalistic radicalism became the most alarming element in the hectic month that preceded the ides of March 1848 in Vienna.

Leaders of reform looked for a program to submit to the Estates. On March 11, 1848, a "Great Petition by the Burghers of Vienna" was adopted by acclamation. In lofty language, it asked for the end of secret fiscal policies, for a united Diet, new press laws, public trials, a new municipal constitution, the establishment of boards of trade and agriculture. If discussed in an atmosphere of calm objectivity, the "Great Petition" could have provided a safety valve against dangerous pressure; if ignored, it might have been shelved among many other well-meant documents. But debated amidst public excitement, it was dangerous.

The government, still wondering what to do about Hungary, Italy, Poland, Bohemia, Moravia, *et al.*, called the Diet of Lower Austria into session on March 13, 1848.

On March 13, nobody who could walk stayed home. The weather favored curiosity. The Estates listened to a flood of oratory, and it seemed a foregone conclusion that the Great Petition would be forwarded to the Imperial government and approved of in principle.

Members of Kossuth's party were present. One of them, Adolf Fischhof, delivered a fiery address in the courtyard of the building of the Estates. Thousands thronged courtyard and corridors, surged into other crowds in adjoining streets and squares. There were chaos, arguments, fisticuffs, but no indication of revolution.

No precautions had been taken. Neither the police nor the mayor dared to make themselves even more unpopular by calling out the militia, and the military did not want to assume responsibility for what they considered civilian business. But when disorder prevailed near the center of the town, heralds of alarm fought their way to City Hall, to the Ministry of Police, to the offices of the garrison commander, to ask for immediate intervention to prevent catastrophe. Everybody was highstrung that day; talk of catastrophe was nonsensical, but it invited disaster. The police did nothing. The civic militia gathered, but very slowly and outside the troubled area. But the military reacted with smart promptness. Several companies, equipped with live ammunition, were rushed to the focal points of the commotion. Few of the soldiers were from Vienna, and the officers had never been taught to handle fundamentally good-natured crowds; besides, they did not believe in good-natured disorderliness.

At 1 P.M. one company forced its way, battering-ram fashion, to the building of the Estates. Officers brandished swords and snarled orders, some people shouted sarcastic remarks. There were more verbal exchanges. The rank and file looked at their officers; their German vocabulary was essentially limited to commands, and they did not know what the shouting was all about. Nobody could tell who then gave the sinister word; perhaps a teen-age platoon commander. Shots were fired. Six persons were hit; but instantly, rumors said that scores had died.

Urged by the panicky mayor, the commanding general of the garrison, Archduke Albrecht, ordered the soldiers back to the barracks. But the streets seethed with clamor for revenge. A subaltern officer or a few uniformed yokels were no satisfactory objects. A great victim had to fall —the greatest of foes, or rather, a superb scapegoat: Metternich.

At seventy-five still the embodiment of all governmental power, the Chancellor was the target of all liberal groups, a man whom hardly anybody loved—a scorner of the post-Napoleonic generation, a derider of progress in public affairs, who stood for everything which champions of perpetual political motion wanted to abolish. The fact that he was an unflinching patriot, a loyal, incorruptible servant of his Emperor, was not held to his credit.

A State Conference was in session in the Imperial town castle, a few hundred yards away from the site of the shooting. Metternich presided. Delegates of the Estates and civic groups appeared, demanding his immediate resignation.

In her memoirs, Princess Metternich wrote: "After Archduke Ludwig had listened to the request, which was presented in the rudest manner by students, professors, burghers, and God only knows whom else, and had seen the threatening attitude of some intruders and the panicky fear of others, he brought himself to tell the man who, for almost fifty years, had been the most solid pillar of the monarchy, that the safety of the capital depended on his resignation."

Prince Metternich, whose word once had shaped the destiny of the continent, resigned without protest—a disillusioned old man who left Vienna the same night for a self-chosen exile. When he returned three years later, he was a mere relic that lived on for another eight years to find that the changed world was not much changed, and hardly improved.

While the Archduke talked to the delegation, looters were on the loose in the suburbs, led on by obscure rabble rousers, who appealed to instincts of hunger. The civic militia could not restore order, and only after university students were armed did the looting grind to a halt.

March 14 saw the establishment of a permanent National Guard and the abolition of censorship. Cheering crowds festooned the monument of Emperor Joseph II and put a black-red-golden flag into its brass hand. Black, red, and gold were the colors of pan-Germany, Model 1848.

On the following day, an Imperial manifesto proclaimed the adoption of a constitution; this was a promissory note, since the constitution was not even drafted. Emperor Ferdinand signed anything his ministers submitted. All he wanted was to be left alone.

He was not left alone, though. His personal popularity and that of various members of his family should serve to cement the shaken regime of his land. Ferdinand and his brother Franz Karl were packed into an open carriage and driven through the city streets. The citizens were delirious with aimless enthusiasm, and their cheers also soared to yet another passenger in the Imperial conveyance, a handsome, slender youth not yet eighteen; Franz Karl's oldest son, Franz Joseph.

That night the city was illuminated. There were manifestations of fervent patriotism. Forgotten were outbursts of looting, scorned were the rabble rousers who had rediscovered the term "communism" from the backlog of the French Revolution. Jubilantly Viennese greeted a millennium the nature of which they could not explain.

Kossuth and more Hungarian deputies arrived, proclaiming that they had come as brethren whose cause was identical with the Austrian. The common slogan was "Freedom." Any variation of freedom. The Viennese cheered.

Playwright Johann Nestroy wrote in one of his unforgettable couplets: "When freedom becomes communism, it ceases to be fun." Poet Franz Grillparzer commented: "Once they called me a radical, now they call me a reactionary. Maybe I'm just sensible." But the meaning of "sensible" was hard to define in mounting sound and fury.

On March 16 the mayor resigned and fled. On March 17 Minister of Police Count Sedlnitzky was out of office and out of town. One month before, when he had still camouflaged his ineptness with a veil of vicious arrogance, he had seemed to be an immense power. Now he was unmasked as a scarecrow blown asunder by a gust of wind.

Also on March 17 a lugubrious celebration took place: some of the wounded in the shooting had died; they received a state funeral, which had a tremendous psychological effect.

On March 18 a responsible cabinet and a municipal committee were appointed. The basic objectives of the liberals seemed achieved, but the emotional dust did not settle.

Archduke Ludwig negotiated with Kossuth, who demanded that Hungary receive full national sovereignty; no bond other than a common ruler should remain between Austria and Hungary, and his prerogatives must be held to a minimum to make the bond nominal. Over the Archduke's opposition, defeatist Ferdinand signed Kossuth's draft. On April 10 he journeyed to Pressburg to sign yet another document: thirty-one Hungarian articles of law by which a new cabinet was set up. It included Count Széchenyi, who, however, felt powerless, went insane, and soon committed suicide. Kossuth held the portfolio of finance.

As of June 5, 1848, Pest became the seat of the new Hungarian government. The monarchy now had two foreign ministries, two sets of finances, two armies. . . . The common ruler was a figurehead; the only obvious ties that remained were economical ones: Austria's manufacturers needed the Hungarian market, and Hungary's agriculture needed the Austrian consumer.

On April 25 the adopted constitution was promulgated. In March the document would have enthused even the most progressive people; but now masses gathered in the explosive suburbs were told that the "goal of the revolution" had not yet been reached.

New waves of excitement rose also in the provinces. Archduke Franz Joseph left Vienna for the headquarters of Field Marshal Count Radetzky in Italy.

On March 17, the day of the state funeral in Vienna, revolution had broken out in Milan and Venice. Austrian Viceroy Archduke Rainer left in less than dignified hurry. On March 22 rebels seized the arsenal of Venice; the civilian governor, Count Zichy, signed an inglorious compact to the effect that all non-Italian troops would be withdrawn and a provisional government established. Venice was again a republic, and Daniele Manin its President.

Street battles raged in Milan. A bombardment would have quenched the outbreak, but Radetzky preferred to abandon the city and to concentrate farther east. Octogenarian Radetzky had long warned the indolent government of widespread unrest. Vienna had respectfully acknowledged his warnings, but sent no reinforcements.

Radetzky's parting proclamation to the Milanese was: "We shall return."

On March 23 King Charles Albert of Sardinia and Piedmont declared war on Austria, certain that his army of 70,000 would accomplish what he and the "Italianissimi" wanted.

The Viennese did not like events in Italy, however. This was not the sort of revolution they wanted. A group of volunteers joined Radetzky.

But as they started on their voyage south, the Archbishop of Vienna was booed by an extremist riffraff, and public gatherings heard orators lament the oppression of Jews, the poverty of the Poles, and high local rents.

King Charles Albert of Sardinia issued a victory bulletin: "On April 7 near Goito, the Austrian army has ceased to exist. Forty thousand prisoners surrendered to the sword of Italy. Radetzky, both his legs crushed, was dragged tied to the tail of his horse, the entire army applauding. Verona has capitulated; all enemy flags, cannon, and baggage are captured. The number of enemy dead is incalculable."

However, the facts of Goito were: two Austrian battalions had fought some rear-guard action at the cost of fifty-five casualties and sixty-eight missing. Radetzky was not there. Verona did not hear a sound of the skirmish, and the Austrians engaged did not have a single cannon.

Twenty-nine days later the first large-scale engagement of the war took place near Santa Lucia. The Austrian victory could not be fully exploited due to the shortage of forces on hand. But twenty-five thousand more soldiers were scraped together from garrisons on the Adriatic east coast, and on July 25, the Italians suffered another defeat, near Custozza. King Charles Albert hoped to hold Milan with forty thousand hastily mobilized, poorly trained "National Guards," but he could not even control the *Barabba,* a riotous mob that terrorized the town and looted the adjoining countryside. The peasants were so angry that they greeted the advancing Austrians with shouts of *"Vengono i nostro* [Our men are coming]," and the Milanese joyfully lined the streets when, on August 6, Radetzky returned.

And all the time a maze of slogans and half-baked ideas kept Vienna and much of the provinces in a state of explosive foment.

Suffrage was granted, but its limitations provided ammunition to both demagogues and true idealists, and there was clamor for guarantees against repeal of any reform. Clubs formed in Vienna, like those in Paris three years before. "Storm petitions" were the vogue, rabid crowds presented demands which they hardly understood, and the procrastinating cabinet said yes, careful not to ask questions.

On May 17 Emperor Ferdinand slipped out of his capital and went to Innsbruck, three hundred miles away, where the atmosphere still had a touch of sanity.

A few Viennese journalists suggested proclamation of a republic, but the crowd which they addressed made mien to hang them on the lampposts.

On May 26, for no obvious reason the government ordered the Academic Legion (armed students) dissolved. The students had not so far sided with elements of disorder, but now they began to erect barricades which were manned by a threatening mob that had nothing to do with the University. And while a deputation of writers traveled to Innsbruck to implore the weary Emperor to return to "the loving citizens of his faithful capital," the Viennese themselves did not quite know what government they had, if any. The printers of the official daily, *Wiener Zeitung,* deleted the Imperial Eagle from the front page of the May 29 issue. Emperor Ferdinand stayed in Innsbruck.

There was an uncontrolled outpour of poetry in Vienna, Frankfurt, almost everywhere on the continent. "For the printers it's a golden year," Nestroy exclaimed.

From Dresden, Richard Wagner made a fourteen-stanza contribution to the poetic accompaniment of confusion, called "Greetings from Saxony." He himself arrived in Vienna early in June. "As I hardly ever undertook anything without a serious purpose," he wrote in his memoirs, "I intended to use my trip to Vienna to introduce effectively my ideas for a theatrical reform."

But the Viennese then had no use for the disgruntled composer-conductor from Saxony. They again hailed Radetzky; and the march which Johann Strauss, Father, a traditionalist par excellence, wrote in his honor and first performed on the "Water Glacis" (now the *Stadtpark*) is the only topical composition from that turbulent year that has survived. Other musical expressions of exuberance—such as the *March of the National Guard,* the *Liberty March,* the *March of the Student Legion,* and a few pieces by Johann Strauss, Son, the later "Waltz King," whom rebellion against his overly strict father turned into a short-term radical—are practically forgotten.

Revolution also had its impact on opera production. When, in July 1848, Giuseppe Verdi's *Macbeth* was performed in Budapest, King Duncan did not enter Macbeth's castle to the music of the composer, then technically an Austrian subject, but to the strains of the *Rákóczy March.*

Radetzky's popularity seemed to augur well for the Emperor's return. Ferdinand reluctantly agreed to go to Vienna, but he was perturbed by bush-fire battles up in various parts of the realm. There had been shooting in Kraków and serious street fighting in Prague. Vienna was unpredictable; and Hungary, a caldron that would have scared even Macbeth's witches, was right at Vienna's back door.

CHAPTER FIFTY-TWO

In Hungary, revolution seemed to be in perpetual motion, new issues constantly bursting into blaze, fanned by wild intolerance as only self-righteous fanaticism can beget. From Hungary, sparks of riot spread in every direction, searing even the Turkish government and making Russia gird for intervention.

Soldiers in Hungary, regardless of origin, had to take the oath on the new constitution. Several Austrian crack units were stationed there. The men's Hungarian vocabulary consisted of *igen* and *nem,* yes and no; they had no idea what they swore to obey and protect, but the inexplicable hypnotic effect of military ceremonial made them robotlike tools.

The new Hungarian Minister of War was Colonel Lázár Meszaros, a parlor radical whom the Hungarian-speaking military had surnamed *as öreg ficzko,* the old fop. Distrustful of professionals, he organized a new militia, *Honved,* from elements that were attracted by lavish rations of wine and a pay that seemed comparatively high in that land where cash was short though in rapid circulation.

The Magyarization of Hungary was championed by magnates, intellectuals, and rabble rousers, most of whom spoke only crude Hungarian. Many civil servants, clergymen, and judicial authorities were helpless; Serbian-, German-, and Rumanian-speaking groups, resentful.

In Transylvania province of Hungary, Rumanians wanted to secede, Magyars to unite with nationalistic Hungary, Germans to stay with Austria; the result was a civil war of repulsive ferocity.

The Serbs in Hungary resolved that they were a free nation, that they should have their own territory and form an alliance with Croatia, Slavonia, and Dalmatia. Count Joseph Jelačić, ban (viceroy) of those provinces, put them under the jurisdiction of Vienna.

Serbs from the Balkans crossed the Danube in small boats for what they expected to become free territory carved out of Hungary. They battled against local Hungarians with obsolete long-barreled muskets, cavalry pistols, and long sharp knives, called yataghans. Prisoners were nailed to church doors or fried at a spit.

Slavs in Hungary argued and struggled among themselves, and the Slavs in the Austrian parts of the tottering realm poured oil in the blaze of disunity. At a Slav Congress in Prague, a lone voice of wisdom, that of historian František Palacký, spoke up: "If the Austrian Empire would not already exist, the interest of Europe, and of all mankind, would require that it be created." The Congress booed him with such vigor that he had to leave.

The paupers of Vienna rioted. The number of jobless rose. The city hired them for digging and carting, and since nothing profitable resulted from the emergency program, daily pay was reduced by the equivalent of two cents, which infuriated the diggers and carters. Late in August, they clashed with the municipal guard and suffered several casualties. The Emperor again left for Innsbruck.

Archduke Johann, who had been late for the Battle of Wagram thirty-nine years before, acted as regent. He was considered a progressive, because he had gone into business as a gentleman farmer, winegrower, and industrialist, and a democrat, because he had married a commoner; but he was inept as a skipper of the floundering craft of state.

When Radetzky had asked for reinforcements, parliamentarians in Pest, still awed by his name, had considered sending soldiers to Italy. But Kossuth delivered a fanatical address that Hungary needed its army for the protection of the Magyar fatherland and that it was not threatened by Italian revolutionaries, but by reaction and by Russia.

Parliament voted to mobilize 200,000 men and to spend 42 million for equipment to protect the fatherland.

Russia also mobilized, not so much at first for an armed intervention in Hungary, but to fish in troubled waters with a mailed fist.

From Croatia and Slavonia came news that Ban Jelačić intended to intervene in Hungary, unless it return at once into the fold of the monarchy. But the Hungarian government refused to recognize Jelačić as a ban, and Vienna did not back this quixotically loyal man.

August 1848 saw the political waters of the lower Danube sufficiently troubled to set the Russian fisherman angling. Riots spread from Transylvania into Moldavia and Walachia. The Turks sent troops to restore order, but when the Russians invaded the provinces as "pacifiers" on their own terms, Turkey did not give battle.

On September 4, Emperor Ferdinand granted unrestricted political powers to Jelačić. Eight days later three Croat divisions and an army corps of Serbian nationals were ready to march up the Danube Valley to Budapest.

Chaos shook the Hungarian government. Rioters, shouting Magyar slogans, dominated the streets. The Emperor dissolved the Hungarian Diet and put Jelačić in charge of all forces in Hungary. Kossuth countered by proclaiming Jelačić a traitor and putting General Moga in charge. In turn, the Austrian Minister of War, Count Théodore Baillet-Latour, released the Hungarian soldiers from their oath to the Pest government, but news of this action never reached the rank and file.

General Moga was an experienced professional; he had only 35,000 soldiers as against Jelačić's 50,000, but through clever maneuvering forced him to veer off to Austria. Moga's Hungarians crossed the border near Hainburg on the Danube.

Emperor Ferdinand packed again; this time he went to Olmütz, Moravia, where all was quiet.

Latour mustered a few battalions of Vienna's garrison to join Jelačić. The first battalion departed under hostile demonstrations, the second mutinied in the barracks and had to be escorted by cavalry to its points of departure. Rioters, joined by National Guardsmen and rebellious legionnaires, blocked its road across the Danube Canal bridges. Latour dispatched a third battalion, some cavalry, and three cannon to Tabor Bridge. A free-for-all resulted. Battalion Two fought Battalion Three, rioters charged the cavalry, and the cannoneers lost their pieces to legionnaires and National Guardsmen.

Somebody ordered the city gates closed, which shut out the rest of the garrison camping in suburban barracks—several battalions under General Count Auersperg. Triumphant rioters fought among themselves for no obvious reason, when a watchword fell, a hated name: Latour.

From St. Stephen's Square masses converged on the Ministry of War only a few hundred yards away, invaded Latour's office, beat the elderly general unconscious, and hung him on the lattice of his window; when the rope snapped they dragged the still breathing man out into the square and strung him up on a lamppost. Nobody had the courage to condemn the murder. Trampling brutes dominated the sordid scene. Authorities made no attempt to restore order.

That same day, the Emperor drove out of Schönbrunn Castle, a nervous wreck. The Hungarians were thirty miles away.

The shutout battalions had left the suburbs. The National Guard remained in the city. It was under the command of Wenzel Messenhauser, a native of Moravia, a poet, and a former first lieutenant, decent, well-meaning, and muddleheaded, who had no idea how to hold a big city against a field army. He found an adviser in "General" Joseph Bem, a native of the Austrian slice of Poland, who had won his military spurs in Poland's ill-fated uprising against the Russians in 1830. Dark-bearded Messenhauser and round-faced "General" Bem spent much of their time on the steeple of St. Stephen's, looking out for the Hungarians, while the National Guard underwent drill and the streets were controlled by a mob led by demagogues.

On October 21, Moga with 30,000 moved upstream, along the route of invasion of the old Magyars. He could have handled Jelačić, but another Imperial army, 40,000 men under Field Marshal Prince Windischgrätz, was on the march. The tall, gray-haired, sharp-featured Prince had full powers to deal with the situation in and around the capital as he deemed fit, and he had no intention of dillydallying.

From Lundenburg (Břeclav), in southern Moravia, he appealed to Vienna to surrender. Nobody in Vienna had the power, nor the courage.

Windischgrätz advanced rapidly, Moga slowly. On October 23, Windischgrätz's army crossed the Danube near Nussdorf, in the vineyards where carefree Viennese used to enjoy their *Heurigen*. While the Prince encamped in the suburb of Hetzendorf, Moga held a war council in Nikolsdorf, east of Vienna. Kossuth, just arrived from Budapest, presided. Moga wanted to wait, even to return to Hungary and gather stronger forces for a showdown with the Imperials. Kossuth insisted that the Hungarians open the way to Vienna at once. The reluctant military were powerless against the stormy civilian.

On October 24, Windischgrätz's troops crossed the Danube Canal, opposed by fighting radicals. Jelačić's Croats turned up in the eastern suburbs and committed untold atrocities.

On October 25, Messenhauser proclaimed a state of siege. From Olmütz, Emperor Ferdinand's decree-signing pen appointed a new government with General Prince Felix Schwarzenberg, Windischgrätz's brother-in-law, as Prime Minister.

The Hungarians had not yet decamped. Kossuth got impatient.

On October 26, Windischgrätz's artillery opened up, causing several fires in the center of the city. Another deputation tried to obtain easier terms, but he would do no more than wait twenty-four hours to give moderates and prudents in Vienna time to subdue the radicals. But moderates and prudents hardly ever subdue the radicals.

On October 28, a general attack opened, in which the rebels fought desperately to gain time. Next morning the Hungarians crossed the Fischa River; by midday they closed in on the city. At Schwechat, Moga's army was shaken by well-aimed artillery fire; from his lookout on St. Stephen's,

Messenhauser saw the Hungarian army falter, break, and run. Only Jelačić's inefficiency saved the Hungarians from annihilation.

Messenhauser asked members of the Municipal Council to plead for twenty-four more hours of grace in which to carry out surrender. They got twelve hours. Meantime, radicals inside the city spread word that the Hungarians had won near Schwechat, and they resolved to make a sortie led by either Bem or Messenhauser. Bem was nowhere to be found, and Messenhauser mustered all his courage to urge them not to interfere with capitulation. He knew that he had forfeited his life, but he wanted to see the city and many more lives spared. His sudden magnificent courage lent power of conviction to his words.

But fanatics did not forgo all further violence. The city gate near the Imperial castle remained barricaded. The army used artillery to force its way into the Inner City, while outlaws set houses afire. At nightfall of October 31, Vienna was in the hands of the army. The complexion of the streets changed as if by magic. The radicals vanished. Jubilant traditionalists hailed the soldiers. The army proclaimed martial law. There was no resistance against disarmament; the dissolution of clubs was a mere formality, everybody disclaiming membership.

Bem escaped. Messenhauser surrendered. He did not plead innocent and remained steadfast to the end that came on November 23, before a firing squad.

Soon Vienna was back to normal. Poet Friedrich Hebbel wrote on November 26: "Vienna is its old *gemütlich* self again. Elegant promenaders jam sidewalks, carriages roll through the streets, shops glitter in accustomed splendor. At windows previously adorned by pictures of the Ciceroes of our own Parliament, a dozen Magyars, and some of our latest pilots of state, we now see the likenesses of Windischgrätz, Jelačić, and Radetzky."

And also by Hebbel is this summary of the 1848 revolution in Vienna: "Liberty was, temporarily at least, overcome by impudence. But most of the ultra-radicals have eventually run away. Less extreme elements try to hide, but they deserve no better than reaction's punishment. Excesses by anarchists must be restrained to prevent complete ruin. History shall determine whether this was done in the proper way, and at the right moment. It is impossible, though, to return to the old track. People should be told: 'Keep from the old times what is good, and add sensible innovations. Thus you will establish an edifice of state the existence of which does not depend on chance.'"

To Viennese dismay, the government did not, at first, return to the city. Frustrated politicians assembled in Kremsier (Kroměříž), a somnolent little town in Moravia, and selected Franz Smolka, a Polish lawyer, as chairman. Smolka was a stanch believer in the Austrian monarchy, a man of tact and intelligence, but even a man of genius could hardly have led the Reichstag to solve the complex problems of the realm. Besides, a rather stupid military and ministerial quasi dictatorship constantly interfered with parliamentary activities.

On December 2, 1848, Emperor Ferdinand made the first decision of his own in a long time: he resigned. His brother, Franz Karl, who would have been next in line, renounced his claim in favor of his own son, Franz Joseph, who became Emperor at the age of eighteen years, three months, and two weeks.

The last act of the great drama of Habsburg began. What came after Franz Joseph I was a brief, melancholy epilogue, and long, sterile, regret.

The change of sovereigns took place in the stately hall of the Kremsier summer palace of the Archbishop of Olmütz. All members of the Imperial House and all cabinet members (except the Hungarians) were present. Ferdinand, aged fifty-five, spoke a few sentences, and hardly listened when a high official read circumstantially worded state papers making the renunciation final. While the official's voice droned on in the stately hall, Prime Minister Prince Schwarzenberg made the announcement to lesser dignitaries elsewhere in the palace.

Chroniclers, anxious to dramatize history, tell how Franz Joseph, overwhelmed by emotion, knelt down before his uncle Ferdinand to receive his blessings. Another version quotes the new Emperor as having said, in French: *"Adieu ma jeunesse"* ("Farewell my youth"). Franz Joseph was not emotional by nature, but the circumstances under which he assumed his exalted dignity were frightening. Nothing but extremely good fortune could help a man to enjoy his youth on the throne, and honest, honorable, straightforward Franz Joseph was not a lucky man. Ferdinand went to Prague and lived at Hradčany Castle, a distinguished, well-meaning, unsophisticated squire, for another twenty-seven years.

Franz Joseph, whose education had been supervised by men whose political views were old-fashioned and whose military science was based on the Napoleonic Wars, signed his first manifesto, drafted by the Prime Minister on the day of his enthronement.

"Firmly resolved to keep the glory of the crown serene, but ready to share Our prerogatives with the representatives of Our peoples, We trust that, with the help of God, and in harmony with the peoples, it will be possible to unite all lands and tribes of the monarchy into one body of

state." This was a pronunciamento in favor of representative government, and "one body of state" seemed to imply that Hungary's autonomy
would be curtailed in favor of centralism. However, there was a long
circuitous way from the manifesto to the next fundamental law, and not
before May 1849 did the young Emperor establish himself in Vienna.

The Reichstag in Kremsier formed a commission to draft a basic
law superseding the Constitution. Most Austrians were indifferent to the
point of apathy. At Christmas of 1848 its first version was ready. It
opened with the statement: "All powers emanate from the people and are
to be exercised in the manner stipulated by the Constitution." Points
provided equality before the law, individual freedom, public trial, in-
violability of the home, privacy of letters, freedom of religion, press, and
tuition, abolition of compulsory military duty.

A nervous government objected to the leading sentence, claiming that
the powers actually emanated from the rights of monarch and Parliament. The drafters protested, then deleted the phrase and proceeded to
other matters. František Palacký had worked out the pattern of a national federation according to which, in his opinion, the country should
be governed. His plan divided the people of Austria and Hungary into
eight national groups: Germans, Czechs, Poles, Italians, Yugoslavs,
Hungarians, Ruthenians, and Walachians. It was a bold pattern, but the
best to emerge from the deliberations. Deputies debated and offered no
real support, and the Imperial cabinet simply did not understand its
merits.

But another draft was hailed in Kremsier. It implied far-reaching centralization: a two-chamber Parliament would be the central legislature;
provincial Diets would exercise very limited powers. Most deputies expected that this version would be unanimously accepted on the anniversary of the March uprisings.

Their expectations were badly frustrated. On March 7, troops invaded the building in which the Reichstag was in session, and the district commissar of Olmütz handed Smolka an Imperial manifesto dated
March 4, 1849, for immediate proclamation: the Reichstag was dissolved, and another constitution was to be introduced by octroi in the
entire monarchy. Smolka refused to proclaim the manifesto. The district
commissar shrugged his shoulders and had it posted on the main square
in front of the general store. This was the end of the 1848 Parliament.

The author of the octroi constitution was not the Emperor, but his
Minister of Interior, Count Johann Stadion. The document still adhered
to parliamentarism. A lower chamber was to be popularly elected, mem-

bers of an upper chamber should be appointed by the ruler. There were no elections, though. All Austrian constitutions were abrogated by Imperial rescript of December 31, 1851.

The Viennese accepted the octroi without grumble; many hailed the end of parliamentarism. Count Auersperg, under his pen name of Anastasius Grün, wrote: "Not within a decade would anything have been accomplished in Kremsier. Constant revolutionizing would have destroyed the achievements of centuries of education, prosperity, propriety, art, and science."

Vienna turned ultraconservative; its people attended a *Te Deum* at St. Stephen's, gala performances in all local theaters, and when somebody arranged a requiem for the victims of March 1848, attendance was small and markedly unenthusiastic.

Austrian deputies returned from Frankfurt, unacclaimed. Pan-Germanism in Austria appeared to have run its unavailing course. A tight union between Austria and the Reich seemed feasible only in the form of a Greater Austria, and the Viennese government did not consider this desirable.

However, while Viennese reveled in loyalism, events in Hungary moved from one crisis to another; revolution ran its course.

The freedom that Hungary wanted became ever harder to define in constitutional terms. It was emotional, a happy dream, that should bring everything to everybody; but all it could bring, at first, was battle, destruction, and disaster.

The people of Hungary had no control over events. The men who assumed leadership were prisoners of their own enthusiasm and of the fighting determination it generated. The Imperial generals assigned to deal with Hungary had come to handle the land that was a traditional part of their Emperor's patrimony like a hereditary enemy.

Right after the battle of Schwechat, Kossuth replaced Moga by General Arthur Görgey. Kossuth had not much love for Görgey, who did not see eye to eye with him on strategic matters, and he considered this an interim appointment.

Meantime, Windischgrätz advanced down the Danube Valley, took Pressburg and Györ against little resistance, told a delegation of the Hungarian Parliament that there could be no negotiations with rebels, and entered Budapest on January 5, 1849.

Kossuth fled east to Debrecen, taking his most ardent followers and the bank-note printing presses along. The rest of the campaign could have been a mopping-up operation had Windischgrätz understood that his task was not fulfilled with the occupation of Budapest and that Kossuth would not give up as long as he could draft men and print money.

Bem had traveled to Budapest, by canoe on the Danube, and Kossuth had appointed him commander of the insurrection in Transylvania. The man who had won no distinction in Austria, excelled in Hungary. As a Pole who did not stand for Magyar supermanhood, he won the Rumanians' favor and restored peace between them and the Magyar nationalists. As an organizer, he succeeded in mobilizing thousands of able-bodied volunteers, and as a military man, he outwitted dull old General Baron Anton Puchner at every turn.

Meantime Debrecen was no longer a precarious haven, but the seat of a government ready to strike out for control of the entire land. A Hungarian Committee of National Defense undertook a full mobilization. One hundred and twenty thousand men and 828 cannon were set afoot. The elite and hard core of this force were twenty former Imperial infantry battalions and ten cavalry regiments, ready to fight their own countrymen with savagely blind dedication. Arthur Görgey was, at last, put in full command. In April, he defeated Windischgrätz, Jelačić, and Schlick in rapid succession. His army performed veritable miracles of courage; the men were carried away by a tempest of temperamental and illogical enthusiasm.

When the octroi constitution was posted, Kossuth went before Parliament, which continued in session in Debrecen. A motion was accepted, declaring that the House of Habsburg, "having perjured itself before God and men," had forfeited its right to rule Hungary and was banished forever. Kossuth, proclaimed Governor of Hungary, was at the peak of his powers, which far exceeded those any Habsburg ruler had ever wielded.

Debrecen, normally a moderately gay, spacious provincial town, was crowded beyond capacity with refugees, politicians, and fortune hunters, who all hailed the Governor and battled for places on his thunderous band wagon.

On May 3, a radiant day, Görgey's superior army arrived under the walls of Buda. The ancient fortress town, which in the turbulent course of history had been besieged by various conquerors from the East, was now under attack by a motley of troops, carrying the Hungarian flag. On May 21, they stormed the ramparts. Again the waters of the Danube were reddened with blood. The Imperial commander held one last fort. When the pressure of the assault became overwhelming, he blew it up himself.

On June 6, Kossuth made his ceremonious entry into the captured city, and Parliament transferred its sessions to the capital. This climax of Kossuth's career marked the beginning of a rapid, dismal end.

Austria might have been unable to restore its kind of order, but Tsar Nicholas I was determined to intervene in strength, since the situation seemed wrought with danger for his own regime. Polish patriots were in a fighting mood again; Hungary's example stimulated their hopes for national independence. Russia hinted to Austria that a request for help would be granted; and the request was made at once. Soon the Hungarians faced 300,000 enemies.

Rapidly moving battle lines ranged crisscross through the country; warfare was most ruthless toward the civilian population, which was dizzy with fear and despair. Russian soldiers again brought the cholera to Hungary, which raged unchecked.

Blow after blow hit the Hungarian forces. June 1849, the month that had witnessed the deceptive triumph of Budapest, also witnessed a series of Hungarian defeats, ushering in total disaster.

On June 28, Emperor Franz Joseph himself saw action, when Győr was recaptured by the Austrians. Riding over the scorched bridge across the Danube, the nineteen-year-old monarch entered the smoldering city. On July 11, the Austrians were back in Budapest. Kossuth resigned his governorship only one month later. He left Görgey nominal dictatorial powers, saying that only a soldier could save the nation. But the only way to save the nation was surrender, which took place on August 13, 1849, on the heath of Szöllös, near the small town of Világos (Şiria).

But the fighting in the tortured land did not stop until October 2, 1849. Kossuth fled to Turkey; with him went several political refugees, soon joined by soldiers, including Polish volunteers. The fugitives were, at first, interned near Vidin on the lower Danube. Later the Turkish government suggested that they adopt Mohammedanism, which would have barred their extradition. Kossuth did not become a Mohammedan, but Bem was converted and joined the Sultan's army. Amurath Pasha, who, in 1850, supressed an Arab revolt in Aleppo, was none other than "General" Joseph Bem!

Kossuth stayed in Turkey for two years, then left for France aboard an American warship. In Marseilles, he was barred from traveling through the country because his passage might have caused demonstrations in favor of revolution. He proceeded to England and spent three weeks there, lionized as the champion of a "magnificent cause." Wherever Kossuth went, legend preceded him. In America, too, where he insisted on being addressed as "Governor," he was hailed and showered with acclamations, but his reputation was marred by other Hungarian exiles, who, according to the Encyclopaedia Britannica, "accused him of arrogance, cowardice, and duplicity."

Kossuth was one of the rare revolutionaries who reached biblical age. He never saw Hungary again. He made various unsuccessful, but widely propagandized, attempts to intervene in wars which involved Austria in the 1850s and 1860s, and in 1867, when another Hungarian Parliament was elected, under a new constitution, he was made an absentee deputy of one district of Budapest. He did not avail himself of a general amnesty to return and take his seat in the lower chamber. When, in 1879, a law deprived of citizenship anybody who had been absent for more than ten years, Kossuth legally ceased to be a Hungarian. He died in Turin, Italy, in 1894, a never forgotten man. Revolutionists who retire under an amnesty are easily scorned; those who die in exile never are. His body was taken to Budapest and he got a hero's funeral. An indestructible Kossuth legend found its expression in the obsequies. Not even the all-out pro-Habsburg textbooks of the kingdom ever attempted to downgrade the man whose "arrogance, cowardice, and duplicity" were undeniable.

In 1849, the Austrian victors showed little leniency toward rebels whom they caught. Military tribunals meted out heavy sentences. Among those who died on the gallows were members of ranking nobility. Large estates were confiscated. But Görgey, whose opposition to Kossuth was appreciated, was spared. He went to Austria and lived there in quiet retirement, while the army would sorely need his talents in the campaigns against Prussia and France.

It is occasionally claimed that Kossuth, before escaping to Turkey, buried the Crown of St. Stephen, the symbol of legal rule in Hungary. Actually, this already mythical relic was hidden by Bartalani von Szemere, in a forest near the Danubian bank. Szemere also reached Turkey. The crown and other hidden regalia were soon recovered, and they figured in the ceremonial under which Franz Joseph was reinstalled as King of Hungary when the last constitution established Austria-Hungary as a dual monarchy.

The present whereabouts of the Crown of St. Stephen are not established beyond doubt. It is said that it escaped the grasp of the Communist regime and was hidden in a safe place, so that one day it may return to a rightful holder.

CHAPTER FIFTY-THREE

The Walachians, whom Palacký had viewed as one of the national groups which should play an equal part in a reorganized Austria, were, in fact, the most backward of all nationalities along the Danube.

Ever since 1526, with short intervals, the Turks had been the dominant power along the lower Danube and in what later became, in 1859, Rumania. Austria, Hungary, and Russia interfered from the fringes of that land, which was a treasure chest by nature's generosity, a backward slum through man's neglect.

After the Tatar flood subsided, practically nothing changed in these regions. Governmental actions hardly affected the primitive plowmen who worked the fertile fields with methods that would have been frowned upon by the ancient Egyptians; the cattlemen who did not know how to improve their herds; and fishermen who braved the waters of the great river to catch sturgeon, sheat, and pike and who were prevented by their taskmasters from enjoying their treasures.

Historians who search archives for documents to prove that there has always been some sort of Rumania can hardly discover more than a report that Michael the Brave "freed and reunited all Rumanian territory." Michael, idol of nationalistic textbooks, ruled from 1593 to 1601, and called himself "Prince of all the lands of Hungro-Walachia, Transylvania, and Moldavia." His regime was never firmly established, and as soon as Turkey tightened the reins again, every vestige of independence vanished.

The lands which Michael is alleged to have ruled had to pay tribute to the Turkish government. Collectors grew rich, even though they were not remarkable for longevity. All along the line from tribute collectors to Grand Vizier, greedy men cheated and were killed by superior grafters. Oriental despotism throve on corruption. Corruption was an industry upon which not only the hierarchy but the national economy depended.

In 1716, an ingenious Turkish government found that hereditary rulership did not bring maximum returns in bribes. The job of voivode, renamed "hospodar" (leading official), was put on sale.

Nothing but hard cash was accepted, a minimum of a million dollars (present currency) for an unspecified term in office. Appointees drew no official salary, but were responsible for the collection of taxes and tributes throughout the provinces.

Methods of taxation were diabolically effective. The peasants had to pay dues for everything they owned, from their dwellings—compared to which a Western pigsty seems luxurious and sanitary—to the rags on their backs, not to speak of such proud possessions as cattle or bees.

In the 1740s a movement of migration started. The peasants began to cross the Danube into Turkey proper (which then included Bulgaria), where official inefficiency made life a little more bearable, and also into the Hungarian districts of Transylvania and the Banat, where a distant Imperial government was paternalistic as compared with the Turkish regime and its upshots. Austrian military statisticians reported that half of the 147,000 peasant families living in Walachia in 1741, left within four years, and almost three fourths within a decade. These figures seem exaggerated, however, since the hospodars would have found ways and means to prevent such a disastrous loss of taxpayers.

The lands became a fertile poorhouse, and occasionally a battleground. Within one century Walachia had a turnover of forty-one hospodars, Moldavia of thirty-six; the Turkish government wanted to collect the appointment fee as frequently as possible, so it recalled hospodars for accounting and often found them derelict in their duties. They had not only to amortize their original investment but to gather reserves to bribe investigators, and, last but not least, to make an exorbitant profit, within an average of less than three years!

Provincial boundaries fluctuated as the power of Turkey's neighbors rose. After Prince Eugene's victories, Austria occupied the land between the Iron Gate, the Carpathian range, and the rivers Danube and Olt. Austrian administrators reported that local taxes had been levied upon bees, wine, pigs, tobacco, horned cattle, sheep, hay, smoked fish, cloth, and chimneys—in that order. The hospodars had collected the taxes several times over by methods which included flogging and torture. Yet so great were the land's natural resources that the Austrians still found 1,000,000 horses, 50,000 head of cattle, 300,000 sheep, and 200,000 beehives. The Austrians reduced dues and were less arbitrary and corrupt in their collection methods, but the soldiers were a rough lot, whose behavior was outright scandalous. Austria ruled the district for twenty years, during which few wrongs were righted.

And all the time, an expansionistic Russia aimed at annexing Moldavia and Walachia and rolling the Turks back to the Balkans and beyond, possibly out of Europe.

Napoleon never went to either Moldavia or Walachia, but Russian and Turkish soldiers continued a fighting side show there, and in 1808, Napoleon and the Tsar, who were just in a spell of friendly relations, signed a document by which the Emperor of the French recognized Russian sovereignty over the two remote provincial territories, with the Danube as a southern frontier.

In 1812, Russian garrisons withdrew to fight the Napoleonic *Grande Armée*. This returned the old administration, but the burden of the Russian superstructure was temporarily removed. Nature proved an indestructible provider but it could not supply cash.

The British consulate reported on those provinces to the Congress of Vienna that meat, bread, and wine were in such abundance, and consequently so cheap, that whole magazines of damaged corn, which had been preserved for wartime, were thrown away, that good wine was sold at a halfpenny a bottle, barley for about two shillings sixpence, a wagonload of hay for one shilling. . . . "This abundance produced upon the character of the lower classes . . . gluttony, drunkenness, natural indolence, and violent sensual appetites. . . . A Walachian peasant (the very poorest) eats regularly four times a day. . . . His wife makes his clothes, and he has no other care (and consequently no incitement) than the repeated demands of the collector of taxes, who is always attended by Albanians armed with pistols, musquets, sabres, daggers, and whips of an appalling consistency. The genuine Walach scarcely ever pays a para (copper) without having previously submitted to as many blows as his posteriors can endure. . . . He finishes by paying not only the original demand, but the Albanians for administering and the collector for superintending the punishment."

In 1825, when Tsar Alexander unexpectedly died, Russia was not all too deeply involved in the affairs of the lower Danube Basin. His brother and successor, Nicholas I, considered the Greeks, who struggled for their independence from Turkey, mere rebels to be dealt with summarily. But in 1828, when Russia attacked Turkey with the tacit consent of England and France, which backed the Greeks, its troops established a strangle hold on the Danube estuary. Russia offered Turkey nominal sovereignty over these regions for ten million ducats and promised to evacuate after payment. Turkey scraped the bottom of its resources to recover its sole bridgehead across the Danube and made several down payments.

With the assistance of a Prussian agent, a "peace" was signed in

Adrianople in 1829. This was the first time in history that Prussia interfered in these regions. A part of the Danube estuary was awarded to Russia, which thus could bottle up the river and block the access from the Central European traffic artery to the Black Sea. Moldavia and Walachia obtained control of their internal affairs (subject to the Russian consul's approval), and the right to establish a lightly armed militia (officered by Russians) and to maintain quarantine stations. Turkish fortifications had to be dismantled; settlements of Mohammedans were prohibited. In 1834, old established Turkish restrictions on trade, industry, and traffic were lifted. With Russian blessings, navigation on the Danube was pronounced free.

Thus, in the budding years of the steamer, the Danube was open from Württemberg to the Black Sea. The effects could have been incalculable, but, in fact, they were not all too important when it happened. Difficulties of navigation along the lower course of the river remained forbidding, and Russia used whimsical chicanery to hamper traffic. Also, general economic conditions did not favor a high volume of trade.

The Russian occupation under local commander Count von der Pahlen had its usual effects upon Walachia and Moldavia: unrestrained requisitioning, forced labor, and deportations. But when General Count Paul Kiselev took over, some improvements were made. First of all, Kiselev reformed the police, who, as long as Walachians could remember, had lived on spoils rather than on salaries, which were rarely paid. A new gendarmery was set up and put on a regular payroll. Crime was reduced. Next came land reform, according to which the land became the boyars' property. The boyars at once raised dues and statutory labor, but the peasants did not rebel. Rebellion was not in their tradition.

Suddenly, to everybody's surprise, navigation on the Danube increased. New merchants flocked into the lands to profit from the low prices of agricultural commodities and business began to prosper. The boyars grew rich and sent their sons to study in Paris, from where they returned by no means erudite, but as epicureans, debauchers, and political wizards. The peasants drank even more than usual and became less subservient.

In 1845, Russia permitted the customs barrier between the two provinces to be lifted; early in 1846, Walachia and Moldavia adopted the joint name of United Principalities.

The United Principalities had no roads or bridges. Hospodar George Bibescu made notable improvements, though using forced labor. Galatz, on the left Danube bank, was expanded; even though situated almost ninety miles upstream, it was considered a seaport and became a center of a grain trade controlled mainly by Greeks and Sephardic Jews until the time of Nazi-German and later Communist rule in Rumania.

The events of 1848 had their repercussions even upon the backward United Principalities, apart from the Austrian, Hungarian, and Russian military operations. From Paris, where they had witnessed the social upheaval, several young boyar offspring, including the brothers Brătianu, hurried back to Bucharest, where they joined with affluent local political hopefuls to organize something revolutionary, the nature of which they had not clearly conceived.

Eventually a realistic program emerged: independence, rule by a Prince freely elected for a five-year term, a Parliament representing all classes, a National Guard, universal education, free press, abolition of capital punishment, emancipation of Jews and Gypsies.

Hospodar George Bibescu first wanted to have all champions of reform arrested, but was badly frightened by an attempt on his life. He appointed a revolutionary cabinet and even signed the draft of a constitution, then ran for safety across the Transylvanian border. Russian consul Kotzebue, a member of the family of Alaska fame, withdrew from Bucharest under a rudely worded protest. Russian officers arrested the revolutionary cabinet, but were, in turn, driven out by an angry mob led by Ion Brătianu. Seven persons lost their lives in the commotion.

On May 1, 1849, while war raged in Italy and Hungary, Turkey and Russia signed the Balta-Liman Convention. Two Princes were to be appointed for the no longer quite united Principalities; Russia and Turkey were to maintain commissars at both capitals to jointly advise them. All assemblies were suppressed. Russian and Turkish troops were to keep the territories under joint occupation until they were "pacified." In 1853, Tsar Nicholas told an illustrious British visitor, Sir Hamilton Seymour: "The Principalities are, in fact, an independent state under my protection, and should remain so."

The Tsar was confident that the interests of Russia and those of Franz Joseph's realm were identical. But in Vienna, Russian expansionism was still viewed as a threat, even after the Tsar's intervention had crushed the Hungarian uprising; the Tsar's expectation of gratitude was badly disappointed.

Austria was plagued by restive nationalities. Serbs, Croats, Slovaks, Rumanians, even Saxons from Transylvania, were still incensed against nationalistic Hungarians. They said that Vienna had let them down in Kossuth's day and that it had requested Russian intervention, which everybody remembered with ill feelings. Demagogues from Pressburg to the Iron Gate appealed to minorities to present claims in the name of nationalism.

Nationalism also became an instrument in the hands of ambitious men high above the level of small-time demagogues.

In France, Emperor Napoleon III, whose personal Frenchness would not have passed a nationalistic acid test, took up nationalism as an instrument to build an imperialistic system with France as its sun and new national states its planets. He who had a great deal of Italian blood in his royal veins was about to establish a united Italy at Austria's expense, and Rumanian students and playboys in Paris, all aspirants for political careers at home, were almost as fascinated by his nationalistic exclamations as they were by the gayer attractions of his capital. Would-be reformers from and in Danubian areas looked for support of their venturesome schemes and received encouraging words galore. Paris turned into a nationalistic Mecca. Vienna, once more caught napping, groped for an effective remedy, and found none.

On February 25, 1856, an international congress convened in Paris to solve the problems of the lower Danube Basin. A special commission was appointed to draft the future status of Walachia and Moldavia. Its French members asked that they be permanently united and independent, according to the people's will.

Lord Henry Palmerston, the British Prime Minister, had misgivings against completely disregarding Turkey's rights in the Principalities. After a lengthy wrangle, Turkish officials arranged "elections" in Moldavia based on a franchise so intricate as only oriental minds could devise. Only 11 per cent actually were admitted to the polls, and the result was a "popular vote" against both union with Walachia and national independence.

Turkey's uneasy sovereignty continued for a short time. But the West considered the rigged elections null and void, and soon the title United Principalities reappeared, even though there was no hint of genuine independence.

The peasants in the fields and the fishermen on the Danube did not know that their lands were being rechristened, that Austria and Prussia made conflicting suggestions about a new flag, and that Austro-French animosities resulted in a *déroute* on the sensitive Paris stock exchange.

The stock exchange rather than the conciliatory attitude of the high parties led to a wordy compromise, which upheld the word "United" and gave the Principalities a Central Commission, but two elected rulers, two cabinets, two elected legislative assemblies.

In December 1858, elections were held in Moldavia. Only people of substance were enfranchised to vote. Five aspirants vied for the office of Prince, and out of the noisy campaigning emerged a surprise candidate, one Colonel Sturdza, commander of Moldavia's so-called army. He was installed on January 17, 1859.

Five days later, Walachia "elected" its assembly. On February 3, it held its first session. It was a house divided in and outside the official building in Bucharest. Right under its windows crowds rioted. A young and rather obscure deputy presented a candidate: Alexander Ion Cuza. Two days later Mr. Cuza was Prince Alexander Ion I, who would soon become ruler of the two principalities.

The streets of Bucharest resounded with well-led cheers, and in Jassy a torchlight procession hailed Napoleon III, represented by the French consul.

Modern Rumania was ushered in, back-door fashion.

Cuza sent a telegram to Paris: "The fate of the Rumanians is now in the hands of Your Majesty."

On February 7, Napoleon addressed the French legislature: "If I were asked what interest France has in the distant lands watered by the Danube, I would reply that the interest of France is everywhere there is a just and civilized cause to be promoted."

Was that "just and civilized cause" unification, or was it the installment of Mr. Cuza as a double Prince? There could be no doubt that Victor Place, the meddlesome French consul in Jassy, had taken a heavy hand in the venture and that some French funds had been invested in it.

Alexander Ion I had been a member of the boyar young set in Paris, an enthusiastic reveler whose oriental handsomeness had won him the brief affection of a substantial number of Parisian belles, but whose record was otherwise undistinguished. He had studied at the Sorbonne but did not graduate, he had been involved in various intrigues, and he had no reputation for integrity. Back home he turned into another political busybody, who wooed both Consul Place and a Turkish agent, Nicholas Vogorides, who was unscrupulous even by Turko-Greek standards, and used him as a front man for various shady ventures. By 1858, Cuza was titular colonel and Minister of War by the grace of the Turks, but the word "gratitude" did not figure prominently in his dictionary, and he deserted Vogorides in favor of Monsieur Place, who now considered him a useful tool.

His establishment as the ruler of the two Principalities surprised various foreign governments, including Russia's, which was displeased to see France pull the wires in a region that could become a springboard for another invasion of Russia.

Cuza dispatched a personal ambassador, poet Vasile Alecsandri, to Paris; the Emperor granted him an audience, then sent a French military mission to Bucharest and had 10,000 latest rifles and a large supply of ammunition shipped there via the Mediterranean, the Black Sea, and the lower Danube. Cuza enlarged the militia of his principalities. The Austrians concentrated one entire army corps along the Rumanian border to guard against surprise raids. This corps was badly missed in Italy, when, on April 26, 1859, another Austro-Sardinian war opened, in which France interfered with decisive effect.

Cuza seemed to be firmly in the saddle; but many boyars distrusted him, and the assemblies came to regret his election, which had not even brought bribes. Cuza, sensing hostility, informed Napoleon III that he would establish a personal dictatorship.

In February 1862, the fusion of Moldavia and Walachia became official; their assemblies merged into one, sitting in Bucharest. Cuza seemed to have clear sailing in his relations with foreign powers, but the boyars remained unfriendly and the peasants grew dissatisfied with mere words. He won the latter's blind allegiance by a bill expropriating the enormous domains of the Greek monasteries for less than nominal compensation.

On May 14, 1864, with French blessings, Cuza staged his dictatorial *coup d'état;* he dissolved the assembly and presented the draft of a constitution, subject to a plebiscite in which all male Rumanians over twenty-five would participate. Roughly 99 per cent of the electorate was illiterate, but the peasants were given to understand that even their small tenure of land depended on their affirmative votes. Cuza's new constitution was accepted by a vote of 682,621 to 1307.

Dictator Cuza hurried to Constantinople to placate the Turkish government, or in his own words: "to place at the Sultan's feet my own homage and that of the entire Rumanian nation."

Foreign consuls were bewildered, but the governmental changes were ratified. Cuza, still in Constantinople, was proud of his achievement; but when he returned home, he found boyar opposition firmer than ever, and peasants, who still waited to take over church domains, no longer blindly loyal. On August 24, 1864, he promulgated another agrarian law, which he expected to make him immortal: it freed the peasants from feudal dues and tithes and allotted them up to two thirds of the landlords' "arable land." But they were saddled with the compensations toward the landlords—state bonds and cash payments over fifteen years—with the result that they were worse off than before, deep in debts the amount of which they could not comprehend.

Cuza's land law was followed by the Public Instruction Law, aimed against the arrogant boyars who wanted the masses to remain illiterate. It stipulated free compulsory education, the establishment of many new primary and secondary schools, and two universities with liberal scholarships. This would have been beneficent in a country with a functioning school system and funds for public education; but in Rumania it remained ineffective for decades.

Cuza was forty-four when he promulgated his laws, a reformer guided by expediency, a debaucher afraid of missing lascivious opportunities, a corruptionist as only insecure power can beget, a man who had only one principle and aim: that of serving his own greedy and lewd purposes. He was surrounded by a clique of foreigners—whom he awarded all sorts of contracts, on terms that constituted a heavy burden for Rumanian generations to come—by political agents who bought favors, by gamblers, glorified panders, and venal women.

Rumanian mores and ethics were below average, but the Prince's behavior was scandalous even in Bucharest. Cuza's enemies exploited scandal by spreading stories about the martyrdom of the Prince's wedded wife. Cuza was said to have had at least half a dozen other women around the palace for more than one year, in addition to many more who stayed only for brief periods. His permanent mistress was Maria Obrenović, whose son Milan was raised by a Gypsy woman and would eventually become the ill-fated King of Serbia.

Cuza relied on the unflinching support of France, but his involvement with Russian agents and his business dealings with Prussians were watched with disfavor, and the French government was ready to forsake its former protégé.

In the summer of 1865, while the Prince was taking the waters in Bad Ems, Prussia, his enemies arranged violent demonstrations in the streets of Bucharest. His foes rallied, including two Ghicas, one Sturdza, two Brătianus, and relatives of the suffering Princess.

Ion Brătianu traveled to Paris, where he had a pamphlet distributed, which wound up: "The Rumanians want the Emperor [Napoleon III] to tell them whom he would view with benevolence as Prince of Rumania."

Napoleon was already pondering the issue. It would take time to find a foreigner of princely blood who would satisfy not only Paris but also other Western capitals.

Back from Bad Ems, Cuza received secret warnings, but he kept reveling and collecting, and trusted his lucky star.

In February 1865, Brătianu was in Bucharest again, and he told his partisans that the time was ripe for a coup. In the small hours of February 23, officers of the palace guard roused Cuza from the bed he shared with Maria Obrenović, forced him at gun point to sign his abdication, and spirited him across the border—whole, well provided for, and after the initial shock was over, not all too unhappy. He lived in Heidelberg, Germany, for another seven years, a foreigner of greater wealth than distinction.

In the afternoon that followed the abdication, the reconvened assembly elected, unanimously, Philip, Count of Flanders, brother of the King of Belgium, as their ruler. Brătianu was caught by surprise, and so was the Count of Flanders, who declined the dignity with almost insulting promptness.

CHAPTER FIFTY-FOUR

Emerged another candidate for the Rumanian throne: Prince Karl Eitel Friedrich von Hohenzollern-Sigmaringen, a twenty-seven-year-old Prussian officer, son of the Prime Minister preceding Bismarck, and a cousin of Napoleon III. Austria did not like his candidacy; Napoleon believed that he would play the French game; Bismarck trusted that he would be willing to promote Prussian economic interests; England would have considered anyone better than Cuza; and Russia was grudgingly noncommittal. Turkey vainly claimed that the resignation of Cuza had voided the union of the Principalities and that the election of a single Prince would be moot.

On March 31, 1865, the ubiquitous Brătianu conferred with Prince Karl at Düsseldorf; and two weeks later, while Karl still hesitated, a provisional government of Rumania proclaimed him Prince. Few Rumanian voters knew what the candidate stood for, but 685,969 ballots were counted in favor of Karl and 224 against him.

Elsewhere in Europe tension was at a peak. War between Austria, Prussia, and Italy was imminent, and the attitude of France was undetermined. Karl was still reluctant to go to faraway Rumania, but Bismarck told him that, having been unanimously elected, he was duty-bound to accept; that the only hostile power would be Austria, which Prussia intended to keep busy elsewhere, and that if the Tsar raised objections, Karl could marry a Russian Princess. Should he run into serious trouble he could always go home and be restored to his military rank.

Karl accepted. In a farewell audience, he told the King of Prussia, who disliked the idea that a Hohenzollern might have to recognize Turkish suzerainty, that he would do so only if inevitable and would free himself later by the force of arms. But he felt increasingly uneasy.

Uneasiness marked the entire venture. Brătianu struck Karl as an outlandish adventurer whose language he did not speak and who puzzled him by his habits, tempers, and sensibilities. He tried to learn Rumanian history in a few easy lessons, but Rumanian history seemed as enigmatic as Brătianu. Karl saw no point of political gravity, no reasonable course to steer. A minor clerk would hardly accept employment under such conditions, but Karl von Hohenzollern-Sigmaringen proceeded to his job as a ruler.

How to get to Rumania was a difficult problem. If he sailed via Constantinople, the Turks would take him from the ship and send him back in disgrace. Something similar might happen if he went via Russia. In Austria he would be arrested as an enemy alien if war with Prussia broke out while he was en route; but Austria had a reputation of inefficiency, and mobilization would create confusion. Eventually, with Bismarck's tacit consent, Karl chose to travel right through the inefficient Austrian lion's den.

In Zurich, Switzerland, he obtained a bogus Swiss passport which gave his name as Karl Hettingen, his profession as a drummer, and his destination as Odessa, Russia. Austrian border guards let him pass. A few miles from Vienna, "drummer Hettingen" was in panic; in the corridor of the train in which he was riding, he ran into some officers whom he had met in the Danish campaign two years before. But after scrutinizing glances which seemed to last for an eternity, they did not recognize him. Several days of discomfort later, he arrived at Báziás, in southern Hungary, from where he was scheduled to continue by Danube steamer. Brătianu had promised to wait for him at Báziás, but neither Brătianu nor the steamer was there. Karl was stranded in the dismal little place, where a foreigner staying overnight became the talk of the town. He had to stay for two nights and was talked about a great deal, but he was not searched, and the local police, who had never set eyes on a Swiss passport, were satisfied with his papers.

At last Brătianu came, but he was careful not to show himself in public with the "drummer." Soon afterward the tardy steamer arrived. The last lap of the voyage was a ride through a gantlet, with Austrians and Turks controlling both banks of the river. Karl had to disembark at Turnu-Severin, the first Walachian town, gateway to Rumania; this was what history required, for Emperor Trajan had set foot on Dacian soil on that same spot. The captain, noticing that the allegedly Odessa-bound passenger was about to leave, tried to stop "drummer Hettingen" and pull him back, but Brătianu helped Karl to break loose and he ran down the gangway into his realm. At the pier Brătianu welcomed him formally in the name of Rumania.

The first Rumanian realities that met the Prince were despicable roads over which he had to ride in an open carriage drawn by teams of eight horses. Settlements all along the way to Bucharest were miserable beyond Prussian imagination. He arrived in his capital on May 22, 1866, in a downpour. The drenched crowds considered this a good omen, for it brought a long drought to an end.

The day of Karl's arrival in Bucharest started a dynastic era in Rumania which was to last for eighty-one years. It brought the country an impressive number of wars and territorial changes, many royal scandals, abdications and comebacks, against the background of fabulous corruption, until Rumania, bleeding from many wounds, became a Russian satellite in 1947.

The first reaction to Karl's arrival came from Constantinople. The Great Vizier, who had said that he would rather see Austria annex Rumania than a Prussian ruler installed, lodged a sharp protest. Turkish troops concentrated along the lower Danube. But already the furies of war descended on the upper Danube Valley, and Karl's rule could establish itself through international neglect.

July 3, 1866, determined the fate of Europe, and eventually of the world, for a long time to come.

On that day, the Austro-Prussian War was decided in a battle at Königgrätz, Bohemia, generally known as the Battle of Sadowa. Due to Austrian tactical miscalculations, corps commanders' arbitrariness, and a rare combination of mishaps and blunders, the Austrian ship of state sprang a leak that was never fully closed. After the Austrian lines dissolved in a maelstrom of panic, Prussia's chief of staff, General (later Field Marshal–General) Helmuth von Moltke, pushed on toward Vienna and the covering line of the Danube. From Linz to Pressburg, people waited for the victors, who, in a single day, had become a hypnotic myth. Field fortifications were improvised; vanguards of Austrian armies that had been victorious in Italy were dispatched to the spot. But it was too little and too late. The Battle of Sadowa weakened the standing of the Danubian monarchy in the Balkans to the benefit of Russian expansion and tied Austrian policies to those of a Prussianized Germany. Sadowa may have saved Karl's rule in Rumania, but it marred the lifetime of several generations.

From Schönbrunn, Emperor Franz Joseph rode on horseback to the Lobau to inspect construction work and boost the citizens' morale. The Emperor was thirty-six, but he looked aged; he was a superb horseman, but he almost dangled in the saddle. Nobody saluted him as he crossed the Inner City.

Napoleon III mediated an armistice. But before it was signed a battle opened in the vicinity of Pressburg, near a village with the poetic name of Blumenau ("meadow of flowers"). It was no big battle, rather a side show staged by two generals eager for last-minute promotion, and it lasted only until noon. Then horn signals and loud shouts announced that hostilities had been suspended.

An Austrian impromptu military party championed resumption of hostilities, arguing that Prussian supply lines were overextended. However, Austrian faith in victory was shattered. Had it not been for the depressing ride through the streets of Vienna, Franz Joseph might have joined the champions of war; but his faith, too, was shaken. When his chief of staff spoke in favor of peace at every reasonable price, the Emperor gave his nod.

The preliminary instrument of peace was signed in Nikolsburg, Moravia, on July 26 (the final peace treaty in Prague, August 23). Austria had to sever its existing ties with Saxony, Bavaria, and all other German states, thus giving tacit consent to a reorganization of Germany in which it would have no part; Prussia would be the leader. The territorial *status quo* was maintained in the North; but in the South, Prussia insisted that the defeated Italians receive Venetia. An indemnity of twenty million thaler, payable to Prussia, was a minor bloodletting under the circumstances, but it whetted Prussia's traditional appetite for "making a plus" and set a dangerous precedent: five years later, a war indemnity of five billion francs (one billion dollars in gold) was imposed upon France, which made the new Germany prosperous enough to develop a dangerous industrial potential in a short time.

Throughout the summer of disaster, Hungarian rebels had been on the move. Elsewhere, provincial Diets clamored for autonomy. Slogans about "unity" found deaf ears. Parochialism prevailed over Imperial policies, soapbox oratory over historical concepts. The little people were excited and bewildered. Wits in Vienna displayed a bitter sense of mediocre travesty.

In Budapest, a new Parliament convened under the intellectual guidance of two moderates, Ferencz Deák and Count Julius Andrássy. On February 27, 1867, the Emperor restored the pre-revolutionary Hungarian Constitution, with Andrássy as Prime Minister. The hallowed spell of the recovered Crown of St. Stephen should forever fasten the ties between the ruling house and Hungary. On May 22, "dualism" was accepted in principle in the monarchy. On June 8, Franz Joseph was crowned King, with medieval pomp and circumstance. On November 14, the realm was rechristened the Austro-Hungarian Monarchy. Relationship between the two parts was based upon the so-called Compromise, which was renewed from decade to decade, with all its glaring imperfections.

The Compromise of 1867 established two governments with partly interlocking competences. The Austro-Hungarian Monarchy had common ministries of Finance, Foreign Affairs, and War, but the army was divided into the "common army" and an Austrian and a Hungarian militia, which were not satisfactorily integrated. And when it came to fiscal matters, there never was harmony between the two parts.

Slavic politicians were angrily dissatisfied. They had wanted at least "trialism"; Bohemia, Moravia, Galicia, and rump-Silesia merged into another kingdom under Franz Joseph. Others even advocated a fourth part, centered on Croatia and Slavonia. Germanophile demagogues, contemptful of all other nationalities, clamored for ever closer association with the new German Reich, which Bismarck created in Versailles in 1871.

The political complexion of the Danube Basin underwent baffling changes. Nothing but a prolonged period of peace could have permitted coagulation and some permanence. The other alternative was muddle and ultimate ruin.

Austrian and Hungarian "delegations" renewing the Compromise convened six times all in all. There was a great deal of debate designed to make edifying reading, but nothing was produced to make the two realms "indivisible and inseparable," as a heraldic aphorism had it. When, roughly half a century after the old Empire became the Dual Monarchy, the existing ties were severed, no legal talent had to be hired for the purpose: union and "compromise" were considered null and void, and a Vienna newspaper rephrased the heraldic aphorism into "invisible and irreparable."

Political storm warnings along the Danube went up in 1869. Napoleon III had hoped to make territorial gains at Prussia's expense, as an Imperial brokerage fee for mediating the armistice of 1866. Bismarck first evaded the issue, and after the Prussian armies were completely disengaged in the Danube Basin, refused the fee in cold, certain terms. Thereupon, Napoleon III proposed to Franz Joseph an alliance against Prussia, which Italy was expected to join. The allies would make Austria again the leading power in the former Reich, reduce Prussia to its ancient status of outsider, and bring France important gains along the Rhine.

Austrian generals, still smarting under defeat, received the suggestion with enthusiasm. In the early spring of 1870, Field Marshal Archduke Albrecht, who, in 1866, had been in charge of the armies in Italy, secretly visited Paris to discuss joint operations. Two months later, French general Lebrun went to Vienna for a similar purpose. But Franz Joseph's confidence in Napoleon was adversely affected by events in Mexico, where his younger brother Maximilian had accepted the Imperial crown on Napoleon's prodding, and had died, abandoned by France, before a firing squad in 1867. Franz Joseph's Foreign Minister, Count Friedrich Ferdinand von Beust, a native of Saxony, did not want to commit himself, and Andrássy was afraid the French plan would upset the balance of power in the Dual Monarchy, to Hungary's disadvantage. In a Crown Council in Vienna on July 18, 1870, he spoke convincingly of the adverse effects of a new alliance on world unity, and his sonorous oratory prevailed over the quiet reasoning of aging Archduke Albrecht. Next morning, Austrian and Hungarian newspapers carried headlines saying that their ruler had decided to maintain a neutral attitude in a conflict between France and Prussia.

This declaration of neutrality immensely strengthened Bismarck's hand. Now he could launch his war against France, another curtain raiser to the twentieth-century holocaust.

Meantime, in the backwoods of Europe, Karl of Rumania found his adopted land shockingly different from what his Prussian mind conceived of as minimum orderliness.

"Through good administration, I must revive a country that is in complete rot, both financially and morally," he told an adventurer who offered to organize an uprising of Rumanians in Hungary.

Shortly after his debarkation he wrote his father that there was not a single copper in the treasury. Karl, who accustomed himself with difficulty to the Rumanianization of his name into Carol, had been told about the marvel of a Prussian-constructed Rumanian railroad; but when he arrived, it had yet to be completed, with the assistance of corrupt and incompetent contractors. Incompetence and corruption were omnipresent.

The army was the Prince's main concern. He found it poorly trained, ill-disciplined, equipped with but a score or two of rifles per company, while sketchy records showed that many modern breechloaders had been ordered, billed, and "delivery accepted." Officers insisted that "looking for lost rifles" was by far less important than cleaning the army of "subversives," meaning soldiers who had been loyal to previous governments. Carol suddenly displayed violent energy and insisted that corruption and feud in the army cease at once and that everything be reorganized after Western models. Rumanian intriguers reported to Paris that their new ruler was more Bismarckian than Bismarck himself and would never play the French game. The Franco-Prussian War had not yet begun when Napoleon III informed Carol that no financial support would be forthcoming.

Carol had been told about the existence of a sound Rumanian school system and modern hospitals.

He found schools inadequate in the few larger cities and nonexistent in rural communities. Not within the lifetime of a generation could Rumania become a country with tolerable literacy.

How long did a lifetime last in Rumania? Statistics did not tell, but there could be no doubt that it was alarmingly short. Infant mortality was enormous. Adults were decimated by cholera. Not a single modern hospital existed, and the pathetically few obsolete installations lacked everything but filth.

Cash was needed, but there was none. Carol accepted his salary in land, whose operations were impeded by mismanagement and inadequate transportation. Several harvests failed and cholera reduced available manpower below the danger point.

Rumania, in the early years of Carol's rule, had a very bad international press. Western newspapers had an eye on the principality ever since Carol's trip had furnished them with good copy. Readers wondered what would happen there next.

Next, Brătianu introduced restrictive measures against the Jews, whom he wanted to be scapegoats for everything and everybody. The Western press denounced him. Diplomatic protests were filed in Paris, London, and Vienna. In Berlin, the Crown Prince spoke of the possibility of throwing cousin Carol to the wolves. Rumania turned into the headquarters of nationalistic plotters and their henchmen, who eventually accounted for the assassination of Mikhail Obrenović, Prince of Serbia, and for an uprising in Bulgaria. A clandestine campaign to revolutionize Rumanians in Hungary continued against Carol's will.

Cousin Carol had not been all napping amidst intrigue. The murdered Prince of Serbia had made a state visit to Bucharest in 1867, and they had discussed throwing off, jointly, what still remained of the historic Turkish yoke. In 1868 they signed a secret alliance, which Greece was expected to join. Only the assassination of Mikhail prevented the immediate outbreak of a Balkan war.

In 1869, Carol paid hat-in-hand courtesy calls on European royalty. Napoleon III was cool, the Tsar contemptuous. In Prussia, he was told to marry a German Princess, Elisabeth von Wied. He obliged, and took his attractive bride, partly by Danube boat, to his shaky princedom, where one of the feuding politicians told him bluntly that Hohenzollern rule could not last much longer.

Early in 1871, when the Prussian colony in Bucharest celebrated the victories in France, mobs threw stones, broke windows, and shouted republican slogans while the police looked on.

Carol's energy was aroused by the very vulgarity of the affair. He called conservative leaders, who had nothing to gain and everything to lose in a republic, and threatened to resign unless they form a cabinet and assume responsibility for the Prince's orders. The conservatives implored him to stay. Their spokesman, Lascăr Cartagiu, formed a cabinet and arranged elections in the time-dishonored Rumanian fashion, which gave the opposition only 6 seats out of 157. Carol's regime was saved, but the country was in a permanent state of unrest, stirred by political mountebanks.

In the 1870s, the fate of Rumania and of all the Balkans was on the razor's edge. Bosnia and tiny Montenegro were in rebellion; Milan Obrenović, the hot-tempered, unbalanced new Prince of Serbia, wanted to be liberator and unifier of the Balkans. Turkey was bankrupt, and shaken by a revolution of May 29, 1876, and Russia expected to become, at long last, its heir.

Russian "volunteers" went to Belgrade and instigated Milan to declare war on Turkey. The undisciplined Serbian army was promptly defeated, but Russia demanded that no retributions be taken against the Serbs.

Turkey was in no mood to yield, and in October 1876, another Russo-Turkish war seemed imminent. This war would be fought along the lower Danube, and Rumania would become the theater of Russian deployment. Carol, not strong enough to safeguard Rumania's neutrality, tried to sell its co-belligerency to Russia, trading his personal command and Prussian military training against a status as Russia's full-fledged ally. But Russia wanted no more than transit in return for an ill-defined compensation for expenses involved, an offer that Carol proudly refused.

"My army is burning to show its worth," Carol wrote his father. Yet, on April 16, 1877, his Foreign Minister granted the Russian army the right of free passage and the use of Rumanian transport facilities and supplies. The Russians promised to respect Rumanian laws and institutions. The Rumanian army was mobilized "to secure respect for the country's neutrality."

From Turkey came a furious summons to resist Russian invasion. The Rumanian reply was a bid for time. The day the reply was made, Russia declared war on Turkey and crossed into Rumania. Prince Alexander Gorchakov, the mastermind of Russia's drive, rejected Rumania's offer of collaboration on equal terms, with the words: "Russia does not need the assistance of the Rumanian army."

Yet, in one way, Carol profited from his humiliating experience. On May 11, 1877, Parliament proclaimed Rumania's complete independence, and ten days later, rupture with Turkey became an accomplished fact.

The Russians crossed the Danube. The Tsar was present for the occasion, and Rumanian troops were permitted to stand by as an honor guard. The crossing of the river, however, did not turn into a parade. Turkish units, small in number but spirited in action, made the passage slow and costly. Prince Carol drew his conclusions. He concentrated every Rumanian soldier and every piece of artillery he could muster (50,000 men, 180 cannon) near the Danube and waited for his opportunity.

The Russians marched south, but ten miles from the right bank they encountered a screen of Turkish defenses, and a few more miles beyond, near Plevna, they were repulsed by the valiant forces of Osman Pasha.

The fortress of Plevna consisted of a sketchily modernized citadel and a number of fieldworks and redoubts that would not have impressed Prince Eugene of Savoy; but Turkish soldiers fought with stubborn fatalism and threw the enemy back time and again, under the eyes of foreign newspaper correspondents, whose sarcastic appraisal of Russia's military power pleased millions of readers who were not favorably disposed toward the colossus in the East. In August 1877, the Russian position became so precarious that the 50,000 Rumanians on the left Danube bank were a factor of major importance, and the Tsar gave Carol to understand that Russia might accept Rumanian co-belligerency. Carol charged his price: personal command of all Russian and Rumanian forces in the Danubian region.

On September 8, the Rumanian army made its debut in the Grivitza sector of Plevna, the press of the West standing by to see what the soldiers of the odd, corruption-ridden principality could do. They did well enough. They could not at once pierce the Turkish defenses, but after a methodical three-month siege, Carol enforced the capitulation of Plevna. This achieved, he resigned from command and left mopping-up operations to the Russians, trusting that Rumanian claims could later be enforced in a peace treaty. He demanded unconditional independence from Turkey, razing of all Turkish fortifications in the Danube Basin, surrender by Turkey of all shipping lanes in the Danube Delta, and an indemnity of 100 million francs (20 million dollars in gold).

But early in 1878, when Russia and Turkey opened armistice talks at Adrianople, Russia refused to consider Rumania an equal partner in the negotiations, until her independence would have been officially recognized by all European governments. A few days later, Prince Gorchakov made it clear that this decision would be revised only if Rumania would "cede" three Bessarabian districts to Russia, in return for "generous compensation in the region of Dobrogea, in the Danube Delta." He added that Rumania must learn to face realities.

The Bessarabian districts had been Moldavian for hundreds of years. In the early nineteenth century they had fallen under the Tsar's domination, but in 1856, in the wake of the Crimean War, they had been returned to Moldavia. The region of Dobrogea was barren land, roamed by Tatars, Gypsies, and remnants of migrating peoples whose national identity was questionable.

Rumania refused, and dispatched memoranda of protest to all great powers. The memoranda rarely reached the foreign ministers' desks, and, adding insult to injury, Russia agreed with Turkey that Russian withdrawal from the Balkans would be carried out across Rumanian territory. Rumania protested to the Tsar, but Gorchakov threatened that if Rumania kept protesting, its territory would be occupied and its troops disarmed.

In Berlin, the great powers were again in conference to settle all questions in and near the Balkans to everybody's everlasting benefit. Carol understood that Bessarabia was lost, but he tried to obtain a better compensation and hoped against hope that Rumania would be admitted to the conference.

All the Rumanians obtained in Berlin was a hearing, to which weightier participants listened with impassive boredom. Gorchakov had not permitted the question of Bessarabia to be put on the agenda. Rumania asked that all Russian transit privileges be voided, that it receive an indemnity, and that it be recognized as both independent and neutral, with a status similar to that of Belgium.

The conferees eventually recognized Rumania's independence (though not its neutrality), and this on condition that the Bessarabian provinces be ceded to Russia. Dobrogea was assigned to Rumania. The Danube Delta became Rumanian. The delta, not quite 1700 square miles of fever-ridden swamps, streams, and lakes, was not even of strategic value, since navigation on the Danube was now internationally regulated and no power could have blocked river traffic without incurring serious risks. All river fortresses had to be dismantled. On October 12, 1878, the Rumanian Parliament ratified the dictum by a comfortable majority.

Carol obtained one concession, however, which amounted to nothing but made him feel a little better: Dobrogea and the delta were not called "a compensation for the loss of Bessarabia," but "a war indemnity freely offered from Europe."

Europe had built its final springboard to catastrophe. Under a benign mask, Bismarck's new German Reich styled itself the honest broker of territories, peoples, and resources, for the benefit of conquerors-to-come. In 1878, Austria-Hungary got a license to annex Bosnia and Herzegovina, where, thirty-six years later, two shots would be fired that killed the heir to the throne and his wife and, in their immediate aftermath, accounted for thirty million war casualties. Also in 1878, Cyprus passed under British control, tearing another stone out of the tottering wall of Turkey and turning, three quarters of a century later, into a thorn in the disintegrating British Empire's side.

The world at large did not recognize, nor would it duly recognize later, that breaking up an empire—even corrupt and decaying, like that of the Sultans; or enshrined in a tradition that stirs the impatience of reformers, like the Austro-Hungarian Monarchy; or mercantile and imperialistic, like Britain's—must result in turning the former realms into playgrounds for demagogues and open highways for tyrannical quacks, representing the modern type of conqueror from the gutter.

CHAPTER FIFTY-FIVE

Austria had lost the war against Prussia. It had lost the rest of its Italian provinces. It had submitted to political surgery. But, as indomitable optimists predicted in poetry, prose, and couplet, the Imperial "Double Eagle" would keep spreading its wings and rise to the highest point of the atmosphere (which then was supposed to be less than fifty miles above sea level). The always merry burghers measured the rise of heraldic eagles in figures of prosperity. The Vienna stock exchange was the source of wealth to many who trusted that it would never dry up and that their wealth would keep growing by leaps and bounds.

Came May 9, 1873, Vienna's Black Friday that dwarfed its counterparts of London, 1866, and New York, 1869—the day on which cash disappeared, on which a thousand millionaires turned paupers, and after which as many bodies of suicides floated in the Danube as there had been dead soldiers floating in the river after the Turkish mass attacks. Dazed contemporaries insisted that the blow had struck out of a clear blue sky.

On May 1, 1873, the Emperor had opened the Vienna World's Fair, but the fifth of its kind in the world, an ostentatious symbol of the Empire's economic welfare. The greatest architects had designed its buildings, one of which, the Rotunde in the Prater, was considered a marvel. Industrialists of many lands vied to display their products; new avenues of trade seemed about to open. Kaiser Wilhelm I came; so did King Victor Emmanuel of Italy, Tsar Alexander II, and, to the delight of the curious crowds, Shah Nasr-ed-Din of Persia, who looked every inch as exotic as the Viennese had hoped he would. Balkan Princes were roaming the grounds, providing food for wisecracks and rubbing shoulders with colorful foreigners whose distinction was determined by the contents of their wallets and who brought a new international flavor to the money-happy town.

The week of the opening had been ushered in by another victorious advance on the only theater of operations that concerned the people, at peace for almost seven years: the "provisional" building of the stock exchange on the Schottenring (opposite the lot on which the permanent building was later constructed).

More millions were added to accounts, more "millionaires" were created. A misanthropic wit has been quoted as saying, "Every cadger who's got a million fancies himself a millionaire."

The skies were blue, and there had been no warning for the multitude that could not or would not read the writing all over the wall: the writing of history and primitive logic. But then as now, writings of history were not favorite reading matter and logic that did not lead to an optimistic conclusion was considered a plain bore.

The Vienna stock exchange was already 112 years old when the bottom fell off in 1873. Maria Theresa had issued the first edict concerning this institution on August 14, 1761; in desperate need of money to keep the caldrons of war boiling, she directed her officials to sign a document announcing the establishment of a locale where buyers and sellers of securities could meet to transact their business through licensed brokers. It was a lengthy document, which, among other things, included flowery greetings to all mundane and clerical authorities and expressions of trust in the public's appreciation of the Empress' beneficence. Maria Theresa's personal signature is not on the document, however.

In the beginning, the stock exchange was a minor, well-disciplined affair. It provided only meager fuel for wars in Bohemia or Silesia; it destroyed no fortunes and created few. The state supervised the operations through a commissar whose annual salary of 600 gulden was less in purchasing power than the top unemployment compensation in the state of New York in 1959, and who was subject to disciplinary action if he took bribes. A military guard stood by to arrest violators who offered securities in an obtrusive manner, calling out rates of exchange or using signals; they were fined 1000 gulden and barred from the stock exchange. Barred also were minors and women, as well as feeble-minded and bankrupt people.

During the Napoleonic Wars the stock exchange failed abysmally to supply the state with cash. Austria had a low, and steadily lowering, credit rating with its security-buying citizens. The years 1811 and 1830 were diastrous ones; untold sums were lost, many suicides committed. Mass arrests of "unauthorized street dealers" only aggravated the calamity.

The big fish survived. They already included several emancipated Jewish financiers, who, some of them recently ennobled and increasingly influential in public affairs, constituted a new upper class. Among them were the Rothschilds (barons since 1823), the Arnsteins, Scheys, Wertheimsteins, and some others whose names are now forgotten even in Vienna but who then could make and break minor millionaires. The year 1848 had, of course, its stock exchange "revolution," a damaging event that quite a few of the 1873 victims vividly remembered.

However, gainers and losers were small in number, as compared with the growing crowd of savers who still did not invest in negotiable items— not so much out of prudence, which was conspicuously missing in the characteristics of the typical Viennese, but out of ignorance of the mechanics of the market. Besides, well into the 1860s the stock exchange's main business was the placement of public loans, and the Austrian public took a dim view of the state's solvency and efficiency. In 1860 the attempt was made to float a 200-million-gulden lottery loan, but no more than 76 million was subscribed.

Also in 1860, it was learned that the military administration had been systematically cheated by crooked suppliers. The Minister of Finance was among those who chose suicide as the best way out. The government was forced to seek loans abroad, under most humiliating terms. And yet, as reliable chroniclers wrote, trade and industry prospered.

Until 1866, only an infinitesimal fraction of the issues listed were stocks of industrial enterprise. Manufacturers did not incorporate their businesses and would not dream of seeing shares pass into the hands of strangers. A few banks, steamship lines in the Danube and the Adriatic, and one early railroad enterprise were listed under the heading of shares; the rest were bonds, most of them the much despised state issues.

Came Sadowa; yet, strangely, the Austrians refused to stay depressed. Actually, a wave of optimism hit the capital, prompted by a strange illusion that disaster on the battlefield and humble pie at the conference table did not have to interfere with gaiety and lavishness at home, as long as there was cash or credit, and a pretense of prosperity, which, if taken for granted, would become a permanently established fact of Viennese life.

Business opportunities seemed inexhaustible. Thousands of miles of new railroads, and requests for water transportation, needed much more shipping space than was available; housing was still primitive, and together with the population, the demand for new construction, and import and export trade, grew. Every increase of business in one field stimulated activities in another, and Vienna bustled with agents, small suppliers, and countless accessaries of a big boom.

The patriarchal businessmen, though delighted by the vertiginous upswing of their markets, could not possibly cope with the demand; and the organs of the state, inefficient, cumbersome, and fumbling as always, drafted ordinances that had little bearing upon the apparently happy circumstances. But the avalanche had started rolling and by 1867 a novel era dawned: the *Gründerperiode* (founder period), or rather that of "the mania for founding bogus companies," as Cassell's German-English dictionary defined it decades later. Those who tapped the money market for honest purposes were snowed under by a motley crowd of confidence men who tricked their victims into hazardous investments and speculation.

The schemes started with some plausible-sounding "business project": some new construction, transportation, export, manufacturing, publishing, or banking firm, of which nothing existed but a bombastic name and a proponent with no more credentials than a letterhead under which he announced that his company-to-be would yield huge, immediate, and superlatively safe returns and that subscriptions of shares at the preferred rate of, say, 120 per cent of the nominal value were still being accepted. Supplied with such papers, a horde of agents convinced small savers that this was their golden opportunity for annual returns of 20, 30, 50 per cent, if they signed and paid up at once. Demand was heavy. People who would not have accepted delivery of a garment without checking the buttons accepted those claims at face value. The wirepullers paid the agents' fees, had shares printed and mailed to the "subscribers" (there existed no law against mail fraud), and set an amount aside to pay the cheated customers an advance on future dividends or an extra bonus. Once he received shares and money, the customer felt like the luckiest man in the neighborhood, and often he, too, would make a fast profit by selling his shares at a fabulous rate to someone who, in turn, would sell it to a third party. So the shares kept circulating, enriching everybody until no further dividends would be forthcoming and the last holder, who discovered that the firm did not exist and the proponent had disappeared, lost every copper. But it took a long time until people grew sufficiently wise to investigate.

Never before, and hardly ever after, had Vienna enjoyed such a boom. Everybody lived high. Coffeehouses, restaurants, theaters, wineries, were overcrowded. Tailors, jewelers, carriage makers, furriers, did not know how to cope with the demand. Orchestras and bands played from afternoon till morning. Art dealers never ran short of collectors.

Money, so tight when the state had needed it, was now bursting into cataracts. Seventy-six million had been all the state could get; 1320 million was invested into stock in 1872 alone.

The number of banks whose shares were traded on the stock exchange rose from 4 to 124 during the *Gründerperiode*. Already in 1871, the number of emissions was so staggering that all liquid funds were inadequate to absorb it. But the bankers and brokers had full confidence in their patrons and allowed them to speculate on margin, arguing that the stream of gold would rise again when Germany, which was about to collect billions from France, would look for investment opportunities on the magnificent Vienna stock market.

There was no recession as yet, but there were setbacks, brief declines invariably followed by recovery. Some people were wiped out; a few banks and small brokers failed. The survivors nurtured the illusion that this was a "big man's" world and bid good riddance to the impotent small fry.

They expected the World's Fair to initiate the big man's boom. Never had Vienna been so pleasure-minded and dance-happy as in the spring of 1873.

April 28 was a day of promise, of new highs. Vienna danced, laughed; not even the sky was the limit. On May 1, cannon salvos greeted the opening of the Fair. Bells tolled; advertisement-loaded papers cheered. The Viennese were either at the stock exchange or in the Prater, and only a privileged millionaire could hope to find a restaurant table that night. Only a fool, a hopeless pessimist, would ponder, wonder, doubt.

Some big bankers were no fools. Scared by the number of margin operations, they requested new deposits. But their patrons needed all their cash for luxuries, amusement. Bankers began to sell.

The tower of rates shook. Some brokers were thrown off balance. More stock was sold, prices declined sharply, and every dip caused more sales.

On May 6, the big board at the exchange began to list the brokers who could not meet their obligations; on May 7, they totaled fifty.

Yet, there being 1300 licensees, this news caused no general alarm. The press was discreet. Many ads were ordered for May 8: buy, buy! May 8 saw sixty more insolvencies.

But there had been bear markets before. On May 9, a leading morning paper carried an editorial on prosperity. All newspapers carried the usual ads on fabulous opportunities; not one printed line expressed doubt. According to the press, the eyes of an admiring world were focused on the Vienna World's Fair.

Yet the voices of optimism sounded hackneyed, too worn to be convincing. There was tenseness in the air, apprehension. Crowds gathered outside the stock exchange, and as the door flung open, a multitude pressed and knocked its way into the big hall.

Vienna had had all sorts of spectacles, sordid, elating, flashy ones. It expected something new, something lurid, or perhaps assuaging, some relief from the nightmare of now openly admitted fear.

The crowd was getting denser by the minute. Hardly anybody intended to buy, but practically everybody expected the next man to be a customer with bulging pockets. Everybody waited. No deals were made as seconds and minutes ticked past, and fear, icy fear, spread. Then a bell rang shrilly: the bell that rang in pronouncements of insolvency. The hall fell silent. A clerk began to chalk a name on the board. Thousands of frightened eyes followed the writing, letter by letter: A-d-o-l-f PETS-CHEK. A cry of horror burst.

Adolf Petschek was kingpin of brokerage, the financial confidant of the cream of society; his clientele read like the *Gotha Almanach* of nobility; his coffers should contain hundreds of thousands, nay, millions of shares that would now be thrown on the market for whatever they could fetch.

The cry of horror was immediately followed by a savage cacophony of weeping, cursing, outbursts of unbridled despair. Into that witches' symphony sounded dull vocal thuds: offers of shares and constantly declining figures drawing no response. Nobody would buy. Money, the impulse, purpose, sole object of the market, had gone. Money, the provider, had deserted its worshiping usufructuaries.

Despair unleashed violence. The self-deceived and the promoters of deception engaged in wild fisticuffs, hunting for culprits where everybody was to blame. Few declarations of insolvency followed. Insolvency was accepted as the rule to which there could be no exception and the clerk with the stylus of white clay wrote no more names.

No telephone existed yet, but the grapevine of frenzy carried the message of ruin all over town with lightning speed. One hour after the ominous writing on the blackboard, names were being called out—names of yesterday's millionaires who had committed suicide.

A broker, disheveled, profusely sweating, his face bruised, stood on a table and delivered a shrieking harangue that the promoters of the most recent fraudulous emission should be lynched. He mentioned names familiar to all. Some of the bearers were present and made for the exit; several were beaten; others, among them Baron Rothschild, barely escaped. While outside the building ruined speculators and investors rushed into voluntary death, there were no fatalities inside.

One floor above the great hall, the "Stock Exchange Chamber" was in session, the government commissar attending. But those hapless people could suggest nothing except to have the hall evacuated by the police. The commissar refused to issue such orders: this was financial revolution, and revolution must be kept off the streets.

The holocaust lasted for a few hours. No business was transacted. Vienna had become a no-money no man's land, with the Fair building sticking out of the ruins like a sore thumb.

On May 15, when the stock exchange reopened after a six-day moratorium, the shrill bell of disaster did not cease to toll. Clerks kept writing names on the board. Quotations defied imagination. The shares of two banks fell from 100 gulden on May 8 to half a gulden on May 15.

For the first time, shareholders, brokers, and bankers checked the background of the gaudily printed shares and found a staggering number of enterprises that had never existed. Many shares disappeared from the market. An ingenuous paper hanger made a business of acquiring the symbols of murderous swindle and suicidal credulousness at a few kreutzer apiece to decorate the walls of surviving customers.

Most of the "founders" were never brought to justice. Many vanished; others were not indicted because of lack of evidence. In the Vienna of 1873, as so often in history, criminal concepts had outpaced legislation.

CHAPTER FIFTY-SIX

In 1878, while Austria was licking its financial wounds, a congress assembled in Berlin made decisions vital for the many countries along the Danubian banks. One was to "regulate," acknowledge, and prolong the existence of the European Danube Commission, which had been formed after the Crimean War to keep the river navigable. Another was to recognize Serbia as an independent sovereign principality.

As an international institution, the Commission was trail-blazing. Neither Austria nor Turkey had been overly navigation-minded, and the Danube had remained a problem child, trafficwise, what with its many shoals, rapids, whirlpools, sandbanks, and the skippers' nightmare and sight-seers' marvel, the Iron Gate. The Turkish pashas embezzled most of the funds designed to keep the muddy Sulina arms open, and the Russians later let them get completely choked and clogged up with sand. Austria, Hungary, Russia, and Turkey were represented on the Commission when it was established at the Peace of Paris, on March 30, 1856; so was Prussia, which elbowed its way into an increasing number of international bodies; so were England and France, and France's budding ward, Italy.

Five years after the Congress of Berlin, in February 1883, representatives of all member nations met in the British Foreign Office to discuss Danubian affairs. The diplomatic mountains began to labor.

Wrangles about competence, delineations of spheres of interest, precedence, and other formal subtleties without any bearing on river navigation continued for weeks. On March 10, the Treaty of London was signed by the plenipotentiaries of the Great Powers. With this 108-article document, the future lines of the power struggle in the Balkans were drawn.

A retreating Turkey, backed by mere words from an England whose policies were getting inconsistent; an Austria-Hungary that might have wanted to expand but for the problem of whether new acquisitions should go to the Austrian or the Hungarian part of the Dual Monarchy;

a Russia which, beset by internal problems, was determined to move into any power vacuum along the enormous peninsula; and the Balkan states themselves, nationally and geographically hard to delineate, selling out to the highest bidder, plotting and battling against one another, vying, arms in hand, for pounds of Turkey's flesh.

The Danube Commission kept functioning until World War I, without noteworthy changes in its statutes or complaints about its operations. The maintenance of an Austro-Hungarian flotilla—small but heavily armed "monitors"—neither violated the London convention nor ever interfered with peaceful navigations. But when war came, a "supreme emergency" for which the convention had made no proviso, the monitors swept hostile craft away from the river and four-inch naval cannon shelled Belgrade, blasting the Commission out of existence.

In 1917, Germany and Austria-Hungary drafted a new convention, according to which control of the Danube would have been confined to riparian states. Their military engineers constructed what became known as the *Treidelbahn* (towing-rope railway) near the Iron Gate, the first up-to-date hauling installation since Roman days. The mile-long track led a few yards away from the riverbank, along a walled canal of perfect navigability for the biggest Danube boats. The very rugged current would have been an obstacle for underpowered craft, but freight locomotives, put to the boats as a relay many hundred horsepower strong, tugged them safely, almost swiftly, through the worst sections of the stream. The *Treidelbahn* still served its purpose after its builder states' long-range plans on the Danube had come to nought.

Nothing was done during World War I to improve shipping conditions in the Danube Delta. From 1915 to early 1918, a front line ran through the delta region. Battle casualties suffered there by Bulgaria, Russia, and Rumania were not high, but disease claimed many victims. No work could be done in the estuary. The peaceful stream flowed on, scornful of man and man's perennial urge for mutual destruction. Every year it carried an average of 200 billion tons of water into the Black Sea, and with the clear water went between 51 and 76 million tons of mud and gravel, unaffected by war.

The 1917 draft of a convention of riparian states was shelved in 1918, and on June 28, 1919, the Treaty of Versailles stipulated the internationalization of the Danube and its tributaries, which also formed national boundaries from Ulm to the Black Sea. Subsequent peace treaties —those of St.-Germain, Neuilly, and Trianon—confirmed the terms of Versailles.

The treaties also demanded that the available river craft be distributed according to the legitimate necessities of the riparian states. This resulted in a great loss to Vienna's *Erste Donau-Dampfschiffahrts Gesellschaft,* the pioneer and undisputed leader of steam navigation on the Danube; but it was not as destructive as the Russian demand more than a quarter of a century later, that the U.S.S.R. receive a share in the company and Danube shipping be turned into the concern of one totalitarian power.

By August 1, 1924, fifteen Danube shipping corporations were operating. Six of them, located in Regensburg, Vienna, Bratislava (Pressburg), and Budapest, formed a cartel operating 202 steamers with a combined engine power of 91,875 horsepower and 881 cargo boats carrying a total of 571,540 tons. Their main problem was that, as they jokingly said, the river was running "in the wrong direction." High-finished products, lighter in weight and heavier in earning potential, went downstream, while the cheap and bulky raw materials had to be shipped up the river, which created a perennial financial problem.

The European Danube Commission resumed its activities in Galatz soon after World War I, but its jurisdiction was confined to a short course of the river near the estuary. The International Danube Commission, located in Bratislava, was created to control navigation between Brăila and Ulm, and a separate authority was set up in Orşova to administer navigation at the Iron Gate. The statutes reiterated freedom of navigation, and stipulated the duties of the riparian states to regulate the river under the Commission's supervision and the Commission's power to undertake overdue regulation work at the states' expense.

CHAPTER FIFTY-SEVEN

The 1878 decision concerning Serbia seemed, at first, of lesser immediate importance than the cumbersome document concerning Danube navigation. But four years later, this stormiest petrel among Austria's Balkan neighbors became a kingdom—not by virtue of achievement, but by the sheer process of self-glorification inherent in small realms carved out of the sore flesh of decaying empires.

After centuries of domination by Turkish pashas or Austrian occupation authorities, the Serbs had had quasi-autonomous Princes since Napoleonic times, pensioners of whoever cared to support their ambitions. The Serbian people, most of them primitive peasants, lived under conditions that would have been considered miserable in medieval England or Germany. Hardened almost beyond belief by want, they grew ever more belligerent in perennial self-defense against brutal and looting authorities. Their code of behavior, based on a retaliatory law of survival —murder for murder, terror for terror—responded to the call of demagogues who glorified violence.

The first spectacular leader in their rebellions against Turkish tyranny can hardly be called a Serb. Ethnically he was a Gypsy from somewhere in Montenegro; the name of Kara George was Turkish for "Black George," Kara (black) referring to his swarthy skin. After a boyhood of stealing, begging, and kettle mending, he entered the services of a Turkish aga, and soon he excelled in squeezing the last bite or copper from the peasantry; but during an insurrection in 1787 he stole equipment from the Turkish arsenals and armed peasant bands against his former masters. The peasants fought with traditional obduracy; at twenty-five, Kara George became a popular hero and called himself "Prince." But in 1791, when the rebellion collapsed, he ran for his life all the way to Austrian territory, enlisted in the Emperor's army with the rank of sergeant, only to turn deserter and return to Serbia, where he became a cattle dealer and cheated the cattle raisers with the skill and ruthlessness of an army-trained Gypsy. At the next insurrection in 1804 he invested some of his ready cash in the affair and this time the insurgents recognized him as their leader. "Karageorge, Prince of Serbia," established his residence in Belgrade and ruled as a choleric despot. But in 1812, when Napoleon's invasion created a second front for Russia and enabled Turkey to withdraw large units from the Russian border and concentrate on Serbia, the peasant troops suffered costly setbacks and the "Prince" fled back to Austria, where he was arrested as a deserter and interned.

The peasants prepared to fight on against all odds rather than surrender. The new leader they trusted was one Miloš Obrenović. Chroniclers with a flair for popular appeal called the Obrenović family Serb peasants, but actually they were titled landowners, their lineage profusely intermixed with oriental blood.

Miloš was close to assassination in 1839, and escaped by abdicating in favor of his son Michael, who, in turn, was on the run a few years later, yielding the deathtrap throne to Karageorge's son Alexander, who, frightened and hapless, watched his supporters and those of the rival "dynasty" butcher each other with zealous impunity. No Serbian court of law, no Turkish governor, made serious attempts at bringing a political assassin to trial.

In 1860, Prince Michael Obrenović returned to the throne. Eight years later, he was murdered.

Those events in Serbia, however, had little bearing upon the attitude of the map makers and kingmakers at the Berlin Conference of 1878. Probably they felt that the powder kegs along the Danube provided auspicious opportunities for schemes and grabs. Serbia's capital, Belgrade, strategically located, was a focal point of traffic on river and road, hub of the entire Balkan Peninsula. Expansionistic, supernationalistic, Serbia became the logical haven for subversive Austrian subjects, a thorn in the monarchy's side.

New-fangled King Milan, Michael's cousin, survived two attempts on his life. He commanded the temporary loyalty of an army he had reorganized and nursed to some vigor, with secret subsidies from Vienna. Milan was an Austrophile, his Russian-born wife, Natalie, was pro-Russian, which may have accounted for some of their conjugal troubles. Sexual conflicts were strong, too. The marriage broke up and Natalie was expelled from Serbia. There were other family quarrels in the Belgrade castle, which would have scandalized a slum neighborhood. The people grumbled, and after six years of kingship Milan resigned in favor of his son Alexander, aged thirteen. A Regency Council was appointed to run the government until the boy came of age. The Councilors were elderly civilians who had been in politics since Turkish days.

Ambitious officers resented them.

The result was a junta, poorly organized and without a concrete program beyond high-sounding phrases and declarations of childish exuberance, but determined to have the King take their orders. The army was the strongest power of the state, but it was a blind power; the other powers were what later analysts would call a corrupt officialdom, and an ignorant and unworthy Orthodox clergy.

Boy-King Alexander was unmanageable from the start. He had been raised in a venomous atmosphere that perverted his body and mind. He was a rabid tyrant at an age when other boys were intimidated by the sight of a police helmet, and a lewd masochist in the earliest stage of his puberty. Haughty and insolent, goaded on by shrewd sycophants who advised him to exercise his royal prerogatives to the limit, he chased the Regency Councilors away when he was seventeen and established a despotism that made the worst phase of Turkish rule appear as an enlightened democracy. Most of the appointments he made were despicable; the way he handled parliamentarians, staged mock elections and plebiscites, dissolved and convoked national representations, was a repulsive travesty, and so were his handling of justice and finance, his patronage and favoritism.

At twenty-six, Alexander married Draga Mašin, an officer's widow ten years his senior, who appealed to his sexual tastes and knew how to make the most of the young King's eccentricities. "The masochist meets his sadist," Serbian officers grumbled, and discontented newspapermen took up the theme with an exhibitionistic lack of discretion. Ex-King Milan, who was living in Belgrade, had tried hard to prevent the marriage, but Draga's straps and whips proved to be more effective than paternal words. Alexander forced his father to leave the country and ordered border guards to shoot the ex-King on sight if he tried to reenter his former realm. Triumphant Draga Mašin and her congenial sisters gave a display of arrogance that no other women had ever dared to give in these regions.

When the hated new Queen launched rumors that she was pregnant, and the rumors proved untrue, a violent wave of scorn surged all over Serbia and regicide again was in the air. But the regicide experts were disunited. They all wanted to do away with the contemptible pair, but some of the officers wanted to cast their lot with Austria, others with Russia; a third faction was still in favor of the Obrenović clan; a fourth wanted an aging Karageorgević, Peter, recalled from modest exile in Switzerland. Also, the older and younger elements in the officers' organization had not completely merged, which resulted in a difference of viewpoint, a certain lack of mutual confidence, and a lack of leadership toward methodical violence.

Enters the most fateful character in modern history, the trigger man supreme: Dragutin Dimitrijević. This son of a civil servant was born on August 17, 1876, graduated from the Belgrade military academy with high honors, was commissioned while still in his teens, and, fascinated by the rabid mysteries of extreme nationalism, displayed such striking talent for leadership that he was chosen for the most urgent "national" task at hand: the elimination of the royal couple and the appointment of his successor.

With the consent of a powerful Russian military clique, he and the junta agreed that Peter Karageorgević should liquidate his petty-bourgeois household in Geneva and prepare for a royal voyage to his capital-to-be. In the early morning hours of June 11, 1903, they broke into Alexander's palace, shot all the guards in their way, dynamited the heavy oak door to the royal suite, where they found the beds empty but the sheets still warm. His leg badly wounded in the process, Dimitrijević limped away to find medical assistance while his henchmen searched for one hour until, in the breaking dawn, they discovered a secret door behind which, trembling, almost nude, holding each other in tight embrace, stood the prey in silent horror. Guns blazed. King Alexander died instantly. Draga, who apparently tried to cover him with her body, still winced when the bullet hit her.

The assassins hit, spit at, trampled on the corpses, then threw them out of the window into the beautiful garden overlooking the Danube bank.

The rest was a triumphal parade of the Belgrade garrison and a laconic official communiqué.

The new cabinet convoked Parliament, a mere formality. Franz Joseph had been so disgusted with the conduct of Alexander and his Draga that his government granted immediate recognition to the new regime. Still in Geneva, but his trunk already packed, Peter drafted his first proclamation:

"Divine grace and the will of a people have called me upon the throne of my ancestors. I herewith declare that I submit to the people's will, and today ascend the Serbian throne. I consider it my first duty to thank God for His grace. . . ."

CHAPTER FIFTY-EIGHT

Captain Dragutin Dimitrijević was still confined to bed when King Peter arrived in Belgrade amidst well-staged outbursts of popular enthusiasm. Dimitrijević had every reason to be satisfied. Among all the great powers only England did not grant immediate recognition to the King who had proclaimed his thanks to God for a grace that was man's bloody doing. When Dimitrijević recovered a few weeks later, King Peter had made him a colonel and the Serbian Parliament had thanked him on behalf of the people and surnamed him the "savior of the fatherland."

The junta was to watch the new King, his government, Serbian press and education—everything pertaining to public life within the still small kingdom. A conspiring body in the permanent session, it would determine the course toward the goal of national aggrandizement.

Assassination was its patent means to political ends. Candidates for assassination successively included King Nicholas of Montenegro, King Ferdinand of Bulgaria, King Constantine of Greece, even Kaiser Wilhelm of Germany—all planned for the greater glory of Serbia. Since the plots were not as simple to execute as the Belgrade murder, and trigger-happy Serbian officers were not easily available abroad, Dimitrijević's clan organized a test school for murder in Macedonia, then part of Turkey (now the Yugoslav-Greek border region). In Macedonia, Serbian, Greek, and Bulgarian insurgents and Turkish gendarmes were engaged in a free-for-all that turned the ancient realm of Alexander the Great into an open highway. Neither the "savior of the fatherland" nor his associates had any scruples; in fact, had anybody told them that they were committing an outrageous violation of international law and Christian ethics, they would have marked that person for extermination.

Disguised as a peasant, a subversive Belgrade officer, Major Voja Tankosić, went to the Macedonian town of Üsküb (Skoplje), which in antiquity had been a center of culture and art, but had degenerated into a primitive, terror-struck Babel. From a mountain hideout near by, Serbian hit-and-run insurgents appealed to their Greek and Bulgarian counterparts to join against the Turkish forces of order and learn the latest guerrilla tactics with the help of brand-new time-fuse hand grenades, just out of Serbian arsenals.

Within a few weeks all of Macedonia was covered by a tight network of ambushes, manned by well-armed ruffians, all graduates of Tankosić's "school." They had been ordered to live on the land. No peasant in Macedonia was safe from the raiders who stole, raped, killed indiscriminately; prowling marauders even ventured into towns and opened fire when the police intervened. Macedonia turned into an inferno as Tankosić's test school flourished. Dimitrijević read his reports with pride and confidence.

In European state chancelleries, however, reports from other sources were read with dismay. In the fall of 1903, an international detachment of gendarmery was sent to the murder ground to establish order.

Tankosić had to return to Belgrade, but his mission was completed. It had been proven that terror organizations could be established, weapons smuggled, killers trained; that the junta's arm could hit its enemies even in neighboring lands and support the army by guerrilla warfare. The stage was being set for wars of conquest in which Macedonia would be but a minor stake.

Dimitrijević was transferred to the general staff. The required tests, usually a candidate's nightmare, were kept within the easiest of limits. No examiner would have dared to make it difficult for the twenty-eight-year-old boss.

Every general-staff officer was entitled to one year of travel to study foreign languages and armies, and Dimitrijević used this privilege for a red-carpet trip through Germany and Russia. On his return he normally would have been assigned to an army corps, but instead was made professor of tactics at the Military Academy of Belgrade. He was not yet thirty, his tactical experiences were limited to Macedonian brigandage, his scientific background was practically nil; yet he was to take charge of an up-and-coming group of officers, future tools for his conspiratorial leadership. Poor orator as he was; defective as his logic remained; repulsive as his concentration on murder as means and objective should have been to the decent elements among officers and students, his crude theories proved to have a portentous appeal. His nationalism inspired young officers and seemed useful to politicians as a propellant for their propaganda mills. Dimitrijević sensed the hypnotic effect of his person and he became convinced of his own vocation, his infallibility, his right to establish his own laws, even if in violation of the Ten Commandments.

The infallible professor, however, suffered a humiliating setback in 1908, when Bosnia and Herzegovina—the former Turkish province occupied by Austria-Hungary—were annexed by the monarchy, with Turkey's consent and without opposition from other Great Powers. Violently indignant, the Serbian radicals claimed that those lands were Serbian, ethnically and historically, even though only 45 per cent of the population gave Serbian as their language. Dimitrijević's ire was savage and impotent. He raged that Vienna ignored him. In his Belgrade office he brooded vendetta.

He did not yet know whom he would kill, and how; but he had many student visitors burning to act. At this point—as at critical points in Hitler's rise to power—the wirepullers took the initiative. They decided on subversive propaganda to undermine their neighbors' internal peace and pave the way for military invasion. On October 8, 1908, the

Narodna Odbrana (National Defense) was formed in Belgrade with Dimitrijević as its clandestine leader. The statutes listed as major aims "awakening of the national spirit, encouragement of national culture, development of physical culture, all in the interest of the realization of national aims and enlightenment in the nationalistic sense."

But domestic operations actually were but a cover for activities in Bulgaria, Macedonia, Bosnia and Herzegovina, and Hungary. Although this did not go unnoticed in those countries, it did not lead to drastic countermeasures. In Austria-Hungary the entire organization was considered a bombastic nuisance and no real threat. Undisturbed, it shipped large quantities of propaganda literature to distribution centers across the border, which blanketed their respective territories with anti-Austro-Hungarian outbursts. To reach the considerable number of illiterates in the rural sections, hundreds of agents roamed the countryside, telling the peasants about the marvels and promise of Serbia and their appalling sufferings under the monarchy.

Strangely enough, the propaganda was effective. It was obvious that economic conditions in an ancient land of over fifty million were much better than in the tiny kingdom of some three million that was just emerging from centuries of corrupt oriental rule. Everybody who read or heard propaganda knew from personal experience that there was no persecution, no organized oppression, no deliberate harassment under Franz Joseph's rule; and yet logic and experience built no dam against untruth and seduction. Propaganda struck a chord when it appealed to frustration, greed, ambition. It addressed itself to youth, to boys who had flunked school or flopped in first jobs. It tried to reach well-established people, to use them as a more decent front. Then as now, there as almost everywhere, those close to the top, who fear never to quite make it, and those at the bottom of the social and economic edifice, are the easiest to subvert.

So Serbian agents talked to merchants, teachers, local officials, and promised unlimited business or promotion to the gentleman candidates if they would organize and supervise the work of tough underlings.

Many joined, while the Serbian government cautiously pulled the brakes; Austria-Hungary had answered their bluster with partial mobilization, and Russia had indicated that it did not want all-out war just yet. Pulling the brakes meant mildly suggesting that Dimitrijević temporize; Prime Minister Nikola Pašić did not want to wind up with a bullet in his chest.

For Dimitrijević, temporizing meant preparing for an emergency.

Marksmen were gathered in "hunting clubs" and "bomb-throwing clubs"; foreign members went to Belgrade to practice on Serbian target ranges, since in their homelands the police might take a dim view of bomb throwing as entertainment. Dimitrijević never met the eager visitors, but cloaked himself in mystery.

It took until June 15, 1910, before his henchmen staged their first action abroad—which was a complete failure. A student with bad marks tried to shoot an Austrian general, but an Austrian guard shot first and killed him instantly. There was practically no investigation; Austria shrugged the matter off too lightly. The Serbian terrorists now had a martyr.

Four more attempts on the lives of Austrian officials failed, and in several other instances they did not even come into assassination range of their targets.

Dimitrijević felt that he was getting too important for his official teaching assignment; he wanted to have his finger on the pulse of both army and government, to make sure that neither would try to dodge his control. But first, with a Balkan war against Turkey approaching, he wanted to revive guerrilla activities.

Early in 1912, he donned peasant's garb, put knives and revolvers under his broad belt, and proceeded first into Turkish Macedonia, then to Albania, which was under Turkish rule, to induce local insurgent leaders to join Serbia in the coming struggle. The insurgent spokesmen asked for weapons, which Serbia promptly supplied, but when war came Albania proclaimed its independence—and neutrality.

Dimitrijević had failed; but this was hushed over, and his legendary prestige remained unscathed, even after yet another experience that would have destroyed the reputation of any professional officer; for this man, who demanded that his chattel stand up even under the most horrible torture, who made death sound like a matter of routine, turned out to be a coward!

In the fall of 1912, when Serbia went to war, Colonel Dragutin Dimitrijević was nominated chief of staff of the Serbian cavalry. This assignment should have given him opportunity to show antique valor in a modernized war, to lead his men into the enemy's rear, to charge over rough terrain, to revive the old tales of which the peasants were fond. But Dimitrijević did not take to horse to ride for his convictions; Dimitrijević reported sick, and his riders had to do their fighting without his leadership. However, his ailment, allegedly contracted in Albania, did not prevent him from accepting a semi-diplomatic assignment to Berlin, where he, who had decreed that his followers must renounce all personal profit, permitted himself to write newspaper articles on military matters for substantial fees.

In June 1913, with the shooting safely over and military articles no longer in demand, Colonel Dimitrijević returned to Belgrade to receive a war medal and assume his newly created post of "Chief of the Information Services of the Great General Staff."

"The Turkish Empire has disappeared; may the God of the Serbs in His graciousness present us with the disappearance of another," one of his chattels exulted in print. The "other" was the Austro-Hungarian arch-foe.

No other means than murder was considered for the achievement of Serbian unification. This would have seemed absurd to a logical mind, for the ties between the Empire and the provinces in which Southern Slavs lived did not depend on any particular person. But Dimitrijević's was not a logical mind; and perhaps the secret awareness of his own cowardice caused him to put up an ever more violent front and to compensate for his unheroic war record by stepped-up terrorism. From the general-staff building, more inaccessible than ever to the small fry, he issued ever sterner orders to conspire, to stab, to shoot.

The government and ranking generals watched his every move. Although Serbia had pledged itself not to interfere with the affairs of Bosnia and Herzegovina after the annexation, Dimitrijević's terrorists were determined to unleash all powers of subversion. In 1913, they staged disorders in Bosnia; the Austrian military restored quiet with unusual efficiency; and when the Bosnian Diet lodged a protest, the provincial military governor, General Oskar von Potiorek, abruptly dissolved it.

Dimitrijević had found a target. A new chapter opened in the book of world history. Its heading reads in blood-red letters: "Sarajevo."

CHAPTER FIFTY-NINE

This chapter is a magazine article which was in my husband's files at the time of his death, ready for publication. The title refers to the day preceding the assassination of Archduke Franz Ferdinand, the Austro-Hungarian heir to the throne, which ushered in World War I.

I am interrupting the narrative to interpolate, with but unavoidable revisions, the story of the pivotal day in modern history, in the manner my husband had chosen for presentation to a mass audience.

A.M.L.L.

THE LAST TWENTY-FOUR HOURS OF PEACE ON EARTH

June 27 was a gloriously peaceful day, one of the most peaceful days in modern history, anywhere, anytime. No war was going on. There was no disturbance of established order. Whatever frictions frilled the smooth surface of national lives seemed minor, ephemeral. But then, on June 28, something came to pass in a town called Sarajevo (pop. 50,000), on the Balkan Peninsula, that unleashed the dogs of war, sent social systems and traditional regimes crumbling, and ever since has kept the world at war, or on the brink of war, in a confusion of insecurity and ruin that dwarfs earlier global disasters, including the big Mongolian invasions, in scope and magnitude.

On June 27, 1914, the Mexican incident appeared to be closing. The ABC press of Buenos Aires expressed satisfaction about the achievements of the conference in Niagara Falls, and commented that "the nations of the Western Hemisphere are able to settle their own affairs without the interference of Europe."

President Wilson called the recession which caused some uneasiness "merely psychological."

John D. Rockefeller donated $2,500,000 to the Medical Research Institute, bringing the total of his diversified gifts to almost 115 million dollars, which, though well below the total donated by Andrew Carnegie, showed what the growth of peacetime economy could accomplish.

In England, the Lord Chancellor proudly reported that the total national income had risen from £860,000,000 in 1868 to a staggering £2,400,000,000.

Suffragist militancy was the only militancy in London. At the fire brigade's parade in Hyde Park, two women jumped on the royal carriage and threw bundles of leaflets at the royal couple's hats. The Queen was indignant, the King smiled, the public was furious.

German newspapers featured the British naval visit at Kiel and spirited official addresses on German-British friendship.

Upon request of the Foreign Office, it was announced, the play *The Horror of the French Foreign Legion* would not be performed in Germany. This should please France.

In Germany, the sharpest note of militancy came from the Association of Men's Underwear Manufacturers, which engaged in a vociferous campaign against retailers who opposed price fixing.

In Italy, calm was restored after several weeks of local riots. Only the oratory in the Chamber of Deputies was still stormy, and the socialist *Avanti* of Milan ran a fierce anti-militaristic editorial written by a young assistant editor, Benito Mussolini.

French newspapers gave little space to a past political crisis, in which a government set a record low of twenty-four hours in office, but abounded with accounts of yesterday's pugilistic sensation, in which world heavyweight champion Jack Johnson and challenger Frank Moran of Pittsburgh, Pennsylvania, had a twenty-round bout in Paris' *Velodrom d'Hiver,* the former retaining his crown.

In Russia, Tsar Nicholas II and Tsarina Alexandra were hosts to the First British Cruiser Squadron at anchor off Kronstadt. Brilliant gala receptions were given. It had been a relatively quiet day in the Russian capital of St. Petersburg, after a brief spell of street fighting in which, as a leading newspaper wrote, "unorganized masses had been thrown defenseless under the yoke of revolutionary agitators."

In Austria-Hungary, Mr. Average Citizen discussed operetta and soccer, and gave little thought to maneuvers in Bosnia province, which they considered a strange wild land, a solid headache for bungling governments, a questionable market for thriving industries.

There, atop a hill near Tarčin in the morning hours of June 27, 1914, a trumpet major sounded the bugle. The two-day maneuvers of the 15th and 16th Austro-Hungarian Army Corps were over. Generals in "field-gray" uniforms gathered at the command post. The giant figure of a slightly graying officer towered over the gathering. A three-star general presented him a document in a leather folder. The big man glanced over the hackneyed generalities about the soldiers' splendid performance and signed: "Archduke Franz Ferdinand, General of Cavalry."

The Archduke would have wanted to leave at once, but routine required that he watch the final parade. After a night of fog and drizzle the skies had cleared. Weary soldiers put their best foot forward. It was high noon when the Archduke took leave of the three-star general, Oskar von Potiorek, army inspector and provincial military governor. He would not see him again until the following morning. Potiorek would go to Sarajevo, the Archduke to Ilidža, where he had a date with his wife.

Franz Ferdinand of Austria-Este, who had been fifty the previous December, was a nephew of Franz Joseph I and Maximilian of Mexico. The death of Crown Prince Rudolf at Mayerling a quarter of a century before, had catapulted him into direct line of succession. Since 1896 he had been heir apparent. He was a well-traveled man. He had even been to America, to visit the Chicago Columbian Exposition and World Congress in 1893. Much of his adult life had been spent waiting. Franz Joseph was nearing eighty-four and still going strong. "I shall never be Emperor," Franz Ferdinand told intimates who wanted to see him installed on the throne, in the interest of their own careers. As heir apparent, Franz Ferdinand had no constitutional powers. Quick-tempered as he was, he would do no more than grumble and toy with ambitious plans for future reforms. His intimates championed reforms, particularly those which would grant the Slavs a greater share in the government, but which Balkan nationalists denounced as annexionistic. Franz Ferdinand disliked making enemies, he disliked controversy, he disliked war. But since the Emperor had made him Inspector General of All Armed Forces, he had to preside over major maneuvers.

The Archduke had intended to excuse himself from the Bosnian affair, but then there had been a mysterious warning of impending danger and he had to go lest he be called a coward.

And now it was almost over. Tomorrow he would pay an official visit to Sarajevo and then return to Chlumetz Castle in Bohemia. Today, at 3 P.M., he would join his wife Sophie, Duchess of Hohenberg, who waited in the idyllic spa of Ilidža, fifteen miles southwest of Sarajevo. It was unusual for an Archduke's wife to follow her husband to distant maneuver grounds, yet practically everything had been unusual in their romance and their morganatic marriage. When Franz Ferdinand met Sophie, she was a lady in waiting of his cousin, one of the Emperor's numerous daughters, whose young daughter, in turn, he was expected to marry. The would-be bride had more self-assurance than charm; the thirty-two-year-old lady in waiting was charm personified. The Archduke, almost thirty-seven, and pampered by eligible female royalty, fell in love head over heels—an outright affront to the Emperor's granddaughter! Franz Joseph was annoyed, the Court aghast. But Franz Ferdinand signed the required act of renunciation of succession to the throne for future offspring of his marriage, married Sophie on June 29, 1900, and was unceremoniously happy. They had three children, whom they brought up so sensibly that in 1938 the youngest son, Ernst, wound up in one of Hitler's concentration camps for having thrown a rock at a picture of the Führer.

In 1909, the forgiving Emperor created Sophie a Duchess of Hohenberg, but the act of renunciation was not rescinded. The Duchess never interfered with protocol, but in June 1914 she could not bring herself to stay behind. She had accidentally entered her husband's private chapel and heard him invoke God's mercy in the case of sudden death. Then only had he told her of the strange warning. He called it ridiculous and insisted that she stay at home. She said nothing, but left Chlumetz a day after him and so informed Franz Ferdinand by wire en route. His reaction was enthusiastic: "Looking forward to reunion. Love." So they would spend their fourteenth wedding anniversary together, after all!

She met Franz Ferdinand's special train at Ilidža Station at 3 P.M., June 27. They would stay overnight. The people, highly patriotic, were exuberant. Sophie had arranged for an official reception at 7 P.M. They would not have much privacy except, they hoped, a walk in the park before supper.

In Vienna that Saturday afternoon, the Minister of Finance left his office in a glum mood. The Minister of Finance was also head of the civilian administration of Bosnia, and thus responsible for whatever happened in those Balkan backwoods. Several weeks before, the Serbian envoy to Vienna had paid an improvised call, talked about ill feelings that Bosnian maneuvers might create among Serbs living at either side of the border, of the possibility that some fanatic youth might put a live instead of a blind cartridge into his rifle; also, he reminded the Minister that June 28 was *Vido Dan,* the anniversary of the Serbs' defeat by the Turks in 1385, which had destroyed their independence for centuries;

Serbian nationals were extremely irritable on that day. He termed the maneuvers dangerous, the Archduke's visit foolhardy. The more he elaborated on the theme, the more cryptic he sounded. The Minister drafted a report that circulated at court—and caused Franz Ferdinand to insist on the trip, come hell or high water.

The Minister directed the Sarajevo authorities to take all necessary precautions, but he had no high opinion of the local police. He wanted the Budapest police, the best of the Empire's security forces, to assign two-score crack detectives to Sarajevo; but this would have required an extra 7000 kronen ($1400), which neither Budapest nor Vienna had available in the regular budget. All they could afford were three detectives. This was cut-rate security! As the liveried doorman saluted him ceremoniously, the Minister confounded his high office and all that went with it.

At about the same hour, in Belgrade, the Prime Minister of Serbia had an apprehensive talk with his cabinet. He was a man of moderation and had lots of trouble with the lunatic fringe of Serbian nationalism, and the most lunatic and ruthless of them all, who had adopted the mythological pseudonym of "Apis," after the sacred bull of the Egyptians. He did not have the power to curb Apis and his gang outright, but he had to go about it in a very clever way. Right now he seemed to have failed in a vital matter. About five weeks before, he had learned that Apis had had three youths trained and equipped in Belgrade for an attempt on the life of the Austro-Hungarian heir to the throne. He directed the Serbian border authorities to keep them from crossing into Bosnia, but allegedly instructions had come too late and the threesome was on the loose. Border guards apparently took Apis' orders, not those of the legal authorities.

Also in Belgrade, a few short blocks away, Colonel Dragutin Dimitrijević conferred with an aide. Both were in high spirits. The thirty-seven-year-old colonel, who in mufti would have looked perfectly nondescript, was none other than the legendary, notorious Apis!

Dimitrijević never had global war on his mind. The range of his political conception never went beyond the Balkans. During his lifetime his name might have passed unnoticed on the shingle of a Serbian green-grocer, and almost fifty years after the most fateful of his foul deeds begot World War I, it is known to only very few people. His complete story was never printed, and this author could find only one picture of him.

This picture shows a thirtyish man of devastatingly vulgar handsomeness—the type of small-town dandy who cheats some lovelorn janitor's widow out of her life's savings.

He was tall and massive, with big, coarse hands; the shape of his round head was quite graceful, his features were repulsively regular, his eyes had an expression of vague pride; his nose was short, straight, and fleshy; a turned-up carefully groomed mustache emphasized moist, sensual lips; his chin was well shaped, with a coquettish dimple. The picture shows him in a colonel's uniform—high cap with tufts of feathers, double-breasted knee-length tunic with brass epaulets, three medals, and a flashy belt restraining a bulging belly.

The father of world wars was rather taciturn, and contemporaries could not explain the reason for his attraction, his magnetism. His ideas were controversial and illogical; but he expressed them in such a flippant tone that his comrades did not realize the gravity of the action he was expecting of them. His sheer presence imposed his will upon other people. One friend described his as "a secret force to which I desire to surrender even if my reason tells me not to do it. He is no chosen leader, yet imposes himself quite naturally and makes us consent willingly to his requests."

Dragutin Dimitrijević seems to have had hypnotic powers. Was this pathologically ambitious coward, catapulted by others into strategic positions, a smiling, soft-spoken Balkan version of Adolf Hitler, who was born thirteen years after him—the Hitler of World War I?

His powers of persuasion must have developed early, as did his talent of getting and keeping people together, of forming nationalistic "cells" that co-operated and started terrorist activities in neighboring Austria-Hungary. His first organization, the "National Defense," had many cells abroad and propagandists in Bosnia and southern Hungary, who championed subversive Serbian nationalism. It promised everything to everybody, once under Serbian rule: lush careers to malcontent intellectuals, higher farm prices, better business, and, last but not least, glorious vindication to all flops. Quite a few youths heeded the appeal. Frustrated boys, who in our day might join street gangs, styled themselves champions of a Greater Serbia and were ready to commit acts of terrorism which make modern juvenile delinquency look like innocent mischief.

But Apis felt too big to keep within the framework of an organization that was not entirely his own. The "National Defense" was getting too clumsy for his taste, too much weighed down by organizational ballast. Without relaxing his control over the group, he founded another even more ruthless one to lead it in deeds of terrorism and provide the cloak-and-dagger element which the "National Defense" lacked. So, on

May 9, 1911, the "Union or Death" sprang into life, also with a pseudonym: the "Black Hand." Its seal showed a clenched fist holding a banner with a skull and crossbones, and also a knife, a bomb, and a poison vial. Apis was leader, head, and soul of this heart- and soulless group of dedicated assassins; yet he had himself listed only as No. 6 on the roster of its ten charter members, the rest being field-ranking officers, one career diplomat, and one newspaperman.

It was the duty of each member to enlist new members and vouch with his life for their conduct. The interest of the organization had to take precedent above all others; by joining, a man was losing his individuality and could not expect personal glory or profit. Betrayal, even if under torture, was punishable by death. New members were initiated in a windowless room lit only by a small candle, before a table covered with a black cloth on which were spread a crucifix, a knife, and a revolver. A masked delegate of the Black Hand's Central Committee put in a theatrical appearance, and before him recruits swore "by the sun that warms me, the earth that feeds me, before God, by the blood of my ancestors, upon my life and honor," to be ready for every sacrifice, and never to quit. The Black Hand's first activities were unsuccessful plots against authorities in provinces it wanted Serbia to annex. In the fall of 1913, the Bosnian military governor became their target.

Apis worked through a distant cell, at the University of Toulouse, France. France was a haven for such rebels because Austria-Hungary had practically no informers there. A number of Serbian and Bosnian student radicals had enrolled in Toulouse. The mellow climate of ancient Western culture had not assuaged the fanaticism with which they debated terrorism, nihilism, bolshevism, and the assassination of Potiorek.

Two loafing students in their late twenties received pistols and went to Bosnia, where they found a willing helper in the person of Danilo Ilić, a tall, pale, ill-tempered youth who had quit teaching school and turned subversive out of rebellion against his frail health and his mother's penuriousness. They could not get near Potiorek, however, and months went by unavailingly.

Then, around Easter, Apis learned of the impending Bosnian maneuvers and decided that the Archduke's death would be a harder blow to the Empire than that of a provincial governor.

The machinery of terror went into motion, slowly, unsteadily, confusingly, but gaining momentum. Reinforcements in terrorists and weapons came via the "tunnel"—an intricate network of conspirators and hirelings that led past inefficient and stupid guards across the border and forwarded contraband, messages, and fanatics. All was quiet in the tunnel on June 27. No traces were left of the shipment of four Browning pistols, six bombs, and three teen-aged boys from Belgrade to Sarajevo. The men who had done the shipping were back in unspectacular fields of peaceful endeavor; one of the boys was at his father's home eleven miles from Sarajevo, the other two were right in town. Hardly anybody had heard the names of these three youths which one day later would be flashed all over the world.

The first boy, not yet nineteen, was Tryphon Grabez, son of a mild-mannered Greek Orthodox pope. "My father taught me religion when I was a child," swarthy Tryphon would later explain, thrusting forward his large head with the piercing black eyes. "But as I grew up I abandoned emotional faith and chose national religion instead. National religion knows no command 'Thou shalt not kill.' "

Pope Grabez had sent his son to the secondary school of Tuzla, Bosnia, not knowing that it was a hotbed of subversion. To impress his schoolmates with a glorious act, Tryphon slapped one of the Austrian teachers and was barred from all schools of the Empire. His father sent the black sheep to Belgrade to finish his studies on a meager allowance; Belgrade schools welcomed exiles from across the border. In Belgrade, Tryphon Grabez patronized The Little Goldfish and The Acorn Wreath, drab coffee shops where you got a cup of coffee and three rolls for a nickel and which kept ultra-radical periodicals for the benefit of like-minded patrons. At The Acorn Wreath he befriended Gavrilo Princip, a fellow flop from another Bosnian school. They considered themselves political exiles, victims of the tyranny of the school curriculum.

Princip, born on July 15, 1895, had been raised by his impecunious widowed mother, who let him drift in an atmosphere which attracted drifters to terrorism. Princip flunked math, hiked to Belgrade, kept drifting, went hungry, remained malcontent and vengeful against Austria-Hungary, which had "let him down."

Also at The Acorn Wreath they met Nedjelko Cabrinović, who had a remarkable record that included slapping his own father, attempted arson, instigation of a strike, work for an obscure printing shop, and occasionally a few days in the cooler. After he had worked as a courier carrying nationalistic pamphlets across the border, to which he added anarchistic literature on his own, the Belgrade National Printing Office hired him as a compositor.

The hangouts of the threesome were also patronized by a strange character who passed as an unemployed waiter but was a Black Hand agent looking for potential terrorists. When Apis ordered reinforcements, the scout got busy. Late in April 1914 he planted a clipping on the coming Bosnian maneuvers on Nedjelko's composing board and wrote in the margin: "Are you ready?"

Nedjelko took the clipping to The Acorn Wreath and showed it to his pals. They warmed up to the common resolve and ranted about "readiness" all the way to The Little Goldfish. There they were drawn into lively conversation by the agent, who then reported to have found "good men."

None of the boys had ever handled a weapon, however.

Next morning the training began at the army rifle range in the outskirts of Belgrade and in a small town several hours away, where bomb throwing was taught. Nedjelko Cabrinović became reasonably good with revolver and bomb; Gavrilo Princip became a fair shot but poor with the bomb; Tryphon Grabez learned slowly. There was no time to waste. After one month their drillmaster told them that they had graduated, using the cryptic formula "Dawn is rising."

On Monday, June 1, the drillmaster saw the boys off at the Belgrade pier. From there a boat took them up the Sava River to Šabac, the first stop. They had received the equivalent of thirty dollars in travel money, which they considered miserly for a four-week venture, and a slip of paper which they should show to a certain major in Šabac, who would arrange for the next lap of their trip. They had the weapons concealed under broad belts like those many Balkan peasants wore.

The major took them on to a border town where a captain would issue further orders. He refused Gavrilo's request for additional funds and the trio reached their goal in a less than exuberant mood. They were put up in the gendarmery building. Gendarmes asked questions about their marksmanship; the boys fired a few pistol shots out of the window, in the direction of Bosnia. Later the gendarmes took them to a dance. A buxom girl scorned the puny Gavrilo but danced a fiery kolo with the solid Nedjelko. A violent spat ensued and threatened to break up the team; next morning the rivals told the captain that they would not go on. The captain had no patience with their story, and when Gavrilo Princip insisted that their ways would have to part, the officer sneered and ordered that he and Tryphon Grabez should go west, while Nedjelko Cabrinović would go south and meet them well inside Bosnia. Princip had to yield.

A Serbian guard was told to arrange the border crossing. The guard sullenly refused. Two other guards insisted that all smugglers' paths were sealed off. The captain roared orders; the guards snapped to attention but would not obey. Only one more guard was at the post! This fourth was a Black Hand man, and he asserted that he would get boys and things across. A peasant from Bosnia rowed them across the border river, past the so-called "Smugglers' Island," toward the Bosnian bank. Had any Austrian guard watched the island he could not have failed to notice the boat. But no Austrian guard watched.

The boys did not know who their next guide would be. They had been briefed to follow peasants they would meet. The oarsman handed them over to a sturdy fellow, and a mile later they were joined by two more rustics, who pointed at their belts, asked for the weapons, and put them into canvas bags. They walked on. Occasionally they had to hide in bushes, when silhouettes of gendarmes appeared in the distance. Rains soaked the trail; they spent one night in an abandoned shack. Next morning it rained even harder. Footsteps indicated the nearness of gendarmes. It could only be gendarmes, for the imprints of their boots with heelpieces of metal were unmistakable. Even the most careless gendarme was bound to search the marchers; but no gendarme saw them.

Soaked and weary, they reached a roomy peasant's hut, another stopover in the "tunnel." The owner hung up their clothes to dry, gave them hot coffee and fat, salty bacon, then cleaned their weapons and wrapped them in cloth. Several hours of sleep later the boys were awakened by the arrival of a man on horseback who impressed them as being no yokel. He took the weapons and ordered the boys to follow him. Docile, subdued, they walked behind the prancing horse. Outside a small town he stopped at another peasant's hut, handed the weapons to the owner, and was off.

It was almost midnight when the peasant harnessed a bony mare to a creaking rack wagon, put the weapons on the wagon, and motioned the boys to jump up. Over bumpy roads they rode. It was pitch dark. Suddenly the clouds broke and a bright moon revealed that they rambled toward a brick building: a gendarmery barrack! The peasant told the boys to jump off and run, bypass the barracks, and wait for him further up the road. They ran like frightened rabbits, made a wide detour, and then waited, fear-struck. The peasant pulled a mat over the arsenal. The odds were a hundred to one; sentinels were under orders to check every man and conveyance. But the sentinel in the guardhouse was sound asleep!

Dawn broke as they reached the outskirts of Tuzla. They were taken to a man whom their guide respectfully called *Gospodin,* which stood for a man of rank.

Approaching middle age, balding, squint-eyed, sporting a black mustache, this Black Hand big shot was a businessman, owner of the city's only movie theater, member of the board of the local bank, a most respectable citizen. The "tunnel" led right through his house. Nedjelko Cabrinović had already arrived. The boys were taken to the railroad station and warned that they were on their own. They rode several hours. Police and gendarmes boarded the slow trains, making spot checks of unusual-looking passengers. The three looked absolutely average. Shortly before Sarajevo one plain-clothes man was supposed to check everybody. This man happened to know Nedjelko Cabrinović and considered him a funny crackpot. They all had a friendly chat and the boys reached their destination without mishap.

In Sarajevo, Danilo Ilić was waiting. He took Gavrilo Princip to his own house, sent Nedjelko Cabrinović and Tryphon Grabez to their families. He told them all to report on June 28, 8 A.M., at a certain confectioner's shop. Ilić loved pastries. He could think of no better meeting place on that day of decision.

Pope Grabez flew into a rage when his son called, but his mother persuaded him to allow the boy to stay. Every new arrival in Sarajevo had to register with the police. Nedjelko and Gavrilo Princip complied, but the police did not check them. Ilić meantime recruited more terrorists.

June 27. It was almost dusk in St. Petersburg, late morning in New York, midafternoon in Sarajevo, when Ilić told Gavrilo Princip: "I need it now." Princip nonchalantly reached under the couch and pulled out a box. "Are you crazy?" Ilić asked. "Didn't you tell me it was so well hidden that nobody could find it?" "It is!" Gavrilo yelled back. "You told me your mother never sweeps under the couch!"

This morning the cleaning woman had been expected; she would have found the box and snooped into its contents. But that Saturday the cleaning woman had a cold and did not come.

Their fates and that of the plot had been on the razor's edge. The recruits received their tools. Ilić explained the handling of the bombs: "First hit the detonator. It takes thirteen seconds until it goes off. Don't throw it too soon." The two promised to remember. They couldn't practice with the bombs, but Ilić wanted to fire a Browning. He took the two youngsters across a meadow to a real tunnel, pulled the trigger, and boasted: "Where it hits there can be no life." And he directed:

"You'll both stand on Appel Quai, one opposite Cumurja Bridge, the other between Lataina Bridge and City Hall. Be there by 8:30 A.M. When he comes shoot or throw, whichever seems best. Then swallow this." He handed them two poison vials; the Black Hand had decided that after "acting" they must commit suicide, lest they be forced to talk. The youngsters were puffed up with pride.

A sentinel at the opposite end of the tunnel had heard the shot but did not investigate. Shooting was common at maneuvers time.

The youngsters took the weapons to a friend, who promised to keep them safe until morning. After they had left, the friend remembered that the Sarajevo police had offered an award of 200 kronen for information leading to the apprehension of plotters. For 200 kronen ($40) you could buy almost anything, including a bicycle. He had always wanted a bicycle. He went to police headquarters. A huge poster offered an award of a full 300 kronen. But he could not bring himself to enter; maybe they wouldn't believe him; maybe they'd cheat him; maybe they'd even put him in jail.

Sarajevoans used to retire early. But the Court of St. Petersburg did not retire early that night of June 27. A gala affair took place in the Tsar's summer castle. In Paris, the English ambassador arranged the most brilliant party of the season. In New York City, Saturday-afternoon shoppers hunted bargains: women's smart footwear at $3.28 at Lord and Taylor's; men's suits at $15 at Wallach Brothers. All over the world harassed reporters tried to dig up some news, but it seemed hopeless. June 27 was a day of perfect peace.

Next morning, at eight, the Archduke's special train waited at Ilidža to take the couple and their small retinue to Sarajevo. Potiorek, his staff, and civilian functionaries would wait at Sarajevo with the automobiles.

At the same hour, a sloppy countergirl at a confectioner's shop in Sarajevo greeted the four customers: Ilić and cronies. Then she arranged her disheveled black hair and paid no attention as Ilić heaped syrupy pastries on four trays, nor when, sitting at a table one minute later, he distributed weapons. She did not listen when Ilić explained basic strategy.

The Archduke would arrive at 10 A.M. He would ride from the station to City Hall, practically all the way along Appel Quai, the main street along the bank of the narrow Miljacka River. Appel Quai, where the conspirators would be lined up, should turn into a deadly gantlet.

Mohammed Mehmedbasić, Ilić's friend from Toulouse, would stand near the bank building opposite Cumurja Bridge. Nedjelko Cabrinović would cover its western approaches. Tryphon Grabez was assigned to Kaiser Bridge. Gavrilo Princip would go directly to Lataina Bridge. Two new boys already had their assignments. Ilić did not intend to make a personal attempt at murder; he would keep inspecting the gantlet, six would-be assassins, yet to be joined by a seventh, concentrated on a stretch of little over half a mile.

By 8:20 the sloppy countergirl was alone. Nedjelko Cabrinović went to a photographer. He wanted to have his likeness preserved for posterity. The photographer was in a hurry; he wanted to see the Archduke ride past. So he did not notice that his customer held a radical paper in his hand and that his coat pocket bulged with a bomb.

It was 9 A.M. when Nedjelko approached his position. The sidewalk was getting jammed. He found himself squeezed in too tightly for action. His bulging pocket bumped into a policeman. He felt a chill in his spine. But the policeman only yelled at him to be gone. He elbowed his way out and ran toward the bridge.

Gavrilo Princip had been at his post since 8:15. He felt lonesome. He had a Serbian tricolor cockade in his pocket, next to the Browning. He put it into his buttonhole. Nobody accosted him. One dull hour had passed when he saw a former schoolmate, son of Sarajevo's chief public prosecutor, Mr. Svara. "Greetings," Gavrilo shouted. Svara looked at the cockade and asked how things were in Serbia. Gavrilo bragged that everything was wonderful, that the country could win any war, and then he stopped abruptly and asked whether the Austrian courts still respected the old law under which the death penalty did not apply to persons under twenty. Svara shrugged and left. He had always considered Princip a fool.

Ilić meantime toured the gantlet. He saw Nedjelko Cabrinović stare into the river with a frightened expression, Gavrilo Princip talk with the prosecutor's son. He had a spell of anger when he noticed that the others were not at their posts and wondered whether he shouldn't call it off. But wouldn't the Black Hand hold him responsible? What if one of the boys would disobey? Pondering, he saw a terrorist old-timer whom he trusted blindly; and he still had one bomb left. A score of seconds and a few hasty words later the last bomb changed hands.

The bells on City Hall struck ten.

The special train pulled into Sarajevo station. The general public was barred from the red-carpeted platform. White-gloved field gendarmes ringed the building. General Potiorek in full kit snarled off the report formula. The mayor of the city, wearing a fez, lifted his hand and tried the deepest bow his belly would permit. The local chief of police gesticulated officiously. The Archduke, alighting from the train, also in full kit, was stern and tense. The Duchess smiled, but her eyes looked worried.

A row of cars waited outside. The police chief's would lead, the mayor's was to be next. The Archduke, his wife, and Potiorek would be in the third car, a big dark-green Graef & Stift double phaeton owned by Count Harrach, who would sit near his chauffeur. Behind their car came the chamberlain, military aides, the Duchess' lady in attendance, some lesser members of the retinue—three more cars altogether. This was no gala array, but everybody wanted to get the visit over with, and the program was arranged accordingly: a ride to City Hall, addresses, inspection of the building, a reception for the ladies of the town; a visit to Konak Castle, residence of the military governor; and perhaps a quick trip to the museum. All the time the special train would wait, steam up.

At 10:15 the Archduke boarded the Graef & Stift. Appel Quai was decked out with black-and-yellow flags. Only a very few houses did not show the Imperial colors. Along the sidewalk people cheered.

The caravan proceeded at fifteen miles per hour. The Archduke would have liked a brisker pace. To distract him, Potiorek pointed out objects of interest. Across the river was a barrack, a sober brick affair but big and brand-new. The Archduke gave it a bored glance. Then he heard a sharp report. The time was 10:18.

As the bells struck ten, Nedjelko Cabrinović had looked for something against which to bump the detonator of his bomb and spotted a lamppost about twenty yards away from the course of the cars. He approached it. People milled about. He had to hold his ground. If he were pushed away he could not hit the detonator and the bomb would be a dud. Seconds crawled past, rounding into minutes that seemed to fly. From far away rose a surf of cheers: Serbian *zivio*'s, German *Hoch*'s. The surf rose; the column came in sight. He did not know in which car his target would ride, but he looked out for green feathers on two-cornered general's hats. He saw them rise out of the third car and also a cart-wheel-sized lady's hat. He grabbed the bomb, banged it against the lamppost, counted, threw—high trajectory, as he had been taught. It seemed to fly with absurd slowness. He watched, spellbound. Somebody obstructed his view. The spell gave way to near panic. He wanted to flee. He did not reach for the poison.

A thunderous crash reverberated from walls and hillsides. Then shrieks and shouts. The youth made for a balustrade, plopped into the shallow river. Blows hit him. Men were jumping on him. They dragged him to the bank, lifted him, twisted his arms, trampled on him, chased him, shoved him up the slope to Appel Quai. He wanted to ask what had happened. Iron fists hit his mouth shut. He couldn't see. They were hitting his eyes, too.

The bomb had hit the folded top of the Graef & Stift, slid off, dropped on the pavement, and exploded in front of the next car. That car was wrecked, its owner-driver slightly injured; one of the passengers, Lieutenant Colonel Merizzi, had suffered major head injuries. Several onlookers had been hit, none fatally.

Nothing seemed to have happened to the Graef & Stift and its passengers, but the Duchess had an uncomfortable feeling on her neck. The car halted. Her whaleboned collar was opened and she showed a red bruise. Apparently she had been grazed by a tiny splinter.

The fifth car took the passengers from the fourth. The two leading cars drove back in reverse. The automobiles were sitting ducks for lurking assassins, but none was around. A physician offered to take Merizzi to the garrison hospital. Nedjelko Cabrinović was just being dragged across Appel Quai. The Archduke did not deign to look at the battered assailant.

Gavrilo Princip was the only one of the conspirators who hurried toward his post as the bomb burst. A breeze carried a faint smell of burned explosive. He was calm—certain that the Archduke was dead. Then he saw the cars, the green feathers standing upright. He reached for his pistol; but, drifting in the crowd, he would not take aim at a target so far away. Next, he saw Nedjelko, soaked, battered. "He didn't take poison," it flashed through his mind. "They'll make him talk, unless I shoot him." But he couldn't get into range and meantime the cars roared away.

The cars continued to City Hall, the leader now doing forty miles per hour. Through a twin lane of people they rode, men and women who all knew that there had been an assassination attempt and tried to cheer vivaciously.

Nothing happened at Lataina Bridge, at Kaiser Bridge, near City Hall. The array of assassins was broken. Ilić was dumfounded. He fretted that he had not called it off. The plot had abysmally failed. Would the "tunnel" take the fugitives back to Belgrade? How would they be received there?

"What are we going to do now?" the Archduke asked Potiorek. "They'll keep throwing bombs and after they've killed me the murderer may spend a few years in prison and be released through some political action. . . ." Potiorek asserted, warily and unconvincingly, that every-thing was under control.

They reached City Hall. As the stunned mayor fumbled for the script of his address, the Archduke burst out: "Mister Mayor: We came to visit the people of Sarajevo and bombs are thrown at us. This is an out-rage!" His voice was high-pitched. The mayor waited, sweating profusely. "You may speak now," the Archduke snarled.

"Our hearts are gladdened by the gracious visit—Your Imperial High-ness can read from the expression on our faces the sentiments of love and devotion . . . unflinching loyalty . . ." The address rattled on, a compendium of fawning epithets. "Sarajevoans filled with joy and pride . . . beloved serene guests . . . God save His Imperial Royal Majesty, our Lord Emperor Franz Joseph . . ."

The Archduke did not conceal his impatience as he reached for his own script and toiled through every syllable of the oratorical brew con-cocted by some speech writer. "With great joy do I accept the protesta-tions of unshakable loyalty . . . I thank you, Mr. Mayor, for the ovations the Duchess and I have received from the rejoicing population." At this point he ad-libbed: "I interpret this to mean that the people are glad about the failure of the assassination attempt," and resumed read-ing, winding up with: "Will you please convey to the citizens of this beautiful provincial capital my cordial greetings and expression of my favor and affection."

From some notabilities came dispirited cheers. Everybody realized that the day was lost and secretly prayed that the visitors would leave soon and without further mishap.

In utter confusion the mayor motioned to the chief of police, who, in rambling official lingo, explained technical details of the bomb. "You seem to think that they'll throw more of the kind?" the Archduke in-terrupted. The police chief, who realized that the best he could hope for was retirement with a pension, mustered all his courage: "I don't know, Your Imperial Highness, but, for God's sake, leave this town!"

Potiorek stepped up, spurs tinkling: "Your Imperial Highness: no un-necessary rides through town! No more than required to leave!" Seeing the Archduke frown, he added quickly: "Maybe we could stop at the museum; that's in the outskirts, controlled by the army. And Her High-ness the Duchess could ride directly to the station."

"I am staying with you," the Duchess said. "Wherever you go I shall go." Her voice was calmer than those of the men. "But Potiorek is right. No unnecessary rides." From outside came cheers.

The Archduke had braved the early warning and did not want to lose face now that it had been proven justified. "We shall visit Merizzi in the garrison hospital," he decided. No objection seemed possible.

Notabilities went into a huddle about how to reach the hospital on the fastest and safest route. They left City Hall as fast as decorum permitted. The Archduke and his wife walked down the staircase, arm in arm.

"*Zivio!*" "*Hoch!*" The Archduke did not acknowledge the ovation.

Again, the police chief's car took the lead and the mayor's followed. Third again was the Graef & Stift. Its chauffeur was ashen-faced and his lips twitched. The Duchess was in the right rear seat. The Archduke sat next to her; in front of her, Potiorek. Harrach jumped on the left running board to cover the Archduke. "That's nonsense," the Archduke objected. "Superfluous," he corrected himself. Harrach did not budge. The police chief's car opened the muffler as if to start a race. The public kept cheering. The column started at 11 A.M.

Ilić still patrolled Appel Quai and side streets. He had never imagined that there would be so many policemen around. At least he was unarmed. But how would the others fare? By 11 A.M. some of the others had managed to leave town. All but Princip had got rid of their weapons.

All but Gavrilo Princip.

When the column had reached City Hall without running into another ambush, Princip suspected that the remaining accomplices had deserted their posts. He felt like a hero. He could hardly have told what mattered more to him: to kill the Archduke or to put the others to shame. Defiantly he pushed his way through the excited crowd, determined to go all the way to City Hall and wait there on the staircase. But soon he reconsidered: he had no chance to stand on the staircase unnoticed. He returned to Lataina Bridge. Maybe the party would drive back along Appel Quai. The crowd was still dense and tense. He heard that everybody was being searched for weapons. The thought of his pistol, the source of pride a moment ago, turned into terror. He had to get rid of it. He would throw it into the river. But how to do so unnoticed? He sneaked toward the balustrade. The grim stare of a fat fellow stopped him in his tracks. Backing away, he considered dropping the thing in the thick of the crowd; but what if it fell on someone's toes? There was no rescue wherever he looked this side of the Quai. He decided to cross over, enter Franz Joseph Street, and dump the weapon in some dark hallway. But as he reached the side street he saw no door open without somebody hanging around. Almost numb with fear, he stared into a shopwindow. The window reflected an empty hallway, but when he reached it there emerged somebody he knew. He greeted furtively and hurried on.

Another door was closed. In the next lingered a janitor. Exasperated, he tried the other side of the street. Some girl smiled at him and stared at his buttonhole. Haunted by the thought of his revolver, he had forgotten the Serbian cockade.

He retraced his steps. Again he heard a surf of cheers. Suddenly an automobile turned the corner: the police chief's car, tooting, exhaust roaring. Princip clenched his weapon, as if in self-defense. A second car: the mayor's. A third: a gentleman standing on the running board, green feathers, general's tunics, a broad-brimmed lady's hat . . . The car stopped, so close that Gavrilo could have touched it.

The time was 11:03.

The police chief's driver had been given a different route, but since everybody seemed in such a hurry, he decided to take a short cut through Franz Joseph Street. The other cars automatically followed him. He turned the corner, switched gears, and was about to step on the gas when he heard Potiorek yell: "What's the matter? Weren't we supposed to drive along Appel Quai?" This was as good as an order. He pulled the brake. The car stopped abruptly, right where Princip stood.

"He gave me an icy stare," Princip later remembered his close view of the Archduke. He lifted the pistol, pulled the trigger—one, two, three—the Archduke, Potiorek, the Archduke again, mechanically, without thinking. He would have emptied the magazine had not an avalanche of people descended upon him, battered him. A policeman's saber hit him. He saw nothing, but heard weird sounds. One of the arresters later insisted that he had shouted something about being under twenty, but Princip denied it and nobody else had heard it.

Actually, the first bullet pierced the body of the car, then hit a main artery in the Duchess' abdomen. The second hit the Archduke's neck, pierced the right aorta, and got stuck in the cervical vertebrae. Potiorek was unhurt. No trace of the third bullet was ever found.

Neither of the shots would have been fatal if the bullets had deviated by one hair's breadth. The Duchess collapsed into her husband's lap. The Archduke sat straight, but Harrach sensed disaster as a thin jet of blood from the Archduke's mouth trickled down on his hand and he heard him whisper: "Sophie, you must live for the children's sake!"

The car turned, raced to the Konak, only a minute's drive away.

But it was too late.

The wires carried the portentous news to a stupefied world. The mills of fate began their ghastly grind.

All over Europe, sabers rattled. There was no choice but war. "If the monarchy must go down, it shall, at least, go down decently," Franz Joseph said.

Three shots, or maybe only two, started a chain reaction which in its first phase, known as World War I, produced twenty million casualties and, in its consequences, keeps spreading ruin decades later. The effects far surpassed the cause in magnitude. Thousands of volumes have been written about the conflagration, but only few of us know how it really began. What would the destiny of the world have been, your life and mine, and the lives of our children's children, if one June night almost half a century ago a border guard hadn't fallen asleep while on duty, or if a cleaning woman hadn't developed a summer cold, or if a certain automobile had not stopped at a certain intersection at a certain split second?

CHAPTER SIXTY

The last decades of Franz Joseph's reign have turned into a radiant legend, the charm of which became ever more irresistible as time went by and a vicious circle of hang-over, collapse, reconstruction, and renewed disillusionment became the gist of human existence in the Danubian regions.

The turn of the twentieth century was like a glorious sunset, the noble decay of a society that relished the splendid hues of dusk, without seriously believing that they marked an end without hope of resurrection through remorseful sentimentality. The aristocracy and socialites enacted their own play of "Life Beautiful" on the most gorgeous stage that nature and architecture could have set. They were good actors, and occasional sham did not interfere with the effectiveness of their show and its appeal to the millions who could never hope to be part of the cast but enjoyed themselves without destructive envy.

Some later historians, using statistics and data provided by malcontents, could prove that the glory of pre-World War I days was fiction, a dreamer's concoction of such ingredients as Johann Strauss' entrancing waltzes, Arthur Schnitzler's sensitive dramas and novelettes, the culinary delights of the Hotel Sacher and the spicy anecdotes of its *chambres séparées;* that there was, in fact, a full measure of instability, that the Emperor was a remote symbol of a vanishing past, that x per cent of the population suffered from chronic diseases, y per cent were poorly housed and unscientifically fed, and z per cent had incomes below the starvation point. But whatever the dissectors' diagnosis, the spirit was there; nostalgia has solid roots.

The old Emperor indeed was a symbol. Franz Joseph was a person of perfect integrity, who considered corruption and disloyalty the most contemptible of sins. He had the highest respect for his office and its exalted dignity. His figure, shorter than it appears from the familiar pictures in full gala, was always trim. His quiet eyes, which seemed to be made of ice-blue china, stared at any breach of etiquette, at the slightest carelessness of attire, in suspicion and dismay. The court ceremonial had hardly changed since the times of the Turkish siege. At the two balls the Emperor attended each season, decorum would not permit him to dance and there is no indication that he regretted the restriction. Empress Elisabeth did not dance either; and as she passed her prime, and her former beauty was ravaged by a ruined complexion, she avoided court entertainment to the limit of etiquette.

Ever since he had ascended the throne at eighteen, Franz Joseph had not had a carefree moment. Habit had turned him rigid, stiff. He was fundamentally shy and no acute thinker, and anything he said could have grave consequences impossible to undo; so every move he made, every word he spoke to a visitor, was laid down by painstaking protocol. Perhaps only one person was permitted to see the gentle human being behind the monarch's mask: his actress friend Katherina Schratt. "We had a large family celebration at Christmas and I received many pretty gifts," he wrote to her; or, "Last night at the theater, when I noticed that you wore no earrings, I liked your performance even better." He commented repeatedly about his dislike of earrings.

However, in matters concerning his own family his attitude was almost medieval. When his son Rudolf died at Mayerling, on January 30, 1889, the afflicted father's first concern was to pledge all those who had been present at the hunting lodge never to reveal what had happened there. And so, to the disappointment of dime-novel readers, and movie and TV fans, the true secret of the relationship between the high-strung Crown Prince and the teen-age Marie Vetsera with the clumsy figure, lovely blue eyes, pitch-black hair, and a brilliantly white complexion, lies buried in the graves of half a dozen decorous gentlemen.

The death of the Crown Prince, whose unpredictable nature had alienated his father, was less of a shock to the Austrian people than might be assumed. The majority gave no thought to a possible change in regime or policies; Franz Joseph had already ruled twoscore years and had become an institution to a generation that hardly remembered any other sovereign.

He was fifty-nine when his son died, sixty-eight when his wife was murdered in Switzerland, nearly eighty-four when the shots fell in Sarajevo. The Serbian commanding general, who for some time had worked with Apis, happened to be in an Austrian spa for a cure, but, on the Emperor's express orders, was not detained; Franz Joseph considered it improper to take unfair advantage of an enemy.

The general's soldiers, however, soon were to inflict heavy losses on Franz Joseph's elegant but inefficient armies that stormed into Serbia, while up north, at the Russian border, pathetically understrength Austro-Hungarian forces withdrawn from the lower Danube arrived late and piecemeal. During the first phase of the war against Russia, Franz Joseph's army lost 100,000 men a week; its cream of only 1,687,000 men on August 2, 1914, went down the drain of vainglorious improvisation that was almost a travesty.

In the alluring light of the days of splendor which suddenly appeared to be the parting with happy greatness, realistic admonishers had been considered warmongers to be beckoned into well-mannered silence. Then, while the war was still in its field-gray, blood-soaked swaddling clothes, pessimism became fashionable in the upper classes and the decency of doom a social command. But the "go down decently" watchword was not accepted by the people at large, who preferred anything to getting shipwrecked. Extremists, demagogues, as well as honest dreamers, devised a variety of schemes to establish themselves as leaders of groups that would set their own course toward Utopia. The elements of subversion had always been dormant in the multi-national realm, but not even the facts established in courts had led the top authorities to realize that the rebellious Hungarians, Poles, Czechs, and even the Slavs of Sarajevo memory, were more than odd types of bombastic delinquents. It came as a horrible surprise to the Supreme Command when, late in 1914, small units began to run over to the Russians and one entire regiment deserted, creating a critical gap in a sector under hard pressure. The men should have been court-martialed according to every military law, but all the Austrians could do was to proclaim the regiment dissolved and order its flag to be preserved in the army museum.

Yet the mills of fate did not grind too swiftly. By 1916, the Italians, who had reneged on their obligations toward Austria-Hungary and Germany, were unable to penetrate their opponents' improvised lines; the powerful Russian armies were badly beaten; so were the Rumanians, who had just declared war on Austria; so were the Serbs. The Rumanian and Serbian campaigns concentrated, in part, in the Danube region, but, though costly, they were but side shows in the general tumult. In the early fall of 1916, the monarchy did not seem doomed beyond reprieve. But that year the harvest failed, and with famine came black-marketeering, corruption, rebellion.

Then, on November 21, 1916, the steadfast symbol of the monarchy vanished. In the evening hours Emperor Franz Joseph passed away after sixty-eight years as a monarch, the second-longest rule in recorded history.

The Emperor died of a cold that would have laid up a younger man for no longer than a few days, but age and grief had sapped his strength. The manifesto proclaiming the declaration of war had started with the words: "It was my ardent wish to devote the years that the Lord in His grace has still intended for me, to works of peace . . ." Franz Joseph, the pious pessimist, must have suffered silent torment as his Empire slid down the road to a doom he could never fully comprehend.

The funeral on November 30, was the last conducted according to the ancient ritual. As the highest dignitaries of the realm carried the coffin from St. Stephen's to the Capuchin vault, the new ruler, twenty-nine-year-old Charles, his wife Zita, and between them their oldest child, Otto, aged four, walked behind. The skies were clouded. A thin, darkish fog blanketed Vienna.

In Austria the new Emperor's ascent to the throne was held down to strict legalism, but in Hungary a solemn coronation as King Charles IV would take place; without receiving the Crown of St. Stephen in the traditional ceremonial, nobody would be recognized as the rightful ruler of the realm. Charles was a timid man, mostly ill at ease even in familiar surroundings, but he felt comfortable in Hungary, where during the mobilization cheering soldiers had carried him on their shoulders along a troop train and where he and Zita had been welcomed with frantic ovations and torchlight processions in 1915. To him, Hungary was the bastion of loyalty, Budapest its impregnable citadel, in a world fraught with dangers.

On December 28, 1916, he and Zita boarded a special train to Budapest. From the Hungarian border all the way to the capital, pageantry, parades, tempestuous homages, marked every whistle stop. In Budapest, the couple rode to Buda Castle in state, with the people shouting themselves hoarse with rapture.

So, in the fall of 1918, when conditions in Austria were taking a turn for the worst and the security of the Imperial couple was threatened, they looked for a haven in Hungary. They went to Gödöllö, a castle not far from the capital, a coronation gift from the Hungarian nation to Franz Joseph and Elisabeth, passed on to their successors. What had been intended as an indefinite sojourn lasted but a few days. The end was at hand.

Moving to Gödöllö, with several hundred attendants, scores of horses, several automobiles, and mountains of luggage, was expensive. Franz Joseph had been a man of great wealth; Charles' personal property chiefly consisted of land and castles, which mostly brought deficits. The young ruler depended on his civil list to defray the costs of his large household, to subsidize the court theaters, to satisfy the hosts of donation seekers. His annual income of 11,000,000 kronen had been the equivalent of $2,200,200 in 1914; four years later its purchasing power had sunk to $700,000, and prices had gone up. In the spring of 1918, the Emperor vainly asked the cabinets for an advance, and an application for a bank loan also was turned down.

It looked as if the Imperial household would have to discontinue payments, like a businessman who had failed. But at the eleventh hour a temporary remedy was discovered, right in the cellar of the Imperial castle: 158,520 gallons of the incomparable wines of Tokaj, stored in special barrels that prevented spoilage. A Berlin syndicate acquired the liquid treasure for almost $800,000. The deal brought the first ray of joy into Charles' life as a monarch. He had failed in his plans for a separate peace; he had failed in his military efforts, as well as in his attempts at preventing political disintegration; but at least he would not fail his family and the few faithful who depended on him for their livelihood.

Had he abdicated, as was expected of him, the sale of the Hungarian wine would have enabled him to live a life of calm and splendor, perhaps to a ripe old age. But he had sworn an oath to protect his country. Duty and emotions told him to stay put.

But when the couple arrived in Gödöllö, they were not received as enthusiastically as they had expected. The many objects of value, no longer as securely protected as they used to be, stirred greedy thoughts.

The last royal duty that Charles performed was the swearing in of the new Hungarian Prime Minister, Count Mihály Károlyi. Then he followed an urgent recall to Vienna, where his throne was also crumbling, while red banners went up on the towers of Gödöllö and loot-minded hordes crashed its gates.

The storm of chaos spread beyond Hungary's shrunken borders. The long trek home of defeated soldiers turned into a road of disgrace. Battery crews sold their horses, offered cannons as premiums, pillaged supply dumps. One regiment, shrunk to 350 men, found a wine depot, killed its administrator, drank themselves into mad, murderous intoxication, staggered out into the muddy village roads, where some collapsed, others fought, yet others crawled on all fours, torn by cramps. Puddles reddened from spilled blood stank from vomiting, and in these puddles collapsed men drowned. This was the symbol of disaster.

The symbol of decency was suicide.

Many officers, Hungarians and Austrians alike, preferred voluntary death to living in shame. *"L'Autriche est ce qui reste,"* Clemenceau was quoted as having said—Austria is what has remained. The ancient land was reduced to what nobody had grabbed, a sad remnant of past grandeur.

Past grandeur was a lost cause. The only busy elements were black-marketeers of shoddy merchandise and peddlers of phony ideals which were not ennobled by having been outlawed a short time before. Once radiant and opulent Vienna looked like a scrap heap, its soiled streets buffeted by gusts of wind, mansions abandoned by their frightened dwellers, traffic reduced to erratic operations of dilapidated streetcars, lights going out at nine, crowds of tattered individuals besieging soup kitchens. Not even in the war year in which the harvest failed had there been so much hunger and so little money to buy whatever was there. Trains loaded to several times their capacity dumped their human cargo on city railway stations. The soldiers who had once left to the accompaniment of cheers, flowers, and enthusiasm were "homecomers" greeted with unprecedented insult in the face of defeat. Howling mobs threw rocks at officers, tore or cut the insignia from collars and caps; pickpockets swarmed around; black-marketeers offered cut-rate prices, wenches their unkempt services for whatever they would fetch.

Every day, every hour piled shame and disgrace on the desolate remnants of the mighty Empire in which once upon a time the sun had never set and which for six and a half centuries had been the glory of the wild, quaint, or placid regions through which Danubius Fluvius had cut its path.

POSTLUDE

"Still filled with constant love for all my people, I do not wish that my person be an obstacle to their free development." Thus started Charles' first and last proclamation, which he signed on November 11, 1918. Leaders of all political parties went to Schönbrunn to witness the signature and to express more or less embarrassed good wishes.

Next day, the Imperial family left for Eckartsau, a lone hunting lodge about thirty miles east of Vienna, on the flats on the left Danube bank. Even in summer the grassy watered plains with their reed grass and small groves have a touch of melancholy; in the late fall, Eckartsau is a lugubrious, desolate place. On November 12, 1918, it certainly fitted the Emperor's mood much better than the castle of Persenbeug, where he had been born when Crown Prince Rudolf was still alive. Eckartsau, away from beaten tracks, should be reasonably free from intruders; but former suppliers of the Imperial household refused to make deliveries for fear of being assaulted, and the discharged court employees who went foraging for their former masters were plundered or summoned for "smuggling food." Then the Empress fell ill and was without medical attention. When rumors of impending assassination of the ex-ruler were heard, the British War Office took charge. There were frequent suggestions that Charles leave for a safer place, but he insisted on remaining, and he also lacked the money to move. On March 16, however, the new government decided that Charles would be interned unless he either abdicated or left; Charles chose the latter.

The countryside in which he had spent the last few months puzzled him with the memories it evoked. A short distance to the east was Pressburg, with the coronation hill from where he and so many of his ancestors had wielded the state sword in all directions to symbolize that they would protect Hungary against attack from every quarter of the globe. He could see the hill through his bedroom window. Was it still in Hungary, or rather in that puzzling new Czechoslovakian republic? Then, a short distance to the left, like a clearing in the vastness of reeds and stooped groves, soaked by the subsoil waters of the Danube, were the plains of the March, where, more than six centuries before, Rudolf von Habsburg had staked it all on one battle. And now the Empire to which the humble count had laid the foundations was gone, and Eckartsau, the friendly little lodge, had become an exile in one's own realm. On clear days, of which there were not many, Charles could see the spire of St. Stephen's, luring, exasperating.

Across that countryside Turks had marched, Swedes had ridden, Napoleon had been there; a little over fifty years before, Prussian vanguards had maneuvered on those grounds when the Empire's fortunes had already run low. Rudolf had founded it, Charles had lost it; but the land, the eternal river, did not change their expression. Nothing material would remain of Charles. They would build no monument to a loser.

Charles and his family traveled to Lake Geneva in Switzerland with no splendor. Some donations by aristocrats enabled them to maintain the externals of a dignified household. Charles kept pondering, sincerely, naïvely, confusedly, about what had happened to him and what was happening to his people. The events of the three short years were too complex to comprehend and arrange in logical sequence, even for an acute analyist, which he was not. He had only emotions to guide him.

His ill fortune did not seem to make sense. He had had the best of intentions, always trying to act according to popular wishes. The people had been war-weary; had he not tried, as hard as he could, to bring about a separate peace? Nationalities were said to have wanted more independence; had he not in 1918 proclaimed all sorts of autonomies? He had been a constitutional monarch; and if he did not have the power to lift restrictive ordinances issued during the war—wasn't this essentially due to the very constitution that had been established long before he was born? Some politicians had been tried and sentenced; he had granted pardons right and left, and some of those who now banished him owed him their lives. He had no mouthpiece to bring those truths before an international forum, and he was not the man to understand that in a contest between simple truth and high-pressure promotion of deception, the former was bound to lose.

Soon after arriving in Switzerland, he resolved to return. He knew that Austria was lost; but in Hungary, Admiral Miklós von Horthy, who called himself "Regent," professed loyalty.

The little band of faithful who shared Charles' exile and privation were men of average intelligence whose political experience had been gained in a bygone era. Then, arriving in increasing numbers were amateurish "kingmakers" with little to lose if their cops-and-robbers schemes failed, but much to gain if they succeeded; and in due course came ex-aristocrats, ex-officials. But during March 1921 the visitors became even more mysterious. They were organizing Charles' surprise departure, his crossing of the Austrian border on a smuggler's path, the 400-mile trip, incognito, through his ancestral realm, to Hungary. The clandestine border crossing was rendered extremely difficult by the principal's poor physical condition.

On March 25, Charles left for a walk. Only the next morning did his wife disclose to her entourage that her husband was on his way home. Nobody in Austria recognized in the pallid, slight, ailing Mr. Kovač, Charles of Habsburg-Lorraine. On March 28, he arrived in Szombathely, just across the Austro-Hungarian border. Excited crowds milled in front of the castle in which the tired newcomer to an ancient home had put up. From Budapest and a few smaller cities notabilities had come to welcome him. But they could not tell him how strong his chances for restoration were; and neither could the local bishop, nor the military commander, a brother of the composer Franz Lehár.

Charles announced his impending visit to Budapest and agreed to an informal meeting with Horthy, who resided in Buda Castle.

Submissive *in modo,* unflinching *in re,* Horthy insisted that Charles leave. At the news of his return, threatening announcements of military preparations had come from beyond the borders, and Charles had no argument beyond his personal hopes. A debate between a tired man tortured by creeping doubts and a man stimulated by power and ambition, and yielding to pressure by wirepullers, ended a vital incident in the history of the Danubian lands.

Charles returned to Szombathely, ill, and as bewildered as the crowds who roamed the stations on his way. A special train took him back into exile, respectfully cheered by a Hungarian military guard of honor; but in a small Austrian town it was met by a howling, threatening mob.

After the international commotion created by what was now generally called "the *Putsch,*" Charles was no longer unconditionally welcome in Switzerland. On May 18, 1921, he agreed to abstain from political activity and to give three days' notice of change of residence.

Residence now was Schloss Hertenstein, on Lake Lucerne, only a short distance away from Meggen, where the ruins of the Habsburg ancestral castle still stood. Charles often walked there to stare at the crumbling walls and meditate. He would not abandon what Rudolf had created, not relinquish what no conqueror had held for any length of time. "I am homesick," he once confided to a companion.

A lengthy letter from Horthy, who warned that Hungary's foreign relations had become extremely precarious due to Charles' visit and that another attempt on his part might cause war, had no effect on the homesick man who lived in the shadow of his family's legend. Charles could not accept the truism that his plans would mature with time; had Rudolf von Habsburg relied on time to dispose of his rivals, he might never have become the founder of a monarchy. Now the monarchy was in decay, almost like the ancestral castle; but one cornerstone still stood: Hungary, beloved mutilated Hungary, whose people had cheered their humiliated King a few short months before.

Charles did not consult his advisers. On the night of October 13, he received a courier from Budapest who carried a complete plan for a second *Putsch* and $10,000 to buy an airplane. The plane would take him from Zurich to Sopron, in Hungary. There, loyal gendarmes, reassembled in defiance of Horthy's orders, would wait for him and escort him to a special train to Budapest. He would ride incognito. During the trip he would don the uniform of a field marshal, and at Budapest step out, draw his sword, and march at the head of his men across the Danube, over the suspension bridge to Buda, and order Horthy to surrender his powers. Zita would be with him. Their papers were made out to Mr. and Mrs. Kowno.

They left on time and arrived in Sopron on the afternoon of the same day. But organization never being Hungary's forte, the preparations for the crucial railroad trip were in a state that would please only comedy writers: there was no train available! This being sugar-beet season, practically all freight cars, in which the gendarmes were supposed to ride, were in use to carry the sweet crop. The gendarmes hung around. Their commander made a snappy report. Mr. and Mrs. Kowno, immediately recognized by growing crowds that had been attracted by the landing aircraft, were cheered wildly. Telephone and telegraph wires started humming. Foreign embassies were assured that Horthy would fight restoration, while from the field near Sopron enthusiastic loyalists accompanied the royal couple to the quaint little town, where the commander of the local garrison arranged that a solemn oath of allegiance be administered to the King. It was all very festive and elating, but incredibly stupid; a kingdom was being lost for the sake of small-town pageantry.

When finally the special train approached Buda, the rails were blocked by Horthy's soldiers; had it not been for the sugar beets Charles might have arrived several hours before them. He refused to have Hungarians combat Hungarians and accepted Horthy's offer of a truce. The train, with its stunned and unhappy crew, waited in the suburbs for two days.

The royal pair took shelter in the nearby castle of Count Franz Eszterházy, and there were rumors of a plot to abduct, even to murder, them. A conference of ambassadors moved to arrest and banish the King. Thirty-five guards were sent to keep the couple in custody; Charles was told to resign, but he still refused.

On October 26, they were moved to the abbey of Tihany, which had been built during the twelfth century atop a grandiose rock on Lake Balaton from where on clear days the view ranges widely over the Hungarian plain. The weather was clear; Charles could give a long farewell look to the land that radiated in the bronze light of the sun reflected by turning leaves. A dozen reverent gray-bearded monks attended their guests.

The terms of the King's banishment provided that he be handed over to the custody of the commanding officer of the British Danube flotilla, which was then stationed in Budapest, and that a statute of deposition be introduced in the Hungarian National Assembly.

Charles had no means to address his people. All he could do was to issue a lame protest against the violation of his rights which the Constitution had entrusted to him as the apostolic King crowned with the Crown of St. Stephen.

The National Assembly yielded to foreign pressure. The royal couple was taken to the anchorage of the flagship *Glowworm*. The Queen was not considered a prisoner, only an expellee. Reception aboard was unceremonious, but along the pier humble people watched and wept. No Hungarian river pilot wanted to serve on the boat that took the King into exile; never before in the tumultuous history of Habsburg rule in Hungary had the little people been so loyal. A non-Hungarian pilot was secured; as a special favor, Count and Countess Hunyádi were permitted to join Charles and Zita.

On November 5, the *Glowworm* steamed downstream.

For the first and last time, Charles saw the full melancholy charm of the great river in the deep fertile plains, the many historical sights on which his ancestors' armies had fought so many battles—all in vain. He passed Belgrade, where a scant eight years before the most fateful plot in human history had been hatched; and, in darkness, he passed the Iron Gate. On December 6, they were in Galatz. Rumanian authorities behaved kindly and arranged a Mass aboard the boat *Principessa Maria* to which the couple and their party were allowed to transfer for the purpose. Charles looked glum and worn. He did not yet know where they would be going. His British custodians only said that the next stop was Sulina.

No Habsburg Prince had ever been to the delta and its lugubrious wilderness. A British destroyer waited there to take them to Istanbul; then they sailed west, on a light cruiser, through the Mediterranean, until, on November 19, Madeira came in sight, the terminal.

When Napoleon was sent to St. Helena, he was to receive an annual £20,000 to maintain his establishment. But the conference of ambassadors had not yet decided how much Charles could spend on his Spanish island. When he contracted pneumonia, he refused to call a doctor, to avoid expenses, and despite the belated arrival of a former court physician, he succumbed on April 1, 1922, at the age of thirty-five.

"I am going home. I should like to go home with you. I am so tired," his secretary and later biographer Charles von Werkmann quotes as his last words.

"Home" was the shores of the Danube for which his ancestors' emblem had been a symbol until a few short years before, which now seemed an eternity. The symbol had gone down to oblivion, while far away in a nebulous future loomed the shadows of the murderous tyrannies that would settle over every square inch of soil of the Danubian regions. The imperturbable waters were to carry the warships and the slavers under the Swastika and the Hammer and Sickle, as they had carried the craft of earlier tyrants who had convulsed the social and political complexions of these variegated lands—leaving nothing unaffected except the grandeur, the drama, beauty and infinity, of the old river itself.

PARTIAL BIBLIOGRAPHY

This is a partial bibliography of source material reconstructed from my husband's notes and supplemented by more recent publications.

A.M.L.L.

Archiv für Kunde österreichischer Geschichtsquellen, Vol. X, Vienna, 1853.

Bogičević, Miloš, *Le Procès de Salonique, Juin 1917,* Paris, 1927.

——, *Le Colonel Dragoutine Dimitriévitch Apis,* Paris, 1926.

——, *Die auswärtige Politik Serbiens,* Vienna, 1928–31.

Bonfinius, Antonius, *Ungerische Chronica,* 1581.

Bourgoing, Jean de, *Briefe Kaisers Franz Joseph an Frau Katherina Schratt,* Vienna, 1949.

Buschbeck, Ernst H., *Austria,* London, 1949.

Cassius, Dio (3d cent.), *Roman History* (tr.), London, 1914–17.

Copybook of the City of Vienna.

Enikel, Jansen (13th cent.), *Gesammelte Werke,* Leipzig, 1900.

Eugene, Prince of Savoy, *Schlachtberichte 1697–1717,* Berlin, 1937.

Gaxotte, Pierre, *Frederick the Great,* New Haven, 1942.

Gervinus, George, *Introduction to the History of the 19th Century* (tr.), London, 1853.

Grillparzer, Franz, *König Ottokars Glück und Ende,* 1825.

Hantsch, Hugo, *Die Geschichte Österreichs,* Vienna, 1959.

Huber, Alfons, *Geschichte Österreichs,* Vienna, 1896.

Katona, István, *Historia critica,* Pest, 1778.

Kleinclausz, A., *Charlemagne,* Paris, 1934.

Koser, Reinhard, *König Friedrich der Grosse,* Stuttgart, 1893.

Kralik, Richard von, *Geschichte der Stadt Wien und ihrer Kultur,* Vienna, 1926.

——, *Geschichte des Weltkrieges,* Vienna, 1915.

——, *Österreichische Geschichte,* Vienna, 1914.

Leeper, A. W. A., *A History of Medieval Austria,* New York, 1941.

Ligne, Prince Charles Joseph de, *Memoirs of Prince Eugene of Savoy* (tr.), London, 1827.

Mailáth, Count Johann, *Geschichte der Magyaren,* Regensburg, 1852.

——, *Geschichte des österreichischen Kaiserstaates,* Hamburg, 1834–50.

Marboe, Ernst, *Das Österreichbuch,* Vienna, 1948.

Mayer, Franz Martin, *Geschichte Österreichs,* Vienna, 1909.

Metternich-Winneburg, Princess Pauline, *The Days That Are No More* (tr.), London, 1921.

Palacký, František, *Geschichte von Böhmen,* Prague, 1836–60.

Pichler, Karoline von Greiner, *Die Belagerung Wiens,* in *Collected Works,* Vienna, 1828–32.

——, *Die Wiedereroberung von Ofen,* in *Collected Works,* Vienna, 1828–32.

Pliny, the Elder, *Natural History,* 77 A.D.

Quin, Michael J., *A Steam Voyage down the Danube,* Paris, 1836.

Reade, Hubert G. R., *Sidelights on the Thirty Years' War,* London, 1924.

Redlich, Joseph, *Emperor Francis Joseph of Austria,* New York, 1929.

Schiller, Friedrich von, *Wallenstein,* 1800.

Seton-Watson, R. W., *A History of the Roumanians,* Cambridge, 1934.

Staël-Holstein, Anne de, *Mémoires,* Paris, 1845.

Stavrianos, L. S., *The Balkans since 1453,* New York, 1958.

Teleki, Count Paul, *The Evolution of Hungary and Its Place in European History,* New York, 1923.

Velleius, Paterculus Caius, *Histoire romaine* (tr.), Paris, 1825.

Weber, Joseph, *Mémoires concernant Maria Antoinette,* Paris, 1896.

Wedgwood, C. V., *The Thirty Years' War,* New Haven, 1939.

INDEX

Aachen. *See* Aix-la-Chapelle
Aargau, 116
Abdurrahman Pasha, 264
Abraham a Santa Clara, 242–43, 259
Achmed Bey, 253
Achsberg, Ernst, 320
Ada Kaleh (Danube island), 155
Adamites, 140, 145
Adrianople, 238, 248, 444, 459
Adriatic Sea, 181, 320, 340–41, 365, 403
Aeneas, 22
Africa, 18, 53
Agnes (King Ottokar's daughter), 123
Aix-la-Chapelle, 67, 75, 165, 298
Akindschi, 174–75
Alani, 31, 58
Alaric, 59–60
Albania, 478
Albrecht, Count of Habsburg (Rudolf of H.'s father), 116
Albrecht, Duke of Habsburg (Rudolf of H.'s son), 124–27, 131
Albrecht V, Emperor, 141
Albrecht, Archduke (15th century), 145–49
Albrecht, Field Marshal Archduke (19th century), 425, 455
Aldringen, Count Johann, 226–27
Alecsandri, Vasile, 448
Alexander the Great, 475
Alexander I, Tsar, 383–84, 388, 390–91, 394, 403, 409 ff., 443
Alexander II, Tsar, 461
Alexander (Karageorgević), Prince of Serbia, 471
Alexander (Obrenović), King of Serbia, 472–74
Alexander Ion I, Prince, 447
Alfons X of Castile, 115
Algiers, 181
Alps, Alpine, 13, 16, 22, 24, 29, 32, 36, 39, 42, 45, 107, 254, 272, 342, 358, 373, 375, 382
Alsace, 116, 118, 159, 216, 234, 371
Alutus. *See* Olt
Amazon River, 18
America, 18, 157, 174, 313–14, 324, 330, 358, 368, 405, 417, 482
Amiens, France, 383
Amurath Pasha, 439

Anabaptists, 185–87
Andrássy, Count Julius, 454–55
Andrews, John, 340, 418
Anhalt-Dessau, Prince of, 290, 294, 300
Anhalt-Zerbst, Sophie. *See* Catherine II
Anjou, 127
Anna of Hungary, 160, 163–64
"Apis," 500 (*see also* Dimitrijević)
Aquileja, 66
Arabia, Arabs, 84, 116, 166, 181, 439
Aragon, 160
Anna, Austrian Archduchess, 189
Anne of Brittany, 159
Argedava, 40–41
Argentina, 417
Argeş River, 17
Ariogaesus, Prince of the Quadi, 49
Arminius, Roman general, 35–37
Arnim, George von, 214
Arno, Archbishop of Salzburg, 72–73
Árpád, Magyar princes, 79–80, 87, 90, 97, 127
Arslan, Pasha of Buda, 182
Artois, 159
Aschach, 12, 224
Asia, Asiatic, 17, 19, 20, 22, 24, 44, 57 ff., 65, 78, 80, 101, 103, 128, 132, 166, 239, 249, 254, 337
Aspern, 398 ff., 403–4
Aspremont, Count, 297
Atelkusu, 78, 82
Attila, 64, 66, 71, 248
Auersperg, 389, 432 (*see also* Grün, Anastasius)
Augsburg, 83, 164
August III, King of Saxony, 315
Augustin (minstrel), 246, 327
Aurelian, Roman Emperor, 54–55
Austerlitz, 390–91, 404
Austria, Austrians, 23, 27, 32, 34, 71–72, 81, 102 ff., 140 ff., 157 ff., 168, 174–76, 181 ff., 196 ff., 208, 214, 220 ff., 250 ff., 276–79, 282, 286–87, 294 ff., 372 ff., 392 ff., 406 ff., 418, 430 ff., 451 ff.
Austro-Hungarian Monarchy, 31, 454 ff.
Avars, 31, 65–67, 73, 128
Ayrendorff, General Kornelius von, 363
Azov, Sea of, 50

Babakai Rock, 17